Contents

Introduction

"Incredible, ain't it?"

When Warner Bros. released its first cartoon in 1930, the intention was to remain ahead of the competition in the field of "talkie" motion pictures, to provide their theaters with fast-moving musical novelties, to promote their Vitaphone Corporation and to plug their popular music library. They accomplished those goals, but at the same time planted the seeds for a longrunning series of animated films which would delight the entire world, creating a menagerie of characters that would surpass Disney's in popularity and win six Academy Awards.

Animated cartoons had always been a popular part of the complete movie program, but never more so than in the early days of sound motion pictures. Walt Disney's Mickey Mouse had caused a sensation. A moving cartoon with synchronized music and funny sound effects was pure magic to the depression-era audiences of the late 1920s.

Warner Bros., having made sound movies popular with *The Jazz Singer*, saw a good thing when producer Leon Schlesinger brought the first all "talk-ink" cartoon character to them. Ex-Disney animators Hugh Harman and Rudolf Ising had created a pilot film featuring their speaking character, a black boy named Bosko. The test film was just that, all talk. Warner Bros. suggested they make the character less ethnic, more like Mickey Mouse, and more musical, incorporating popular songs from the studio's new feature musicals. With that, Looney Tunes and Merrie Melodies were born. And though the road was a bit bumpy in the 1930s, the films eventually settled into a style which nurtured many top animation talents (Friz Freleng, Chuck Jones, Tex Avery, Bob Clampett, Frank Tashlin, Bob McKimson, etc.) and created many superstars (including Bugs Bunny, Daffy Duck, Porky Pig, and the Road Runner) and hundreds of lesser lights (Egghead, Charlie Dog, Marvin Martian, et al).

Most importantly, the studio created an *attitude* in animated films. From the late Thirties onward, there was only one kind of Warner Bros. cartoon—*funny* ones. Disney may have had the beauty and polish, but Warners had the laughs. A sense of humor in writing and drawing, even in the music and sound effects was the bottom line goal. More often than not, that was the result.

It was also the key to their popularity. Leon Schlesinger was not interested in the little details of cartoon production, but the overall product, and his philosophy was humor. "The public still likes to laugh and the cartoon is still the perfect mediuim for comedy," Schlesinger said in 1940. "Our policy has always been laughs—the more the better." Schlesinger didn't care what his boys came up with, as long as there were plenty of jokes in it.

Sadly, the cartoons produced by this studio between 1940 and 1960 represent a situation which may never occur again: a group of zany artists given total freedom to make funny cartoons and invent funny characters— with complete access to the talents and facilities of a major motion picture studio.

The studio produced cartoons because there was a market for them, and because they needed product for their new theaters. This was a time when the general public regarded animated cartoons as they did newspaper comic strips—good clean fun for *all* ages. And when unique talents behind the screen—writers, artists, and musicians—cared about making good funny films and dared to push this medium to extremes.

Carl Stalling, the musical director from 1936 onward, was invaluable. Formerly with Walt Disney and Ub Iwerks, and before that a Kansas City theater organist, Stalling took the scoring of each cartoon as seriously

LOONEY TUNES™ and MERRIE MELODIES™

A Complete Illustrated Guide to the Warner Bros. Cartoons

by JERRY BECK & WILL FRIEDWALD

An Owl Book
A Donald Hutter Book
HENRY HOLT AND COMPANY
NEW YORK

Published by Henry Holt and Company, Inc.,
115 West 18th Street, New York, New York 10011.
Published in Canada by Fitzhenry & Whiteside Limited,
195 Allstate Parkway, Markham Ontario L3R 4T8.

Library of Congress Cataloging-in-Publication Data
Beck, Jerry and Will Friedwald.
Looney Tunes and Merrie Melodies
A Complete Illustrated Guide to the Warner Bros. Cartoons
"A Donald Hutter Book"
1. Warner Bros. Cartoons 2. Animated films—United States—
History and criticism   I. [Title]
NC1766.U52W3737n.1989   741.5'8'0979493   89-1373
ISBN: 0-8050-0894-2 (An Owl Book: pbk.)

Henry Holt books are available at special discounts for bulk purchases for sales promotions, premiums, fund-raising, or educational use. Special editions or book excerpts can also be created to specification.

For details contact:
Special Sales Director
Henry Holt and Company, Inc.
115 West 18th Street
New York, New York 10011

First edition

Produced and Prepared by Sammis Publishing Corp. and Layla Productions, Inc.

Typesetting by LCR Graphics, Inc.
Manufactured in the United States of America
10 9 8 7 6 5 4 3

as he had a Buster Keaton two-reeler or a Tom Mix western.

And where would Warner cartoons be without its ensemble cast of voice actors. Led by Mel Blanc, the one man responsible for the majority of starring character voices (Bugs Bunny, Daffy Duck, Porky Pig, and more) and joined by Arthur Q. Bryan (Elmer Fudd), Stan Freberg (Junior Bear, Pete Puma) Bea Benaderet, Daws Butler, June Foray, and others—this talented troupe gave these cartoons a unique sound and fury.

Of the many great art talents—including layout and background artists effects and character animators—there are five directors who deserve special mention: five different styles, five different approaches, five who set the standard we have come to expect from a Warner cartoon. *Tex Avery* brought the satirical edge to Warner cartoons in the late 1930s and experimented with new screwball characters seen in such cartoons as *Porky's Duck Hunt* and *A Wild Hare* and stretched the cartoon boundaries with films such as *Page Miss Glory* and *Porky's Preview*. *Robert Clampett* defined the personality of Porky Pig, created Tweety, and found animators to create animation as funny as the jokes they were trying to tell, especially in films as great as *Book Revue* and *Coal Black*. *Friz Freleng* masterfully combined music and humor in such cartoons as *Back Alley Oproar* and *The Three Little Bops*, and created Yosemite Sam as well as masterpieces like *You Ought to Be in Pictures* and *Tweety Pie*. *Frank Tashlin* brought a live action director's sense of perspective to the Looney Tunes universe, a frantic energy in cartoons including *Porky's Romance*, *Porky's Pig Feat*, and *Stupid Cupid*. *Chuck Jones* experimented with stylized art, backgrounds, and movement and created characters like Pepe Le Pew, the Road Runner, Wile E. Coyote, Inki, Marvin Martian, Charlie Dog, and the Three Bears, and acknowledged classic cartoons such as *What's Opera, Doc?*, *One Froggy Evening*, and *Duck Dodgers in the 24½ Century*, to name but a few.

About this filmography: Yes, we have watched every cartoon listed in this book—and it has been a labor of love. Our biggest problem was obtaining all the screen credits, a chore made difficult by the old Warner Bros. policy of reissuing earlier cartoons and replacing the original credits with a new "Blue Ribbon" main title. For example, almost all prints of the Looney Tune *Book Revue* (1946) that exist today are "Blue Ribbon" prints—which call the film a "Merrie Melodie," list no credits, and misspell the title as *Book Review*. We found a print with original titles at the UCLA Film Archive in Hollywood and thanks to the University are able to provide the credits for this film and many others (but not all). By the way, the "Blue Ribbon" reissue print also removed the Porky Pig "That's all, Folks" end tag as well. If credits are missing from an entry, then it was *nowhere* to be found.

The credits that are listed here have been standardized. For example, Carl Stalling's credit on the cartoons varied from Musical Supervision to Musical Direction to just plain Music; we've listed him under "Musical Direction." Robert Clampett has been billed as Bob Clampett, Frank Tashlin occasionally used the name "Tish Tash." We have tried to remain true to the on-screen titles, but some standardization was necessary for convenience.

Many cartoons of the 1930s and 1940s contain characters and situations which today would be considered racist and/or sexist. Films like *Bugs Bunny Nips the Nips* and *Coal Black and de Sebben Dwarfs* play on ethnic stereotypes, a common practice in comedy films of that period. Many of these cartoons are no longer shown on television, but history cannot be ignored. In our efforts to be complete, we have included these entries, and we hope that you will view them in their proper historical context.

Will Friedwald wrote of the cartoons of the 1930s and 1950s, Jerry Beck covers the 1940s and 1960s and compiled the sections on TV series, specials, feature films and miscellaneous information. Obviously, this book could not exist without the cooperation of Warner Bros. Inc,, and particularly the Warner Bros. Animation Department. We are grateful to Steven S. Greene and Kathleen Helppie-Shipley for encouraging this project. Their staff was especially helpful and we would like to thank Chris Walsh, Rick Gehr, Jim Champin, Terry Lennon and Greg Ford for their knowledgeable assistance.

The UCLA Film and Television Archive was an invaluable source in researching many of the pre-1948 titles, and special thanks are due to Jere Guldin and Ed Carter, who shared their enthusiasm during our many marathon cartoon screenings.

For helping us fill in the gaps, providing stills, films, and general moral support, we would like to thank Gary Schwartz, John Cawley, Tony Eastman, Dwayne Dimock, Mark Mayerson, Rick Scheckman, Kit Parker, P.A. Carayannis, Herb Graff, John Kricfalusi, Bruce Goldstein, Jim Korkis, David Mruz, Harry Fisk, George Woolery, Paul Merle Wise, Jim Benson, Harry McCracken, Mike Kazaleh, Will Ryan, John Sammis, Lori Stein, Don Hutter, David Wilkerson, Bill Lorenzo, Susan Neri, Libby Simon, "Uncle" Wayne Daigrepont, "The New York Cult," and the gang in *Apatoons*.

Special thanks to Chuck Jones, Friz Freleng, Leonard Maltin, Steve Schneider, and Richard H. Thomas, true experts on the history of Warner Bros. cartoons, who provided answers to our most trivial questions.

And finally, for special efforts above and beyond the call of duty, we are indebted to some good friends without whom this book would not be as complete. We are thankful for the research assistance provided by Mark Kausler, Greg Duffell, Collin Kellogg, Steven "Doc" Ferzoco, and Kevin Wollenweber.

A last note: watching over 1,000 Warner Bros. cartoons *is* educational. We learned four rules which have enriched our lives and we will never forget:

#1: Hippety Hopper is *not* a giant mouse.
#2: *Always* get a warranty from ACME.
#3: *Never* let Bugs or Daffy shave you!
#4: The little light—it stays *on!*
Jerry Beck
Will Friedwald
April 1989

Note: In the credits in the following filmography, "LT" denotes Looney Tune and "MM" denotes Merrie Melodie. "2/C" stands for Two Strip Technicolor (red and green hues), used in 1934-1935 Merrie Melodies; "3/C" indicates Three Strip Technicolor (full color) which was used from 1936 onward. Hugh Harman and Rudolf Ising supervised all cartoons unless otherwise credited through 1933. Frank Marsales, likewise, scored the music.

1930

SINKIN' IN THE BATHTUB

Bosko, Honey; Sept; LT; Supervision by Hugh Harman and Rudolf Ising; Animation by Isadore Freling; Music by Frank Marsales.

We open on Bosko, the Talk-ink Kid, allegedly bathing, but really giving far more attention to music-making than to cleaning himself, as he turns his feet, his nose, and streams of shower water into musical instruments. Even Bosko's bathtub gets into the act and does a gay dance with the towel and toilet paper (to Mendelssohn's "Spring Song")! After dressing, Bosko summons his car from the outhouse and the two go tip-toeing through the tulips over to see his girlfriend, Honey. She, too, is singin' in the bathtub, and modestly closes the blinds and dresses when Bosko calls to her. Despondent when a goat consumes the tulips he has brought his sweetie, Bosko bawls until Honey reassures him "Ah still loves yo'" and he serenades her with an ad-hoc saxophone and her front steps used as a giant xylophone. Then they're off together for a ride that starts out unpleasantly as they encounter a fussy bespectacled cow whose powerful expectorations threaten to annihilate their engine. The ride soon becomes downright harrowing when a bump knocks Bosko out of the car as they start to climb slowly up a mountain. Eventually, they reach the top, but the car starts rolling down. Bosko chases after it as Honey screams, "Ooh, Eee, Ah! Ooh! Eee! Ah! Ooh! Eee! Ah!" Bosko grabs onto a rope extending from the car, only to have his crotch dragged over a succession of boulders, trees, and telephone poles. Eventually car, Bosko, and Honey wind up plummeting off the mountain, luckily landing in a lake below, which immediately becomes an enormous bathtub for them to sing in—lily pads and ducks joining in.

CONGO JAZZ

Bosko; Oct; LT; Animation by Max Maxwell and Paul Smith; Music by Frank Marsales.

Bosko, first shown with pith helmet and elephant gun, goes stalking wild game in the jungle, although any intention of hunting the jungle animals soon vanishes as Bosko makes music with them. First he produces a flute in the face of a hungry tiger. Then, once the beast is sufficiently charmed, he kicks it off a cliff. Next, a father gorilla (addressed by our hero as "Mr. Ape") catches Bosko spanking one of his offspring, and Bosko cools him down by turning chewing gum into a harp string and plunking out a tune. Soon, Bosko finds himself conducting an entire orchestra of not-so-wild animals, each playing either an instrument, a piece of jungle scenery transformed into an instrument, or another animal whose body is used as an instrument. Fade out on Bosko laughing merrily with a trio of hyenas.

The animators seem uncomfortable with quadruped animals, so most of the congo critters walk around on their hind legs. "When the Little Red Roses Get the Blues for You" serves as the chewing gum harp solo.

HOLD ANYTHING

Bosko, Honey; Nov; LT; Animation by Isadore Freleng and Norm Blackburn.

Bosko as a riveter on a construction crew consisting mainly of Mickey-like mice, all of whom show more interest in music than in their labors. Bosko whistles and operates his machinery in time to the score, the mice march in musical formation, and when Bosko discovers the sound a mouse makes bouncing on a saw, he proceeds to use the mouse and saw as an instrument, still smiling cheerfully as he decapitates the helpless rodent. He hollers to the crew (the re-capitated mouse and a goat) to send up a beam, and just when we think he's actually going to do some work, he turns the wire cables into harp strings and calls out to Honey, typing away in the office of a nearby building. She responds by typing, "Gee You're Swell!" and Bosko goes into a tap dance on the swaying beam. Far from being afraid of falling, he continues his terpsichory on a line of musical notes that appear. He then converts Honey's typewriter into a piano as Honey tap-dances and scat sings on the ledge. When the goat swallows the steam whistle and inflates, Bosko uses him as both a balloon and an instrument as Honey continues her dance. The goat-balloon carries Bosko into the air, and he falls onto a brick wall, breaking into a half-dozen miniature Boskos (Fred Astaire would do this in live action in *Blue Skies*), who dance in a chorus line, turning the bricks into piano keys. They reassemble into one normal-size Bosko, who tips his hat.

THE BOOZE HANGS HIGH

Bosko; Dec; LT; Animation by Isadore Freleng and Paul Smith.
Barnyard humor. Bosko and miscellaneous smiling cows, horses, and pigs engage in a bizarre juxtaposition of musical interludes and gross gags: a horse's behind becomes an arco bass fiddle; a family of skipping ducks interrupt their merry prancing about so that one little duckling can go to the bathroom; a trio of swine wallowing in a particularly disgusting trough of slop happen upon a bottle of hooch, get thoroughly plastered, and the biggest, most drunken porker vocalizes as he regurgitates (a gag cut from most TV prints). Though the score (and selection of specific tunes) is hardly tangential to any of the Harman-Ising Warner films, here it supplies the film's strongest point of humor. The soundtrack consists almost entirely of quotes from *Song of the Flame*, a rather bourgeois Oscar Hammerstein operetta, filmed by Warners in 1930, concerning the French Revolution. The cartoon climaxes in the basso profundo intoxication aria, "One Little Drink," reducing it to a series of piggy squeals and oinks. We end on Bosko and the pigs doing a cossack-dance to "Song of the Flame." It opens when the blackness of the title card becomes the back of a cow's udder, as in Disney's 1928 *Plane Crazy*, which Harman and Ising had also worked on.

1931

BOX CAR BLUES

Bosko; Jan; LT; Animation by Rollin Hamilton and Max Maxwell.
Bosko and a fellow hobo, a cute but sleazy-looking fat pig with a banjo, are bumming on a train, entertaining each other with "Cryin' for the Carolines." The train's somewhat perilous ride supplies most of the story line when it goes uphill. The train becomes an inchworm that scurries up the back of the mountain; then it becomes human and its "pants" start to slide off. On reaching the top, the last box car breaks off from the rest of the train and goes rolling down with our hapless heroes aboard. On top, Bosko yells for help as the car rolls topsy-turvy over treacherous hills (getting his head temporarily lopped off in the sliding door at one point), in and out of pitch-black tunnels, though even fear of death doesn't prevent him from going into an impression of Jolson doing "Mammy!" The boxcar tangles with a cow on the tracks and Bosko finds himself being dragged over the same boulders, trees, and telephone poles as ᵢn *Sinkin' in the Bathtub*. After a crash, which results in several minutes of falling rubble, Bosko and the pig end up once again on a handcar with their banjo. They continue their singing.

Appropriately, the music in the opening shots is "Alabamy 'Bound."

BIG MAN FROM THE NORTH

Bosko; Feb; LT; Animation by Isadore Freleng and Robert Edmunds.
Bosko is a rather sheepish Northwest Mountie whose short-tempered Sargent orders him "Get your man!" He mushes his dog sled over a few hills until it crashes into the side of a building (merging all three dogs into one three-headed conglomerate pooch). Bosko enters after reaching into his pocket and drawing out two guns, each as big as he is. He is in a saloon, and the delighted Bosko discovers Honey entertaining therein (scatting the 1930 pop song "Chinnin' and Chattin' with May"). As you might expect, Bosko temporarily abandons his "Get your man" mission to join Honey in enter-

taining the crowd, a mixture of bearded prospectors and beavers. Bosko then starts to play a piano solo, abetted by beavers and pelicans who emerge from a spittoon, but is interrupted by the peg-legged villain whom he has been assigned to apprehend. Summoning up his courage, Bosko pulls his pistol; it fires only a cork and a string. Thinking quickly, Bosko douses the lights with some well-aimed saliva and the darkness blazes with gunfire. When the lights come on, Bosko has a machine gun to use on his adversary and tricks him into getting caught up in the saloon's swinging doors. Bosko then delivers the finishing blows, a jab deeply and violently in the rump with a sword, then a huge rifle blasting off the villain's fur, leaving one rather scrawny animal behind to run off to the other other animals' applause.

Other song: "Looking For the Love Light in the Dark."

AIN'T NATURE GRAND?

Bosko; Mar; LT; Animation by Isadore Freleng and Norm Blackburn.
Kindhearted Bosko goes fishing but is much too humane to subject his worm to the hook and lets it go free (while his story is interrupted by a lengthy bird-chasing-worm episode). Bosko catches a fish only to fondle it as he asks the audience, "Ain't dat cute?" In return the fish spits in his eye. Bosko continues frolicking in the great outdoors, gaily following a butterfly, admiring and joining a pair of dancing bees in front of a waterfall, then doing a chorus line with four gung-ho frogs who emerge from the mouth of a pelican. Other woodland creatures get into the act, including a spider whose body turns into a maypole. Two little bugs convert a dragonfly into a bombing warplane from which they drop rocks and shoot bees at the screaming Bosko who ducks into a fountain for safety, posing like a sprouting statue for the fadeout.

UPS 'N DOWNS

Bosko; LT; Supervision by Rollin Hamilton and Paul Smith.
Music by Frank Marsales

It's the day of the big horse race and the animals are arriving in droves. Bosko is a hot dog vendor with dancing weinies. He sells one to a dog character who recognizes it as his long lost "Sonny Boy," and the two go off together to the tune of the Jolson song. While the other horses train for the race like boxers, Bosko produces his own steed, a mechanical horse. The gun goes off and Bosko's horse goes in reverse, crashing against a wall. Bosko repairs him by mixing him up in a cocktail shaker. Once this mechanism gets going, there's practically no stopping it, even when the bad guy's black saliva threatens to reverse Bosko's horse-rider relationship. Bosko wins the race by stretching out the robot horse's neck in front of his adversary.

DUMB PATROL

Bosko; May; LT; Animation by Isadore Freleng and Max Maxwell.
An explosion here, a burst of gunfire there, and the screen is filled with warplanes, soaring, shooting, flaming. We dissolve to Bosko, the Talkink Kid, cheerfully whistling "Get Happy" in the middle of the war as he lovingly oils his little airplane (and blows its nose). When one particularly gnarly enemy flyer nearly kayos them with a bomb, Bosko and plane take to the air and follow in hot pursuit. Bosko takes aim on the villain, but the cad reduces Bosko's plane to rubble with shots from a monstrous cannon. Bosko crashes in the ruins of a house where he encounters Honey, no more upset about the war or the destruction of her home than Bosko, and the two "parley-voo." She's indignant when he steals a kiss, so he makes up for it by entertaining her at the piano. Their merrymaking gets interrupted by more death from the skies. Bosko improvises an airplane from a broomstick, a board, and a dachshund, and turns a fence into a

3

machine gun which hurls planks at his adversary who fires real bullets back. Our hero sends both bullets and a bomb speeding back, reducing the enemy to a bunch of little flies.

With Bosko losing some of his timidity, his creators have begun to expand the range of possibilities. The plot has become more fleshed out and the visual effects, using black-and-white and the same Bosko-style pie-cut eye design are quite impressive. Background music includes "Shuffle Your Feet" and "Just Roll Along."

YODELLING YOKELS

Bosko; June; LT; Animation by Rollin Hamilton and Norm Blackburn.
Now we have alpine antics, Bosko gleefully yodelling and playing his concertina as he frolics when he encounters an owl who can out-yodel him. Bosko's answer is to shoot the bird and laugh uncontrollably at the singed, featherless creature. Bosko and Honey yodel back and forth for a while, then they go out to play. As he leaves her, a little mouse eeks timidly out of his hole. Now the cartoon becomes a sort of animated *Intolerance*, cutting back and forth between two stories: Bosko and Honey on skis falling down a snow-covered alp, the mouse sneaking across the floor; Honey in a giant snowball that smashes against a boulder and sends her flying, the mouse using a piece of swiss cheese as a golf course with a pea as a ball; Honey landing on an iceflow in an icy river and heading towards the falls as Bosko and a convenient St. Bernard dog speed to the rescue, the mouse still trying to play golf with the cheese.

BOSKO'S HOLIDAY

Bosko; July; Animation by Isadore Freleng and Paul Smith.
Bosko, asleep in bed, is awakened by the telephone clobbering the alarm clock, which in turn pounds on Bosko's bedpan and jabs him with its pointy arm. It is a call from Honey. Hysterical dialogue follows; the upshot is Honey inviting Bosko to a picnic. Leaping into his clothes, he calls his car from the garage (it's followed by a litter of baby cars that Bosko tells to "Go Home").

He drives over to Honey's, strumming his banjo. It is in need of a new string so Bosko grabs the tail from a mouse that happens to be posing as his hood ornament. He takes Honey out for a ride. Her little white dog follows, and the unwelcome pooch distracts Bosko just when he's trying to push the car over a hill. The dog inflates as it bites into one the auto tires. The two go on their picnic, skipping to a pond that shines with their reflections. In the woods, Bosko whispers a fresh suggestion in Honey's ear and she is indignant until he makes a great show of liking her sandwiches ("Dat sho' is fine!"). Just as he's won her over again, the pesky pooch licks her right smack on the behind, and Honey, thinking Bosko is responsible, gives him a rocking slap and leaves in a huff. Bosko faces the camera disgruntedly.

Music includes "I Can't Give You Anything But Love, Baby" and "It's a Little String Around Your Finger."

THE TREE'S KNEES

Bosko; Aug; LT; Animation by Isadore Freleng and Rollin Hamilton.
Bosko returns to the forest primeval (as in *Ain't Nature Grand*) but here it's trees who beg for humanity, with surprising combinations of the cute and the grotesque. A family of baby trees silently begs Bosko not to chop down their mother. Instead of killing them, Bosko whips out his harmonica and plays a tune for the trees (each now with two legs) to dance to. When one baby tree razzes Bosko, he rips off its bark, but then returns it to the tree, which continues to slight him. "Well shut my mouth!" exclaims Bosko, finding a mother bird and a tree that rockabyes out buckets. Then Bosko chases after a butterfly and turns a bunch of small trees into harp strings on which he plays "Dancing with Tears in My Eyes." A stately older tree makes like a concert violinist; other trees, especially the weeping willow, bawl hysterically and pussy willows meow in tempo. One mouse saves another from drowning, then the two of them form an impression of a phonograph player as another tree goes into a Spanish dance. "Trees" also turns up on the soundtrack.

LADY PLAY YOUR MANDOLIN

Foxy; Sept; MM; Supervision by Frank Marsales; Animation by Rollin Hamilton and Norm Blackburn; with Abe Lyman and His Brunswick Recording Orchestra.

A jazz-hot cartoon set in a south-of-the-border saloon. The music is so hot and infectious that all distinctions are blurred as pertain to morality and sobriety. Lyrics keep dwelling on the line "When you sing your song of sin/ I'm a sinner, too." The whole joint dances to the music, even hat racks, tables, and a customer's beard. Foxy, a new character resembling Mickey Mouse with pointy ears and a bushy tail, gets ticked at his horse for wanting to prance around on two legs and whoop it up with everyone else. The horse gets woozy from Foxy's blow to his head with a hooch bottle and staggers about the place in a stupor, making noises like a live trombone and hallucinating nightmarish monsters in mirrors. His antics get so hot he spontaneously combusts, burning much of his body to an ash. Meanwhile, Foxy does Jolson impressions and sings Frank Crumit's "The Gay Caballero" while his girlfriend on stage does her act as the original lady with the mandolin. A shimmying ape waiter is determined to fill every open mouth with liquor.

SMILE, DARN YA, SMILE

Foxy; Sept 5; MM; Animation by Isadore Freleng and Max Maxwell; Music by Abe Lyman and His Californians.

Foxy dreams he is the Toonerville Trolley engineer, urging his passengers to smile, darn ya, smile. First he picks up a lady hippo so obese she can't fit in the car. Foxy obligingly deflates her with her own hat pin. Next his girlfriend boards the car, and the two indulge in a chorus of the title song, accompanied by the train's advertising, which comes to life. The obstacles they must surmount as the train trudges across the countryside begin with a stubborn cow, lazily chewing its cud on the tracks, and a quartet of hobos who mock him with a chorus of the same song (when their partially cooked chicken joins in the music, one of the bums entreats it to "Boil, darn ya, boil!"). The ride becomes more perilous as the car gets away from Foxy, carrying his girlfriend over a treacherous mountain pass. When Foxy is unable to stop it, he wakes up from his dream and clobbers his radio, which is in the middle of a final rendition of "Smile, Darn Ya, Smile!"

This early Merrie Melody is more valuable for its historic significance than as a cartoon, and for its theme-song inspiration to *Who Framed Roger Rabbit*.

BOSKO SHIPWRECKED

Bosko; Sept 19; LT; Animation by Rollin Hamilton and Larry Martin.

The plot thickens. Although there's nothing wrong with purely visual and musical cartoons, the animated cartoon in the talkie era generally developed toward fuller narratives, more believable characters, and graphic realism (or at least a particular interpretation of realism). For once there's precious little song and dance, as Bosko gets washed up on a deserted island by a terrible storm. As he naps, a couple of monkeys engage in amusing antics with his hat, until they accidentally spill an egg on him, which inspires a wiseguy parrot to crack, "The yolk's on you." A lion comes lunging after Bosko (he sees the shadow first), who high-tails it to a lagoon. Bosko leaps onto what he thinks is a rock but turns out to be a crocodile. Unwittingly, the lion leaps into the croc's mouth; Bosko is saved. Finding a rowboat, Bosko tries to anchor to a piece of land that turns out to be a hippo that drags him to a native camp. Burning his behind on a red-hot caldron, Bosko flees the tribe of cannibals coming after him. Bosko drives on to what he thinks is a boat, but discovers is a rhinoceros. No matter, the beast gives Bosko armored protection from the natives, helping him get away.

ONE MORE TIME

Foxy; Oct 3; MM; Animation by Isadore Freleng and Paul Smith; with Abe Lyman and His Brunswick Recording Orchestra.

The song is about a separated sweetheart who pleads "One more time/let me do the things that I used to do/let me sit down to some tea for two." Here the lyric is altered to describe Foxy's dilemma as a police officer walking his beat, constantly harassed by nervy law breakers. In tempo with "One more time," he vows that the next guy who doesn't watch his step will get it but good. The transgressors range from gangsters who ambush Officer Foxy with machine guns out of garbage cans to the lady hippo (from *Smile, Darn Ya, Smile* and *Bosko's Soda Fountain*) hauled in by Foxy on an automobile charge. The hippo weepingly pleads in song with Foxy not to be given "One more fine." Soon after, Foxy runs into his girlfriend and her dog, and the two stage an impromptu concert, using a piano as well as the dog's teeth. The music is interrupted by the noise of tiny bird hoodlums robbing a wealthy hippo at machine gun point. Foxy and a wagonful of cops go after what soon is a whole carload o' crooks. Foxy is nearly done in by one of the bad guy's rather nasty expectorations. When the cads make off with Foxy's gal, he chases them on a robot horse and cleverly tricks them into jail. One gets away and pops out of a manhole to use a machine gun on Foxy's behind.

BOSKO THE DOUGHBOY

Bosko; Oct 17; LT; Animation by Rollin Hamilton and Max Maxwell.

Explosions! Death! The whirr of bullets tearing flesh! Troops marching into battle with bayonets poised! Soldiers, bullets piercing their bodies, keeling over. For Bosko the Doughboy, it's all cheerful on the Western Front. There is some plot, meaning any nonmusical interlude. One battalion of infantrymen

charges this way, another attacks that way, and it's deliberately unclear who's fighting whom and which side Bosko's on. The whole point of the film is getting off on the way the cute and round Harman-Ising approach circa 1931 surprisingly suits the horrors of war, the Bosko philosophy, as well as the visual style. Their standard elements, in fact, assume new meaning in this setting: Bosko's ability to make music in any situation becomes intense when he and a pal timestep together in a foxhole bombarded by a rain of bombs. In every Harman or Ising film up through the 30s, characters are always finding uses for objects that are very different from what the objects were intended for (improvising). In this cartoon, you realize these cartoon characters are devising funny and cute li'l ways to kill each other, it becomes morbid humor in the true sense. It almost seems like a parody when inanimate objects mimic the human action of dying.

Whether the best parts of the film's humor are intentional or otherwise, this remains one of the strongest of the Boskos. "Am I Blue" figures on the soundtrack.

YOU DON'T KNOW WHAT YOU'RE DOIN'

Piggy; MM; Oct 21 Animation by Isadore Freleng and Norm Blackburn; Music by Gus Arnheim's Brunswick Recording Orchestra.

Bosko and Honey are reincarnated as Mickey and Minnie-like pigs called Piggy and Fluffy, who go to a vaudeville show (the stuffy doorman outside scoffs at them until their backfiring motorcycle transforms him into a blackface Jolson). The band sounds pretty good to the audience at large (now as then), but Piggy takes umbrage with the musicians, telling them they don't know what they're doing and engaging in a talking instrument conversation with a trombone-toting horse. On stage, it's Piggy's turn to be heckled; three drunks who become a vocal trio take on the assignment. They and Piggy sing the title song back and forth at each other. One wino falls out of his box and onto the stage, and his breath instantly intoxicates Piggy. The two go off drunkenly joy-riding together on a wild surreal binge in which the entire city sways to the music. Streets bob and curve and bounce every which way, cars breathe fire (the "voice" of the car is supplied by Arnheim's vocal trombonist, Orlando Slim Martin), Piggy gives everything the raspberry and vice versa; the entrance to a sewer becomes the mouth of a monster of the mind, and finally the whole thing climaxes when both Piggy and the drunk get picked up by an anthropomorphic pick-up truck, which dumps them in the trash, as they yell "Whoopee!"

The definitive Harman-Ising Warner film: the characters are cute, the humor is gross, the visuals are uninhibited, and the music is red hot.

BOSKO'S SODA FOUNTAIN

Bosko, Honey; Nov 14; LT; Animation by Isadore Freleng and Rollin Hamilton. Music by Frank Marsales
Bosko as a soda jerk is happily constructing ice cream concoctions for his cartoon clientele. Once again, animals who happen to be handy suggest various plots. A little Mickey-type mouse who squeals "Oh boy! Oh boy! Oh boy!" unwittingly finds himself recruited as a surrogate egg beater when Bosko attempts to serve a sundae to his "old school teacher, Miss Pitty" (a grossly fat hippo who gets most of it on her face). A dachshund has the misfortune to devour a row of five-cent sandwiches and becomes an accordion (Bosko plays "Where, Oh Where Has My Little Dog Gone?" on him). Cut to Honey giving a piano lesson to a bratty little cat (identified in another film as "Wilber") who refuses to follow the rules of western tonality until he gets an ice cream cone. Honey orders one from Bosko via phone, who has a tough time biking over and not spilling it. He is rewarded by Wilber screaming "I don't like vanilly!" and blowing it in his face. Bosko then chases Wilber around the house. This is truly a lad after Bosko's heart; he's even crueler than Bosko, kicking him in the face and arranging for him to slide down a bannister with no bannister so all the supports go into his crotch and Bosko

goes flying out the window and into a wash basin, from which he emerges with underwear on his head and a dumb look on his face.

HITTIN' THE TRAIL TO HALLELUJAH LAND

Piggy; Nov 28; MM; Animation by Isadore Freleng and Paul Smith; Music by Frank Marsales.
One of the more event-packed Merrie Melodies, with more plot going for it than the usual boy-girl-villain formula. Piggy is a riverboat captain whose boat is the stage for a band of black musicians and dancers. Piggy picks up his girlfriend, who was driven to the dock by the old reliable servant Uncle Tom. Piggy's dance on the boat rail ends when he falls into the river where he gets knocked about by the paddlewheel and then tangles with a crocodile. Meanwhile, Uncle Tom has problems of his own; he's accidentally bumped into a cemetery ("Holy Mackerel!") where three evil dancing skeletons leave their graves and threaten to send Uncle Tom to hallelujah land. He flees and dives in the river, and starts to drown. While Piggy jumps in to help ("I'll save Uncle Tom!"), a black-hatted villain tries to. get fresh with the girl ("Me proud beauty!"). Piggy catches him on a hook suspended from a crane and for punishment lowers him onto a buzz saw.

BOSKO'S FOX HUNT

Bosko; Dec 12; LT; Animation by Rollin Hamilton and Norm Blackburn.
A pack of dogs followed by animals (and Bosko) on strange horses chase after a happy-go-lucky Mickey Mouse-like fox who prances and merrily trips across the forest, the central thread in this collection of horse-and-hunt gags. Bosko's on a droopy horse whose middle sags under his weight. Bosko, showing his usual selflessness, shoves a log down the horse's throat to prop him up. The fox avoids the pack of dogs and hunters by dodging into a hollow log. When he sees Bosko on his trail he arranges for hero and horse to go splashing into a muddy puddle. The horse walks off, but Bosko is undeterred. A lovable mutt not only

befriends him (it turns out to be Bosko's dog-to-be, Bruno) but points him in the direction of his prey. Producing an enormous rifle out of nowhere, Bosko fires on the fox, as Bruno chases after it. Bruno sniffs the trees in search of the fox but one tree kicks him for fear that Bruno will ... The fox turns the tables on his hunters, biting Bruno in the rear and twisting Bosko's gun so he fires on himself. The fox hides in a dark cave, and Bosko goes in after him, soon coming out with what he thinks is the fox but is really a colossal wild boar with nasty-looking tusks. Now it's Bosko's turn to be chased. It all ends up in another cave. Bosko exits victorious but gets accidentally clubbed on the head by Bruno. Even if Bosko doesn't get the fox at the end, he's made an important new friend.

Background numbers: "Many Happy Returns of the Day" and "(With You On My Mind) I Can't Write the Words."

RED-HEADED BABY

Dec 26; MM; Animation by Rollin Hamilton and Max Maxwell.
The routine of the plot never interferes with the peppiness of the visuals and the music in this midnight-in-a-toyshop opus. You can guess what happens: the toymaker goes to sleep, and all the little characters come to life and go into a production number. Carmen-like, the Red-Headed Baby doll of the title finds love in 32 bars with "Napoleon," the commander of a troop of toy soldiers. A monstrous spider tries to carry her off on a toy train and knocks the stuffing out of a plucky soldier trying to defend her. The soldier inflates himself and arranges for the "Lousy Scoundrel" to get a hot foot—but not on his foot, no sir! Then the Red-Headed Baby and the other toys go into a reprise of the title song, so infectiously hot that even the toymaker wakes up and gets in the act.

The Red-Headed (in black and white no less) Baby comes off like a 30s counterpart to Bette Midler, especially when shaking her thighs wildly ("Snake-hips!" the appreciative Napoleon yells) or in the final number in a trio

backed by two Black dollies. The Boswell Sisters-inspired arrangement they sing, however, is hipper than anything Midler's done. For a couple of toys, these two have a pretty adult relationship.

1932

BOSKO AT THE ZOO

Bosko, Honey; Jan 9; LT; Animation by Isadore Freleng and Larry Martin.
"Won't it be fun, Bosko?" asks Honey as the two are about to enter the zoo. Of course, Bosko is going to have a good time with an entire menagerie of animals to abuse and entertain, but these round, smiling beasts give as good as they get. A vignette in the fish tank (shown from inside, with Bosko and Honey on the outside rendered in squiggly lines to indicate water distortion) sets up the usual parallel of the cute and the crude: cute little fishies playing leap frog and using an obliging octopus for a maypole dance share their tank with a snarling, sharklike fish that growls at both our heroes and the audience. An ostrich then swallows Bosko's derby and he rather roughly forces the big bird to return it by laying an egg that contains the hat. Bosko then cheers up the dejected bird with a little tune on his flute, which sets off a brief musical episode wherein beavers beat their tails in tempo and two little monkeys scratch to the beat. This leads to a gross scene in which the monkeys greedily eat one of the bugs and stab each other with forks, for which Bosko scolds and spanks one of them. An enormous gorilla, presumably a parent, catches Bosko in the middle of thrashing his offspring, and Bosko high-tails it out of there! Running from the ape, everything goes wrong for Bosko. He grabs a snake instead of a vine and falls onto a lion. Soon the lion is chasing after him as well, while the ostrich and a seal get in the act. It ends with the ostrich, the seal, and the lion crashing into a brick wall and emerging from the accident mish-moshed into one bizarre, chimera-like amalgam with three heads.

More sophisticated visuals: the gorilla and the lion moving towards the camera with the background moving in perspective behind them. In the beginning, Bosko and Honey la-la-la "Ta-Ra-Ra-Boom-De-Ay" on a bicycle.

PAGAN MOON
Jan 31; MM; Animation by Rollin Hamilton and Norm Blackburn.
Happy Hawaiians! A ukulele-playing boy (who also scats like Cliff Edwards and Bosko) and a hula girl are our heroes. As they dance and sing the title number, other tropical fauna (a chimp who plays coconut percussion, a little bird who has to go the outhouse) and flora (a femme tree with coconut breasts) get in the act. The boy saves his uke from a hungry croc and then gets the razz from a turtle. When the instrument falls in the lagoon, he dives to the bottom (avoiding the hungry fish from *Bosko at the Zoo*.) To appease an angry octopus, he plays an underwater piano on a shipwreck and is soon surrounded by fish trumpeters, trombonists, and clarinetists, with a spittoon serving as a snare drum. Not only does the octopus like music, he plays piano himself and sings in a basso voice. Then a carnivorous fish comes by, scaring the boy and all his new fish pals away. The boy escapes in a bubble that carries him above the surface and into the air, where his hula girl rides a pelican to his rescue.

BATTLING BOSKO
Bosko, Honey; Feb 6; LT; Animation by Isadore Freleng and Paul Smith.
If there's brutality in Bosko's music (such as his use of animals as instruments), then, all things being equal, there's also music in his brutality. A boxing match between Bosko and the champ, the gorillalike "Gas-House Harry," is as much a musical event as a sporting competition. There is the rhythm of the crowds approaching the stadium and their cheers, Bosko's boasting in song of his macho prowess to both Honey and the crowd at large, his tap dance on the ropes, and an interruption by the referee (an ostrich), which becomes a gay "Dance of the Cuckoos." Honey, seated at her piano, listens nervously to the broadcast, reacting as though she can actually see Bosko being clobbered. When the ref starts to count Bosko out, Honey and her dog run to the arena and manage to make it to Bosko's side while the count is still going (although by that point it's reached 13 instead of ceasing at the customary ten). She implores Bosko to get up and fight, but he declines, wrapping himself up in the canvas as though it were a blanket and yelling, "Ah utsnay!"

Other music: "Turkey In the Straw" and "The Shanty Where Santy Claus Lives."

FREDDY THE FRESHMAN
Feb 20; MM; Animation by Isadore Freleng and Paul Smith.
Another "period" location, the vigorous college atmosphere depicting the Harold Lloyd-ian 20s (Freddy wears genuine "Joe College" glasses). There's not a villain in this one, just a party sequence, with the expected quota of singing and dancing, and a football game. The game is clever, Freddy winning by carefully circumnavigating the various duck ponds and clotheslines covering the field (in the days before astroturf). The musical number is the highlight, with the irresistibly peppy title song being broken down line by

line to be sung by various entities, from four cats who comprise Freddy's "raccoon"-skin coat to a little Mickey-influenced mouse who pops out of a spittoon and sings in falsetto. On campus, a couple of owls cheer about Night School.

Other music includes the Warner's perennial "It Looks to Me Like a Big Night Tonight" and several college cheers, among them Harvard ("Boola, Boola") and Georgia Tech ("A Heck of an Engineer").

BIG-HEARTED BOSKO

Bosko, Bruno; Mar 5; LT; Animation by Isadore Freleng and Rollin Hamilton.
Not three men and a baby, but a man, his dog and a baby. Bosko and Bruno amuse themselves atop a frozen pond, with Bosko doing stunts while Bruno tries (without success) to avoid getting doused in the ice water. The two stumble on a mysterious yowling basket that turns out to contain an orphaned baby. They take it home, and the objective becomes to pacify the lad's caterwauls somehow. Bosko's violin solo, performed as Bruno gently rocks the babe in a cradle (fortunately, Bosko happened to have a cradle), does no good. Bruno accidentally sits on a stove and sets his fanny afire, temporarily turning the orphan's cries into shrieks of laughter. Finally, Bosko resorts to what his fans knew would work all along: he sits down at the piano and breaks into a hot jazz number. Bruno gets in the act by slipping on a lamp shade and making like a shimmy dancer. Bosko then dances about the house, the cartoon ending when he bumps into a goldfish bowl that lands on his head.

CROSBY, COLUMBO AND VALLEE

Mar 19; MM; Animation by Rollin Hamilton and Max Maxwell.
Disappointing in that the title song, though perhaps not a very good song, could certainly have been given better treatment. In a war dance, a tribe of Indian braves complain about the three paleface crooners who get their women all upset. Meanwhile, a little boy brave and his sweetie "Minniehaha," communing with a forest-full of smiling-

and-bouncing animals get off on the new music via a cathedral radio. There also is a babbling brook that sounds like Bing ("Many Happy Returns of the Day") and a bear that does a Rudy Vallee impression ("This Is My Love Song"). Soon all the other Indian kids join in the fun, which is interrupted only when the brave takes a few seconds off to play Smokey the Bear and put out a runaway fire by spitting on it.

Other music: "Pale Moon."

BOSKO'S PARTY

Bosko, Honey; Apr 2; LT; Animation by Isadore Freleng and Larry Martin.
While Honey puts on her makeup and dresses, Bosko and friends prepare a surprise party. She applies her cake mascara (with a little saliva) on her false eyelashes and tastefully dresses behind a transom. Meanwhile, downstairs, funny animal types of all description (but usually round and with pie-cut eyes) scurry about looking for hiding places. Bosko helps an obese swine cram his carcass under the bed (where he discovers a little animal hiding in a chamberpot) by deflating him, and then shoves a flower pot on top of the little cat character (named "Wilber" in *Bosko's Dizzy Date*). They all "duck" before Honey enters the room and then surprise her with a chorus of "Happy Birthday." Bosko presents Honey with her gift, a ukulele, which she uses as backing for a duet on "Sugar" (not the jazz standard but a '31 pop tune with the same name), as the other animals cheer. Unnoticed in their revelry, Little Wilber has been unable to get out from under the flower. When he finally succeeds he goes straight into a mousetrap. Through a Rube Goldberg set of circumstances, the little cat winds up falling into the cake and splashing Bosko with icing.

GOOPY GEER

Apr 16; MM; Animation by Isadore Freleng and Rollin Hamilton; Music by Frank Marsales.
In a crowded nightclub, everyone is asking for Goopy Geer, the star performer. Goopy, a piano-playing dog character, comes on stage and performs the number "I Have Not Studied

Music." He sees three cats eating spaghetti and accompanies them to the tune of "The Sidewalks of New York." Goopy next performs "Tiger Rag" four handed—his two hands and his two gloves!

A waiter orders a bowl of soup, which is prepared by a chicken that swims in a pot. Goopy is joined on stage by a girl singer who croons, "I Need Lovin'." Goopy then does a soft shoe that starts the whole club dancing, including a performance by a pair of coat racks that dance with hats and canes. A horse gets drunk, looks in the mirror, and starts to see horrible images of monsters. The horse begins to spit fire, which destroys Goopy's piano, ending the cartoon.

No story, just music and dance. This was Harman-Ising's way to end the depression blues. The crowd scenes are lifted from *Lady Play Your Mandolin* (1931).

Goopy Geer

BOSKO AND BRUNO

Bosko; Apr 30; LT; Animation by Rollin Hamilton and Paul Smith.
Bosko, whistling a happy tune, and Bruno, messing about with some fleas, are our two heroes, happy-go-lucky tramps walking down the railroad tracks. Will their adventures never cease? First, they have to avoid an oncoming train, with Bruno's leg caught in the track. The dog takes the opportunity to fake Bosko out (as he had previously done in *Big-Hearted Bosko*) and make Bosko think he's been killed. They then wander into a tunnel and are scared witless by train-like noises that they soon learn emanate from a cow. Next, they trespass into a farmyard, allegedly to swipe a

few eggs. This escapade soon escalates into Bruno chasing a chicken riding a lawnmower. Suddenly, the irate farmer comes charging after them with his shotgun. The two get away by leaping onto a box car, which turns out to be the same free-wheeling, no-stopping-it box car that had given Bosko such a hard time in *Box Car Blues* (1930). They hold on for dear life as the car goes tearing around a treacherous mountain pass. Protagonists, train, and a foldable cow crash into a tree and the cartoon abruptly ends.

IT'S GOT ME AGAIN ACADEMY AWARD NOMINEE

May 14; MM; Animation by Isadore Freleng and Thomas McKimson.
Nine years later, an Ising-produced cartoon (Puss Gets the Boots M-G-M) would give birth to Tom and Jerry; this more primitive cat-and-mouse episode has appeal of its own. The mice share Mickey's circular ears and bulbous shoes, but notably they're more interested in making music than in stealing food: instruments, phonographs, and metronomes serve equally as attractions, musical devices for the rodents (a piano serving as a backdrop for an Apache dance, the tune plunked out by the dancers' feet). All have a fine time until a cat appears and breaks up the party. When he corners a rodent it squeaks out the title song, a Jolson singspiel in falsetto. From there on we get the standard bunch-of-little-guys-throwing-stuff-at-the-big guy bit, as the mice use the instruments as implements of cat punishment. Violin bows become bows for arrows, harp strings hurl projectiles, a phonograph and its needles serve as a machine gun and a blow-torch, well, it remains pretty effective in its original function! The cat beats it and the mice cheer.

The mouse chorus line from *Hold Anything* shows up again here.

MOONLIGHT FOR TWO

Goopy Geer; June 11; MM; Animation by Isadore Freleng and Larry Martin.
Square dance shenanigans: hillbillies Goopy and his girlfriend meet, perform a duet, and then head for the local dance. There, they go into a few steps, both the music and the dance deriving

more from Tin Pan Alley than the Ozarks. The point becomes moot as the scene is quickly stolen by, of all things, a pot-bellied stove that becomes the most important character in the flick! The stove dances around, and when the usual last-minute villain finally arrives, the stove saves our hero and heroine by burning the bad guy's behind and breathing fire on him.

BOSKO'S DOG RACE

Bosko; June 25; LT; Animation by Rollin Hamilton and Norm Blackburn.
The opening sequence has Bosko (singing "Are You from Dixie?") frying an egg on a campfire and chasing after a Mickey Mouse-ish squirrel that has made off with the egg. Bosko and Bruno come across a poster advertising a "Whippet Race" with a purse of $5,000, and Bosko declares, "Bruno, you're gonna run in this race and you're gonna win!" Dissolve to Bosko putting Bruno through the paces of "training" (a knife-sharpener rigged up like a belt-vibrating machine), although Honey is skeptical about his chances. Comes the day of the big race, Bruno still isn't up to the competition: he drags his tail and even leaves the track upon spotting the egg-stealing squirrel. The selfsame squirrel, however, tactfully drops a beehive on Bruno's behind, and Bruno runs like the dickens, rampaging through a basket of laundry (the clothes flee the bees) and back onto the track, with a pair of lace panties on his head. "Oh, look at Bruno!" the announcer cries, "He's coming down the field like a streak of lightning!" The bees are still behind him, but after Bruno crosses the finish

line (the force of which temporarily breaks him into a half-dozen mini-Brunos) and wins, they mysteriously disappear. Bosko, Honey, and Bruno pose cutely for the iris out.

More music: "Whistle and Blow Your Blues Away."

THE QUEEN WAS IN THE PARLOR

Goopy Geer; July 9; MM; Animation by Isadore Freleng and Paul Smith.
As with most of the Ising Merrie Melodies, we get some gags based on the locale (a medieval castle with kings and knights), a song, and then the usual boy-saves-girl-from-villain plot. As usual, the "plot" doesn't merit distracting us from the music and the shtick. The first bit involves the unpretentious pig king, who arrives in his castle on the back of a donkey, inquires as to the whereabouts of his missus and is answered by a trio singing the title song. Annoyed by her failure to show up, the king consoles himself with court jester Goopy Geer's entertainment. When Goopy produces a Rudy Vallee-in-a-box, the king comments, "I'd rather hear Amos n' Andy." Goopy obliges with an impression thereof, and this gradually dissolves into an episode wherein Goopy takes on the villainous Black Knight.

BOSKO AT THE BEACH

Bosko; July 23; LT; Animation by Isadore Freleng and Rollin Hamilton; Music by Frank Marsales.
Bosko is selling dancing hot dogs at the beach. An octopus and a group of sea horses dancing on the beach become a seaside merry-go-round. Disaster strikes as Bruno gets a nail stuck in his paw, but Bosko pulls it out. Meanwhile, Honey and Wilber are running along the seashore. Honey stops to sing and play her ukulele, while Wilber attempts to take a dip in the ocean. Bosko sees Honey in her bathing suit and exclaims, "Hot Dog!" Honey gets dressed to be with Bosko; she brings a bra and panties into the changing room, but emerges from the locker braless, topless, and flat-chested—her normal attire!

Bosko and Honey sing, "Ain't We

Got Fun." During the course of the song Bruno interrupts several times. Each time Bosko throws a stick, the dog returns with a larger piece of wood: a branch, a log, and finally a huge tree. Wilber goes into the ocean and is carried off on a wave. Bosko dives to the rescue. Bruno rides out to Bosko and Wilber on a log with an electric fan attached for propulsion. They ride back to shore, a triumphant ending.

I LOVE A PARADE

Aug 6; MM; Animation by Rollin Hamilton and Tom McKimson; Music by Frank Marsales.
Fun and frolics at a circus opening on a quartet of ecstatic onlookers who happily harmonize on Arlen and Harburg's marchlike "I Love a Parade" as they watch the circus parade go by. A tumbling clown appears several times as a sort of visual reference point, though the focus is on the musicians and an unenthusiastic street cleaner who would rather their parade were rained on. The next segment dwells on the acts in the sideshow, which include a savage wild man, "Gumbo, the India Rubber Man," who can transform himself into a tire and jews harp, piggy Siamese twins who do the old joke about one inhaling on a cigar and the other blowing out smoke, a tough, then effeminate tattooed man, an exotic-dancing lady hippo, and the "Skinny man from India," Mahatma Ghandi. Inside, the horse of Mam'selle Fifi the bareback rider (another of those obese lady hippopotomi that Harman and Ising often employ for humor) eventually turns the tables on her while a Honey-like girl cat walks the high wire while singing how she, too, loves a parade. Then, the lion tamer sticks his head in the big cat's mouth, and the lion does the same. The lion then has trouble with some unscratchable fleas, who finally go away when he removes his teeth and puts them on this tail.

BOSKO'S STORE

Bosko; Aug 13; LT; Animation by Isadore Freleng and Bob McKimson.
Shenanigans in a grocery store with Bosko as proprietor: a dachsund eating sliced baloney becomes an accordion, a little mouse with big round ears phones Bosko (by riding around on the dial), asks if the store has dried fish, and then demands, "Well, why don't ya give 'em a drink?" but mainly it's Bosko taking care of business in time to the music. Honey and Little Wilber show up across the street, and she suggests, "Let's make whoopee, Bosko!" But as they execute a unison dance to a player piano version of "How Can You Say No (When All the World Is Saying Yes?)" Wilber proceeds to demolish the store. Bosko tries to stop him, but only gets a banana in his face, his body stuck in a mess of molasses and, in the concluding gag, barbed wire scraped across his torso.

BOSKO THE LUMBERJACK

Bosko, Honey; Sept 3; LT; Animation by Isadore Freleng and Max Maxwell.
First, a succession of animals-chopping-down-trees gags, then Bosko-chopping-down-trees gags, then Bosko having lunch with Honey (the same messy chomps as in *Bosko's Holiday* 1930). Then we then get around to the chase melodrama: Bosko has to rescue Honey from the clutches of a hulking French-Canadian lumberman who's just as brutal as he is big. Thrown backward on to one of those enormous Pearl White-style conveyor belt saws, Bosko nearly gets his backside sliced in two, is knocked down all the rungs of a ladder, and has a treeful of sap shpritzed at him, as the villain carries Honey off in a canoe. He hides in a cabin, and Bosko fires his rifle through the standard stuffed wild game animal head mounted on the wall, to make for a truly bizarre image. Forced to confront the brutal villain, Bosko catches him with a barrel. He gets a kiss from Honey and then looks stunned when a painting falls off the wall onto him, thereby putting his head on Napoleon's body for the closer.
The action sequences have a good sense of momentum and timing. On the soundtrack: "I Wish I Had Wings" and "How Can You Say No (When All the World Is Saying Yes?)."

YOU'RE TOO CARELESS WITH YOUR KISSES

Sept 10; MM; Animation by Rollin Hamilton and Larry Martin.
A domestic comedy about a comic drunkard husband and his plucky wife who has to go out and bring home the bacon when he comes home sloshed at the crack of dawn. Unfortunately, both the musical angle (a dreary waltz whose only distinction is this film) and the boy-girl-villain triangle interfere with a potentially more sophisticated story line. Husband and wife are bees, and the villain is a monstrous spider (who informs the audience, "They tell me I'm crazy, but I'm not ... much!"). The spider chases the girl bee all over his haunted house when she comes in from the rain. Luckily, her ne'er-do-well husband, still in his top hat and spats, hears her shrieks, snaps out of his intoxicated stupor, and rallies all the other insects to her rescue.

The old drinking song "The Bear Went Over the Mountain" serves as theme music.

I WISH I HAD WINGS

Oct 15; MM; Animation by Rollin Hamilton and Paul Smith; Music by Frank Marsales.
Harman and Ising on the farm, where the cock o' the walk crows and then goes about waking up the other birds, including a rack of geese that he soon has doing a goose step as he chants, "Ein! zwei! drei!" As the various farmyard fowl go about their business, a chicken couple takes part in a domestic drama as the hen reveals her egg about to hatch and he fetches the stork. Doc Stork soon delivers a peppy baby boy chick ("Hi pop!") who loses his enthusiasm for living when he realizes how much pushing and shoving he's going to have to do to get at the food, and then, in song, bemoans the fact of his not having wings (yet) to get on the other side of a fence. However, he finds a lady's corset and uses that to flap up to the top of the fence and a pair of panties to parachute down. There's all the peas he can eat on the other side, but immediately a monstrous scarecrow starts chasing him. Using his ingenuity again, he maneuvers the scarecrow to a kerosene lamp and burns its stuffing.

A GREAT BIG BUNCH OF YOU

Nov 12; MM; Animation by Rollin Hamilton and Thomas McKimson; Music by Frank Marsales.
It's junkyard jive, with a wonderful song used as the basis for a swell production number that consists of seven minutes of dancing refuse in a junkyard led by a discarded department store mannequin in 1890's clothes. The mannequin comes to life when the junkman tosses him into the city dump and immediately does a Bosko step and sits down at the piano (using a set of bedsprings in place of the original strings). Other junk gets into the act as he sings (including a pair of shoes that stick their tongues out at each other), and the junk characters applaud wildly when he does impressions of Maurice Chevalier and Ted Lewis. A grandfather clock does a spry dance with the picked-clean skeleton of a chicken in a pot and a sextet of baby clocks, and then a miniature troop of toy soldiers fires their pop guns at discarded bottles and sinks the ship in a painting of Washington crossing the Delaware. The mannequin flies around on a bathmat-cum-magic carpet and leads a mannequin orchestra in "Happy Days Are Here Again," leading into a trio of dressmaker dummy-ettes who go back into "Great Big Bunch of You." One enterprising mannequin improvises a trap drum kit out of garbage while two hat racks do a soft shoe. The main mannequin converts a vacuum cleaner into a set of bagpipes and resumes playing the piano just before a load of rubbish falls on his head. He emerges and asks, "Is everybody happy?"

Who says animation has to have a plot? All it needs is a good tune and pep!

1933

THE SHANTY WHERE SANTY CLAUS LIVES

Jan 7; MM; Animation by Rollin Hamilton and Norm Blackburn; Music by Frank Marsales.
Christmas bells ring as a ragged little street urchin trudges wearily home, unhappily watching other little kiddies celebrating Christmas, feeling all the more dejected when he finds his Christmas stocking empty. He hears the sound of sleigh bells and says, "Santy Claus!" just as jolly old Saint Nick bursts through the door, singing the title song. When they get to the bridge the kid sings, "Oh Boy! I'd like to go with you," and Santy answers, "You've been so good, you'll have that wish come true!" They ride off together in Santy's sleigh to his North Pole workshop where dozens of "living" toys entertain him (and us) with an irresistibly peppy version of the title song, bounced back and forth between a female trio (*Red-Headed Baby*-like dolls) and a hot band, represented visually by a wind-up "Sambo jazz band." For a bit of tension near the end, the Christmas tree catches fire, and all the toys cooperate to put it out, and the kid douses the flames by rigging up bagpipes to a hose.

Harman and Ising are at their best. There are also celebrity caricatures (like a doll who inflates herself into Kate Smith) and a nice juicy rhumba thrown in the middle for a little relief from "Shanty."

RIDE HIM, BOSKO!

Bosko; Jan 16; LT; Animation by Isadore Freleng and Norm Blackburn.
Framed visually by the light of the pale western moon and musically by howling coyotes, our cowboy hero Bosko croons, "While the Bloom is on the Sage." He rides into Red Gulch, a rough, tough town described by an intertitle card as "Where men are men, nine times out of ten." Bosko's friends are so tough they "welcome" him by riddling his hat with bullets. In a comparatively tame saloon (for Red Gulch) Bosko does a soft shoe dance in spurs ("Comin' 'Roun' the Mountain"), while the piano player downs a drink so devastating it reduces him to a simpering sissy. Bosko takes his place at the piano as the others square dance. Meanwhile, the "free wheeling" Deadwood Stage (so named because no axles or spokes are shown), containing Honey as its sole passenger is besieged by a bunch of blood-thirsty bordertown bandits. To make things more harrowing, they chase the coach down a precarious mountain pass. Word gets to Bosko of the attack. Mounting his trusty steed, he's off the save his sweetie. After a few cross cuts between the screaming Honey, the persistent Bosko, and the snarling bandits, the scene pulls back to reveal Bosko on a small TV-sized screen, surrounded by three live animators. "Say! How's Bosko gonna save the girl?" asks one. Says another, "I don't know. Let's go home." And they exit, leaving a thoroughly deflated Bosko on screen.

THREE'S A CROWD

Jan 17; MM; Animation by Rollin Hamilton and Larry Martin.
Warner's first literary variant on the midnight-in-a-toyshop format with historical and fictional characters leaving their books to indulge in music and comedy, applauding one another. Alice (of Wonderland fame) turns on the radio to hear Art Jarrett singing Johnny Green's "Three's a Crowd," his chorus followed by one of the Three Musketeers and Robinson Crusoe's Man Friday, who join forces to become a surrogate set of Mills Brothers. Then Marc Anthony (the Roman, not the bulldog) introduces Emperor Nero, who

fiddles accompaniment to a genuinely sexy dance by none other than Cleopatra, and Uncle Tom offers a mournful "Got the South in My Soul." Next it's time for the villain, in the form of the apelike Mr. Hyde, to make his appearance and then make off with little Alice. The other characters gang up on him, using human-sized desk paraphernalia as weapons: pipes, paper clips, fountain pens, pencil sharpeners. They eventually do the bad guy in and ceremoniously dump his body in the waste basket.

More music: "One Step Ahead of My Shadow."

ONE STEP AHEAD OF MY SHADOW

Feb 4; MM; Animation by Isadore Freleng and Max Maxwell; Music by Frank Marsales.

A first-rate Warren and Dubin song that got pretty much crowded out of *Footlight Parade,* here at last is given the chance to be featured in a full production number. Another location picture, like most of the other Merrie Melodies, this opens with general gags on topical American cultural references placed irrespectfully in an exotic setting (old China, but with American-style traffic cops, outhouse-rickshaws, Toonerville Trolleys, and Amos 'n' Andy impersonators). Our boy hero paddles up to his girl's house on his miniature junk, singing the title song in a mock-Chinese accent. Upon greeting each other they swing it, not musically, but on a real swing in the backyard. Cut to a Mandarin approaching the house on a rickshaw. Although his treatment of people is barbaric (he treats his driver like a horse), his ideas on music are quite modern. Upon hearing a tradi-

tional Chinese band, he decides to show them "'melican way!" As the boy and girl come inside, the Mandarin and band go into a mock-Chinese-cum-hot version of "One Step Ahead of My Shadow," with nonsense syllables that serve both as scat phrases and phoney Chinese talk. Meanwhile, nearby, a captive dragon breaks out of his cage by melting the bars with his fire breath and sneaks up on our party, chasing them all over until the boy gets the wise idea of shoving a box of fireworks in the dragon's mouth, leaving a skeleton that gallops away.

BOSKO'S DIZZY DATE

Bosko, Honey; Feb 6; LT; Animation by Rollin Hamilton and Bob McKimson.

For once, no elaborate settings or occupations, just a sort of slice of life, Bosko style. Honey, getting nowhere with a bratty little kid (identified as "Wilber") to whom she is giving violin lessons, telephones Bosko. On the other end, Bruno answers and, at Honey's request, wakes up Bosko by dragging him out of bed. Honey entreats Bosko to "come on over," and, following a slightly turbulent bike ride, he arrives at her doorstep. They go into one of their famous duets, "(We've Got To) Put that Sun Back in the Sky." They then go off bicycling together, Bosko pedaling and Honey atop the handlebars. They travel through a farmyard, and Bosko laughs hysterically when Honey gets caught on the back of a cow. When a storm besieges them and Bosko gets drenched, it's her turn to laugh at him.

Other music: "Shade of the Old Apple Tree" and "It Ain't Gonna Rain No' Mo'." Gags of note: Bruno getting struck by lightning directly on his butt and Bosko's song climaxing in his nearly getting drowned by a bucketful of soapy washwater hurled at him by the obnoxious Wilber.

BOSKO THE DRAWBACK

Bosko; LT; Animation by Isadore Freleng and Bob McKimson.

There's plenty going on here, the football match itself only a small part. In the beginning, it is the noisy exuberance of the stadium before a big game, spectators noisily crowding in, the marching band and cheerleaders getting everybody in that rah-rah spirit. Inside, Bosko, the football hero, receives a killer rub-down. Bosko leads the team onto the field and the referee fires the gun (or rather fires out an egg that contains a bird who blows a whistle) and the game begins. The game action serves only as a centerpiece for other activity: cheering fans in the bleachers, a nervous sportswriter who pounds his typewriter so hard it finally punches back. When the writers can't think of good visual football gags (how many players does it take to tackle each separate section of a centipede?), they resort to puns that will appeal to sports trivia fans. Eventually, they cut to a running gag about an eagle who sits atop a flagpole and hatches the tip.

Music: "This Is the Missus," "One Step Ahead of My Shadow."

YOUNG AND HEALTHY

Mar 4; MM; Animation by Rollin Hamilton and Larry Martin; Music by Frank Marsales.
In 18th-century France, fat King Louis is bored to tears with the doddering old fogies who comprise his court ("balls, parties, and picnics, bah!"). A Jimmy Durante-in-a-box provides his only amusement. When the Durante doodad dies ("Am I mortified!"), the king walks dejectedly to his balcony and finds what he's looking for, a group of ecstatic little kiddies frolicking joyfully in the royal yard. "Oh, boy! Oh, boy! Oh, boy!" He slides down a bannister and joins them, being thoroughly delighted with their playful pranks. All go into the *42nd Street* number, and then he gives them the run of the palace to romp and play in, getting a big kick out of their terrorizing the old hag-queen. Finally, they accidentally knock him down the main steps, and he rolls into the pond in front, squirting water and fish out of his mouth.

In addition to chorus after chorus of "Young and Healthy," you also hear "Let's Put Out the Lights and Go to Sleep," sung by the King, and "Am I Blue?"

BOSKO THE SPEED KING

Bosko, Honey; Mar 22; LT; Animation by Isadore Freleng and Paul Smith.
If you were told there was a Bosko cartoon with an auto race theme, you could easily imagine this one almost gag for gag. That doesn't make it any less exciting a cartoon. Bosko finds himself in an auto race, his principal competition being an especially vile cur who takes cruel delight in scarring the polished finish on Bosko's car. Many of the gags are at least original, even if they're not side-splittingly funny, the best being Bosko's "tuning up" of his car as if it were an instrument and his transformation of a cat into a jack to hold his car up when he changes tires. We also get a trio of offbeat "fourth wheel" substitutions: one car hobbling on a crutch where the fourth wheel ought to be, another (piggy) driver using a roll of salamis in place of the tire, and the next carrying the fourth wheel along in a wheelbarrow. The villain knocks nearly every car off the road with a well-tossed box of tacks, but Bosko's car cleverly bites the villain's vehicle on the behind and zooms ahead to victory!

All draped in Harman and Ising's increasingly sophisticated visual style, the cartoon gives us the onslaught of the automobiles from all sorts of interesting angles. The villain is even smarmier than usual, so one takes particular pleasure in his downfall. Music: "Meow."

BOSKO'S WOODLAND DAZE

Bosko; Mar 22; LT; Animation by Isadore Freleng and Paul Smith.
A plotless romp in the forest with Bosko and Bruno. Bruno gets too turned on by certain trees, and Bosko still gets vines and other nasty things dragged across his bottom. There is a Rip Van Winkle-like dream in which gnomes fete him with bubbles rather than booze and a trio of semi-realistic femme fairies harmonize. Bosko lands on a giant piano and performs a vigorous ragtime solo by waving his hands and feet all about and swimming across the keyboard. All at once, a gruesome giant appears and chases Bosko across

the floor of a cave, catches him, and shoves him between two giant slices of bread, dousing him with mustard. Bosko wakes up just in time to grin broadly into the camera for the iris out.

BOSKO IN DUTCH

Bosko, Honey; Mar 22; LT; Animation by Isadore Freleng and Thomas McKimson.

The setting dictates the narrative: a duplistic effort, cramming in as many Dutch cliches as possible and, at the same time, offering a full supply of the usual Bosko (albeit doused in Hollandaise sauce). The central scene takes place in a windmill instead of the customary cottage, and Bosko and Honey's tap dance is replaced by a wooden-shoed clog dance, while their duet is something called "When It's Tulip Time in Holland." This sequence is preceded by an opener with lots of animals-on-ice gags (another little baby duckling who has to go to the outhouse, which is, naturally, a miniature windmill), followed by an episode in which Bosko rescues two little ice-skating cats that have fallen in a river. For the record, there are no gags concerning Dutch cleanser, Dutch doors, Dutch uncles, Dutch elm disease, my old Dutch or Dutch Reagan. It's up to the viewer to determine if this effort ranks as a Dutch treat or a Dutch cheese.

Goopy Geer makes an unbilled guest appearance, ice-dancing to his theme song. Title music: "Ach Du Lieber Augustine."

THE ORGAN GRINDER

Apr 8; MM; Animation by Rollin Hamilton and Tom McKimson; Music by Frank Marsales.

Foreign locales are not the only ones subject to ribbing: here are parodied local American ethnicities, mostly Italian-Americans. The Italian organ grinder and his monkey slowly stroll down the street, entertaining the nice people and passing the cup as they go. First, the grinder charms two middle-aged housewives who interrupt their washes to sing a refrain or so of the title song. When neighborhood kids crowd around the organ man for cheap thrills, the monkey gets hot with some more

modern entertainment, shaking his "little can" (both the real and the tin one) in a dance that also involves doing impressions of Harpo Marx, and Laurel and Hardy and playing two pianos at once. This is followed with a one-man-band performance of "42nd Street" and ends with a nonmusical interlude that becomes musical again, as the monkey gets stuck in a car that goes out of control, crashing into an Italian's fruit wagon and a Chinese man delivering laundry. Then it lands in a music store, and the monkey and the organ drive out with the car having been transformed into a sort of mobile mechanical orchestra.

BOSKO IN PERSON

Bosko, Honey; Apr 10; LT; Animation by Rollin Hamilton and Bob McKimson.

No plot, no setting, no costumes, just Bosko and Honey on stage doing their vaudeville act. It's quite an act, opening with Bosko at the piano playing his theme, "Whistle and Blow Your Blues Away." Honey enters, and the two duet on "Hello, Baby," first as a vocal with Harry Barris-like scat interjections galore, then as a precision tap dance. Next, in an Eddie Cantor up tempo number, Bosko defines his relationship with Honey ("I Love Her and She Loves Me/And Everything's Okay, You See?"). Back at the piano, Bosko demonstrates some tricks that would shame even Chico Marx as he rolls off his glove and goes into a Senor Wences-type act, the glove bashfully reciting "Mary Had a Little Lamb" via a squeaky violin for a voice. More comedy: Bosko trying to execute a particularly difficult shuffle step and landing on his backside. Time for a few quick impressions: Honey, in a sheer, transparent gown, does Aunt Jemima (Tess Gardella) asking the musical question, "Was That the Human Thing to Do?" and Greta Garbo in oversize shoes. Bosko next sticks out his lower lip to do a Chevalier impression (singing, "Whistle and Blow Your Blues Away") and affixes a balloon to his nose to mimic Jimmy Durante ("I know I'm not good-lookin', folks, but what's my opinion against a million?"). Is there no end to his talents? He grabs a trumpet and plays a hot solo on "Sweet Georgia Brown," leaps around the stage in a feat of acrobatic skill, plays a drum solo with his feet while standing on his hands, swims across the floor while simultaneously playing chimes and the whole percussion kit, makes like Ted Lewis in a clarinet solo, buck-and-wings into a kettle drum (Honey, meanwhile, undulates her body and her tonsils and dances in front of strobe lighting). For a conclusion a bass drum with the image of President Roosevelt holding a stein of beer to celebrate the end of prohibition exits the stage as Honey waves the flag.

WAKE UP THE GYPSY IN ME

May 13; MM; Animation by Isadore Freleng and Larry Silverman; Music by Frank Marsales.
Although Harman studied Pudhovkin, he and Ising probably never realized how well the Merrie Melodies format suited Russia as a potential background. It's easy to perceive the little guys who gang up on the villain as true Soviet mass-heroes! But that's getting ahead of our story. First, the Russian peasants make merry and do Cossack dances over what is basically 1933-style American hot-pop (one of the musicians uses a herring for a balilika pick). A Paul Whiteman caricature leads a few Ruskies in "Rhapsody in Blue." The quartet that sings the title number feels no need for even a minor bow to authenticity, their number being joined by a little gypsy gal, tambourine in hand. Meanwhile, cut to some antics by funny anarchists instead of funny animals, an assassin who tries to sneak up on Rice-Pudin' the Mad Monk, who (in addition to playing with a jigsaw puzzle and cheating) in turn has one of his Cossack cronies capture our heroine. Just as he corners her, he finds that the peasants are revolting (!), and with their hammers and sickles, they oust the Mad Monk from his palace and run him out of town, shoving a bomb in his pants for good measure. The force of the explosion turns him into a Ghandi caricature.

BOSKO'S KNIGHT-MARE

Bosko; June 8; LT; Animation by Bob McKimson and Robert Stokes.
Bosko dozes off reading a book of medieval lore and dreams of being a knight in King Arthur's day, although his fantasy includes too much '30 cartoon shtick to convince us that Bosko is completely committed. Atop his steed in a suit of armor he gives out with "Young and Healthy" (his voice in this one being more tenor than falsetto) and does a rhumba ("Peanut Vendor") without having to remove his armor. Arriving at the castle, he greets his fellow Knights of the Round Table—you know, Groucho, Harpo, Chico, Zeppo, Ed Wynn, Jimmy Durante, Mahatma Ghandi, Oliver Hardy (Bosko obliges with a Stan Laurel impression and a few Cab Calloway slogans). After a few obligatory stanzas of some chivalrous, stately-sounding "Knights Were Bold," Bosko goes into a tap dance to "42nd Street" accompanied by various suits of armor, both inhabited and otherwise! Cut to the evil Black Knight trying to get friendly with the damsel-about-to-be-in-distress Honey. She resists ("Poo! I don't like that old meanie!"), but the villain comes after her, so she yells for help. Bosko comes running (authentic olde-English dialogue: "Stop! You mug!") but the bad guy makes off with her. Bosko follows them to the Black Knight's, there showering the no-good-nik with bullets from a convenient machine gun, but all to no avail. About to be pummelled senseless by his foe, Bosko awakens from his dream. Still dizzy, he smashes his own suit of armor, sings "Let's Put Out the Lights and Go to Sleep," and jumps in bed (clothes and all), which retracts into the wall, revealing a chamberpot underneath.

I LIKE MOUNTAIN MUSIC

June 13; MM; Animation by Isadore Freleng and Larry Martin; Music by Frank Marsales.
This follow-up variant to *Three's a Crowd*, the original books-come-to-life cartoon, has magazine covers (midnight in a magazine rack) replacing literary characters, and villains and famous fictional characters initiating the every-

body-gang-up-on-the-bad-guy theme. Cowboys from a western mag (including one with gay guns and another who rides a concertina like a bronco) do the title number, interrupted by gags from Eddie Cantor and Will Rogers. A relatively realistic ice ballerina skates on a mirror for ice and talcum powder for snow, followed by Hawaiians who dance and sing, "It's Time to Sing 'Sweet Adeline' Again," while a svelte coed in a diaphanous dress from the cover of "College Rumor" flirts with a Swiss yodeler from the cover of "Travel." When they get around to the robbery and chase bit, a bunch of fugitives from the cover of "Crime Stories" loots the cash register, pursued by Sherlock Holmes and Watson. Then comes the worst impression of Edward G. Robinson ever heard. After that, it's everybody: squad cars from "Police Gazette," fascist troops under the command of Mussolini, and, lastly, the giant ape "Ping Pong" from "Screen Play," who makes short work of the bad guys, trapping one under the soda fountain and relentlessly squirting razz-berries at him.

BOSKO THE SHEEP-HERDER
Bosko; June 14; LT; Animation by Rollin Hamilton and Max Maxwell.
Here's a promising premise: Bosko minding a flock of sheep and unable to suppress his urge to use them as musical instruments. A few minutes are used with a little lamb chasing after and devouring a couple of insects (the second is a grasshopper that chews tobacco and uses a flower for a spittoon). Bosko and the lamb frolic. Unafraid of the consequences, he converts a

beehive into a bagpipe, and they have lunch, reusing the sandwich sequence from *Bosko's Holiday*. A wolf stalks the flock. Donning a convenient piece of sheep's clothing, the wolf infiltrates the flock and makes off with a lamb. Bosko and Bruno rally to the rescue, chasing the wolf into a cave. Off-screen a tremendous fight ensues, and Bosko comes out carrying the sheep and leaving us to wonder how Bruno will make out against the wolf. When the figure of the wolf emerges, Bosko thinks the worst has happened. But it turns out to be Bruno wearing the skin, once more faking Bosko out. Ending: both Bruno and the lamb lovingly licking Bosko's face.

Background music includes the ever-popular "I Like Mountain Music."

BEAU BOSKO
Bosko; July 1; LT; Animation by Rollin Hamilton and Norm Blackburn.
Death to the infidels! This is Harman and Ising's most serious adventure cartoon at Warner's, possibly the only one with no singing, dancing, or impressions, a well-balanced mixture of adventure and comedic elements in a Foreign Legion setting. We open with a funny series of "reveille" gags: the gnarly-looking troops greet their sergeant with an effeminate chorus of "Good Morning to You," Bosko's uniform having to wake him up when he doesn't hear the bugle. In formation, Legionnaire Bosko opens the backpack of the soldier in front of him as it contains a faucet and sink for him to wash in. The commandant orders Bosko to apprehend the Desert Scourge, Ali Oop. Bosko mounts his camel and rides into a nearby city. After a bit of local color (they can't resist having a snake indulge in a scat break), Bosko encounters Honey in see-through harem-girl garb just in time for Ali Oop and his band of cut-throats to attack the town. A shoot-out follows, and, though the bullets seem real enough, there's more dropping ceramic jugs on people than bloodshed. Finally, Bosko catches Ali Oop by throwing spears around him that become an ad-hoc cage. We end with Bosko, Honey, and camel carrying off their prisoner.

SHUFFLE OFF TO BUFFALO

July 8; MM; Animation by Isadore Freleng and Paul Smith; Music by Frank Marsales.

Here's a novel setting: Heaven, although never strictly named as such, the place where babies come from. An Old Man (who could be Father Time) processes the requests for children that come from couples around the world. When Mr. and Mrs. Nanook order a pair of twins, our Old Man retrieves a couple of baby Eskimos from the refrigerator and gives them to the stork (in an upper and lower "birth" instead of berth) to carry to the North Pole. The next request, written in Hebrew, is passed along to the stock room. Back comes a little baby with curly black hair and big nose (would you believe "Abie Baby"?) on whose diapers he stamps "Kosher for Passover." Together, Old Goy and Baby duet on the title number (from *42nd Street*). Moving into the nursery proper, they're joined by a whole choir of inkblot babies, including a pint-sized Chevalier. Then we see the baby factory in action, with an assembly line operated by bearded gnomes washing, drying, powdering, and diapering the babies. In the nursery one gnome tries to appease the yowling brats who demand, "We want [Eddie] Cantor!" They get Cantor (doing his *Palmy Days* razz), and the musical antics including Ed Wynn, "The Gold Dust Twins" and a final hot chorus of "Shuffle" by a gnome jazz band for the ecstatic toddlers.

WE'RE IN THE MONEY

Aug 26; MM; Animation by Isadore Freleng and Larry Martin; Music by Frank Marsales.

At midnight, the old nightwatchman turns off the lights in the department store and leaves. When he's gone, all the toys come to life, run to the music department, and play, "We're in the Money." There's lots of merriment here: toy soldiers pump air into a trumpet to play it; a beaded doll does a xylophone solo; socks jump rope using shoestrings. Even the store cash register opens, and the heads on the coins sing, "We are the money."

A mannequin rolls around the store, accompanying himself with a trio of mirror images. The dummy then plays every piano in the store, spins around, and finally knocks himself out as he crashes into a shelf, and dozens of hat boxes fall on him.

BUDDY'S DAY OUT

Sept 9; LT; Supervision by Tom Palmer; Animation by Bill Mason; Musical Supervision by Norman Spencer and Bernard Brown.

Opening title cards introduce Buddy, our hero; Cookie, his girl; Elmer, the baby; Happy, his dog (credited as "Buddy's Pal"). Warner's first cartoon without Harman and Ising is a typically crude cartoon of the early '30s. Basic plot: Buddy, Cookie, and friends go on a picnic.

Cookie is washing the naked little Elmer; Buddy is washing his car. Cookie shouts, "Yoo-hoo Buddy, I'm ready!" Buddy's car goes in reverse, smashing though a greenhouse and covering the car with flowers, which delights Cookie. They travel to the country and set up their picnic. Buddy asks Cookie, "Wugee, Wugee, Wugee?" (which must mean "Wanna neck?"); Cookie replies, "No Wugee, Wugee, Wugee! The birds, bees, and frogs are having the same luck. Baby Elmer teases pet Happy and gets food all over himself. Elmer gets into car and accidentally starts it going. Buddy and Cookie chase after it in a baby carriage. The car goes out of control and lands on a railroad track headed straight for an oncoming train. The baby carriage gains wings after crashing into a house, and Buddy flies it to the scene. Using a ladder as spare train track, he veers the locomotive into a barn. Rejoining Elmer, Buddy asks, "Wugee, Wugee, Wugee?" The baby squirts him with milk! End title: Buddy says, "That's all, Folks!" arising from behind a fence with the "Looney Tunes" logo on it.

BOSKO THE MUSKETEER

Bosko, Honey; Sept 16; LT; Animation

by Rollin Hamilton and Robert Stokes.
Bosko is a song-and-dance man who
flashes back to the France of Alexander
Dumas's time. He duels with about four
opponents at once, then heads for the
local pub to join his buddies, "The
Three Musketeers" (so identified by an
intertitle), Porthos, Amos, and Andy.
Though the Musketeers hold swords,
they're good for little more than scat
singing and quaffing the ale that Bosko
pours into their mouths (actually, one
drinks it, the second licks his lips, and
the third burps). When Bosko has to
defend Honey from the usual villain,
his pals are nowhere to be found. The
fight itself is a highlight: the plume on
Bosko's hat is revealed to be part of a
live chicken. When the bad guy breaks
his sword, he yells for the caddie to
come in and replace it, and Bosko fixes
his sword point in a pencil sharpener.
Bosko finally does him in by hurling
hot coals into the seat of his pants. In
the wind-up, Bosko and Honey flash
forward to the present, and when
Honey doesn't believe any of this story,
Bosko responds, "Was you dere,
Charlie?"

When Honey cleans the house at the
beginning, she dusts off her goldfish
and does an impression of Mae West
("You can be had!"). In the pub she
introduces herself with "Here I am, you
lucky people!" her dance looking as if
it were lifted from *Bosko in Person*.

BOSKO'S PICTURE SHOW

*Bosko; Sept 18; LT; Animation by
Isadore Freleng and Max Maxwell.*
Bosko is a combination organist/emcee
for a program of shorts and a feature at
a movie house. First, he leads the audience in a sing-a-long to "The Goldig-
ger's Song" (from *Goldiggers of 1933*)
with the lyrics on screen to follow
along. The program begins with the
"Out-of-Tone News (Sees All—Hears
All—Smells All)," a pretty lame bunch
of blackout gags, one being a dog race
scene taken from *Bosko's Dog Race* in
which the Marx brothers appear as dog
catchers, and one intertitle that
announces "Famous Screen Lover on
European vacation," before cutting to a
hysterical shot of Jimmy Durante being

chased by an ax-toting Adolf Hitler.

This is only the beginning, Bosko
tells us. Next up is a short comedy,
"Haurel & Lardy in 'Spite of Everything,'" wherein the title is better than
either the gag or the caricatures.
Finally, we get the feature presentation,
"T-N-T Pictures Present 'He Done Her
Dirt (And How!)." Apparently, a gay
90s melodrama, with audience participation. For the first part we keep cutting to Bosko's reaction to the
characters and events. Honey rides
along on a bicycle, accompanied by the
Marx Brothers (again!) as a chorus of
admirers sings "Bicycle Built for Two,"
unknowingly followed by the cur, Dirty
Dalton (described by Bosko as "The
dirty fox"). The villain runs off with
the girl, shouting, "Aha! me proud
beauty!" as he takes her on top of a
train. She cries for help, and Bosko
responds, "I'll save you!" He leaps into
the screen, and when we expect to have
him enter the action a la Buster Keaton
and *Sherlock Junior,* he tears right
through the screen itself, which produces the desired effect of stopping the
bad guy.

I'VE GOT TO SING A TORCH SONG

*Sept 23; MM; Supervision by Tom
Palmer; Animation by Jack King; Music
by Bernard Brown and Norman Spencer.*
A gently-satirical paean to the most
effective means of world communica-
tion: commercial radio programming.
Hands all over the world turn on their
radios first thing in the morning, from
all walks of life; even such world leaders as Shaw (George Bernard, not
Artie) and Mussolini do their exercises
in time to it. Chinese police tune it in
and tune it out, African cannibals getting ready to dine upon Wheeler and
Woolsey listen to it for recipes, Arctic
whales swim happily to the beat, and
Arab sheiks prefer the antics of Amos
n' Andy to their scantily-clad harem
girls. Movie stars also need the radio.
Jimmy Cagney and Joan Blondell push
each other around a la *Blonde Crazy*,
Ben Bernie and "Cros Bingsby" croon
"Why Can't This Night Go On Forever?" A gang join forces for the title

Gold Diggers of 1933 ballad: the Boswell Sisters (closer visually than vocally), Garbo (for once they lay off her pedal extremities), Zasu Pitts, and Mae West all sing a torch song. Only the ending falls flat, Ed Wynn getting blown through a roof and landing in a bed containing his Wynn-like wife and kiddies.

THE DISH RAN AWAY WITH THE SPOON

Sept 24; MM; Animation by Rollin Hamilton and Bob McKimson; Music by Frank Marsales.

Here the cast consists of chinaware and cutlery. We open on the happy little plates and silverware swimming and bathing in the sink, washing the soap off in meat grinders, using seltzer as showers, and drying themselves in a waffle iron and a toaster. A bushy duster uses a case of knives as a piano; ceramic salt, pepper, and sugar shakers sing in a trio, Mister Spoon proposes to Miss Dish in song (using "Shuffle Off to Buffalo"). When she accepts, he expresses his rapture by playing a percussion solo on a row of baking tins as a chorus line of tea cups dances, and a bottle of bluing, joined by a potato with tears in all of his eyes, sings "Am I Blue." If that isn't enough, an egg falls and breaks, releasing a newborn chick, which sings, "Young and Healthy." Revelry is interrupted by a doughy behemoth who consumes yeast to make him grow and tries to make off with the dishy heroine. Then it's the usual collective heroism, lots of little guys ganging up on the big bad guy. In this case, dishes throw other dishes at the monster, graters grate at him, other utensils hurl popcorn missiles and flatten him with a rolling pin. Eventually, he falls into an electric fan that chops him up and distributes the dough into tins for baking cookies and cakes. All the kitchen characters cheer as Mister Spoon takes a bow.

BOSKO'S MECHANICAL MAN

Bosko; Sept 27; LT; Animation by Isadore Freleng and Thomas McKimson.

This was Warner's entry in the cycle of '30s robo-toons, following on the heels of Fleischer's *The Robot* (1932), Iwerk's *Techno-Cracked,* (1933) and Disney's *Mickey's Mechanical Man* (1933). There was also a sub-cycle of robot cow cartoons, including Lantz's *Mechanical Cow* (1932) and Clampett's *Porky's Poppa* (1938).

"Oh, Bosko, you fulfill my wishes," Honey tells Bosko, "You're just in time to do the dishes!" They wash and dry the chinaware (Honey trying to sing "Ain't We Got Fun" but forgetting the words). Bosko winds up dropping and breaking the entire lot. Undaunted, he stumbles across a newspaper that headlines, "Robot Will Do Work of Hundred Men Say Technocrats," which gives him the idea of building a mechanical man out of pipe and a pot-bellied stove, powered by an automobile engine. Unlike most other cartoon Frankensteins, this one doesn't even wait for something to happen before it goes on a berserk rampage. Bosko and Honey are occasionally able to pacify the monster through musical means. At one point, Honey turns it gay by spraying it with perfume, causing it to exclaim "Oh swish!" do a little spring dance with a roll of toilet paper. Soon it's chasing Bosko and Honey all over the place. Honey inserts a phonograph and record of "Mary Had a Little Lamb" into its hollow torso, which works until the record skips! It chases Bosko and Honey out of the house and down the street, finding time to electrocute Bruno on the way. Bosko finally stops the monster by hurling a load of explosives into its open mouth.

The final Harman-Ising film for Warner's, this was certainly a respectable showing, with enough good gags and spirit to make up for trend-following unoriginality. A peppy sound track contains "One Step Ahead of My Shadow," "From Me to You," "I Like Mountain Music," "Let's Put Out the Lights and Go to Sleep."

BUDDY'S BEER GARDEN

Buddy; Nov 11; LT; Supervision by Earl Duvall; Animation by Jack King and Tish Tash; Music by Norman Spencer.

What better way to celebrate the end of Prohibition than with your favorite cartoon character adopting a German accent and passing out huge steins of beer to customers, with a dachshund serving pretzels? While a tough customer downs one glass after another, the evening's entertainment includes a German band playing oom-pah music and a trio harmonizing "It's Time to Sing 'Sweet Adeline' Again." The customers play with their food. After the tough guy tries to get fresh with cigarette girl Cookie, she goes into her act, a red-hot rhumba done in a diaphanous skirt that reveals her legs, inspiring the place's piano to get up and dance as well. Finally, we get the concluding act, a Mae West impressionist singing, "My Good Time Slow Time Baseball Man (He's Game for Anything That You Can Plan)," who is revealed, in the final shot, to be none other than our hero in elaborate drag.

Buddy is not only Warner's greatest pre-Bugs Bunny authority on cross-dressing, in this particular film he's the closest thing the '30s have to Pee-Wee Herman.

BUDDY'S SHOW BOAT

Buddy; Dec 9; LT; Supervision by Earl Duvall; Animation by Jack King and James Pabian; Music by Bernard Brown.

Buddy's the happy-go-lucky captain of a musical riverboat, swaying down the stream as four minstrels sing a swing version of "Swanee River." After landing at the harbor, Buddy leads a group of animals in a marching band through town to announce the riverboat entertainment.

The minstrels perform "Sweet Georgia Brown" as customers rush in to see the show. Cookie perfumes herself in the dressing room, throwing a kiss at a poster of her man, "The Famous Capt. Buddy." One of the deckhands has a crush on Cookie, and he sits in his bunk, perfumes himself, blowing a kiss at the poster of "Mlle. Cookie, the Showboat Star." Buddy calls Cookie and kisses her through the phone wires. When the deckhand tries the same thing, the phone slaps him.

At showtime, Buddy and Cookie perform "Under My Umbrella," and do a soft-shoe routine while a chorus line of scantily clad dancers high kicks. Buddy then presents the next act, Chief Saucer-Lip, a Zulu native, who imitates Maurice Chavalier. The deckhand kidnaps Cookie and fights with Buddy. Buddy knocks the villain into the seal cage and the sea lion tosses the rowdy into the ship's hold. Buddy hoists him on a hook and places him over the riverboat paddle, giving him the spanking he deserves.

SITTIN' ON A BACKYARD FENCE

Dec 16; MM; Supervision by Earl Duvall; Animation by Jack King and Don Williams; Music by Norman Spencer.

Late at night, everything, is snoring including the alarm clock, the phone, and teeth in a glass. A female house cat sings "Am I Blue?" to a tomcat on the backyard fence and joins him for a midnight stroll. On the billboards, Bull Dernem tobacco sings the title song to the contented cows of Ternation Milk. Long johns perform a high wire act, while the cats play music using junkyard items.

A scavenger cat with an eye-patch asks to dance with the girl, making her new boyfriend jealous. He hurls a brick at One-eye, and that starts a chase all over the city. A great moving background shot occurs when the two cats, attached by a rolling pin, ride the telephone wires. They land in the doghouse, the dog knocks them out. The girl struts past her suitors with a new boyfriend and kittens.

On end title, girl cat says, "So long, folks," with a particularly grotesque mouth movement.

1934

BUDDY THE GOB

Buddy; Jan 13; LT; Supervision by

Isadore Freleng; Animation by Jack King and Ben Clopton; Music by Norman Spencer.
Buddy's first adventure film rates as the most successful in the series; Freleng is enough of a showman to keep music and comedy integral elements. A U.S. Navy battleship docks in China, and Buddy the Gob goes ashore. He gets a gander at the quaint Oriental customs, then takes in a Chinese New Year-style parade. Though it includes American elements (Western brass instruments, a drum major and mask-images of Dressler and Durante) it has what filmmakers thought was a distinctly Chinese center attraction: "A beautiful girl will be sacrificed to the (sacred) dragon."

Buddy follows the girl to the temple where the sacrifice is scheduled to take place. Just as the dragon comes after her, Buddy and girl escape through a window and get away in a rickshaw, an angry crowd coming after them. They elude the mob by crossing a chasm and cutting the ropes of the bridge behind them.

Most of the music is, appropriately, "Shanghai Lil."

PETTIN' IN THE PARK

Jan 27; MM; Supervision by Bernard Brown; Animation by Jack King and Bob Clampett; Music by Norman Spencer.
A plotless series of musical gags set in the city park in the spring. Two lovebirds neck, two woodpeckers peck a heart in a tree, and a policeman steals a kiss from a nursemaid as birds sing the title tune.

The nurse slaps the policeman and takes her charge to the sidewalk, where she promptly joins man listening to the title song on his car radio. The policeman follows, but is slapped again, and the car with the nurse and child drives off.

Meanwhile, the birds hold their Annual Water Carnival, in which all the park fowl compete in a water race. Pelicans, geese, and ducks are among the entrants, but the competition is won by a penguin in a bathtub.

HONEYMOON HOTEL

Feb 17; MM; Supervision by Earl Duvall; Animation by Jack King and Frank Tipper; Music by Bernard Brown; Processed by Cinecolor, Inc.
A trio of bug bill-posters on a scaffold invite us to Bugtown in song (new lyrics to the verse of "Honeymoon Hotel," painted on the wall as they sing). "We will show you insects that are living/ just the same as me and you." As they sing we watch mini-scenes of Bugtown life, including a "Little Alimony Dodger/in the Bugtown county jail." "And Bugville even has a park ..." Here we focus on a bug couple who canoe (in a peapod) into the blue lake (accompanied with "By a Waterfall") where an embrace fades into a wedding, and the newlyweds go off in their "Merry Oldsmobile" to the "Honeymoon Hotel," which receives so many requests for Bridal Suites the registration desk has a rubber stamp with the names "Mr. & Mrs. Smith." Once in their room, their love-making (to the tune of "You're Getting To Be a Habit with Me") is constantly interrupted by a nosy house dick and a chorus of maids and bellhops. Even the Moon sticks his face in, singing, "Ah, the Moon is Here ... I can see everything that you do." Their amorous activities raise the temperature so much that the Bugville Fire Department has to extinguish the burning building. Our couple tries to escape the waterlike flame, and jumps in a Murphy bed. After an explosion reduces the hotel to rubble, they merely leap back in, showing a winking picture of a big buggy baby (not a baby buggy) on its underside.

BUDDY AND TOWSER

Buddy; Feb 24; LT; Supervision by Isadore Freleng; Animation by Jack King and Bob McKimson; Music by Norman Spencer.

"Here Towser," Buddy tells his round white dog, "Keep your eye on those chickens tonight." While the fowl attempt to sleep (and do the last of the little-chick-called-by-nature gags) their henhouse is invaded by a hungry fox. They shoo him out by heaving their eggs at him (unhatched off-spring!), and then Towser, still attached to his doghouse chases the fox around the yard, the noise waking up Buddy who runs out in his hunting garb. They chase the fox through the woods, accidentally disturbing a bear who soon becomes three angry bears. Buddy and Towser cleverly zip them up in a cave. The two chase the fox through a tree (Towser accidentally blasted on his doggy bottom) and up a snow-covered hill, where he starts to roll backward, forming a huge snowball. Rolling down the hill, it gets bigger and bigger and swoops up our two heroes, who, trying to hit the escaping fox, club each other upon dizzily stumbling out.

On the soundtrack, John Green's "There's a Ring Around the Moon."

BEAUTY AND THE BEAST

Apr 14; MM; Supervision by Isadore Freleng; Animation by Jack King and Rollin Hamilton: Music by Norman Spencer; Words and Music by Kalmar and Ruby; Processed by Cinecolor, Inc.

"It's time little girls were asleep," the Sandman tells our heroine, a blonde Buddy-in-drag, as he douses her in gravel. As she dozes she levitates into the fairyland scene on her wallpaper, finding a storyville castle that beckons her inside. There, dozens of nursery rhyme characters (or rather the same six repeated several times) cheer her, and a trio of gnomes sing, "Welcome, Little Girl," warning her to "be careful of the big bad Beast." After watching a marching exhibition by the *Red-Headed Baby* toy soldiers, she becomes attached to their leader and kisses him. Humpty Dumpty finds this so hilarious he tumbles off his wall and smashes

into a half-dozen toy skating ducks. Together, the soldier and the girl (still in her pajamas) stroll into Fairytale Land, famous for its big books. They open the volume "Beauty and the Beast" and duet on the song. The book comes to life, and the Beast leaps off its picture on the page and attacks the girl. It's up to the toy soldier to save her, but his toy airplane gives the Beast only a punk haircut, and the cannon whimpers like a dog and puts out its fuse. Just as the Beast is throttling her, the girl wakes up and jumps under the covers, sticking out her little bare bottom under the iris out.

BUDDY'S GARAGE

Buddy; Apr 14; LT; Supervision by Earl Duvall; Animation by Jack King and Sandy Walker; Music by Bernard Brown.

In most of the '30s cycle of gas station toons (*At Your Service* (Lantz, 1935, with Oswald), *Mickey's Service Station* (Disney, 1935), *So Does An Automobile* (Fleischer, 1939, with Betty Boop), the starring characters function less as mechanics than as doctors or shrinks for the humanized autos. This one runs out of garage jokes early on, and rather than flog a dead horse (although Buddy would no doubt try that), the point of the picture switches entirely to a chase, after a burly criminal enters the joint and makes off with Cookie (still a brunette at this point). Buddy tails them in the station's tow truck, not caring how many houses he demolishes (in one, his towing device latches onto the bed of a couple of elderly people and drags them out into the street). He finally uses the tow to extract Cookie from the villain's car and then removes the villain as well, sticking him in the back of the truck, where his punishment is to breathe the exhaust.

Buddy whistles "Woodenhead Puddin' Head Jones" and plays "By a Waterfall" on a row of tempered files. "California, Here I Come" also turns up as a background to the chase.

THOSE WERE WONDERFUL DAYS

Apr 26; MM; Supervision by Bernard Brown; Animation by Paul Smith and Don Williams; Music by Norman Spencer; Black & White.
The opening number establishes the premise: "Those were wonderful days," an affectionate enough description of the gay '90s, with each line punctuated by a bell-ringing expectoration into a convenient cuspidor. Throughout this largely nonnarrative gallery of bygone images, nostalgia and satire undercut and support each other. The music, whether danced to by a chorus of Keystone Kops ("Put On Your Old Gray Bonnet") or la-la-la'ed by a line of talking mugs, supplies the connecting link. Along the way they put down or glorify such outdated fashion items as bustles and Victorian bathing suits. For the second half they serve up a spoof on a '90s mellerdramer in which a mustachioed, top-hatted villain tosses TNT under the seesawing hero (a muscular boy, interchangeable with the Fleischer's Fearless Fred in *No, No, A Thousand Times No* or Terry's Strongheart in *The Banker's Daughter*) and makes off with our full-figured heroine in a balloon. The good guys win only by abusing the law of gravity, reserving one little twist ending for the iris out.

Goodies but oldies: "Oh, You Beautiful Doll" and "In the Shade of the Old Apple Tree."

BUDDY'S TROLLEY TROUBLES

Buddy; May 5; LT; Supervision by Isadore Freleng; Drawn by Ben Clopton and Frank Tipper; Music by Norman Spencer.
In this amplification of 1931's *Smile, Darn Ya, Smile!*, Buddy has replaced Foxy as the engineer on the trolley line, joyfully picking up his passengers (including a human version of Foxy's obese hippo dame) and giving them a little song and dance amid singing advertisements. His favorite customer, needless to say, is Cookie, whom he picks up from her fourth-story flat via a hydraulic lift (or the '30s Rube Goldbergian equivalent to hydraulics) that raises his entire car. Unfortunately, it also causes a traffic jam that gets Buddy in dutch with a tough copper, see? As the car leaves the city, Buddy and Cookie run into the same old meanie who gave them such a hard time in *Buddy's Beer Garden* and *Buddy's Garage*. Here he is playing an escaped convict. Again he makes off with the vehicle and Cookie, Buddy following close behind in a hand car. Buddy, clever fellow, eventually manages to swing on the trolley and off againwith Cookie, sending the bad guy straight for a truckload of dynamite that happens to be resting on the tracks. Buddy loses his trolley but saves Cookie and captures the convict.

Background music includes "Why do I Dream Those Dreams" and "Woodenhead Puddin' Head Jones."

GOIN' TO HEAVEN ON A MULE

May 19; MM; Supervision by Isadore Freleng; Animation by Rollin Hamilton and Bob McKimson; Music by Norman Spencer. B&W
Black people are picking cotton in the Deep South. Gags here include a fellow using a lawnmower to pitch cotton into bales and cotton being put into a machine that manufactures 100 percent wool suits. A lazy boy sleeping near a stable awakens to drink some gin. His "angel" conscience warns him against it, his "devil" approves. They fight while the boy drinks and dreams of "Goin' to Heaven on a Mule." In "Pair O'Dice" he can do whatever he wants. In the swinging heavenly nightclub, the Milkyway Cafe, he eats a huge watermelon!

Other heavenly gags: a "Buller Brush" man knocks on the pearly gates and has the door shut on him; angels play halos like xylophones. When our boy drinks gin from a tree of "Forbidden Fruit," he is taken to the "Chute to Hades." He wakes up from his dream and throws away his bottle—then gives it a second thought a second later and races around the house to catch it!

BUDDY OF THE APES

Buddy; May 26; LT; Supervision by Ben Hardaway; Animation by Paul Smith and Sandy Walker; Music by Bernard Brown.

Buddy stars as a slick-haired, smiling Tarzan in a film that presents the idea that jungle animals, here quite "civilized," are preferable to natives, who walk around nearly naked (one reads a paper called *The Nudist News*) and attack Buddy and his pals for cannibalistic purposes. The animals retaliate in cartoon-like fashion: an elephant turns himself into a machine gun, a gloved kangaroo uses one of the natives as a punching bag, a hippo becomes a cannon. Finally, the tribal king is humiliated by getting porcupine quills in his rear and is then beaten up by Buddy.

The cartoon is appealingly drawn and animated, with Buddy *almost* having a personality, but even *Coal Black* and *Tin Pan Alley Cats*, with their more overt, deliberate use of racial stereotypes, are easier to take. The first of three Buddys involving black caricatures, the others being *Buddy's Circus* (1934) and *Buddy in Africa* (1935). Theme music: "My Old Man," a song closely associated with Leo Watson and the Spirits of Rhythm.

HOW DO I KNOW IT'S SUNDAY

June 9; MM; Supervision by Isadore Freleng; Animation by Frank Tipper and Don Williams; Music by Bernard Brown. B&W

Extending the words-come-to-life tradition beyond books (*Three's a Crowd*) and magazines (*I Like Mountain Music*), this takes in the merchandise at a general store, mainly vegetables (an onion and multi-eyed potato sing the title song) and the familiar labels and boxes of nationally-known consumer goods. Tamales and a Mexicali lobster rhumba (a piece of footage you'll be seeing again and again), Old Dutch cleanser ladies clog dance in their wooden shoes, two Morton salt girls with umbrellas sing "By a Waterfall" and are joined by two Uneeda biscuit boys in raincoats for a double duet on "How Do I Know It's Sunday." On top of this the "real story" starts: a bunch of carnivorous flies come in the window and threaten to break up the romance of a cookie girl and an Eskimo Pie boy. Soon it's a battle between flies armed with bows and arrows (converted safety pins) and matchstick torches (the Planters' peanut douses the flames with seltzer). The package insignia characters glob syrup onto the flies and then fire popcorn on the mess, turning it into a popcorn ball (which goes on sale with other popcorn balls). The Eskimo boy catches the remaining flies in a bottle.

A magical cartoon. And a good song helps.

BUDDY'S BEARCATS

Buddy; June 23; LT; Supervision by Jack King; Animation by Ben Clopton; Music by Norman Spencer.

Generally speaking, the baseball episodes of any '30s cartoon series are the weaker entries, but this manages to stay lively. First are nervy gate crashers and clever stadium vendors in a pre-game sequence. We remain distracted with musical routines (the ref introducing both teams, the Battling Bruisers and Buddy's Bearcats in 2/4 time) until there's enough suspense to let the game take over by itself. As the star hitter, Buddy scores the first hit for his team by sliding into the plate with a roller skate foresightedly fixed to his back. As pitcher, his screwball (preset with a corkscrew) is all but unhittable. However, in the last half of the ninth with the score tied, Buddy is too nervous and sheepish to go on until he gets the proper encouragement from Cookie. He even comes through, winning the game amid a rain of hats tossed by his admiring audience.

Joe E. Brown is caricatured, vocally and visually, as the announcer. The most repeated theme: "Is My Baby Out for No Good?"

WHY DO I DREAM THESE DREAMS?

June 30; MM; Supervision by Isadore Freleng; Animation by Rollin Hamilton and Robert McKimson; Music by Norman Spencer. B&W

Rip Van Winkle and his dog are thrown out of their home by Mrs. Winkle (the dog returns to razz the missus). Rip leaves town singing, "Nothing Worries Me," followed by admiring children, to the county line. Rip stops by a lake to fish, putting his bait in a mousetrap at the end of his line. He then takes his fateful nap.

While Rip sleeps, the "little men" sing and dance their theme song, a variation of the title tune "If You Will Dream These Dreams." They find Rip and explore his belongings, accidentally shooting off his gun and waking him. The men run off and hide, but Rip finds their kegs and takes a sip. He shrinks to tiny size and his dog chases him off a cliff into a spider web. As the spider is about to attack, Rip wakes up from his nap. He is now an old man. His dog joins him—followed by a litter of puppies!

THE GIRL AT THE IRONING BOARD

Aug 23; MM; Supervision by Isadore Freleng; Animation by Frank Tipper and Sandy Walker; Music by Bernard Brown. B&W

An underwear-comes-to-life cartoon. This film begins with a behind-the-scenes look at the laundry women singing the title tune while washing and ironing. We see the "Button Breaking Department" while the NRA eagle comes to life and blows the whistle for everyone to go home.

That night, a nice man and woman drop off their laundry in the chute. Their underclothes come to life and sing and dance to a sold-out crowd of clothes. The long johns skate, using irons as feet, and then do a soft shoe. A "villain" drops off his laundry, and immediately his underwear kidnaps the "girl" and escapes riding a galloping ironing board. The "hero" underwear catches the crook and throws him in the washer for a happy, and clean, ending!

For the end title, a long john marches out, and a human head pops out of the neck to say, "That's all, Folks!"

THE MILLER'S DAUGHTER

Oct 13; MM; Supervision by Isadore Freleng; Animation by Rollin Hamilton and Charles M. Jones; Music by Norman Spencer. B&W

Two statues (a boy and a girl) sit atop a table in a living room. A cat enters the room and tries to jump on the birdcage, but falls on the table, breaking the girl statue. The lady of the house puts the broken statue in the attic. The boy statue, a shepherd, comes to life and, with his sheep statue, walks up to the attic and repairs the girl statue with glue. All the stuff in the attic comes to life to sing and dance. A "See No Evil, Speak No Evil, Hear No Evil" trio, take-offs of the Three Stooges, sings the title tune. Girl figures on a lamp shade do a chorus line; cocktail shakers shake a mean conga; the boy statue leads the clock chimes in a concert of "The Blue Danube," and a silhouette picture of a couple comes to life and (in rotoscope) dances a waltz. The sheep statue says hi to a lion statue, which comes to life and chases him. The boy statue uses a Cupid statue's arrow as a weapon, which causes the lion to smash against the attic door. The boy and girl slide down the bannister and return to the table, accidentally knocking over a potted plant. The lady of the house blames the cat for the damage.

SHAKE YOUR POWDER PUFF

Oct 17; MM; Supervision by Isadore Freleng; Animation by Bob McKimson and Bob Clampett; Music by Bernard Brown. B&W

Onstage and offstage antics at your

local funny animal vaudeville theater, the overture being an all-animal orchestra playing "Zampa" (including two little mice dancing on a xylophone and one bandsman who apparently does nothing but gargle and spit). The main act is a trio of female rabbits of rather loose morals who do a number ("Shake Your Powder Puff") about picking up sailors played by three Donald-esque ducks. Next two hick goats come out and do a close-unison clog dance, with stiff legs and no arm movement at all. Then, as a trio of obese pigs reprise "Powder Puff," the show's only interruption is caused by a drunk dog in the audience, who, after being thrown out for heckling, sneaks up to the roof and douses the whole crowd in pepper. When he falls on the stage they stone him with vegetables.

The return of the drunk dog from *You Don't Know What You're Doin'* emphasizes Freleng's lack of interest in this Harman-Ising plotless "stage" musical, in contrast to the infectious spirit he garners for his "own" genre, package labels come to life (as in *How Do I Know It's Sunday?*)

BUDDY THE DETECTIVE
Buddy; Oct 17; LT; Supervision by Jack King; Animation by Paul Smith and Don Williams; Music by Bernard Brown.
Neither Buddy nor Cookie gets much attention here, for the real star is the villain, the bearded, Svengali-like "Mad Musician." He has a greater gift for hypnotism than for music. His madness is not liking jazz, preferring instead a heavy-handed performance of "Moonlight Sonata." Desiring inspiration, he hypnotizes Cookie, courtesy Ma Bell ("Come to me, my little Cookie!") and summons her over to his haunted house. Cookie's dog is on the case and summons Buddy, who arms himself with magnifying glass and deerstalker cap. Buddy braves the terrors of the skeletons and spooks, and, upon finding the bad guy, wrestles him to the ground. He and Cookie then force the fiend to listen to her hot music.

Rich in atmosphere (good spooky stuff) and some original gags (a portable door of the sort Avery would use in *Little Rural Riding Hood*,) you can't help feeling someof this effort should have gone into developing a worthier character for the lead.

BUDDY THE WOODSMAN
Buddy, Cookie; Oct 20; LT; Supervision by Jack King; Animation by Paul Smith and Don Williams; Music by Bernard Brown.
You want lumberjack gags? We got lumberjack gags! Lazy lumberjacks who can slice trees in half even as they sleep, effeminate lumberjacks who chop down wimpy trees, Jewish lumberjacks who slice wood as if it were salami, and Buddy, the manager of the place, displaying his usual concern for the feelings of others when he chops down a tree containing a cute little family of birds at its top and when he goads a goat into unwittingly trisecting a couple of logs for him. Buddy is provided with a a Chinese cook who serves the hungry singing woodsmen spaghetti. The smell of the food entices a bear in the camphouse, and he breaks up the meal, Cookie being the first to try shooing it. The bear gets a piece of pipe stuck on his snout, which Buddy fills with powder. The result: bear runs around sneezing all over everything while the undaunted Cookie fires on him, until Buddy ejects the beast with a hydraulic piano stool.

"I'll String Along With You" is heard as a soundtrack instrumental, "The Bear Went Over the Mountain" is sung two times.

BUDDY'S CIRCUS

Buddy; Nov 8; LT; Supervision by Jack King; Animation by Bob McKimson and Ben Clopton; Music by Norman Spencer.
At Buddy's circus, most of the freak-show attractions are African natives exploited in cruel ways and described as "Ubangis." Although it includes a black fire eater and a pliable India-rubber man, the highlight of his show is the acrobat finale. However, a little baby somehow gets caught up in the aerial action, and before long both the baby's gawky mother and Buddy are climbing the ropes trailing after the baby who is, in turn, following the acrobats, until they eventually find the lad in the mouth of a hippo. For those of you Bosko fans still into animal abuse for musical purposes, Buddy performs on an xylophone that consists of the tusks of a row of elephants, a device that is bannered as "20 Tons of Tunes."

One black caricature with enormous lips, described by the racially tolerant Buddy as a "Ubangi Phone," plays a record of "Why Do I Dream Those Dreams?" in his mouth.

THOSE BEAUTIFUL DAMES

Nov 10; MM; Supervision by Isadore Freleng; Animation by Paul Smith and Charles Jones; Musical Score by Bernard Brown. 2/C
One of Warren & Dubin's most adult numbers is perverted into the most juvenile of premises, a poor little orphan wearily trudging home through snow to the squalor she lives in. Bereft of food and heat, she dozes off, and the place is invaded by dozens of little toy dolls and animals who paint and redecorate, put in wallpaper, rugs, and furniture. When she wakes up, the seedy shack has been transformed into a charming little cottage, and the toys throw a big party for her. They treat her and us to two choruses of "Dames," the first by three dolls who've rewritten the lyrics to describe dolls (the toy kind, not the Damon Runyon kind) instead of dames, danced by a wind-up minstrel "Jazzbow" dancer. The second comes from a phonograph decorated by dancing bears who have to repeat the

same step over and over when the record skips. For the finale, all the little toys throw her a grand banquet and booby-trap her ice cream with a jack-in-the-box.

A sex-change rehash of *The Shanty Where Santy Claus Lives,* except that they make no mention of either Christmas or Santa Claus.

POP GOES YOUR HEART

Dec 8; MM; Supervision by Isadore Freleng; Animation by Frank Tipper and Sandy Walker; Music by Norman Spencer. 2/C
The song, from *Happiness Ahead* (1934), emphasizes the cyclical nature of romance; the cartoon dwells on the cyclical seasons of nature. When spring comes to the woods, would-be naturalistic forest animals go about their business: turtles teach their young to swim, grasshoppers show their offspring how to spit, spiders play the plug tune on web-harps, as worms in apples form the limbs of a humanoid figure (the apples being the torso) and dance. The song is sung by a trio of tenor frogs, while a fish-eating swan is, in turn, eaten by a fish, a worm turns the tables on a hungry little bird, and beavers play tennis with tails. A bully bear attempts to attack the beavers (after being spooked by a growling turtle). Acting as a team, the beavers douse him in honey and a hive of bees attacks him. Running from them, he rolls through a field of hay, which sticks to him, and gets loaded into a confused farmer's hay-baling machine in the end.

VIVA BUDDY

Buddy; Dec 12; LT; Supervision by Jack King; Animation by Frank Tipper and Ben Clopton; Music by Norman Spencer.

Singing "Monterey," Buddy, the Mexican troubadour, heads to the Cantina Del Moocher in time to awaken the sleeping and snoring locals from their siesta. Upon opening their eyes, they immediately go into a musical number that seems deliberately concocted to sound like a bunch of gringos making like Mexicans ("We sing-a and play all day long-a/and-a we hope-a you like-a our song-a"). The villain/revolutionary/bandito (Wallace Beery caricatured as Pancho Villa) and his gang ride into town, shooting everybody and everything in sight and laughing hysterically. Our heavy carries on the same activity in the cantina, keeping his good humor even when Buddy retaliates to being shot at by squeezing a banana into his kisser. Pancho has Buddy play the piano for him while a senorita (not specifically identified as Cookie) dances. When the big lug makes a pass at her, Buddy fights back by shooting him with an arrowlike fork and plugging up his six-shooters. The fight continues with Pancho using his whip to bring Buddy to him, spinning him around, not considering that Buddy would grab onto a lighting fixture, generating enough force to crash the two into a table. Arising from the wreckage, the Beery character says, and I quote, "I was only foolin', Buddy."

1935

MR. AND MRS. IS THE NAME

Jan 19; MM; Supervision by Isadore Freleng; Animation by Ben Clopton and Cal Dalton; Music by Bernard Brown. 2/C

"On an island/far away/mermaids and fishes are at play," sings a trio of topless

mermaids on the ruins of a shipwreck in the South Seas. The classic Merrie Melody unities of song-then-story, with a reprise somewhere in the second half, are still relevant. After more undersea antics, including some Latinate clams and the same old rhumba-dancing lobster who must be in a half-dozen Merrie Melodies, we cut to a little mermaid boy (Buddy with fins) and girl (less mature than the well-endowed beauties in the opening). Playing tag, they investigate the shipwreck and try out the various items in its treasure chest, among them a cane and bowler that allow the lad to become an amphibious Chaplin and jewelry that the girl uses to make like Mae West. Finding a piano that functions underwater, the girl bangs out another chorus of the Warren & Dubin "Flirtation Walk" number, as skull and crossbones dance and a Harpo Marx lobster sings in baritone. The girl then gets abducted by a monstrous blobby octopus. The boy follows with the aid of a motorized propeller. He goes at the beast with a pointed stick jabbed at its soft underside and finally traps it in a section of pipe.

RHYTHM IN THE BOW

Feb. 1; MM; Supervision by Ben Hardaway; Animation by Rollin Hamilton and Ben Clopton; Musical Score by Norman Spencer. B&W

Hobos riding box-cars provide the initial laughs. A tramp rides atop the train, honking at traffic with a goose. Under the train, a vagrant sharpens his knife on the train's wheels, cuts a bun, and serves himself a hot dog heated by friction. Inside the train, a hobo washes daintily from a pail, pulls out his violin, and plays the title tune while the other tramps join in song.

The conductor throws the violin player off the train, but the happy-go-lucky fellow dusts himself off and whistles "Arkansas Traveler" as he walks down the road. The hobo meets a dog and plays the violin for him. He teases the dog and locks him in a yard, then visits a hobo camp to rest his feet. The tramps there join him in a reprise of the title song.

The dog breaks free, chases the violin player to the railroad tracks, and gets caught on the train trestle. The hobo saves the dog at the last moment, and they dive into the water below as the train passes. They become best friends.

THE COUNTRY BOY

Feb 9; MM; Supervision by Isadore Freleng; Animation by Bob McKimson and Paul Smith; Musical Score by Norman Spencer. 2/C

Even before the titles are over, the chorus of insipid feminine voices behind the credits tells us that this is going to be a cute little bunny-wunny cartoon. The nose-blowing joke in the first scene and the sardonic quality of the singing in the main musical number reveal that their hearts can't deliver cuteness without spiking the punch a bit. Mommy Rabbit sends her little bunnies to school, taking special care to warn her most mischievous lad, Peter Rabbit, to stay out of trouble. A lot of good it does. He heads straight under the farmer's fence, but three other little rabbits (each, male and female, with a particularly cloying Bernice Hansen voice) catch and stop him with the warning song, "Naughty Boy" (they pronounce it "new-tee boy"). Instead of going to school, he makes himself a veritable banquet in the farmer's vegetable patch. In uprooting a row of radishes, he accidentally dumps a cow in a well. The farmer hears the commotion and chases after Peter. The rabbit makes his escape on the farmer's lawnmower, demolishing the poor man's flower garden and much of his crops. Peter's come-uppance seems rather mild: the mower charges through a hen-house, leaving the rabbit covered with feathers.

BUDDY'S ADVENTURES

Buddy, Cookie; Mar 5; LT; Supervision by Ben Hardaway; Animation by Bob McKimson and Don Williams; Music by Bernard Brown.

Buddy and Cookie set sail in a hot-air balloon. Cookie is frightened as lightning strikes and winds punch them around, making them both dizzy. A rattle-snake cloud with a lightning tongue bursts their balloon. They crash in a strange land and are chased by a giant bird into Sour Town ("No Laughing, No Singing, No Dancing, No Jazz Music, Absolutely No Merriment or Happiness of Any Kind!"). Inside, they see that Laurel and Hardy are in a stockade for laughing and smiling. At the Pessimists' Club, the members drink vinegar and sing "Life Is Just a Bowl of Lemons." Buddy defies the law and picks up a guitar to sing a cheerful skat song. A policeman puts Buddy under arrest, and he is brought to King Sourpuss (who squeezes lemons on his head). Buddy and Cookie are sentenced to a spanking machine, but Buddy pulls out his harmonica, and Cookie gives out with some fancy hoofing. Soon everyone is feeling bouncy, and in the finale, even the king is swinging: "It's got me, pal!"

BUDDY THE DENTIST

Buddy; Mar 5; LT; Supervision by Ben Hardaway; Animation by Rollin Hamilton and Jack King; Music by Norman Spencer.

Of all the recurring themes of '30s short-subject comedy, tooth-extraction has to be the least funny. (Actually, its very unfunniness is what made it so funny in the Fleishers' 1934 *Ha! Ha! Ha!*.) Buddy's dog Bozo gets a painful toothache (one of those with a little devil hammering on his root canal). Buddy looks for homespun ways to yank out the aching bicuspid. He tries giving the dog gas from the wall, which succeeds only in inflating him like a doggy blimp. Finally, Buddy resorts to what they all get around to sooner or later: tying one end of a piece of string to the ailing tooth and the other to something else, usually a doorknob. Here, Buddy shows Bozo

that it doesn't hurt by affixing the other end to one of his own teeth; immediately Bozo spots a cat and gives chase, dragging Buddy all over town. They end up, coincidentally, at Cookie's house, where they all crash into her hammock. The chase over, Buddy holds up the dog's extracted tooth, but then Cookie points out that Buddy's tooth has been removed as well. They all laugh hysterically at the end.

I HAVEN'T GOT A HAT

Porky Pig and Beans; Mar 9; MM; Supervision by Isadore Freleng; Animation by Rollin Hamilton and Jack King; Music by Bernard Brown. 2/C
The characters are introduced as in a Warner Bros. feature: Miss Cud, the school teacher (a cow); Beans, a mischievous little cat; Porky, a stuttering pig; Oliver Owl, a snooty little egghead; Ham and Ex, two troublesome pups. The occasion is a school musicale, emceed by Miss Cud. It opens with Porky Pig's recitation of "The Midnight Ride of Paul Revere," read in a rather unpleasant high-speed stutter, illustrated with props, dramatic gestures, and sound effects (and modulating into "Charge of the Light Brigade"). Next, it's another poem from a cute li'l tyke with a funny voice, "Little Kitty" (Bernice Hanson), doing "Mary Had a Little Lamb." As she gets more and more nervous, she starts forgetting her lines (the teacher tries to give her a hint by tossing snowlike corn flakes in the air, but she misses the point and describes the lamb as having fleece as "white as corn flakes") and talks faster and faster, fidgeting like she has to go to the bathroom. No matter, it's the next "act" that we paid our two-bits to see: Ham and Ex, those cutesy twin puppies, who sing "I Haven't Got a Hat" in a harmonized falsetto, but with one doing basso treble interjections, amusingly scatted ("bo bo bo bo!"). Then we're back to the rest of the cartoon. "We have with us today a very competent musician, Master Oliver Owl." He and Beans have already started sneering back and forth at each other. After being introduced, Owl plays an elementary exerciselike

tune. Beans, from outside the window shows him up in front of the class, depositing a cat and dog in the keyboard. All of a sudden, the piano starts playing the fingerbustingly-difficult "Overture to Zampa." The class and parents can't see what's happening, so Oliver is quick to take a bow for the performance, until the animals come out, at which point everyone boos. Beans laughs hysterically, so Oliver squirts him with green fountain pen ink. Beans falls back on a bouncing bench that hurls both Beans and a can of red paint into the schoolroom. Covered in red and green, the two grin sheepishly and shake hands in front of the kids.

Still looking for a star, the studio here tries out a gang of kiddie characters; and who could have guessed that the one given the least attention (the pig in the opening act, in fact) would be the one to make it?

BUDDY'S PONY EXPRESS

Buddy; Mar 9; LT; Supervision by Ben Hardaway; Animation by Ben Clopton and Cal Dalton; Music by Bernard Brown.
In one of those lawless western towns where life is cheap and cartoons ain't human (and undertakers need only walk into the streets to find their customers) news of a pony express race is posted, with the grand prize to be a mail contract. Buddy makes the mistake of bragging that his horse is the fastest in the county within earshot of his rival. The villain switches horses on Buddy, taking Buddy's mount and giving him a glue-factory reject that he inflates and paints open eye pupils on

its closed lids. Even with his bum steed Buddy takes the lead until the bad guy uses more dirty tricks. Riding over a mountain pass, the meanie shakes the wood-and-rope bridge just as Buddy is on it. Buddy gets out of it by transforming the whole thing into a treadmill and rolling forward, but he crashes off a cliff and hangs at its side. The bad guy hurls a rock down at him. Fortunately, it bounces off a branch and returns to knock its thrower off the cliff. Buddy, the bad guy, and their horses fall into a lake. The bad guy gets ahead with the faster horse, but it starts to rain, and a lightning bolt to the posterior of Buddy's tired nag gives it the energy and inspiration to win.

The race stuff works, but Cookie and Buddy's musical number at the beginning ("Oklahoma Cowboy Joe," sung by Bernice Hanson) falls flat. Other participants in the race include a dogsled and a man with a broken leg.

BUDDY'S THEATRE

Buddy; Apr 1; LT; Supervision by Ben Hardaway; Animation by Don Williams and Sandy Walker; Music by Norman Spencer.
Not quite Buddy's remake of *Bosko's Picture Show,* since Buddy manages the theater and runs the projector while Bosko only plays the organ and acts as emcee. Buddy gags include a baby who swallows a roll of tickets and is recruited as a human ticket dispenser and carrying a precarious stack of film cans up to the booth. As in the Bosko flick, we get a newsreel parody, "The Passe News," with the most interesting gag referring to a fascist Italian dictator "Mausoleum" (and, like the Bosko epic, the fact of the gag is funnier than the gag itself).

Next, we get a load of trailers in which the gags are, for a change, funny. "James Bagknee in Here Comes the Gravy," "15 Features! Come Spend a Quiet Weekend With Us!" and *Eight Girls in a Boat* with *The Thin Man.* The main plot stars Cookie, already established as a movie star and the object of Buddy's affection. When the dear girl is assaulted by a gorilla, Buddy, again with Sherlock control, changes the

scenery into a back alley via the projector and then apprehends the gorilla in a set of long underwear hanging on the line. It ends with the hero sticking his head through the screen.

BUDDY OF THE LEGION

Buddy; Apr 4; LT; Supervision by Ben Hardaway; Musical Score, Bernard Brown; Animation by Bob Clampett and Charles Jones.
Buddy, working in a bookstore, daydreams while reading that he is a French Foreign Legionnaire marching with his troops across African desert sands. They don't know it, but nearby lurks a fortress full of burly, mother-in-law like Amazons, who lure soldiers into their clutches with a hypnotized hotcha dancing girl. Circe-like, she makes them take leave of their senses, and once captured, the big tough dames force their hapless prisoners to do their domestic bidding. Buddy is never quite subdued, however, and fights back against the role-reversalists, as the other other captives cheer, "Vive La France!" We'll never know how he makes out, though; before the story has concluded, Buddy is awakened and fired by his Amazonian lady boss.

This is the most original plot of Warner's toons-and-sand legionnaire epics (everybody made at least one), though not the best as a cartoon. Having Clampett and Jones working behind Hardaway reminds one of *Forty-Second Street* with Ginger Rogers in the chorus and Ruby Keeler the "star."

ALONG FLIRTATION WALK

Apr 6; MM; Supervision by Isadore Freleng; Animation by Bob McKimson and Paul Smith; Musical Score by Norman. 2/C
A college setting with a football theme and humanlike chicken students. It opens at a dance on the night before the big game, with couples dancing to a funny animal band and then listening to a glee club duck quartet harmonizing on the title number (from the Powell-Keeler flick *Flirtation Walk,* released by Warner's in December '34). The "camera" pans across the campus to show us a romantic fowl couple

spooning on a park bench. Comes the big game, and it's Plymouth Rock College versus Rhode Island Red University. The concept of athletic competition has been translated into chicken terms all too literally. Instead of a football game, these cheering crowds have crammed the stadium to witness an egg-laying contest! Apart from the minor distinction, the rest of the standards of college sports flicks (as defined by Harold Lloyd's *The Freshman*) have been preserved: the home team doing badly in the first half (the opposition, we learn, cheats by consuming billiard balls beforehand), the enthusiastic pep talk by the coach at half-time, and the eager young benchwarmer, pleading with the coach to be sent in until given his (her?) chance in the final 15 seconds and winning the game. In the last shot, he (she) is carried off as a hero (heroine) by a worshipping crowd.

More music: "Fare Thee Well, Annabelle" from *Sweet Music* (released by Warner in February '35).

MY GREEN FEDORA

May 4; MM; Supervision by Isadore Freleng; Animation by Chuck Jones and Robert Clampett; Music by Bernard Brown. 2/C
A good-try adventure cartoon made memorable by its opening musical sequence in which a boy rabbit tries to silence his yowling baby brother, Elmer, by donning a baggy old coat and green-plaid hat and singing, "I'm wearin' my green fedora/fer Dora." It works better on the audience than on the kid, who continues his bawling and

obnoxious Joe Penner laughing impressions. The boy rabbit disgruntedly leaves the house. This gives a fiendish weasel the chance to make off with the baby rabbit by burrowing through the ground right through their floorboards. When the big brother remembers that he promised Mother he'd watch the brat, he returns home to find Elmer missing, then stumbles into one of the weasel's tunnels. A long chase follows in which the boy rabbit chases the weasel (carrying Elmer in a sack) through tunnel after tunnel, the rabbit getting outfoxed until the weasel detours him up to the surface. Elmer uses a garden hose to fill up the tunnels with water, and both baby brother and weasel come floating out, the weasel landing in a cactus patch.

The tunnel bit almost becomes monotonous, but there's a sense of real terror in a snarling tight close-up of the weasel (Freleng pulled off the same thing with the cat in *Billboard Frolics*) and in a shot of the weasel holding the little baby bunny in a frying pan directly over the flames!

BUDDY'S LOST WORLD

Buddy; May 18; LT; Supervision by Jack King; Animation by Rollin Hamilton and Sandy Walker; Music by Norman Spencer.
Lots of activity around the fringes occasionally compensate for the lack of anything remarkable in the center (i.e., a memorable character), as Buddy and his dog Bozo travel off on a motorized raft in search of the "Lost World." They discover an uncharted island inhabited by prehistoric monsters and primitive white people.
Buddy and Bozo become separated. Buddy is swallowed by a giant carnivorous plant whose entrails lead to an underground city of cavemen (Spencer plays "Lullabye of Broadway," as if to demonstrate that Stalling wasn't the only musical director with a sense of humor). The cavemen play a strange form of croquet. Bozo finds that people here covet and bury bones just as dogs do back home. Finally, Buddy finds

Bozo, but he's the bait in a trap set for them by Three Stooges-like cavemen. The tribe drops our hero in a pot of boiling water, but he is rescued by a brontosaurus. It ends with both dino and doggie licking Buddy's face.

INTO YOUR DANCE

June 8; MM; Supervision by Isadore Freleng; Animation by Cal Dalton and Ben Clopton; Music by Norman Spencer.
The locals cheer over the arrival of the Showboat, piloted by the popular Captain Benny. As they buy tickets and go aboard, a minstrel quartet sings "Go Into Your Dance" (with blackface in honor of the song's originator, Al Jolson). Captain Benny introduces their conductor, the world's most popular orchestra leader, a pig version of Paul Whiteman, popular with neither the audience, which greets him by throwing tomatoes, nor his musicians, one of whom affixes an electric socket on his tail (for no discernable reason) so that he conducts at super-fast speed. Next, Captain Benny announces the start of amateur hour, with the first contestants an operatic cow and a tough-looking mug who recites poetry with offstage sound effects. Next comes a cretinous stutterer who makes both audiences endure his "G-G-Go In Your Dance," by swiping the gong and stuffing it in his trousers. Having cost Captain Benny his audience, the oaf is chased down the street by the showman, who swacks at the gong in his pants.
Also heard: "Alabamy Bound."

BUDDY'S BUG HUNT

Buddy; June 22; LT; Supervision by Jack King; Animation by Bob McKimson and Paul Smith; Music by Norman Spencer.
Buddy is chasing a butterfly. Luckily, it flies into the headquarters for his insect collection, "Buddy's Bug House." After nabbing the butterfly, Buddy inspects a spider under a microscope. Getting a whiff of ether, Buddy passes out, giving the spider a chance to escape the microscope and free the other insects. While the spider restrains Buddy with his web, the other insects force him to take a reducing pill

that makes him bug size. The bugs laugh and sing "We've Got You Where We Want You!" They march Buddy to a Supreme Court where he is tried for cruelty to insects. The witnesses the judge calls include a grasshopper whose leg has been removed by Buddy and a spider, made a widow by Buddy's cruel experiments. The jury finds him guilty, and they seat him on a cigarette lighter. Buddy awakens and sets all his bugs free. Just in time, too. As he slams the door on his "Bug House," it falls apart. Buddy watches as two frogs play seesaw with a loose board.

BUDDY IN AFRICA

Buddy; July 6; LT; Supervision by Ben Hardaway; Animation by Don Williams and Jack Carr; Music by Norman Spencer.
To darkest Africa, where savage natives mow the grass tops of their houses instead of their lawns and use the rings in pygmies' noses (with the pygmies attached) for games of horseshoes. Buddy brings his mobile "Variety Store" to a native village to trade his goods with the locals for fruit (at least it looks like fruit). He then offers them "a drink that'll cure your jitters/Buddy's famous jungle bitters." The stuff inspires four natives to give out with an impression that's as good as the real thing of the Mills Brothers doing "Love Song in My Heart." A little monkey tries to swipe a bottle of Buddy's cure-all and gets spanked. The little monk persuades a big ape to crash the gate at the village and give Buddy a hard time. However, after both Buddy and gorilla have a house crash down on them, they realize the monk is the instigator of their misfortune, ending the cartoon with a shake of hands.

THE COUNTRY MOUSE

July 13; MM; Supervision by Isadore Freleng; Animation by Don Williams and Jack Carr; Musical Score by Bernard Brown. 2/C
Elmer the country mouse sings and boasts of being "The Strongest in the County" to all the barnyard kids. Granny Mouse reminds him to finish his chores and demonstrates her

37

strength by chopping a tree into clothes pins—with her fists! Elmer wants to be a fighter and that night sneaks off to the city to make good. As the "Hickville Threat," Elmer encounters the champ, the "Run-Some Bulldog," in the boxing ring. To the tune of "La Cucaracha," they fight. Granny listens to the fight on the radio. Becoming concerned, she bikes into town. Granny knocks out the champ and teaches Elmer a lesson: she spanks him in the ring.

This film features the second appearance of the Warner cartoon "Our Gang" (previously in *I Haven't Got a Hat*) as the barnyard kids in the beginning of the film. A Porky-like character also appears as a boxing second near the end. Someone was grooming that pig for stardom.

BUDDY STEPS OUT

Buddy; July 20; LT; Supervision by Jack King; Animation by Charles Jones and Robert Clampett; Music by Bernard Brown.

A promising title, but, alas, if only this one were about stepping out. Instead, while Buddy and Cookie step out, we have to stay home and watch the lamest stuff-comes-to-life cartoon yet conceived. As our hero, we get an ersatz Buddy (as if the real one weren't boring enough), from a wallet-sized photo of him that comes to life. The film dwells far too long on a going-nowhere plot peg in which the miniature Buddy and a statuette of the Greek Titan Atlas open the window and save Cookie's little bird from the snowstorm outside. Once the bird is inside and revived, we get the animated package labels and playing cards going into "A Quarter To Nine," and while the sequence has a few ringers (such as a pig on the label of a package of ham who croons in pig Latin), it hardly seems worth the viewing. When Buddy and Cookie return home, all the little characters scamper back into place.

THE MERRY OLD SOUL

Aug. 17; MM; Supervision by Isadore Freleng; Animation by Rollin Hamilton and Riley Thompson; Music by Norman Spencer. 2/C

Old King Cole marries the Woman in the Shoe. He meets all the kids and is soon doing the wash and bathing the babies via a modern factory conveyor belt method. He floats each clean baby via balloon to the diaper table and rocks the kids to sleep with a sewing machine hook-up. Two mischievous kids, Nip and Tuck, rock the babies out of their cribs. The cartoon ends with babies and Cole crying into the night.

Not the usual story—no villain, just music and factory gags.

BUDDY THE GEE MAN

Buddy; Aug 24; LT; Supervision by Jack King; Animation by Sandy Walker and Cal Dalton; Music by Norman Spencer.

The Department of Justice assigns Federal Agent Buddy to "conduct [a] secret investigation as to the treatment accorded prisoners by warden [Otto B. Kinder] at Sing Song Prison." Donning a false mustache, he infiltrates the big house by climbing on board the back of the car incarcerating notorious gangster Machine Gun Mike. Inside, he takes notes on what he sees, starting with the warden's motto, "All Work and No Play," which calls the shots for his attitude toward the inmates: he silences their singing, prevents laughing (when Machine Gun receives a chain letter instead of the expected love note from "me goil"), and makes sure their rockpile labor is hard. He seems quite mild compared to many real-life wardens, but after Buddy's suggestions are put into effect, Buddy is made warden, and the place is turned into such a heavenly haven (with free ice cream and cigars for the prisoners) that men are trying to break into prison!

The story had some potential for absurd comedy, but neither the director nor the star had anything resembling a sense of humor. This was Buddy's swan song anyway; the next Looney Tunes tried to make stars of the Beans gang. On the track, "Lulu's Back in Town" is both played and sung, interrupted only by a few bars of "She's a Latin from Manhattan."

THE LADY IN RED
Sept 7; MM; Supervision by Isadore Freleng; Animation by Robert McKimson and Ben Clopton. 2/C
In a closed Mexican cafe, the cockroaches make themselves at home. Some use food for sport. Bowling olives knock over radish ten-pins. Tennis is played with peas, while spectators sit on egg crates. At the Roach Nite Club, dancing and musical entertainment are provided by Senorita Cockroach, "The Lady in Red." Meanwhile, a parrot escapes his cage and captures the Lady. A heroic roach pursues the parrot and gets a chance to set its tailfeathers aflame when it stops by the stove. "The End" is spelled out in smokey sky-writing by the wounded parrot.

And the roaches live happily ever after.

A CARTOONIST'S NIGHTMARE
Beans; Sept 21; LT; Supervision by Jack King; Animation by Don Williams and Paul Smith; Musical Score by Bernard Brown.
When it's quitting time (six o'clock) at an animated cartoon studio, all the sane and the normal head home, except one animator trying to finish a scene on deadline. He draws Beans being menaced by the Beast of *Beauty and the Beast*, and then protects him by drawing jailbars between the two characters. When the cartoonist falls asleep, the Beast reaches off the drawing board and hauls him into the scene. Laughing maniacally, he drags him into a rogue's gallery room of "Cartoon Villains," among them the Mad Musician from *Buddy the Detective*, the Octopus from *Mr. and Mrs. Is the Name*, and some originals like Spike the Spider

and Battling Barney the killer kangaroo. This gang beats up on the animator, singing "The tables are turned/and now you are in our clutches" (copping the melody of "Teddy Bear's Picnic"). They push him into a deep alligator pit that they make him draw. Beans breaks out of the bars with a saw from a loaf of bread, distracts the villains out of the room, and helps the cartoonist escape the pit by dropping down a pencil to him. After Beans sends all the villains sliding into the pit with a grease gun, the animator erases it. He and Beans shake hands before he wakes up from his nightmare and rewards Beans (on the drawing board) with three feet of ice cream and a spoon.

LITTLE DUTCH PLATE
Oct 19; MM; Supervision by Isadore Freleng; Animation by Paul Smith and Robert Clampett; Music by Norman Spencer. 2/C
The usual boy-girl-and-villain plot here, in a standard variation on a setting—a kitchen full of characters in a little cottage by the Zeiderzee. The little Dutch boy (a salt shaker) loves the girl on the little Dutch plate. Three other girls on little Dutch plates form a vocal trio for the title number, as various kitchen characters do a wooden shoe dance. After the boy sings the mock-ethnic "My Boopshin" to the girl in her little Dutch mill, the vinegar-bottle villain (Billy Bletcher) enters and threatens to foreclose on her mill unless she marries him. The villain gives the boy until noon to come up with the dough. The piggy bank is empty, but the boy gets the idea of swiping the gold fillings out of a set of dentures belonging to the people who own the house. When he returns, the old meanie has already stolen the girl, taking her inside a grandfather clock that he uses as a sawmill and tying her to a log. The boy sets her free and starts pummeling the villain, knocking off his vinegar bottle stopper head. The villain reaches around for a new head and accidentally puts a different head on his shoulders, one with a blonde pretty-boy face. The girl takes one look

39

at him, coos, "You handsome man," and goes off arm in arm with him, leaving the boy standing with a dumb look on his face.

HOLLYWOOD CAPERS

Beans; Oct 19; LT; Supervision by Jack King; Animation by Rollin Hamilton and Charles Jones; Music by Norman Spencer.

Beans is a Hollywood hopeful who crashes the gate at a big studio by using a balloon to disguise himself as Oliver Hardy. Inside, big-shot director Oliver Owl is attempting to shoot a gay '90s musical meller with Little Kitty in the lead and a turtle who can play two pianos at once (the camera is more animated than anyone). Beans gets the director's goat by messing up a shot, and the irate director tosses him onto a nearby set. There, Beans accidentally "turns on" the Frankenstein monster, portrayed as a robot, and the metal man goes on a rampage. In one imaginative moment, he consumes a movie camera, shown to us from inside that self-same camera! Beans finally hacks the monster with a giant fan/wind machine.

Caricatures of W. C. Fields (surprisingly svelte) and Charlie Chaplin (in a car with wheels that skid along in the fashion of Chaplins famous turns) also appear.

BILLBOARD FROLICS

Nov 9; MM; Supervision by Isadore Freleng; Animation by Cal Dalton and Sandy Walker; Music by Bernard Brown. 2/C

This starts out as another swell entry in the it-comes-to-life cycle, this time it's posters (don't worry, they get the Dutch cleanser in there)—gets bogged down early in a routine of bird-chasing-worm ("My Ami") and cat-chasing-bird antics. These advertising come-to-life creatures are a faithful lot, however, willing to take up arms for one of their comrades. They gang up on the attemptedly-realistic cat, the RCA "Nipper" dog, and the Arm & Hammer baking soda emblem. Before that, luckily, caricatures of "Eddie Camphor" (Cantor) and "Rub 'Em Off" (Rubinoff), on a poster advertising an in-person appearance, duet on the "Merrie Melodies" future theme song, "Merrily We Roll Along." We also get to hear the song done as a rhumba, danced by a Cookie-esque Cuban cutie on a travel poster.

FLOWERS FOR MADAME

Nov 20; MM; Supervision by Isadore Freleng; Animation by Paul Smith and Don Williams; Music by Norman Spencer. 2/C

Flowers and vegetation: on a basic level, part of the Warner's stuff-comes-to-life series, this really has more in common with the '30s toon tradition of pageantry (most often used by Disney and Columbia), i.e., a flower parade is the central event. We open on a series of flower chorus lines, the last a bevy of Floral Flora Dora Girls (that's one pun they missed) who dance to "Oh, you Beautiful Doll," as played by a dandelion Harpo Marx. For a plot, it's the "Casper" formula, a cactus looking like a pickle as the ostracized outsider (whose parade float is jeered by the judges and crowd) who saves everybody and becomes a hero when a fire breaks out. It is one of those insidious fires that knows enough to turn off a sprinkler, though not to stay away from a watermelon.

Trivia: the toon's "plug tune" (the title song) has one other claim to fame—it was recorded by Bob Crosby.

1936

GOLD DIGGERS OF '49

Porky and Beans; Jan. 6; LT; Supervision by Fred Avery; Animation by Bob Clampett and Charles Jones; Musical Direction by Carl W. Stalling.

Little Kitty is the girl, Porky Pig (the original weight-watchers' poster boy, who would just as soon yell "Whoopee!" as look at you) her father, and Beans the trusting hero, who, upon discovering gold in the hills, broadcasts the news all over town. Everyone drops what he's doing to head for the hills. There are Chinamen who get covered in car exhaust and become Amos n' Andy, and a barbershop quartet that abruptly returns to finish the last line of "Sweet Adeline." Once they make it to the gulch, no one seems to find any more gold (only numerous gags on the subject, such as a treasure chest containing a book called "How to Find Gold"). Excitement arises from a shady character who swipes a priceless parcel of Porky's, and the obese stutterer promises Beans his daughter if he'll retrieve it. In the chase that ensues, new Schlesinger director Avery plays fast and loose with cartoon conventions of speed and time (not to mention historical detail—after going to great pains to explain this is 1849, he provides Beans with an automobile) as villain and hero zoom about the desert firing at each other. The pace picks up after Beans runs out of gas; he refuels with that magical potion, liquor, enabling the car to knock the bad guy for a loop, swoop him and Porky up, and head for town where the contents of the valuable sack are revealed.

I WANNA PLAY HOUSE

Jan 11; MM; Supervision by Isadore Freleng; Animation by Cal Dalton and Sandy Walker; Music by Bernard Brown. 3/C

Two mischievous little bears, one brown and one black, play hide and seek. The black bear finds a gypsy wagon to hide in. Inside, he discovers food and drink and soon becomes drunk on cider. He puts on a hat and croons to himself in the mirror "I Gotta Sing 'Cause I'm Gay." The brown bear finds his playmate, but the wagon breaks loose and starts to roll along a cliffside road. The wagon crashes near their dad, who punishes the lads accordingly.

This unremarkable cartoon has the distinction of being the first Warner Bros. cartoon to have the famous "circles/bullseye" opening, which has become as much a trademark of the studio as "That's all, Folks!"

THE PHANTOM SHIP

Beans, Ham, and Ex; Feb 1; LT; Supervision by Jack King; Animation by Paul Smith and Don Williams; Music by Bernard Brown.

Haunted-house antics set on a ghost ship that aviator-adventurer Beans and his stowaway nephews, Ham and Ex, discover in a "Hunt for Haunted Treasure Up North." For the first part of their experience, they have to deal with supernatural opposition, various skeletons who are as spooked by Ham and Ex running around covered in a sheet as vice versa. For the second, Beans discovers a couple of undecayed crew members whose bodies have been preserved by the cold (Beans exclaims, "Frozen stiff!"), and, rather stupidly, defrosts them. As Beans and the kiddies toss the ship's treasure out the window and onto their plane, the pirates awaken, and now it's their turn to chase our heroes. There are genuine thrills, as the peg-legged captain pursues Beans and the knife-wielding first mate climbs the mast after Ham 'n Ex. They fall into Bean's airplane, just as the captain hurls a keg of gunpowder at Beans, which blows up the ship. Somehow, they manage to catch him and go flying off to safety.

This genuinely effective adventure in film-making goes off track only when the characters try to be cute or funny.

THE CAT CAME BACK

Feb 8; MM; Supervision by Isadore Freleng; Animation by Robert McKimson and Ben Clopton. 2/C

A momma mouse warns her children to beware of cats, while a momma cat trains her kittens to attack all mice. One mouse and one kitten sneak out of their lessons, meet, and become friends. Then their mommas pull them away. Later, the baby mouse invites the cat to listen to music on a record player, which inspires a very fey dance that leads to both animals falling down a sewer drain. The little mouse uses his tail to rescue the kitten from a whirlpool. They return to their grieving parents, and all the cats and mice rejoice. As the film ends, both cats and mice (don't ask why) go back to their feuding ways.

This was the last Warner cartoon produced in two-strip Technicolor.

BOOM BOOM

Porky and Beans; Feb 29; LT; Supervision by Jack King; Animation by Cal Dalton and Sandy Walker; Music by Norman Spencer.

After a series of foxhole and bomb gags that aren't really tasteless enough to be funny (war has gotten more namby-pamby in the years since *Bosko the Doughboy*), we zero in on Porky, a cowardly infantryman who wishes he'd stayed on the farm, and Beans, who tries to bolster his sidekick's spirits with braggadocio ("Take it easy, Porky old boy!"). When a carrier pigeon brings them news that General Hardtack is "being held prisoner by enemy in old farmhouse," Beans motorcycles off at once to the rescue, dragging the reluctant Porky beside him in his sidecar. Braving bombs that have minds of their own, and traveling part of the way in a portable trench, they finally discover their general being given a hot foot by the Billy Bletcher-acted enemy leaders. Using a rocket to tie up the other guys in barbed wire, Porky, Beans, and the general make their escape in a convenient airplane, which nearly gets done in by the unceasing rain of bombs. After they land amidst an explosion, we cut to the three characters bandaged beyond recognition in a hospital bed. The general passes along one of his medals to Beans, who gives half to Porky.

The ending is almost cloying enough to make the film.

MISS GLORY

Mar 7; MM; Supervised by Tex Avery; Words and music by Warren & Dubin; Modern Art Conceived and Designed by Leodora Congdon. 3/C

The whole town of Hicksville, small as it may be, is a-buzzin' about the imminent arrival of a genuine celebrity: the famous Miss Glory! Abner, the hick bellhop in the town hotel, is so excited that he's been "prac-ticin'" bellhop stuff to impress her. While waiting for her to show up, he dreams of a super art deco hotel, the kind of place Miss Glory normally frequents, done up in high-gloss. Like everyone else, Abner is trying to page the beautiful, the charming, the lovely, the adorable, the one and only Miss Glory for her dozens of wealthy admirers. As Abner dashes in vain about the hotel, frustrated by uncooperative elevators and other pitfalls, in search of America's sweetheart, we get a remarkably well-balanced mixture of music and gags, mostly framed in musical-comedy format; i.e., song, plot, and comedy, then reprise of song, end scene. The two performances of the song, each by a male chorus, are the stunners: the first by three sophisticated looking inebriates, decorated by a montage of cocktail-hour imagery. When Abner finally falls off the roof of the skyscraper hotel and wakes up from his dream, he is back in Hicksville to meet the real Miss Glory, a little girl (Bernice Hanson again) who remarks "Boy, do I slay 'em" when Abner faints from surprise.

Even more than Iwerks' *Merry Mannequins* and Disney's "Pastoral Symphony" from *Fantasia*, this remains an outstanding use of art deco in cartoons, especially the reprise of the number wherein a chorus of top-hatted and tailed John Held-like thin men prance around the fashion plate "dream" Miss Glory, shown from high and low in a series of Busby Berkeley-derived angles. Lush and lovely, but also

42

remarkably well-directed. Inside stuff: the "Cosmopolitan Hotel" refers to Hearst's same-named film company, which produced the Warners feature *Miss Glory* with Marion Davies and Dick Powell. Keep an eye open for the figures of Avery, Bob Clampett, and Chuck Jones awaiting Miss Glory outside the hotel near the end.

ALPINE ANTICS

Beans; Mar 9; LT; Supervision by Jack King; Animation by Riley Thompson and Jack Carr; Music by Norman Spencer.

"She Was Only an Acrobat's Daughter," sung by a trio of snowmen with the profession changed to "Ice Skater," provides the theme, musically as well as textually, for the opening sequence of animals on ice gags. Beans and Little Kitty read a sign announcing a big ski race with a purse of $100,000 in prizes or $2.00 in cash. The race is directed with just enough zip to help us forget we couldn't care less about the main character. Although Porky Pig (in another nonspeaking, even nonstuttering role), riding on a rocking horse utilized as a makeshift sled, as well as a couple of ducks riding dachshunds also participate, Bean's only real rival is an obnoxious Billy Bletcher-voiced bully, not above using foul means to succeed. The bad guy trips up all the others with a rope strung between two trees. Beans gets it to backfire and wrap around the villain. Later, they're racing along with the nogoodnik somehow affixed to the top of Bean's shoulders, but an extended tree branch first stops him and then flings him though the ice

so beans can ski ahead to victory.

Soundtrack music includes one of Billie Holiday's favorites, "What a Little Moonlight Can Do."

THE FIRE ALARM

Ham and Ex, Beans; Mar 9; LT; Supervision by Jack King; Animation by Bob McKimson and Ben Clopton; Music by Norman Spencer.

The crew seems to be working extra hard to make Ham and Ex, here left to wreak havoc in a firehouse where Uncle Beans works, a mixture of cute and obnoxious, but the two are even more obnoxious when they're cute. Left to their own devices, they think nothing of practical jokes that might cause life-and-death situations. Instead of being regretful after sending the firetrucks out on a false alarm (Disney would have them caught in a burning building as punishment), they indulge in an amoral little song: "Oh! How We Like To Fool the Firemen." Other cute li'l hi-jinks include wrapping an engine and bouncing joyfully on the firemens' bunks. For a climax, they take a firetruck around the city in a rampage of destruction, knocking entire rows of telephone poles to the ground and leveling parks and houses. For punishment, they are spanked.

THE BLOW OUT

Porky Pig; Apr 4; LT; Supervision by Fred Avery; Animation by Charles Jones and Sid Sutherland; Music by Bernard Brown.

Every time he turns around, the little guy is there. No matter where he tries to run and hide, the little guy is always there. This is the germ of the idea that Avery developed into *Dumb Hounded* (MGM, 1943). Here, it is set up like this: a mad bomber, newspaper headlines inform us, has been terrorizing the city. Meanwhile, Porky Pig has discovered he can earn the pennies necessary to purchase an ice cream soda by picking things up for people and handing them back to their owners. He sees the bomber leave behind a clock, and not knowing it contains a time bomb ("that'll blow up an entire city") he tries to return it to him, coyly stretching his hand out for the gratuity. The fiend runs up to the top of a building, and the little guy is there. He ducks to the bottom of a manhole, and the little guy is there. When a couple of police officers realize what's going on ("The little fella's got plenty of nerve to tackle a mug like that!"), the bomber escapes to his hideout and locks about five doors behind him. Somehow, the little guy is there too, and when he runs into the paddy wagon to get away from Porky, the pig shoves the bomb in at the last second. It explodes in close contact with its maker. We end on the gleeful Porky enjoying his reward ecstatically filling his face with one ice cream soda after another in rapid-fire succession.

The first real Porky Pig cartoon (though not his first appearance) and the first Avery villain who talks to the audience: "Now I'll fix the little pest so he'll be blown to pieces, whether you people like it or not!" Porky's happy-go-lucky theme is "The Fella with the Fiddle."

I'M A BIG SHOT NOW

Apr 11; MM; Supervision by Isadore Freleng; Animation by Jack Carr and Riley Thompson; Music by Bernard Brown.

The setting is Birdville, and after seeing some of the more genteel citizens at work and play, we move over to the rougher part of town, the Birdville Saloon, where our antihero hangs out. He's a nasty-looking yegg and wears the prerequisite '30s mug outfit to prove it, a striped turtleneck plus Beagle Boy cap and eye mask. Flipping a coin a la George Raft, he sings a number that could have been written for Edward G. Robinson in a musical version of *Little Caesar*: "I used to be a softie/But I swore I'd be a toughie/And I did it—baby, and how!/I'm a little big-shot now!" To demonstrate this, he thrashes a cop and puts away 1-2-3-4-5 slugs of hooch. He and his tough-guy-big-shot pals then heist a bank and get away from the bird bulls, laughing at the wanted posters ("Reward: 500 worms"). A cop on his beat spots him when he briefly leaves his birdhouse hideout and he and the police clash in a

violent shootout. The police shoot at him with every kind of gun and from every angle, including from bird-planes overhead and while swinging Tarzan-style from a vine on a nearby tree. In the last shot, he sings to us from a prison cell, "I'm just a jailbird now."

WESTWARD WHOA

Porky and Beans; Apr 25; LT; Supervision by Jack King; Animation by Paul Smith and Ben Clopton; Music by Norman Spencer.

The unmourned demise of the Bean's Gang cycle, after nine months and as many films. They're in charge of a wagon train of would-be settlers, heading west across Injun territory singing "Those Covered Wagon Days." When they break camp in a safe-looking spot, most of the troupe watches Porky square dance in drag, but Ham and Ex go into the woods, where they're soon up to their old mischief. They find a turkey with Indian-like plumage and use it to give the rest of the camp a good scare. Beans warns them, "Some day an Indian'll catch ya, and off goes yer head!" Their mock-Indian ululations attract the real thing. This time, when they try to warn the camp, everyone assumes they're crying wolf. The stuttering Porky is the first adult to spot the Indians, but he takes too long to get out his warning, and the Indians get the jump on the palefaces. Gradually, the tables are turned on the attackers. Beans uses a bear trap on an Indian who's about to rid the world of Ham and Ex. In the wind-up gag, Beans gives the li'l rascals a dose of their own Indian noise medicine just to see how they like it.

Porky loses his pants at one point, thereby inaugurating a career-long fashion trend.

PLANE DIPPY

Porky Pig; Apr 30; LT; Supervision by Fred Avery; Animation by Sid Sutherland and Virgil Ross; Musical Score by Bernard Brown.

Porky plays a lad keen on joining the Air Corps. His first problem is to express this desire to the recruiting officer in spite of his anti-communicative stutter (when the officer gives him a chalk board to write on, even his handwriting stutters). Porky is recruited, handed a feather duster, assigned to clean a robot plane that obeys orders spoken into a microphone. Unfortunately, its monkey scientist inventor leaves the control box on a window sill near where a bunch of kids from Porky's old neighborhood (mainly Bernice Hanson's "Little Kitty") are demonstrating tricks a little dog can do. The plane responds to the orders and it rolls over, plays dead, and shakes all over the place with the hapless Porky aboard. It crashes through a circus and splashes underneath the ocean, destroys a clock tower, chases an anthropomorphic cloud-person, and turns a wagonful of straw into a wagon of straw hats. Once back on terra firma, Porky decides he wants no more of airplanes and immediately enlists in the infantry.

Instrumental themes include "I'd Love to Take Orders from You" and "When I Yoo-Hoo."

LET IT BE ME
May 2; MM; Supervision by Isadore Freleng.
Poor Bing Crosby. Because he's the greatest and most popular singer ever, they've got to portray him as a cad (here as in *Bingo Crosbyana*). And what a cad! All over the countryside of this chicken universe, hens go crazy for the crooning cock o' the walk, Mr. Bingo (imaginative name, that!). Women flock around his door, huddle around radios, and covet his photo (away from their insanely jealous boyfriends). With all these women after his autograph and more, you'd think that the strutting peacock would have enough to chase without bothering our heroine, Emily. But no. He drives past her cottage with his bu-bu-bu'ing horn (just as her hick boyfriend comes a-courtin'), takes a gander at her gams and instantly sweet-talks her into a joy ride. Cut to a decadent cabaret where the swine tries to get her drunk so he can have his way with her and quickly dumps her for the club's entertainer, a shapely Fifi D'Orsay-like capon who gives out with the 1930 "I've Got My

Eye on You." After he has the waiter kick Emily out (and she's got the footprint to prove it), "Time Staggers On." She's reduced to selling violets in the snow. Meanwhile, boyfriend Lem clobbers the radio and then Mr. Bingo himself, finally finding Emily on the street. Time passes again, and we see the couple years later. When one of their little chicks tries to bu-bu-bu, they throw the book at him–literally.

Heard instrumentally: "I Wanna Woo."

I'D LOVE TO TAKE ORDERS FROM YOU
May 18; MM; Supervision by Fred Avery; Animation by Bob Clampett and Cecil Surry; Music by Norman Spencer.
A cute li'l tyke of a scarecrow considers it his mission to frighten animals, and even prays to be made "a big scarecrow just like my dad." When his dad comes home from a hard day of scaring crows in the cornfield, he practices scary poses with him, their frightfulness being undercut by Avery's having allotted this sequence to the musical number. In addition to singing, the scarecrow family bobs up and down and flaps collective arms in a charleston variation. Comes the dawn, the lad sneaks out of the house to try his hand at terrifying the local wildlife and has success with a rooster, a squirrel and a rabbit. A huge roc-like crow ignores him, but then gets mad and chases the little fellow down the field. He tries pose after ineffective pose. All of a sudden, one pose turns the crow white with fear. It turns out to be his Pops', for he is standing behind him. That night, when Junior is boasts to his Ma about how he "wasn't a bit afraid of that old crow," Dad lets the wind out of his sails by scaring him with a phony crow shadow.

The premise isn't thrilling, but you've got to admire the thoroughness

with which Avery works it out, down to imaginatively posed "scare" takes and an effective birds-eye shot of the crow swooping down on the running boy scarecrow.

FISH TALES
Porky Pig; May 23; LT; Supervision by Jack King; Animation by Bob McKimson and Don Williams; Musical Score by Norman Spencer.

It's a tad flatly directed, and the character of Porky doesn't yet have the personality he will in a year or so, but this is potentially one of the most effectively gruesome cartoons ever made. Porky, fishing on the open sea, bites into a donut, which is revealed to be bait set by a giant fish, who, in a frightening role reversal, reels Porky in, grabs him by the feet, and takes him home to be eaten by his family. There the fish "scales" Porky by scraping his clothes off with a huge knife, garnishes him by forcing an apple into his mouth, and sticks him in an oven, flames dancing all around him. Escaping the oven, the hapless pig is chased all over the ocean by no end of frightening sea creatures, among them eels, octopuses, and a swordfish. Waking from his dream, Porky, not surprisingly, recants and tosses overboard all the fish he has caught, as well as his gear.

BINGO CROSBYANA
May 30; MM; Supervision by Isadore Freleng; Animation by Cal Dalton and Sandy Walker; Music by Norman Spencer.

The household pests of last year's *The Lady in Red* return, this time as flies rather than cockroaches. All the senoritas are excited about Bingo Crosbyana, the crooning caballero cucaracha, who not only thrills them with his crooning and singing and one-string guitar playing, but performs a thrilling demonstration of aerial acrobatics in which he shows up all the other men (and literally leaves them with their pants down). He finally gets his comeuppance when a nasty spider attacks the buggy community and the ladies learn what a cad and coward Bingo really is.

Disappointing in that while it mimics the Crosby voice, it doesn't do anything with either his image or his screen/radio persona, which, as later W.B. toons proved, were both ripe subjects for the short cartoon medium. Crosby's attorneys didn't think it was funny either. "A potential threat to cartoon producers who caricature stars," was how the *Hollywood Reporter* (August 5, 1936) described the legal action. "The Crosby corporation has demanded that Warners cease distribution and exhibition of the reel. The demand states that the Crosby voice is imitated and the character of BINGO CROSBYANA is shown as a 'vainglorious coward.'"

SHANGHAIED SHIPMATES
Porky Pig; June 26; LT; Supervision by Jack King; Animation by Paul Smith and Joe D'Igalo; Music by Norman Spencer.

Another Jack King "laugh riot." A sadistic villain of a sea captain, hearing that his crew has jumped ship en masse, decides to shanghai a new crew from the dockside inn where Porky and his pals are having a jolly time. He forcibly impresses them into his service, and once he has them in his power on his boat, he treats them in a way that makes Simon Legree look like Tinkerbell. The whip-wielding captain not only makes Porky swallow a bar of soap, he shoves the little pig's head in a bucket of water until he squeals in agony. He denies the crew food and allows them to eat only the leftover bones of his meal (making a great show of eating in front of them). Finally, Porky rallies his courage to voice their demand for food. When the captain refuses, they attack! His cowardice forgotten, Porky leads the charge against the evil captain, brandishing a scimitar. The Captain tries to turn a cannon on them and blows up the ship. The ending has the crew on a makeshift raft being towed by the defeated captain under the command of Porky's whip.

"Don't Give Up The Ship" serves as all-purpose theme song.

WHEN I YOO HOO
June 27; MM; Supervision by Isadore Freleng; Animation by Bob McKimson and Don Williams; Music by Norman Spencer.

46

The caste system of Hickory Holler does not distinguish between human-type animals and animal-type animals. The only lines are drawn between the two feudin' families, the Weavers and the Matthews. A lanky goat yodels the title song (later to become a Stalling staple), accompanied by the clog dancing of his Clarabelle Cow/Miss Cud sweetheart, as a prelude to a minute of so-so feud gags (one firing a rifle with his feet, etc).

The sheriff drives into the midst of the battle and posts the following notice: "For the peace of the county, the Weavers and the Matthews are hereby notified to settle their feud by a rooster fight to be held at Higgins' barn. Loser *will leave the county."* Comes the night of the cock fight, staged like a boxing match, with the sheriff serving as referee and announcer. He introduces the crowd to "Squawk-in-the-Face" Weaver and "Cock-of-the-Walk" Matthews, in a fight to the finish. They mix it up good. The Matthews' rooster gets the edge on his competitor when he chugalugs a little corn whiskey. He pummels the Weaver's bird so that he bounces back off the ropes and both get knocked out. When the Ref declares the Weavers' bird the winner, the Matthews start shooting at him, the same thing happening the other way around. The Ref then declares the match a draw; both families jump in the ring and start scrapping as the two roosters watch from the stands.

PORKY'S PET

Porky Pig; July 11; LT; Supervision by Jack King; Animation by Cal Dalton and Sandy Walker; Music by Norman Spencer.
When Porky receives a telegram from a big-time Broadway producer that he has a spot for Porky and his pet ostrich, Lulu, in his new show, the two set out for New York. However, no sooner do they attempt to board a train than an irate conductor yells, "You can't bring no buzzard on this train!" Porky has to *sneak* the ostrich past the conductors, hauling her in through the train window and stuffing her under

the seat. The durn fool bird has the durn fool habit of eating everything that comes within reach of her mouth. When she swallows a concertina, the noise it makes inside gives away her hiding place. Porky shoves her into a guitar case. She starts squawking again just as the conductor comes by, and he throws them both off. Porky and Lulu make do with a handcart that they tie to a cow who moves faster than the train.

I LOVE TO SINGA

July 18; MM; Supervised by Fred Avery; Animation by Charles M. Jones and Virgil Ross; Music by Norman Spencer.
Professor Fritz Owl, music instructor, hangs his prejudices out in front of his tree on a sign: "teacher of voice, piano & violin, *BUT - NO JAZZ!*"

Most of his newly-hatched kiddies, born in jackets with tails and instruments in their hands, go along with this (an infant tenor singing "Lucia" is a "Caruso," a violin prodigy is a Fritz Kreisler). The last to hatch, however, explodes out of his egg with "I Love to Singa!" "Mama," the prof. consoles his fainting wife, "if he must sing, ve vill teach him to sing like ve vant him to!" Iris in on Mama trying to teach "der little feller" how to sing an ancient tune suitable in polite society, "Drink to Me Only with Thine Eyes." Every time she turns the page he succeeds in getting in a few bars of his kind of music: "I Love to Singa!" His Pop catches him at this. "Ach! Enough is too much! Outa my house! You hotcha! You croona! You jazz singa!" Mama Owl quickly phones the police to look for her errant boy, who is delighted at the chance to walk through the forest singing his song. He quickly comes to a radio station holding an amateur contest where "Jack Bunny," the emcee, is giving one untalented musical hopeful

after another the gong. Our hero (identified by his card as "Owl Jolson") is a shoo-in for the prize money and a radio career. His parents hear him on the radio. Seeing them outside the control booth, our hero switches to "Thine Eyes." This will get him the gong, until Pops breaks in and gives his approval to "Go on and singa/'bout the moona and the juna and der springa" as parents and siblings form a chorus line behind him.

PORKY THE RAINMAKER

Porky Pig; Aug 1; LT; Supervision by Fred Avery; Animation by Cecil Surry and Sid Sutherland; Music by Norman Spencer.

A heat wave threatens the welfare of Farmer Pig, his son Porky, their animals and crops. Papa Pig gives Porky their last dollar to buy some feed in town, but Porky spends the money on a box of weather pills from a traveling salesman. The pills include Rain, Snow, Ice, Lightning, Thunder, Earthquake, Wind, Cyclone, and Sun. Back at the farm, Papa is mad at Porky for bringing home pills and throws them into the yard. The hungry animals eat them, with the expected results. A chicken eats the Lightning pill and becomes a feathered bolt of electricity; a horse eats Fog and soon his horseflies are reporting "No visibility, ceiling zero." Each animal performs violent gyrations. A goose eats Thunder, a chicken eats Cyclone, and another chicken gobbles up Earthquake. A goose almost swallows the Rain pill but shoots it out of his mouth into the sky, bringing life-restoring water to the crops. In the last shot, the barnyard characters strike a final "happy ending" pose, but suddenly go into their wild weather contortions.

SUNDAY GO TO MEETIN' TIME

Aug 8; MM; Supervision byIsadore Freleng; Animation by Bob McKimson and Paul Smith; Music by Norman Spencer.

Our hero Nicodemus's woman tries to show him the virtues of righteousness, but even when she drags that fool by the ear from a crap game to the lord's house, don't you know that fool has done sneaked out and is soon stealin' chickens again. A blow on the head from the farmyard fence helps him to see the error of his ways. He dreams that he is up before the big judge, who has his life writ on a page in his big book, detailing his crimes, such as watermelon theft. The judge sends him plummeting into the inferno, falling off a large cliff onto a giant pinball machine that delivers him to a whole mess o' torturous little devils and one really nasty *big* devil. All of them sing "You've Got to Give the Devil His Due" as they start to give Nicodemus "the works." When he wakes up, his feets do their stuff, and he heads straight fo' church.

You're never sure if this animated *Cabin in the Sky* is entertaining because of or in spite of its prejudice. Some of the "jokes" are a bit much, especially all the gags about shining black babies' heads like shoes and then using a brassiere as a double-barreled baby bonnet. Heard: "The Swingin'est Man in Town" and "Shout All Over God's Heaven."

PORKY'S POULTRY PLANT

Porky Pig; Aug 22; LT; Supervision by Frank Tash; Animation by Don Williams and Volney White; Musical Direction by Carl W. Stalling.

First cartoons aren't supposed to be this good, even from someone who's been around. As if to shout in capital letters that a great director had arrived, he opens on a long pan over a farmyard, zeroing in on a henhouse door out of which strut Porky's prize poultry. Ever the diligent animal tender, Porky lovingly makes sure all of his chickens, ducks, and geese are well fed (when worms hide underground, Porky snake-charms them out of their holes). These jolly scenes fade to a bleaker image: Porky bemoaning deaths in his fowl family due to "Public Chicken Enemy No. 1, The Hawk." A wanted poster shows the villainous bird dissolving to the real thing, eyeing the landscape in search of victims. Porky sees his shadow and sounds the hawk alarm. He fires on the villain, but the hawk makes off with one little chick. Porky takes off after him in his Bee plane. The aerial battle that follows between Porky and a flock of ferocious hawks is thrilling, with Tashlin having replicated the angles and editing of live-action aerial adventures, and funny, as when the chase becomes a literal metaphor for a football game, with the chick used as the football that Porky catches (just in the nick of time) when the enemy fumbles. Porky does away with the hawk and returns to the farm triumphantly. In the last scene, the fowl are spooked by a hawk shadow that turns out to be a weather vane.

Both Tashlin and Stalling (in his first released film for Warners) are already past masters. The only room for improvement is in Porky's really awful voice.

AT YOUR SERVICE MADAME

Aug 29; MM; Supervision by Isadore Freleng; Animation by Don Williams and Cal Dalton; Music by Norman Spencer.

Ah, yes, my little chickadees, this all-pig picture opens at two different locales, the first a cozy little house where the widow pig Mrs. Hamhock endeavors to bring up her children, including the uncontrollable "Piggy" who can't seem to do anything like the others. The second introduces us to our antihero, a dignified bum, specifically W. C. Fields reborn as a pig, who breaks his elegant stride to dash for a discarded butt of a stogie on the other side of traffic. He becomes interested in Mrs. Hamhock when the paper tells him she's inherited a fortune. The giggling, unbecomingly-girlish widow is so love-starved that practically as soon as he walks in the door, he's making love to her. He sings of how he's at her service, Madame. While she distracts herself with the piano, he very smoothly empties out her safe. Luckily, little Piggy catches on to what he's doing and gets his siblings to gang up on the gigolo. At first, Mrs. Hamhock is shocked and embarrassed. They put him through a cartoon-style torture anyway, winding up with getting him repeatedly stuck on the wall with his suction-cup nose and finally having the evidence shaken out of him with a vibrating machine. He walks off coolly,

still vibrating, muttering "Good night, my little chickadee."

TOYTOWN HALL

Sept 19; MM; Supervision by Isadore Freleng; Animation by Bob McKimson and Sandy Walker; Musical Direction by Carl W. Stalling.

Most '30s cartoon fairylands are populated by a mixture of peoplelike animals, talking toys, and star caricatures. This one rationalizes by having our dreaming protagonist, a cute Berenice Hanson-voiced baby boy forcibly put to bed in the middle of listening to the radio (Ben Bernie on KFWB). His hallucination consists of toys mimicking radio stars. The plot peg legitimizes the cannibalization of old animation galore, as virtually every performance here is an encore from a recent Merrie Melody, the original drawings touched up to turn the caricatures into toys: Fred Allen, emceeing, the Bing Crosby bird from *Let It Be Me* (1936, not a caricature at all, really), Eddie Cantor from *Billboard Frolics*, Rudy Vallee (again with "Sweet Music"), the Mexicali Trio and the Lady in Red from *The Lady in Red* (1935; all, thankfully, no longer cockroaches), the rabbit doing the Joe Penner impression from *My Green Fedora* (1935), the wind-up colored band, the lighting-expert elephant and other toys from *Those Beautiful Dames* (1935). For the big conclusion, the kid wakes up (ho-hum).

MILK AND MONEY

Porky Pig; Oct 3; LT; Supervision by Fred Avery; Animation by Charles Jones and Virgil Ross; Musical Direction by Carl W. Stalling.

To pay off the Viper landlord who's threatened to foreclose on his Papa's farm, Porky and his horse try tomake good inthe city, where they answer a want-ad for a man with a horse as a milkman. As if they don't have enough problems with cats who consume the quarts as soon as Porky leaves them, the horse's old nemesis Hank Horsefly gives him such a sting that both wagon and bottles are smashed against a street light. They get fired. Trudging around dejectedly, the horse is attracted by a bucket of oats that leads him onto a race track. Porky decides to make a try for the $10,000 purse. The horse just stands there until the horsefly bites him again. This time his bite is beneficial; it inspires the nag to zoom around the track in a blur and win.

PORKY'S MOVING DAY
Porky Pig; Oct 7; Supervision by Jack King; Animation by Paul Smith and Joe D'Igalo; Musical Direction by Carl W. Stalling.
The situation of full of potential. Miss Cud's house is perched on the edge of a cliff hanging over the ocean, ready to fall at any moment. She phones "Porky's Moving Van" to remove the furniture. The major new character is a dumb ape sidekick for Porky named Dopey who keeps throwing punches when he hears a bell and saying, "Okay bosssss." Porky tosses out a mattress to protect the piano he's about to throw, but it crashes right through to the ground anyway. Meanwhile, Dopey removes the entire fireplace and chimney and carries it out while Lulu the Ostrich gets caught up in a carpet that Porky rolls up with his feet. Lulu then swallows an alarm clock that goes off and causes Dopey to start swinging just when he's carrying the china. Ultimately, waves come surging through the house, washing all the stuff into the van.

BOULEVARDIER FROM THE BRONX
Oct 10; MM; Supervision by Isadore Freleng; Animation by Paul Smith and Cal Dalton; Music Direction by Carl W. Stalling.
There's more than a ballgame at stake here. When the big city team comes to play the local lads, the swaggering braggart star pitcher and hitter, Dizzy Dan, cozies up to our hero Claude's gal (the selfsame "Emily" chicken, so easily seduced by slickers, be they ball-

players as here, crooners as in *Let It Be Me* or movie moguls, as in *A Star Is Hatched*). Besides pushing the railway station over to match the train when it overshoots the mark, the town also sends out a brass band ("Big Time Tonight") to welcome the visiting team and to accompany the loud-mouthed Dan as he brags of his prowess in (the title) song. Dan wants to show up Claude in front of the town and his girl. Dan and his team pull all sorts of underhanded dirty baseball tricks, chiefly a dachshund who can send his front legs to run ahead for the next base while his hind legs remain safe on the previous one. In the last inning, pitcher Dan walks "three men just to get at Claude." Claude gets a hit on the third pitch (after the draggy slow ball). It's a home run that wins the game, giving him the chance to crow in the slicker's face.

DON'T LOOK NOW
Nov 7; MM; Supervision by Fred Avery; Animation by Robert Clampett and Joe D'Igalo; Musical Direction by Carl W. Stalling.
A Freudian parable portraying the two halves of the human personality as distinct characters: Dan Cupid, whose arrows grow like roses in his garden and make everybody feel all lovey-dovey; and a Li'l Devil, who's happy only when he's making people miserable. St. Valentine's Day is the big day for both. They make a test case out of a couple of bears. Just when the male is trying to get romantic, along comes the devil and whispers insults in the female's ear. A well-aimed shot from Cupid makes everything alright. In fact, the bears decide to get married. Comes the wedding day, as the bridegroom shows up on the bride's doorstep, the devil decorates him with telltale evidence of another woman: lipstick and phony blonde hairs (and ladies stockings in his pocket). Cupid smoothes over everything again, but after wrestling with devil (and shooting his pointy tail into a tree) Cupid learns the devil has one more dirty trick up his sleeve: when the ceremony starts, he hires two bear cubs to run into the

church screaming, "Daddy!" Finally, Cupid beats the devil by arrowing him directly, the power of love being so strong not even the devil can resist it.

LITTLE BEAU PORKY

Porky Pig; Nov 14; LT; Supervision by Frank Tash; Animation by Robert Bentley and Nelson Demorest; Musical Direction by Carl W. Stalling.

In the first of Porky's several Middle-Eastern visits, he's a much-abused Foreign Legionnaire who's humiliated in front of his comrades by the stern commandant (Bletcher trying out his accent Francais). He is ordered to scrub the commandant's camel, which dodges Porky's brush while the pig makes Oliver Hardy expressions. When word is received of the whereabouts of desert riffraff Ali Mode, the whole fort prepares to attack (in an effective montage sequence), all except Porky, who is cruelly told, "We need men, not camel-scrubbers." Alone in the fort, Porky sour-grapes that if he were to meet Ali Mode, "I'd punch him in the jaw, the big sissy!" He soon gets his chance. The sneaky sheik tip-toes up to the fort and tries to doubletalk his way in ("I'm a poor little sheik/with no place to sleep."). Then the pig-Latin speaking desert thugs with Ali Mode attack, and Porky has to defend the fort single-handedly. In an ingeniously-edited battle sequence Porky semiaccidentally kicks the bad guy onto his camel, who pummels him with his slapping humps and dumps him into a barrel of syrup. In the pay-off shot, Porky struts out his chest covered with as many medals as the commandant had at the opening. The camel is similarly decorated.

THE COO COO NUT GROVE

Nov 28; MM; Supervision by Isadore Freleng; Animation by Bob McKimson and Sandy Walker; Musical Direction by Carl W. Stalling.

Movie stars mingle at the posh Hollywood nightspot, the Coo Coo Nut (a ribbing of "Coconut") Grove. Bandleader·Ben "Birdie" entertains, W.C. Squeals cozies up to horse Katharine Heartburn, monocled turtle George Arliss dances with lovebird Mae West, Monkey Laurel and Pig Hardy

exchange thin and fat roles, drinking out of straws from a coconut, Edna Mae Oliver does a mean rhumba with a rose in her teeth (causing Clark Gable to shake his castanet ears), the Dionne Quintuplets sing about their old man (the Spirits of Rhythm number "My Old Man"), Mrs. Weismuller rescues Tarzan from a mouse, Harpo Marx (as a bird) repeatedly pursues a girl whose face is off camera. Lastly, a very sincere Helen Morgan causes everyone to blubber uncontrollably with "The Little Things You Used To Do." Even such real tough guys as banana-eating Wallace Beery and mean mugs Edward G. Robinson and George Raft sob. Collectively, they cry a river and float away at the conclusion.

Also on the soundtrack: "About a Quarter to Nine."

THE VILLAGE SMITHY

Porky Pig; Dec 5; LT; Supervision by Fred Avery; Animation by Cecil Surry and Sid Sutherland; Musical Direction by Carl W. Stalling.

A narrator recites the verse about "The Village Smithy," and everything in the poem appears. The spreading chestnut tree plops into the scene, as does the "smithy" with "large and sinewy hands," and roaring bellows.

The blacksmith puts a horse in a chair and takes his foot measurement, as in a modern shoe store. Porky Pig, his assistant, climbs a ladder to get the box with the right size. Porky pounds the rubber horse shoe, but his hammer bounces off, giving him a black eye. The rubber shoe starts bouncing and won't stop bouncing, so the Smith puts it in a vise and shoots it dead! Porky hits the horse with a hot shoe and the horse speeds off, with the Smithy in tow, running through town so fast the bank is uprooted (a safecracker is at work inside). The action freezes so the Smithy can comment, "What A Buggy Ride!" The horse keeps running until he bounces into a fence, which, like a rubber band, pushes the horse in reverse (the Smithy even comments again, in reverse!). Returning to the blacksmith shop, the Smithy asks Porky, "How did this happen?" Porky demonstrates, causing the horse, with Smithy, to run again!

PORKY OF THE NORTHWOODS

Porky Pig; Dec 19; LT; Supervision by Frank Tash; Animation by Volney White and Norman McCabe; Musical Direction by Carl W. Stalling.

Porky's animal pals applaud as he posts signs around his game reserve forbidding hunting, trapping, and fishing. An unseen, off-camera villain with a French accent (Bletcher) just ignores them, even shooting the signs. As a result, little Betty Beaver (Hanson), lured by an apple hanging suspiciously from a tree (off for the middle of winter) gets her tail caught in a bear trap and tells her friend, "Go get Porky! Go get Porky!"

Porky frees her and a slew of other poor critters trapped by the unseen villain, who gets really mad when he learns someone's let the animals out of his traps. He finds Porky tending to a long line of broken animals, attending to their bent bodies with an iron. Stepping in, the brute irons Porky's curly tail straight, sticks him onto a table, and thrashes him with a whip and snowshoes. Don't despair, help is on its way! In *Birth of a Nation*-inspired crosscutting, the "cavalry" comes, dozens of Porky's animal buddies: bears, marching turtles, skunks and others. They break down the door and chase the villain out, tripping up the bad guy as he flees. He lands head first in the snow and the cute li'l beavers use his upturned skis as a teeter-totter.

One of the superb cartoons, tightly-written and solidly directed, succeeding on all counts of comedy, action, and cuteness. Music includes "Little Man You've Had a Busy Day' and "In the Shade of the Old Apple Tree."

1937

HE WAS HER MAN

Jan 2; MM; Supervision by Isadore Freleng; Animation by Paul Smith and Cal Dalton; Musical Supervision by Carl W. Stalling.

An abusive and unpleasant melodrama, but the fact that its central character is a despicable antihero at least shows someone is trying to come up with more than the usual boy-girl-villain plot lines. Frankie worships Johnny, thinking him a mouse Clark Gable, although he makes her sell apples in the snow all day, fork over the dough, and then cook him dinner. To top it off, he beats her up for laughs. Even after he leaves her for a dancehall dame she forgives him when he walks through the door with his current flame. He feels the same way about her—rotten —and thrashes her about some more in an especially abusive dance. This is the last straw. She grabs a nearby pistol and fires on the lout. It only grazes him, but the shot has altered the nature of their relationship. Cut to Johnny hustling apples in the snow while Frankie, for a change, has it soft.

Music: "Fancy Meeting You," "I'd Love to Take Orders From You" (hummed by Frankie), and "He Was My Man," sung by Frankie with a voice that I would bet is really Wini Shaw (Warner's junior league Helen Morgan, who sang the famed "Lullaby of Broadway").

PORKY THE WRESTLER

Porky Pig; Jan 9; LT; Supervision by Fred Avery; Animation by Charles Jones and Elmer Wait; Musical Direction by Carl W. Stalling.

"Extra! Extra! Capacity Crowds to Witness Champion Wrestling Match Tonight! Everybody's Going!" First we get hitch-hike jokes, which conclude when Porky, on his way to the big event, is given a lift by the Challenger, who sports a Polish name that which is repeated many times for comic effect.

When the car pulls up to the stadium, the promoters fail to see the real wrestler fall into an open manhole and mistakenly assume Porky is the challenger. Before he can protest, they've got him in the ring with the bearded ferocious champ, "Man Mountain." The cartoon gets mileage out of the champ's brutal infantilism: he compresses the pig into a ball and plays with him, stupidly twisting his own legs around Porky's neck. Upon swallowing a customer's pipe, he plays choo-choo train and enrolls Porky and the ref in his shenanigans (someone opens a window and is startled to see railroad-style moving scenery). Next the brute uses the "Airplane Spin" (identified by a subtitle) on Porky. When he clobbers Porky on the head, the pig comes rebounding back from the other direction, thereby knocking out the champ and winning.

PIGS IS PIGS

Jan 30; MM; Supervision by Isadore Freleng; Animation by Bob McKimson and Paul Smith; Musical Direction by Carl W. Stalling.
This little Piggy is obsessed with the idea of food. While his brothers and sisters play, he dreams of chickens, watermelons, and corn on the cob. To kill time while waiting for dinner, he swipes and swallows one of his mother's pies. No sooner does she catch and scold him than his mind drifts again to thoughts of food. At chow time, his mother serves spaghetti. While all are saying grace, he ties everyone's pasta together so that he can consume it all with a single slurp! That night he dreams he's in the clutches of a hicupping scientist (Billy Bletcher), who for no reason has a mania for force-feeding the hungry little pig (not that he needs much forcing). The scientist devises new techniques for shoving food in the pig's mouth: automatic soup spoon twirlers, banana-openers, ice cream cone emptiers, automatic sandwich makers (the earliest known use of Friz's perennial "hold the onions" gag), a pie "jukebox," and others (all combined into a montage). They all leave Piggy an obese blubbery mess who refuses to learn any moral. When the scientist releases him,

he immediately shoves a chicken leg into his mouth and explodes! Or rather, he wakes up, but it's time for breakfast, and again he starts eating like it's going out of style.

Piggy's dreaming of food theme: "When My Dreamboat Comes Home." Mother's (Mrs. Hamhock) quaint Germanic theme: "My Boopshin."

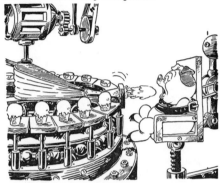

PORKY'S ROAD RACE

Porky Pig; Feb 6; LT; Supervision by Frank Tash; Animation by Robert Bentley and Joe D'Igalo; Musical Direction by Carl W. Stalling.
"All the characters in this picture are strictly phony. Any resemblance to any actual living person is the bunk." A deft merger of auto-race setting and gags plus quite droll movie star caricatures. Also original, even when resorting to Garbo's feet: the tootsies are shown sticking out from under her auto. "At last I am alone!" Laurel and Hardy inflate tires with a seesaw pump, Charlie Chaplin accidently wrenches W.C. Fields's nose, and then Fields helps Edna Mae Oliver ("My little wallflower") by filling her gas tank with hooch.

When the race commences, the villain "Borax Karoff" (a combination of the mad scientist and the monster), sinks Charles Laughton's floating power engine with a flying torpedo. Laughton cries, "It's mutiny!" The villain then douses the road in glue, causing most of the cars to stick to one another. Porky (whose wheels have been converted into tank-treads through a fortunate accident) gets through. Now it's just Porky and

Karoff, our hero gaining the advantage when they zoom over a drawbridge, causing Porky to fly overhead. Porky wins, but Edna Mae Oliver, whose vehicle has been gradually scaled down to a kiddie scooter and whose clothing has been obliterated down to her bloomers, gets the crown.

Other movie celebs: Gable hitch-hiking as in *It Happened One Night,* and the Cheerio special containing George Arliss, Leslie Howard, and Freddie Bartholomew, who drink tea with their pinkies extended.

Soundtrack: "At Your Service, Madame" (theme for Fields), "In My Merry Oldsmobile," "Don't Give Up the Ship," "Love and War."

PICADOR PORKY

Porky Pig; Feb 27; LT; Supervision by Fred Avery; Animation by Charles Jones and Sid Sutherland; Musical Direction by Carl W. Stalling.
Three gringos blow into a fiesta-mad Mexican village. Porky and his two pals get the wise-guy American idea of fleecing the natives out of a thousand-peso prize by having Porky pose as a matador who pretends to fight the other two in a bull costume. The plan backfires when the two pals get crocked, and a real bull comes into the ring. Porky boldly battles the bull thinking it's his two chums. When they stagger out in the middle of the ring, Porky realizes he's fighting a real bull! When the stooges come to their senses, they clobber the beast, take his place, and pretend to keel over so Porky can collect the loot. The bull then re-enters and chases them off.

A sturdy comedy plot serving as a framework for gags that exploit the possibilities of animation. There is Porky making the bull disappear into his handerchief and running up and down the borders of the screen. Mel Blanc does his earliest work for Warners as the drunk singing "La Cucuracha."

More soundtrack: "In Caliente," "Lady of Spain," "Lady in Red."

I ONLY HAVE EYES FOR YOU

Mar 6; MM; Supervision by Fred Avery; Animation by Bob Clampett and Virgil Ross; Musical Direction by Carl W. Stalling.
A literate story that first introduces us, through a background chorus, to an all-bird cast. The hero is a spoonerism-spouting, buck-toothed iceman, trying to avoid an ungainly old maid who's forever trying to seduce him with her cooking. The object of his affection is Katie Canary, who repeatedly rejects him on the grounds that "I'm saving my heart and my love for a radio crooner. Some day, some way, I shall marry one, and I know we shall be so terribly happy, really I do!" The situation's hopeless until the iceman comes across Prof. Mockingbird, ventriloquist and imitator. Learning that he can croon, the hero sticks the bird in the back of his ice truck. Cyrano-like, he lip syncs to the Prof.'s performance of the 1934 "Dames" number, fooling Katie, who instantly snuggles next to him on the front seat. The jig is up when the ventriloquist starts shaking from the cold, shivering until he sneezes the truck apart.

The last scene reveals Katie taking care of the sick Prof. while moving men replace her radio with an icebox (electric!). Our hero is resigned to eating the old maid's edibles for the rest of his days.

THE FELLA WITH THE FIDDLE

Mar 27; MM; Supervision by Isadore Freleng; Animation by Cal Dalton and Cal Howard; Musical Direction by Carl W. Stalling.
When he sees his grandchildren acting greedy, Gramps Mouse tells them a cautionary story about how a money-hungry mouse was done in by his lust for gold. Begging on the streets, he makes a fortune pretending to be blind and playing a violin. He lives in a luxurious mansion, which has been elaborately doctored to look like a poor shack. When the Tax Assessor comes around the fancy furniture rolls over and is replaced by seedy stuff. At one point the taxman catches the house in mid-metamorphosis but doesn't believe his eyes. It isn't taxes that does this

mouse in, it is death. A hungry cat approaches his shack/palace and, realizing the mouse's lust for bucks, tempts him into his mouth by putting gold coins in it. The trick works, though not before the mouse has accidently pulled out a tooth instead of the gold. This same tooth becomes important after the story is told. Seeing this tooth on Grampa's vest, one of the little mice realizes that Gramps is actually the fella with the fiddle and that he wasn't done in by his own greed after all.

PORKY'S ROMANCE

Porky Pig, Petunia Pig; Apr 3; LT; Supervision by Frank Tash; Animation by Don Williams and Volney White; Musical Direction by Carl W. Stalling.
Tashlin doesn't just direct cartoons, he conducts symphonies, and *Porky's Romance* is a perfectly orchestrated concerto for heartstrings. Flowing seamlessly beginning to end, this is a tale of Porky who (after a suicide attempt gives him a dream-inducing blow to the head) hallucinates about marrying his lady love, "Leon Schlesinger's New Cartoon Star: Petunia Pig." Tashlin reveals his mastery of tempo (of the overall film) and timing (of individual gags) as well as an eagle eye for the million little details that make the difference between a potboiler and art. Tashlin anticipates both Speilberg and Mel Brooks, using a given vocabulary of genre elements, and out-does both of them in making you feel along with the characters, then pulling out the rug, reminding you that this is a movie. All of this is established through the contrast of heightened realities: the idyllic wedding and honeymoon, separated by a title card ("Time Munches On"), frantic nightmarish wedded life wherein the obese shrew Petunia clouts her henpecked hubby with a Maggie-and-Jiggs rolling pin for not properly taking care of dishes, cooking, ironing, and washing, as well as their dozens of Katzenjammer kids. Porky wakes up from his dream and not only flees from Petunia and marriage, but gives her obnoxious dog a much-deserved kick that sends him flying through the iris out.

SHE WAS AN ACROBAT'S DAUGHTER

Apr 10; MM; Supervision by Isadore Freleng; Animation by Bob McKimson and A. C. Gamer; Musical Direction by Carl W. Stalling.
This year's installment in the long, long series of "theater" cartoons is one of the funniest. This movie house's program consists of a newsreel and a feature. The first is punnily named "The Goofy-Tone News." There is a story about a mad dog's bite that causes the good people of Boondoggle to go about on all fours and bury bones (it's narrated by Lew Lehr, aka "Who Dehr," and the animal audience doesn't laugh either). The main attraction is "The Petrified Florist," a rib-tickling parody on the play, complete with on-the-money caricatures of Leslie Howard and Bette Davis. But the gags come from the audience, too, including a look at the screen from widely distorted angles. There's solid choreography in a scene where virtually everybody switches seats before the lights dim. An obese hippo annoys all when he wants to get up and sit down again, and talky nuisances such as the donkey who offers refreshments in the middle of the picture and a little goose who refuses to stop gabbing dumb questions and ends the program by screwing up the projector. Best of all, a singalong of "Acrobat's Daughter" illustrated by Milt Gross-inspired drawings, with one wrong slide getting in by mistake so the entire crowd sings "Please do not spit on the floor."
    More music: "Woodenhead Puddin'-head Jones," "Nagasaki."

PORKY'S DUCK HUNT

Porky Pig, Daffy Duck; Apr 17; LT; Supervision by Fred Avery; Animation by Virgil Ross and Robert Cannon; Musical Direction by Carl W. Stalling.
Stop the presses! No discovery in western civilization can compare with this one: Warner toonists hit upon ideas that will really put them on the map. Porky and his dog-of-the-week go hunting ducks in the marshes where they encounter no end of screwy wildlife, not the least of which are dozens of fel-

low hunters, who down planes (mistaking them for ducks) and commence firing on Porky when he tries out a duck call. A quintet of inebriated fish harmonize on "Moonlight Bay" (and, more remarkable, hiccup on key and in tempo!). They win my booby-prize. You can tell the director's heart is most with a brilliantly inane little black duck who ululates hysterically as he bounces across the marsh. When Porky points out a move that isn't in the script, the duck insists that he's just a crazy darn fool duck. When Porky gives up and trudges wearily home (his dog "Rin-Tin-Tin" having swallowed the duck call), he finds a bevy of "sitting" ducks performing acrobatics outside his window. To conclude, the star duck reprises his *danse d'idiot* over the "Looney Tunes ... That's All Folks" end title!

AIN'T WE GOT FUN

Apr 17; MM; Supervision by Fred Avery; Animation by Charles Jones and Robert Clampett; Musical Direction by Carl W. Stalling.

The first of three ultracute Avery mouse cartoons (followed by *A Sunbonnet Blue* and *The Mice Will Play,*) this one uses a decade-old ditty for a plug tune. The plot consists of a triangle between a doddering old fool who likes to curl up in his easy chair and smack his cat when he finds him there, the cat, who's always putting up with the man's abuse, and a community of mice (in stylish bell-bottomed trousers), who wait for the cat to sleep so they can transform the pantry into a veritable department store for mice (a dumbwaiter serving as elevator). The mice use food for sport as well as nourishment, assigning a sentry to warn them at the approach of the cat. The crackers the

sentry consumes prevent him from whistling his warning and the cat breaks up the act. They leave him holding the food (and covered in a roast chicken) so the old man thinks he's been eating him out of house and home. The toothless old geezer throws the cat out in the snow, shouting, "Give you a home and what do you do? You eat it!" The cute li'l rodents immediately throw a mouse party. It gets underway with a smooth trio performance of "Ain't We Got Fun" and climaxes with dozens of mice pelting the oldtimer with food. He begs the cat to return, but the cat holds out until the mice tease him. He reward for scaring them right out of the house is getting to recline in the old man's chair, while the old man has to curl up on a rug!

Background themes include "Gee, But You're Swell," "Love and War," "Meow."

PORKY AND GABBY

Porky Pig, Gabby Goat; May 15; LT; Supervision by Ub Iwerks; Animation by Charles Jones and Robert Clampett; Musical Direction by Carl W. Stalling.

Only one season into the Porky series proper and already they're saddling him with co-stars. While the obnoxious and unlovable Gabby Goat wouldn't last much longer than Lulu the Ostrich, elements of his voice and personality would soon be assimilated into Daffy Duck. His debut consists less of plot than of camping episodes designed to display his single character trait, hot-headed impatience. From start to finish, it's rare that Gabby stops fuming and screaming. For starters, Porky and Gabby tangle with a slow-moving truck that won't get out of the way of their car. ("Excited? Who's excited?") The episode ends in Gabby getting mushed into a murky mud puddle. Gabby also burns when they have to push their car over a hill. A bee messes up Porky's attempt to pitch the tent. For the longest sequence, they're not faced with inconvenience so much as violent death! Gabby accidently starts an outboard motor (unconnected to any boat), which goes flying through the air, its propeller slicing the tent and gear to shreds and threatening to do the same to Porky and Gabby. When they drive away from this flying instrument of death, they crash into the same truck that gave them grief in the beginning.

CLEAN PASTURES

May 22; MM; Supervision by I Freleng; Animation by Phil Monroe and Paul Smith; Musical Direction by Carl W. Stalling.

Harlem good times, with drinking, gambling and carryin' on, causes the stock of Heaven (Pair-o-Dice Pre-ferred) to plummet, as that of the other place, Hades, Inc.'s, soars. St. Peter doesn't know what to do. His first attempt at converting the heathen, a shiftless Stepin Fetchit angel, proves ineffective in getting the highlivin' Harlemites to abandon their sinful ways at ginjoints like "The Kotton Club." However, St. Pete is flanked by a group of more modern angels, exem-plifying the new black man of the future, represented by the musical geniuses who would play a major role: Louis Armstrong, Fats Waller, Jimmie Lunceford, and Cab Calloway. They preach to Peter that "to get the folks to Pair-o-Dice, you really have to mod-ernize." He gets the idea. When these slick-looking up-to-date cool black angels show up on Lenox Avenue, com-bining their talents in an exuberant "Swing for Sale," the folks just come 'a runnin'. Soon not only is there a parade of ex-sinners following the Cal-loway angel up to the Pearly Gates, Lucifer himself wants to get in!

An appealing all-black cartoon and a forerunner of the classic *Coal Black* and *Tin Pan Alley Cats.*

More music: "Old Folks at Home" (tapped by Bojangles Robinson), Jolie loving to singa to his dummy Jewish/black sonny boy, "Half of Me," "Sweet Georgia Brown," "Save Me Sister," "Rhythm," and "Golden Slippers."

UNCLE TOM'S BUNGALOW

June 5; MM; Supervision by Fred Avery; Animation by Sid Sutherland and Virgil Ross; Musical Direction by Carl W. Stalling.

The story of Uncle Tom's cabin, paro-died with modern touches such as Simon-Simon Legree (pronounced see-moan-seemoan) selling Uncle Tom to Topsy and Little Eva like a used car and then repossessing when they fail to keep up with the installments. Labori-ous and plodding: Avery goes through a tedious introduction of the characters ("and last but not leashed, the hounds") and is unable to make a joke out of their being bored with the old Uncle Tom story, an idea he would work out beautifully in *Red Hot Riding Hood* (MGM, 1943) Anyhow, after Legree comes to collect Uncle Tom, the chase over the ice floes begins, the narrator becoming a horse-race announcer (Liza is "the dark horse in this race"). How-ever, Uncle Tom is able to pay off Legree with the money he made shoot-ing craps (he grabs the dice over the iris out as it starts to close). "My body might belong to you, but my soul belongs to Warner Bros."

PORKY'S BUILDING

Porky Pig; Jun 19; LT; Supervision by Frank Tashlin; Animation by Volney White and Norman McCabe; Musical Direction by Carl W. Stalling.

"This is indeed a malignant situation." Contractors Porky and his nogoodnick competitor, Dirty Diggs, submit identical bids for the job of erecting a new city hall. The city building commissioner devises a rather elaborate means of settling the ques-tion: both companies are to erect build-ings, and whoever finishes first wins the contract. The whole plot is laid out like a college football story. As in most such stories (from *The Freshman* on, including *Along Flirtation Walk*) it's the eager young bench-warmer, in this case a falsetto'ed rabbit ("How 'bout me, Porky?") who, when finally put into the game, saves the day. Porky's crew also includes a camel who mixes cement by rhumba-ing with cocktail shakers on his humps and one little fellow who can't get the crowd to keep away from him when he's using explosives and finally decides the heck with it and blows them all up. It looks like Dirty Diggs is going to win with his gosh darn fast brick laying machine. Porky's hare reveals himself to be a super-colossal brick layer. He uses his ears to construct walls as fast as the machine and gets the advantage when Dirty Diggs's doodad gets stuck in reverse and deconstructs his building before it explodes. Porky and the rabbit pose victoriously atop their new city hall.

Background tunes include "Organ Grinder's Swing" and "Let's Put Our Heads Together."

STREAMLINED GRETA GREEN

Jun 19; MM; Supervision by Isadore Freleng; Animation by Cal Dalton and Ken Harris; Musical Direction by Carl W. Stalling.
A slice-of-life episode in a world of automobiles making like people with no humans present (save one service station attendant). Human and auto paraphernalia are freely interchanged. A gas station becomes a bar, a garage a home, and the term "Taxi Dance Hall" takes on new meaning. Cars also experience the human cycle of life. Our juvenile protagonist (another boy with a Bernice Hanson voice) is at that awkward stage where he has imagined a frivilous, fun career as a taxi (his world's equivalent of a cowboy, one supposes) while his mother has in mind for him the life of a touring car (businessman). Instead of going to school, he drives into town to play in the dangerous big city traffic. A slug of powerful gas gives him the nerve to try to outrace a speeding locomotive, his trick being to zoom cross the tracks just in front of the oncoming express train. It works two times, but he doesn't know when he's run out of gas, and gets stuck on the tracks. Pow! Human auto doctors repair him, but even after this

accident and his mother's scolding, he heads right back for the train tracks. This time, instead of being wrecked by the railroad car, it's more the other way around.

On the soundtrack: "Streamlined Greta Green" sung by a quartet impersonating the Mills Brothers, "My Little Buckaroo," of Broadway," "Little Man You've Had a Busy Day," "Shuffle Off to Buffalo."

SWEET SIOUX

Jun 26; MM; Supervision by Isadore Freleng; Animation by Bob McKimson and A. C. Gamer Williams; Musical Direction by Carl W. Stalling .
Black-out gags on an Indian reservation leading up to the tribe's attack on a wagon. Freleng obviously loves opening with a majestic shot of the stoic noble savage just so he can deflate it with a shot of "Chief Rain-in-the-Face" with a miniature storm going off in his kisser. More gags: a Joe College Indian wearing his teepee like a racoon skin rug (wearing *Freddie the Freshman*'s glasses and singing his song); a lazy lug Injun bums a ride by leaping on a passing squaw. After they spot the oncoming palefaces ("Calling all Braves ..."), the tribe does a war dance, led by a big-breasted Martha Raye caricature, and interpolates the Russian cossack dance. The best gags (not to mention a much reused sequence of Injuns riding toward the camera) come during the battle sequence. Indians become a merry-go-round, then a college football team (subs warm benches while the crowd chants, "Give 'em the axe! The axe!"). There also is a Yiddish Indian who looks like Mel Brooks in *Blazing Saddles*. Only the morbid ending, which implies that both Injuns and settlers have been wiped out, falls flat. One brave clubs another just so he can be the last of the Mohicans.

PORKY'S SUPER SERVICE

Porky Pig; July 3; LT; Supervision by Ub Iwerks; Animation by Charles Jones and Robert Clampett; Musical Direction by Carl W. Stalling.
Porky the gas station owner/attendant and his customers. One drives a mod-

ern vehicle so newfangled it's impossible to find the gas tank. Another, upon learning he has a flat, cries, "Why don't somebody tell me these things!" In trying to remove a dent from one car, Porky hammers it away but it repeatedly pops up in different places. Finally, it eggs Porky into breaking the guy's windshield. The *piece de resistance* only marginally involves the gas station setting. Porky battles with the meanest of mean little kids (you know you're really in for it when they wear baby bonnets), who constantly gives Porky a hard time when he's not looking. The lad sticks the air hose in Porky's pants and sends him skyward. Eventually, the kid's equally awful mother finds the two of them squirting grease guns at each other. In the windup, just when you can't decide who's the more irritating, the brat or his royally asinine mom, the terrifying toddler decides for you by tying a gas hose to their departing car and pulling the entire station down around Porky.

Background music: "Little Old Fashioned Music Box," "My Little Buckaroo," "Gee, But You're Swell."

EGGHEAD RIDES AGAIN

Egghead; July 17; MM; Supervision by Fred Avery; Animation by Paul Smith and Irvin Spence; Musical Direction by Carl W. Stalling.

Though the title and the main character (repeatedly) tell us that Buck Egghead rides again, this represents the first time out for Egghead, an Alfred E. Newman-like twerp who also assumes the personas of Joe Penner, Daffy Duck, and Barney Rubble. He's a lad obsessed with the west whose dadburn landlord throws him out for making too much dadburn noise while playing dadburn cowboy, dadburn it. He stumbles across (literally) a want ad from the Bar None Ranch in Wahoo, Wyoming, and mails himself there via the pony express. He announces to the ranch hands, "I'm a rootin', tootin', shootin', high falutin' cowboy ... and I want the job because today I yam a man!" They tell him he's got to "shoot straight and ride hard" to qualify. He can't quite hack the cowboy tests they put him

through. When told to brand a calf, he brands everybody in sight but that calf. Told to catch it and he'll get the job, he chases the calf across the prairie and hills, and winds up being roped and tied by the calf. In the conclusion, he gets the job all right, but it's not what he thinks!

The western-oriented score includes "My Little Buckaroo."

PORKY'S BADTIME STORY

Porky Pig; Gabby Goat; July 24; LT; Supervision by Robert Clampett; Animation by Charles Jones; Musical Direction by Carl W. Stalling.

An early attempt at slow-burn "frustration" humor, which seems as exasperating to do properly as any action of the on-screen characters. Porky and Gabby race to work so fast they pull their garage inside out. In the central slow sequence, the two try to sleep so they can make it to work on time the next morning and not lose their jobs. The elements conspire against them to keep them awake, starting with a yowling alley cat who throws shoes back at Porky, an annoying bee, and a windowshade that engages the Pig in a graceful ballet of rolling upwards (and letting in moonlight) whenever he's not looking. Worst of all, a rainstorm comes through their leaky roof and nearly drowns the two of them (having been reduced to sleeping in a common bed). Comes the dawn, and our heroes awaken from the chest of drawers they've taken refuge in (their beds having been obliterated), and high-tail it to work. The punchline: it's Sunday and the place is closed.

Lots of music, very little dialogue: "When My Dreamboat Comes Home," "Woodenhead Puddin'head Jones," "How Could You?" "By the Light of the Silvery Moon," and "September in the Rain."

PLENTY OF MONEY AND YOU

July 31; MM; Supervision by Isadore Freleng; Animation by Cal Dalton and Phil Monroe; Musical Direction by Carl W. Stalling.

This cartoon is about an ostrich that likes to eat things; that's about the extent of his personality. He's hatched out of a chicken's egg at the start with no explanation, although the row that Mama and the other hens make informs us that this is not a routine occurrence. The Mother Hen attempts to raise him as if he were just another chick, but while they're scratching for worms and doing all sorts of cool chicken stuff, he's devouring all kinds of unchickenish vittles like fish and auto jacks. A villainous rodent, described by a title card as "The Weasel (The Rat)," apprehends the ostrich with the idea of eating him for a change (turnabout is fair play). As he seasons the bird (wearing a chef's hat) he sings (Mel Blanc) the plug number from *Golddiggers of 1937*, changing the word "money" to "gravy." It was the ostrich's ceaseless consumption of inedible objects that got him into this fix, it is that that gets him out. He swallows a load of fireworks, and in a few very painful shots, gets stuck live in a red hot oven. You might predict that the heat would set off the fireworks, but who could have guessed that the shots of the ostrich regurgitating explosions all over the room would be so gross? Or that the ground in the nearby farmyard would shake earthquakelike from the bird's firework belches. When the weasel at last tosses him out, his mother hen embraces him, but she too gets turned off by the ostrich's internal explosions.

PORKY'S RAILROAD

Porky Pig; Aug 7; LT; Supervision by Frank Tashlin; Animation by Joe D'Igalo and Robert Bentley; Musical Direction by Carl W. Stalling.

As in 1938's *Porky's Poppa*, the pig plays the sentimentalist defender of old traditions that come into conflict with new ways. Opening titles introduce us to two locomotives, the 30th Century Limited, described as a "crack train" and the 5th Century Limited. Porky is in the train he affectionately calls "Toots" (also a crack train—everything is cracked, including the engineer). The train is too feeble to make it up a mountain until Porky sprinkles pepper into its furnace and it sneezes its way up.

After Porky tangles with a stubborn cow and an angry bull on the tracks, he gets word that he and Toots are to be replaced by an art deco, souped-up streamline train called "The Silver Fish." When the taunting engineer of the rival train calls Toots a percolator on a roller skate, Porky mumbles under his breath how his train can easily beat the other. The guy takes him up on it. When it looks like the bad guy will win, Porky chugs past the same bull he had tangles with earlier, and the irate beast butts the front car clear over his competitor. After Porky wins, he gets to engineer the "Silver Fish," with Toots on board as a passenger ("headin' for the last roundhouse").

Lots of offbeat, rarely used camera angles (particularly Porky's aside to the audience). The score includes "California Here I Come."

A SUNBONNET BLUE

Aug 21; MM; Supervision by Fred Avery; Animation by Sid Sutherland and Virgil Ross; Musical Direction by Carl W. Stalling.

In the Snobby Hatte Shoppe one night, a boy mouse peers out of a mousehole, looks around and shouts, "Is anybody here?" Finding no response, he calls out all his friends from the mousehole, including his girl and a green-skinned "villain" rat. The boy and girl take center stage, sing a love song about a "Sunbonnet blue and a yellow straw hat" (the hats come to life and enact a marriage and family life) to the all-mice audience. They are followed by "The Three Ratz Brothers" (a Ritz Bros. spoof) who sing a medley that includes "I Haven't Got A Hat," "An Old Gray Bonnet," and "The Lady in Red" (with marvelously looney animation by Irven Spence).

The villainous rat kidnaps the girl. The boy mouse finds the mouse police chief under a helmet, and they call out the troops. Under each cap in the shop is the appropriate hero mouse: the fire hat, cowboy hat, football helmet, etc. The boy mouse puts a flattened top hat under the rat, and it springs the villain into an iron mask from a suit of armor. The boy and girl mouse get married. A wedding present is brought out in a large hat box. Inside, a live-action still of a baby bonnet.

GET RICH QUICK PORKY

Porky Pig; Aug 28; LT; Supervision by Robert Clampett; Animation by Charles Jones; Musical Direction by Carl W. Stalling.

"Get Rich Quick Sale—This lovely lot contains lots and lots, oh! just oodles of oil!" A mustachioed villain named Honest John rigs up a worthless city lot to look like it's dripping with oil, then parts a couple of fools, Porky Pig and Gabby Goat, from their money by selling it to them. They grab a couple of tools from a nearby street repair site and begin digging. Meanwhile, a goofy-looking dog with a perpetual cross-eyed smile and an elastic body tries to bury his bone in the lot, but the oil keeps squirting back at him. Gabby, digging with a pneumatic drill, gets carried underground. The dog encounters a wide-eyed gopher who forcibly ejects the bone from the hole and does a magician-style disappearing act with it. Porky discovers the villain's land trick, and the crook offers to give him a "nice crisp one-dollar bill" in exchange for the deed. Meanwhile, Gabby, riding underground on the drill, runs into a pocket of real, honest-to-gosh oil! The stuff comes gushing out of the ground just as Porky is handing the deed back to Honest John, and the two struggle for the paper atop the gusher. Porky gets the edge when Gabby rides the pneumatic drill into the villain's pants (you can see how that would give him the advantage). Porky discovers he's holding the dog's bone instead! Luckily, the gopher offers to give back the paper, half of it rather, provided they agree to split the proceeds "Fifty-fifty, even-steven."

SPEAKING OF THE WEATHER

Sept 4; MM; Supervision by Frank Tashlin; Animation by Joe D'Igalo and Volney White; Musical Direction by Carl W. Stalling.

Magazine covers come to life. First a crime story is enacted, a re-do from *I Like Mountain Music* (1933), this time with added attractions. First music: Leopold Stokowski, on the cover of "Etude" magazine, starting to conduct the "Storm" movement of "William Tell," then within a single frame trucking and breaking into "Speaking of the Weather" (scatting in a thick Blanc-style Russian accent!). After the number, sung by trios of both femme vocalistes and tongue sandwiches, we get into the mini-mellerdrammer: Crook from "The Gang" magazine uses torch from "Popular Mechanics" to open safe on cover of "Wall Street." Crook is caught by Charlie Chan from "Detective" and delivers a "True Confession," then is sentenced by the "Judge" to "Life" but soon escapes to "Liberty."

It's in the chase finale that the gags really start coming fast and furious. Everyone joins in from the Boy Scouts on "American Boy" to Tarzan on the cover of "Jungle Stories." In the chasing-the-villain bit are animals from "Nature," sailors from "Sea Stories," battleships from "Our Navy," banditos from "Wild West," along with William "Thin Man" Powell (from a book: one assumes they couldn't think of a magazine) and his dog Asta from "Dog World," who scare the Mug disguised as a "Better Baby" (although Powell must blindfold Asta as they walk past "The Saturday Evening Post"). Everybody gets into the act, even Greta Garbo ("Photoplay"). Crook ultimately lands in the book, "Twenty Thousand Years in Sing-Sing."

PORKY'S GARDEN

Porky Pig; Sept 11; LT; Supervision by Fred Avery; Animation by Sid Sutherland and Elmer Wait; Musical

Direction by Carl W. Stalling.
Porky and his Italian next-door neighbor compete for a cash prize ($2,000 less $1,999 tax) for the largest home-grown product at the upcoming county fair. Porky's entry is his jumbo vegetables, which he grows big and juicy with the aid of "Quick Grow Hair Tonic." The neighbor plans to enter his chickens by spiking their feed with vitamins. When they spit out the vitamins, he plays dirty pool and sicks 'em on Porky's produce the moment he goes inside. For a few minutes we get chickens-eating-veggies gags (spinach transforms a weak little chick into Popeye, the sailor). By the time Porky discovers the damage, it's too late, and the neighbor isn't all that helpful ("I canna make-a da chickens talk."). However, Porky has one huge pumpkin left and must get it past the chickens straight to the fair, although the big chickens seem like a shoo-in for the prize. Unfortunately for them, they swallow a medicine-show man's reducing pills and shrink just as they're about to take the prize away from Porky's pumpkin. As the twin irises start to close, Porky grabs the prize from the Italian over the iris black.

Music: "Pretty Baby," "Carolina in the Morning," "Am I Blue."

DOG DAZE
Sept 18; MM; Supervision by Isadore Freleng; Animation by Bob McKimson and A.C. Gamer; Musical Direction by Carl W. Stalling.
Dog show gags, only thinly connected. First we check out various breeds on display, all of them puns. A bird dog is in a canary cage, an Irish setter hatches pups out of eggs, a spitz expectorates. On a stage we get what amounts to doggie-vaudeville, varying between musical acts. Scotties do the highland fling, wolf hounds do a cossack dance, a trio of prairie dogs does "My Little Buckaroo" with new lyrics, "Dog Eat Dog," a little pup consuming a frankfurter, and "Little Man You've Had a Busy Day," an exhausted pup who has just done what doggies will do to a row of telephone poles. As a running gag, a great clumsy St. Bernard

slides around on roller skates and lets a flea circus attack one little Bernice Hanson pup re-enacting "Mary's Little Lamb" from *I Haven't Got a Hat*; the pup then gets sowsed on the St. Bernard's supply of brandy. None of the gags is bad, but we could do with a bigger wind-up gag for the finish.

I WANNA BE A SAILOR
Sept 25; MM; Supervision by Fred Avery; Musical Direction by Carl W. Stalling.
This starts with a potentially cutesy cautionary tale, slipping in many wise-guy gags (preferably the kind where someone gets to talk to the audience). Little tough guy Petey Parrott wants to be a sailor, his mother wants him to be a cute li'l "Polly want a cracker"-type. Both for the same reason: his father was a sailor, "that high-seas home-wrecker, that sea-goin' slob, that rum-soaked old seagull who couldn't stand bein' anchored in one harbor for five minutes."

Petey transforms a barrel into a "play" boat in which he intends to put out to sea because today he is a man! The uninterruptedly verbal Gabby Goose ("Ain't I the talkin'est little guy") comes along for the ride as Petey sings "I am the Captain's Kid!" Petey only talks a good fight. When a thunderstorm breaks and the waves sink their precarious craft, he yells for mother, who comes running out to them (shouting "I'm coming! I'm coming!" then "'Cause my head is bending low."). Petey is saved by swimming-type bird Gabby (who calls him a "Big Sissy!"). In the last gag he's asked if he still wants to be a sailor, and he sobs sadly but says, "Yes!" Ma does a take and faints, asking the audience, "Now what would you do with a child like that?"

Overheard: We're Workin' Our Way Through College" and "September in the Rain."

ROVER'S RIVAL

Porky Pig; Oct 9; LT; Supervision by Robert Clampett; Animation by Charles Jones; Musical Direction by Carl W. Stalling.

Porky, full of enthusiasm about a book of "New Tricks to Teach Your Dog," is anxious to try them out with his dog Rover, an ancient doddering old hound (whose entrance is underscored by "Old Black Joe"). Rover can barely hear Porky's instruction. and is far too arthritic to tackle any of the tricks. A brash young pup comes along who can and does know the tricks, not only showing up Rover in front of Porky, but constantly insulting him as well. "You're finished, through, washed up ... you're one of them there used-to-wases!"

While playing fetch the stick (Rover accidently leaves his dentures on it at one point), the young pup accidently retrieves a stick of dynamite from a nearby construction site. Old Rover has brains enough to dash to the dictionary and look up the word "dynamite," while the pup keeps chasing after the hapless Porky and handing him the sticks. Self-sacrificing and stoic, Old Rover finally manages to grab the TNT from the pup and runs off with it. After the explosion, the pup and Porky think poor Rover is finished. The little dog is at last apologetic and humble. "Why, shucks, Rover, you're the best little stick bringer-backer that ever was!" On hearing this, Rover recovers, sits up, and asks, "Do ya mean it?"

THE LYIN' MOUSE

Oct 16; MM; Supervision by Isadore Freleng. Story by Tedd Pierce; Animation by Ken Harris; Musical Direction by Carl W. Stalling.

Freleng's tenure as a Warner director may predate Avery and Tashlin, but he contributes to the development of wacky rowdyism as much as anyone. That's by bold, broad strokes as well as by subtler though no less insidious means. Instance: the ridiculing of cartoon elements taken seriously such as Bernice Hanson's cutey-cute voice. Here, the voice belongs to a little mouse caught in a trap and about to be sacrificed to a hungry cat's (Blanc) appetite. Pleading with the cat to spare him, he tells a story about a ferocious lion (Bletcher: "I'm the rip-snortin'est, Edward Everett Horton'est, Charles Laughton'est, you ain't heard nort'in'est lion in the whole jungle") with a killer roar that terrifies animals and rolls up the jungle carpet floor. He catches a mouse (the same) and sets it free, because he's more interested in food he sees in traps set by lion-catcher Frank Cluck. One contains a live lamb who silently begs the lion to eat him. The lion ends up in a circus where a tamer thrills the crowd by first putting his head in the big cat's mouth then reversing roles. Later, the mouse frees the lion by gnawing through his wooden cage. Back to real life, the blubbering cat releases the mouse, who, just before ducking into his hole, turns to the cat and yells, "Sucker!"

The grand-daddy of later lion-mouse flicks such as Jones's *From Hand to Mouse* and Avery's *Slap-Happy Lion*.

Music: "Congo," "Little Old Fashioned Music Box," "How Could You?" "Too Marvelous for Words," "Am I Blue?" "Old King Cole."

THE CASE OF THE STUTTERING PIG

Porky Pig, Petunia Pig; Oct 30; LT; Supervision by Frank Tashlin; Story by Melvin Millar; Animation by Volney White; Musical Direction by Carl W. Stalling.

In this amazingly directed horror-parody, the mystery elements work well enough to be taken seriously. All shot composition and editing represent a cartoonization of a James Whale or a Tod Browning gothic. Kindly lawyer Goodwill informs the nieces and nephews of the late Solomon Swine (Porky,

Petunia, Peter, Percy, and Portus) that they're to inherit his fortune, but that if anything happens to all of them, this same lawyer is next in line to the property. When the gentle lawyer leaves he ducks downstairs to the cellar, and there drinks a bottle of "Jeckle and Hyde juice," instantly turning into a maniacal monster. He announces his intentions to the theater audience; "I'm going to get rid of those pigs, and you can't help them either, you bunch of softies! Yeah, you in the third row!" Upstairs, the light switches off and on, each time one of Porky's brood disappears. Then, when Porky and Petunia gingerly tip-toe through the halls in search of them, the fiend substitutes himself for Petunia. When Porky realizes whose hand he's holding, he split-second dashes upstairs. Upon seeing who he's talking to, he dashes down into the basement. There he discovers the others held in a wooden trap. The villain breaks through the door and starts coming after them as they cower helplessly in a corner. A chair hits the bad guy and knocks him into the trap. "Who did that?" they ask in unison. "Me," an off-camera voice answers. "Who are you?" the villain asks, and the voice tells him, "I'm the guy in the third row, ya big sourpuss!"

LITTLE RED WALKING HOOD
Egghead; Nov 6; MM; Supervision by Fred Avery; Story by Cal Howard; Animation by Irven Spence; Musical Direction by Carl W. Stalling.
A storybook opens to page one and "Once upon A time," a modern version of the fairy tale "Little Red Riding Hood" is told. The wolf is in the pool hall playing pinball when he spots Red walking by. He hops into his sports car and tries to pick up the walking hood (a combination of Bette Davis with a Kate Hepburn voice). She gives him a literal cold shoulder (with icicles!). The wolf talks to her from his car in song, "Gee, But You're Swell," until he hits his head on a mail box. Egghead gives him directions to Grandma's (Egghead pops up all through the picture whistling "The Organ Grinder's Swing"). Though Granny won't open her locked

door to anyone, Egghead walks right in. The wolf breaks the door down, running through the house to the back-yard. He opens the back door by pulling on the knob and playing pinball with it. The wolf chases Granny around the house, while she keeps him at bay by declaring "King's Ex!" Granny gets a phone call from the general store and orders her long list of groceries (including a case of gin) while the wolf waits and complains, "Aw, come on, Gran'ma!" When Red arrives, the wolf dons a nightie and jumps into bed. Red makes comments like "What a large 'schnozola' you have!" The wolf chases Red, stopping only for some people in the audience to be seated. The wolf finally asks Egghead who he is and what he's doing in the cartoon. He responds with a mallet to the wolf's head stating, "I'm the hero in this picture!"

The backgrounds are rendered with colored pencils, perhaps an attempt to give it a more "storybook" look.

PORKY'S DOUBLE TROUBLE
Porky Pig; Nov 13; LT; Supervision by Frank Tashlin; Story by George Manuel; Animation by Joe D'Igalo; Musical Direction by Carl Stalling.
The Killer, a criminal pig, escapes from Alcarazz Prison. Meanwhile, his gang awaits him at their hideout, the "Katz School for Girls." A Mae West-type comes to the hideout door and it turns out to be the Killer in disguise (with a barbell as breasts). Reading about his escape in the paper, the Killer spots an item about Porky Pig ("From janitor to bank teller in 15 easy years!"), and notices a resemblance ("He could be me twin brother!"). Meanwhile, Porky is on duty at the Worst National Bank and is too shy to accept a date from sultry Petunia Pig.

On his way to lunch, Porky helps "Mae West" with her car— and gets kidnapped. Brought to the hideout, the Killer puts on Porky's "sissy clothes." Inside Porky's teller station, the Killer takes all the money and jewels given to him. When Petunia comes, the killer steals a kiss. "Why wait till tonight, baby!" Realizing this isn't the Porky she knows, Petunia rings the alarm. Racing back to his hideout, the Killer and his gang are soon surrounded by the police. Porky breaks free and fights with the Killer. The police break in, and only Petunia can identify the real Porky Pig (of course the Killer has been clearly unshaven throughout the cartoon). Petunia moans, "How that killer can kiss!"

THE WOODS ARE FULL OF CUCKOOS

Dec 4; MM; Supervision by Frank Tashlin; Story by Melvin Millar; Animation by Robert Bentley; Musical Direction by Carl W. Stalling.

A really wonderful idea: where *Coo Coo Nut Grove* and *Hollywood Steps Out* take the likenesses of Hollywood stars and transfer them to cartoon imagery (whether as funny animals or people), this cartoon constructs dozens and dozens of characters based on the names, voices, and personalities of radio stars, without, except in one or two cases, giving a hang about what these people look like! (Actually, it's the same idea that would create Foghorn Leghorn ten years later.) A radio revue program serves as the format, so funny (and so beautifully drawn) that it's only a minor irritant that many of the stars of this bygone era are now completely obscure (for instance, there's a long but funny spoof on the forgotten "Community Sing" program). There is the ever-feuding Ben "Birdie" and Walter "Finchell," the Happiness Boys, Billy Goat (Jones) and Ernest Bear (Hare) who lead the crowd in a singalong on "The Woods Are Full of Cuckoos (and my heart is full of love)." Fred Allen is a Red Fox, Eddie Gander, Sophie Turkey (Last of the Red Hot Gobblers), W.C. Fieldmouse, Dick Fowl, Fats Swallow, Deanna Terrapin, Fred McFurry, Bing Crowsby, Al Goatson (the singing kid, yet!), Ruby Squealer, Grace Moose and Lily Swans (two dickering divas who try to out-sing each other in a long-neck high-note contest), Joe Penguin (reprising "My Green Fedora" in animation from the 1935 cartoon), Moutha Bray (yeah-

man-ing "How Could You?"), and Louella Possums introducing Jack Bunny, Mary Livingstone, and Andy Bovine in a two-second sketch from their forthcoming Warmer Bros. picture.

PORKY'S HERO AGENCY

Porky Pig; Dec 4; LT; Supervision by Robert Clampett; Animation by Charles Jones; Musical Direction by Carl W. Stalling.

Porky falls asleep reading a volume of ancient Greek legends, and dreams he's a classical hero, "with nothin' to do but slay monsters and rescue damsels" all day. He even has a rate card of his fees for various heroic acts. The Greek coffee shop-like emperor of the place summons Porky (here called "Porkyakarkus") to hear a fireside chat about the scourge of the Gorgon, an evil witch bent on turning one citizen after another into stone. In fact, the emperor's audience consists entirely of statues that he's rigged with puppet-strings to give a fascist salute. Assigned to stop the Gorgon, Porky flies off with his Mercury-like winged feet. The Gorgon's place resembles a photographer's studio ("why go someplace else and get yourself chiseled, the Gorgon will turn you to stone cheaper with her marvelous photographic eye. If not satisfied, you will be brought back to life with her life-restoring needle ... maybe!"). The ugly Gorgon has her subjects pose in front of her. Covering his porky carcass with a hero's stone bust, Porky cozies up to the Gorgon, grabs her life-restoring needle, and runs off de-petrifying the statues he passes. He gives Venus De Milo Popeye arms and allows the discus thrower to hurl himself out of the scene. The Gorgon eventually grabs Porky and tries to force him to open his eyes just as he wakes up in his mother's arms.

SEPTEMBER IN THE RAIN

Dec 18; MM; Supervision by Isadore Freleng; Story by Tedd Pierce; Animation by Cal Dalton; Musical Direction by Carl W. Stalling.

That rare product-labels-comes-to-life without even the usual vague hint at a plot. In some cases that would be an asset: here, the film seems without a center and ends abruptly. The standard high caliber of visual gags and punchy puns with zingy music helps you not notice. Much material has been reprised from *How Do I Know It's Sunday* (and *Flowers for Madame* and *Billboard Frolics*), in terms of gags as well as reused "colorized" animation, like the "Old (Dutch) Maid" cleanser chorus line, the bottle of blueing that sings "Am I Blue?" the "Mon Ami" chick devouring a jumpy worm, the Morton salt girl-with-umbrella doing "By A Waterfall." Most of the new footage consists of black characters (explaining why most every print of this around is severely edited), mainly a longish-treatment of Jolson in blackface (on the "Dream of Wheat" package) singing "September in the Rain" to his Mammy (on a package of "Aunt Emma [Jemima] Pancake Flour"). Following this, Fred Astaire and Ginger Rogers climb off cigarette boxes and dance to the tune (via partially-rotoscoped footage from *The Gay Divorcee*). Lastly, the whole thing winds up with caricatures of Fats Waller and Louis Armstrong (as "The Gold Rust Twins") reprising "Nagasaki" from *Clean Pastures*.

1938

DAFFY DUCK AND EGGHEAD

Daffy Duck; Egghead; Jan 1; MM; Supervision by Fred Avery; Story by Ben Hardaway; Animation by Virgil Ross; Musical Direction by Carl W. Stalling.

A combination that can't miss: Avery's two star discoveries of the previous year, the Duck (in his second, though first color and starring appearance) and the Twerp (here a Joe Penner impression, in his only hunting film, support-

ing the theory that he evolved into Elmer Fudd). Because they're both nuts (literally, they're introduced out of nuts at the start), the not-yet-standard format of hunting-and-heckling doesn't really apply, and the picture becomes a battle of half-wits. A Parkyakarkus-imitating turtle (Blanc does the voice better than the actor himself) serves as referee for a duel of pistols at ten paces. When Egghead repeatedly misses at embarrassingly close distances, Daffy slaps a "blind" sign, dark glasses, and tin cup of pencils on him. The best bits are individual: Egghead firing on the silhouette of a guy (probably posed by Tedd Pierce) in the audience who does death throes as outrageous as any cartoon character; Daffy's bravura show-stopper of the new Looney Tune theme, "The Merry Go Round Broke Down" (with special lyrics). Daffy spends much of his time hopping insanely on the surface of the lake. In the end a duck in a white jacket comes to take him off. All three characters heave a Looney-Tuney fit into the horizon, but Daffy isn't crazy, folks, he just doesn't "give a darn."

Music: "Dawn" ("William Tell"), "Lady in Red," "Bob White."

PORKY'S POPPA

Porky Pig; Jan 15; LT; Supervision by Robert Clampett; Animation by Charles Jones; Musical Direction by Carl W. Stalling.

Clampett really knows how to open a cartoon: a male chorus sings "Old MacDonald" with lead-in lyric alterations "Porky's Poppa had a farm/E-I-E-I-O/And on that farm he has a pig/Porky Pig you know." The off-camera song serves to introduce the characters, each with some sort of noise and here a whatever, there a whatever, everywhere a whatever, reiterating the song until the characters object to having to repeat their noises. The song closes with "and on this farm he has a mortgage, oh, oh, oh ... " This fades into an announcer announcing, "And so tday, as it must to all men, debt comes to Porky's Poppa, 48." His problems: no milk, no money. The poor old cow, Bessie, is quarantined with "hoof 'n mouth" disease (pun) so Porky's Poppa orders a mechanical cow from a local airmail-order outfit. Porky, sentimentally attached to Old Bessie, encourages the flesh-and-blood cow to eat her hay, to "show that tin-can cow who can make the most milk." Porky helps Bessie to produce bottles of milk like babies ("quart-uplets") and tactfully pretends not to notice when Bessie gives birth to a black bottle of chocolate milk. The robot turns out milk like a mass-production assembly line, and, with the flick of a switch, can produce various cheeses (each with its own visual pun). After Porky finally removes the cow's hooves from her mouth, the robot cow douses Bessie's hay with vanishing cream so that it fades away. It then starts consuming all the hay in sight, transforming into a vacuum cleaner and sucking it all up. Finally, Porky and Bessie go after the "Last Straw" and, just when Poppa declares the robot cow the winnah, her metal casing turns out to contain none other than Old Bessie.

MY LITTLE BUCKAROO

Jan 29; MM; Supervision by Isadore Freleng; Story by Tedd Pierce; Animation by Robert McKimson; Musical Direction by Carl W. Stalling.
A western with comedy taking a backseat to seven straight minutes of virtually uninterrupted chases and gunfire. "The year, 1872, the town of Boiled Beef, Texas. For the past two years, this little border town has been terrorized by a notorious desperado known as the Terror," a Mexicali bandito so ratlike that he'll put anybody on the spot for $7.50, mother-in-law for $2.50!

The sheriff and his posse are helpless; one time they can't chase him because their horses are on strike ("No feed—No steed"), another time he slides past the border and the umpire calls him "safe." "Then, one day, out on the sun-baked range, there appeared a half-baked ranger": our hero, Andy Devine transformed into a cartoon pig. He happens to be standing nearby when the Terror makes his getaway and chases him over a mountain pass (his

horse getting a special thrill out of sliding down), finally reeling him in with a lasso-gun.

Freleng knows how to handle both the action (through shadows, straight frontal shots) and the comedy (mainly visual puns such as the bad guy having a slot machine in his gun) so that they both play well. The Devine character's whining, off-key (but thankfully brief) vocal on the title tune seems like a deliberate attempt to confound the publishing department that stood to benefit from the song plug.

PORKY AT THE CROCADERO

Porky Pig; Feb 5; LT; Supervision by Frank Tashlin; Story by Lew Landsman; Animation by Volney White; Musical Direction by Carl W. Stalling.
The Crocadero night club hosts a guest night: "Famous orchestra leader in person directing the Crocadero band. Hear them play 'Little Man You've Had a Busy Day,' 'In the Shade of the Old Apple Tree,' with 'The Lady Who Couldn't Be Kissed.'" Porky Pig is excited about hearing his favorites and vows to be like them someday. He shows us his diploma from the "Sucker's Correspondance School of Music." He imagines himself to be famous like Stokowski, Rudy Vallee, and Benny Goodman (and imitates each to prove it). His hopes are dashed when he spots the price "$25.00 per plate, $25.50 with food." He notices a "Help Wanted" sign and runs in to apply. He gets the job: washing hundreds of dishes. When Porky tries to swat a fly, his boss (a walrus) sees him waving a spatula and figures he has his mind more on music than dishes. He throws Porky out, telling him, "Today you are a ham!" The walrus receives word that the star musicians are delayed. The patrons are demanding music, and in a fit of panic the walrus remembers "that swing dishwasher! I must get him back!"

Porky is given the bandleader's job, and the rest of the film is an entertaining musical with Porky imitating Paul Whiteman, "Guy Lumbago and his Boiled Kanadians" singing "Summer Nights" and "Cab Howlaway and his Absorbent Cotton Club Orchestra" with

Porky in blackface singing "China Town." A running gag involving a penguin waiter whose drink is being slurped by the trombone player is resolved at the end when the penguin downs the drink himself and razzes the trombone.

JUNGLE JITTERS
Feb 19; MM; Supervision by Isadore Freleng; Story by George Manuell; Animation by Phil Monroe; Musical Direction by Carl W. Stalling.
You've got to give them points for trying. The opening sequence works well as a mood-and-location establisher, showing a village of cannibals in the middle of a war dance (beating African drums but yowling like American Indians) with a few typically grotesque ring-in-the-nose jokes and a musical interlude wherein the ceremony is likened to a merry go round (set to the new Looney Tunes theme, "The Merry Go Round Broke Down") which breaks down.

Unfortunately, we then meet our protagonist, a completely unsympathetic stuttering slob of a door-to-door salesman, who, when he finally gets 'em to open one of the doors, incessantly babbles this pat sales spiel in an attempt to sell the natives some darn thing or other. The cannibals envision him as a giant squab and soon have him boiling in a pot (Friz's first use of the the "Hold the Onions" sign gag) Through a subtitle we are introduced to the queen, a homely spinster who takes one look at the ignoramus salesman and sees both C. Gable and R. Taylor, and they're immediately married by a native judge. However, when he realized he's going to have to kiss the bride, the hero decides he prefers the cooking pot and dives in, saying to himself, "I hope they all get indigestion, I hope, I hope." The queen sings a little of Rudy Vallee's hit "Vieni, Vieni."

WHAT PRICE PORKY
Porky Pig; Feb 26; LT; Supervision by Robert Clampett; Animation by Charles Jones and Bob Cannon; Musical Score by Carl W. Stalling.
The first war relived and the second anticipated. The conflict between Porky's chickens and a gang of hoodlum ducks over a few ears of corn escalates into full-scale western front-style warfare with trenches, goose-steppers, flying death machines, battleships, and Porky repeatedly being caught in no-man's land (fortunately he has a portable foxhole). Dirty tactics: one mean duck pretending to be the Easter bunny besieging the naive Porky with booby trapped (though not explosive) eggs; a row of attacking ducks who get caught behind a curtain of fog, so they transform it into a stage curtain and start doing a chorus-line routine. Porky ultimately defeats the enemy almost singlehandedly, with a washing machine-cum-machine gun firing corn at their warplanes and rounding up the ducktator in a stockade.

Certainly one of the more elaborately-produced Looney Tunes, with heavy emphasis on effects animation and dozens of ducks that look and act like Daffy but talk like Donald! Amid the gunfire: "Mademoiselle from Armentieres" and "Workin' Our Way Through College."

THE SNEEZING WEASEL
Mar 12; MM; Supervision by Fred Avery; Story by Cal Dalton; Animation by Sid Sutherland; Musical Direction by Carl W. Stalling.
A bunch of cute li'l chickies, who go out bright and chirpy (literally) in the morning to eat worms, lose one of their clan who pursues a worm (who resists being eaten) and gets caught in a storm. He comes down with a cold and his mother hen's decision to go for the doctor is overheard by a slinky laughing weasel who, in talking to the audience, identifies himself as the villain. He gains access to their unguarded domicile by posing as the doc, but his disguise gets blown off with the first chicken-sneeze, and the chicks engage in standard bunch-of-little-guys teaming-up-against-the-big-bad-villain antics (firing popcorn is always effective). Ultimately, germ warfare saves them for when the chick achoos in the villain's face, he becomes the sneezing weasel, and the force of his gezundheits rearranges the furniture, to say the

least! They also leave him helpless for repeated clobberings (the chicks even revive him with smelling salts so they can mallet his head again).

Hysterical stuff, made funnier by the presence of the cute-but-obnoxious chick lead (he's like both the cutesy squirrel and the lead in M-G-M's *Screwball Squirrel* at once), and the very-full-of-himself weasel, who never stops laughing at his own cleverness (and who signifies one of Tex Avery's first appearances as a voice actor).

PORKY'S PHONEY EXPRESS
Porky Pig; Mar 19; LT; Supervision by Cal Howard and Cal Dalton; Story by Melvin Millar; Animation by Herman Cohen; Musical Direction by Carl W. Stalling
In an old western town, the mail is scooped up into a vacuum cleaner and put in a sack for the Pony Express. Porky Pig is an office boy at the Pony Express office, sweeping floors and licking stamps. It's his dream to ride the mail someday.

A rider comes in complaining he can't get through the Red Gulch, too many Indians. The boss concocts a plan: they'll send Porky ahead with a sack of horse shoes to decoy the Indians, while the real rider rides free. The plan immediately backfires and Porky grabs the sack with the real mail. The Indians spot Porky and chase him. An arrow opens his mail bag and the letters go flying, the pig retrieving the mail with a butterfly net. After a series of chase gags, Porky makes it to Red Gulch and becomes a hero. In the last scene, Porky is the new manager of the Pony Express, his ex-boss now licking stamps.

A STAR IS HATCHED
Apr 2; MM; Supervision by Isadore Freleng; Story by Tedd Pierce;

Animation by Bob McKimson; Musical Direction by Carl W. Stalling
The same territory as 1936's *Let It Be Me*. Instead of a rooster that sounds but doesn't look like Bing Crosby, the lead is a hen who sounds but doesn't look like Katharine Hepburn. A hopelessly star-struck movie nut, the hen hitch-hikes to Hollywood when the big shot director "J. Megga Phone" proffers a card with the sincere inscription, "If you want to get in pictures, look me up"; 1,600-plus miles later, she arrives in Los Angeles, where she witnesses famous actors in their day jobs (W.C. Fields as a traffic cop, Freddie Bartholomew hawking papers, big-eared Clark Gable as a street car conductor). Sneaking into the studio at Super Colossal Pictures Corp., hen goes past the casting office (men with fishing rods), while on stage seven, the director shoots a production number clap-boarded as *Broadway Broadcast* (Directory: Buzzard Berkelee; Star: Dick Fowl) that consists of Powell carica-tured in a military medley, "Love and War," "Shovin' Right Off for Home Again," "Don't Give Up the Ship," each separated by a quick change. When our heroine makes it to the employment office, she can't get anywhere near Megga Phone as dozens of small-town girls with the same card flock around him. Sometime later, after she's settled down with her hick boyfriend, one of her little chicks does a Kate Hepburn. Ma gives her such a smack!

Instrumentals: "Bei Mir Bist Du Schoen," "California Here I Come," and "Vieni Vieni."

PORKY'S FIVE AND TEN
Porky Pig; Apr 16; LT; Supervision by Robert Clampett; Animation by John Carey and Charles Jones; Musical Direction by Carl W. Stalling.
Newspaper headline: "Porky to open 5 & 10 store on Tropic Isle." A school of thieving fish see Porky coming and use a sword fish to saw open the bottom of his boat to rob the bewildered Porky of all his merchandise. From here on the toon becomes a series of gags concerning the uses the fish find for all the human consumer products. First, one

swallows a radio and has to react to the sound effects on the gangster shows. As the stuff covers the ocean floor, it becomes an underwater equivalent of the Hollywood Hotel nightclub, with an electric eel for a neon sign. Inside, fish versions of film stars (Laurel and Hardy, Mae West, and Garbo with big feet) watch a boxing match between two fish atop a typewriter (their feet hit the keys that type out the letters that describe the fight). A chorus line of dancing legs all turn out to belong to one multilegged mollusk. It's in the middle of dancing that the radio announces that a giant waterspout is heading toward their island. Said waterspout turns out to be a boon for Porky, as it picks up all the stuff and whooshes it all back into Porky's boat. For the wind-up, Porky squirts one nasty little fish with seltzer.

THE PENGUIN PARADE
Apr 16; MM; Supervision by Fred Avery; Story by Ben Hardaway; Animation by Paul Smith; Musical Direction by Carl W. Stalling; Words and Music by Byron Gay.
Ace animated antics originating at an Antarctic nightspot, penguins and the occasional walrus comprising most of the patrons as well as the talent. A double-talking emcee (doing comedian Cliff Nazarro's bit, as in *You'll Never Get Rich*) introduces the acts, beginning with a marching line of penguins who walk up each other's feet, then on to "our popular crooner, Bon Crispy," who makes an effective ballad out of "When My Dreamboat Comes Home." This leads into a Jimmy Lunceford-inspired trio arrangement of the number in which the glee clubbing, trucking penguins pull a stop-time break, a freeze framing on three highly silly faces. The rest of the show is strictly instrumental. There is a penguin band that includes inspiring clarinet and trumpet soloists as well as the legendary Fats Walrus on piano, all getting really hot on "Dreamboat" and "Bei Mir Bist Du Schoen," the latter modulating into "Merry Go Round Broke Down." In the end, this way-out band tells us in unison that they can't keep this up all night and retreat from the stage.

PORKY'S HARE HUNT
Porky Pig; Apr 30; LT; Supervision by Ben Hardaway; Story by Howard Baldwin; Animation by Volney White; Musical Direction by Carl W. Stalling.
A group of rabbits are eating corn in a field when Porky the hunter comes by. Porky frightens them all except one screwball white bunny. First, the wacky rabbit sends a wind-up decoy bunny to confuse Porky's dog, then loads Porky's gun with pepper, forcing the rifle to sneeze. Drinking "Whizz Hare Remove," the rabbit becomes invisible and gives Porky a swift kick.

The hare heckles Porky's dog, pretending to be a bullfighter and the dog a bull. Then he makes the dog disappear in a magician's handkerchief. The rabbit spins his ears like a helicopter and buzzes the pair. Porky corners the rabbit in a woodpile but the hare gives him a sob story. Porky isn't falling for it and tries to shoot, but his gun is jammed. This gives the hare time to heckle the pig, tear up his hunting license, and fly off. Using a well aimed rock, Porky knocks the hare into a haystack. When Porky joins him, the rabbit fakes a death scene, then gets up, declaring, "Of course you realize this means war!" He marches off, playing Yankee Doodle on his fife. Porky chases the hare to a cave and lights a dynamite stick, but it explodes on him. Later in the hospital, bandaged and bruised, Porky is visited by the hare, who makes his recovery a nightmare.

NOW THAT SUMMER IS GONE
May 14; MM; Supervision by Frank Tashlin; Story by Fred Neiman; Animation by Bob McKimson; Musical Direction by Carl W. Stalling.
The female chorus sings how busy little squirrels gather and store nuts for win-

ter (deciding whether or not they're kosher—oy vey!), while showing us a series of squirrel-and-nut gag scenes. From the general to the specific, one father squirrel looks around for his son and finds him shooting dice for nuts, singing, "Those boys must be tetched in the head/to keep working till you're almost dead/this is the way to gather nuts for winter now that summer is gone." Pop gives him a smack! "So! Gambling again, eh!" After a montage of more squirrely diligence contrasted with Junior's ill-gotten gains, the next time Dad catches him, he smacks himself . Then, one day, Dad tells Junior to "Get our supply of nuts from the bank and get back before the snow falls. And remember, no gambling!" He goes off to the first Nutional Bank and retrieves their satchel, but gives in at the first invitation to "indulge in a little game of chance" with a black-mustached stranger. In another Tashlin montage, he quickly loses the whole pile of nuts at cards, dice, and roulette. By the time he gets home (in the midst of the snowstorm) he has concocted a cock-and-bull story about "A gang of bandits! They jumped me, they robbed the nuts! Oh, I put up a terrific struggle ..." Dad puts on his phony mustache and suit and reveals that he was the gambling stranger. Has Junior learned his lesson? Well, when Pops is about to give him ten lashes that he won't forget, Junior offers, "Look, I'll flip ya, Pop, double or nothing!"

INJUN TROUBLE
Porky Pig; May 21; LT; Supervision by Robert Clampett; Animation by Charles Jones and Izzy Ellis; Musical Direction by Carl W. Stalling. (Remade in color by Clampett in 1945 as Wagon Heels.)
Back in the early days of this country, the one thing preventing American expansion westward was Injun Joe, a man-mountain of a red-skinned savage, ornery enough to bite a bear trap back and send it simpering like a dog and to out-grizzly a monstrous bear and convert it into a cowering cub. As a scout for a wagon train ready to brave Injun Joe's territory, Porky rides up ahead and finds the burned ruins of an earlier

train. He encounters a fear-crazed pioneer with crossed eyes, a white beard, and arrows sticking out of his clothing. The pixilated pale face's name is "Sloppy Moe," and he has a secret he won't tell, though Porky asks him again and again. When Injun Joe sees Porky's wagon train coming, he flies toward them, and forms a one-man attack around the circle of covered wagons. Both the pioneers and their coonskin caps shoot at him, but Injun Joe merely eats their bullets. Porky tries to put up his dukes against I.J., but the redskin starts swinging his tomahawk (in his patch he chops out a Statue of Liberty). Just when he has Porky hanging off a cliff, Sloppy Moe appears and reveals his secret: "Injun Joe is ticklish!" The goon starts tickling the now-helpless Injun Joe who likes it so much that he asks him to "Do um some more" before the iris out closes.

THE ISLE OF PINGO-PONGO
May 28; MM; Supervision by Fred Avery; Story by George Manuel; Animation by Irven Spence; Musical Direction by Carl W. Stalling.
The first of Avery's (and Warner's) spot-gag travelogue parodies. An ocean liner leaves the port of New York for Pingo-Pongo, "the pearl of the oyster islands." Gags along the way include the Statue of Liberty acting as a traffic cop, the ship passing the Canary Islands (pictured as a giant bird cage), the Sandwich Islands (a hot dog), and the Thousand Islands (a jar of dressing). Egghead is the film's running gag, appearing regularly to ask, "Now, boss?" Meanwhile, we dock at Pingo-Pongo and notice the birds: a hummingbird (who hums), a mocking bird (who mocks the narrator), and a tiny baby canary (who screams "MAMA!"). Among the animal life on the island is a spotted Giselle, who slows down to show us, a la a fashion show, her beautiful spots. We meet natives who sing "She'll be Comin' Round the Mountain"; natives eating at the "Dark Brown Derby" who are served ham and eggs on a plate, actually their big Zulu-stretched lips. Next we see a live-

action shot a horse race, for no reason at all (an in-joke). The native celebration includes a waltz, which segues into a jazz rendition of "Sweet Georgia Brown," with a skat singing "Fats Waller." The natives play swing music and dance to the rhythms. The narrator calls for the sun to "sink slowly in the West." When it doesn't, he calls on Egghead to shoot it down.

PORKY THE FIREMAN

Porky Pig; June 4; LT; Supervision by Frank Tashlin; Story by Melvin Millar; Animation by Robert Bentley; Musical Direction by Carl W. Stalling.
Porky the fire chief tries to water down a fire at Mr. Twerp's Theatrical Boarding House. Among the problems are his helper, a hard-of-hearing dog, and the wacky tenants inside. Among the victims of the fire: Mabel, the fat lady, who is tossed out the window by the fire dog; an old-timer who instructs them to "save Grandpa!"; Lucy the bearded lady; and acrobatic divers who jump from the windows, landing in such a way to form the Warner Bros. shield.

Porky has problems with a fire hydrant. Everywhere he sticks the hose, water spurts from another spout. As the building finally burns to the ground, the firemen surround to douse the final flame, and the flame grabs the hose and sprinkles the firemen!

KATNIP KOLLEGE

Jun 11; MM; Supervision by Ben Hardaway and Cal Dalton; Story by Dave Monahan; Animation by Joe D'Igalo; Musical Direction by Carl W. Stalling.
Are you hep to this jive? All the students at Katnip Kollege are in the groove; especially those groovy gators in the Swingology class. Man, when that peckin' professor asks 'em to lay a little of that history jive on him, do they give out! Each indulges in hot harmony on "Let That Be a Lesson to You," a piece of hysterical historical histrionics, attributing the demise of some mighty heavy cats (Columbus, Napoleon) to their inability to swing. These are all real gone cats except

Johnny, whose sonnets sound like Kostelanetz. I mean, brother, this icky's idea of hip is like with a flask (you dig?), he thinks boop-oop-a-doop and vo-do-de-o-do are the latest. So the Prof rightfully makes him wear the dunce cap, and his cute li'l girlfriend Kitty returns his pin. But dig this, a swingin' clock gives Johnny the beat, and he takes it and runs with it right down to where the cats are havin' a session. He makes with the rebops all right, singin' and tootin' a little torrid tempo he calls "Easy as Rollin' Off a Log." This really sends the cats, including his kitten. Well all reet, well all root, well all right!

If a cartoon can succeed on pure spirit, this is it. Some unbilled playing and singing by Warner contractee Johnny Scat Davis. Also on the track: "We're Working Our Way Through College" and "You're an Education."

PORKY'S PARTY

Porky Pig; June 25; LT; Supervision by Robert Clampett; Animation by Charles Jones and Norman McCabe; Musical Direction by Carl W. Stalling.
It's Porky's birthday so he throws himself a party, for some unexplained reason not inviting either his girlfriend, Petunia, or his usual sidekick, Daffy Duck. The first present that arrives is an Oriental silkworm (with glasses and buckteeth) who "does his stuff" whenever you say "sew" and who confuses that instruction with the word "so." Second plot thread: Porky's current dog, Black Fury (unlike Bosko or Buddy, Porky seems unable to keep a dog for more than one picture), who mimics his master by dabbing hair grower on his head. He finds that the

stuff has a kick to it, and starts guzzling. Porky's guests arrive; apparently knowing they're not going to last beyond this cartoon, they take their hostility out on Porky. The first, a penguin, offers a quick "Happy Birthday, Porky" as he dashes to the table where he immediately starts feeding his face. The second, a cross-eyed, smiling bird identified as "Goosey," waddles to the table and hands Porky a phone arm bearing the device "Happy Birthday, Fat Boy!" "He's so silly," comments Porky, and the little worm starts producing lingerie, which comes rolling down Porky's front. Porky tosses the worm away, and it lands in the penguin's ice cream. As soon as he says, "so/sew," the worm knits a top hat inside the penguin's head. We get a few minutes of Goosey and Penguin trying to restore the shape of his head to normal by banging him against the wall like a battering ram and clobbering him with a huge mallet. Black Fury staggers out of the john, not only drunk and covered with human hair (the dual effects of the tonic), but, having tried to shave himself, with shaving cream on his face. The kids assume he's a mad dog and start running to get away. When they discover, "It's only old Black Fury after all," the penguin says "so" again, and the silkworm immediately produces a few garments covering the penguin up in mummy wrapping.

HAVE YOU GOT ANY CASTLES?

Jun 25; MM; Supervision by Frank Tashlin; Story by Jack Miller; Animation by Ken Harris; Musical Direction by Carl W. Stalling.
Classics, illustrated. Part of Tashlin's 1937-38 books-come-to-life musical mini-series (along with *Speaking of the Weather* and *You're an Education*) and of the magazine/book musical crime story trilogy (*I Like Mountain Music, Weather,* and *Book Revue*). Here the plot is the least followable, as "The Three Musketeers" let loose "The Prisoner of Zenda" for no reason other than to give these literary layabouts something to do. Though we don't get the exact same "Judge," "Life," and "Liberty" gags, the whole thing still

winds up in everybody chasing the villain. Plot seems such a minor thing to pout about, though, when we have such great music, gags, graphics, and chutzpah to revel in! For starters, The Bookshop "Town Crier," a caricature of radio's Alexander Wolcott, calls on famous book characters to come to life and perform. Four fictional fiends ("Frankenstein," "Mr. Hyde," "Phantom of the Opera," and "Fu Manchu") snarl out and do pansy dances; the "Good Earth" prays, while the "Invisible Man" and "Topper" (only their top hats, gloves, and spats are visible) tap dance to "Vieni, Viene," joined by Bojangle Robinson on "The 39 Steps" and big-footed Greta Garbo on "So Big." Then Cab Calloway and assorted blacks on "Green Pastures" reprise "Swing for Sale" from *Clean Pastures.* "Heidi" gives out with a heap of hi-de-ho, and William Powell's "Thin Man" puts on a little weight. The two central numbers, the historic-rhythmic "Old King Cole" and "Have You Got Any Castles?" come from Warner's *Varsity Show.* The first is done with verse (yet!) by "Little Women," "Little Men," a drumming bulldog (pun), "The House of Seven (Big-Eared) Gables," Paul Muni as "Louis Pasteur," and Charles Laughton in "Mutiny on the Bounty." "Uncle Tom" (of Cabin fame) beats up "Rip Van Winkle" for messing up his Afro. Upset by his caricature, Warner's removed the Wolcott introduction and ending in all reissue prints. You get the idea. By the time of the "Castles" number, sung by the Musketeers as a vocal trio, which leads directly into the jailbreak and chase, the gags and book titles come so fast and furiously that it almost defeats the purpose to catalogue them. One can clock about three dozen of these super-closely-cut gags in a space of about 90 seconds! Funny, funny, funny.

LOVE AND CURSES

Jul 9; MM; Supervision by Ben Hardaway and Cal Dalton; Story by Melvin Millar; Animation by Herman Cohen; Musical Direction by Carl W. Stalling.
Foreword:"To those unswung villains

who were too gay in the gay '90s, this picture of dastardly doings and daring deeds is dedicated. Please do not hiss the villain ... Much!" The 30s were never less funny than when they made fun of the 1890s (the one flat number in *The King of Jazz* for instance). Parodying the boy-girl-villain melodrama works even worse than doing it straight. The gray-haired Harold and Emily 'reminisce about their old nemesis of 40 years earlier, the snakelike Roger St. Clair. In a flashback, the villain kidnaps her off a swing, and Harold, stouthearted lad that he is, spends six months trailing her to a den of iniquity (in time to hear a barbershop quartet go through "All Is Not Gold That Glitters"). The snake sneaks off with her again, tying her to the track in front of an oncoming train. Our hero, in addition to constantly spouting pithy epithets, is also a superman strong enough to lift the train, break a sawmill blade with his head, and bounce bullets off his body. When the flashback ends, we learn that the villain is still around and after the girl.

On the positive side, we have an attractive and realistic heroine. Overall, it's hard to believe this is the same studio and premise as *The Dover Boys* (1942), especially as there's zero '30s Warner shtick (as in "I Beeeetcha" and "I Do Mean You"). Also heard "Put on Your Old Grey Bonnet."

CINDERELLA MEETS FELLA
Egghead; July 23; MM; Supervision by Fred Avery; story by Tedd Pierce; Animation by Virgil Ross; Musical Direction by Carl W. Stalling.
This time the pumpkin-and-glass-slipper bit gets the razz. Even the royal invitation to the ball concludes with an ad for a local cheeseburger joint. Avery can't let so much as a few seconds go by without a gag, whether it pertains to Cinderella or not. When the fairy godmother fails to appear on time, Cindy phones the police, and they put out a calling-all-cars alert, assuring Cindy over one of those talking back radios (like in *I Love to Sing*a) that they'll "search every beer joint." Sure enough, when the paddy wagon brings her, she

whips out a bottle of gin instead of the expected magic wand. After traveling to the ball in a western stage coach (the best the inebriated godmother can´produce), Cindy and Prince Charming (Egghead to you and me) immediately dance and fall in love, in a rather suave love scene deflated only by the prince's audience-directed gushing, "Look, fellas, I'm dancin', see I'm dancin'!" It is cut short by the clock striking midnight, Cinderella being sure to leave one glass slipper behind. Instead of getting girls to try on the slipper, our Prince Charming finds Cinderella's house fairly easily (about five neon signs advertise it). She, however, grows tired of waiting, goes to a Warner Bros. show, and is in the audience watching this very cartoon. Reunited, the lovers decide to stay in the theater and catch the newsreel.

Egghead is funnier as Joe Penner than Penner himself ever was. Music includes "Please Be Kind," "About a Quarter to Nine," "The Blue Danube" and something called "Boy Meets Girl."

PORKY'S SPRING PLANTING
Porky Pig; July 25; LT; Supervision by Frank Tashlin; Story by George Manuell; Animation by Joe D'Igalo; Musical Score by Carl W. Stalling.
A follow-up to *Porky's Garden* (1936) with the pig again trying to defend his much-adored vegetables from a neighboring bunch of hungry chickens, the story itself rarely strays from the ingenious angles Tashlin devises to shoot it from (it should be the other way around, but no matter). This is the most attractive Porky Tashlin's yet devised. As Porky plows the seemingly-endless garden, his slow-moving dog, Streamline (who keeps murmuring unintelligible one-liners under his breath), digs

tiny seed holes with his tail and then lets the seeds roll down the entire length of his doggy carcass before dropping into the ground. As soon as Porky and his dog leave, hungry chickens from next door convert the place into a cafeteria. Porky's efforts to vacate them prove useless, for each time he swings at one with a broom, another chicken appears, and when he tries a scarecrow, the coat is swiped by an Orchard Street kosher chicken who admits it's a good material. After they beat up poor Streamline, Porky is ready to talk turkey with the chickens: "Let's you and me get together, you stay out of my garden, and I'll plant a garden just for you and grow anything you want." He then quizzes them on what veggie they want, and when he hits upon corn, they respond with an en masse Martha Ray impression, "Oh, yeaaahhh!"

On the soundtrack: "Peckin' With the Penguins," "Little Man You've Had a Busy Day," "April Showers," and "Bob White."

PORKY AND DAFFY

Porky Pig, Daffy Duck; Aug 6; LT; Supervision by Robert Clampett; Animation by Robert Cannon and John Carey; Musical Direction by Carl W. Stalling.
Basically standard boxing gags framed in a standard two-reel comedy plot. Manager Porky gets fighter Daffy a bout with the champ, who looks like a scrawny weakling until he gets in the ring, when his chest and muscles expand to the point where he becomes a man-mountain (or rather chicken-mountain). Freshness and wacky exuberance give the cartoon its charisma. For instance, there's the sight of Daffy hopping and hoo-hoo-ing round the ring, clad in boxing gloves and oversized trunks and miming an invisible bicycle that he can actually ride. He explains, "I'm so crazy, I don't know this is impossible." More laughs derive from the pelican referee, given a hysterical Blanc voice that might be described as an antecedent of Chuck Jones's little Martian character from the '50s, whose rubbery bill gets a lot

of gag space. Unfettered wackiness serves Daffy as well as the film itself. When the ref is about to count him out, Porky revives the Duck with his customary method of banging a metal pan on his head. Daffy then goes flying about the ring raining blows on his adversary, turning the match into a baseball game—and winning.

THE MAJOR LIED TILL DAWN

Aug 13; MM; Supervision by Frank Tashlin; Story by Richard Hogan; Animation by Phil Monroe; Musical Direction by Carl W. Stalling.
I say! In this jolly good cartoon, an old Colonel Blimp-like major tells wild hunting stories to a little spot of a lad (who looks like Freddie Bartholomew, don't you know). He tells of a fabulous safari wherein he acquired all the animal heads currently mounted on his walls. As the major, his butler, and their crew of natives travel deeper in Africa, they pass American-style highway numbers on a stick-shift elephant as well as antelopes on pogo sticks. Eventually, they arrive in lion country (you can tell by the lodge signs). Failing to shoot the big cat, our major steps into the boxing ring with the lion where he bests the mangy critter at fisticuffs. Tarzan appears and summons every bloody beast in the jungle to gang up on the major. Luckily, he knows enough about Popeye to realize that spinach will supply him with the muscle power to annihilate the animals and turn them into fur coats, luggage, and pianos.

One of the only '30s cartoons to make fun of the English. We also get a blimey running gag about a curious chap, an elephant trying to remember something, which he does in the last shot.

WHOLLY SMOKE

Porky Pig, Aug 27; LT; Supervision by Frank Tashlin; Story by George Manuell; Animation by Robert Bentley; Musical Direction by Carl W. Stalling.
Warner's brush with conventional cartoon morality ends in a draw. In *Pigs is*

Pigs, the errant progagonist is punished, but refuses to learn his lesson. In *Wholly Smoke,* he claims to learn it, but the final shot negates this by deliberate over-sacchariness. Traditional values of the sort glorified in Disney films are afforded even less respect than the naughty stuff the film pretends to expose. When a local punk calls Porky a "puny puss," Porky is forced to prove his masculinity with cigar-smoking stunts that are too much for the pig. Wandering into a tobacco shop, Porky experiences a way-out musical nicotine fever dream that combines all the cartoon paraphernalia in a smoking motif. Packages and graphics come to life with celebrity caricatures of Crosby and Vallee as "Crooner" as opposed to "Corona" cigars. To prove to Porky that little boys shouldn't smoke, pipes and cigars chant a propagandistic antismoking jingle, using the melody of "Mysterious Mose" (which ought to be revived by the American Lung Association). They force smoke into Porky's lungs in a manner anticipating *A Clockwork Orange.* When he revives, he dashes to church, realizes he doesn't have a nickel, dashes out again, clobbers the bully and retrieves his coin, and makes it back to his pew just in time to put it in the collection plate, vowing "I w-w-w-will never smoke again."

Most of the music is "Mysterious Mose," the vocal version with new lyrics.

A-LAD-IN BAGDAD
Egghead; Aug 27; MM; Supervision by Cal Howard and Cal Dalton; Story by Dave Monahan; Animation by Volney White; Musical Direction by Carl W. Stalling.
Egghead (Joe Penner again) as Alladin in a topical spoof of "The Arabian

Nights," winning the fabulous magical lamp in an arcade game, thereby spiting an evil turban-head who's been after it for some time because it contains a big black genie who can grant any wish. Egghead happens upon a crowd gathering around a poster from the sultan offering, "To the cleverest entertainer I will give my daughter's hand in marriage." He summons a magic carpet (with an outboard motor yet!) to the palace, where the contestants are doing their stuff. First is "Ali Baba Breen—Boy Wonder," a hulk who recites "Mary Had a Little Lamb." Next, "The Slap Happy Boys," who start into the Happiness Boys' theme song ("How Do You Do"). The sultan reacts with a gong and a gun. When it's Egghead's turn, he and the Sultan's daughter fall for each other at first sight. Egghead does a chorus of "Bei Mir Bist Du Schoen," but his magic art has been sabotaged by the bad guy, who's switched lamps on him. Don't worry, Egghead, yelling, "I've been swindled!" socks the fink and grabs the lamp back from him, making off with the princess on a magic carpet. She too feels she's been swindled, and uses the lamp to summon up Robert Taylor.

Generally superior to most of the Hardaway/Dalton films, the non-Avery Eggheads make him more sympathetic.

CRACKED ICE
Sept 10; MM; Supervision by Frank Tashlin; Story by Jack Miller; Animation by Bob McKimson; Musical Direction by Carl W. Stalling.
My little ham hock, ah, yes, 'tis said that a St. Bernard and his gin are soon parted. When our ice-skating friend "W. C. Squeals" (Fields as a pig) learns that this pooch carries hooch (he sees him mix a cocktail to restore a petrified pelican), he sets about devising ingenious ways to purloin "two fingers of that alpine cure-all," because he's not a well man, and never touches the stuff, "except for its medicinal value (why I can almost feel pneumonia embracing me in its icy grip)." Simultaneously bantering with an unseen Charlie McCarthy in the audience (a

reference to the Fields-McCarthy radio feud), his idea is to draw the canine comrade to him by using a magnet to pull his plate of bones. The plan goes awry, and both the magnet and some of the liquor get dropped in the drink, so W. C. has to contend with a drunken fish wearing a magnet. His underwater careening coincidentally coincides with a skating contest on the surface of the ice. The magnet pulls our porcine protaganist's skates in such a way that he wins said contests. W. C.'s first move is to fill the victory cup with gin, but the fish's magnet pulls it away from him.

Music: lots of "Little Brown Jug" and "Little Dog Gone."

A FEUD THERE WAS

Egghead; Sept 24; MM; Supervision by Fred Avery; Animation by Sid Sutherland; Story by Melvin Millar; Musical Direction by Carl W. Stalling.
Peaceful Ozark mountains and sublime yodeling harmony aren't enough for these hillbillies, who awaken at the sound of a jug popping open. They go about their interfamily feud as routine business. The constant flying back and forth of bullets even helps one family's Maw drill holes in her coffee pot so she can pour five cups at once. As in a sports match, going a yard or so over one's boundary line is an offense more serious than murder. One gets his beard shot off and puns, "The old gray hair ain't what she used to be," and, failing to get a laugh, murmurs apologetically, "Well, it sounded funny at rehearsals, anyway." Although they blast their enemies both on the screen and in the theater, ("Is there a Weaver in the audience?"), the guy they really hate is Egghead (riding a motorcycle inscribed, "Elmer Fudd, Peacemaker") who has the temerity to suggest to each side that they should "let there be an end to this meaningless massacre." Ultimately, the showdown is between both families against the peacemaker. When the smoke clears, the harmless-looking twerp has kayo'd the lot of them. He goes yodeling off, but the plot has the Weaver in the audience shoot Egghead!

PORKY IN WACKYLAND

Porky Pig; Sep 24; LT; Supervision by Robert Clampett; Animation by Norman McCabe and I. Ellis; Musical Direction by Carl W. Stalling.
"Welcome to Wackyland: It Can Happen Here." Clampett's tour-de-force of multiplied screwiness, using Lewis Carroll's Wonderland idea as the excuse for the setting and the standard Warner's chase theme as the plot. Aviator Porky is on the trail of the incredibly rare Do-Do bird, believed to be extinct and so valuable it requires more zeros than can fit on the newspaper headline to list its worth. For once given the chance to indulge in super-screwiness for its own sake, without even having to bow to the limits of cartoon logic, Clampett comes up with pip after pip, most of the gag-characters being sly comments on the wackyland known as real life. A growling behemoth up close turns out to be a simpering sissy, the sunrise is actually five guys on a totem pole (accompanied by a one-man band playing the "Dawn" from the "William Tell Overture"), a goon in convict's stripes holds a prison window in front of his face, demanding to be let out, a cross-eyed rabbit sways on a swing suspended by his own ears, one black-faced entity with enormous white lips travels by switching bended knees across the ground and murmuring "Mammy!" a peacock has playing cards for plumage, one beast has a dog on one end and a cat on the other, a three-headed wierdo who takes after Moe, Larry, and Curly because "His mama was scared by a pawnbroker's sign"—all this and more than we describe here being part of a long panning shot across the wackylandscape, before Clampett has to return to the McGuffin of the chase plot. Over the course of said chase, the Do-Do (bird head, banana feet, and arms that appear and retract as needed), repeatedly escapes through his mastery of wacky logic. He can simply take out a pencil and draw a door to dash in any time he likes, or he can lift the backdrop and replace it with a brick wall for Porky to crash into, and he can hop in

an elevator that's drawn as sort of a hole in the scenery, popping back into frame atop the "WB" shield logo. Porky finally catches him using a wacky disguise of his own, but is he really the last of the Do-Dos?

The Do-Do's theme is "Feeling High and Happy."

LITTLE PANCHO VANILLA

Oct 8; MM; Supervision by Frank Tashlin; Story by Tedd Pierce; Animation by Bob McKimson; Musical Direction by Carl W. Stalling.
The idea ain't to be authentic, it's to make ersatz culture fun. "Pancho! How many times have I tell you not to read the book of the bool fighting? You will never be bool fighter! You will always be Mamasita's good little muchachito, remember!" To this, little Pancho says, "Phooey!" When three leetle Senorita-chitas come by and admire a bool-fighter on a poster (bearing the likeness of Gable as a matador), Pancho brags that he is an even greater toreador. The girls, they laugh and say he is only throwing the bool. In fact, at the arena, they won't let Pancho come in with the amateur matadors ("Only toreadors allowed in here, no leetle shreemps like you."). The others take on the bool at once, but he makes short work of all of them, one of them landing on the other side of Pancho's haycart. On the rich-ochet, the leetle feller finds himself in the ring. A rough fight follows between Pancho and the bool, including lots of running around the arena, bouncing, and butting (at one point the bull gets dizzy and sees multiple, swirling images of Pancho). After being tossed in the air, Pancho lands on the bool's head and knocks heem out. The referee declares Pancho the weener and pre-sents him a not-so-modern washing machine for Mamasita.

Authentic Mexican music: "In Cal-iente," "When Yuba Plays the Rhumba on the Tuba."

PORKY'S NAUGHTY NEPHEW

Porky Pig; Oct 15; LT; Supervision by Robert Clampett; Animation by Robert Cannon; Story by Warren Foster; Musical Direction by Carl W. Stalling.

"Cartoon Animals: OUTING. Main Event: SWIM RACE. P.S.: Elephants Must Wear Trunks While Swimming." Porky tries to relax on the beach, com-pletely exposing himself to his naughty little nephew Pinkie, a cuddly, baby-bonnet-clad little piggy with a killer instinct and the ability to move from any given violent act to simply standing there and looking innocent. After Porky gets his face poked repeatedly with a shovel and covered by an irre-movable starfish and his body covered by a pick-up truck full of sand, the swim race begins. As soon as the gun goes off (it fires a traffic light that sig-nals "Go") all the other cartoon ani-mals run off for water vehicles. Only Porky attempts the race completely on his own. Water race gags follows, chief among them Eddie Cantor's fatherly adoption of one of the "buoys." Pinkie whips out a toy sailboat that makes like a shark fin, which scares Porky into swimming so fast he wins the race. When Pinkie tries to show his uncle that it's only a little toy sailboat, it turns out to be a real shark.

To make Pinkie cute bordering on the obnoxious, he is given a squeally Berenice Hansen voice. When he plays with sand, Stalling underscores the action with "Japanese Sandman."

JOHNNY SMITH AND POKER-HUNTAS

Egghead; Oct 22; MM; Supervision by Fred Avery; Story by Rich Hogan; Animation by Paul Smith; Musical Direction by Carl W. Stalling.
The Capt. John Smith story doesn't contain quite the cliches as do Cinder-ella and Red Riding Hood, but Avery finds plenty and surrounds them with bits ribbing the conventions of narra-tive fiom. When we are introduced to Egghead as Capt. Smith (who's going to be famous because he came over on the *Mayflower*) the clod accidentally leans on his subtitle and knocks the letters over. When the Pilgrims land and are attacked by scalpers (peddling tickets to the Rose Bowl), the theater manage-ment informs us that "Due to the length of our program, it will be neces-sary to cut short this thrilling chase

between Capt. Johnny Smith and the Indians."

Next, the Indians have Smith on the chopping block, the "jeering section" is yelling, "Give 'em the axe! The axe! The axe!" (it was funny in *Sweet Sioux,* but it's funnier here). They are about to chop with golflike strokes at Egghead's neck, which has a dotted line and instructions to cut along it. Then Poker-Huntas hears what's going on from Walter Winchell on the radio and races off to his rescue in her car. The Injuns pursue (after counting to 50) in their roadsters. "Now don't you people out there get excited," Poker-Huntas starts babbling, "because you see the Indians don't ever catch us and we escape on a ship . . ." Although Egghead stops her from telling the whole story, that's what happens, and we cut to the happy couple years later offering their brood of little papooses and eggheads as evidence of the dubious validity of the book, *The Last of the Mohicans.*

PORKY IN EGYPT

Porky Pig; Nov 5; LT; Supervision by Robert Clampett; Animation by Norman McCabe; Story by Ernest Gee; Musical Direction by Carl W. Stalling.
For locale-establishing shots, we get the Middle East trivialized via American pop-culture references. A group of Arabs in prayer suddenly become Amos 'n' Andy shooting craps, a sexy harem girl in a veil holds it aside to reveal an ugly old spinster face, a sightseeing tour is barkered as "See the homes of the mummy stars." A group of staff caricatures board the herd of camels and pull out with the tour, leaving Porky behind. He follows on his camel, Humpty Bumpty, the hot sun working doubly hard to wear them both out. Eventually, it knocks out the camel, which hallucinates on a grand scale. The film's center is a bravura monologue in which the camel has caught what he describes as "The Desert Madness!" It's a magnificent hodge-podge of every imperial adventure cliche in the book, from Kipling and Tennyson on down. Echoey voices cry his name as the scenery starts spin-

ning, and he goes into the "Charge of the Light Brigade" ("cannons to the right of me ..."). Imagining troops approaching, he hysterically cries, "The camels are coming, the camels are coming!" At once he appears with a kilt, tartan, and bagpipes, playing the Scottish desert theme, "The Campbells Are Coming," intercut with a jig. Further grand illusions include mirages and impressions of Lew Lehr ("Camels is da cwaziest peoples") and the Lone Ranger. A blow on the head apparently restores the camel's sanity; he hears the voices once and runs back to town, carrying Porky. Locking the door behind him, he comments on their being safe at last, but we learn the Desert Madness has warped Porky's brain too. Iris out over Porky indulging in the now-established signs of cartoon character insanity, dangling tongue, crossed eyes, skittering feet, and Napoleon hat.

YOU'RE AN EDUCATION

Nov 5; MM; Supervision by Frank Tashlin; Story by Dave Monahan; Animation by A. C. Gamer; Musical Direction by Carl W. Stalling.
The climax of Tashlin's come-to-life trilogy of '37-'38. Midnight in a travel agency with scenes of brochures first functioning as individual tableaux, then interacting in a musical number, then getting all mixed up in a crime story. The opening minute contains about a dozen different country scenes, each with a gag and an appropriately mock-exotic location song. We get such extended numbers as "When Yuba Plays the Rhumba on the Tuba," played by a Cuban tubist, Lawrence "Tibbet," and a trio of pudgy, cherubic black babes (representing the American South, and inspired.by the Peters

Sisters, perhaps) who then go into the title plug number, rewritten as "Food's an Education." This escalates the pun concept on another level. Now we have travel, music, and food gags (Hungary, Sandwich Islands, Twin Forks, Montana, Hamberg(er), Chile, Java, Turkey). The final thread, the chase plot, has the Thief of Bagdad using the Florida Keys to rob the Kimberly diamond mine and trying to sell his booty to the Pawnee Indians. He is chased by soldiers and police from all countries, finally getting away by forming what Lennie Bruce would call an "unnatural" alliance with the Lone Stranger ("Well, you're not alone now, Beeg Boy!").

THE NIGHT WATCHMAN
Nov 19; MM; Supervised by Charles M. Jones; Story by Tedd Pierce; Animation by Ken Harris; Musical Direction by Carl W. Stalling.
The regular night watchman is too sick to mind the kitchen, so his son, Little Tommy Cat (a Sniffles antecedent) subs for him. This fact delights the local hoodlum mice no end, each being bigger than the kitten, whom they cruelly push around. Not only do they immediately start devouring food in humorous ways (assuming the shapes of a banana, a pretzel, and a jar of olives), they bully the little feller into serving them. The floorshow consists of a mouse trio hepping up "Shade of the Old Apple Tree" (accompanied by an orchestra of tough mice playing funnels and pipes).

Tommy Cat walks away whimpering

and crying, but his conscience gets him to remember his poor old daddy who trusted him and asks, "Are you a cat or are you a mouse?" He gets back in there and fights, knocking off dozens of rats with one blow apiece, and then settles a special score with their head man.

Notable only for being the first cartoon Jones directed, even the production number has no charm. There's pain in watching the little guy take it, but no particular cathartic pleasure in watching him dish it out. Behind the eating sequence: "The Latin Quarter."

THE DAFFY DOC
Daffy Duck, Porky Pig; Nov 26; LT; Supervision by Robert Clampett; Animation by John Carey and Vive Risto; Musical Direction by Carl W. Stalling.
High Warners-style opening, with the titles given over a speeding ambulance a la any number of the studio's inner-city gangster/hospital/reporter pictures (*Night Nurse,* for one). This leads us to think we're getting a spoof of medical movies, but anyone could rib those cliches. Clampett has undertaken the more satisfying task of adapting them to his characters and then letting the parody grow out of the situation. The plot itself, however, has more in common with a horror movie. A surgeon's assistant, humiliated by his boss and evicted from an operation, tries to one-up him by sawing open a patient of his own. Next thing you know, he's after the hapless Porky, and the giant mallets and axes he chases him with are just warm-ups for what he'll do if he ever gets Porky on the operating table! Clampett addresses specific doctor-flick iconography in directly daffy style: the duck gets tossed into an artificial lung which causes different parts of his body to inflate, and calls a "consultation" by clobbering himself, seeing triple and conferring with the two blurry images of himself that appear. A thermometer sticking out of Porky's mouth turns out to be a lollypop. Then Daffy pursues Porky all over the place with a saw and a Daffy expression which, apparently, masks a homicidal maniac.

DAFFY DUCK IN HOLLYWOOD

Daffy Duck; Dec 3; MM; Supervision by Fred Avery; Story by Dave Monahan; Animation by Virgil Ross; Musical Direction by Carl W. Stalling.

Having seen the ruckus Daffy can raise with just one single hunter to heckle, imagine what he can do with an entire movie studio, Hollywood's "Wonder Pictures" ("If it's a good picture, it's a wonder"). He first bursts through the door of producer I. M. Stupendous (asking, "Do you need a good duck actor?") as the producer phones in a demand to his adjacent director, Mark Hamburger, "That picture you're working on ... it better be good and you'd better finish it today or else!" The director (you can tell by his Teutonic rolling r's, beret, pencil-thin mustache, and jodphurs) has little chance of achieving this.

Daffy drenches everyone by plugging the sprinkler system into the lights, loads a round of machine gun fire into a hand-cranked camera ("This isn't a gangster-r-r pictur-r-re!" the director sobs), cuts in on the middle of a love scene with another Katharine Hepburn chicken, and makes a surprise appearance in the director's turkey. While the crew has lunch, Daffy wanders into the stock footage library and decides to give 'em a real feature, a goofy newsreel compendium of absurd live-action shots with mis-matching narration (including two seconds from *Gold Diggers of 1933*). Daffy switches with the director's film as he's about to screen it for the producer, and the producer likes it so much that in the next shot Daffy is a pompous foreign director and Mark Hamburger is heckling him with wacky antics.

PORKY THE GOB

Porky Pig; Dec 17; LT; Supervision by Ben Hardaway and Cal Dalton; Story by Melvin Millar; Animation by Gil Turner; Musical Direction by Carl W. Stalling.

As a sailor in the U.S. Navy, Porky's troubles have less to do with the enemy than with his screwball captain, who repeatedly singles out Porky for abuse. When ordered to batten down the

hatches, Porky tells the captain that he already has, and the captain comes back with, "Well batten 'em down again! I'll teach those hatches!" A wire comes in offering a $50,000 reward for the capture of a much-feared pirate sub. The wacky captain summons all hands on deck, and they all fly off in search of the sub, except Porky, who is told, "Get out! You're rockin' the ship, and I do mean rocking!" As soon as they're gone, Porky must defend the battleship from the pirate sub and its deadly torpedoes. Porky fires the ship's cannons at it and gets his chance to catch the bad guys when they climb out of the sub. He swings Tarzan style, knocking them out, then hoists the sub up with a common bathroom plunger. The last scene has Porky being decorated for valor by the admiral, a ceremony interrupted by the mess call, but not before Porky dashes back for his sack of reward money.

One imaginative bit has the zany captain declare, "Last one in the mess hall's a softie," and then ordering his men to halt so that he can get in first. Porky and chorus sing "Shovin' Right Off for Home Again" at the opening.

COUNT ME OUT

Egghead; Dec 17; MM; Supervision by Ben Hardaway and Cal Dalton; Story by Melvin Millar; Animation by Herman Cohen; Musical Supervision by Carl W. Stalling.

Country bumpkin Egghead receives some junk mail from the ACME Correspondance School of Boxing. The letter asks, "Are you a man or a mouse? Fight your way to success. Learn to Box!" Egghead sends for the lessons via airmail (an airplane in his mailbox) and receives an immediate response: a package full of boxing equipment and ten recorded boxing lessons. After a few gags with his wise-guy recorded boxing coach (Mel Blanc), Egghead earns his diploma, exclaiming, "It's amazing!"

In the ring, Egghead challenges the champ, Biff Stew. He brings his player and final record to the match. The recording urges him to "Fly into him," but the champ proceeds to beat him up. "Remember, you're fighting for dear old ACME," the record shouts. Another round, and Egghead becomes so dizzy he sits on the champ's leg, a Charlie McCarthy. The champ smashes the record player, and Egghead is ready to give up, but the champ won't let him. Getting beaten to a pulp, Egghead wakes up. It was just a dream! As he throws out his recordings and fighting equipment, a boxing glove gives him one more sock.

Some historical notes: this was the first use of ACME in a Warners cartoon; Egghead is at his most Penner-ish in this film; and Tex Avery supplies the voice and comic laugh of the fight referee.

THE MICE WILL PLAY

Dec 31; MM; Supervision by Fred Avery; Story by Jack Miller; Animation by Sid Sutherland; Musical Direction by Carl W. Stalling.

On one level Avery wants to make a cute late-'30s-style cartoon, but he pounds on the table and shouts, "I can't do it, I tell you I can't do it!" A group of little boy mice wander into a laboratory and immediately get into funny-mousey uses for the doc's scientific tools. Their antics intercut with shots of a cat slowly creeping up on them and with shots of helpless Susie Mouse, trapped in a cage in the next room, yelling at the top of her breath for help. She finally gets word to Johnny Mouse via a paper airplane, and he dashes over to free her. When they're safe, he wants to know what's eatin' her. She stands in front of the x-ray machine, which reveals that she loves him. Cut to a musical wedding ceremony, wherein a full mouse orchestra accompanies a trio transforming "Here Comes the Bride" into "Don't Spare the Rice" as the bride and groom speak their vows on clarinets before a trumpet-toting preacher. By now, the cat has finally reached them and is about to pounce when Susie babbles," By and by maybe there'll be lots and lots and lots of fat little mice." The cat decides to wait.

Very effective cross-cutting throughout, not to mention "zooming" back and forth within these quick shots. Music includes "Garden of the Moon."

1939

THE LONE STRANGER AND PORKY

Porky Pig; Jan 7; LT; Supervision by Robert Clampett; Animation by I. Ellis and Robert Cannon; Musical Direction by Carl W. Stalling.

Not just another cartoon western, but Hollywood's all-time most effective western parody, which scathingly satirizes the genre (particularly the cowboy serial with a costumed hero). As it opens, an effeminate narrator (who later gets plugged by the villain for calling him a punk shot) reads off a standard serial intro almost straight, describing the "Robber bands [that] stretched from town to town, snapping up their ill-gotten loot." But then, "as things looked darkest, a ray of hope broke through the gloom striking terror into the black hearts of the scoundrels. A masked rider of justice, on a fiery horse with speed of light and a cloud of dust and a hi-yo Silver, the Lone Stranger rides again!"

Asleep after a hard day of nick-of-time rescues, the Lone Stranger is awakened by his faithful Indian Scout Pronto who summons him (from his masked house) to the aid of Porky Pig. Porky's shipment of gold is under attack from a mustachioed villain and his mustachioed horse. The Lone Stranger and the bad guy battle it out, their slugfest being intercut with end-of-chapter-type titles, "Will the Lone Stranger be smashed on the rocks below? What about it, audience?" Hardly, but what's really surprising is that, in the meantime, the good and bad guys' horses have fallen in love, gotten married and sired a herd of ponies.

The Lone Stranger offers a great non-sequitur: "Come on Silver, old girl, get moving. Movies are your best entertainment!"

DOG GONE MODERN

Jan 14; MM; Supervision by Charles M.. Jones; Story by Rick Hogan; Animation by Phil Monroe; Musical Direction by Carl W. Stalling.

The first of Jones's "Two Curious Dogs" series, in which canines function as straight men while the setting supplies the interest. Here, the big brown boxer and the little spotted puppy wander into "An electric model home [of the future], open for inspection, visitors welcome." Jones plays them against a series of machines that cannot distinguish between the dogs and the objects they're designed to deal with. The big dog immediately gets into the clutches of an electric dishwasher, which repeatedly soaps and scrubs him, while the little pup gets folded into a napkin-ring and then runs afoul of a robot housecleaner that sweeps up anything that falls on the floor. In between bouts with the sweeper, he also messes with a futuristic mechanical orchestra (which plays and sings "The Little Old-Fashioned Music Box"). Finally, the dogs make an exit through the garbage disposal and clobber the robot-sweeper, which goes into some very human death throes.

A great score, if "At Your Service, Madame" happens to be your favorite song and you like hearing it over and over.

IT'S AN ILL WIND

Porky Pig; Jan 28; LT; Supervision by Ben Hardaway and Cal Dalton; Story by Melvin Millar; Animation by Herman Cohen; Musical Direction by Carl W. Stalling.

Porky and his ever-chattering Pal Dippy (the Gabby Goose character from *I Wanna Be a Sailor*) go fishing at a deserted waterfront, followed by a friendly but nevertheless unwanted dog. They are forced to seek shelter in an abandoned yacht club when a terrible storm breaks out. The place looks haunted, but no real spooks inhabit it. There are only the storm, an occasional animal, and each other, but our heroes think that spooks are after them. In one scene, Dippy gets hold of a fishing reel and winds up pulling on Porky in another room. When the hook lands on a bearskin rug on a wheeled chair, Dippy thinks a bear monster is coming after him. Meanwhile, the dog, who has also wandered in, gets spooked by a turtle and falls into a diving helmet with his tail caught in a trap. Covered in chains, he unwittingly spooks Dippy, the two sticking their heads out at each other in a succession of barrels. At the end, when all is revealed, Dippy says of the dog to Porky, "Boy, did he scare you!" and the dog runs back into the place to clobber the turtle.

HAMATEUR NIGHT

Egghead; Jan 28; MM; Supervision by Fred Avery; Story by Jack Miller; Animation by Paul Smith; Musical Direction by Carl W. Stalling.

It's Amateur Night at the local "Warmer Bros. Theater" (where they are showing *"Four Daughters* with selected shorts"). The orchestra members lead their conductor, a one-man band. Contestants include: Maestro Paderowski who plays "The Merry-Go-Round Broke Down" on his player piano; an operatic bird who gets the trap door; the Hindu mystic Swami River with a failed basket trick (his volunteer, Egghead, gets his money back); Teeny Tiny Tiney Tinny Tinny Tin, an insect who recites "Mary Had a Little Lamb"; Fleabag McPoodle and his trained dog, a "realistic" pooch, who, when asked to speak, begins a thunderous political dialogue; a Shakespearian wolf who tries to perform "to be or not to be" without being hit by a tomato; and a pair of chickens performing the balcony scene from *Romeo and Juliet.*

Running gags: Egghead rushing on stage every so often to perform "She'll Be Coming Round the Mountain" and getting the hook; a hippo with a big laugh (voiced by Avery) disturbing members of the audience and some of the performers.

In the end, Egghead gets the prize, for the entire audience is made up of cheering Eggheads!

ROBIN HOOD MAKES GOOD

Feb 11; MM; Supervision by Charles M. Jones; Animation by Robert McKimson; Story by Dave Monahan; Musical Direction by Carl W. Stalling.

Three cutesy little squirrels get the idea of playing Robin Hood. The smallest and puniest of the three is the one that gets forced into playing the villain. He receives a thrashing from the two "heroes," who are lured into a trap by the voice of Maid Marion (they don't know who she is until they look up the name in their storybook and find she's supposed to be Robin Hood's sweetheart). They're rather unhappy to learn the voice is really a hungry fox who likes "little fat juicy squirrels! With potatoes and onions, doesn't that just make your mouth water?"

Luckily, the third squirrel thinks quickly, and using sound effects and different voices, convinces the fox that a party of hunters is breaking down the door. The fox runs out screaming. When the two bigger squirrels walk out they too expect to see hounds and hunters and instead find the smallest squirrel asking, "Whooooo's gonna play Robin Hood?"

Berenice Hanson, doing all three squirrel voices, has one good number, but the vocal highlight is Mel Blanc as the cowardly fox, doing one of those great hysterical death monologues: "Look, fellas, get me out of here! I'm young, strong, healthy! Don't let 'em kill me ... I'm afraid to die!"

PORKY'S TIRE TROUBLE

Porky Pig; Feb 18; LT; Supervision by Robert Clampett; Story by Warren Foster; Animation by Norman McCabe; Music by Carl W. Stalling.

The central sequence, a funny pantomime by a quadruped dog, could almost be a Disney Pluto-on-the-flypaper soliloquy. This dog has fallen into a vat of rubberizing solution. He wobbles around thoroughly rubberized, stretching his doggy form into one bizarre shape after another (including the likenesses of Edward G. Robinson , Edna Mae Oliver, Gable, and Hugh Herbert).

The story surrounding this classic scene consists of the dog, name Flat Foot Flookey, already bizarre beyond belief (and wearing two pairs of shoes), following Porky to work. The pig tries to keep him out of sight of his tough walrus boss (Bletcher), who hates dogs and doesn't allow them at his factory. Porky ties F.F.F. to a car to keep him out, then Porky and his grumpy boss attempt to go about with his work, which consists of the walrus operating a steam shovel that chews up rubber trees into gooey masses that Porky waffle-iron presses into tires. The mutt tunnels into the plant, dragging the car along with him. When the boss encounters Flat Foot Flookey, he summarily tries to eject him, but the rubberized rascal keeps bouncing back. He even pops through a steel door and knocks the boss into the tire-press, transforming his torso into a tire.

On the soundtrack: "You Must Have Been a Beautiful Baby," "Mutiny in the Nursery," "The Panic Is On."

GOLD RUSH DAZE

Feb 25; MM; Supervision by Ben Hardaway and Cal Dalton; Story by Melvin Millar; Animation by Gil Turner; Musical Direction by Carl W. Stalling.

A city slicker looking for gold stops at a desert gas station and is told by the attendant of the perils of prospecting. What follows, in flashback, is a series of spot gags on one man's quest for gold in 1849.

Arriving in San Francisco, our hero is suckered into a crooked card game. Trying to stake his claim, he is beaten to it by competing stakes (signs reading "I Saw It First!" "Finders Keeper!" etc.). Mining for gold gags include panning for goldfish, cooking a pot of Gold Bullion soup; and miners singing a chorus "My Sweetheart Needs Gold for Her Teeth." In a final frenzy, our hero covers the globe in search of any gold claim. Back to the present, the gas attendant has sworn off prospecting, but a shout of "Gold in the Gulch!" has him giving the station to the city slicker and taking his auto into the sunset.

PORKY'S MOVIE MYSTERY

Porky Pig; Mar 11; LT; Supervision by Robert Clampett; Animation by John

Carey; *Story by Ernest Gee; Musical Direction by Carl W. Stalling.*
A parody of the late Mr. Moto series of films starring Peter Lorre. "Any resemblance this story has to the one it was stolen from is purely coincidental." A mysterious phantom is causing trouble at the Warner Bros. studio. All the movie villains are quizzed by police, including Frankenstein, shown biting his nails.

The phantom climbs a circular staircase to his dressing room where it is revealed that he is the Invisible Man, angry because Hollywood starred him in only one movie. The police call in Mr. Motto (Porky Pig), who is vacationing on a deserted island reading his ju jitsu book. When he gets the call, he attaches an outboard motor to the island and speeds back to the mainland. Mr. Motto enters the police station in a helicopter, smashing through the ceiling. He investigates the movie studio, but the phantom spots him and chases him with an axe. Motto uses ju jitsu and throws the Invisible Man. Using his anti-invisible juice, the phantom is revealed as—Hugh Herbert!

A DAY AT THE ZOO

Egghead; Mar 11; MM; Supervision by Fred Avery; Story by Melvin Millar; Animation by Rollin Hamilton; Musical Direction by Carl W. Stalling.
"Here we are at one of the country's most interesting zoos …" Ah, yes, the gags come fast and furious. A wolf in his natural setting (at someone's door); camels smoking cigarettes; a greyhound bus; two bucks and five "scents" (skunks); two friendly elks (lodge members going, "Hello, Bill!").

The gags are grouped according to species, mainly the monkey cage (one little chimp yells at a little old lady who tries to feed him); and the bird house (which contains the Alcatraz jailbird, who talks like Edward G. Robinson). Along the way we encounter, to name just a few, a skunk reading "How to Win Friends and Influence People," multiplying rabbits, winged pink elephants left over from the last New Year's party, and, in a running gag, Egghead, as a wise guy who insists on

teasing a lion. When scolded by the narrator for this, he replies, "I'm a baaad boy," indicating that Lou Costello's catch phrase was already nationally known before Abbott and Costello had broken into the movies.

PREST-O CHANGE-O

Mar 25; MM; Supervision by Charles Jones; Story by Rich Hogan; Animation by Ken Harris; Musical Direction by Carl W. Stalling.
In *Dog Gone Modern*, two dogs confront and confound the highly logical magic of technology. For their second film (of three in one year), they're up against the surreal illogic of stage magic. Fleeing the dog catcher, they wander into Sham-Fu the Magician's house. The brown boxer encounters a rabbit that appears and disappears at unexpected moments, vexing him by magically producing a vase, popping a pop gun at him, and making a Christmas tree grow out of nowhere. The rabbit vanishes and returns from behind a cape, then turns a door into a chest of drawers.

The little black-and-white pup tangles with a Hindu rope trick that repeatedly clouts him with objects it makes appear with a magic wand. When the pup swallows the wand, balloons appear out of his mouth when he hiccups. The dogs encounter each other again after the pup swallows a balloon that deflates and sends him flying backward, pushing the rabbit into a heap of rope. The boxer locks the rabbit in a succession of larger and larger safes, but he appears out the pup's next balloon. This time, the big dog gets hold of the rabbit and gives him a shiner.

Magic theme: "Umbrella Man."

BARS AND STRIPES FOREVER

Apr 8; MM; Supervision by Ben Hardaway and Cal Dalton; Story by Jack Miller; Animation by Rod Scribner; Musical Direction by Carl W. Stalling.
"Stone walls do not a prison make . . . but they sure help." Once you have a setting, you can either think of some really funny spot gags and dispense with the narrative or you can put in Porky Pig or Daffy Duck so the location becomes secondary. For this romp on life in the big house, they did neither, assembling instead a low-key day in the life in prison that leads into a musical jailbreak. Spot gags include a visit with "Warden Paws" (a Hugh Herbert caricature); a musical jail-break with the escapee singing "I'm Going to Scram From Here!" leading to a wild shootout which land the convict back in solitary confinement; and a running gag about a little convict who takes the rap for a bigger convict.

With a weak story and direction (except one scene of a prisoner going to the electric chair) we can still enjoy the unadorned Warner-isms, such as Blanc doing impressions of both Jerry Colonna and Hugh Herbert.

CHICKEN JITTERS

Porky Pig; Apr 1; LT; Supervision by Robert Clampett; Animation by Robert Cannon and Vive Risto; Musical Direction by Carl W. Stalling.
A typical morning on Porky Pig's Poultry Farm. The rooster wakes the barnyard fowl when he spots the sun rising through his binoculars and yells, "wake up, fella!" The chickens and ducks include the Jones Family, the Hardy family, Blondie and Dagwood and Mother Carey's Chickens. Porky inspects the eggs and plays "snake charmer" to get worms for the chicks. Meanwhile, outside the fence, a fox is salivating, rubbing his paws and thinking of dinner. When the fox grabs a little black duck, Porky chases him with an axe. The fox blasts the axe into a tiny one, but the ducks come to the rescue, flying in formation and dive attack. The fox punches Porky, but the ducks drop a dressmaker's dummy over him, then bomb the animal, leaving a fox fur on the dummy torso.

DAFFY DUCK AND THE DINOSAUR

Daffy Duck; Apr 22; MM; Supervision by Charles M. Jones; Story by Dave Monahan; Animation by A. C. Gamer.
Opening title reads: "For no particular reason, our story is laid in the 'Stone Age'—millions and billions and trillions of years ago—probably before any of you were even born!"

Caspar Caveman, a Jack Benny caricature, wakes up, calls Fido, his dinosaur, and they go out to hunt up some breakfast. They spot Daffy Duck in a lake and decide to bean him with a rock. Daffy puts on a traffic-cop hat and whistle and directs the rock onto Fido's head. Caspar tries to dive in after the duck, but Daffy's "Positively No Swimming" sign stops him. Daffy paints a self-portrait on a rock, and Caspar clubs it, causing him to vibrate. Daffy settles him down and gives him a card: "For the biggest, most luscious duck you ever tasted—200 yards." Caspar and Fido follow a series of signs leading to a giant duck, actually a balloon Daffy has inflated. When Caspar stabs it with his knife, it explodes. Floating to heaven on a separate cloud, Daffy reconsiders, "Maybe that wasn't such a good idea after all."

PORKY AND TEABISCUIT

Porky Pig; Apr 22; LT; Supervision by Ben Hardaway and Cal Dalton; Story by Melvin Millar; Animation by Herman Cohen; Musical Direction by Carl W. Stalling.
Thirties horse-race cartoons rely on two essential precepts: that the horse has got to win by extra-physical stimulation (the lightning in *Buddy's Pony Express*, the horsefly in *Milk and Money*) and that said horse must be the saddest, most miserable, hasn't-got-a-chance nag in the race. Porky's dad, stuttering hay-and-grain dealer Phineas Pig, sends him to the track to deliver some feed and to collect eleven dollars in payment. Unfortunately, Porky stops in front of an auction on the way back. The auctioneer happens to be asking eleven dollars for an old nag just as Porky is yelling the time (11 naturally) to a deaf old geezer. When Porky learns that the immedi-

ately upcoming steeplechase pays $11 ($10,000 minus taxes), he decides to enter his nag. The horse, we learn, has both pros and cons: on the negative side, he's overly fascinated with the movement of a slide trombone, and when he hears one playing he has to stop and listen to it. On the plus side, when he hears a balloon pop, he runs like crazy and beats anything on four legs. After he wins, the disgusting, snorting, wheezing, glue-factory reject tries posing cutely with a slip-horn.

On the soundtrack: "She Was an Acrobat's Daughter" (flim-flam theme), and "Ride, Tenderfoot, Ride," and a malapropism-dispensing announcer who predates Doodles Weaver.

THUGS WITH DIRTY MUGS

May 6; MM; Supervision by Fred Avery; Story by Jack Miller; Animation by Sid Sutherland; Musical Direction by Carl W. Stalling.

Say! Looky here, you mugs, this one of the real Avery classics, one of the funniest cartoons ever. Although it utilizes gangster-plot cliches, the main targets are the conventions of Warners crime films.

We open with the typical Warner feature-style actor introductions: F. H. A. (Sherlock) Homes as Flat Foot Flanigan with a Floy Floy and Ed. G. Robemsome as Killer Diller. The killer's succession of bank robberies, starting with the First National and working up (skipping past the 13th; "Killer Superstitious") to the point where 87 banks are robbed in a day, is depicted in a montage of newspaper headlines and quick-cut, unusual-angled bank-job shots (one overhead). Behind a glass door we see Officer Flanagan in silhouette, apparently grilling a suspect and threatening, "I'm gonna pin it on ya." He turns out to be playing pin the tail on the donkey. An agent calls the cop. Shown in a diagnol split screen, the officer leans over from one half of the screen into the other. But crime does not pay, and, finally, the killer, who has been doing Robinson for the whole picture (apart from "showing off" his Fred Allen), is caught when a guy in the audience who has seen the picture before tips off the police, who catch the

villains in the act of opening a wall safe that's behind a radio dial. The "Long Sentence" that the killer gets in the end is "I've been a naughty boy."

KRISTOPHER KOLUMBUS. JR.

Porky Pig; May 13; LT; Supervision by Robert Clampett; Animation by Norman McCabe and I. Ellis; Musical Direction by Carl W. Stalling.

The comedy visuals serve to illustrate the narrator's straighforward telling of the Columbus story, with the cute, smiling Porky in the lead. In "1492, when even the most learned of astronomers believed that the world was flat as a pancake ..." Porky/Chris first persuades the king and the queen that the world is round by heaving a baseball in one direction and having it come back in another covered with travel stickers. Since his crew chickens out (when he asks them if they're men or mice, they metamorphize into the latter), "Columbus faced the vast ocean alone ... out into the uncharted sea where no man had dared sail before." He sails by the stars (they form signs) for 40 days and 40 nights (which blink on and off), and past sea serpents, although Porky exclaims, "There's no such thing as a sea serpent." He runs into one with a Charlie Chan accent who in turn is spooked by an even bigger monster. When all is darkest, Porky spots land and finds a cigar-store Injun version of Manhattan whose inhabitants throw him a ticker-tape parade. A few original Americans also return with Columbus to show the queen "their native ceremonial dance, never before seen by white man." It turns out to be a lindy hop circa 1939.

Theme music: "Let That Be a Lesson to You."

NAUGHTY BUT NICE

Sniffles; May 30; MM; Supervision by Charles M. Jones; Story by Rich Hogan; Animation by Phil Monroe; Musical Direction by Carl W. Stalling.

They call him Sniffles because that's what he does. For his debut, his sniffling is attributed to his having a cold. For this particular episode his malforming nostrils aren't his most distinguishing characteristic: here he's a drunk. You heard me, drunk! He's gone to the drugstore in search of a cold medicine and wound up drinking a 125-percent alcohol remedy. Plastered, he befriends an electric shaver and passes along both conditions, the cold and the inebriation. Soon a cat is after our intoxicated mouse and tries to hoist him out of an arcade-style toy steam shovel game. When the shaver sees what the bad ol' cat is doing to his pal, he lets him have it! It ends with a cold drunk mouse sneezing himself backward into the toy steam shovel.

POLAR PALS

Porky Pig; June 3; LT; Supervision by Robert Clampett; Story by Warren Foster; Animation by John Carey; Musical Direction by Carl W. Stalling.
The cartoon opens on the Eskimo pig waking up in his igloo bed of fur-blankets that turn out to be living polar bears. Clampett's cuteness and his mean streak are flip sides of the same record. First he indulges in a happy and peppy production number with dozens of smiling polar pals cavorting to "Let's Rub Noses (Like the Eskimoses)," Porky trucking in front of an ice bank that distortedly reflects his figure like a funhouse mirror. Then the director takes equal delight in what amounts to a production number of an animal massacre, caused by a slaughter-happy fur-trapper named I. Killem. With machine guns and cannon he reduces penguins to bowling pins and transforms bears and deer into rugs and mounted heads. Porky, the two-gun conservationist, fights back, blasting the villain with a musket that spits out buckshot and explosives. The bad guy's defeat is accelerated by his fleeing in a kayak that he learns to his dismay is actually a whale.

More music: "Deep in a Dream," "Singing in the Bathtub," and "Tain't No Sin."

BELIEVE IT OR ELSE

June 25; MM; Supervision by Fred Avery; Story by Dave Monahan; Animation by Virgil Ross; Musical Direction by Carl W. Stalling.
Mr. Ripley gets the rib this time, with one ludicrous strangely-believe-it gag after another, periodically interrupted by Egghead as a doubter strolling across the screen carrying an "I Don't Believe It!" or "It's a Fake!" sign or voicing his disbelief to the off-screen narrator. Some of the bits are just blackout gags, others specifically Ripley trademarks (like a dopey match-game optical illusion, "try it on your friends").

A few highlights: actual pictures of life on Mars that reveal space hero Buck Dodgers posing effeminately and talking in Blanc's voice ("Don't miss me in next Sunday's funny paper. Boy! It's a killer thriller!"); the actual "berth" (get it?) of a baby; a man who builds ships in bottles—only he's in the bottle and the full-sized ship is outside. Funny names are also a highlight, among them a certain Mr. Holstein Cud, who has consumed 50 quarts of milk a day for the last two years. For the finale, Egghead, (still in his Joe Penner phase) putting his doby where his mouth is, tries to prove that the magician, Mr. Horace Buzzsaw, is a fake, and volunteers to be sawed in half. "It's all done with mirrors!" he exclaims, only to discover his lower half walking away without him.

Familiar themes: "Umbrella Man" (for Egghead), "Beautiful Baby," and "Over the Waves."

HOBO GADGET BAND

June 17; MM; Supervision by Ben Hardaway and Cal Dalton; Story by Jack Miller; Animation by Richard Bichenback; Musical Direction by Carl W. Stalling.
The collective hero, a group of tramps led by one particularly seedy-looking gent with Pinto Colvig's voice, arises and goes about its daily routine, showing us something of its life and habitat, presented as a parody of "normal" living. For instance, the group has constructed an Our Gang-like hobo train station for the purpose of free-loading rides on passing trains. However, the train engineer has a few devices up his sleeve as well, one of which, labeled "Hobo Eliminator," shakes the train like a cracking whip, tossing bums off in the middle of a

polka. They roll down a hill, find a sign advertising "Amateur Musicians Wanted for Radio Broadcast," and head for the radio station. Using a vocal trio and an orchestra comprised entirely of jugs, cigar-box mandolins, "pots and pans and old tin cans," they stage a production number that both the station announcer and audience really dig. They are offered a radio contract and a "life of luxury." The head tramp accepts, but as soon as they hear the first train whistle blow, they're outa there!

Opening scene music: "Deep in a Dream."

SCALP TROUBLE

Porky Pig, Daffy Duck; June 24; LT; Supervision by Robert Clampett; Animation by Norman McCabe; Story by Ernest Gee; Musical Direction by Carl W. Stalling.

Daffy, comically outfitted with giant swordsheath and Napoleon hat (here both a sign of screwiness and authority) is the stern commander of a frontier fort in the rear of Injun territory. When he orders his men to fall in for reveille, they come barrelling out of the barracks, trampling Daffy—all but Porky, who slumbers on. Daffy gets so tuckered out trying to wake Porky that he, too, hits the hay. When Porky accidentally bounces backward on Daffy's over-sized sheath, the two embrace, and Daffy says coyly, "I didn't know you cared!" They don't have much time for such antics, for the entire Sioux nation is soon attacking the fort. One Sioux walks through the wooden wall by guzzling fire water and breathing a hole in it. One paleface keeps score of his hits by chalking them up and singing, "One little, two little Indians." By the time he gets to "Ten little Indian boys," one of the redskins has gotten to him, while a Jerry Colonna Indian suggests, "Greetings, mate, let's scalpitate!" Daffy turns the tables when he accidentally swallows a load of ammunition, which then detonates with burps and hiccups. Porky seizes advantage of the opportunity to utilize his commander as the first machine gun. Soon Daffy's inflating and explosive

stomach disorders have scattered the savages. At the windup, Daffy sighs, "I'm sure glad that's over!" just as his stomach begins a repeat performance.

OLD GLORY

Porky Pig; July 1; MM; Supervision by Charles M. Jones; Animation by Robert McKimson; Musical Direction by Carl Stalling; Uncredited narrator voice of Uncle Sam by John Deering; Arrangements by Milton Franklin.

The spirit of Uncle Sam demonstrates to Porky why it's important to learn the pledge of allegiance by showing him (rotoscoped) scenes from American history. This begins with the Pilgrims who "came to this great unknown country in search of freedom, instead they got ... "OPPRESSION! UNFAIR TAXES! TYRANNY! UNFAIR LAWS! INJUSTICE! INJUSTICE! INJUSTICE!" fading into Patrick Henry's "Liberty or death" spiel. It goes from there to the Midnight Ride of Paul Revere (I think Porky did it better in *I Haven't Got a Hat,* don't you folks?). The marching feet of Revolutionary soldiers then become a pounding gavel at the signing of the Declaration of Independence and the marching musicians of the *Spirit of '76*; the Liberty Bell rings over George Washington's signing of the Constitution. "G-G-Gee, that's wonderful!" exclaims Porky. "Then what happened?" Then, Porky, "began a vast movement to the west with incredible hardships, magnificent sacrifices by these gallant pioneers which might have been in vain had it not been for a great American." Porky looks over to a statue of A. Lincoln, with the last part of the Gettysburg Address recited over a heavenly choir humming the "Battle Hymn of the Republic." Porky wakes up, removes his hat, salutes the flag, and starts to recite, "I pledge allegiance to the flag ..."

PORKY'S PICNIC

Porky Pig, Petunia Pig; July 15; MM; Supervision by Robert Clampett; Animation by Robert Cannon and Vive Risto; Musical Direction by Carl W. Stalling.

Cutesy-wootsy Porky and Petunia go on a picnic together, with the threat of heavy violence lurking just under the surface, supplied by Pinkie (returning from *Porky's Naughty Nephew*), whose ultra-cute countenance, baby outfit, and Berenice Hanson voice belie the most sadistic little kid ever in cartoons. Pinkie's favorite pastime is annoying Porky, not to mention numerous attempts to decapitate a squirrel. Eventually, Pinkie wanders into a nearby zoo, where Porky must rescue him from a snapping alligator and a mother lion whose offspring he teases. Best is the way Clampett and crew parody the conventions of Porky's character, much as they would later do for Bugs Bunny and Elmer Fudd. For instance, Porky "combing" his bald head, getting caught up in the middle of a stammer and telling the audience, "I sound like a motorboat." Unable to pronounce the name "Goldilocks" when telling a fairy tale to Pinkie, he describes her instead as "a little peroxide blonde."

DANGEROUS DAN MCFOO

July 15; MM; Supervision by Fred Avery; Story by Rich Hogan; Animation by Paul Smith; Musical Direction by Carl W. Stalling.

"A gang of the boys were whooping it up at the Malibu Saloon/And the guy that tackled the ivories was playing swing time tune." "The shooting of Dan McGrew" is parodied line by line with spot gags and topical references galore, beginning with "at the back of the house in a solo game was dangerous Dan McFoo." The game turns out to be pinball, and our hero is a little nimrod with Elmer Fudd's (Arthur Q. Bryan) voice. When the heavy enters and takes one look at the "girl who's known as Sue," he immediately visualizes her as Bette Davis, even though she talks like Katharine Hepburn ("I hope Dan mows you down, really I do").

The climactic fight sequence begins at once, as a referee appears from nowhere, and a train comes through the door to ring the bell signifying the start and finish of rounds. The bad guy's glove contains not only four horseshoes, but also the very horse they came in on. "For the benefit of the fight fans in the audience, we will stop the camera at intervals to enable you to see the blows as they land." Each freezed frame reveals a below-the-belt blow. "Hey, you mugs," the narrator says, "you aren't getting anywhere. Here, take these [pistols]. Let's get this thing over with." They reach for their guns, the lights go out, a woman screams, and two guns blaze in the dark. When the lights go on, Dan is lying on the floor, Is he? Hmmm, could be.

SNOW MAN'S LAND

July 29; MM; Supervision by Charles Jones; Story by Dave Monahan; Animation by Ken Harris; Musical Direction by Carl W. Stalling.

A little nebbish of a mountie (Pinto Colvig) gets assigned to apprehend the "scourge of the north, Dirty Pierre." Pinto's the only one not to run away when the captain asks for volunteers. Quite the dopiest of the mounties, Dutch doors are too much for him to deal with, and he doesn't recognize the object of his search even when Dirty Pierre is standing next to one of his own wanted posters. Pinto finally gets wised up when D. P. pounds him into the ground like a spike. When the villain tramps into a log cabin, the dim-witted mountie threatens to break the door down. He breaks everything, but the door, into rubble. The fiend gives Pinto another kick in the pants to send the mountie rolling. Unwittingly, he rolls himself into a snowball that not only engulfs Dirty Pierre but also kay-oes the entire police cabin.

Jones's first out-and-out comedy underscores how remarkable his comic masterpieces of the '40s and '50s are.

WISE QUACKS

Porky Pig, Daffy Duck; Aug 5; LT; Supervision by Robert Clampett; Animation by I. Ellis; Story by Warren Foster; Musical Direction by Carl W. Stalling.

The Warner characters come of age in a manner of speaking, this being our first encounter with one of their wives, let alone offspring. Porky reads (in another Clampett newspaper, *The Barnyard Bulletin*) that Mr. and Mrs. Duck are expecting a blessed event. Delighted, he exclaims, "My pal Daffy a father! I can hardly believe it! Why, we were kids together." He strolls over to pay a visit. As Mrs. Daffy heats up her bottom to hatch the eggs, the highly-strung father to be, far from passing out cigars, tries to unwind with generous slugs of corn juice. By the time both the babies and Porky arrive, he's good and plastered. Unfortunately, out of the sky comes a hoodlum buzzard who makes off with Daffy's youngest. When Daffy chases him, our villain summons his whole gang of roughneck birds. Daffy gets them to release the chick, and Porky catches him by sliding through the marsh. The buzzards corner Daffy in a shed, and Porky and Mrs. Daffy creep timidly in to discover that Daffy has reduced the whole flock of pursuers to a bunch of slap-happy drunks by being generous with his jug.

Daffy's youngest is a real scene-stealer, forever shaking his head yes when he means no (and the other way around): when dropped by a buzzard, plummeting toward certain death, he baby-talks, "I'm flying!"

HARE-UM SCARE-UM

Bugs Bunny; Aug 12; MM; Supervision by Ben Hardaway and Cal Dalton; Story by Melvin Millar; Animation by Gil Turner; Musical Direction by Carl W. Stalling.

Ironically, the director(s) most responsible for both the name and basic story format (the rabbit hunt) of Warners greatest cartoon star never quite mastered the "high" Warners style. There's much of the classic Bugs here, yet it seems light years behind Avery's *A Wild Hare*, the definitive Bugs Bunny film to come. For one thing, Bugs spends the cartoon heckling a short-tempered hunter who has gone hunting to procure his own meat and thus combat high meat prices. For another, this

heckling includes appearing in various guises (not necessarily dis-guises). Many of these, as would become typical of the series later on, involve the participation of props that aren't there. A door opens in the side of a cliff; Bugs announces the floor's merchandise as though he were a department store elevator operator; a highway cop pantomimes an "air motorcycle." Other elements that anticipate the later series include Bugs's cross-dressing (putting on a "female dog" costume) and his pathetic begging the hunter not to shoot him near the finish. However, it takes off only when he's not the rabbit of tomorrow, but the rabbit of yesterday, doing Daffy Duck impressions a la his debut (*Porky's Hare Hunt*), anticipating another Hardaway star, Woody Woodpecker.

DETOURING AMERICA

ACADEMY AWARD NOMINEE

Aug 26; MM; Supervision by Fred Avery; Story by Jack Miller; Animation by Rollin Hamilton; Musical Direction by Carl W. Stalling.

"All states depicted in this photoplay are fictitious. Any similarity to actual states, either Democratic or Republican, is purely coincidental." This "educational tour of the United States" begins in New York, establishing a recurring theme concerning a human fly trying to climb the Empire State Building (it's funnier along the way than the final punchline). Jerry Colonna is a Texas cow-puncher using fisticuffs on a confused steer; an old squaw Indian carries her fully-grown papoose on her back; Indian snakes dance; the geyser "Old Reliable" erupts into a spittoon; prairie dogs, instead of the urban variety, go wacky over trees.

Not on the same level as the follow-up from the next year, *Cross-Country Detours*, very few gags here (like the Indian sequence and the bit with the giant sequoias) are worth repeating.

Cut to Colonna telling the narrator, "Ah! So you're wondering too!" Old reliable themes: "Umbrella Man" and the "Pilgrim's Chorus" from Tannheuser (later known as "Return My Love").

PORKY'S HOTEL

Porky Pig; Sept 2; LT; Supervision by Robert Clampett; Animation by Norm McCabe and John Carey; Musical Direction by Carl W. Stalling.
Situation comedy: Porky as owner-proprietor of a small-town hotel where he and his sidekick, Gabby Goose, try to please their only customer, a wheelchair-confined, irritable and irritating gout-plagued geezer named Gouty Goat, who's come to the hotel for peace and quiet. With the obnoxious Gabby around, Gouty hasn't a chance. The goose's endless blabbering, repeatedly punctuated with "I betcha," is sheer torture. The audience is on Gouty's side when he yells, "Boo!" at the little goose and makes him cry. Things get really dicey when a fly enters and Gabby goes running around the room trying to swat it with a hammer that you know is going to end up slamming the old goat's gouty leg. The inevitable finally happens after Porky serves him lunch (goat gags: he throws away the food and eats the plate). The goat does just what we'd like to do by chasing Gabby all over the hotel (still in his wheelchair, yet!) with intent to kill. It ends in a comic crash.

So many Warner toon characters are hyperthyroid, it's about time we ran into one who's legitimate. "Honeymoon Hotel" serves as a much-used background theme, first vocally behind the establishing scenes as cooed by a syrupy choir (eight bars) and almost unceasingly through the rest of the film as an instrumental.

LITTLE BROTHER RAT

Sniffles; Sept 2; MM; Supervision by Charles M. Jones; Story by Rich Hogan; Animation Bob McKimson; Musical Direction by Charles W. Stalling.
And you thought Sniffles was at least unique! Here it's revealed that he's only one of a race of snivelling girl-voiced rodents, a bunch of which are throwing a party that includes a scavenger hunt, as in *My Man Godfrey.* Sniffles gets the jump on the competition when he returns with a cat's whisker, but the next item is a toughie: an owl's egg. To make things dicier, Sniffles doesn't know that a certain revenge-minded, whiskerless cat is on his path. The eloquent, brawny father owl catches Sniffles red-handed trying to make off with his unhatched offspring and tosses him out of the birdhouse. He lands on the cat underneath and bounces right back. Making another attempt to swipe the egg, he trips and cracks it open, hatching a baby owl. Now his problem is that the owl-ette won't stop following him (even when he ties him back in the shell!). He even follows Sniffles down to the ground, where the cat is waiting to pounce on both of them. Sniffles grabs the owl chick and runs, and Papa Owl, witnessing this, swoops down on the cat and deposits him in a nearby chimney. "And, as a token of our gratitude," the father owl tells Sniffles, "we want to give you this egg." "Gee willikers!" says Sniffles, as the baby owl once more pops out of the shell.

SIOUX ME

Sept 9; MM; Supervision by Ben Hardaway and Cal Dalton; Story by Melvin Millar; Animation by Herman Cohen; Musical Direction by Carl W. Stalling.
"The worst drought in a decade has descended upon the Indian people at Hangnail, Oklahoma. Crops are burned to a crisp, streams and rivers are drying up. There is no relief in sight from the scorching winds ...These unfortunates are faced with certain disaster unless they get rain." We start with a few heat and dryness gags (corn popping, etc.) and cut to the Indian

chief watching helplessly as the tribe animals go on strike. He calls on the local rainmaker, a fellow named J. Q. Drizzlepuss, and demands, "My people, they starve, my animals, they die. You make 'em rain, savvy?" The rainmaker leads the tribe in a production number, "We Want Rain," that juxtaposes the traditional Hollywood notion of what Indian music sounds like with 30s college cheers. But, nada. It turns out the trick he connived for faking rain (a hose in the trees) has gone dry, so he gives his son beads to trade for a barrel of water in town. The lad instead brings home a box of weather pills sold by a slick-talking medicine-show man. His disbelieving pop hurls the pills aside. Indians and animals eat them, putting lightning in a turtle and making a a squaw and papoose experience internal earthquakes. After the rain pill is rescued from a vulture, the long-awaited storm finally starts.

JEEPERS CREEPERS

Porky Pig; Sept 23; LT; Supervision by Robert Clampett; Animation by Vive Risto; Story by Ernest Gee; Musical Direction by Carl W. Stalling.
There are two kinds of scary house movie comedies. The kind where real ghosts are shown (Disney's *Lonesome Ghosts*) and the ones where the elements contrive to make the progagonists think there must be ghosts (Hugh Harman's *The Old House*). This is a combination of the two, as policeman Porky investigates a haunted house where a sure-enough ghost dwells, one who employs such bits as frogs-in-shoes. The ghost, portrayed vocally by Pinto "Goofy" Colvig, first treats us to a chorus of "Jeepers Creepers" (from Warners' *Going Places*) with new spooky lyrics all the while performing ghostly feats for our amusement (such as bathing in a '30s washing machine and wringing himself out). The next highlight is an outstandingly realized chase, of the everywhere-I-run-he's there variety, wherein Porky dashes back and forth, up- and downstairs, trying to get away (he's so scared the floorboards stick to his feet), even doing one of those gags where he leaps

into the arms of his pursuer without realizing who it is ("What's a matter, baby?" the ghost coos; "Look out, here I go!" yells Porky). For the wind-up, Porky's cop car backfires in the ghost's face, leaving him to do a Rochester impression: "My, oh, my! Tattletale gray!"

LAND OF THE MIDNIGHT FUN

Sept 23; MM; Supervision by Fred Avery; Story by Melvin Millar; Animation by Charles McKimson; Musical Direction by Carl W. Stalling.
The *Airplane!*of the '30s: straight story in a very strict genre, a newsreel covering a trip to the frozen wastes of Alaska, crammed with blackout gags. Few are individually memorable, but taken one after the other (as they were meant to be) they collectively pummel you into a silly sensibility. After dozens of "silly Eskimo" bits (such as an Eskimo gal putting lipstick on her nose), Avery takes us inside "The Brass Monkey Night Club" and proceeds to impose western culture on the natives, from a (largely rotoscoped) femme Eskimo doing an ice dance a la Sonja Henie to a schmaltzy waltz. "And so, with heavy heart, we bid a reluctant farewell to the land of frozen splendor ..." It winds up with the ship being caught in a fog and docking on top of the World's Fair trylon.

Most off-color gags: the gay "ferry" boat, the puking passengers making the trip "by rail."

The score includes "Umbrella Man" and other perennials.

NAUGHTY NEIGHBORS

Porky Pig; Oct 7; LT; Supervision by Robert Clampett; Animation by I. Ellis; Story by Warren Foster; Musical Direction by Carl W. Stalling.
When you see an opening title card

that reads "Our story unfolds in the quiet old hills of old Kentucky where, in contrast to the troubled outside world, the hill folk live in peace and harmony," you know the next shot is going to be a tableau of mountain warfare. Fade to a newspaper headline, "Feud Ends," teling us that the leaders of the two families, Porky and Petunia, have decided to call a cease-fire. From there on it's the usual brilliant Clampett mixture of the cuddly and the bloodthirsty, every deliberately-overdone shot of Porky and Petunia making goo-goo eyes at each other being undercut by images of other members of the two families trying to make nice but oh-so-obviously wanting nothing more than to slaughter each other. While Porky and Petunia scamper off doing their cutesy-pie duet (Harry Warren's "Would You Like To Take a Walk") the other Martins and McCoys (mostly ducks and chickens) engage in seemingly innocent dances that, without warning, break out into Apache-like wrestling. A simple game of patty-cake between the old geezers threatens to explode into World War III. In fact, it does. The explosions of the rekindled feud jar Porky and Petunia out of their lovey-doveyness, but Porky has already planned a solution that will satisfy Clampett's flip-side-of-a-coin urge for the ultracute and ultraviolent: a dainty-looking hand grenade (inscribed "Feud Pacifier") with an explosion that has enough force to transform the whole lot of macho mountaineers into simpering sissies and (the ultimate sign of docility) maypole dancers.

LITTLE LION HUNTER

Oct 7; MM; Supervision by Charles Jones; Story by Robert Givens; Animation by Philip Monroe; Musical Direction by Carl W. Stalling.
Hunting with his spear, Inki, a little black jungle boy, narrowly misses a parrot, a giraffe, and a butterfly. He then pursues a black minah bird, who appears and disappears mysteriously throughout this adventure. When the minah bird drops into a hole, Inki reaches in and pulls out a skunk. When he stalks a turtle through a hollow log,

the minah bird pops out and walks over the jungle boy.

Inki puts his ear to the ground to listen for game. A large lion finds him in this position. Inki is unaware of his presence, so the lion pounds the ground to give him a clue. Inki is then chased and uses a tree stump as camouflage. The minah bird comes to the rescue, ties up the lion, and lures Inki out of hiding, giving him a swift kick in the rear.

The first of Jones's Inki cartoons, this is subtle, relying on facial expression and nuance, a Jones trait in years to come.

THE GOOD EGG

Oct 21; MM; Supervision by Charles M. Jones; Animation by Ken Harris; Story by Dave Monahan; Musical Direction by Carl W. Stalling.
An ostracized outsider has to prove himself worthy of everybody else's company. Here it's a baby turtle in a barnyard full of chickens; he gets there when his adopted mother hen stumbles across his unhatched egg when she goes down to the river to drown herself in a fit of childless depression. The little chicks cruelly snicker at the turtle when he tells them he's a chicken and laugh when he falls on his face, but change their tune when they have an accident while playing pirates. Their boat falls apart and the chicks start drowning. Our hero leaps in the pond and saves them, then carries them all home on his shell. In the end, both mother and child are accepted, although you get the feeling he's valued only for services rather than his inner worth.

Jones has come up with high-speed squeals for the chicken voices that are even better than Berenice Hanson, if that's possible.

Chickeny music: "(Ho-Ole-Ay) Start the Day Right," "Umbrella Man," and the chick-saving theme, "Don't Give Up the Ship."

FRESH FISH

Nov 4; MM; Supervision by Fred Avery; Story by Jack Miller; Animation by Sid Sutherland; Musical Direction by Carl W. Stalling.

Title card: "Any resemblance to the poor fish either living or at Santa Anita is purely coincidental." Narrator: And now come with us on an educational cruise aboard our glass-bottom boat to view the wonders of marine life in the South Seas ..." Blackout gags about funny fish intercut with a linking story peg concerning the renowned Professor Mackerel Fishsticks, eminent authority on denizens of the deep. Equipped with his modern diving bell, the professor will be sent to the ocean floor in search of the rare wim wam whistling shark never before captured by man."

In between shots of the professor in the bathysphere, we get mainly puns based on "combination"-type names of fish. We get dogfish, tigersharks, taxi crabs, and movie star references such as Ned Sparks as an old crab and Katharine Hepburn as a star fish. The most bizarre is a polite bucktoothed creature with heads on both ends in search of Mr. Ripley (believe it or else!). The funniest is Lionel Barrymore as a teacher of a school of fish who gets hooked when showing his students what *not* to do.

Theme music: "Forty-Second Street," "You Oughta Be in Pictures," "Fingal's Cave," and "Ride of the Valkyries."

PIED PIPER PORKY
Porky Pig; Nov 4; LT; Supervision by Robert Clampett; Animation by John Carey and Dave Hoffman; Musical Direction by Carl W. Stalling.
Distinctly lesser Clampett, with the idea of Porky as Pied Piper fading before routine cat-and-mouse antics. The opening newspaper headline gives us the background data that P.P.P. has rid the town of rats, as Porky demonstrates (to the tune of "Mutiny in the Nursery") for an off-camera female chorus, by hypnotizing them with his clarinet. However, there's one little rat left in Hamelin, a wise guy rodent with a Rochester voice, who is not only immune to the Piper's horn but climbs up Porky's torso and breaks the thing. So, Porky takes out a box marked "Old-Fashioned Mouse Trap" that contains a cat Porky calls "Slapsy Catsy."

The cat is at first afraid of the rat (making like a woman holding up her skirt on a chair), but then steels his courage and gives chase. However, the cartoon cat slams head-on into a wall, knocking him out and darn near killing him. The nine lives start to leave his body, until Porky (remember him?) rallies them back with a strong shot of catnip that turns the pussy into a supermacho he-tiger cat. The muscle-covered cat charges into the rat's hole, and the noise of a tremendous struggle can be heard from inside. It's the rat, not the cat, who emerges victorious, covered in "Gen-u-ine ermine."

Porky's rat-mesmerizing theme is "Umbrella Man."

FAGIN'S FRESHMAN
Nov 18; MM; Supervision by Ben Hardaway and Cal Dalton; Story by Jack Miller; Animation by Rod Scribner; Musical Direction by Carl W. Stalling.
A little kitten nicknamed Blackie gets punished by his overly-strict mother for the easily understandable desire to listen to a cops-and-robbers radio show rather than participate in their inane singalong of "the three little kittens/ They lost their mittens." He's sent to bed without supper, but even in his dream he doesn't actually do anything except discover a training facility for budding gangsters. He watches the students demonstrate their techniques in close harmony (the school song, "We're Working Our Way Through College") as well as in heisting and picking pockets. Before he's had the chance to do something he'd regret, the place is raided by cops and he's whimpering he wants to go home. Just when you're thinking you'll see some action at last, the shoot-out is interrupted by a phone call from Officer Hogan's wife asking him to pick up a pound of butter. We don't even see how it comes out. Blackie wakes up from his dream, and (as opposed to the heroes of *Pigs Is Pigs*, *I Wanna Be a Sailor*, and *Streamline Greta Garbo*, who immediately revert to their sinful ways) zooms downstairs to join his family at the piano, apparently vowing to be a sissy from now on.

PORKY THE GIANT KILLER

Porky Pig; Nov 18; LT; Supervision by Ben Hardaway and Cal Dalton; Story by Melvin Millar; Animation by Gil Turner; Musical Direction by Carl W. Stalling.

"All giants depicted in this photoplay are fictitious. Any similarity to actual giants living or in the national league is purely coincidental." Another weak-sister Hardaway-Dalton effort, in which even the way they draw Porky makes you yearn for Tashlin or Clampett. Porky joins a group of villagers on their way to invade the giant's castle just as the big guy is putting his baby to sleep. At the first sound of the giant, the others turn tail and run, leaving Porky alone in the castle. Trying to avoid the giant, Porky ducks into the baby's nursery, where he finds himself entertaining the five-foot-seven-inch toddler to keep him quiet. In playing with him, Porky gets pat-a-caked across the room. He amuses the babe further by showing him how to make his baby bottle nipple pop in and out. The pig then silences the tot by sitting at his toy piano and playing "The Alphabet Song." The giant busts in and pursues Porky across the castle, eventually chasing him onto a ledge, where he falls into the moat. The giant quickly drinks the water, catching Porky. It ends with Porky being forced to play the infantile song over and over like a Good-Humor wagon.

Also heard: "You Must Have Been a Beautiful Baby."

SNIFFLES AND THE BOOKWORM

Sniffles; Dec 2; MM; Supervision by Charles M. Jones; Story by Rich Hogan; Animation by Robert McKimson; Musical Direction by Carl W. Stalling.

Sniffles, asleep on a bookshop shelf, is discovered by a bespectacled bookworm. Terrified, the worm seeks help from his friends, the characters in books. In pantomine, he tells one a huge monster has invaded the shop and the worm's description of the trespasser leads to the summoning of a Viking-type guy to help. Relieved to discover it's only a mouse, the book characters produce clarinets and go into a musical number involving all the Mother Goose characters. Their revelry is interrupted by Frankenstein's monster, who leaves his coffinlike book to stalk the terrified nursery-rhyme characters. When Sniffles sees the monster about to attack the helpless bookworm, he yells, "Stop!" which sends the monster after him. Sniffles cleverly trips him and sends him flying off the shelf, earning himself a peck on the cheek from the bookworm.

Stiff and stodgy stuff—who needs a serious books-come-to-life cartoon? Jones doesn't even let us enjoy the film's potentially great musical number; he denies us that pleasure by cross-cutting to the oncoming bad guy.

SCREWBALL FOOTBALL

Dec 16; MM; Supervision by Fred Avery; Story by Melvin Millar; Animation by Virgil Ross; Musical Direction by Carl W. Stalling.

"Good afternoon, ladies and gentlemen, we are here at the famous Chili Bowl football classic, the biggest game of the year . . ." Complain, if you like, that this blackout opus is up to neither Avery's nor Disney's '40s sports classics, but there are still enough goodies to please fans of both the gridiron and screwiness.

At half time, the players crowd around the coach and give him a stern pep talk, and the *audience* changes sides. A desperate cheerleader makes an impassioned plea for yells from the crowd, only to receive a mild whisper from the one guy left in the stands. In the second half an important touchdown is interrupted when the radio has to take time out for a commercial. The suspense mounts, but the "gun that ends the game" comes from the bleachers, where a little baby takes revenge on the big lug who's been swiping licks from his ice cream throughout the game.

The players include Stinkovich, Palookavich, Stubblevich, Scramovich. You get the idea. The music incorporates the usual sports-and-college fanfare.

THE FILM FAN

Porky Pig; Dec 16; LT; Supervision by Robert Clampett; Animation by Norm McCabe and Vive Risto; Musical Direction by Carl W. Stalling.

Everyone loves the movies, coming from far and near to see them via the efficient Los Angeles mass-transit system. Even a snooty dowager, who claims she never goes to the movies, gets dragged in by her excited pooch when he learns it's a film about trees (perhaps it's an Avery cartoon). Little Porky Pig, whose mother sent him on a quick errand to the grocery, can hardly believe his eyes when he sees the sign, "Kids admitted free today only." Dashing into the theater, Porky takes in the day's program, beginning with a newsreel already in progress. Porky changes his seat (to look at the bizarre underangle of the running horse from *She Was an Acrobat's Daughter*). Then it's mainly trailers: "If you want to laugh, *Four Feathers* will tickle you. Special Double Feature: *Honeymoon in Bali* with *The Old Maid* ... *Gone with the Breeze*." Lastly, it's a preview of the serial *The Masked Marvel*, which uses a little footage from *Lone Stranger and Porky*. It's mainly the masked cowboy and his horse Sterling agreeing to take the high and the low road and breaking out into "Loch Lomond." Porky's rapture comes to an end when the management receives a phone call from Mrs. Pig that occasions an usher to announce, "If there is a little boy in this theater, that was sent to the store by his mother, he'd better get home right away!" At this, the entire theater empties out.

CURIOUS PUPPY

Dec 30; MM; Supervision by Charles M. Jones; Story by Robert Givens; Animation by Phil Monroe; Musical Direction by Carl W. Stalling.

In this follow-up to *Dog Gone Modern*, the two dogs become more naturalistic. Any lack of cartooniness is compensated for by the inclusion of a chase element, supplying tension between the dogs themselves as well as between them and the setting. Said location is an amusement park after hours into which the little black-and-white pup meanders (attracted by the image of a cat). The entire place, including lights, rides, and attractions, can be turned on by the flick of a single switch. The big brown boxer, the park's watchdog, gets most of the footage as the animators struggle to convey his personality, using "slow burn" humor despite a doggy face and no voice. The watchdog slowly pursues the little pup through a house of mirrors where they do the Marx Brothers (*Duck Soup*) mirror routine, a "phunny-photo" stand, an automatic popcorn machine that butters and salts the pup, a high-angled slide into a pool, a rack full of toy dogs each identical to the pup (the boxer tears the stuffed animals to shreds). He then sees the pup on the other side of the park exit. His frustration mounts to the point where he starts bawling hysterically.

Gentle humor accompanied by a little of "Oh, You Crazy Moon" and a lot of "Little Dog Gone."

1940

PORKY'S LAST STAND

Porky Pig; Jan 6; LT; Supervision by Robert Clampett; Animation by I. Ellis; Story by Warren Foster; Musical Direction by Carl W. Stalling.

Porky and Daffy are short-order cooks at a lunch wagon out in the middle of nowhere. After the establishing scene/production number—"(Ho-De-Ay) Start the Day Right," sung by another sticky-sweet female choir —the cartoon veers off in two directions: while Porky tries to fry a couple of eggs, one of which hatches into a baby chick who gets an instant hot foot, Daffy deals with a tough customer who wants a good hamburger and fast! Discovering that the mice have left him a note, "Greetings, Gate, you're a wee bit late," Daffy goes looking for something to make a hamburger out of. He gets an idea: clobber a small calf he spies outside (singing "With Plenty of Gravy on You"). Instead, he finds himself up against a monstrous bull who chases after both Daffy and Porky. A well-directed, clear, and suspenseful chase (including one of the earliest uses of the "heart" gag, Porky's valentine-shaped heart pounding in his chest). The bull charges right through the lunch wagon and eventually totals it. The final gag has chickens on a wheel transformed into a mini-merry-go-round, with the bull's nose ring as the gold ring you have to grab.

THE EARLY WORM GETS THE BIRD

Jan 13; MM; Supervision by Fred Avery; Story by Jack Miller; Animation by Robert Cannon; Musical Direction by Carl W. Stalling.
Mrs. Blackbird puts her three little children to sleep. One has other ideas. Reading in a book that "The early bird gets the worm," this little blackbird decides to wake up early and try it. His mother scolds him, warning about the mean old fox, but the little bird is not afraid and sets his alarm clock.

The bird goes out, finds the worm, and chases it into its hole. The fox appears and grabs the little feathered boy. The fox puts the blackbird between two pieces of bread and is about to garnish his meal with ketchup when the worm dispatches an angry bee to sting him. Dropping the bird and spilling the ketchup on himself, the fox runs away, thinking he's bleeding.

Later that morning, the mother bird asks her children what they'd like for breakfast. The birds want worms, except for our early bird, who'd rather not. His new friend, the worm, adds, "Neither does I, Mammy!"

AFRICA SQUEAKS

Porky Pig; Jan 27; LT; Supervision by Robert Clampett; Story by Dave Hoffman; Animation by John Carey; Musical Direction by Carl W. Stalling.
A narrated spot-gag cartoon on jungle life, with guest star Porky Pig. Into the heart of Darkest Africa goes explorer Porky with native guides. The group encounters Spencer Tracy as "Stanley," who presumes the pig is Dr. Livingston.

We see many interesting specimens of wildlife, including a sleeping ostrich with its head in the ground, but sleeping on a pillow; two lions chewing bones, making a wish on the wishbone; a brooklyn gorilla; natives blowing darts to put meat on their table, winning it in a carnival game!

Meanwhile, Porky can't sleep because of the jungle noise. "Stanley" looks under rocks and in kangaroo pouches for Livingston. An elephant is thrown out of a boarding house, and the landlord keeps his trunk until he pays the rent. A vicious condor flies overhead and preys on some baby deer—who scramble into the bush and shoot the bird with a cannon. A native tells Porky of a white man in the jungle, and they take "Stanley" to meet his Livingston. It is "Cake Icer" (Kay Kaiser) and his Kollege of Musical Knowledge who gets the jungle jumping to his swing music. The narrator bids Africa farewell, and the Dark Continent responds, in blackface, "Good bye!"

THE MIGHTY HUNTERS

Jan 27; MM; Supervision by Chuck Jones; Story by Dave Monahan; Animation by Ken Harris; Musical Direction by Carl Stalling.
"Once upon a time, many, many years ago, there lived in the great Red Rock Canyons of Arizona a fierce tribe of wild Indians. So savage were these ferocious warriors that the very birds and animals of the forest fled in terror when their deep, throbbing war drums filled the air."

Indians dancing around a fire, their huge shadows shown silhouetted against the cave wall, turn out to be a group of Indian children. The kids run outside to play hunt. One young Indian is pulled aside by a parent and saddled with a papoose on his back. Two others, with bow and arrow, try to hunt a squirrel. Still another Indian has a rough time trying to mount a stubborn mule.

The papoose, who is eating a striped candy cane, is followed by a hungry bear. The bear scares the two hunters and the boy with the papoose, causing them to back up toward a mountain ledge. Forced to hang from the ledge, one of the Indian boys loses his pants completely. The bear tries to reach for the candy cane and falls, landing on a branch below with the candy cane. As the "mighty hunters" say good night, one little Indian is still out, still trying to sit on the mule.

Based on Jimmy Swinnerton's cartoon feature, "Canyon Kiddies," in *Good Housekeeping* magazine.

ALI-BABA BOUND

Porky Pig; Feb 17; LT; Supervision by Robert Clampett; Animation by Vive Risto; Story by Melvin Millar; Musical Direction by Carl W. Stalling.
Yet another Porky-of-the-Legion premise: in this one, no less a personage than George Raft is a nasty spy (name of Tattle-Tale Gray). He slips Legionnaire Porky the secret message that Ali Baba, the Mad Dog of the Desert, and his Dirty Sleeves, are planning to attack the legion fort. Porky borrows a little camel he calls "Baby Dumpling" and rides off to the fort. It's deserted, for all the troops (including General DeLivery) have gone off to the Legion Convention in Boston. It's up to Porky to defend the fort from hordes of unsavory-looking Arabs all by himself. Those heathens are relentless, but Porky holds his own, assisted by the baby camel's mother (whose lock of yellow hair gives her the right to be named Blondie). Finally, one midget Arab with a huge bomb tied to his head (identified as a "suicide squad") charges the fort. Porky opens the door on one end, the camels open the door at the other, and the little squirt storms right through and blows up the Arabs at the opposite side. The

attackers land in a succession of tents with the banner, "Ali Baba's Auto Camp."

"Girlfriend of the Whirling Dervish" gets a lot of use on the track, as sung by Porky and, instrumentally, there are "Merry Oldsmobile" and "Snake Charmer."

BUSY BAKERS

Feb 10; MM; Supervision by Ben Hardaway and Cal Dalton; Story by Jack Miller; Animation by Richard Bickenback; Musical Direction by Carl Stalling.
In an old village, Swenson the town baker can't complain about business. "There ain't none!" Additionally, he has virtually no flour or other ingredients. When a blind man wanders in asking for any spare bread, Swenson gives him his last donut.

The blind man returns to his windmill home, removes his disguise, and calls his helpers, who sing their theme song, "The Happy, Slappy Little Baker Man." While the baker sleeps, they perform a series of spot gags on baking and pastry making and fill the store with cakes and pies. Swenson awakens and sees the busy bakers as they leave his now fully-stocked shop. The townspeople buy the pastries, leaving Swenson with plenty of gold. The blind man returns and asks again for something to eat. The baker gives him a pie, but reminds him there is a five-cent deposit on the pie tin. The baker gets the pie in his face and laments, "That's gratitude for you!"

This is an unusual cartoon for Warners in 1940—the story and character designs are more like something Freleng would have done in 1936. It's a handsome cartoon, but a backward step considering the direction Warner Bros. was then taking.

ELMER'S CANDID CAMERA

Bugs Bunny, Elmer Fudd; Mar 2; MM; Supervision by Charles M. Jones; Animation by Bob McKimson; Story by Rich Hogan; Musical Direction by Carl W. Stalling.
Reading up on "How to Photograph Wild Life" and armed with camera, tripod, and film, Elmer Fudd heads out

to the woods. Finding a sleeping bunny, Fudd sets up his camera. Looking through his viewfinder he sees the rabbit's rear end. Elmer readjusts, but the wise-guy rabbit (not quite the Bugs Bunny to come, but close) asks the photographer what he's taking pictures of. Elmer is surprised as the bunny walks away. Next, Elmer sets up near a realistic squirrel. The rabbit reappears, pulls the camera lens out, and it snaps back, pushing Elmer into a tree. The photographer is pummeled by falling apples. Elmer next tries to photograph birds. When the hare asks him if he'd like to photograph a rabbit. Elmer is too mad to speak and drops a net on the bunny. The rabbit performs a classic death scene ("Gimme air! I can't breathe!"). Elmer begins to feel sorry for the rabbit: the bunny revives and drops the net over Elmer. Elmer goes insane, yelling, "Wabbits! Wildwife! Wabbits!" and jumps into the lake. Bugs rescues the amateur photographer, dries him off, and asks him how he feels. When Elmer says okay, the rabbit kicks him back into the water. A copy of his photography book plops on his head.

PILGRIM PORKY

Porky Pig; Mar 16; LT; Supervision by Robert Clampett; Animation by Norman McCabe; Story by Warren Foster; Musical Direction by Carl W. Stalling.
"The time is 1620: The place; Plymouth, England, a quaint little seaport town of a thousand souls ... and a few heels." Captain Porky orders all aboard, and soon a crew of gooney-Clampett Pilgrims get the ship under way. The crew of the *Mayflower* spot a group of flying fish (in airplanes with an "Eat At Joe's" advertising banner in tow). White caps, literally, appear. The ship encounters a storm and an iceberg, which opens like a drawbridge. Running gag has narrator ask the black cook for some fresh fish. The cook jumps into the sea, periodically asking, "How's dis, boss?"

When the ship reaches the New World, it passes the Statue of Liberty (at age 3); the *Mayflower* docks via parallel parking. The welcome is delivered by Chief Sitting Bull. A giant fish emerges from the sea and asks, "How's dis, boss?" opening its mouth to reveal the smiling cook inside.

CROSS COUNTRY DETOURS

Mar 16; MM; Supervision by Fred Avery; Story by Rich Hogan; Animation by Paul Smith; Musical Direction by Carl W. Stalling.
Another spot-gag travelogue spoof. Gags include a visit to Yosemite National Park, where a tourist, despite posted warnings, feeds a bear. The bear is a stickler for the rules ("Listen, stupid! Can't you read!!"). A shy little deer does a Mae West impression; a park ranger races to a discarded lit cigar butt and smokes it. In the frozen wastes of Alaska, a polar bear complains "I don't care what you say, I'm cold!" A ferocious bobcat is going to pounce on a poor, helpless baby quail but sobs, "I can't do it, I can't!" There is a classic close-up of a frog croaking—he takes out a gun and kills himself. A lizard sheds his skin as a strip tease. To prove Warner Bros. cartoons are for adults as well as children, the next gag splits the screen: one side, for grown-ups, shows a hideous gila monster, the other side, for children, shows an innocent little girl reciting "Mary Had a Little Lamb." The little girl frightens the gila monster. A Grand Canyon tourist tries to hear his echo and gets an operator who responds, "I'm sorry, they do not answer." Beavers build a concrete dam. Finally, the film's running gag: an Eskimo dog sees a sign "California 5000 miles" and runs until he reaches giant redwoods, joyously shouting, "Thousands and thousands of trees and they're mine, all mine!"

CONFEDERATE HONEY

Elmer Fudd; Mar 30; MM; Supervision by I. Freleng; Story by Ben Hardaway;

Animation by Cal Dalton; Musical Direction by Carl W. Stalling.
"Our story is laid in the Bluegrass country of old Kentucky. The year is 1861 B.C.—Before "Sea Biscuit." At the mansion of Colonel O'Hairoil, a real Southern blueblood (with blue skin, singing "Am I Blue?"), we meet his slaves picking his cotton and his daughter, Crimson O'Hairoil. Crimson is in love with Ned Cutler (Elmer Fudd). Ned parks his horse and goes up to Crimson and begins to pop the question. Just then, bombs burst and the Civil War starts. Ned goes off to fight, and Crimson vows to keep a light in the window for him, scanning a huge spotlight over the skies. A Hugh Herbert caricature is a Confederate captain. Elmer defends his men by shooting a cannon like a pinball machine. Years pass, and Ned returns from the war, rushing home to Crimson. He finally asks that burning question, "Will you validate my parking ticket?""

SLAP-HAPPY PAPPY

Porky Pig; Apr 13; LT; Supervision by Robert Clampett; Animation by John Carey and I. Ellis; Musical Direction by Carl W. Stalling.
Time to caricature Hollywood celebrities as barnyard chickens, using as the dominant theme the much-milked fact that Eddie Cantor had four daughters while Bing Crosby had four sons—an instantaneous source of humor in those days (even more than Crosby's horses). Porky reads in another one of those newspapers that turn up in virtually every Clampett cartoon (this one is a pip, is called "Cluck, the Poultry Picture Paper") that Mr. and Mrs. Eddie and Ida "Cackler" are expecting a son. A pan over to the house shows the heartbreak Eddie experiences when his missus's eggs hatch into five more girls. Bing Crosby passes by, pushing a baby carriage full of little roosters and singing "I've Got a Lot of Beautiful Babies/ And Each and Every One Is a Boy." Cantor/Cackler runs out and demands to know the secret of Papa Bing's male hen fruit. "Well, Eddie, old man, I'll tell you." Bing demonstrates that his masculine style of singing causes the impregnated females to generate male

offspring. "It's a very simple matter." Cackler dashes into his own henhouse and lays a little "If I Could Be With You" on her, and then we get a real treat in the form of an exuberant, well-captured animated interpretation of a Cantor song-and-dance. For the finish, Ida hatches an androgynous little chick who, when Papa Eddie asks, "Tell me, is it really a boy?" answers, "Hmmm, could be." Just born and already he knows his Warner toon cliches!

More music: "Am I Blue." More caricatures: Kay Kyser and Ned Sparks.

THE BEAR'S TALE

Apr 13; MM; Supervision by Fred Avery; Story by J.B. Hardaway; Animation by Rod Scribner; Musical Direction by Carl W. Stalling.
"Miss Goldilocks appears courtesy of Mervyn LeBoy Pictures." Once upon a time, in a beautiful green forest, there was a quaint little cottage inhabited by the Three Bears, Papa (voiced by Tex Avery), Mama, and Baby Bear. Their porridge is so hot, Papa has to race to the kitchen sink and put his mouth to the spigot. He makes matters worse when he turns on the hot water instead of the cold. The bears decide to go out on a bicycle built for three while their breakfast cools. Meanwhile, cute little Goldilocks knocks on the door of Grandma's house, where the wolf is expecting Red Riding Hood. The wolf sets her straight and tells her to scram, but Goldilocks asks, "What's Red got that I haven't got?"

Red Riding Hood finally arrives and finds a note from the wolf "Dear Red, Got tired of waiting. Went to the Bears' house to eat Goldilocks." Red phones Goldilocks, and the split screen allows her to hand Goldie the note. The bears return home to their porridge, which has been eaten. The wolf sneezes in the bedroom, causing the bears to suspect robbers. Papa goes upstairs to investigate, knowing he'll find Goldilocks because he "read this story last week in *Reader's Digest*!" He encounters the wolf and becomes scared: "so over the hill went the three bears, the Papa Bear, the Mama Bear, and the l ittle bear behind."

THE HARDSHIP OF MILES STANDISH

Elmer Fudd; Apr 27; MM; Supervision by I. Freleng; Animation by Gil Turner; Story by Jack Miller; Musical Direction by Carl W. Stalling.

A grandpop complains about a radio retelling of the courtship of Miles Standish. "Did it *reeeally* happen that way, Grandpa?" asks his grandson. It was more like this: At Plymouth, in the year 1621 1/2, the Town Crier bellows, "Flash! What maid is *that way* about a certain captain?" Priscilla (caricature of Edna Mae Oliver) is in love with Miles Standish (caricature of Hugh Herbert). Miles tries to write a love letter but is distracted by the sexy calendar from the John Alden Singing Telegraph Service. Before you know it, John Alden (Elmer Fudd) is racing over to Priscilla's to sing "You Must Have Been a Beautiful Baby." Suddenly the Cleveland Indians attack.

Indian-attack gags include Priscilla trying to get her wash off the clothesline, and boasting, "You didn't even touch me!" while her backside is full of arrows. Elmer's hat is shot off by the Indians, each time replaced by another headpiece (a straw hat, a coonskin cap, etc.). A cross-eyed Indian accidentally hits the head of another Indian, who clearly lip syncs the words "God damn, son of a bitch." This keeps up until one of the Indians smashes Priscilla's front window, and John comes out angry. "One of you fellas has got to pay for that glass!" They run, leaving Priscilla in love with her hero, John Alden.

PORKY'S POOR FISH

Porky Pig; Apr 27; LT; Supervision by Robert Clampett; Animation by David Hoffman; Story by Melvin Millar; Musical Direction by Carl W. Stalling.

A little card announces, "This screen play is an adaptation of the world famous book Twenty Thousand Leaks Under The Ceiling." At "Porky's Pet Fish Shoppe— under new *mis*-management," the owner sings his theme song, "I Am Porky the Pig," while we see a collection of fish gags. Little Shrimps with big muscles; 14 karat gold fish; three l'il fishes (in an itty bitty bowl); two electric eels—A.C. and D.C.; a holey mackerel, and so on.

When Porky leaves for lunch, a hungry cat walks in, preparing to feast. As he reaches for a fish, the word goes out. The electric eels spell out the words "The Cat" and a turtle rides a sea horse shouting, "To arms!" The hammerhead shark bops cat, the electric eels zap him, the mussels sprout Popeye-like arms and punch the pussy out the door so fast Porky only feels a draft as he reenters the store.

SNIFFLES TAKES A TRIP

Sniffles; May 22; MM; Supervision by Charles M. Jones; Story by Dave Monahan; Animation by Phil Monroe; Musical Direction by Carl W. Stalling.

Sniffles sings about how "the great outdoors is calling me," walking along the train tracks, his belongings tied in a handkerchief carried on a stick. He comes to Country Meadows "for a restful vacation" and is taken with nature. Admiring the trees, the birds, and flowers ("I'm *reeelly* out in the country!"), he makes a hammock and tries to take a nap. He is disturbed by a woodpecker pecking the tree his hammock is tied to. Sniffles ties his hammock to another secure location— between the legs of a stork! Sniffles awakens to find himself underwater. The little mouse runs out on the stork's head, looks him straight in the eye, and slides off his beak. Back in the water, Sniffles is frightened by a frog he mistakes for an alligator.

That night, by campfire, Sniffles contemplates the peace and quiet. "It's sure nice and dark, all right." Silhouettes of inchworms, quails, grasshoppers, and menacing trees with eyes in them scare the mouse, who runs back home to the city.

YOU OUGHT TO BE IN PICTURES

Porky Pig, Daffy Duck; May 18; LT; Supervision by I. Freleng; Story by Jack Miller; Animation by Herman Cohen; Musical Direction by Carl W. Stalling.
A combination of live action and animation. Only Porky and Daffy (and Porky's car) are animated. At the Warner Bros. cartoon studio, an artist is shown drawing a picture of Porky Pig. Someone calls, "Lunch!" and everyone runs out of the studio at high speed. A picture of Daffy Duck comes to life and convinces Porky to quit cartoons and try features.

Daffy goads Porky into producer Leon Schlesinger's office, and the pig timidly asks out of his contract ("What's Errol Flynn got that I haven't?"). Leon gives in to his star pig, shakes his hand, and wishes him good luck. As soon as he leaves, Leon confides, "He'll be back!" Porky drives to the feature lot and encounters the guard at the gate (Michael Maltese dubbed by Mel Blanc) who throws him out. Porky sneaks in disguised as Oliver Hardy. The pig wanders into a live set and sneezes, knocking over film cans. A stage hand throws him out. The guard chases Porky into a western town where a stampede is in progress. Porky decides to get his old job back. Meanwhile, Daffy is trying to convince Leon to give him Porky's old slot by singing "I'll Be Famous on The Screen." Porky gets wise to Daffy's scheme and takes him outside and beats him up. Leon has not torn up the real contract, and tells Porky to get back to work. Daffy, now in bandages, suggests another job "opposite Greta Garbo" and gets a tomato in his face.

A GANDER AT MOTHER GOOSE

May 25; MM; Supervision by Fred Avery; Story by Dave Monahan; Animation by Charles McKimson; Musical Direction by Carl W. Stalling. Technical Advisor; Mother Goose.
Spot gags on nursery rhymes (for the most part). Mary, Mary, quite contrary, how does your garden grow. As Kate Hepburn, she replies, "Confidentially, it stinks!" Humpty Dumpty falls without a scratch, until he walks away and we see a "crack" at his rear end. Jack and Jill go up the hill, but don't come down. Finally Jack comes down with kisses all over his face, joking, "The heck with the water!" Little Miss Muffet is so ugly she scares the spider away. The Three Little Pigs combat the wolf's huffing and puffing with a bottle of Histerine mouth wash. A dumb dog recites "Starlight, Starbright" and wishes for a tree. The Old Lady in the Shoe takes care of all the kids while the Old Man sits in his chair reading the paper and gives us a high sign. Little Hiawatha shoots an arrow into the air. An eagle returns it: "Listen Doc! Be a little more careful where you shoot these things! The Night Before Christmas, not a creature is stirring, not even a mouse, except for a little one, who whispers, "Merry Christmas" to another, who shouts back, *"QUIET!"*

THE CHEWIN' BRUIN

Porky Pig; June 8; LT; Supervision by Robert Clampett; Animation by Norman McCabe and Vive Risto; Musical Direction by Carl W. Stalling.
On a rainy night, Porky listens to an old-timer tell a story of how he came to catch the bear whose head is mounted over the fireplace. "He was a mighty peculiar critter, had a hankerin' for chewin' tabaccy. That bruin was *wacky for tabaccy!*" In flashback, the hunter is in the woods with his dog, observing animals like a reindeer with beautiful "horns." A bear follows the pair, causing the dog to literally freeze (with icicles) when he sees it. The bear is following the chewing tobacco sticking out of the hunter's back pocket. The hunter runs back to his cabin, withdrawing his "Welcome" mat and setting a bear trap. The bear bites the bear trap, sending it running, and opens the side of the house like a garage door, scaring the hunter's gun, which faints! The bear wrestles the hunter for his tobacco, and that really gets the hunter mad. The hunter beats him dead with his bare fists, and tells Porky, "He never got my tabaccy!" The bear head comes to life, chewing: "Oh yeah?" he asks, spitting at the old-timer!

CIRCUS TODAY

June 22; MM; Supervision by Fred Avery; Story by Jack Miller; Animation by Sid Sutherland; Musical Direction by Carl Stalling.

Spot gags at the Jingling Bros. Circus include a balloon salesman who is ten feet off the ground, Gamer the Glutton (referring to effects animator A.C. Gamer), who eats pots and pans which then rattle inside his stomach: Hot Foot Hogan (referring to storyman Rich Hogan) who walks over hot coals in his bare feet, and Captain Clampett (refering to director Bob, caricatured to look like him as well), who shoots out of a cannon only to return with decals applied to his rear.

We meet many circus animals, including a monkey who apprehends a culprit who disobeyed the rules by feeding the simian; a stork who gets calls from Eddie Cantor pestering him for a boy; a gorilla, 2000 pounds of hate and fury, who innocently asks, "How do you do?"; and a dancing horse who does a box step!

But wait, there's more! We meet The Flying Cadenzas, an acrobatic trio who fly to the trapeze, a trick rider who loses her teeth trying to grab a handkerchief; Clyde Binder (referring to studio executive Henry Binder), a lion tamer who gets so much applause the lion sticks his head in the man's mouth; elephant trainer Prof. Ignatz Ignatzavich who lets 13,000 pounds of pachyderm sit on his head: the elephant cries, "I can't do it." And Count Morris Leapoff, who has jumped from a great height into a small tank of water off screen, has the circus bandleader playing "Taps."

TOM THUMB IN TROUBLE

June 8; MM; Supervision by Charles M. Jones; Story by Rich Hogan; Animation by Robert Cannon; Musical Direction by Carl W. Stalling.

Once upon a time in the dark forest lived a woodchopper and his tiny son, Tom Thumb. Tom is so small that he can take a bath in his dad's cupped hands. When dad goes to work he leaves Tom to do the housework, cleaning dishes to the tune of an original song. Tom accidentally slips on the soap and almost drowns in a pan. A little bird crashes through the window and pulls Tom to safety. Tom's dad returns and finds the bird over the unconscious Tom. He chases the bird out, then nurses Tom back to health. Tom is unable to explain that the bird saved his life. That night, Tom leaves a note for his dad and goes out into the snowstorm to find his feathered friend. Dad awakens and calls for his son. The little bird hears dad's calls and flies to Tom, bringing him home. Dad, crying over the loss of his son, looks up to see Tom and the bird. That night, Tom is safely asleep in the pillow, the little bird nestled in dad's beard.

Although the Warner cartoon staff had tried to mimic Disney in the past, by 1940 they had pretty much given up that ambition in favor of the gag approach with which they would soon achieve popular success. This film is a deliberate, last time effort to figure out the Disney formula. Disney would be used only as a source of satire in the future.

PORKY'S BASEBALL BROADCAST

Porky Pig; July 6; LT; Supervision by I. Freleng; Animation by Cal Dalton; Story by J.B. Hardaway; Musical Direction by Carl W. Stalling.

Apart from the absurd idea at its center—that the heavily stuttering Porky has somehow gotten a job as a radio announcer— this one has little to offer. There are dozens of puns and spot gags you've seen before, accompanied by Stalling sports fanfares (including "In Caliente") that had become inseparable from the subject matter as early as 1940. For a running gag, a rather restrained English-butler type roams the stadium in search of his seat, with a double punchline: he doesn't find it until the very last exciting play, which he misses because the seat turns out to be directly behind a post.

Few gags bear singling out, but the overall spirit of the cartoon makes it worthwhile. Freleng would develop this specific attitude more successfully in

Warner's finest sports cartoon, *Baseball Bugs* (1946).

LITTLE BLABBERMOUSE

July 6; MM; Supervision by I. Freleng; Story by Ben Hardaway; Animation by Richard Bickenbach; Musical Direction by Carl W. Stalling.

Spot gags, with music, in a department store. A "W.C. Fields" mouse is selling tickets for a basket-seat tour of the store. While pointing out the amazing sights to behold he is constantly annoyed by one little passenger, a talkative little boy with a big curiosity. Among the sights: Vanishing Creme that actually vanishes; a bottle of Reducing Pills that gets thinner; Sleeping Powder boxes that are sleeping; Smelling Salts that sniff around like a dog; Cough Medicine having a coughing fit; The largest giant in captivity—a giant malt; a Shaving Brush that shaves.

The music begins with the "Rubber Band": elastic bands that play musical instruments. There are clocks which warble, "Sing While You're Dressing." An order pad sings "I'd Love to Take Orders from You." Powder Puffs: "Shake Your Powder Puff." The heads of coins in the cash register sing "We're in the Money." Pink Pills "I'm the Cure for What Ails You." 50/50 pipe tobacco sings "Half of Me Wants To Be Good." Bath salts: "Singing in the Bathtub." Greeting cards greet the mice going by, and mousetraps scare the mice off. One of them is a real cat! The mice all race back to their mousehole and bolt the door. Little Blabbermouse won't shut up, so "Fields" puts alum in his mouth—which puckers it!

THE EGG COLLECTOR

Sniffles; July 20; MM; Supervision by Charles M. Jones; Story by Robert Givens; Animation by Rudolf Larriva; Musical Direction by Carl W. Stalling.

In a bookstore at night the little mouse Sniffles and his silent friend, the bookworm, are reading about egg collecting, in particular, the eggs of barn owls. Barn owls are harmless, feeding mainly on small rodents. Figuring a rodent is a flower, Sniffles follows the worm ("You mean you *reeeely* know where there's an owl's nest?") to a church loft.

They find an owl's egg resting in its little nest bed (marked "Junior"), and Sniffles takes the egg, with its little occupant who's just hatched. The worm discovers they're not alone and is scared stiff realizing he's standing next to the huge owl. Sniffles brags to the bookworm how he snatched the egg "from under the nose of that stupid old owl." The owl responds to Sniffles, "Stupid old owl?" and the little mouse continues, "Yeah! A big fat stupid old dumb owl." Owl tells the mouse, "That's a fine way for a rodent to talk! Owls also eats worms." The bookworm passes out. The little owl hoots, giving Sniffles time to drag the worm and run back to the bookshop. The worm awakens and his first sight is a terrifying picture of the owl in the egg collecting book.

A WILD HARE ACADEMY AWARD NOMINEE

Bugs Bunny, Elmer Fudd; July 27; MM; Supervision by Fred Avery; Story by Rich Hogan; Animation by Virgil Ross; Musical Supervision by Carl W. Stalling.

The classic cartoon that solidified the personalities of Bugs Bunny and Elmer Fudd and became the blueprint for their future encounters.

Elmer is hunting for "wabbits." Sticking his rifle into a rabbit hole, the gun barrel gets tied in a bow. Bugs Bunny emerges and asks "What's up, Doc?" Elmer describes the kind of rabbit he's looking for, and Bugs tells the confused hunter, "Confidentially, I *AM* a wabbit!" Sneaking up from behind, Bugs and Elmer play "guess who?" After a few wrong guesses, "Heddy Lemarr, Owivia De Haviwin," the screwy rabbit gives him a kiss. Elmer sets his "wabbit twap," which captures a skunk instead. Bugs, willing to show he's a good sport, gives Elmer a good shot at him. Standing under a tree, Bugs tells Fudd to "Hold It," as he moves from the path of chirping birds above. Elmer shoots, and Bugs gives a classic death scene. "It's getting dark! Goodbye, pal!" Elmer cries over killing the poor fuzzy bunny. Bugs lines up

Fudd's backside and gives him a swift kick in the rear. Elmer goes mad, shouting, "Wabbits, Wabbits!" and walks away in disgust. Bugs concludes, "I think the poor guy's screwy!" and marches back into his rabbit hole, playing "Yankee Doodle" on an imaginary fife.

GHOST WANTED

Aug 10; MM; Supervision by Charles M. Jones; Story by Dave Monahan; Animation by Bob McKimson; Musical Direction by Carl W. Stalling.
A little ghost is practicing haunting and scaring. He scans the "Saturday Evening Ghost" for the "Haunt Ads," and finds a situation available at 1313 Dracula Drive. At the spooky house, a jolly fat ghost (voiced by Tex Avery) interviews him for the position and then decides to spook the little ghost for fun.

The fat ghost chases the little one around the house, turning up everywhere, laughing and shouting, "Boo!" The fat ghost grabs some fireworks and drops a firecracker next to the little ghost. The fireworks in his back pocket ignite, turning the fat ghost into a fireball that chases the little ghost out of the house. The fat one ends up cooling himself off in the well.

The innocent little ghost is a cute idea, a precursor to Casper, the Friendly Ghost, which Paramount's Famous Studios would develop in the later forties. One of the very few cartoons in which Avery provides a voice for a film he didn't direct.

CEILING HERO

Aug 24; MM; Supervision by Fred Avery; Story by Dave Monahan; Animation by Rod Scribner; Musical Direction by Carl W. Stalling.
Spot gags on air travel include a pilot who has just received his license (shown with license plate attached to his rear end), a six-propeller airplane whose wing takes off without the plane; the launching of a rocket ship that explodes into fireworks reading, "Eat Tony's Hot Dogs"; a modern cabin cruiser (a log cabin airplane), and a China Clipper (a slant-eyed cockpit window), a pilot bailing out of a plane, his parachute reading "Good to the

Last Drop!" stunt pilots tying a knot with their skywriting, and more.

Final extended gag has a test pilot (from the motion picture of the same name) fly straight up, passing Los Angeles city limit road signs and forming ice on its wings that attracts polar bears, then dive straight down and crash. The narrator asks, "Is he hurt? Is he killed?" The pilot climbs out and responds, "Hmmm ... could be!"

PATIENT PORKY

Porky Pig; Aug 24; LT; Supervision by Robert Clampett; Story by Warren Foster; Animation by Norman McCabe; Musical Direction by Carl W. Stalling.
Adapted from a novel, *The Pains Came*. Before we get to the plot, there's a collection of hospital spot gags. On the paging system: "Calling Sir Gery, Calling Dr. Cyclops." An elevator operator informs patients of the diseases cured on each stop: "Going up! First Floor, Asthma, Anemia, Arthritis, Aches." A chart of "Today's Births" indicates "Cats 5, Dogs 2, Rabbits 490." The latter is corrected to 491 in a cameo by Bugs Bunny. Dr. Christian, an owl, looks at one patient's leg through an X-ray, and observes the bones knitting. Herbie Hippo has swallowed a piano, so a crazy cat in the next bed plays his tummy. Porky Pig comes in with a stomach ache. "I had a birthday party and I guess I made a pig of myself!" The crazy cat pretends to be a doctor, young Dr. Chilled Air, and takes Porky on a wild ride through the hospital halls, atop a wheeled bed, singing, "I Want to Be a Surgeon" (to the tune of "We're Working Our Way through College"). The cat wants to operate on Porky with a saw, but the pig runs and is chased around the medical center by the phony feline physician. The cat catches Porky in a hospital bed and lifts his gown to find a sign on his stomach, "Do Not Open Till Ximas." The cat jumps into the bed, stating, "I'll wait!"

MALIBU BEACH PARTY

Sept 14; MM; Supervision by I. Freleng; Story by Jack Miller;

Animation by Gil Turner; Musical Direction by Carl W. Stalling.
Jack "Bunny" invites us to a beach party at his home. We have a collection of spot gags with Hollywood caricatures. Celebrities include Bob Hope, Bette Davis, Kay Kaiser, George Raft, Baby Snooks, James Cagney, Alice Fay, Phil Harris, Fred Astaire, Ginger Rogers, Deanna Durbin, and Mickey Rooney.

Gags worthy of mention include Spencer Tracy as Stanley, greeting Mary as "Miss Livingston, I presume?"; Clark Gable swimming with his ears; Greta Garbo sailing on her big feet; John Barrymore reciting, "I come to bury Caesar" as he buries Caesar Romero with sand; and Ned Sparks being called an old crab by an old crab!

Jack plays the violin as a finale, as the celebrities leave one by one.

CALLING DR. PORKY

Porky Pig; Sept 21; LT; Supervision by I. Freleng; Animation by Herman Cohen; Musical Direction by Carl W. Stalling.
At New Rightus Hospital, "We Take Pains—We Have Lots of Patients," a drunk comes in looking for a doctor. While he's waiting, the drunk tries to escape a trio of pink elephants. Meanwhile, Porky Pig, M.D., gives pills to a dizzy man with a literally spinning head.

The drunk asks for Porky's help, and the pig prepares a prescription while the drunk waits. The elephants examine the lush and decide to operate. They put him in a chair and give him the third degree as though he were on trial. The drunk is screaming to leave as Porky returns with a tonic. The medicine cures the drunk, but, leaving the hospital, he sees a circus parade including a line of elephants with the pink ones in tow! He dives back into a hospital bed; the pink elephants kick him out!

STAGE FRIGHT

Sept 28; MM; Supervision by Charles M. Jones; Story by Rich Hogan; Animation by Ken Harris; Musical Direction by Carl W. Stalling.
Two dogs, one orange and one white, are fighting over a bone. Their feud takes them backstage at a vaudeville theater, where their bone lands in a magician's top hat. The hat's inhabitant, a small tough bird, returns the bone to the two clumsy dogs. The bone is tossed up to the high wire. The orange dog goes up after it. Walking on the wire shakes the bone down to the seal's water tank. The white dog goes underwater to get it. The orange dog returns to the stage, but knocks into the magic hat, causing the bird to give the dog the eye. The seal sends the bone into the magician's hat. Pulling it out gets the orange dog a sock in the face from the tough bird, who then backs the pooch into the water tank. The seal twirls and tosses the dogs, the white one lands near the bone, but is too dizzy to pick it up. Just as he's about to, the orange dog lands on top of him, shooting the bone again into the magic hat. The little bird comes out, breaks the bone in two, and shoves one half in each dog's mouth.

PREHISTORIC PORKY

Porky Pig; Oct 12; LT; Supervision by Robert Clampett; Animation by John Carey; Story by Melvin Miller; Musical Direction by Carl W. Stalling.
This cartoon is set "One Billion Trillion B.C. (a long time ago)," when dinosaurs (and cave-pigs) ruled the earth. A mean, snarling dinosaur comes toward us then smiles and greets us as Kate Smith with "Hello, Everybody!" A vulture sings, a la Jerry Colonna "These Are Wonderful Days."

Caveman Porky calls his pet dinosaur, Rover, over for a bone. The dino is so delighted he wags his giant tail, rattling the armor off other dinosaurs, causing landslides, hatching eggs, etc. Porky gets his mail, which includes *Expire*, the magazine for cavemen. Reading about the new spring fashions, Porky decides to go hunting for a new suit. In the jungle, Porky grabs a little spotted leopard and tries him on (posing as a female fashion model). The leopard clubs Porky in the shins. Meanwhile, a ferocious black panther checks his watch and sees it's dinner time. He pounces on Porky. Porky's club is of no help—the panther eats it, spitting it out as clothespins! The panther chases Porky and corners him. Porky explains he meant no harm, just wanted to get a new suit. The panther stops growling and says, "Why didn't you say so? I can get it for you *wholesale!*"

HOLIDAY HIGHLIGHTS

Oct 12; MM; Supervision by Fred Avery; Animation by Charles McKimson; Story by Dave Monahan; Musical Direction by Carl W. Stalling.
Spot gags based on American holidays. New Year's Day an infant Baby New Year shouts, "Happy New Year!" Valentines Day pictures a little boy and girl who passionately make love. Washington's Birthday recreates the scene of George and the cherry tree. When his dad asks him if he chopped it down, the pint-sized father of our country replies, "Hmmm ... Couldst be!" Arbor Day shows a man getting precise instructions on where to plant a tree from a dog. Easter has a fuzzy-wuzzy Easter bunny approached by a vicious fox, who meekly asks for an easter egg. For April Fools' Day the picture is blank! The theatre manager puts on a slide "Tain't Funny, McGee!" Mother's Day has a mother and son enjoying a reunion after 22 years apart who simply say "hello." Graduation Day shows a little fellow graduating and taking his place in society, right behind the headmaster in the bread line. Halloween is marked by a witch flying a banner advertising "Dollar Days" attached to her broom. Thanksgiving Day has the turkey saying grace at the head of the table. Christmas reveals Santa Claus to be a "Good Rumor" ice cream man. On New Year's Day we witness a group of children gathering around the float of the Lone Ranger along with a group of dogs gathering around the float from California: big trees!

GOOD NIGHT ELMER

Elmer Fudd; Oct 26; MM; Supervision by Charles M. Jones; Story by Rich Hogan; Animation by Philip Monroe; Musical Direction by Carl W. Stalling.
11:00 p.m. Elmer puts down his book, takes his candle, and goes into the bedroom to retire.

First, he can't take off his jacket, because he can't find a place to put his candle. He leaves it on a window sill, and the flame blows out. Putting it on his head only gives him a problem of where to put his hat. Finding a shelf at last, he can't get the candle holder off his finger.

Next, Fudd goes to bed (with his hat on!), but can't blow out the candle. Each time he tries, the flame starts up again; he puts a book over the candle, but the flame goes right through it. Putting a stack of books between him and the flame only causes the flame to get bigger; breaking the candle in two creates two flames! Elmer takes an axe and chops everything in his bedroom to pieces. By the time he is able to get some rest, the sun is coming up outside his window. Elmer cries in frustration.

So does the audience. One of the most irritating cartoons ever made. There was no reason to animate this, everything in this cartoon could have been easily filmed in live action. Chuck Jones's early super-slow timing at its most brutal (hard to believe that this man would later make the super-speed Roadrunner cartoons). And Elmer is *so* stupid it's painful!

THE SOUR PUSS

Porky Pig; Nov 2; LT; Supervision by Robert Clampett; Animation by Vive Risto and Dave Hoffman; Story by Warren Foster; Musical Direction by Carl W. Stalling.
The rest of the cartoon has a hard time topping the first minute when Porky reads in the paper (another Clampett newspaper gag) that the fishing season opens tomorrow. Porky prods his lethargic cat into guessing what they're going to have for dinner soon. The cat guesses chicken and does an impression of one, but Porky counters with a hysterical shot of a pig imitating a fish.

This is followed by the cat doing an ecstatic dance all around the room (he kisses a mouse out of sheer joy, causing a startled canary to observe, "Well, now I've seen everything" in Jack Benny's voice and then shoots himself). "And so to bed." While Porky counts sheep, the cat counts fish leaping over a post. Comes the dawn, our heroes think they've landed a flying fish, but what they've hooked instead is a screwball character who makes like Daffy Duck hopping and hoo-hooing all over with a lunatic vibrato in place of Daffy's Schlesingerian lisp. He constantly comments on his own comic talents: "Gee, ain't I a card though? Oh, boy, I'm killing me! Gosh, am I funny! I'm a panic!" The wacky fish relentlessly heckles our heroes, uses the pussy's nose as a punching bag, pretends to let Porky hook him and then imitates a yo-yo (all the while telling the audience things like "I'm a yo-yo! I'm a yo-yo!"). When the cat falls in the drink, the fish directly asks us, in that bizarre voice of his, "Where did the pussycat go?" For the conclusion, the fish tries to scare them by mimicking a shark, and when the Sour Puss calls his bluff, he pulls a real shark out of the water! While Porky and pussy high-tail it, the shark does a Lew Lehr impression: "Pussycats is da cwaziest peoples!"

WACKY WILDLIFE
Nov 9; MM; Supervision by Fred Avery; Animation by Virgil Ross; Story by Dave Monahan; Musical Direction by Carl W. Stalling.
Spot gags involving animals in the wild. A timid little fawn takes a drink at a pond, slurping it down like a slob; a vicious reptile hypnotizes a bird to walk into its mouth ("If you think I'm going in *there*, you're crazy!"); a skunk whose shadow holds its nose; an alligator with a small body ("Well, I've been sick!"); a bird mother chirping furiously at her young chick ("Oh, lay off the bird talk, Ma! What's on your mind?"); a sexy leg of lamb; a pig wallowing in mud ("All right, so I ain't neat!"); a camel who walks through the scorching desert without stopping for a drink ("I don't care what you say, I'm thirsty!"); and, of course, a wild dog who points out what makes him wild: loggers are cutting down the last tree in a forest.

What would an Avery spot-gag cartoon be without a dog/tree gag? This film is a close prototype of the "Speaking Of Animals" series Avery developed at Paramount in 1941.

BEDTIME FOR SNIFFLES
Sniffles; Nov 23; MM; Supervision by Charles M. Jones; Story by Rich Hogan; Animation by Robert Cannon; Musical Direction by Carl W. Stalling.
Carolers are singing on the snowy street below. Above, in his little sardine-can house, Sniffles the mouse is cleaning up and singing "Jingle Bells" as he awaits the arrival of Santa Claus.

In one hour and thirty-three minutes Santa will be here, so Sniffles makes some "Haxwell Mouse Coffee" and dances a waltz with music on the radio to stay awake. The radio begins playing a lullaby, "Sleep, Baby, Sleep," which makes Sniffles tired. Soon he falls asleep on a hair brush, but he catches himself and awakens with the brush teeth having made holes on his face (making him think he's got measles). He washes his face to stay awake, then stands in the frozen cold doorway. The coffee isn't working; his "Good Mousekeeping" magazine opens to a tire ad "Time to Retire"; and his bed beckons him. Slowly Sniffles climbs into bed and goes to sleep, just as Santa flies by.

This is the flip side of *Good Night, Elmer*, a cartoon about trying to stay awake. This has the early Jones charm and a wonderful situation we've all known personally.

PORKY'S HIRED HAND
Porky Pig; Nov 30; LT; Supervision by I. Freleng; Story by Dave Monahan; Animation by Richard Bickenbach; Musical Direction by Carl W. Stalling.
The Cornstalk Employment Agency sends Porky Pig (c/o Porky's Chicken Ranch) one "Gregory Grunt," a witless lunkhead (with Blanc's voice) who, they believe, will prove to be a

reliable watchman. Or a reasonable facsimile. The agency feels obliged in the letter of introduction to add a PS: "All right! So he ain't neat!" Cut to Porky making Gregory repeat his orders, "Keep your eyes open and watch out for that fox, he's been gettin' too many of my chickens lately. He's a sly devil, he is, and ... don't go to sleep!"

When the fox does come sneaking in (telling the audience, "I'm the guy they can't catch"), he fills his sack with Porky's hens and chicks. Gregory intercedes and tells him to "put 'em back where ya got 'em." The fox, sly devil that he is, hoodwinks the clod into letting him keep the sack by promising to go into partnership with him: "Gregory and Fox." "Won't be long now, Gregory, you'll have your own office and private secretary to sit on your lap." However, upon leaving, the Fox goes through the wrong door, walking into the incubator room and locking himself in. After another hysterical Blanc "death" monologue, Porky arrives, and out comes a steam-reduced midget fox. "Just look at me, I'm a ruined man! You'll hear from my lawyer."

OF FOX AND HOUNDS
Dec 7; MM; Supervision by Fred Avery; Story by "Draft No. 1312"; Animation by "Draft No. 6102"; Musical Direction by Carl W. Stalling.
Dawn at "Ye Fox and Hound" hunting lodge. The hunters sound the trumpets and all the hounds take off—all but a big dumb St. Bernard named Willoughby. He's so dumb, he finds the fox, named George, and asks *him*, "Which way did they go? Do you know where the fox is?" The fox gives directions: "Ya see that tree stump down there? You turn right till you come to a rail fence. The fox is right on the other side.

Ya can't miss him!" Willoughby runs over the fence, falling off a cliff, and crashing into a pile of logs. The dog gets wise and realizes that was the fox. Returning to the scene of the crime, the dog meets another hound (the fox in costume) named "George," who gives the dumb dog the same directions. Willoughby crashes again.

George has Willoughby follow him. He goes through a log, ripping his costume off, running out the other end as the fox. Willoughby corners the fox in a cave, blocking the entrance with a large rock. A grizzly bear follows Willoughby and chases him up a tree. The fox escapes from the cave and saves the dog by giving the bear a hot foot. Willoughby shares his doghouse with the fox, and the next day, when the hounds take off, he asks, "Which way did they go?" Getting the usual directions, he falls again. this time lands on a mattress, "Ya know, I ain't so dumb."

THE TIMID TOREADOR
Porky Pig; Dec 21; LT; Supervision by Robert Clampett and Norman McCabe; Animation by I. Ellis; Story by Melvin Miller; Musical Direction by Carl W. Stalling.
"Bullfight Today," a poster in a small Spanish/Mexican town advertises. "See the World's Greatest Matadors, Toreadors, Picadors and Cuspidors!" Porky plays a hot-tamale vendor whose overt gringo-ness is never queried by the locals, and whose tamales become a sort of rite-of-passage for those who consider themselves fanciers of Spanish food. A chicken downs one and is summarily fried. At the bullfight, "The greatest matador of all time, Punchy Pancho!" gets quickly done in by the bull "Slapsy Maxie Rosenbull," as does a picador who has only to laugh at Slapsy Maxie before the bull compresses him into his horse, turning him into a centaur (a la *Fantasia*, another Clampett/Disney reference). Without any explanation, Porky turns up in the stadium looking the bull straight in the face. He runs and even tunnels underground to try and get away from the bull. The beast is about to do him in when he discovers Porky's merchan-

dise, "Hot tamales? Hot? Who's afraid of hot?" The bull makes the mistake of consuming the entire box of tamales and goes exploding away as the cheering crowd showers their sombreros on our triumphant hero (who throws in an Oliver Hardy impression to leave us with).

Stadium fanfare includes "The Gaucho Serenade," "La Cucaracha," and "In Caliente."

SHOP, LOOK AND LISTEN

Dec 21; MM; Supervision by I. Freleng; Story by Dave Monahan. Animation: Cal Dalton; Musical Direction by Carl W. Stalling.

A direct sequel to *Little Blabbermouse*, featuring the same characters and almost the same plot. At J.T. Gimlets Dept. Store, they are having a closeout sale. Signs read "Everything must go—including Gimlet; Through these Portals Pass the Most Talented Shoplifters in the World." The "W.C. Fields" mouse starts a tour of the store, with gags that include hosiery with no runs, no hits, no errors; shoes, including red and green Mules; paintings, such as Whistler's Mother (who whistles "She'll Be Comin' Round the Mountain"). The Thinker contemplates his 1940 Income Tax form (saying, "Confidentially, I Think!"), The Hunter's hound goes wild for the Lonesome Pine and The Last of the Mohicans.

Robotics are in at Gimlets: an automatic ashtray utilizes a robotic boot; the 100% Automatic Poker Table shuffles, cuts, deals, and plays poker. It also cheats! An automatic ribbon clerk really impresses little Blabbermouth, who says (at a mile a minute), "That's better than the telephone. Did Don Ameche invent that too? Do it again, Mister, do it again." W.C. has Blabbermouse wrapped up and stuck with a "Do Not Open Till Xmas" label on his mouth!

1941

ELMER'S PET RABBIT

Bugs Bunny, Elmer Fudd; Jan 4; MM; Supervision by Charles M. Jones; Story by Rich Hogan; Animation by Rudolf

Larriva; Musical Direction by Carl W. Stalling.

Singing "Strolling Through the Park" while walking down the street, Elmer spots a timid rabbit in a pet shop window. He purchases the pet and deposits the bunny in a wire pen in the backyard. The rabbit (introduced as Bugs Bunny for the first time in the opening titles, but with a different voice) complains about his food and lodgings. Inside the house, Elmer finishes a good "weg of wamb" and settles in to catch up on Dick Tracy. Bugs Bunny barges in, turns on all the lights and the radio, then dances with Elmer. Fudd throws him out and goes to bed. Elmer is stopped from going into the bathroom by the rabbit (with a magazine), who asks him to wait his turn. Elmer throws the rabbit out of the shower and into the tub. Bugs fakes drowning, and Elmer pulls him out. Bugs feels bad about "All the things I've done to him in this picture" and asks Fudd to give him a good swift kick in the rear. When Fudd complies, the rabbit states, "Of course, you realize this means war!" and slaps Fudd with his glove. Fudd goes into his bedroom and is told to "Turn off that Light!" by the bunny in his bed. Elmer chases him out of the house. Returning to his bedroom, he flips on the light. Again he is shouted at by the rabbit to "Turn off that light!"

PORKY'S SNOOZE REEL

Porky Pig; Jan 11; LT; Supervision by Robert Clampett and Norman McCabe; Story by Warren Foster; Animation by John Carey; Musical Direction by Carl W. Stalling.

Porky Pig is the newsreel host of "Passe News, the eyes, ears, nose, throat, of the world." It is a spot gag collection that includes an Elks parade, a tax expert from behind prison bars advising *not* to pay income tax, and the new battleship of the Swiss navy. It is full of holes! Porky, as Lew Lehr, shows us the dogs at the annual dog show, including a bird dog who flies and chirps to a bird-dog house, a Coney Island hot dog, and a Doberman pincer, who pinches the other dogs.

Other gags include National Defense,

on land: a new tank crashes through everything, then gets caught in a mouse trap; at sea: a mine is eaten by a jelly fish and explodes—becoming six delicious flavors!; in the air: airplane motors *hum* "Aloha," and there is a literal "dog" fight in the air. Lowlights in the World of Sports include a horse race with a photo finish, the horse and jockey posing and smiling; a swim race in "Goon Lagoon, Florida" with human divers going in and alligators coming up!

THE FIGHTING 69th 1/2

Jan 18; MM; Supervision by I. Freleng; Story by Jack Miller; Animation by Gil Turner; Musical Direction by Carl W. Stalling.

A picnic lunch left unattended is claimed by two ants, one red, one black. They fight over an olive ("Aww, no you don't!" "Oh, yes I do"). When the olive smashes over the black ant, he declares, "Of course, you realize this means war!"

The bugle is blown and the troops, the "Ants In Your Pants Division," "The Royal Flying Ants," tramp through the mud. Supplies include Insect Powder and Absorbent Cotton, brought to the front lines. The air above the picnic setting is filled with bursting bombs and rockets. The red general goes over the blueprint for the attack: approach from the rear of the potato chips to grab the hot dog. The red ants approach the hot dog, but are ambushed by the black ants under the bun. They get the hot dog, and a "black" black ant remembers the mustard. The ants grab what they can: slices of cake, watermelon, and berries. The red ants construct a dagwood sandwich and receive an order to "Hold the onion!"

The battle rages until the shadow of a human comes forth. The woman picks up her picnic leftovers and leaves a large piece of cake behind. The ants call a peace conference to divide the cake, but a fight breaks out over who gets the cherry on top!

SNIFFLES BELLS THE CAT

Sniffles; Feb 1; MM; Supervision by Charles M. Jones; Story by Rich Hogan; Animation by Ken Harris; Musical Direction by Carl W. Stalling.

Sniffles and his mouse friends are chased into their hole by the house cat. Discussing how softly the cat walks gives Sniffles an idea. If only the cat had a bell around his neck, the mice could hear him coming. Sniffles becomes the volunteer for the job and is forced out of the mouse hole with a bell.

Sniffles practices ways of asking the cat to put on the bell. The cat is sitting there watching his performance. Sniffles catches on that the cat is waiting to pounce. Running frantically, Sniffles winds up resting on top of the cat's nose! Sniffles runs again, and this time the cat follows. Sniffles hides in a coffee cup. The cat plays the old shell game, carefully picking up each cup, looking under each one slowly (excellent animation by Bob McKimson). Sniffles sneaks out, and again the cat chases him. The bell gets caught on the cat's neck. Back in the mouse hole, his friends ask how he did it. Sniffles boasts of his bravery. ("Look here, Mr. Cat, you put this old bell on before I get mad ...") He crosses his fingers behind his back.

THE HAUNTED MOUSE

Feb 15; LT; Supervision by Fred Avery; Story by Michael Maltese; Animation by Sid Sutherland; Musical Direction by Carl W. Stalling.

A starving cat walking through the desert comes upon the billboard for "Ma's Place—Home Cooking. 3 miles." He runs toward it, entering what has all the signs of a ghost town; "The Waldorf Ghostoria," a "U.S. Ghost Office," and a billboard for "Old Ghost Cigarettes." A movie theater is playing "Mr. Smith Ghost to Washington." The cat enters the restaurant, which is empty except for a ghost mouse, who decides to get even for all the troubles cats gave him.

The mouse leaves a ghost plate of milk, which disappears as the cat tries to drink it. The wise-guy mouse drives the cat crazy with gags. He tickles the cat's ribs, plays drums, then beats the cat's head with the drumsticks. He gives the cat a hot foot, making him jump out the window, crashing below. The mouse rejoices, "The slug had it comin' to him. That's one cat that won't bother me any more!" The cat reappears at the window as a spirit. The mouse screams, "A Ghost!" and runs out of town, stopping only to change the population sign from 100 ghosts to 99.

THE CRACKPOT QUAIL
Feb 15; MM; Supervision by Fred Avery; Story by Rich Hogan; Animation by Robert McKimson; Musical Direction by Carl W. Stalling.
A goofy dog is admiring the sleek pointer on the billboard for Barko Dog Food. The dog takes off to hunt quail but crashes into "a tree!" Hearing a razzing noise, the dog encounters a wise-guy quail trying to keep his top knot from falling on his face. The quail has many characteristics of Avery's Bugs Bunny, including calling the dog "Doc." When the dog gets wise that the little bird is a quail, the feathered friend shouts, "You're right," pulls his nose, and blows in his ear. The dog chases the quail all over the forest, the dog continuing to crash into trees (the film's running gag). The dog follows the quail tracks into the lake. Underwater, he sees fish swim by, including the quail! The bird uses his top knot as a periscope, spots the dog, and runs back on land. Now the top knot acts like a windshield wiper to remove water from his face. The dog corners the quail, but the bird gets him to "fetch the stick." The dog fetches, but gets wise when the quail disappears. Running furiously toward the bird, the dog smashes through bushes, trees, and a log cabin, destroying them all and winding up beneath them. The dog points out, "Ahh, lots of trees!"

Censorship note: The bird's razz noise, made during his efforts to keep his top knot up, was redubbed in later years to a cute whistle.

THE CAT'S TALE
Mar 1; MM; Supervision by I. Freleng; Story by Michael Maltese;

Animation by Herman Cohen; Musical Direction by Carl W. Stalling.
A cat chases a mouse around a house, but the mouse is fed up. "What am I, a man or a mouse?" Having a showdown with the cat, the mouse explains, "I'm gtting sick and tired of this chasing business! Everywhere I go, you chase me!" The cat explains that "Cats have always chased mice, dogs have always chased cats." The mouse goads the cat into telling the bulldog, Spike, to quit chasing him.

The cat approaches Spike and tries to explain the new thinking, but the dog ignores him and eats his bone. "There's really no sense in this chasing business." When the cat puts his foot down, it topples the dog dish on Spike's head, and the dog chases the cat.

The mouse is filing his nails, resting in the cat's bed when the cat returns, wearing bandages. Explaining to the mouse that Spike "just couldn't see it your way," the cat resumes the chase. Back in the mouse hole, the rodent thinks again, "Am I a man or a mouse?" and decides, "I'm a mouse!"

JOE GLOW, THE FIREFLY
Mar 8; LT; Supervision by Charles M. Jones; Story by Rich Hogan; Animation by Philip Monroe; Musical Direction by Carl W. Stalling.
Joe Glow is a firefly, which means he's a fly with a fireman's hat and a lantern. The fly explores a camper's tent, landing on the sleeping hunter's head, resting on his cheek, examining his watch, and slipping on his fingernail. Flying to a table, the fly tries to walk on saltine crackers, gets caught in a flood of salt, sneezes in a pepper shaker, and rescues a ketchup bottle from crashing to the floor. Flying out of the tent, the fly remembers something. He returns to the man's ear and shouts "Good Night!"

An interesting and successful experiment by Chuck Jones, using one of his favorite themes, the world from the point of view of a tiny insect. The gags are kept to a minimum, as we follow Joe Glow and imagine from his perspective what it would be like to explore a giant world of objects we take for granted. Excellent realistic black-

and-white backgrounds add to this film, one of the few Warner Bros. cartoons that can actually be labeled "charming."

TORTOISE BEATS HARE

Bugs Bunny; Mar 15; MM; Supervision by Fred Avery; Story by Dave Monahan; Animation by Charles McKimson; Musical Direction by Carl W. Stalling.
Bugs Bunny walks out during the main titles and reads the credits. When he gets to the cartoon title, he becomes furious ("Why these screwy guys don't know what they're talkin' about! Why, the big bunch of jerks, and I oughta know, I work for 'em!"). He rips the titles away and confronts Cecil Turtle, challenging him to a race (for ten bucks).

The race begins, and Bugs zooms away. Cecil calls his cousin Chester, asking him to call the boys and give the slicker rabbit "the works." All along the course Bugs encounters the turtle always ahead of him. Cecil confides to us, "We do this kind of stuff to him all through the picture!" Bugs puts up barricades, cuts bridges, climbs trees. Everywhere there is the turtle. Bugs runs hard to cross the finish line, but the turtle is already there. "Hey, Speedy, what kept ya?" Bugs pays up the ten dollar bet and walks off, wondering, "If I've been tricked?" Ten turtles reply, "It's a possibility!" and kiss the bunny.

PORKY'S BEAR FACTS

Porky Pig; Mar 29 LT; Supervision by I. Freleng; Story by Michael Maltese; Animation by Manuel Perez; Musical Direction by Carl W. Stalling.
On his farm, Porky Pig is happily plowing the land, singing "As You Sew, So Shall Ye Reap." Meanwhile, Porky's neighbors, a lazy bear and his dog, are sitting on their porch, strumming "Working Can Wait." The bear's lazy cow is reading "Ferdinand The Bull," the chickens play scrabble, and the mouse reads *Of Mice and Men.*

The months pass, cold December arrives, and the bear has no food. The bear describes a delicious meal to his dog, who rummages through the empty cans. They find a bean in one can, but

as they say grace, a mouse steals the bean. The bear cries hysterically, and the dog wonders, "I wouldn't be surprised if he tried to eat me." The bear walks toward the canine with fork and knife, following the pooch outside the house, past Porky's window, where the pig is about to feast on a large turkey. The bear and dog appear at his door, and Porky tells them, "You've buttered your bread, now sleep in it!" and slams the door. Then he spots a "Love Thy Neighbor" sign and invites them in.

Fattened and full, the bear vows not to be caught cold and hungry next winter. But, spotting spring about to arrive, the bear jumps back to his porch singing "Working Can Wait."

GOOFY GROCERIES

Mar 29; MM; Supervision by Robert Clampett; Story by Melvin Miller; Animation by Vive Risto; Musical Direction by Carl W. Stalling.
It is late at night in a grocery store, and all the products and character labels come to life. Among the many gags: a contented cow from Carnation sings "If I Could Be With You One Hour Tonight"; a crab (Ned Sparks); Jack Bunny; a dog from Barker Dog Food ushers characters into Big Top Pop Corn to see Little Egypt; Billy Posies Aquacade, which includes U-Know Biscuits singing "By A Waterfall"; and a tomato can-can.

The plot starts half-way through when a gorilla escapes from a package of Animal Crackers. Navy Beans come to the rescue, as do turtles from Turtle Soup who use their shells as tanks. Jack Bunny chases the ape with an axe, as a dozen eggs hatch chick cheerleaders. ("Give 'em the axe, the axe, the axe!") The gorilla grabs Bunny and threatens with dynamite. A goofy Superman from Superguy Soapchips comes alive, but is reduced to a cry baby by the gorilla. Suddenly, the gorilla is called by his mother and scolded. Jack Bunny is caught in a dynamite explosion, as Rochester exclaims, "My, Oh my! Tattletale gray!"

Bob Clampett's first cartoon in color. Another first is the Superman gag. The first Max Fleischer Superman cartoon was still in production when this film was made, making this the superhero's first screen appearance (albeit a spoof of the character).

TOY TROUBLE

Sniffles; Apr 12; MM; Supervision by Charles M. Jones; Story by Rich Hogan; Animation by Robert Cannon; Musical Direction by Carl W. Stalling.
Sniffles and his pal the bookworm explore the toy section of Lacy's Department Store. The bookworm knocks into a wind-up jazzbo band, and Sniffles warns him "Stick with me or you'll get into trouble!" Unfortunately, the bookworm next encounters a kookie Quack-Quack toy duck rolling out of control. It chases the worm to an electric train set. The set is turned on, and the railroad cars chase the worm around the track. Meanwhile Sniffles is walking among the stuffed animals and passes a real cat, who awakens and chases the little mouse. Sniffles hides among a row of Porky Pig squeak toys. The cat pokes them, but the mouse fools the feline. The bookworm runs from the train track to the top of the cat's head. Seeing Sniffles down below, it waves to him. The mouse tries to warn the worm, shouting, "The cat!" The cat goes for Sniffles, but the Quack-Quack toy comes toward the cat, chasing him on the railroad (past alphabet blocks that spell "Zoom"). Sniffles finds his friend the worm with a glass test tube over his head.

PORKY'S PREVIEW

Porky Pig; Apr 19; LT; Supervision by Fred Avery; Story by Dave Monahan; Animation by Virgil Ross; Musical Direction by Carl W. Stalling.
All the animals are buying tickets for Porky's Picture Show. A skunk doesn't have the five cents to buy a ticket: he only has one *scent* (get it?). Porky introduces a program of his own animated cartoons, drawn in stick-figures.

The program includes a circus parade in which the animals are followed by a stick-figure sanitation man, a choo-choo train going up and down a mountain, marching soldiers walking toward each other and up to the sky, a horse race that has Crosby's horse running last at Santa Anita, dances that include a hula dancer whose skirt falls off, a Mexican dancer who gets scribbled on until Porky draws it right, a chorus line with one tiny member, and a ballet dancer who does a split.

When Porky returns to the stage, he finds his audience has run out. Only the skunk remains, applauding wildly.

THE TRIAL OF MISTER WOLF

Apr 26; MM; Supervision by I. Freleng; Story by Michael Maltese; Animation by Richard Bickenbach; Musical Direction by Carl W. Stalling.
The case of the Big Bad Wolf vs. Little Red Riding Hood is presented to a jury of wolves. Red Riding Hood is a snobby Katharine Hepburn imitation, with "guilt" literally written all over her face. The Wolf tells his story, which begins with him as an innocent schoolboy communing with nature. The evil Red Riding Hood sneaks around the trees, pretending to need the Wolf's aid in locating Grandma's house. Grandma loves fur coats and hides them when the Wolf and Red approach. Grandma pretends to be ill ("She has a teriffic hangover," says Red). While Red bolts the door, Grandma asks the Wolf, "My, what a beautiful fur coat you have!" The Wolf is also impressed. "My, what a big mallet you have!" Grandma chases the Wolf around the house. Each door the Wolf opens has Grandma on the other side, first with a knife, then a machine gun, then, in the basement, with a cannon. Finally, the wolf gets the mallet, but Grandma chokes him. "It was only through a miracle that I escaped with my life," he tells his peers. They don't believe him. "And if that ain't the truth, I hope I get run over by a street car." The Wolf is immediately pummeled by a trolley crashing through the courtroom wall.

PORKY'S ANT

Porky Pig; May 10; LT; Supervision by Charles M. Jones; Story by Rich Hogan; Animation by Rudolph Larriva; Musical Direction by Carl W. Stalling.

In the African jungle, Porky Pig, the explorer, and his pygmy native guide are seeking the rare "pygmy ant of Central America," valued at $150,000. Meanwhile, the pygmy ant has spotted Porky's pygmy and follows him, trying to get the bone from his top knot. Tugging at Porky's guide, he knocks over the native. Porky sees the rare ant and chases him to his ant hole. Porky tries to bait the ant with chocolate candy near a piece of flypaper. The speedy ant grabs the candy and avoids the paper. Porky chases the ant and reaches for him under a bush. The ant is resting next to a sleeping lion's paw. While Porky tries a string trap, the ant ties the string to the lion, and dances around the beast, confident that Porky won't try anything for fear of waking the lion. Unknown to the ant, the lion wakes and walks off. Porky crawls closer and closer to the ant. The lion spots the pygmy native and chases him. The native leads the lion to Porky, and soon they are both being chased. The ant throws the flypaper on the lion, who gets stuck with it. Porky is grateful to the ant for saving his life and rewards him with the native pygmy's top-knot bone!

FARM FROLICS

May 10; MM; Supervision by Robert Clampett.

After the hand of the artist draws an opening shot of a farm, many spot gags about the animals who live here are presented. These include a championship horse who shows off his talents by doing a gallop and a canter, the latter being an imitation of Eddie *Cantor*; a watchdog who fetches the newspaper and reads the funnies ("I can hardly wait to read Dick Tracy!"); a weasel steals eggs and is scared by the chicks inside who hatch abruptly, yelling "Don't ever *do* that!"; Birds who build a birdhouse "financed by FHA"; a field mouse with huge ears who says, "I just keep *hearing* things!" We also are given a closer look at the strange relationship between a cat and a mouse. The rodent confides, "Get me out of here!" A running gag involves piglets watching a clock, running to their mother at dinner time. The exasperated mama hog tells us (a la Zazu Pitts), "Oh dear, every day it's the same thing!"

HOLLYWOOD STEPS OUT

May 24; MM; Supervision by Fred Avery; Musical Direction by Carl W. Stalling.

A "Hollywood caricature" spot-gag cartoon that begins with a shot of Hollywood at night, the spotlights swaying to the conga beat. We truck into Ciro's, where dinners are $50. "Six months to pay, small down payment!" Gags and celebrities include Cary Grant who says "If I ever told *My Favorite Wife The Awful Truth*."Greta Garbo selling "Cigars, cigarettes, butts ... ," lighting a match on her big shoes; Edward G. Robinson greeting the "Oomph Girl"; Leon Schlesinger and Henry Binder with reserved seats; Johnny Weissmuller checking his coat and dining in his leopard skin; James Cagney, Humphery Bogart, and George Raft pitching pennies; Harpo Marx giving Garbo a hot foot. Bing Crosby comes out to host the entertainment, beginning with Stowkowski playing (in a juke box) a conga. Jimmy Stewart is too shy to dance with Dorothy Lamour. Gable pursues a sexy blonde (the film's running gag). Sonia Hennie dances with Tyrone Power. Frankenstein does the conga, while the Three Stooges poke and slap in rhythm. Oliver Hardy dances with two girls and Mickey Rooney (as Andy Hardy, dating Judy Garland) talks to Judge Hardy about the dinner bill. Bing introduces Ann Rand, the bubble dancer, and Kay Kaiser calls his "students." They are William Powell, Spencer Tracy, Douglas Fairbanks, Errol Flynn, Wallace Beery, and C. Aubrey Smith. Peter Lorre has "never seen such a beautiful bubble"; Henry Fonda is called by his mother; "G" Man J. Edgar Hoover can only say, "Gee! Gee! Gee"; a "stoneface" table of Boris Karloff, Arthur Treacher,

Buster Keaton, Mischa Auer, and Ned Sparks. Jerry Colonna shares his binoculars with Yahoodi. Harpo bursts Ann's bubble, revealing she's wearing only a barrel. Gable catches the girl, who turns out to be Groucho. She says,"Fancy meeting you here!"

A COY DECOY

Daffy Duck, Porky Pig; June 7; LT; Supervision by Robert Clampett; Story by Melvin Millar; Animation by Norman McCabe; Musical Direction by Carl W. Stalling.
Set in "Ye Book Shoppe" at midnight when all decent books "come-to-life," we pan across a live action table full of books as Porky Pig sings "Ride, Tenderfoot, Ride" from the cover of *The Westerner.* Daffy Duck jumps off the cover of *The Ugly Duckling* to serenade us with "Git Along Little Doggie" and to ride *Black Beauty* (a black "Aunt Jemima"). Meanwhile *The Wolf of Wall Street* hides behind *The Green Bay Tree* to spy Daffy in *The Lake.* The Wolf uses a decoy to lure the duck, a sexy girl that has Daffy's eyes bugging out. He exclaims, "Beat me Daddy, eight to the bar!" Daffy makes out with the decoy, blindly grabbing the Wolf's snout and feels his long sharp teeth. Daffy, frightened of the Wolf, tries to discourage him, "I'm not even a mouth full, I'm skin and bones! I've got spots before my eyes!" He also shows off his coated tongue, dandruff, B.O., flat feet and rejection by the Army. Daffy runs to *Escape,* but the wolf blocks it. Chasing Daffy to *The Bridge at San Luis Rey* (a bridge of teeth), the wolf is caught in a *Hurricane,* with *The Storm* and *Lightning.* The wolf dies on the cover of *For Whom the Bell Tolls.* Daffy returns to *The Lake* with his decoy, while Porky laughs, "Everybody knows

that they can never possibly mean anything to each other!" The pair produce a family of decoy ducklings, and Daffy gets the last laugh, "You and your education!"

HIAWATHA'S RABBIT HUNT [ACADEMY AWARD NOMINEE]

Bugs Bunny; June 7; MM; Supervision by I. Freleng; Story by Michael Maltese; Animation by Gil Turner; Musical Direction by Carl W. Stalling.
Bugs Bunny is reading "Little Hiawatha" and realizes that the "mighty warrior" is going to hunt him. Meanwhile, the goofy little Hiawatha is preparing a large kettle for his dinner. The warrior tracks rabbit footprints to the pot where Bugs is taking a bath! Bugs helps the native put logs under the kettle; he'd like a good hot bath. The Indian puts carrots into the bath, but Bugs eats them. Then he gets wise to the fact the Indian is making rabbit stew. He escapes to his rabbit hole.

Hiawatha plans to tie the rabbit with rope, but Bugs laughs that off, ties up the Indian, and conga dances into the woods. Bugs tries to fool the native disguised as an Indian brave, but Hiawatha puts an arrow to the bunny's head. Bugs challenges the Indian to hop after him, which lands the Indian at the bottom of a cliff. As the sun sets in the west, Hiawatha canoes into the distance. Bugs recites the last lines of the famous story, but the Indian paddles back to give the rabbit a "wacky" kiss.

PORKY'S PRIZE PONY

Porky Pig; June 21; LT; Supervision by Charles M. Jones; Story by Rich Hogan; Animation by Ken Harris; Musical Direction by Carl W. Stalling.
At the County Fair, Porky Pig is a jockey readying his prize pony for the steeplechase and the $10,000 prize. Meanwhile, a clumsy horse, looking for a new owner, spots Porky. The horse catches Porky's eye with his "Take Me Home Free" sign and his "Good Horsekeeping Seal of Approval." He tries to demonstrate his posture, but his tail keeps getting in the way. He then follows Porky, who isn't interested, and carelessly smashes into a tractor and falls into the water trough.

The horse tries to help Porky with a

water bucket, but trips, and the bucket lands on Porky's head. Next, the horse demonstrates his ability at the steeple-chase. He runs, then jumps, but crash lands in the barn. The horse tries again and again knocks the water bucket on Porky's head. Porky throws the pail on the horse's head. The horse gets the pail stuck on his hoofs, and hops after Porky, knocking into the stable and causing Horse Liniment (125% Proof) to fall into the water bucket. By the time the race begins, Porky's pony is dead drunk. Seeing this, the clumsy horse grabs Porky, and they run around the track like a locomotive. The horse is such an oaf, he causes the other horses to miss their jumps and fall into the water traps. The horse, with Porky in tow, crashes into the trophy case with all four feet stuck in the first place cup!

THE WACKY WORM

June 21; MM; Supervision by I. Freleng; Story by Dave Monahan; Animation by Cal Dalton; Musical Direction by Carl W. Stalling.
A determined crow comes across the wacky worm, a "Jerry Colonna" type, resting in an apple tree and singing. He sees the crow ("My word, a bird!") and hops into an apple. The crow boasts he knows where the worm is. The worm hides in a toothpaste tube, which the crow squeezes. The worm pops out and lands in a record player in a junk yard. The crow thinks he has the worm trapped, but the mustachioed insect blasts music into his foe's ear. They chase around a toaster, and the worm hides in a bottle containing 110% alcohol. The worm gets drunk and boldly faces the crow, "Listen crow, you better go!" He challenges the crow to a fist fight, but the crow chases him back to the apple tree. The worm hides in an apple, and the crow decides to eat every one until he finds the character.

A short time later, the green-faced crow is sick, but happy, "Now I gotcha!" Just as he is about to grab the last apple, a woodpecker knocks a dozen others from the tree. "Oh well, who wants a worm, anyhow!"

MEET JOHN DOUGHBOY

Porky Pig; July 5; LT; Supervision by Robert Clampett; Story by Warren Foster; Animation by Vive Risto; Musical Direction by Carl W. Stalling.
Draftee Porky Pig is showing a war-time newsreel "chock full of military secrets!" Porky asks, "If there are any Fifth Columnists in the audience, please leave the theater right now." The newsreel begins with "Porky Pig Presents" as a spoof of the RKO main title. First we see a wartime factory literally "humming"; a British Spitfire airplane spits fire; a newsreel quotes citizen Sugar Cane as saying, "Our Open Door policy is responsible for the Draft!" The film shows our army traveling on its stomach, literally.

Other spot gags include two artillery gunners comparing cigarettes. "Mine's longer than yours!"; a new weapon, a super-fast land destroyer zipping around the battlefield, stopping, and we see Jack Benny and Rochester in their Maxwell automobile; the Statue Of Liberty defending the nation by spraying enemy planes as though she were spraying insects.

THE HECKLING HARE

Bugs Bunny; July 5; MM; Supervision by Fred Avery; Story by Michael Maltese; Animation by Bob McKimson; Musical Direction by Carl W. Stalling.
A dopey dog, sniffing for game, comes across a rabbit hole. Bugs Bunny raises his ears and feels the dog's teeth with them. The dog digs into the rabbit hole, while Bugs spins out to observe. He asks, "Umm, What's up, Doc?" and leaves. The dog gets wise and chases him. They meet face to face, Bugs imitates his snarling gestures. Soon the dog is imitating the bunny's funny faces (Bugs holds a sign: "Silly, Isn't He?"), and the rabbit slugs the dog with a baseball bat. Bugs runs to the lake, puts on a bathing cap, and dives in. The dog pursues underwater, but loses him. Coming out of the water, the dog shakes off the water, Bugs secretly on his back. Pondering his next move, the rabbit starts scratching the dog, who turns around and gets a big kiss on the lips from Bugs. Using the dog's tail

as a diving board, Bugs jumps up into a tree. The dog reaches for the rabbit, but Bugs teases his paw with a stick then drops a tomato in it. The dog squashes the tomato and thinks he has killed the rabbit. The dog brings flowers to his rabbit hole, and Bugs accepts them. "For me, Doc? Oh you darlin'!" The dog digs into Bugs's hole and almost falls through, cliff side. He walks away, carelessly falling off the cliff. Bugs remarks, "Too bad, but he had it comin." He steps into his hole, which now drops him. He falls along with the dog until they apply the brakes and land gently, "Fooled ya, didn't we!"

This film ends abruptly for a reason. Avery originally had the two characters fall through another hole, ending the film with Bugs stating, "Here we go again!" Leon Schlesinger, who normally stayed out of the creative end, objected to the idea of his newest star ending in death. He ordered the final 40 feet cut, which caused an argument between Schlesinger and Avery. Avery was suspended, then fired.

INKI AND THE LION

Inki; July 19; MM; Supervision by Charles M. Jones; Story by Rich Hogan; Animation by Phil Monroe; Musical Direction by Carl W. Stalling.
Little jungle boy Inki is hunting with his spear. After a series of loud crashing noises, the minah bird appears from the brush (to the tune of Fingal's "Cave Overture") and Inki throws his weapon at him. The bird walks over his spear and into a hollow tree trunk. Inki reaches in for the bird but pulls out a skunk.

Inki comes across a cute little lion cub playing, and is about to spear it when its "Daddy" comes along and chases Inki into a hollow log. Inki runs and hides, but is accidentally on top of the big lion. Climbing down from his head, Inki feels the lions teeth between his toes. The jungle boy races to a tree stump to hide. The lion runs past it, and Inki is safe, emerging from the stump with the minah bird on his head. Inki follows the minah bird to a cave, the lion follows the boy. Inki intends to

trap the bird, putting boulders in front of the opening, but unintentionally tries to place the lion's backside there as well. Inki runs inside the cave to escape the big cat, but meets him eye to eye inside. He then races outside, where the cat demands the jungle boy walk into his mouth. Inki is about to comply when the minah bird walks past and ties the hungry lion's tail to a tree. Inki wants to shake hands with the bird who's saved his life, but the minah bird spins him around and smashes him to the ground.

AVIATION VACATION

Au. 2; MM; Supervision by Fred Avery; Story by Dave Monahan; Animation by Sidney Sutherland; Musical Direction by Carl Stalling.
This Avery spot-gag opus takes us on a trip around the world by airplane. As we depart via a plane that takes off like a bird, running and jumping into the sky, we leave sunny California "where the sun is always shining," a sun pictured surrounded by a wall of clouds. The plane follows a train track, its shadow averting obstacles on the ground, retracting its wings to go in a tunnel, etc.

We pass Mount Rushmore and admire the presidents, which include the Republican and Democratic nominees for 1941. On the Emerald Isle, Patrick serenades us with "When Irish Eyes Are Smiling," during which a hair gets caught in a the gate of the projector running the cartoon. He stops his song to shout out, "Hey, you, up there! Get that hair outa here!" A silhouette of a hand plucks it out.

In Darkest Africa, natives beat jungle drums to black cartoon stereotype natives who ask, "What did he say?" Answer: "Boop-ditty-boop-ditty-boop-boop-de-boop!" We see an ostrich who can't find his friends when their heads are buried; and cocoons from which

119

emerge beautiful butterflies with one exception. "Well, I've been sick!"

Back in New York, visability is poor. The clouds lift, and our tour plane is seen attached to a ride at Coney Island. Iris out.

WE, THE ANIMALS SQUEAK

Porky Pig; Aug 9; LT; Supervision by Robert Clampett; Animation by I. Ellis; Story by Melvin Millar; Musical Direction by Carl W. Stalling.

At Radio City in New York, Porky Pig hosts a radio program in which animals tell their life stories. After listening to a rabbit's "hare-raising story," Porky introduces a "Pussy Cat with an unusual *tail.*" Kansas City Kitty tells of her mouse-chasing days, then meeting Tom Collins and starting a family. The mice plan to kidnap Kitty's kitten. They take her kitten hostage and threaten to hurt the kitten if Kitty does anything to them. The result: the mice romp and play in front of the miserable cat. They raid the refrigerator and use Kitty's face for a workout, building up their muscles by stretching her whiskers and using her nose as a punching bag. The kitten escapes, and Kitty chases the mice. Porky congratulates Kitty on her story and gives her a present, a mouse, causing her to jump on a stool and scream!

SPORT CHUMPIONS

Aug 16; MM; Supervision by I. Freleng; Story by Michael Maltese; Animation by Gerry Chiniquy; Musical Supervision by Carl Stalling.

Spot gags "bringing you low lifes in the world of sports." An archery expert hits the bullseye every time: the camera pulls back to reveal the sportsman standing a foot away. Billiard balls travel in same set across table. A swimming demonstration includes the crawl, the jack knife dive, the swan dive, and another popular dive, Sloppy Joe's.

Other sports spoofed include ping pong, skiing, track and field, baseball, football (played at "Avery Memorial Stadium"), and auto racing. During a gag for bicycle racing, the racers go round and round "Madison Round Garden," stopping to say, "Monotonous, isn't it?" Yes, indeed!

THE HENPECKED DUCK

Daffy Duck, Porky Pig; Aug 30; LT; Supervision by Robert Clampett; Story by Warren Foster; Animation by John Carey; Musical Direction by Carl W. Stalling.

"I want a divorce!" cries everyone in Judge Porky Pig's courtroom. Daffy Duck is the first case, and his wife is screaming for a divorce. In a flashback, we learn that Daffy is a truly henpecked duck, responding to every one of his wife's wishes with a sour, "Yes, my love." She's going to her mother's, and leaves Daffy to sit on her egg and keep it warm. When she leaves Daffy plays magic tricks with the egg, making it disappear with the magic words, "Hocus Pocus Flippety Flam, Razz-a-matazz, Alakazam!" His trick works too well. He can't make it reappear, and tries all day, wearing himself out. In a mad panic for a replacement egg, Daffy leaves a door knob in the nest. His wife sees the door knob and screams for a divorce. Back in the courtroom, Daffy asks the judge for one more chance. Porky approves, the duck speaks his magic words, and the egg returns! A chicken (a la Zazu Pitts) laments, "Alakazam and you get an egg! Oh, dear, and for fifteen years I've been doing it the hard way!" The Daffy duckling hatches and, with gavel in hand, calls, "Case dismissed, step down!"

SNOWTIME FOR COMEDY

Aug 30; MM; Supervision by Chuck Jones; Story by Rich Hogan; Animation by Robert Cannon.

Chuck Jones's "Two Curious Dogs" chase a bone in a snowy wilderness setting. Both dogs have separate adventures on ice, with both bumping into the film's running gag, a beaver trying to build his dam. The yellow pup is trying to escape a widening crack in the ice that pursues the pooch up a tree and splits it. The larger brown hound gets his rear end and legs encased in ice and has trouble removing it. The yellow dog chases the elusive bone down a ski jump, becoming covered with more and more snow as he slides back to the ice pond. He becomes a giant "snow dog" and crashes into the beaver's barricade, creating a snow-covered Hoover Dam. The cartoon ends with our two heroes popping out of the snow bank, the bone sticking out of the snow-covered head of the yellow dog.

ALL THIS AND RABBIT STEW

Bugs Bunny; Sept 13; MM; Supervision by Fred Avery (uncredited); Story by Dave Monahan; Animation by Virgil Ross; Musical Direction by Carl Stalling.
A lazy hunter is shuffling through the woods, singing to himself, "I'm gonna catch me a rabbit." He encounters a rabbit hole and orders the bunny below to put his hands up and march out. The rabbit hole moves at gunpoint to the side of a tree. The hunter shoots, destroying the tree and leaving Bugs Bunny perched atop his rifle barrel. Bugs takes off, "swimming" away in the ground. The hunter uses a bathroom plunger to pull out the rabbit, but Bugs tickles him and escapes into a cave. The hunter pursues and grabs at the first pair of white eyes he sees. Bugs points out he's holding a grizzly bear. Escaping the cave, the hunter shoots at Bugs, his bullets chasing the rabbit around the woods. They are scared off by a skunk! The hunter chases Bugs through a hollow log that the bunny maneuvers so that each time the hunter steps out, he is standing in mid-air—eventually falling. Bugs watches him then turns around to see the bandaged hunter pointing his rifle in his face (Bugs gives a terrific take, as his limbs separate in a mid-air jump). Bugs offers to play dice with his pursuer. They go behind a bush, the hunter draws snake eyes. Bugs wins all his clothes and gun and emerges from the bush imitating the lazy hunter. The hunter is now naked with only a fig leaf in place, but Bugs pulls *that* off and displays it for us at the iris out.

NOTES TO YOU

Porky Pig; Sept 20; LT; Supervision by I. Freleng; Story by Michael Maltese; Animation by Manuel Perez; Musical Direction by Carl W. Stalling.
While an alley cat sets up a sheet music stand on the backyard fence Porky goes to sleep. Starting with "Figaro," the cat keeps Porky awake all night with a concert performance.

Porky gets his gun and goes out with a milk dish as bait. The pig falls asleep while waiting, and the cat drinks the milk, leaving an empty bottle with a note "Please leave two quarts tomorrow!" Porky chases the cat around a fence, and as he corners the feline, the cat serenades the pig to sleep with a soft rendition of "Rock-a-Bye Baby." The cat places Porky back in his bed, then abruptly wakes him up by turning on the radio. Porky locks the cat out, who goes back on the fence to sing medley of "Umbrella Man," "Jeepers Creepers," and "Make Love With a Guitar." Porky shoots the cat, who dies singing "Aloha Oe/Farewell to Thee." Porky is sorry to have killed him, but a ghostly chorus of the cat's nine lives sing Donizetti's Sextet from "Lucia."

Remade and improved in 1948 as *Back Alley Oproar* with Elmer Fudd in Porky's role and Sylvester as the musical cat.

BRAVE LITTLE BAT

Sniffles; Sept 27; MM; Supervision by Charles M. Jones; Story by Rich Hogan; Animation by Rudolf Larriva; Musical Direction by Carl W. Stalling.
Sniffles is singing and motoring through the countryside. Suddenly his little wind-up toy car breaks down and falls apart. Storm clouds start to brew and Sniffles seeks refuge in an old windmill. The mouse makes himself at home by resting on a hay stack and is soon visited by the lighthouse keeper, Batty, a little talkative bat who wears wooden shoes. Sniffles explores the lighthouse with Batty, and they encounter a cat. Sniffles is trapped by the feline, but Batty flies to his rescue.

Not many gags or much story. Batty looks almost exactly like Sniffles except for his Dutch costume and bat wings. His talkative personality would be transferred to Sniffles in later cartoons such as *The Unbearable Bear* and *Hush My Mouse.*

THE BUG PARADE

Oct 11; MM; Supervision by Fred Avery; Story by Dave Monahan; Animation by Rod Scribner; Musical Direction by Carl W. Stalling.
Spot gags based on little-known facts in the world of insects. Bug gags include a housefly with suction cups on his feet; a slow horsefly who's been hanging around Bing Crosby's horse; a sexy wasp who loses her girdle; a queen bee who lays a million eggs; a spider who captures a cow in his web; fireflies, including one who didn't pay his light bill; two caterpillars who meet and shake each of their hands ("Glad to meet ya, hi, glad to know you too!"). A moth with a flame causes an insect to shout, "Hey, stupid! What are you trying' to do, start a fire?"; a cootie comes to an army camp and is overjoyed by "Millions and millions of soldiers, and they're mine, all mine!"; a termite saws down the tall trees, until he hits the "Petrified Forest"; silk worms picket the nylon products company; an evil spider "just *loves* little flies!"

Other insects spoofed include Red and Black ants, grasshoppers, centipedes, and snails.

ROBINSON CRUSOE, JR.

Porky Pig; Oct 25; LT; Supervision by Norman McCabe; Animation by Veve Risto; Story by Melvin Millar; Musical Direction by Carl W. Stalling.
Norman McCabe's first cartoon as director has all the pluses and minuses most of the films in his two-year stint had. There is good art and animation, but weak gags.

Porky Pig is a sailor on a tall ship. When the order is given, "All ashore that's going to shore." A daddy mouse tells his "baby Snooks" something Porky doesn't know, "Confidentially, it sinks!"

After nine weeks of smooth sailing, a hurricane blows the ship with Porky to a deserted island, where a man Friday is already waiting with a "Welcome

Robinson Crusoe" sign. They create an island paradise, to the tune of "I Love Coffee, I Love Tea." Porky goes exploring, finding a tropical bird, he asks, "Polly want a cracker?" The bird responds, "I'm waiting for the $64.00 question!" Porky observes animals around a watering hole, a modern water cooler! Porky finds a telescope to observe monkeys playing bridge and trying to climb a "slippery" elm. Porky next finds footprints and follows them into a cave. The group of cannibals inside spots the pig and chases him back to his hut. Porky grabs an axe and chops a log into a motorboat. The natives drop their spears when they see an American flag. Friday holds a "V" for Victory sign as they speed away.

ROOKIE REVUE

Oct 25; MM; Supervision by I. Freleng; Story by Dave Monahan; Animation by Richard Bickenback; Musical Direction by Carl W. Stalling.
Weak gags on military life, including soldiers snoring to the tune of "You're in the Army Now." The bugler puts a nickel in the jukebox to play "Reveille," a mess hall includes caricatures of director Tex Avery and executives Henry Binder and Ray Katz. A new artillery weapon is a giant pop-gun. Airplane pilots play aerial games in tic tac toe fashion. A general gives specific coordinants to gunners manning a large gun. They fire, destroying headquarters and giving the general a black eye ("I'm a baaad general!").

SADDLE SILLY

Nov 8; MM; Supervision by Charles M. Jones; Animation by Philip DeLara.
Opening title card: "This picture is dedicated to the Pony Express Co., *without* whose whole-hearted co-operation this picture was made."

A collection of spot gags on the Pony Express. Examples: the Pony Express rider gives airplane-pilot-like landing instructions to "Phoney Express Station 13"; horses pass the rider from one to another like racers passing the baton in a relay race. Running gag has a little mustachioed hitchhiker trying to get a lift. Horse and rider encounter water problems in the river stream, and in

Indian territory are attacked by Wild Bill Coty. Finally making it to Fort V-8, the rider brings the parcel to the general. Inside the pouch is the little hitchhiker with a sign "Thanks for the ride, bub!"

THE CAGEY CANARY
Nov 22; MM; Supervision by Tex Avery and Bob Clampett; Story by Michael Maltese; Animation by Robert McKimson; Musical Direction by Carl W. Stalling.
This was one of the films in production when Avery left the studio. Bob Clampett completed it and *Crazy Cruise*, neither film released with a supervision credit.

A cat aims to catch and eat the canary, but Granny tells the bird to whistle if the cat tries anything, and she'll throw him out in the rain. Among the gags: the cat traps the canary in a jar, but a fly buzzes by, distracting the feline. The bird shows a sexy picture to the cat, causing him to whistle. The cat offers crackers to the canary, who eats them then can't whistle until he swallows. The bird heckles the cat by sticking out his tongue at the feline, hits the cat with a mallet, and pulls out his tongue, which flaps back into his mouth like a window shade.

The cat puts ear muffs on Granny, then chases the bird unafraid. The canary turns on every noise device in the house, then clobbers the cat with an ironing board. The cat finds the bird at Granny's door. Granny gets wise to their hijinks, and both are sent out in the rain. The bird asks, "Ladies and gentlemen, would any of you in the audience be interested in a homeless cat and canary?"

PORKY'S MIDNIGHT MATINEE
Porky Pig; Nov 22; LT; Supervision by Charles M. Jones; Animation by Robert Cannon; Musical Direction by Carl W. Stalling.
Singing "I Ought to Be in Pictures," Porky is working as care-taker backstage after the show. He encounters a caged little black ant with a bone in his top-knot. He lets the little fellow go, but soon discovers it's Prof. McGurk's Trained African Pygmy Ant worth

$162,422,503.51 (plus sales tax). The stuttering pig spends the rest of the film trying to undo his good deed.

Porky chases the ant into a magician's trunk and out to the high wire. The ant next runs into Porky's lunch. Porky gets his hand caught in the mustard jar. With the ant's assistance, the pig breaks the jar. In pain, he puts the mustard covered hand in his mouth, burning his mouth. The ant hands him a bottle of turpentine to drink and then escapes.

Porky tries to lure the ant with a candy cane. The ant replaces it with a stick of dynamite. Porky throws the dynamite, which explodes near the ant, landing him back in his cage. The ant gives a big black-face grin to end the film.

RHAPSODY IN RIVETS
ACADEMY AWARD NOMINEE
Dec 6; MM; Supervision by I. Freleng; Story by Michael Maltese; Animation by Gil Turner; Musical Direction by Carl W. Stalling.
At a construction site downtown, the workers applaud the arrival of the lion foreman, who "conducts" his builders to the tune of Liszt's "Second Hungarian Rhapsody." Most of the gags are of characters hammering rivets and nails and laying bricks to classical music. Big guys with little hammers, little guys with big hammers. As the music reaches its climax, the builders go higher and higher (going so fast, they build around a cloud in the way). They finish the building, and a worker closes the front door, causing the skyscraper to crash down into a pile of rubble.

WABBIT TWOUBLE
Bugs Bunny, Elmer Fudd; Dec 20; MM; Supervision by Wobert Cwampett; Story by Dave Monahan; Animation by Sid Sutherwand; Musical Direction, Carl W. Stalling.
Elmer Fudd's vacation in Jellostone

National Park, "A Restful Retreat." Fudd's car chugs through the Grand Canyon doing a conga. Bugs Bunny spots him and posts a "Camp Here!" sign. Elmer's tent is pulled into Bugs's rabbit hole. Fudd grabs it and has a tug of war, getting it back tied in knots! Elmer tries to grab the rabbit, but when he removes his hands from the rabbit hole, his fingers are tied in knots! Elmer nails a board over the hole with the mistaken impression "that'll hold him, all right! Heh-eh-eh-eh!" Bugs walks out of his trap and imitates the portly camper. As Fudd rests in his hammock, Bugs paints his glasses dark blue and sets his alarm clock to a nighttime hour. The alarm goes off and Fudd thinks it's late. He gets into his pajamas and goes to bed. He sleeps for a few seconds, then Bugs imitates a rooster crowing. Fudd gets up and washes his face. Bugs holds his towel away from him, making Elmer walk off a cliff. Wiping his face, he admires the view, gets wise, and runs back—into Bugs's arms. Elmer chases Bugs, but runs straight into a grizzly bear. Pulling out his handy copy of "Bear Facts," Fudd is advised to "remain absolutely motionless." The bear sniffs him ("P.U.") and walks away. Bugs decides to imitate the bear and abuse Elmer's nose, asking, "Funny situation, ain't it?" Elmer tries to clobber the rabbit with his rifle, but hits the grizzly instead. The bear chases Fudd among the tall trees to the tune of the "William Tell Overture." Fudd grabs his gear and races from the park, stopping only to chop up the welcome sign for which a park ranger sends Fudd to prison. "At least I'm rid of that screwy rabbit." Sharing the cell with him *is* the rabbit and the bear, who both ask, "How long ya in for, Doc?"

PORKY'S POOCH
Porky Pig; Dec 27; LT; Supervision by Robert Clampett; Animation by I. Ellis; Story by Warren Foster; Musical Direction by Carl W. Stalling.
In New York City a hungry Scotty dog named Sandy is watching a cook toss pancakes. He spots his friend Rover in a big car. Rover tells Sandy how he got himself a master. He simply walked up to the apartment of Porky Pig and rang his bell. Porky listened to a classic sales pitch: "Hello, bub! You ain't got no dog, and I ain't got no master. Let's moige!" (Brooklyn for "merge").' Rover showed off his talents: affection, by kissing Porky's head; playing dead (and imitating rigor mortis). Porky dumped him down the staircase, but when he returned to his apartment, Rover was there, doing his Carmen Miranda imitation. Porky threw him out again, but the dog came back, shouting, "You don't want me! I can take a hint!" Giving the pig a sob story, he threw himself out the window (photo backgrounds of New York skyscrapers). Porky went to look: the dog was on the ledge. Porky locked the window. The dog on the ledge fell off. Porky raced downstairs and held the fallen dog, pleading for it to "Speak to me!" Rover revived, saying, "Gosh! I didn't know you cared!"

1942

HOP, SKIP, AND A CHUMP
Jan 3; MM; Supervision by I. Freleng; Story by Michael Maltese; Animation by Cal Dalton.
Grasshopper Hopalong Casual introduces himself to us and to a pair of Laurel and Hardy-like crows trying to catch him. They try to get him in a bag, but the grasshopper substitutes an angry bee in his place. The bee chases the comic duo underwater.

The crows then chase the hopper into a junkyard, where, among other gags, the crows are trapped in a piano while the grasshopper plays "The Storm" on the keyboard. In the end, the hopper jumps through the iris out, boasting about not being caught—but one of the crows pulls him back in for more.

PORKY'S PASTRY PIRATES
Porky Pig; Jan 17; LT; Supervision by I. Freleng; Story by Dave Monahan; Animation by Gerald Chiniquy.
Outside Porky's bakery a little fly is drooling over the cakes. A "Cagney" bee comes along and invites the fly to

watch how he can eat anything in the shop. Threatening Porky with his stinger, the bee eats marble cake, cheese cake, and limburger cheese cake (which he spits out). Candy is taken from the pants of a gingerbread man, and the trousers fall down, revealing striped underwear! The bee calls Porky over and splats eclair creme in his face. Porky tries to use his swatter, but the bee electrifies it.

The bee helps the fly disguise himself as a bee, with a metal nail for a stinger. The fly dives into a cake, swimming in its icing. Porky spots the insect and boots him out. "Get out and stay out, you unsanitary old fly." The bee returns for a snack, but gets smacked with the swatter. This time it's the fly doing the swatting.

THE BIRD CAME C.O.D.

Conrad Cat; Jan 17; MM; Supervision by Charles M. Jones; Animation by Ken Harris; Musical Direction by Carl Stalling.

Conrad Cat, errand boy for the Arctic Palm Co., delivers a potted plant to a vaudeville theater. First, he can't get it through the door because the leaves are too spread out. Once inside, Conrad falls down the staircase. Replacing the plant on stage, Conrad spots the magician's hat and decides to pretend doing magic. He really pulls a rabbit out of the hat, then a little gray Henery Hawk-like bird, who pokes him in the eye. Conrad tries to get rid of the hat, but it boomerangs back to his face. The bird gives the cat the eye and backs him into the orchestra pit. Trying to get out of the theater, Conrad falls into a set of magic hats, releasing a flock of birds that surround him, abuse him, and return to their top hats.

Another Chuck Jones excercise in frustration. "Says You, Says Who, Says I" is heard on the soundtrack.

ALOHA HOOEY

Jan 30; MM; Supervision by Fred Avery (uncredited); Story by Michael Maltese; Animation by Virgil Ross; Musical Direction by Carl W. Stalling.

On a steamship, the S.S. *Sabotage*, two American birds meet up as stowaways. One is Cecil Crow from Oakville, Illi-nois, the other Sammy Seagull from Brooklyn. In the tropics, they spot Lelani hula dancing on the beach. Sammy swims toward shore, picking up a pearl to give her as a gift. Cecil gets a pearl too, but the oyster reclaims it. Sammy skywrites, with cigar smoke, a heart with an arrow across it. Cecil tries to blow smoke, but falls into the ocean. Sammy tries to impress Lelani with a trick sky dive. Cecil tries one and almost gets eaten by a shark, is attacked by a turtle, and kicked in the butt by a starfish.

A gorilla with a red sweatshirt (which reads "The Villain, As If You Didn't Know!") grabs Lelani. She is rescued by Cecil and he becomes her hero. In the end, they fly off waving goodbye to Sammy, their children in tow.

WHO'S WHO IN THE ZOO

Porky Pig; Feb 14; LT; Supervision by Norman McCabe; Animation by John Carey; Story by Melvin Millar; Musical Direction by Carl Stalling.

Spot gags featuring the animals in the Azuza Zoo, with Porky Pig as the zoo-keeper. Gags include a pan shot of the timber wolf, the gray wolf, and the Hollywood wolf who sings, "You Ought To Be in Pictures." There are absorb-ent cotton-tailed rabbits, march hares who actually march; a down-and-out bum steer; a bald eagle with a toupee ("O.K., Blabbermouth, so I am bald!"), and a running gag about a lion waiting for the ice-cream truck.

PORKY'S CAFE

Porky Pig, Conrad Cat; Feb 21; LT; Supervision by Charles M. Jones; Animation by Rudolph Larriva; Musical Direction by Carl W. Stalling.

Restaurant gags with waiter Porky and Conrad Cat the cook. Making pan-cakes, Conrad has problems with an ant who gets caught in the batter. Serving a little mustashioed man, Porky prepares the meal using a typewriter to generate letters for alphabet soup. He makes a T-bone steak by cutting it into the shape of a "T" and cooks an egg in a Rube Goldberg mechanical machine. Conrad chases the ant and crashes into Porky, who was about to serve a large wedding cake. Porky ends up on a platter with an apple stuffed in his mouth, Conrad and the customer landing inside the cake. The ant ends up atop the pastry, holding the bride.

CONRAD THE SAILOR
Daffy Duck, Conrad Cat; Feb 28; MM; Supervision by Charles M. Jones; Animation by Ben Washam; Story by Dave Monahan; Musical Direction by Carl W. Stalling.
Conrad Cat is in the navy, swabbing the deck and singing "We're Shoving Right Off for Home Again" (sung by Pinto Colvig). Daffy Duck is watching him and comments, "Is that guy awful!" Daffy replaces Conrad's water bucket with a can of red paint, and admonishes him, "Very sloppy, Roscoe! You're a slovenly housekeeper!" He throws the mop on Conrad's head, the Duck heckles, "Very petite, Betsy!"

Conrad chases Daffy around the ship with various gags including one where Daffy becomes Conrad's telescope, "Swell view, eh, Doc?" He hides in an artillery gun, gets blasted into the sky, and leads the explosive shell back to the ship. Conrad, Daffy, and the explosive salute the little bearded captain (the film's running joke), then resume the chase as the cartoon ends.

CRAZY CRUISE
Mar 14; MM; Supervision uncredited; begun by Fred Avery, completed by Robert Clampett; Story by Michael Maltese; Animation by Rod Scribner. Musical Direction by Carl W. Stalling.
Yet another travelogue spoof with spot gags from across the globe. Gags include a tobacco plantation where we meet an auctioneering tobacco bug. The 1939 World's Fair symbols, the trylon and the perisphere, sit in the Sahara Desert next to the Sphinx, which asks, "Monotonous, isn't it?"

There is a tour of "Veronica Lake" and giant cannibals who are fond of white hunters in regular and king size. End gag shows cute realistic bunnies about to be attacked by a vicious Japanese vulture. They scamper into a bush and fire a heavy artillery gun. One of the rabbits turns toward the camera, revealing he's Bugs Bunny in a war helmet, and gives us a thumbs up. His ears get caught in the iris out, forming a "V" for Victory.

THE WABBIT WHO CAME TO SUPPER
Bugs Bunny, Elmer Fudd; Mar 28; MM; Supervision by I. Freleng; Story by Michael Maltese; Animation by Richard Bickenbach. Musical Direction by Carl Stalling.
Elmer Fudd and his dogs are hunting for Bugs Bunny in the woods. Bugs pretends to be be one of Elmer's dogs, but the hunter gets wise and is about to shoot the rabbit when a telegram is delivered. His Uncle Louie is leaving him three million dollars on condition that he doesn't harm any animals, especially rabbits. Elmer lets Bugs go and returns home, but finds the wacky wabbit in his shower (singing "Angel in disguise"), powdering himself, and shaving his armpits. Elmer is about to shoot him, when Bugs holds up a sign, "What would Uncle Louie think?" Elmer pleads with the rabbit to leave, but Bugs wants food. Elmer leads him to some out the front door. Outside, Bugs performs a classic death scene ("Hey, this scene ought to get me the Academy Award!"). Elmer opens the door to the dying rabbit and attempts to nurse him back to health, singing "Rock-a-Bye Baby." Bugs asks him to "Swing it." Elmer is informed that Uncle Louie has kicked the bucket, but an itemized list of his inheritance taxes leaves Fudd owing $1.98. Elmer chases Bugs around the house. Passing the grandfather clock as it strikes midnight, the rabbit tricks Fudd into thinking it's New Year's Eve. Bugs runs into the basement ("Don't go down there, it's dark!"); and finally outside. A delivery man brings Elmer Easter greetings, a hollow egg filled with little Bugs Bunnies asking, "Eh, what's up, Doc?"

HORTON HATCHES THE EGG

Apr 11; MM; Supervised by Robert Clampett; Animation by Robert McKimson. From the story by Dr. Seuss.
Told in rhyme, this is the tale of Horton the elephant who is asked by "that lazy bird, Maisie" (a spoof of Ann Southern) to mind her nest and sit on her egg while she takes a vacation. Through rain and snow, Horton remains atop the nest. "I meant what I said, and I said what I meant/An elephant is faithful, one hundred percent!" Three hunters encounter the elephant and aim their rifles "right straight at his heart" (his rear end). They take Horton to America and sell him to a circus. Maisie drops in and demands her egg back (after 51 weeks). When the egg hatches, out flies an elephant bird. Horton and son go back to the jungle and happily sing "The Hut-Sut song."

Bob Clampett and Dr. Seuss—what a combination! Seuss-inspired backgrounds, green skies, pink elephants, and blue polka-dot birds. Clampett is able to inject his style, and contemporary Warner Bros. humor, and still remain faithful (100%) to Dr. Seuss.

SAPS IN CHAPS

Apr 11; LT; Supervision by I. Freleng; Story by Sgt. Dave Monahan; Animation by Manuel Perez. Musical Direction by Carl W. Stalling.
Spot gags about cowboys and the Wild West. A narrator tells of the western pioneers who crossed the nation when it was young (even the presidents on Mt. Rushmore were babies), across the *literal* backbone of the nation.

Other gags include a thirsty desert wanderer who fills up at Custer's Last Stand; wagon trains that are just that, covered locomotives; western towns where everyone, including the cats and mice, are bow-legged; brave Texas Pete who laughs at danger and can't stop while he's getting shot ("Ha! Ha! You're *Killing* Me!"); a Rodeo trick rider who gets stage fright; and a running gag involving a Pony Express rider who can't seem to get on his horse.

DOG TIRED

Apr 25; MM; Supervision by Charles M. Jones; Animation by Phil Monroe; Musical Direction by Carl W. Stalling.
Two dogs digging a huge hole are scared by an automobile. They jump over a nearby wall and into the county zoo. the brown pup lands in the kangaroo's pouch; the white dog lands in the fountain pond. The white pup observes two love birds (wonderfully animated) who tell the pup to "Scram, stupid." Whitey runs past the film's running gag, a frustrated stork determined to stand on one leg. Meanwhile, Brownie is getting a tour of the zoo via the kangaroo. He finally sneaks out of the hopping kangaroo's pouch, but continues to bounce uncontrollably and straight into a tight metal pipe. The dog pulls himself out, landing in a tree. Under the watchful eye of a laughing hyena, he slides down onto a porcupine. The white pup encounters a lion, and buries his bone near a sleeping ostrich who steals the bone, losing it to a turtle. The white dog eventually must go into a hippo's mouth to get it back, and runs with it at such a speed, he crashes into the brown dog, having troubles with a pelican and the kangaroo. The two dogs end up in the kangaroo's pouch, joined by their biggest fan, the laughing hyena.

DAFFY'S SOUTHERN EXPOSURE

Daffy Duck; May 2; LT; Supervision by Norman McCabe; Story by Don Christensen; Animation by Vive Risto; Musical Direction by Carl W. Stalling.
Daffy Duck decides *not* to fly south and to check out "this winter business!" While Daffy is impressing *us* with his wacky water antics, cold weather arrives and Daffy crashes onto the sud-

denly frozen pond. Titles read, "Through wind and snow and thirty below, we find our hero—gosh, we *can't* find our hero ...." Frozen and starving, Daffy imagines a tree to be a giant T-bone steak. Smoke from a cabin beckons the duck. Inside are a hungry wolf and his weasel sidekick who are sick of beans and dying for a duck dinner. They disguise themselves as spinster sisters, invite Daffy inside, and chase the looney duck around the cabin. There are many chase gags, including a rendition of "The Latin Quarter." The chase continues outside and up a tree, the spruce carved into a totem pole. Daffy runs south. When we last see him, he's happily living within Carmen Miranda's fruity hat.

THE WACKY WABBIT

Bugs Bunny, Elmer Fudd; May 2; MM; Supervision by Robert Clampett; Story by Warren Foster; Animation by Sid Sutherland; Musical Direction by Carl W. Stalling.

Elmer Fudd is prospecting for gold in the desert, singing "Oh Suzanna" with modified lyrics ("Don't you cry for me/ I'm gonna dig up lots of gold/V for victory!"). Bugs Bunny, wearing an animal skull, joins Fudd in a duet. Elmer digs a hole and drops a stick of dynamite in it, but it gets thrown back at him. Each time he throws it in the hole, it's tossed right back to him. Fudd zippers the hole and hides behind a cactus, but Bugs finds him and hands him his dynamite. Elmer hides his eyes, but the stick is a dud. Bugs makes up for it by yelling, BAM!, then putting Fudd's head in a kettle and banging on it. Bugs excitedly tells the angry Fudd that gold has been discovered. When Elmer asks, "where?" Bugs points— into his mouth, where he has a gold tooth. Elmer shows Bugs his gold tooth, then chases the rabbit to his hole. Fudd raises his pick axe to attack the rabbit, but it gets caught in the mountainside. Bugs takes a scissor and cuts Elmer's pants off, revealing his girdle. Fudd scolds us, "Don't laugh! I'll bet plenty of you men wear one of these!" Elmer jumps into Bugs's rabbit hole, but Bugs pops out and starts burying Fudd, noting, "Gosh, ain't I a stinker?" Elmer came for gold and he's gonna get it—he wrestles Bugs to the ground, coming up shouting, "Eureka! Gold at last!" holding a golden tooth. As Elmer and Bugs smile at us, we see that Elmer has pulled his own tooth!

THE DRAFT HORSE

May 9; MM; Supervision by Charles M. Jones; Story by Ted Pierce; Animation by Robert Cannon; Musical Supervision by Carl W. Stalling.

A farmer's plowhorse, upon spotting a recruiting poster, "Horses Wanted For U.S. Army," sees his patriotic duty, kisses the farmer goodbye, and rushes down to the draft board to enlist. With the plow still tied to his back, he rushes over a wooden bridge turning it into a small cabin (with an F.H.A. sign in front); plows through the farmhouse and silo; crashes into the recruiting sergeant ("Major, you got yourself a horse, Major!"). The horse gives a wild demonstration of how he'll perform under fire. This patriotic soliloquy ends with his mock death and a performance of "Taps," that has the sergeant in tears— until he realizes it's just an act. The seargeant orders the horse to strip, and the animal performs a strip-tease. Finally removing his only clothing, his harness, he gets a rubdown from Pvt. Snafu (in a rare unbilled cameo). The horse is then given a physical examination, which includes an eye test to the tune of "You're in the Army Now."

The horse is classifed 44-F and rejected. Walking back to his home, he wanders into a field where a very realistic sham battle is going on. With bombs bursting everywhere, he runs back to the farm. Next day, the horse is at home knitting "Bundles for Bluejackets." He holds up a finished sweater, with a big "V" for victory stitched on front.

NUTTY NEWS

May 23; LT; Supervision by Robert Clampett; Story by Warren Foster; Animation by Virgil Ross; Musical Supervision by Carl W. Stalling.

A newsreel spoof narrated by Arthur Q. Bryan in his Elmer Fudd voice. Topics include Hunting Season: A moose hunter uses a "moose call" to lure his prey, while a moose uses his "Hunter call" ("Yoo-hoo" in a sexy voice) to bop the sportsman; barbers have a new invention to get children to sit still in the barber chair—a jack-in-the-box Hitler that scares the kids stiff; inventions: a man (a caricature of Ray Katz) demonstrates a rear-view mirror to protect his hat and coat from theft, while unattended during dinner—but his pants get stolen; fireflies have an air raid blackout; Frank Putty, artist of "Putty Girl" fame, shows off his latest painting—his thumb!; ducks with gooney, mindless expressions go swimming; traffic signs down south like "No U-All Turns"; A baseball pitcher throws a dollar across the Potomac River, proving that a dollar doesn't go far these days; workers protest department-store construction site with pickets that read "This Store Will Probably Be Unfair!"; and battleships pass in review during a storm, except U.S.S California which sails in sunshine.

LIGHTS FANTASTIC

May 23; MM; Supervision by I. Freleng; Story by Sgt. Dave Monahan; Animation by Gil Turner; Musical Supervision by Carl W. Stalling.
Musical spot gags on Times Square, a spoof of the lighted neon billboards and animated advertising signs. The film opens with a live action shot of the Manhattan thoroughfare, and on to a few nightspots: Yahoodi Cafe, "No Cover Charge, No Minimum, No Entertainment, No Nothing!"; and Strand Theater, now playing "Caught in the draft with selected shorts."

Other gags include a Chinatown bus tour powered by rickshaw; a free eye test by Dr. I.C. Spots; a stick figure quartet, the Four Noses, sing "My High Polished Nose" ("My Wild Irish Rose); the mascot of "Clown cookies" singing "Laugh, Clown, Laugh"; "Face and Sunburn" coffee cans do a can-can; to the tune of "The Blue Danube," little light bulbs and neon swirls alight an elaborate sign—just to say "Eat At Joe's"; and finally all the signs join in to do the "Conga."

HOBBY HORSE-LAFFS

June 6; LT; Supervision by Norman McCabe; Story by Melvin Millar; Animation by Cal Dalton.
Spot gags on people and their hobbies. The gags include a man who subsists on carrots removes his hat for the camera and reveals a pair of rabbit-sized ears; a magician who makes himself disappear; Prof. Blooper and his invisible musical instruments, music provided by a record player strapped to his back; air pilots who fly like birds without airplanes; inventors whose devices include an eye-poker for people who read your newspaper over your shoulder and an anti-hot-foot shoe.

Poor Norman McCabe! He seems to be sabotaged by the poor scripts, loaded with old, unfunny jokes. The animation drawings are, as usual, top-notch, but they can't save this weak entry.

HOLD THE LION, PLEASE!

Bugs Bunny; June 13; MM; Supervision by Charls M. Jones; Story by Ted Pierce; Animation by Ken Harris; Musical Direction by Carl W. Stalling.
The hippo, giraffe, and monkeys agree: the lion is a has-been. They mock his title, "The King of the Jungle." The goofy lion decides to catch a rabbit to prove them wrong. The Lion finds some rabbit tracks, and soon Bugs Bunny rides by like a locomotive train, snatching the carrot bait from the lion's hand. The lion informs Bugs of his plan to catch him, to which the bunny pretends to be frightened and runs off ("Shriek! Shriek! Scream! Scream!"). The lion finds Bugs picking carrots in the field, wearing a sun bonnet and singing. The lion chases Bugs back to his hole, where the rabbit puts up a door. The lion knocks on the door, and Bugs laughs at the lion, now wearing the sun bonnet. The laughter is contagious and while the lion laughs, Bugs

puts the door behind the big cat and slams it shut. The lion beats on the door trying to get "out," then runs to break it down. Bugs opens it at the last second causing the lion to crash. The Lion grabs Bugs, but then the phone rings. It's the lion's wife, Hortense, who orders him to come home. Bugs laughs at the henpecked lion, boasting that he wears the pants in his family. Mrs. Bugs Bunny appears and proves *she* wears the pants.

GOPHER GOOFY

June 27; LT; Supervision by Norman McCabe; Story by Don Christensen; Animation by I. Ellis; Musical Direction by Carl W. Stalling.

A farmer, proud of his beautiful garden, is invaded by two "Brooklynesque" hobo gophers. Virgil, the big dumb gopher, wants to go back to Central Park, while the small gopher, with a derby hat, has a plan. The farmer tries to listen, but they shout into his ear, "Let's not get nosey, Bub!" When the farmer sticks his gun barrel right in their faces, the gophers ask, "What's dis? The Holland Tunnel?" They escape and hit him with their "Be Kind To Gophers Week" sign. The farmer tries to gas the rodents, causing them to float into the sky. They fall into a tomato patch, where the farmer thinks he has them cornered. The farmer reaches for them and squashes a tomato, thinking he mashed a gopher. The gophers begin to dig up the garden, but now the farmer tries to flood them out. Virgil holds the hose until it grows and is about to burst. The water explodes, and the farmer lands in the lawn fountain—his head sticking through the top and water gushing out his ears. The gopher's note, "Something new has been added!"

DOUBLE CHASER

June 27; MM; Supervision by I. Freleng; Story by Michael Maltese; Animation by Gerry Chiniquy; Musical Direction by Carl W. Stalling.

In a nutshell: a cat chasing a mouse is chased by a bulldog.

The cat leaves a piece of cheese in front of a mouse hole, the scent of which seduces (in female shape) the mouse into coming out. The mouse grabs the cheese and runs into the yard toward the sleeping bulldog, which frightens the cat. The cat tries luring the mouse again, this time putting the cheese on a string. The mouse drags the sleeping dog with him. The dog wakes up and walks away, allowing the cat to chase the mouse into a hole in the ground. The cat digs up the hole, but digs up the dog! The dog chases the cat into the henhouse, where the mouse is hiding. The cat inspects the chicken eggs and finds the mouse in one. The dog comes into the henhouse, but the cat disguises as a rooster. The eggs hatch, and the mouse pretends to be a chick. The cat grabs the mouse, the dog grabs the cat, and the chase continues outside. The mouse pulls the "He's in here" gag on the dog, whistling and pointing to all the cat's hiding places—until the dog jumps behind a bush, landing in a junk pile with a cuckoo clock on his head. No longer trusting the mouse, the dog whistles "He's in here" to the cat, and they both chase the mouse. The mouse paints an apple to look like a bomb to scare them away. Unfortunately, it explodes—sending the mouse to heaven with an apple core in his hand.

WACKY BLACKOUT

July 11; LT; Supervision by Robert Clampett; Story by Warren Foster; Animation by Sid Sutherland; Musical Direction by Carl W. Stalling.

Spot gags on how the war affects animals and insects on the homefront. Blackouts include a cow who gives 5000 quarts of milk a day says emotionally, "*Gives* nothing! They come in and take it from me!" Her calf replies, "What a performance." A running gag involves a wacky woodpecker who is a riveter at Lockheed; a turtle who thinks he's a jeep; a goofy dog who only gets kissed during a blackout; a caterpillar who got a retread; an early, sickly-looking version of Tweety as a bird who wants to be a dive bomber;

and veteran carrier pigeons who vow "we did it before and we can do it again." The film ends with the pigeons saluting a live-action U.S. flag.

BUGS BUNNY GETS THE BOID

Bugs Bunny, Beaky Buzzard; July 11; MM; Supervision by Robert Clampett; Story by Warren Foster; Animation by Rod Scribner; Musical Direction by Carl W. Stalling.

Mama Buzzard instructs her children to bring back some meat for dinner. One bashful buzzard, Beaky (in this film named "Killer"), is reluctant. Mama kicks him out of the nest, telling him to bring back a rabbit. He spots Bugs Bunny reading "Hare Raising Stories," and swoops down for the kill. Bugs radios landing instructions to the buzzard, causing a crash landing. "What's up?" The buzzard tells him he's supposed to bring home a rabbit for dinner. Bugs goes below to "tidy up a bit," but when Beaky takes a peek in his rabbit hole, the bunny, in a shower cap and feminine manner, scolds the buzzard, "You naughty, naughty boy," and whips him with his towel. Beaky chases Bugs, but Bugs sneaks up on the bird, grabs his top knot, and tickles his Adam's apple. The buzzard grabs Bugs and flies him into the sky. The rabbit tickles the buzzard, and the rabbit is dropped—into the skeletal remains of a mule. Thinking the bones are his, Bugs starts crying, "Gruesome, isn't it!" Bugs lifts himself out, but Beaky grabs him again. They go into a jitterbug, and Bugs spins Beaky into the bones. Beaky's momma comes to the scene and asks, "What's happened?" Bugs pulls Beaky from the bones—and receives a kiss from momma buzzard, who calls the rabbit her hero. Bugs, imitating Beaky (a take-off of Mortimer Snerd),replies, "Oh no, no, no ..."

FONEY FABLES

Aug 1; MM; Supervision by I. Freleng; Animation by Richard Bickenback; Story by Michael Maltese; Musical Direction by Carl W. Staling.

Spot gags on storybook characters. The narrator opens a book of "Fairy Tales," and on each page is an new story and another gag. Sleeping Beauty: the prince quietly slips into the room, approaches the dreaming princess and shouts: "Wake up! Wake up, ya lazy good fer nuthin'!" Tom Thumb: a big gooney Tom is asked how he got that way—with Vitamin B-1. The Grasshopper and the Ant: when asked why he's not working, the grasshopper shows his war bonds. Jack and the Beanstalk: a two-headed giant chases Jack, but has to rest because "He's been sick!"; The Wolf in Sheep's Clothing: "The 5th Columnist of his day" preys on unsuspecting sheep, encounters another in disguise. Aladdin and His Lamp: sings "I Dream of Genie with the Light Brown Hair," but to no avail—a picket sign arises from his lamp, stating "Genie On Strike!" The Goose that Lays the Golden Eggs now lays aluminum eggs for National Defense; Old Mother Hubbard shows her poor dog she has none, until the pooch opens the cupboard himself and exposes the doublecrossing food hoarder; This Little Piggy is sung to a little baby who complains (in dialect) "For crying out Pete Sake, Mother! Be Careful! My Corn!"; The Boy Who Cried Wolf is the running gag, and is warned by the narrator to stop. The film ends with his cries of "Wolf!" and laughter—coming from a well-fed wolf seen picking his teeth.

THE DUCKTATORS

Aug 1; LT; Supervision by Norman McCabe; Story by Melvin Millar; Animation by John Carey; Musical Direction by Carl W. Stalling.

In a happy barnyard, Mr. Duck is handing out cigars to announce the arrival of a new chick in the family. Mama Duck's black egg hatches, and out pops a Hitler mustachioed, swastika arm-banded duck shouting "Sieg Heil." Time passes, and the Duck's artistic ambitions only lead to hanging swastika wallpaper. The duck gives public speeches, which many gullible geese listen and agree with, especially one Mussolini-like goose (a title card appears apologizing to all the "nice ducks and geese who may be in the audience"). The Hitler Duck reviews his troops, which include a black duck from the south, and a deathly ill "*Sick*

Heiler." His Storm Troopers literally march through a rain storm, while a dove of peace laments, "What has come to so erase/All thoughts of peace about this place." At the Peace Conference, Hitler duck shreds his agreement and begins to fight. Meanwhile, a Japanese duck rows in from the east, singing "I'm a Japanese Sap-Man." When the dove tries to reason with them, the Ducktators march over him. The dove rolls up his sleeves and begins to beat them up—and the other farm fowl join in to beat the Axis poultry. The dove mounts the Ducktators heads on his wall. A title card ends the film: "If you'd like to make this true, this is all you have to do: For Victory Buy War Bonds and Stamps," closing on the famous Minuteman wartime poster.

THE SQUAWKIN' HAWK
Henery Hawk; Aug 8; MM; Supervision by Chuck Jones.
Little Henery Hawk won't eat the worm his mother is trying to feed him (to the delight of the nervous worm). The junior chickenhawk wants chicken, and his frustrated mother sends him to bed without dinner. Henery can't sleep; he counts sheep that turn into chickens. He sneaks out of his house to get some fowl and immediately crashes into a rooster weather vain. Falling from the henhouse roof, he lands under a sleeping chicken named Hazel. He lifts the bird and walks it out. The rooster discovers Henery, and a chase ensues. Henery's mother rescues her son from the rooster's wrath. Back home, the worm starts making out his last will, but Henery *still* wants chicken—resulting in a big kiss from the worm.

EATIN' ON THE CUFF
Aug 22; LT; Supervision by Robert Clampett; Animation by Virgil Ross;

Story by Warren Foster; Musical Direction by Carl W. Stalling.
A live-action piano player tells us, in rhyme, the story of the Moth and his Flame, a Honey Bee. It's their wedding day, and the Moth goes out to get some breakfast. First, he eats all the clothes in the closets, to the tune of "Yankee Doodle" (shaving the fur off a fox stole, leaving a Hitler mustache and haircut), then down to the bar where he eats all the pants of the men at the counter. His bride is waiting at the altar and, realizing the time, the Moth tries to leave, but is caught in a trap left by an ugly Widow Spider. The man-hungry Spider disguises herself as Veronica Lake (especially difficult due to her bulbous nose) and chases the Moth all over the bar: over sandwiches; on hands playing poker ("Play your Jack!"); finally landing in the drink. Consulting a book, the Spider finds out moths are attracted to flames. The Honey Bee enters just as the Spider gets her hands on the Moth. They duel with their stingers ("Confidentially, she stings!"). The Moth and Bee escape and live happily ever after, but the piano player confides to us, "I could never understand what that cute little Bee ever saw in that Moth. What a dope!" The Moth responds by eating his pants—forcing him to run through the studio in his underwear!

FRESH HARE
Bugs Bunny, Elmer Fudd; Aug 22; MM; Supervision by I. Freleng; Story by Michael Maltese; Animation by Manuel Perez; Musical Direction by Carl W. Stalling.
"WANTED by the Mounted Police: Bugs Bunny, Dead or Alive! (Preferably Dead!)." Elmer Fudd is a Mountie who is following rabbit tracks in the snow. He leaves a carrot by the rabbit's hole, and when the bunny reaches for it, handcuffs him. Bugs turns the tables and cuffs the Mountie to a bomb. Bugs also has the keys, but is too late to prevent the explosion. Elmer arrests Bugs and reads him the charges, which include assault and battery, going through a boulevard stop, triple parking, and conduct unbecoming to a wab-

bit. While he's reading, Bugs swipes his hat and pretends to be his superior—stripping him of his rank and his uniform. Fudd chases Bugs through the snow banks, eventually finding the rabbit insulting a snowman surrogate of Fudd. Bugs punches Elmer in the nose, smashing him into an ice wall rear backward (creating a lovely heart shape in the ice). Unable to follow Bugs into a cave opening, Elmer picks up the rabbit pretending to be his rifle and receives a big kiss. Elmer cries about being a "diswace to the wegiment," and feeling sorry for him Bugs gives himself up. Put to a firing squad, and given one last wish, Bugs sings "I wish I were in Dixie" then goes into a chorus of "Camptown Races" as he, the firing squad, and Elmer become black-faced minstrels. "Fantastic, isn't it?"

THE IMPATIENT PATIENT

Daffy Duck; LT; Sept 5; Supervision by Norman McCabe; Story by Don Christensen; Animation by Vive Risto; Musical Direction by Carl W. Stalling. (The credits for this film, like a doctor's prescription, are in the artists' own handwriting.)
In the swamp, Daffy Duck is a telegram delivery boy with hiccups (and an appropriate gooney hat). Trying to deliver a message to "Chloe," Daffy decides to see if the local M.D., Doctor Jerkyl, can cure his hiccups. Daffy creeps around the haunted house, while the doc is downstairs in the lab making coffee thru elaborate test tubes.

The doctor straps the hiccupping duck to his examination chair, while he drinks a formula consisting of moth balls and pen ink, among other things. Dr. Jerkyl becomes a big goofy monster named Chloe. "Let's you and me *rassle!*" Daffy reads Chloe his telegram, "Happy Birthday to you, signed Frank N. Stein." Chloe chases Daffy around the house. Daffy gets even by spraying Chloe with a formula that turns him into a baby. The baby grabs a hammer, Daffy grabs a mallet, and they both confide to us, "He don't know me very well." Their weapons crash off camera, as a cuckoo clock bird holds up a sign "He Dood It!"

FOX POP

Sept. 5; MM; Supervision by Charles M. Jones.
A Fox sneaks to a farmhouse, steals a radio, and chops it up with an axe. Two crows witnessing this scene, ask him 'why?' In a flashback we learn that the Fox overheard on the radio that ladies will be having foxes around their necks this year. The Fox tries to get into the Sterling Silver Fox Fur Farm. He pretends to be caught in the trap, but the trapper tells him they only want silver foxes—and throws him into the junkyard. There he finds a can of silver paint, and after painting himself, he is quickly accepted at the farm. That night in his cell bunk, his neighbor informs him of a jailbreak that night. He reluctantly goes along with the escape, and when everyone gets out, he goes back. Returning to his cell, he realizes that he's about to be skinned (for Mrs. Van Dough). He uses the key he got from the others to open his cell and escapes again, this time he's pursued by dogs. He runs through the lake, removing his silver color, but the dogs catch him and beat him up anyway. The crows help the fox destroy the radio.

THE DOVER BOYS

Sept 10; MM; Supervision by Charles M. Jones; Story by Ted Pierce; Animation by Robert Cannon; Musical Direction by Carl W. Stalling.
The full on-screen title of this film is THE DOVER BOYS AT PIMENTO UNIVERSITY or THE RIVALS OF ROQUEFORT HALL. Besides being a hilarious spoof of gay 90s dime novels and melodramas, it is also a landmark experiment in limited animation. The characters pop from pose to pose, with a few frames of "smear" action between each position—resulting in a new cartoon "logic" that would be used in Warner cartoons for the next 15 years, making them faster and funnier.

"Pimento University! Pimento U. Good Old P.U." Out and away the most popular fellows at old P.U. are the three Dover Boys: Tom, the big blond fun-loving member of the trio; Dick, a serious long-nosed lad of eighteen summers; and Larry, the roly-poly youngest of the three jerks. They are playing hide and seek with Dainty Dora Standpipe, which gives that blue-skinned coward, bully, cad, and thief Dan Backslide a chance to kidnap Dora for his own. In Backslide's mountain cabin hideout, the Dover Boys beat him to a pulp—but Dora walks off with an old-timer in a bathing suit who has been doing a funny walk (as a running gag) all through the picture.

THE HEP CAT (First Color Looney Tune)

Oct 3; LT; Supervision by Robert Clampett; Story by Warren Foster; Animation by Robert McKimson; Musical Direction by Carl W. Stalling.
This predecessor to Clampett's masterpiece *A Gruesome Twosome* (1945) also uses violence and sex as interchangeable commodities. A dog chasing a cat who considers himself a ladies' man (a feline Victor Mature, in fact) exploits the cat's horniness and tries to lure him with phony sexual bait. After establishing the chase premise, the cat flies into a song and dance explanation of his lust: "I Love Da Goils and Da Goils Love Me" (presumedly a Clampett-Foster original). The central gag is the dog's luring the cat with a hand-puppet of a cute li'l gal kitty. Upon kissing the "kitty," his whole body stiffens into a giant erection, and upon caressing "her," his discovery of the dog's nose in back provokes him to imitate Jerry Colonna declaiming, "Well, something new has been added!" Freud would have a ball with this one, but no more so than the audience.

The cat represents an in-heat but no less musical version of the star of *Notes to You*, (1940) and the dog is almost Willoughby, and almost the *Hare Ribbin'* (1944) and/or the *Ding Dog Daddy* doggies. More music: "Five O'Colock Whistle," "Umbrella Man," "Spring Song (Mendelsohn)." Incidentally, now that (some) Looney Tunes were in color and no longer have to have continuing characters, the distinctions between this and the Merrie Melodies series ceased to be relevant.

THE SHEEPISH WOLF

Oct 17; MM; Supervised by I. Freleng.
A flock of sheep is guarded by a talkative sheepdog who must stay alert to prevent an attack by the wolf. Meanwhile, a Shakespearian wolf is also watching the flock, imagining them as lamb chops and steaks. The wolf disguises as a sheep, mingles with the flock, and lures a lamb with a carrot. He catches the sheepdog instead, who scolds the disguised wolf and kicks him back into the flock. The wolf in sheep's clothing tries to lure another lamb, but a black sheep (with an appropriate southern accent) tells on the wolf and brings the sheepdog running. The dog uses a "wolf call" that brings the wolf running to him, in love. Coming to his senses, the wolf runs, with the sheepdog in pursuit. The wolf disguises as an old grandma, and the dog disguises as Red Riding Hood, and they go through the "What a big nose you have" bit. The dog chases the wolf through the farmer's bales of hay, but the dog gets caught in the stacking machine. Finally, the dog grabs the wolf, boasting to the sheep, "Look fellas, I caught him, I caught him!" The sheep shed their disguises (they're all wolves in disguise) and say "Well, how do you like that?" in unison.

THE DAFFY DUCKEROO

Daffy Duck; Oct 24; LT; Supervision by Norman McCabe; Story by Melvin Millar; Animation by Cal Dalton; Musical Direction by Carl W. Stalling.
Daffy Duck is a Hollywood singing cowboy who leaves Tinseltown to vacation in the real West. Says Daffy, "I want to be a lone ... Ranger." Riding west on his burro, with trailer attached, singing "My Little Buckeroo," he accompanies himself with guitar, piano, and trombone.

He comes across an Indian reservation and falls in love with Daisy June, a pretty duck squaw with a Brooklyn accent. Her giant Indian boyfriend, "Little Beaver," is very jealous and chases the dude. Daffy disguises as an Indian maid, and they "pitchem woo." After a few kisses, his hair piece falls off and the chase resumes. Daffy steals a kiss from Daisy June, while Little Beaver watches—at which Daffy replies, "Oh, well, *you* too," and kisses the Indian brave! They chase through the literally painted desert and the petrified forest. Little Beaver corners Daffy at his trailer and calls for the other Indians to attack. They circle his vehicle and strip his tires, using the rubber for a motor-scooter. The cartoon ends with the patriotic reminder to "Keep It Under 40."

Despite a weak end gag, this is one of McCabe's best cartoons. Social scientists please note: Daffy displays some outrageous bi-sexual behavior in this film.

THE HARE-BRAINED HYPNOTIST

Bugs Bunny, Elmer Fudd; Oct. 31; MM; Supervision by I. Freleng; Story by Michael Maltese; Animation by Philip Monroe; Musical Direction by Carl W. Stalling.

Elmer Fudd is reading "Stalking Wild Game" while walking in the woods. A bear knocks him down, but Fudd uses hypnotism on the grizzly, transforming him into a canary. The bear flies away. Elmer encounters Bugs Bunny and begins to hypnotize him. The rabbit hands Fudd a helium balloon which sends the hunter into the sky, passing the bird-brained bear. Bugs offers to catch Fudd, who crashes to earth, falling through the bunny's open-bottomed basket. Fudd chases Bugs to his hole, and they have a tug of war with his rifle. This frustrates Elmer, who begins to cry "How can I hypnotize you if you don't cooperate?" Bugs relents, but turns the tables on Fudd by hypnotizing the hunter into thinking he's a rabbit. The plan works too well—Elmer suddenly becomes "wacky," resuming the rifle tug of war. Bugs asks, "who's the comedian in this picture?" Elmer sneaks up behind Bugs and force feeds him carrots. Bugs chases the screwball hunter underground, where a hypnotic battle takes place. Fudd returns to normal and runs off, while Bugs takes off— into the air. "I'm due at the airport—I'm the B-19!"

A TALE OF TWO KITTIES

Tweety, Babbit and Castello; Nov 21; MM; Supervision by Robert Clampett; Story by Warren Foster; Animation by Rod Scribner. Musical Direction by Carl W. Stalling.

A slicker cat, Babbit, urges his gullible partner, Catstello, to "get the bird."

Catstello climbs a ladder, which slowly falls apart, eventually walking on two "stilts." Babbit then puts his patsy in a box with a large coil spring, then releases him, causing him to bounce near a sleeping Tweety. For the very first time, Tweety "tawt" he "taw a puddy tat." Each time Catstello pops up, this particularly violent Tweety bird uses various weapons to bat, smash, poke, water squirt, and dynamite the feline. Tweety laments, "Poor puddy tat, he 'crushed' his little head!"

Catstello is next dynamited toward the bird nest. Tweety grabs an apple out of his hand as he flies past, pulling out a worm and eating it (Yecch!). Catstello falls on a barn roof, sliding to a clothes line where he hangs upside down by his toes. Tweety comes along and plays "This Little Piggy," and Catstello falls. Tweety has a heart, however, and throws him a rope—attached to an anvil, which smashes the cat against the ground. Catstello is next fitted with two wooden "wings," and, propelled by a huge elastic band, becomes "A spitfire!" Tweety calls for the Air Raid Warden, who orders the cat shot down. Catstello crash lands on Babbit, but they sneak up on Tweety—who shouts them back, "Turn out those lights!"

MY FAVORITE DUCK

Daffy Duck, Porky Pig; Dec 5; LT; Supervision by Charles M. Jones; Story by Michael Maltese; Animation by Rudolph Larriva; Musical Direction by Carl W. Stalling.

Porky is camping out. Rowing through

the lake singing "Moonlight Bay," he is joined by another voice—Daffy Duck. Porky finds a campsite, but every spot he picks to pitch his tent is occupied by Daffy, who informs him via signs and billboards that hunting season is closed, "No Duck Shooting—Don't Even *Molest* A Duck!" The only free spot Porky finds is under the lake. Back on dry land, Porky makes breakfast. The pig opens an egg left by Daffy which contains a baby eagle. The father eagle smashes a pan over Porky's face and retrieves his child. Daffy reminds Porky there is a $5000 fine for touching a duck. Porky goes fishing and catches a nap in his rowboat. Daffy turns the boat upside down, then flies upward, yanking the string. Porky "dives" into the air, "swimming" upside down. Porky chases Daffy into a cave, and decides to smoke him out using two TNT sticks the duck provides. After an explosion, Porky gets his rifle, but Daffy pulls out the hunting signs again—but now "Duck Season Is Open!" Porky chases Daffy around a mountaintop, when suddenly the film breaks! On a white screen Daffy walks out to explain how the picture ends, with him beating Porky to a pulp. A hook pulls Daffy off screen, and Porky soon marches across—a beaten Daffy in tow.

DING DOG DADDY

Dec 5; MM; Supervision by I. Freleng; Story by Tedd Pierce; Animation by Gerry Chiniquy; Musical Direction by Carl W. Stalling.
A shy, but goofy dog (voiced by Pinto Colvig) is watching two love birds ("Let's not get nosey, bub!"), and decides its time to get himself a girl. After being rejected by an Afkan, he goes after another female—a garden statue he mistakes for a girl named "Daisy." He kisses the statue, just as a lightning bolt hits it. He's never had a kiss like that and becomes madly in love. Meanwhile a vicious bulldog makes his presence known and kicks the lovelorn mutt out. The dog tries to sneak back in, but at every turn is the bulldog. He gets near the statue, but kisses the bulldog instead. He tries to tunnel under the garden, but comes up

under the bulldog and rides him on his back. This gives him a headache, and the dog takes two aspirin. Finally getting near the statue once more, the dog kisses "Daisy," and lightning strikes twice!

The statue is taken away by men collecting scrap metal for Victory. He follows their truck to a muntions factory. He watches "Daisy" become an artillery shell, but loses track of her. Surrounded by hundreds of ammunition supplies, "Daisy" falls into his arms. He returns her to the garden and gives her a kiss, which explodes in his face. Overjoyed, the dog exclaims, "She hasn't changed a bit!"

CASE OF THE MISSING HARE

Bugs Bunny; Dec 12; MM; Supervision by Charles M. Jones; Story by Ted Pierce; Animation by Ken Harris; Musical Direction by Carl W. Stalling.
At the Bijou theater, Ala Bama, the world renowned magician, begins his show today. The fat magician is personally posting signs for the show and puts one over Bugs Bunny's hollow tree home. The rabbit asks, "Look, Doc, do I go around nailing signs over your house?" The magician offers the bunny a blackberry pie—in the face. "Of course, you realize this means war!"

Ala begins his show by pulling a rabbit out of his hat, but Bugs pops out of his shirt collar, fuming, "You didn't expect to see me again, eh Svengali?" Bugs helps out by pulling himself out of the top hat, kissing the magician, and tying his mustache into a braid. Bugs disguises a little boy volunteer from the audience to participate in the next trick—to sit in a basket while Ala puts swords through it. Bugs makes painful noises as each sword is pushed through the basket. The magician gets wise and chases the bunny with a large sword. Bugs stops him by playing "Red Light, Green Light, 1-2-3." They perform a fencing match, but Bugs is up in the balcony applauding the action on stage. Ala shoots the rabbit, but the bunny pops out of the magic hat on stage, gives Ala an exploding cigar, then smashes a fruit pie in his face ("If I dood it, I get a whippin'—I dood it!"). The rabbit sings "Aloha Oe" as he lowers into the magic hat.

1943

COAL BLACK AND DE SEBBEN DWARFS

Jan 16; MM; Supervision by Robert Clampett; Story by Warren Foster; Animation by Rod Scribner; Musical Direction by Carl W. Stalling.

Coal Black is a Bob Clampett masterpiece, and certainly one of the greatest Warner Bros. cartoons ever made. A blackface parody of Disney's *Snow White*, told in rhyme, updated with wartime themes, sex, and hot jazz.

A mammy tells her child the story of "So White," beginning with the Wicked Queen who is hoarding sugar, coffee, auto tires, and scrap metal. With a family crest consisting of dice and switchblades, she asks her magic mirror "to send me a prince, about six feet tall." Prince Chawmin' (who has a pair of dice as his two front teeth) thinks the queen "sure is a fright/but her gal So White is dynomite!" The prince jitterbugs with the sexy So White (voice of Vivian Dandridge), leading the Queen to call Murder Inc. to "blackout So White." Murder Inc. kidnaps So White (truck reads: We rub out anybody $1.00; Midgets 1/2 price; Japs FREE!), but leaves her in the woods unharmed. She finds the seven dwarfs are now in the army. The queen visits their army camp, selling a poisioned candied apple to So White. "There's only one thing that'll remedy this/and that's Prince Chawmin' and his dynamite kiss!" The prince gives her his special "Rosebud" kiss, which doesn't work. The little "dopey" dwarf awakens So White with his special hot kiss, but "that is a military secret!"

CONFUSIONS OF A NUTZY SPY

Porky Pig; Jan 23; LT; Supervision by Norman McCabe; Story by Don

Christensen; *Animation by I. Ellis; Musical Direction by Carl W. Stalling.*

From "Ye Towne Cooler" (20 degrees cooler inside), Constable Porky Pig and his dog Eggbert follow the trail of the spy "Missing Lynx," a master of disguise.

Porky questions a disguised Lynx, while Eggbert finds his disguise kit (which includes a Hitler mask). Lynx plans to blow up a bridge, but Eggbert grabs the bag with the ticking bomb. The dog follows Porky and Lynx into a cave where the bomb seems to fizzle out until Lynx, in disgust, hits it. Dead, in the clouds on his way to the afterlife, Lynx falls over, his feet making the "V" shape on the iris out.

This film spends its first three minuts devoted to visual gags: the Fingerprint Dept. has dirty handprints all over it; Exhibit "A" is a large letter "A" with a tag on it; "Crime Club" is a "club" hung on a wall; wanted posters include one with a pin-up girl, noted "And We Ain't Kiddin', Brother! signed U.S. Army!"

PIGS IN A POLKA _{ACADEMY AWARD NOMINEE}

Feb 2; MM; Supervision by Isadore Freleng; Musical Supervision by Carl W. Stalling.

A parody of the "Three Little Pigs" set to classical music a la *Fantasia*. A "Deems Taylor" wolf introduces the story and music, mainly from Brahm's *Hungarian Rhapsody*.

The Pigs build their houses (of sticks, straw, and bricks) to the music. The wolf enters the scene disguised as a gypsy woman who lures pigs 1 and 2 behind a rock. After a fight, the pigs emerge dancing in gypsy garb. The wolf chases them and sets the straw house on fire, then knocks the house of sticks (matchsticks) over. The wolf chases the pigs to the brick house.

When the wolf uses his breath to blow the brick house down the pigs send out a bottle of mouthwash. The wolf pretends to be a homeless old woman playing violin in the snow. Pigs 1 and 2 let the "woman" in, but smart Pig 3 gets wise and flips the violin record attached to the wolf's back. Suddenly, the wolf is doing the Hungarian kick dance, and his disguise comes off. The wolf chases the pigs around the house, finally knocks himself out, and falls down the elevator shaft.

TORTOISE WINS BY A HARE
Bugs Bunny; Feb 20; MM; Supervision by Robert Clampett; Story by Warren Foster; Animation by Robert McKimson; Musical Direction by Carl W. Stalling.
One of Bob Clampett's best and one of Mel Blanc's most frantic voice jobs. The cartoon begins with stock footage of the race in *Tortoise Beats Hare* (1941), which Bugs is reviewing on his movie projector. Bugs is frantic: "A turtle beating me, a rabbit! Why, I'm in the pink! I'm an athlete! I've got an athlete's legs! I've even got athlete's foot!" Disguising himself as an old-timer, Bugs visits Cecil the turtle and asks him how he does it. The turtle recommends his "air-flow chasis." Bugs goes home, builds a streamlined metal turtle shell, and challenges the turtle to another race. The gambling ring says, "We're betting everything we got on the rabbit to win. In fact, we don't even think the turtle will finish!" As the race begins, Bugs runs to a hollow tree where he slips into his "turtle-shaped" streamlined shell. The rabbit gangsters mistake Bugs for the turtle and clobber him. Disguised as a rabbit, the turtle passes the bunny. Bugs breaks free and runs, but the rabbits bombard him with bullets and bombs. Bugs freaks out ("Look, folks! I'm in the lead! I'm gonna win! Look at me go!"). The gangsters pin him down, letting the disguised turtle win. Bugs rips off his shell and screams, "YOU FOOLS!! WHAT ARE YOU DOING? I'M THE RABBIT!!" sticking his cotton-tail in their faces. The gangsters reply in unison, "Now he tells us" and blow their brains out!

TO DUCK OR NOT TO DUCK
Daffy Duck, Elmer Fudd; Mar 6; LT; Supervision by Charles M. Jones; Story by Tedd Pierce; Animation by Robert Cannon; Musical Direction by Carl W. Stalling.
Daffy Duck is swimming and bicycling through the sky over the swamp where Elmer Fudd is hunting fowl. Elmer shoots, Daffy fakes being shot and falls. Elmer introduces himself to the duck as a "great sportsman." Daffy heckles him about that: "You don't know the meaning of fair play... You and your bullets, and your shotgun, and your knife, and your duck call. What protection have I got? A bullet-proof vest," opening his chest to reveal a steel lining. Daffy challenges Elmer to a boxing match, which is immediately set up for an audience of ducks. The referee introduces Elmer ("laughing hysterically, "He's a dog. You can have him") and Daffy ("Good to his mother"), and he tells them to fight clean. The crowd roars, "Oh, brother!" as the referee and Daffy knock Elmer out while demonstrating all the things you *can't* do in the ring. In the bleachers, Elmer's pooch observes, "There's something awfully screwy about this fight, or my name isn't Laramore. And it isn't!" When the referee asks them to shake hands, Daffy mallets Fudd. As round one begins, Elmer is already out cold. Daffy is declared the champ, but Elmer laments, "I thought you said no rough stuff." Elmer gets his turn to kick, punch, and poke the two birds.

FIFTH COLUMN MOUSE
Mar 6; MM; Supervision by I. Freleng. Musical Direction by Carl W. Stalling.
When the cat's away, the mice do play. Here, the mice are swimming in the sink to the tune of "Ain't We Got Fun." The cat bursts in and attacks the mice. The cat tempts one mouse with cheese and offers the rodent all he wants if he will organize the others to be his slaves.

The next day, the mice are shown waiting hand and foot on the cat. When the cat has a craving for a "nice, fat, tender mouse," the mice run and organize an army, to the tune of "We Did It Before and We Can Do It Again." The mice construct a mechanical bulldog to chase the cat. One mouse shaves the cat, leaving only the dot-dot-dot-dash pattern (the V for Victory in Morse code). The cat runs from the house, and the mice claim victory: "We dood it!"

FLOP GOES THE WEASEL

Mar 20; MM; Supervision by Charles M. Jones; Musical Direction by Carl W. Stalling.

A black mammy chicken is knitting and singing when she feels a tapping from her egg in the nest below. In Morse code, it reads, "Kill de fatted worm, yo is practically a mammy!" The delighted momma chicken runs out of the hen house, "One fatted worm comin' right up!" Meanwhile, a weasel steals the egg and brings it to his kitchen, where he is preparing an egg breakfast. When he cracks open the egg, the baby chick comes out and thinks the weasel is his mother. The weasel still plans to eat him, but goes along with the gag. He shows the chick his baby picture and tells him it's a mirror. First they play hide and seek, and the weasel hides the chick in the oven—but the chick gives the weasel a hot-foot. Next they play tag, the weasel trying to tag the chick with an axe. The chick tags first—with a mallet! The chick offers the weasel some pepper to pour on his tail to catch him, but the weasel inhales it, becoming a sneezing weasel. Confused, the weasel sticks his finger in an electric socket. His sneezing becomes so strong, he backs himself into the stove, which forms a throne. Sneezing again, he falls into the washer, waving a flag of surrender in the spin cycle. In his real home at last, the chick tells his story, but mammy doesn't believe him. The weasel, in bandages, backs him up, "He ain't just whistling *Dixie*, mammy!"

HOP AND GO

Mar 27; LT; Supervision by Norman McCabe; Animation by Cal Dalton; Story by Melvin Millar; Musical Direction by Carl W. Stalling.

Bouncing into the picture, singing "Hippety Hop," is a kangaroo, Claude Hopper (voiced by Pinto Colvig), the "world's champeen hopper." Overhearing his claim of being "the best durn hopper in the whole world" are Andy and Sandy, two Scottish rabbits who decide to "take him down a peg or two."

Claude shows the bunnies a certificate to prove himself (it reads "This Guy Is A Goof!"). They challenge him to a long distance hop. When Claude jumps, the rabbits hitch a ride on his tail, then hop off ahead of him. Frustrated, Claude empties his pouch of its pots and pans and jumps again. The bunnies stick his tail in an adhesive, causing him to crash into his own junk pile. The rabbits drive Claude crazy, making him jump all over a field and then landing in a lake. They help Claude by coaching him. They stuff a huge box in his pouch as ballast, and propel him via a seesaw high into the sky, past army planes, and smashing the "price ceiling." Heading downward, Claude lights a match to see where he is, bringing on air raid searchlights and aerial bombs. Claude then notices the box he's carrying is full of dynamite. He crash lands and the box explodes, destroying Tokyo! "I guess we know who's champeen now!"

SUPER RABBIT

Bugs Bunny; Apr 3; MM; Supervision by Charles M. Jones; Story by Tedd Pierce; Animation by Ken Harris; Musical Direction by Carl W. Stalling.

A spoof of the Superman character and the popular Paramount Superman animated cartoons.

"Look, up there in the sky! It's a bird...Naw, it ain't no bird, it's a dive bomber. It's Bugs Bunny, the Super Rabbit, the rabbit of tomorrow!" The origin of SuperBugs is retold, beginning in the lab of Prof. Canafrazz, where Bugs is a laboratory animal and the doctor is preparing a "super-vitamized, locked-in flavorized," modern, super carrot! Bugs takes a chomp and can now, "leap the highest buildings, etcetera, etcetera..." Noting a newspaper story on Cottontail Smith, a Texas rabbit hater, Bugs goes into the phone booth to change. First coming out as Mary and her little lamb, Bugs quickly changes into a blue caped sweatshirt with a flowing red cape ("Ta-daaa!"). He flies to "Deepinahata, Texas." "The better to carry out my mission, I shall assume the disguise of a mild-mannered forest creature"— with glasses, natch! Bugs hops alongside Smith and his horse. With each hop, they exchange places with each other. Smith gets wise to the rabbit and fires his gun, leaving only a rabbit-shaped pile of bullets. Bugs offers to have Smith try a cannon on him. The bunny uses the cannon ball like a basketball. Bugs transforms Cottontail and his horse into cheerleaders ("Bricka-Bracka Fire-cracker, Sis-Boom-Bah, Bugs Bunny, Bugs Bunny, Rah! Rah! Rah!"). Cot-tontail chases Bugs in an airplane, but Bugs has them bailing out. In need of a recharge, Bugs drops his super carrots and falls back to earth. Cottontail Smith and his horse have eaten the fallen carrots and are ready to eat the bunny. But Bugs runs into a phone booth and emerges as "a real Super-man," a U.S. Marine. "I'm sorry, fellas, I can't play with ya anymore. I've got some important work to do!"

THE UNBEARABLE BEAR

Sniffles; Apr 17; MM; Supervision by Charles M. Jones; Story by Michael Maltese; Animation by Robert Cannon; Musical Direction by Carl W. Stalling.
Four plot elements make up this car-toon. 1. An English burglar fox has entered the home of Police Officer and Mrs. Bear. 2. Mr. Bear, just returned home from being out late drinking with the boys, does not want to wake his wife and is trying to catch the fox very quietly. 3. Mrs. Bear, his nagging wife, is sleepwalking. 4. Sniffles returns to the screen as a noisy, fast-talking blab-bermouth who won't shut up.

Highlights include the burglar telling Sniffles he's Robin Hood (which evokes a classic "Are you reeeeally Robin Hood?") and letting the mouse assist him in "robbing the rich." Sniffles turns on the radio, almost waking the house. When Mrs. Bear starts sleep-walking, she grabs the fox, washes him, and hangs him to dry. In the end, Offi-cer Bear hits his wife, thinking she's the burglar, with an umbrella in which the fox was hiding. The blow wakes her from her sleepwalking. She thinks her husband just handed her a fox stole and forgives him though Sniffles almost spills the beans!

THE WISE QUACKING DUCK

Daffy Duck; May 1; LT; Supervision by Robert Clampett; Story by Warren Foster; Animation by Phil Monroe; Musical Direction by Carl W. Stalling.
The duck at his daffiest! Mr. Meek has the job of killing Daffy Duck for tonight's dinner with Mrs. Meek, "Sweetie Puss" ("If I don't roast a duck, she'll cook my goose!"). Sneaking up on the fowl, he raises his axe, but the duck surprises him, shouting, "Watch it, Bub!" Chasing Daffy behind a haystack, Mr. Meek takes another swing with the axe blade, provoking the duck into throwing ketchup and screaming, "He broke my little head!" Pushing his head into his collar, the duck writhes around like a headless chicken ("Gruesome, isn't it?"). Inside the house, Mr. Meek is depressed over the killing. Daffy offers him a fresh cup of coffee ("Buck up, B-B eyes. Have a swig of swamp water!"). Daffy gives him a few "lumps," and some cream, on his head, and Meek chases him around the house. Daffy dive bombs the man with eggs, smashing dishes, simulating an air attack. Meek burns up (frying an egg on his bald pate). Daffy runs for it, but smashes his beak into Meek's gun. Giving up, Daffy does a strip tease (revealing his boxer shorts) and kisses Meek, causing him to blush. Daffy escapes, returning to the front door disguised as a "Jerry Colonna" swami who paints Meek's palm red and reads the "bumps" on his head. Daffy runs around the house, smashing his beak again into Meek's rifle ("Oh, no! Not twice in the same picture!"). This time Meek blasts Daf-fy's feathers off, shoves him in the oven, and turns up the heat full blast. Hearing the duck's hideous scream, Meek opens the oven and finds Daffy basting himself. "Now you're cooking with gas!" he shouts.

GREETINGS BAIT   ACADEMY AWARD NOMINEE

May 15; MM; Supervision by I. Freleng; Story by Tedd Pierce; Animation by Manuel Perez; Musical Direction by Carl Stalling.
A sequel to *The Wacky Work* (1941). A fisherman lowers his line into the water, with the Wacky Worm (a Jerry Colonna

caricature) as bait. The worm puts on a bathing cap, goes to the bottom of the lake, and sets up "Joe's," the worm attracting fish by lying down between two pieces of bread.

The worm tries to lure a goofy fish with a show of aerial acrobatics. He urges the fish to try it. ("Don't be so reluctant, Dragon!") When the fish tries it, he's pulled up right away. Dressed as a mermaid, the worm lures another fish (singing "Trade Winds"). A crab chases the worm, and the wiggler ties the crustacean's extended eyes around a treasure chest. The worm later eludes the crab by disguising itself as a sea horse.

The worm challenges the crab to a fight. For the benefit of those in the audience "with faint hearts, weak stomachs, and 4-F ratings" the camera moves above the surface. The fisherman, Jerry Colonna, pulls up his beaten worm and states, "Ah, yes! Embarrassing, isn't it?"

TOKIO JOKIO

May 15; LT; Supervision by Cpl. Norman McCabe; Animation by I. Ellis; Story by Don Christensen; Musical Direction: Carl W. Stalling.
The film begins with scratchy lines on a blank screen, indicating that what we are about to see is a captured Japanese newsreel. What follows is an unfunny spot-gag newsreel spoof about the latest in Japanese warfare, sports, and homefront activities. The whole joke here is in the offensive Japanese caricatures, which presumably were a laugh riot in 1943.

"Nippon News" has its own "Pathe" rooster, who warbles "Cock-a-doodle doo, please!" Japan's Finest Air Raid Siren is shown as a Jap getting pins in his behind and screaming. Honorable Air Craft Spotter puts "spots" on planes! Fire Prevention Headquarters is burned down! A warning about incendiary bombs shows a Jap roasting weenies in flames, then literally "losing face"! Kitchen Hints: Prof. Tojo shows us how to eat a ration card sandwich. Fashion Styles of the Week: Japanese Victory Suit with no cuffs, no pleats, no lapels, no suit! The World of Sports presents the Japanese King of Swat,

who misses hitting a fly (housefly). During an air raid a skunk wears an air mask when next to a Jap. Flashes from the Axis is a visit to celebrated ruins including Mussolini. Inside a submarine, the Japs are playing pinball and looking at peep shows. A mine sweeper (with broom) explodes, leaving sign "Regrettable incident, please!"

JACK-WABBIT AND THE BEANSTALK

Bugs Bunny; June 12; MM; Supervision by I. Freleng; Animation by Jack Bradbury; Story by Michael Maltese; Musical Direction by Carl W. Stalling.
"Once upon a time, on top of the beanstalk in Giantland, there was a garden. In this garden grew a certain vegetable that a certain rabbit had heard about. So..."

The Giant catches Bugs Bunny in the act of chopping carrots in his victory garden. Instead of running, Bugs slaps the dopey giant with his glove and challenges him to a duel with pistols. Bugs tricks the giant into 20 paces; unfortunately, 20 giant steps brings the goofy colossus all the way around the world. The giant captures the bunny under a glass. Bugs gets his attention with a demonstration of his latest scientific discovery, "The Little Gem Glass Cutter." The rabbit escapes, leaving a notice "Back in 15 minutes." The giant awaits the next demonstration, then catches on. "They can't outsmart me 'cause I'm a moron." When the giant grabs Bugs, the rabbit reads the lines on his palm ("I'll bet you're a regular Don Ju-wan!"). Climbing into his ear to give him some pointers, Bugs abuses his ear drum, walks through his head, and runs into his hairline, where he starts a fire. Bugs makes a run for the beanstalk, which has an elevator in it. Pretending to be an elevator operator, he instructs the giant to use the stairs. The giant falls from Giantland, creating a hugh canyon on the earth below. The giant gets up, telling Bugs to watch that first step, "It's a lulu!"

THE ARISTO CAT

Hubie and Bertie; June 19; MM; Supervision by Charles M. Jones; Story by Tedd Pierce; Animation by Rudy

Larriva; Musical Direction by Carl W. Stalling.

Meadows, the butler, is charged with looking after Pussy, the pampered and spoiled cat who has his own room in the mansion. The cat abuses Meadows by squirting grapefruit in his eye and leaving soap on the floor for him to trip on.

Fed up, Meadows leaves the cat to fend for himself. A book falls from the shelf, "Behavior of Cats by F. E. Line," and Pussy reads it, learning that cats eat mice. He encounters Hubie the mouse and is frightened, not realizing this is a mouse. Hubie and his sidekick, Bert, take advantage of this situation by raiding the house of it cheese. They help the cat find a mouse by pointing out a bulldog in the yard as a big one. Pussy tries to eat Rover with two pieces of bread, but gets punched into the library. The book falls down again, opening to a page with pictures of a dog and a mouse. Getting wise, the cat chases the mice, but runs into the dog, who beats him up.

The cat wakes up in his giant bed, relieved. "What an incredible dream!" The bulldog and the mice, also under the covers, agree. "Yeah, wasn't it?" Heavily stylized abstract backgrounds highlight this cartoon.

YANKEE DOODLE DAFFY

Porky Pig, Daffy Duck; July 3; LT; Supervision by I. Freleng; Animation by Richard Bickenbach; Story by Tedd Pierce; Musical Direction by Carl W. Stalling.

Porky Pig, a talent agent for Smeller Productions, is trying to sneak out to go on vacation. Daffy Duck pushes the Pig back into his office and forces him to give his client, a little black duck with a large lollypop named Sleepy Lagoon, an audition.

Daffy tells Porky how he'll open the act with "I'm Just Wild About Harry," then do a banjo solo ("Three Cheers for Father"). Porky tries to slip out, but at every turn Daffy is demonstrating another part of Sleepy's act. Daffy does Carmen Miranda, but Porky slams the door in his face. Opening each door in his office, he finds Daffy

in another guise: Pagliacci singing "Laugh, Clown, Laugh," bronco-busting while singing "I'm a Cowboy." Porky locks the duck in a safe and escapes to the airport. He discovers Daffy is his pilot, singing, "We watch the skyways..." Porky jumps from the plane, but Daffy is his parachute, singing "Angel in Disguise." Landing on a roof, Daffy pursues Porky down the fire escape, singing the "William Tell Overture." Back in the office Daffy performs a wild acrobatic finale that includes juggling, riding a unicycle, etc. Porky gives in and lets Sleepy perform. Strange ending has the little duck performing an opera solo, then going into a coughing fit.

WACKIKI WABBIT

Bugs Bunny; July 3; MM; Supervision by Charles M. Jones; Story by Tedd Pierce; Animation by Ken Harris; Musical Direction by Carl W. Stalling.

Two castaways, one thin, one fat, are adrift on a raft. They are so hungry they imagine each other as food. Just as one of them offers his foot for a snack, they spot an island. They swim to it. The first food they see is Bugs Bunny, and they chase Bugs, who does a native dance and asks, "What's up, Doc?" in native tongue. His wild jungle gyrations cause the pair to join the dance. The rabbit slips away. Referring to a book of native customs which says that natives dive for coins, the castaways drop a coin in a stew pot, but Bugs steals the whole pot! They find the rabbit bathing in the pot, singing "Tradewinds." The castaways set their dinner table while singing "We're gonna have roast rabbit!" Bugs sneaks off to his tree-top abode where he takes a chicken, attaches strings to it, and returns it to the stew pot. The castaways serve the bird, which Bugs brings to life with his puppeteering skills. The castaways tug on the strings, bringing Bugs out of hiding. He and the chicken escape. The castaways spot an ocean liner in the distance and are euphoric. Bugs comes by to wish them "Bon voyage." They become so confused they are soon wishing Bugs "Farewell." The bunny sails off on the ship. The castaways chase each other, one imagining his companion as a hot dog, the other as a hamburger.

PORKY PIG'S FEAT

Porky Pig, Daffy Duck; July 17; LT; Supervision by Frank Tashlin; Story by Melvin Millar; Animation by Phil Monroe; Musical Direction by Carl W. Stalling.

"Any similarity between this hotel and other hotels, living or dead, is purely coincidental." In the Broken Arms Hotel, Porky Pig is reading the itemized bill for the room he and Daffy Duck have been sharing. The bill includes charges for "One Louie XVI Bed (without Louie)," "Air (for Breathing)," and "Goodwill." The poor duck has just lost all their money gambling with the hotel's porter. Porky tells the manager that Daffy will be right back with the money. "I hope so," says the manager, with Daffy outside the door. The duck leaps to his own defense. "Insulting my integrity, ay fatso! Insinuating I'd flee this flea-bitten dump, any fatso? Intimating I'd abscond with your financial renumerations, ay fatso?" He shoves his head deep into the manager's face. "Hey, look! A Dick Tracy character, Prune Face!" The manager locks the two in their room, "until you pay." Daffy pulls the rug from under the manager, sending him falling down the spiral staircase. Porky and Daffy tie sheets together and slide to the sidewalk. Porky gets a hot-foot that sends them rocketing back. They try a rope, swinging to another building, but the manager swings them back. Months later, they are still prisoners. They call their hero, Bugs Bunny, who asks them which gags they pulled. They've tried them all. Bugs, chained next door, concurs. "Don't work, do they?"

TIN PAN ALLEY CATS

July 17; MM; Supervision by Bob Clampett; Story by Warren Foster; Aniamtion: Rod Scribner; Musical Direction by Carl W. Stalling.

A "Fats Waller" cat shuns the advice of the Uncle Tomcat Mission, which warns him away from that den of iniquity, the Kit Kat Club. He will be "tempted by wine, women, and song," but the skat cat replies, "Wot's de matter wit dat?" Inside, the joint is jumpin' to a jazzy version of "Nagasaki." A trumpet player offers to send him "out of this world" with his hot licks. The cat gets higher and higher, finally landing in a colorized version of "Wackyland," updated with caricatures of Hitler, Stalin, and Japanese enemies. He also meets a tiny elastic "Rubber Band." Screaming to leave ("Gabriel, blow that horn!") the cat returns to the swing club, bolts out the door, and joins the Uncle Tomcat Mission band. The preachers are puzzled: "Wot's de matter wit him?"

SCRAP HAPPY DAFFY

Daffy Duck; Aug 21; LT; Supervision by Frank Tashlin; Animation by Art Davis; Story by Don Christensen; Musical Direction by Carl W. Stalling.

At Daffy Duck's Scrap Pile, the duck is yodeling and climbing mountains of metal trash, boasting in song, "We're In To Win."

Meanwhile, in Germany, Hitler is screaming with anger over Daffy's patriotism and orders his troops to "Destroy that scrap pile!" A submarine fires a torpedo containing a hungry, metal-eating goat. Daffy encounters the hiccupping goat and gives him a bromo seltzer. Spotting his swastika, Daffy learns that "This tin-termite is a Nazi!"

The goat chases Daffy and butts him into a tree. Daffy is weakened from the battle, the spirits from his patriotic past recount their heroic deeds and remind him, "Americans don't give up!" Inspired, Daffy rockets into the sky and becomes a "Super American" (complete with cape and boots), defeats the goat, and fights back the German submarine heavy artillery. Suddenly, Daffy awakens: "It was all a dream!" But above him, a chorus of German soldiers shout, as they sit in their sub on top of the scrap heap, "Next time you dream, include us out!"

HISS AND MAKE UP

Sept. 11; MM; Supervision by I. Freleng; Animation by Gerry Chiniquy; Story by Michael Maltese; Musical Direction by Carl W. Stalling.

Roscoe the dog and Wellington the cat are fighting again. Granny lays down the law. If they fight once more, they will be thrown out in the snow. Granny goes to bed with the warning, "Not one peep!"

Roscoe sets a dozen mechanical mice loose around the house and awakens Granny, but Wellington covers before she can notice anything. Wellington marks the house with hundreds of dirty dog paw prints (to the tune of Raymond Scott's "Powerhouse"), then rings for Granny. The dog, in an air raid warden helmet, orders Granny, "Put out that light!" before she can spot the mess.

Roscoe puts feathers in Wellington's mouth and hides the canary. Granny is shocked and beats the cat until the canary reappears. Wellington puts foam on the dog, and Granny yells, "Mad dog, mad dog!" while she hits the mongrel. The cat and dog resume their fighting, stopping only when they hear Granny approaching. The canary has had enough and creates a ruckus, causing Granny to come downstairs. Wellington and Roscoe try to stop the bird, but Granny blames the mess on the two fighting pets. Thrown out in the snow, the dog asks the cat, "How can you smile?" Wellington opens his wide grin. The canary is trapped in his mouth!

A CORNY CONCERTO

Bugs Bunny, Elmer Fudd; Sept 18; MM; Supervision by Robert Clampett; Story by Frank Tashlin; Animation by Robert McKimson; Musical Direction by Carl W. Stalling.

A parody of Disney's *Fantasia*, set in "Corny-Gee Hall." Elmer Fudd (a la Deems Taylor) introduces "A Tale of the Vienna Woods" in which we listen to the "whippering whythm of the woodwinds, as it wolls awound and awound... and it comes out here!"

Porky and his dog (a pointer) are hunting for "that *!?@# rabbit!" Throwing carrot remains into his "Rabbit Rubbish" receptacle is Bugs Bunny, who instructs Porky's pet, "It ain't polite to point!" Porky chases Bugs until an angry squirrel gets the pig's rifle and shoots. All three characters take a fall, Bugs pretending to be shot. Removing the rabbit's paws from his chest reveals the bunny's brassiere! Now in a ballerina leotard, Bugs ties the two boobs (Porky and his dog) with his bra and pirouettes into the horizon.

The "Blue Danube" tells an "ugly duckling" story of a little black duck who tries to join a family of swans. A vulture watching the clan kidnaps the swans and rejects the duck giving him a 4-F rating. The black duck uses a "cartoon license" to rescue the birds, handing the vulture a keg of gun powder. He removes the cloud he's resting on, dropping the bird to an exploding finale.

FIN N' CATTY

Oct. 23; MM; Supervision by Charles M. Jones; Animation by Ben Washam; Story by Michael Maltese; Musical Direction by Carl W. Stalling.

This cartoon is summed up in its introduction. "As everyone knows, goldfish must have water in order to exist. Goldfish hate cats. On the other hand, cats hate water, but need goldfish to exist. So..."

So a wild chase ensues between a water-hating cat, who must run to the paper towels if he gets even a drop on him, and a clever goldfish who wears a derby. The cat tries to suck water out of the goldfish bowl, but the fish has his finger in the hose. The fish puts flypaper over the paper towels, causing a sticky situation for the cat. An unguarded moment out of his fish bowl traps the goldfish, who becomes delirious and runs a gamut of stylized backgrounds to the cat's mouth. He thinks he's in a swimming pool. He escapes the jaws of death and flies to the bathroom shower. The cat follows, accidently locks himself in the water filled chamber, and begins to like it! We end on a shot of the cat sleeping in the fishbowl, the fish living in a drinking glass.

FALLING HARE

Bugs Bunny; Oct 30; MM; Supervision by Robert Clampett; Story by Warren Foster; Animation by Rod Scribner; Musical Direction by Carl W. Stalling.
At a U.S. Army air field, Bugs Bunny is sitting under an airplane reading "Victory Through Hare Power," and laughing over the thought of gremlins, which the book says are those little men who wreck planes with "dia-boli-cal saba-togee." The bunny hears a noise, and upon investigation spots a little orange man with a mallet, hammering a blockbuster bomb. Bugs grabs the mallet and takes a swing, then realizes his mistake ("What am I doing?"). The little man disappears. Bugs speculates, "Hey, could that have been a gremlin?" The little orange character shouts a reply, "I ain't Vendel Villkie!" Bugs chases the gremlin into the airplane and gets knocked about. The gremlin starts the plane, then teases the bunny from the outside. Bugs runs to break down the door, the gremlin gives way, and the rabbit finds himself standing in mid-air. Running back into the plane, Bugs slips through the fuselage on banana peels and goes out the other door. The rabbit chases the gremlin, but is caught in the bomb bay as the gremlin steers for a skyscraper. Bugs takes control of the plane and pulls it straight up, then forces it into a dive. The rabbit turns white and flattens against the floor. The plane sputters and stops just before hitting the ground. The gremlin apologizes, "Sorry, folks! We ran out of gas!" Adds the rabbit, "You know how it is with these A-Cards!"

INKI AND THE MINAH BIRD

Iniki; Nov 13; Inki; MM; Supervision by Charles M. Jones; Animation by Robert Cannon, Shamus Culhane; Musical Direction by Carl W. Stalling.
Inki is hunting in the jungle and, while chasing the minah bird, meets up with a hungry lion. The lion chases Inki into his little hut. He tries to stop the beast by throwing a steak at him. The mysterious minah bird is inside the lion's mouth and catches and eats the steak!

The lion chases the minah bird into a haystack—which walks off, getting smaller and smaller, until only two strands of straw remain and then disappear! Meanwhile, Inki, hiding from the lion, accidentally backs into his mouth! Inki runs out of the lion's jaws, with the big cat's false teeth. Chasing Inki, the lion finds two pieces of straw, which magically become the minah bird. The lion chases Inki and the bird in and out of rabbit holes and barrels until the minah bird tosses the lion, turning him into a haystack and making him disappear. Inki is relieved and extends his hand to the black bird, who hands the little hunter two pieces of straw. They magically become the lion. The lion chases Inki into the sunset, while the minah bird smiles, the lion's false teeth in his grinning beak!

DAFFY—THE COMMANDO

Daffy Duck; Nov 28; LT; Supervision by I. Freleng; Story by Michael Maltese; Animation by Ken Champin; Musical Direction by Carl W. Stalling.
In a Nazi foxhole, German commandant Von Vulture receives a message from the "Gestinko Gestapo." "If vun more kommando gets through, it's your ka-rear!" Hearing a plane overhead, Von Vulture calls his silent second-in-command, Schultz, to aim a spotlight into the sky. Falling via parachute is Daffy Duck (singing in Cockney accent "She Was Poor But She Was Honest"). Daffy shouts, "Put out those lights!" and uses the spotlight to do hand shadows including a chorus line that has Schultz whistling. Daffy lands and makes a gooney face that scares Von Vulture. The vulture chases Daffy all around the foxhole, with many gags, including Daffy asking the vulture for the time—to set a time bomb. He dodges enemy aircraft, causing them to destroy each other in "a Mess of Messerschmidts!" Daffy hides in an artillery cannon, becoming a human cannon ball blasted to a Third Reich rally, where a realistic (rotoscoped) Hitler is giving a speech. There, Daffy takes care of Adolf, crowning him with a mallet!!

145

AN ITCH IN TIME

Elmer Fudd; Dec 4; MM; Supervision
by Robert Clampett.

Elmer is reading a LT comic book, his
dog sleeping peacefully by his side. A
flea hops into the house and scans the
room with his enormous telescope
(which he keeps inside the front of his
pants). Seeing the pooch's ample rear
end, the flea shouts "T-BONE!"
Bouncing to the tune of "Food Around
the Corner," the flea lands on the dog's
head, whispering the lullaby "Go to
Sleep" into his ear. The flea prepares
to eat by spreading salt, mustard,and
ketchup on the dog's skin, then bunches
up some of the flesh under two pieces
of white bread. The dog feels an itch
and bites at the flea. The flea sticks
some of the dog's skin between the pursuing teeth. The dog jumps up and
Elmer gives him relief with some flea
powder (the flea "ice skates" in the
snowy scene). Elmer threatens to give
the dog a bath if he scratches one more
time. Meanwhile, the flea prepares a
major dig in the dog's "rump roast"
The dog wants to scratch, but Elmer is
watching. Turning shades of blue, red,
polka-dot, and plaid, the dog gets the
cat to scratch him. The flea ignites a
ton of explosives, causing the dog to
drag his rear end all over the house
(stopping only to confess, "Hey, I better
cut this out. I may get to like it!").
Elmer drags the dog to a bath, but the
flea jumps on him. The dog takes
Elmer to the bath, slipping on a bar of
soap. They land on the flea's "Blue
plate special". The cat, looking on,
says, "Well, now I've seen everything!"
and shoots himself!

PUSS N' BOOTY

Dec 11; LT; Supervision by Frank
Tashlin; Story by Warren Foster;
Animation by Cal Dalton; Musical
Direction by Carl Stalling.

Dickie bird is missing. When Rudolf,
the house cat, hiccups, feathers pop out
of his mouth. The feline helps his mistress look for Dickie in the trash can, in
envelopes, under postage stamps, all to
no avail. Rudolf imitates bird chirps,
and waves goodbye out the window, sig-
naling to his mistress that another bird

should be ordered from the pet shop.

Rudolf awaits the pet store truck,
getting more frantic as each one passes
by. Soon, a new bird, Petey, joins the
family. When the two are finally alone,
Rudolf attacks the bird cage. Petey
lifts his cage, and the cat flattens
against the wall. Rudolf ties the cage in
place and attacks it once more. This
time, the bird opens both front and
back doors, and the flying cat lands in
the flower pond. That night Rudolf
strikes again. The next day, Rudolf is
missing. When Petey hiccups and the
cat's bowtie pops out.

This is the last black-and-white Looney Tune. Warners certainly had the
classiest looking black-and-white cartoons. Tashlin's night sequence uses
odd angles and shadows to heighten the
danger to Petey bird, working to great
comic effect. The scene of Rudolf
awaiting the pet store truck is a classic
of animated anxiety.

1944

LITTLE RED RIDING RABBIT

Bugs Bunny; Jan 4; MM; Supervision
by I. Freleng; Story by Michael Maltese;
Animation by Manuel Perez; Voice
Characterizations by Mel Blanc; Musical
Direction by Carl Stalling.

A teen-age bobby-soxer, Red Riding
Hood, is taking Bugs Bunny to Grandma's house, singing "The Five O'Clock
Whistle." Meanwhile, the wolf sneaks
over to Granny's, where a note for Red
indicates she's working the swing shift
at Lockheed. "P.S. Leave rabbit under
door." The wolf gets into Granny's bed
and awaits Red. Red arrives and
screams, "Hey Grandma! I brought a
little bunny rabbit for you—to have"
The wolf rushes Red out of the house
so he can eat. Red reappears, asking,
"That's an awfully big nose for you to
have" and "What big ears ya got!" The
wolf disguises himself as a door, but
Bugs knocks on his head, yelling,
"Anybody home?" Bugs, imitating a
stool pigeon, whistles and points to various rabbit hiding places. The bunny is
actually in one of them. Bugs distracts
the wolf by making him sing "Put On

Your Old Grey Bonnet." The rabbit hides under the wolf's grandma nightie and sticks a hot coal to his rear end. The wolf jumps and lands perched between a table and chair, hot coals below his bottom, while Bugs loads weights and heavy objects in his arms. Red makes another annoying appearance, and Bugs decides to put Red in the wolf's situation over the coals. Bugs and the wolf share a carrot.

WHAT'S COOKIN' DOC?

Bugs Bunny; Jan 8; MM; Supervision by Robert Clampett; Animation by Bob McKimson; Story by Michael Sasanoff; Musical Direction by Carl W. Stalling.
"Hollywood, land of make-believe," says a narrator, taking us on a tour of Hollywood's famous sights, via technicolor live-action stock footage (mainly from 1937's *A Star Is Born*). We see the Chinese Theater, the Trocadero, and a Hollywood wolf. It is the presentation of the eighth annual Academy Awards, and the narrator asks, "Who will win the Oscar?"

Bugs Bunny assures us, "It's in the bag!" as he greets his pals Cecil B., Edward G., Jerry Colonna, and Bing Crosby. He imitates each one. Bugs goes up to get his award, but James Cagney has won. Bugs gets angry ("I demand a recount!"), pulls down a screen, and throws a bunch of film cans up to Smokey, the projectionist. "I'll leave it to youse intelligent people in dis audience whether I deserve the Oscar or not." Smokey rolls the first reel, a stag film, and corrects it to a clip from *Hiawatha's Rabbit Hunt* (1941). After the clip, Bugs becomes a one-man band, with "Let Bugs Have It" and "Give It to Bugs" written on the drum. The audience decides to "give it to him" and pelts the bunny with fruit. Bugs pops out of the pile as Carmen Miranda and is hit again, this time with a gold "Booby Prize Oscar" shaped like Bugs Bunny. The rabbit loves it, promising "I'll even take youse to bed wit me every night!" The statue responds, "Do you mean it?" kisses the bunny, and strikes an effeminate, hands-on-hips pose!

MEATLESS FLYDAY

Jan 29; MM; Supervision by I. Freleng; Animation by Jack Bradbury; Story by Michael Maltese; Musical Direction by Carl W. Stalling.
A hungry spider (voiced by Tex Avery) tries to catch a fly. First he ties a string to a sugar cube, but gets pulled off his web. The fly heckles the spider by performing a trapeze act without a trapeze! "Look at him!" says the spider. "A poor man's Bugs Bunny!" The spider joins the act, but the fly gives him a hot foot. Falling in flames, the spider laughs. "Look! I'm a Zero!" (referring to the suicide planes). Next, the spider paints candy color on buckshot and leaves them on a plate. The fly eats them and, when the spider appears, cannot get away, weighted down from the buckshot. The spider uses a magnet to control the fly, but it also attracts the kitchen knives and every other sharp utensil in the house. Playing atop a wedding cakes, the fly pretends to be the bride. The spider appears next to the fly as the groom. The tricky fly escapes and leaves a dynamite stick disguised as the bride: it explodes. The spider chases the fly through a neon sign (a la *Lights Fantastic*). An air raid warden shouts, "Put out that light! The spider finally catches the fly and sharpens his knife, singing, "Would you like to take a walk." The fly points out the date. It's "Meatless Tuesday." The spider panics, "No! You can't do this to me!" He runs to the Capitol in Washington, shouting, "You can't! you can't!"

TOM TURK AND DAFFY

Daffy Duck, Porky Pig; Feb 12; LT; Supervision by Charles M. Jones; Animation by Ken Harris; Story by "The Staff"; Musical Direction by Carl W. Stalling.
Daffy is singing "Jingle Bells" and building a snowman when the sound of gunshots disturbs him. A turkey (Tom Turk) pleads with Daffy to hide him from Pilgrim Porky Pig. Daffy helps his friend by stuffing him in the perfect place, inside his snowman. The turkey is grateful ("What a pal, what a pal, what a pal...").

When Porky comes by, the pig describes the delicious meal he had planned to eat ("Chestnut dressing, cranberry sauce, mashed potatoes, green peas, and candied yams"). The duck breaks down and literally becomes a stool pigeon, crying, "The yams did it!" posting a dozen "He's in there!" arrows toward the snowman. The turkey puts a few of his feathers on Daffy, and Porky chases the duck. Daffy throws a variety of snowballs at the pig, malleting him from inside one. Daffy also uses frozen water creatively, creating heavy ice objects, a shield, and a bridge, all to aid his escape. Daffy runs toward Tom Turk, who's now completing the snowman, and pleads to be hidden. His friend Tom complies ("Try in here! No in here! Hide in here!"), throwing the duck up into a tree, into the frozen lake, etc.

BUGS BUNNY AND THE THREE BEARS

Bugs Bunny; The Three Bears; Feb 26; MM; Supervision by Charles M. Jones; Animation by Robert Cannon; Story by Tedd Pierce; Voice Characterization by Mel Blanc; Musical Direction by Carl W. Stalling.
Once upon a time there are three bears, Papa (voiced by Mel Blanc), Mama (voiced by Bea Benaderet), and Junior (voiced by Stan Freberg), who are sitting around bored out of their skulls. Papa comes up with a plan for dinner: they'll lure Goldilocks with their hot porridge and "Wham!" Mama can make only carrot soup for bait, which lures Bugs Bunny, who gets wise to their plan early on. Bugs drinks their soup and goes up to bed (singing "King for a Day"), where the bears pounce upon him.

Mama corners Bugs, but he romances her ("your eyes, your lips, they're beautiful"). Papa and Junior chase Bugs, but Mama defends him ("Tell me more about my eyes!"). Bugs is smothered by the love-sick bear. Bugs opens a series of doors, trying to escape. Behind each one is Mama in another sexy pose, a negligee, as Veronica Lake, and in a bathtub! Bugs runs to his rabbit hole, where he is smothered in kisses by Mama waiting inside. Bugs runs in horror into the distance.

I GOT PLENTY OF MUTTON

Mar 11; LT; Supervision by Frank Tashlin; Animation by I. Ellis; Story by Melvin Millar; Musical Direction by Carl W. Stalling.
One snowy night a starving wolf is reading a newspaper that reads. "O.P.A. Ruling: No Meat For Wolves— Hollywood or Otherwise." The wolf sets up a stew kettle, secretly dipping his only bone in the broth. Mice drink the broth down to the last drop. He then prepares a steaming plate of pea (one), slices it, and listening to it fall into his empty stomach. The newspaper also reports on "Dogs for Defense," noting that the local sheepdog has joined the WAGS. The wolf immediately runs down the snowy mountain toward a flock of unattended sheep. He runs head to head into "Killer Diller, the wolf destroying ram." The ram backs the wolf into a tree stump and butts it out of the meadow.

The wolf disguises as a sexy ewe to lure the ram from his post. The plan works too well. Killer falls in love and performs a classic love scene with the disguised wolf ("Where have you been all my life?"). The wolf lures the ram to a trap, a bank safe dropping on his head. Killer opens the safe from the inside and continues to make love. The wolf tries an artillery cannon, but the ram is in the gun barrel. The lovesick ram chases the ewe/wolf into the night until the wolf finally breaks down and admits, "I'm not a sheep! I'm a Wolf!!" The ram confides, "So what? So am I!"

THE WEAKLY REPORTER

Mar 25; MM; Supervision by Charles M. Jones; Story by Michael Maltese; Animation by Ben Washam; Musical Direction by Carl W. Stalling.
A World War II newsreel spoof on the topic of homefront unity.

The nation's solidarity during wartime is shown with the Statue of Liberty wearing an air raid warden's arm band, the heads on Mt. Rushmore in air raid warden helmets, and the state of Florida with a "We Love California" sign stuck in it. There are numerous other homefront gags. After an auto accident, the ambulance picks up the rubber tires. A woman asks a butcher if he has porterhouse steak. She can afford only to smell it at a cost of $1.19. Hoarding is a thing of the past, but you can't hoard too many War Bonds. A beauty shop shows a woman trying on a new blow torch mask ("It sure certainly does things for you, dearie!"). Bandits rob an alarm clock from a jewelry shop. A factory grinds to a halt while a woman repairs the machinery with her bobby pin. The sign on Henry J. Kaiser's door says, "Out to Launch."

If this film doesn't sound funny, it's because it isn't. Its humor, topical in 1944, seems hopelessly dated today. The bridging sequences between gags are handled with stylized backgrounds and animated stick figures, predating a stylized look UPA would make famous in the 1950s.

TICK TOCK TUCKERED
Porky Pig, Daffy Duck, Apr 8; LT; Supervision by Robert Clampett; Story by Warren Foster; Animation by Tom McKimson; Musical Direction by Carl W. Stalling.
A remake of Clampett's *Porky's Badtime Story* (1937). Porky and Daffy are roommates who have a problem getting to work on time. They ignore their alarm clock and have to sneak into work late every day. At the Fly-By-Night Aircraft Company, Daffy tries turning the time-clock at the job backward, but the alarm goes off, permitting their live-action boss to catch them ("Well, well! If it isn't the Dover Boys!"). The boss gives them an ultimatum: if they're late one more time, they're fired.

That night, they are determined to go to bed early. At first, the cats in the alley disturb Porky, who throws an old shoe at them. They throw the shoe back, so Porky throws a book ("The Falcon"), but that comes back as well (as "The Falcon Returns"). Next, the window shade won't go down, and Daffy finds the moonlight too bright— so he shoots it out of the sky ("Unbe-

lievable, isn't it?"). At 2:00 a.m., it begins to rain, and a leak develops over their bed. Daffy opens an umbrella (Porky warns, "It's bad luck!"). A lightning bolt destroys umbrella and bed. Sleeping in a chest of drawers as the morning alarm goes off, they awaken, rush to put their clothes on, and speed down to work only to find that it's Sunday. They return home and to bed. Porky shoots the clock, which dies a dramatic death.

BUGS BUNNY NIPS THE NIPS
Bugs Bunny, Apr 22; MM; Supervision by I. Freleng; Story by Tedd Pierce; Animation by Gerry Chiniquy; Musical Direction by Carl Stalling.
"Somewhere in the Pacific," Bugs Bunny is adrift in a wooden crate, singing "Trade Winds," and waiting for the "island that inevitably turns up in this kind of picture," to turn up. He is washed ashore on a South Pacific paradise, "so peaceful, so quiet," until bombs start exploding, and he finds the island inhabited by the Japanese. Bugs encounters an angry soldier hiding in a haystack and outsmarts him by dressing as a Japanese general. The soldier gets wise and recognizes Bugs from the movies, addressing him, "What's up, Honorable Doc?" Bugs escapes and challenges him in the air. Bugs flies by (in a Japanese aircraft) and hands his parachuting opponent an anvil. "Here's some scrap iron for Japan, Moto! Happy landings!" Back on the island, Bugs encounters a mammoth Sumo wrestler. Disguised as a Japanese maiden, he mallets the brute. Bugs watches the arrival of more "Japs! Hundreds of 'em!" The bunny deceives them as a Good Rumor Man, selling ice cream pops with grenades inside. "Here's one for you, Monkey-face. There's plenty for all. Here you are, Slant-eyes." "Business is BOOMing!" says Bugs. The island is once again peaceful, too peaceful for the bunny. Bugs soon discovers another presence,

a beautiful sarong-clad female rabbit, and chases her into the sunset.

THE SWOONER CROONER _{ACADEMY AWARD NOMINEE}

Porky Pig; May 6; LT; Supervision by Frank Tashlin; Story by Warren Foster; Animation by George Cannata; Musical Direction by Carl W. Stalling.
Dawn at the Flockheed Eggcraft Factory. The chickens, each with lunch pail, show their I.D.s and punch in at the time clock. Each chicken is strapped onto a conveyor belt and required to drop eggs, one at a time, into a basket. Suddenly, the chickens stop laying and leave their post to see and hear Frankie, a skinny crooning rooster.

Manager Porky Pig finds "absentee" signs in the nests and looks under every barrel, rock, and water pump on the farm. He finally finds them fainting, melting and passing out over Frankie. Porky places a want ad: "Rooster Auditions: singing rooster needed to keep hens producing." He auditions a Nelson Eddy rooster singing "Shortnin' Bread," a Jolson singing "September in the Rain," a Durante singing "Lullabye of Broadway," a Cab Calloway hi-de-hoeing "Blues in the Night," and finally a Crosby, crooning "When My Dreamboat Comes Home." The chicks begin to lay eggs again. The skinny rooster Frankie challenges the Crosby rooster, and in a contest that includes "Trade Winds," "You Must Have Been a Beautiful Baby" and others they have the farm filled with mountains of eggs. Porky asks them how they do it, and they croon a little in his direction, causing Porky, himself, to lay eggs.

RUSSIAN RHAPSODY

May 20; MM; Supervision by Robert Clampett; Story by Lou Lilly; Animation by Rod Scribner; Musical Direction by Carl W. Stalling.
"Once upon a time, way back in 1941..." A fleet of Nazi bombers fails to reach Moscow. The headlines ask, "Could It Be Gremlins?" and the headlines answer, "Hmmm ... Could Be!" The Fuehrer is furious as he rants and raves at a "New Odor" rally:

"Stoopnagle hamburger, vit der frandkurter und der sauerbraten. Vit der Zoot Suit, mit der Reet Pleet ... Stup Fritz Freleng vit der Henrich Binder und der Vat's Cooking Doc! Pumpernickel vit der Sauerkrauten from der Delicatessin vit liver wurst und hassen pheffer und der chatten-ooga choo-choo..." A card is held over the screen: "Silly, isn't he?"

To bomb Moscow, Hitler vows to send his greatest pilot, "The greatest Superman of all time!" A party member ask "Who's dat? YOU, Fuehrer?" Adolf responds with a Yiddish accent, "Who else?"

The newspaper headline reads, "Our Adolf to Bomb Moscow in Person." As Hitler sits in the cockpit, hundreds of Technicolor Gremlins invade the plane (most are caricatures of the Warner cartoon staff) to the tune of "We Are Gremlins from the Kremlin." They smash his controls, saw through the wings (with burping "Termite-skis"), and change his C gas ration card to an A card. When Hitler gets wise, they stick his nose in an electric socket—zapping Mein Fuehrer into a glowing swastika, a skunk, and a jack-ass. Hitler chases them with a knife, but a mask of Stalin makes him faint. They drop him out of the plane, then crash the plane atop the dictator, the aircraft's wings becoming his tombstone. Hitler arises from his final rest to imitate Lew Lehr: "Nutzis is de cwaziest people." The Gremlins pound him back under with a large mallet.

DUCK SOUP TO NUTS

Porky Pig, Daffy Duck; May 27; LT; Supervision by I. Freleng; Story by Tedd Pierce; Animation by Richard Bickenbach; Musical Direction by Carl W. Stalling.
Filing his nails amid the realistic ducks in the lake, Daffy notes "I kinda stand out in a crowd, don't I?" A gunshot causes the other ducks to fly off, but Daffy puts on his bathing cap and dives

underwater. Hunter Porky Pig points his rifle at Daffy, who emerges from the water demonstrating his talents by singing, dancing, acting. "I got a contract at Warner Bros.!" He enacts a play, casting himself as the villain, chasing Porky around a rock. Next, Daffy distracts Porky by making bumps on his head. Porky sticks his rifle at the duck point blank, but Daffy looks in the barrel and peeps a pin-up girl. When Porky looks inside he sees Daffy! Shooting Daffy out of his gun and into the lake, Porky pursues him underwater with his diving helmet. Porky returns to the surface, grabs a bucket, and begins to bail the water out of the lake. When the whole lake is drained, Daffy remains flopping around like a dying fish. Porky doesn't believe he's a fish, so Daffy doesn't believe he's a pig. Daffy convinces Porky he's an eagle. To prove it, Porky jumps off a tree branch and crashes! Porky blindfolds Daffy and is about to execute him. The duck says goodbye to his family, but Porky can't pull the trigger. Daffy's family are revealed to be his buddies in disguise. Porky gets even with them … in the end.

ANGEL PUSS

June 3; LT; Directed by Charles M. Jones; Story by Lou Lilly; Animation by Ken Harris; Musical Direction by Carl W. Stalling.
Li'l Sambo is singing "Mammy's Little Baby Loves Short'n Bread" on his way to the disagreeable job of having to drown a cat (for which he was paid four bits). The wise guy cat escapes the sack and decides to torment the boy by pretending to be his conscience. The cat goads him into dropping the sack into the river. Feeling guilty after performing the act, Sambo walks home sad and frightened. The cat disguises himself as an angel, and when Sambo wanders into a graveyard, the cat appears in a ghostly fashion, with halo and harp, causing Sambo to through into a series of scare "takes."

The boy runs into an old house and blocks the door, but turns around to find himself face to face with the cat. Sambo runs from the house, the cat

chasing him and luring him back in with rattling dice. When the boy gets close enough, the cat says, "Boo!" and Sambo runs again. This time both of them fall into a pond. The cat's disguise comes off. Angry at being tricked, Sambo gets his rifle and shoots the cat, whose nine ghostly lives march out, "And this time, brother, we ain't kiddin'!"

SLIGHTLY DAFFY

Daffy Duck, Porky Pig; June 17; MM; Directed by I. Freleng; Story by Michael Maltese; Animation by Virgil Ross; Musical Direction by Carl W. Stalling.
An almost exact color remake of Robert Clampett's *Scalp Trouble* (1939). Porky Pig is a cavalry soldier helping defend his fort against a tribe of wacky Indians. General Daffy Duck accidentally swallows the ammunition and becomes a living machine gun. In the end, "Yanks Beat Indians, 11-3!"

Most of the animation is reused from the previous picture. Differences include the picture of Petunia hanging next to Porky's bunk bed replaced with a sign reading "Buy Bonds" and a few new Indian gags.

HARE RIBBIN'

Bugs Bunny; June 24; MM; Directed by Robert Clampett; Story by Lou Lilly; Animation by Robert McKimson; Voice Characterization by Mel Blanc; Musical Direction by Carl W. Stalling.
A red-haired Russian-dialect dog (a take-off on Bert Gordon's "Mad Russian" character on the Eddie Cantor radio program) is looking for a rabbit, sniffing every object in the woods. He stops at Bugs Bunny's armpit and asks Bugs if he's seen a rabbit, giving the bunny a chance to abuse the dog while describing himself. The dog gets wise and chases the rabbit to a lake. The rest of the cartoon takes place underwater.

Bugs dresses as a sexy mermaid and drives the dog wild by singing "Would It Be Wrong?" "Let us play games," the dog suggests. They play tag, with Bugs batting him about the lake bottom with his dorsal fin. The dog, hungry for a rabbit sandwich, corners Bugs, stating, "I think I'll have dinner right now!"

Bugs imitates a French waiter and chokes the dog with his dinner napkin. Claiming to be out of "rabbit." the bunny imitates Elmer Fudd and goes hunting for "wabbits." The dog grabs Bugs and demands his sandwich. The bunny lies between two huge pieces of bread, bunching up his legs as the dog takes a bite. Bugs screams and performs a classic death scene. The dog mourns for the rabbit, yelling, "I wish I were dead!" Bugs asks, "Do you mean it?" pulls a gun and shoots him dead. (Two versions of this scene exist; the other has Bugs handing the dog a pistol to shoot himself.) Bugs puts a lily in the hound's hand and pirouettes into the distance. The dog holds back the closing iris, commenting, "This shouldn't happen to a dog!"

BROTHER BRAT
Porky Pig; July 15; LT; Direction by Frank Tashlin; Story by Melvin Millar; Animation by Art Davis; Musical Direction by Carl W. Stalling.
This cartoon begins with a brief prologue that explains the new role of American women in the workplace, how women are working in all lines of war production, making the weapons of war—guns, tanks, planes—to supply the needs of our fighting men. Our nation has created a "Super Woman" who has overcome all obstacles and difficulties except one: where the heck to put the kids while she's working! One musclebound female worker from Blockheed recruits Porky Pig to daycare her kids. She asks him, "You want those planes to roll off the assembly line, doncha? You want those Nazis and Japs bombed off the earth, doncha?" She leaves him with a book to help, "Child Psychology," which suggests he ask the child its name. The baby, Butch by name, is playing solitaire and hands Porky an anvil that crashes him into the basement. The book recommends, "Give baby a cat and watch his little puss light up!" Butch uses the cat as a jump rope. When Porky tries to divert Butch's interest, the baby bites his finger and won't let go. Finally shaking the brat free, Butch lands in a mountain of pots and

pans and, as Winston Churchill, declares "This means War!" The baby chases Porky with an axe. The mother comes home and shows Porky how she uses the book: to give him a spanking.

HARE FORCE
Bugs Bunny; MM; Directed by I. Freleng; Story by Tedd Pierce; Animation by Manuel Perez; Voice Characterization by Mel Blanc; Musical Direction by Carl Stalling.
On a cold, snowy night Granny leaves her dog Sylvester cozy near the fireplace. Knocking on the door is a frozen Bugs Bunny; he is brought in to thaw by the kind-hearted old woman. Granny instructs her dog to take care of the bunny, but while she goes up to bed, the hound can think only of ways to kill the rabbit.

The dog throws the hare out of the house, but Bugs performs a classic death scene ("I'm catching pneumonia!"), while constructing a bunny made of snow. The dog goes out to investigate and returns with the snow rabbit, wich melts in front of the fireplace. Worried about what Granny will do when she finds the puddle on the floor, the dog looks to Bugs for a place to hide. The rabbit suggests behind the front door, but when the dog is outside, Bugs slams the entrance shut. When Granny checks on her two pets, Bugs brings the frozen pooch inside to "pose" for a sketch. When the dog thaws, he kicks Bugs when his back is turned. He apologizes, but Bugs abuses the dog by retaliating ("All you did was this!" POW! "Now if you had done this," BOP "or this" SMACK! "I'd have gotten sore and done this!" WHAM!). Bugs tricks the dog outside ("How's the weather out there, John L.?"). Bugs rests, roasts a carrot by the fireplace, and hears the poor dog's moan. Going out to check, the rabbit finds a note in a snowbank, "Don't you wish you were inside, like me?" The two adversaries take turns throwing each other out. Finally, Granny comes down and they toss her out. In the end, Bugs and the dog are resting by the fireplace. The bunny admits, "Ain't I a stinker?"

FROM HAND TO MOUSE

Aug 5; LT; Directed by Charles M. Jones; Story by Michael Maltese; Animation by Robert Cannon; Musical Direction by Carl W. Stalling.

A mouse is caught in the grip of a lion and begs for his life. "Spare me! Spare, me and someday I might be able to save your life!" The gullible lion lets him go, and as the mouse gets to his hole, he shouts, "Sucker!" Feeling stupid, the lion pounds his head against a tree. Later, the mouse gets caught in a mouse trap. When the lion approaches, the mouse "reminds" him of his promise to help him escape. The lion lets him go, and the mouse again yells, "Sucker!" The lion beats his head again.

Next day, the lion jumps the mouse, but the rodent crawls within the lion's fur creating an itch. The lion combs the mouse out of his mane, but the little pest has a "12 points" ration tag and asks, "Got your ration stamp, bub?" Lion lets mouse go, and the rodent rubber stamps "Sucker" on the lion's behind. Later, the mouse gets caught in the mouse trap again, but the mouse disguises himself as a mini-lion, and the lion releases him. The mouse persuades the big cat into thinking that he's a mouse. The lion begs to be let go but soon gets wise. Next, he finds the mouse disguised as an Indian—"Him go that way"—later, as a Zulu native. A gorilla grabs the lion, but the mouse saves him by handing the ape a bomb. The mouse and the lion walk off together as friends, the mouse letting the lion walk ahead, off a cliff. The lion yells at himself in a mirror, "Sucker! Sucker! Sucker!"

BIRDY AND THE BEAST

Tweety; Aug 19; MM; Directed by Robert Clampett; Story by Warren Foster; Animation by Tom McKimson; Musical Direction by Carl W. Stalling.

A cat creeps toward a nest located in a tall tree. He stares, drooling, at the little bird (Tweety) sleeping inside. The bird wakes and notices the feline. "I taught I taw a putty tat." Tweety flies off the tree, the cat follows, not realizing he is out of the tree. Tweety points

that out. "The poor putty tat! He fall down, and go BOOM!" Tweety hides in a bulldog's food dish, requiring the cat to dig through the food. The dog chases the cat away. Meanwhile, Tweety, wondering where the "putty tat" is, wanders into the cat's mouth. He lights a match to help him see, and the cat passes out. Tweety dons a fire hat and sticks a hose into the cat's now flaming mouth. Tweety turns on the liquid (it is gasoline), causing the cat to explode. "The poor putty tat got hot as a firecwacker. He blow up and go boom!" Tweety does a little whistling "theme-song" dance and encounters the cat again. He has disguised his mouth as a nest (with a "Home, Sweet Home" sign). A chicken comes along and lays a dozen eggs in the nest. The cat gets up, displaying the eggs in his mouth as though teeth. Tweety points and says, "I like him, he's silly!" and smashes the mouthful of eggs. The cat chases Tweety back to his nest, reaches for the bird, but grabs a grenade, destroying the cat once and for all. "You know, I lose more putty tats dat way!"

BUCKAROO BUGS

Bugs Bunny; Aug 26; LT; Directed by Robert Clampett; Story by Lou Lilly; Animation by M. Gould; Voice Characterization by Mel Blanc; Musical Direction by Carl W. Stalling.

The Masked Maurauder strikes again! His crime: stealing the carrots from all the victory gardens. Only one man can save us. He is "out of the west, Brooklyn's famous fighting cowboy, Red Hot Ryder." Ryder is so stupid, the only way he can stop his "horsie" is to pull a huge club from his pants and knock him unconscious. Bugs sees the twerp and decides to bother him. Wearing a hankerchief over his face, Bugs sticks a carrot into his rear end and shouts, "Stick 'em up or I'll blow your brains out!" Using a magnet, the rabbit pulls off all of Ryder's metallic items, causing his pants to fall. Ryder meets Bugs, unmasked, and asks him if he's seen the Maurauder. The rabbit asks if he robs you like this, repeating the magnet gag, this time leaving Red naked below the waist (except for a fig leaf).

Bugs checks his watch and asks Ryder to wait while he robs the 5:15 train (he fakes it with elaborate sound effects). Ryder rides after the thief, with Bugs pointing to various getaway routes, each one a larger chasm, until the cowboy and horse blindly leap into the Grand Canyon. They fall, landing deep below the ground. Red finally catches on. "You know, I think our friend is really the Masked Maurauder." Bugs burrows in, announcing, "That's right! You win the $64 question!" and gives Ryder a big kiss!

GOLDILOCKS AND THE JIVIN' BEARS

Sept 2; MM; Directed by I. Freleng; Story by Tedd Pierce; Animation by Ken Champin; Musical Direction by Carl W. Stalling.

A piano player tells the story of the three black bears, the King-Size Bear, the Middle-Size Bear, and the Wee Little Bear, a hot swing trio who hold a jam session. When their instruments get too hot (Little Bear on Bass, Middle Bear on piano, Big Bear on horn), they decide to take a walk to let them cool.

Meanwhile, the Big Bad Wolf of "Little Red Riding Hood" is disappointed. Red is working at Lockheed as a riveter. He spots sexy Goldilocks entering the Three Bears' place and joins her in bed! The wolf is chasing Goldie as the Bears return, but they mistake the pair for "Jitterbugs," return to their instruments, and give out. Goldie gets into it, bouncing the wolf all over the dance floor. The wolf tries to escape the dance-crazed Goldie, but she has boarded up the doors and windows.

Later the wolf rests at Grandma's house, just as Red shows up. Red is surprised the wolf isn't chasing her, but he shows her his red, burning feet. The bears show up and start jamming. Grandma, hiding in the closet, forces the wolf to jitterbug with her. The wolf laments a la Durante, "Umbriago! Everyone wants to get into the act!"

PLANE DAFFY

Daffy Duck; Sept 16; LT; Directed by Frank Tashlin; Story by Warren Foster;

Animation by Cal Dalton; Musical Direction by Carl Stalling.

At carrier pigeon headquarters, the flyers are worried about a comrade, Homer Pigeon. ("That his buddies are worried is really a shame, because Pigeon 13 is A.W.O.L. with a dame!") Homer has fallen into the clutches of the queen of spies, Hatta Mari, a Nazi se-duck-tress. The only person who can help is Daffy Duck, the squad's woman-hater.

Daffy, military secret in his pouch, flies out on his secret mission, but Hatta Mari's leg attracts the duck. Going inside her bird house, he melts at her kiss. Hatta tries to take his secret, but Daffy pulls it back and runs like a rocket (except for daintily walking up and down stairs). Behind every door is Hatta with a knife, or machine gun, or artillery cannon. Daffy hides in a narrow umbrella stand. After Hatta fires a musket at it point blank. Daffy pops up, "Missed me!" Daffy flies out of the apartment, but zooms right back with "It's scary out there!" Daffy hides in the ice box and discovers a secret. "Well, what do you know! The little light stays on!" The sexy spy corners the duck, who swallows his military secret. Mari straps the duck to an X-ray and, via television, broadcasts the secret to Hitler, Goering, and Goebbels. It reads "Hitler is a Stinker" but "That's no secret!" His aides reply, "Yah, everybody knows that," and kill themselves. Daffy hoo-hoos, "They lose more darn Nutzis that way!"

LOST AND FOUNDLING

Sniffles; Sept 30; MM; Directed by Charles M. Jones; Story by Tedd Pierce; Animation by Ben Washam; Musical Direction by Carl W. Stalling.

High on a mountaintop tree branch, a hawk is sleeping on her nest. One egg rolls out and falls below, rolling down the mountain onto the highway, where it misses being crushed by trucks. It rolls over logs, through the river and into Sniffles's home, stopping under the mouse's rear end. Sniffles wakes up, wonders, and consults a book. "No, silly! Mice don't lay eggs!" The egg hatches, and Sniffles adopts the little bird, thinking it is a chicken. He plays piggy back with the little bird, and, in a montage representing time passing, we see the bird getting bigger and bigger and bigger. By winter time, it's a big, dumb giant named Orville who rides Sniffles's back, yelling, "Hi-yo Silver!" Sniffles pulls out his reference book to find out what kind of chicken he is and discovers he is actually a hawk. Hawks eat rodents. Suddenly, the bird is no longer goofy, but sly and hungry. Sniffles offers the hawk some food, but the bird puts the steak sauce on the mouse. The hawk pretends to go to bed, and Sniffles does too, with a large stick pin as a weapon. The hawk sneaks out of bed and tries to attack the mouse. Sniffles gets up, turns on the lights, the radio, drinks 12 cups of coffee, and reads "Wake Up and Live." The hawk changes the radio to a station playing the lullabye "Go to Sleep," makes him some ovaltine, and prepares a soft bread bed. The hawk is about to eat the rodent, but has second thoughts and cries, "I can't do it, I can't." The reference book lands on the table, and the hawk discovers that "A certain superior hawk does not eat rodents. This is marked by a red mark under his arm." He wakes Sniffles and shows him his mark. They go out playing "horsie," a can of red paint in the hawk's back pocket.

BOOBY HATCHED

Oct 14; LT; Directed by Frank Tashlin; Story by Warren Foster; Animation by I. Ellis; Musical Direction by Carl W. Stalling.

A cold winter day on the farm has a mother duck freezing and trying to keep her eggs warm. She holds her eggs to the light and sees, in silhouette, one chick warming himself by a stove, another one sneezing, and another skiing. She gathers the eggs together (with a pool rack), and takes the collective temperature ("Cold as a brass monkey"), then heats her rear-end over a flame. About to place her red-hot bottom on top of the eggs, the chicks hatch in unison, screaming, "Don't do it! We'll come out!" The mother duck takes her ducklings down to the lake

for a swim, except for one., Robespierre hasn't entirely hatched (just his feet stick out of the egg). He's still cold and searches for a warm place to hatch. The mother duck, taking a head count ("Franklin, Eleanor, Winston, Leon" are some of their names), realizes Robespierre is missing and shouts his name all over the countryside. Still in his egg, Robespierre is walking through a storm, yelling for help ("This is the saddest part of the picture, folks!"). The egg is found by a hungry wolf, then hides under a hibernating bear. The wolf uses T.N.T. to extract Robespierre. The mama duck finds the wolf, and they have a tug-of-war over Robespierre, with mama poking the wolf's eye to bring home her son. Mama accidentally grabs an egg-shaped doorknob; the wolf begins to boil the real egg. When she finally rescues her baby from the boiling caldron, the duckling complains, "Aw, Ma! Just when I was getting warm!"

THE OLD GREY HARE

Bugs Bunny, Elmer Fudd; Oct 28; MM; Direction by Robert Clampett; Animation by Robert McKimson; Story by Michael Sasanoff; Voice Characterization by Mel Blanc; Musical Direction by Carl W. Stalling.

Elmer Fudd is sitting by a tree, crying because he is unable to catch that wabbit, Bugs Bunny. The voice of God (Mel Blanc) tells Elmer to "try, try again." But how long will it take? The voice asks Elmer to look far into the future, "past 1950, 1970, 80, 90 ... When you hear the sound of the gong it will be 2000 A.D." An old wrinkled Fudd picks up a newspaper: "Smellovision Replaces Television" (subtitled

"Carl Stalling says it'll never work!"). Instead of a rifle, he has a "Buck Rogers Lightning-Quick Rabbit Killer." An old Bugs Bunny pops, up asking, "What's up, Prune Face?," and chokes the elder Fudd. Elmer shoots his ray gun and knocks the bunny out. Bugs performs a classic death scene, taking out a photo album of memories. The two reminisce about their very first meeting, as babies!

A cute little Baby Elmer finds little Bugsy Bunny drinking carrot juice in a bottle, which he smashes over Fudd's head. Elmer chases Baby Bugs, they take a nap, and resume the chase. Bugs hides behind a tree. As Elmer sneaks around it, the bunny razzes him with a tuba. Elmer pulls out his baby carriage racer, but Bugs, pretending to be a traffic cop, pulls him over. When little Elmer gets wise, Bugs shouts in his face, "You ain't just whistling *Dixie!*"

Back to the future, the old Bugs starts to dig his own grave (with a "Rest in Pieces" tombstone). He bids his friend goodbye, they both cry, and, before you know it, Bugs has tricked Fudd into the grave ("So long, Methuselah!" as Bugs shovels dirt over his old foe). Buried alive, Elmer is just glad to be rid of that rabbit. Bugs hands Fudd a farewell gift, a bomb that explodes after the fade out, shaking the "That's All Folks!" title card.

THE STUPID CUPID
Daffy Duck, Elmer Fudd; Nov 25; LT; Directed by Frank Tashlin; Story by Warren Foster.
Elmer Fudd is a stupid Cupid who uses rubber suction-cup arrows on his helpless victims. First he attacks a bluebird, who zooms to his love, building a honeymoom cottage as their bird nest. Next he zings a fighting dog and cat, who stop their feud and neck. A stunned feline remarks, "Now I've seen everything!" and shoots his nine lives.

Cupid spots his old friend Daffy Duck taking a bath in the barnyard water tub. Daffy confronts the Cupid and tells him to lay off. "You shot me last year and look what happened," showing a photo album of his shotgun wedding and six kids (including one

with two heads). Daffy blames Cupid for making him a henpecked duck. Daffy takes Cupid and shoots him like an arrow through his bow. Cupid retaliates by using a giant arrow to get Daffy, smashing him into a tree. The duck becomes love happy and chases a chicken throughout the barnyard, much to the dismay of her husband, the rooster. Daffy begs forgiveness of the rooster, blaming "that stupid Cupid." The rooster lets the duck go, but Cupid shoots Daffy again and he zooms right back between the two fowl lovers.

STAGE DOOR CARTOON
Bugs Bunny, Elmer Fudd; Dec 30; MM; Directed by I. Freleng; Story by Michael Maltese; Animation by Jack Bradbury; Voice Characterization by Mel Blanc; Musical Direction by Carl W. Stalling.
Using a fishing rod with a carrot attached for bait, Elmer Fudd hunts Bugs Bunny. Bugs attaches the hook to Elmer's backside, and the hunter pulls himself in. Bugs laughs, "What a zany, what a knucklehead, what a dolt." Elmer chases Bugs into the city and backstage of a vaudeville theater. The sight of a can-can chorus stops Fudd, who admires the legs. He notices the rabbit among them and waits for the bunny offstage. Bugs decides to stay on, doing a tap dance number. Elmer sneaks onstage in a piano and Bugs uses this opportunity to perform a piano solo, knocking Fudd about with the key-hammers. Bugs then forces Elmer to perform a high dive into "an ordinary glass of water."

Chased into a dressing room, the bunny dresses Fudd in Shakespearian togs and forces him back on stage. There, Bugs coaches him in a series of funny faces. This results in Fudd being pelted with a tomato. Bugs gets behind Fudd and forces the hunter to perform a strip tease. Bugs disguises himself as a western sheriff and arrests Elmer for

indecent exposure. Meanwhile, on screen, a Bugs Bunny cartoon begins, and they stop to watch. In the film, Elmer sees Bugs dress up as the sheriff. Fudd tries to pull off the rabbit's disguise, but it's a real sheriff ("You'll swing for this!"). Bugs, disguised as Leopold, is leading the orchestra and confides, "I've got a million of 'em!"

1945

ODOR-ABLE KITTY
Pepe LePew; Jan 6; LT; Directed by Charles M. Jones; Story by Tedd Pierce; Animation by Robert Cannon; Musical Direction by Carl W. Stalling.
An orange tomcat decides the only way to get respect, and some food, is to disguise himself as a skunk. The plan works too well. He attracts the attention of Pepe LePew, a hot-blooded skunk who pursues his newfound love all over the countryside. The high point of the chase has the cat, disguised as Bugs Bunny, asking Pepe, "What's up, Doc?" In the end, "Pepe's" wife and kids appear and bring the odorous Casanova home. The tormented tabby happily returns to his former identity, a hungry and abused alley cat.

This hilarious cartoon features the first appearance of the skunk who became world famous. Jones had no long-term commitment to this new character, identified here as Henry, with his accent a put-on and with a family. It should be noted that Pepe is chasing a disguised male cat. Future pseudo-skunks were to be decidedly female.

HERR MEETS HARE
Bugs Bunny; Jan 13; MM; Directed by I. Freleng; Story by Michael Maltese;

Animation by Gerry Chiniquy; Musical Direction by Carl W. Stalling.
Nazi General Herman Goering is "soothing his jangled nerves" with a hunting trip in the Black Forest. Bugs Bunny, making a wrong turn in Albequerque, winds up in Germany. When Bugs asks for directions he gets a gun in his face. The bunny admires the officer's medal and observes that it is made of cheap tin! This causes Goering to curse "that Hitler swine!" Bugs disguises himself as the Fuerher and berates him, then dresses as the blond-wigged Brunhilde. Goering performs as Siegried and gets a shield bashed in his face.

Goering commands his hunting falcon to catch the rabbit, and the bunny gets sacked. Bugs is taken to Hitler's office. When Adolf opens the bag he finds the rabbit disguised as Stalin, puffing on an enormous pipe, asking, "Does your tobacco taste different lately?"

DRAFTEE DAFFY
Daffy Duck; Jan 27; LT; Direction by Robert Clampett; Animation by Rod Scribner; Story by Lou Lilly; Musical Direction by Carl W. Stalling.
At home, Daffy Duck is reading in the newspaper, "U.S. Army announces a smashing Frontal attack on enemy Rear!" This bit of news causes Daffy to cheer, wave his American flag, and sing, "Hooray for the red, white, and blue!" Daffy receives a phone call informing him that a letter from the president is on the way. When he realizes it's "the little man from the draft board," he starts crying. Looking out the window he sees the little man is already here, letter in hand ("Howdy doody, son!"). Daffy puts everything in the house in front of the window, ties it with barbed wire, then runs like a rocket upstairs. "I guess he's gone now," says Daffy as he peeks out the upstairs window. "Well now, I wouldn't say that!" responds the little man at the window. Daffy races all around the house. At every turn, there is the little man with lines like "What's all the hub-bub, bub!" and "Is this trip really necessary?" The duck finally traps the

man in a safe, builds a wall around him ("So long, Dracula, you dope!"), then heads for a rocket on the roof marked "Use in case of induction only." The rocket crash-lands deep within the earth in a firey inferno. It must be none other than Hades. The duck shrugs off his situation and confides to the Devil, "Anyway, I sure put it over on that dope from the draft board!" The Devil removes his mask. He's the little man! "Well now, I wouldn't say that!"

THE UNRULY HARE
Bugs Bunny, Elmer Fudd, Feb 10; MM; Directed by Frank Tashlin; Story by Melvin Millar; Animation by Cal Dalton; Voice Characterization by Mel Blanc; Musical Direction by Carl W. Stalling;
Elmer Fudd is a surveyor, disturbing Bugs Bunny's peace by singing "I've Been Working on the Railroad" ("That sounds like an unreasonable facsimile of Frankie Sinatra!"). As Elmer looks through his survey viewer, Bugs holds sexy pin-up pictures, causing Fudd to pant. Bugs puckers his lip-sticked mouth and asks Fudd, "Is you is or is you ain't my baby?" Elmer chases Bugs back to his tree stump and fires a record number of bullets. Returning to his viewer, he sees the forest on fire (actually Bugs holding a lit match in front of the equipment). Elmer yells "Fire!" and Fireman Bugs squirts him with seltzer. Elmer gets wise, but Bugs lights half-a-dozen explosive cigars in his mouth. Elmer chases the rabbit back to the tree stump. Wondering if Fudd is still there, the rabbit sticks a decoy Bugs Bunny head (on a stick) up. It gets crowned. Bugs sits atop Elmer's tripod and kisses the surveyor again. Fudd again points his gun at the rabbit, who turns around, stating, "Only a big, fat rat would shoot a guy in the back!"

Elmer shoots, boasting, "So I'm a big, fat rat!" Bugs emerges from the gunsmoke, "Ahh, have some cheese, rat!" and stuffs a large wedge of Swiss in his face. Elmer drops a stick of dynamite down Bugs' hideout. Bugs runs from the scene, hands Elmer the stick, as if in a relay race. Elmer throws the stick back to Bugs, who receives it like a baseball catcher. Bugs runs with it into the gunpowder shack where it explodes, laying all the railroad tracks. A train passes Elmer, with Bugs on board waving goodbye. As he jumps off the train (rather painfully), he is reminded that "none of us civilians should be doing any unnecessary traveling these days!"

TRAP HAPPY PORKY
Porky Pig; Feb 24; LT; Directed by Charles M. Jones; Story by Tedd Pierce; Animation by Ken Harris; Musical Direction by Carl W. Stalling.
Porky Pig, asleep at a tourist lodge called Uncle Tom's Cabin ("Boarders taken—for all they've got!"), is awakened by crashing noises. Two mice are breaking dishes in an attempt to crack a walnut. Porky sets a trap, but his bait is stolen by a mouse "only three-and-a-half years old!" The other mouse shows off by basketball-dribbling an olive. Porky asks, "How am I gonna get rid of those mice?" A cat knocks at the door with the sign, "Does this answer your question?" The cat sets up a Rube Goldberg-like invention that clobbers the pests. Porky returns to bed, but soon is awakened by a gang of drunken cats singing "Moonlight Bay" (what else?).

Porky brings a bulldog home, and leaves the canine to chase the cats. Instead, the dog joins them in "When

Irish Eyes Are Smiling." Porky gives up and figures if you can't beat them, join them. He does.

LIFE WITH FEATHERS ACADEMY AWARD NOMINEE

Sylvester; Mar 24; Sylvester; MM; Directed by I. Freleng; Story by Tedd Pierce; Animation by Virgil Ross; Musical Direction by Carl W. Stalling.
A love bird has had a major fight with his wife. Since he cannot live with love, the bird decides to end it all. After considering shooting himself, jumping from a window, and letting a train run him over, he decides to let a cat eat him.

Sylvester is rummaging the trash for food when the bird whistles for his attention. The cat is delighted. "Sufferin' succotash! Squab!" Sylvester sneaks up on the bird, the parakeet waiting blindfolded. Sylvester is suspicious, thinking the bird may be poisonous, and refuses to eat him. The bird tries a series of gags to get into Sylvester's mouth. He mallets the cat's foot, flying into his mouth when he screams; pretends to be Santa Claus; and tempts the starving cat with an audio and visual bombardment of delicious food images. Sylvester is about to give in when a telegram arrives telling the bird that everything is going to be alright at home. Sylvester now decides to eat the love bird and chases him, but falls off the porch. The bird goes back to his cage and finds that his wife has gone home to mother. She changes her mind and comes home. The bird now chases Sylvester, shouting, "Here kitty, kitty ... "

BEHIND THE MEAT BALL

Apr. 7; LT; Directed by (uncredited) Frank Tashlin; Story by Melvin Millar; Animation by I. Ellis; Musical Direction by Carl W. Stalling.
Fido is sleeping, dreaming of all manner of steaks, roasts, and chops. A hamburger appears, he shakes his head, and a hand removes the onion. His mistress calls him for dinner, and he's so happy he does an Indian war dance around his dinner bowl. When he examines the contents, however, his mood changes. All vegetables ("Bugs Bunny food!"). He finds a dog food can and eats its contents. Something tastes funny. He reads the contents label and finds it is loaded with carbohydrates, proteins, dextrose, calcium, vitamins, "But No Meat!" He spits out the food, flattens the can, and cries, "I want meat! You've had this feeling before, haven't you, folks?" He imagines a tree stump to be a roast, a tennis racquet to be a T-Bone steak, and finally sees a real steak fall from a meat market truck. The dog thinks this too may be a mirage. When a little dog picks up the juicy steak and walks off with it, his brain cells tell him, "That was real meat, YOU DOPE!" A large bulldog enters the contest, and the steak becomes the object of a three-dog tug of war. They chase around the neighborhood, and while the bulldog punches out Fido, the little dog eats the meat. Fido mallets the bulldog and himself. He observes, "We can dream, can't we?" and both dogs imagine a parade of meats passing by.

HARE TRIGGER

Bugs Bunny, Yosemite Sam; May 5; MM; Directed by I. Freleng; Story by Michael Maltese; Animation by Manuel Perez, Ken Champin, Virgil Ross, and Gerry Chiniquy; Layouts and Backgrounds by Paul Julian and Hawley Pratt; Musical Directed by Carl Stalling.
Bugs Bunny is traveling west on the Superchief when the train is held up by the notorious bandit Yosemite Sam, "the meanest, roughest, rip-roarin'est, Edward Everett Horton-est, hombre that ever packed a six-shooter." When Sam challenges Bugs to draw a gun, the rabbit produces a pen and paper and sketches a pistol. Sam tries to draw one, but Bugs tells him "it stinks!" Sam chases the rabbit around the train, at one point Bugs opening a door to an adjoining car to find a live action saloon. "Now that's what I call deluxe accommodations!" Bugs and Sam exchange gunfire: the rabbit's bullets wait patiently for Sam to show his face before they blow his hat off. When Bugs douses Sam's head with red ink, the hombre thinks he's been shot. After

a mock funeral, Sam gets wise and chases Bugs to the live-action railroad car, where a saloon brawl is in action. Bugs throws Sam into it, roughing up the cowpoke. In a daze, Sam is loaded up with luggage by Bugs disguised as a porter. Sam yanks the bunny to the top of the train, where he ties up the rabbit, intending to throw Bugs from the moving locomotive. A cliffhanger ending asks, "Is this the end of Bugs Bunny?" Bugs walks in front of the title card, stating, "He don't know me very well, do he?"

AINT THAT DUCKY
Daffy Duck; May 19; LT; Directed by I. Freleng; Story by Michael Maltese; Animation by Gerry Chinquy; Musical Direction by Carl W. Stalling.
Daffy Duck is singing and taking a bubble bath when he is interrupted by a little yellow duck crying and clutching a briefcase. "Well, rustle my hair and call me Frankie!" Daffy inquires, "What's all the hub-bub, bub?" The little duck's response, "Ah, keep your hands off, Mr. Anthony!" Meanwhile a hunter (the voice and caricature of actor Victor Moore) comes along, singing, "A Hunting I Will Go." Daffy tries to protect the little duck, but the duckling can protect himself, telling the hunter, "Eh, shut up!." Daffy assumes this hunter is a push-over and tells him to pick on "somebody your own size." The hunter obliges by pulling out a frying pan to measure Daffy. "Oh, I'm afraid you're the right size!" The hunter chases Daffy to a barnyard, where Daffy notices something missing. "There's supposed to be a barrel here. It says so right in the script. Someone's been lying down on the job. J. L. will hear of this!" The hand of the artist paints a barrel and Daffy hides inside. The hunter finds the duck, and they chase around a fence and to a mountainside. The little yellow duck is

at every turn, sobbing over his briefcase. Daffy and the hunter team up and swipe it. Reading the paper inside, the hunter remarks, "This is awful." Daffy agrees. "It's worse than that. It's Fantasmagorical!" They show us the page, which has written on it "The End."

A GRUESOME TWOSOME
Tweety; June 9; MM; Directed by Bob Clampett; Story by Warren Foster; Animation by Robert McKimson, Manny Gould, Basil Davidovich and Rod Scribner; Layouts and Backgrounds by Thomas McKimson, Michael Sasanoff; Effects Animation by A.C. Gamer; Voice Characterization: Mel Blanc; Musical Direction Carl W. Stalling.
Two cats (one a caricature of Jimmy Durante, the other a dumb, pot-bellied goof) are rivals for a sexy female feline who will tells them "Whoever brings me a little bird can be my fella." They both sneak up on the "naked genius," Tweety (at his most vicious), who beats them with a sledgehammer, sending them crashing to the ground ("Aw! The poor putty tats! They faw down and go BOOM!").

The cats team up disguised as a horse (in the phoniest-looking pantomime pony suit you ever saw; just how a horse is supposed to attract Tweety is another question). Tweety pulls a bumblebee out of his pants, slaps it around, and shoves it in the horse costume. This creates a bucking bronco that Tweety rides like the Lone Ranger. Tweety then steals the bone from a vicious bulldog and throws it in the

horse suit, getting the dog to destroy the cats once and for all. Says Tweety, "I get wid of more putty tats dat way!"

A TALE OF TWO MICE
June 30; LT; Directed by Frank Tashlin; Story by Warren Foster; Animation by Art Davis; Musical Direction by Carl W. Stalling.
Two mice, Babbit and Catsello, try to steal some cheese from under the nose of the house cat. The cat chases Catsello into his mouse hole, where Babbit gives him a pep talk. "Where's your courage? Some of the greatest names in history have been rats!" "Yeah, and I know one of them!" responds the portly mouse.

Babbit makes a diagram and talks his pal into walking out to get the cheese. Babbit locks the door behind him. Running to break the door down, Catsello is propelled by an elastic band at the doorway toward the cat! "My mother told me there would be days like this!"

Other attempts to get cheese include Catsello in a model airplane that crash lands, Babbit raising Catsello by a rope and pulley with the cheese over the sleeping cat, Catsello walking on the cat's paw to get cheese and discovering how his claws work by dancing on them. The cat tosses the fat mouse in the air to catch him in his mouth, but the rodent clobbers the cat with the ironing board and runs back to his roommate with the cheese. Babbit protests, "You know I don't like Swiss!" Catsello stuffs it in his mouth. "Well, you're gonna like it now!"

WAGON HEELS
Porky Pig; July 28; MM; Directed by Robert Clampett; Animation by Rod Scribner, Manny Gould, I. Ellis, and C. Melendez; Layouts and Backgrounds by Thomas McKimson and Michael Sasanoff; Voice Characterization by Mel Blanc; Musical Direction by Carl Stalling.
A color remake of Clampett's earlier *Injun Trouble* (1938). In 1849, Injun Joe the "Superchief" dominated the Old West. Injun Joe is so powerful, his every step shakes the ground; he scares off bears and bites bear traps! Porky Pig leads the wagon train west, scouting ahead into "Injun Joe Territory." Porky finds a massacred wagon train, with a blue-skinned survivor, Sloppy Moe, who runs around singing, "I know something, I won't tell … " to the tune of "London Bridge."

Sloppy Moe heckles Injun Joe, thinking, "Him screwball." Injun Joe takes on Porky's wagon train, using his mouth as a cannon. He catches Porky and is about to do him in when Sloppy Moe comes by and taunts, "I know something, I won't tell." Moe is forced to reveal his secret: Injun Joe is ticklish. The Injun laughs so hard he falls off a cliff.

HARE CONDITIONED
Bugs Bunny; Aug 11; LT; Direction by Charles M. Jones; Story by Tedd Pierce; Animation by Ken Harris, Ben Washam, Basil Davidovich and Lloyd Vaughn; Musical Direction by Carl Stalling.
Bugs Bunny is part of a department-store display window depicting a woodland scene. A store official (a caricature of radio's Throckmorton P. Gildersleeve) tells Bugs he's being transferred to the Taxidermy Department, adding that he'll "look very nice, after you're stuffed." Gildersleeve chases the rabbit around the store, stopping only to help a lovely female customer (Bugs in disguise), who asks, "I'm looking for something nice in a pair of bedroom slippers." "Confidentially, so am I!" he replies. Continuing the chase, they run into every department, dressing appropriately in each section: the boys' section (shorts and a Little Lord Fauntleroy suit); the Turkish bath (towels and slippers); Sports (Bugs in a rowboat, Gildersleeve on skiis); the costume shop (front and back of a horse costume); and, running out of the lingerie department, a wolf-whistling Bugs chasing a negligee-clad Gildersleeve. After some elevator gags, they wind up on the roof. Cornered, Bugs tries some small talk, telling the storekeeper about a scary book he just read. The rabbit describes a suspenseful scene happening behind him, and when Gildersleeve turns around, Bugs makes

a horrible face. Gildersleeve is so frightened he jumps off the building to his death. Bugs makes the scary face in a mirror and hurls himself from roof!

FRESH AIREDALE

Aug 25; MM; Directed by Charles M. Joens; Story by Michael Maltese; Animation by Ben Washam, Lloyd Vaughan and Ken Harris; Music Direction by Carl Stalling.

A parable on success and fame with a moral: if you are in the right place at the right time, and give the right impression, you will succeed no matter what back-stabbing you've done to get there.

A dog named Shep is treated like a king by his master. At dinnertime, Shep gets a large meaty bone, the cat a small leftover fish. Shep steals and eats the master's steak. The master thinks the cat has done it and throws him out. Shep offers up his dog bone. The master rewards Shep with another steak. When the master goes off to work, Shep is bribed by a burglar to let him into the house. The cat attacks the burglar, but when the master returns, Shep makes it look as if he had chased the crook away. Shep is hailed in the newspapers as a "Heroic Dog." Another item in the paper about the "No. 1 Dog" gives Shep, that night, a surreal nightmare in which Shep hops a train to the "No. 1 Dog," with the cat following. When Shep is about to attack the dog, the cat clubs Shep into the river. The "No. 1 Dog" rescues Shep, but when reporters come by, Shep makes it look as if he had rescued the pooch. Shep is honored with a ticker-tape parade, while the cat gets mud in his face on the sidelines. The cat pounds his fists against the statue of justice until the scales fall on his head.

THE BASHFUL BUZZARD

Beaky Buzzard; Sept 5; LT; Directed by Robert Clampett; Story by Michael Sasanoff; Animation by Robert McKimson; Voice Characterization by Mel Blanc; Musical Direction by Carl Stalling.

Mama Buzzard instructs her progeny each to bring home something for dinner. They all take off like fighter planes, except the shy Mortimer Snerd bird, Beaky (nicknamed "Killer"). "At least go out and get a butterfly, or a little worm, or something." He follows his brothers, who raid a farm, smashing into a rooster weather vane. Mama rescues Beaky. "My little killer, the spitting image of his papa. Patooie!" Beaky tries again, and attacks a flock of sheep, pulling the wool of a little lamb. Mama is delighted with what her boys are bringing home: a cow, complete with a farmer still milking, a dog clinging to his hydrant, a horse and buggy with two lovers aboard ("When I'm with you I feel like I'm way up in the clouds"), and a parade of circus elephants, including one little pachyderm with a sign reading "I am NOT Dumbo!" Beaky, on the other hand, is "bringing home a baby bumblebee." Its parent stings Beaky, who races to a water hole to relieve the pain. A little creature laughs at Beaky, and the buzzard picks a fight. The creature turns out to be a giant winged dragon who chases Beaky into a cloud.

When Beaky returns, Mama scolds him for not ever coming home with one "teensy-weensie piece of meat." The dragon whose tail is in Beaky's hand, responds, "Well now, I wouldn't say that!"

PECK UP YOUR TROUBLES

Sylvester; Oct 20; MM; Directed by I. Freleng; Story by Michael Maltese; Animation by Ken Champin; Musical Direction by Carl Stalling.

A hungry Sylvester chases a silent little woodpecker. The cat uses a leafy twig attached to his head as camouflage and climbs the tree where the woodpecker has made his home. The bird greases the oak, causing Sylvester to fall. The cat tries chopping down the tree, but a bulldog pressures Sylvester into repairing the damage with wood stucco. Sylvester tries stilts, which the woodpecker pecks. Sylvester hangs on a branch. The bird pecks a dotted line, then cuts along it.

Sylvester tries tightrope walking on the electric wires, but gets zapped. He then flies to the woodpecker's home via a kite. When Sylvester reaches into the tree, the bird places a tomato in his paw. The cat thinks he's crushed the feathered fellow. The woodpecker dresses as an angel and offers Sylvester a gun to end it all. Feeling guilty, the cat almost does until he recognizes the tobacco brand on the back of the bird's angel costume. Sylvester makes a few more attempts to get the bird, then realizes and holds up a sign that reads, "Anything is possible in a cartoon!" He runs in to the bird's house and is caught in a tight branch. Sylvester strings the tree with dynamite, but the dog's presence changes his mind. The woodpecker causes the dynamite to explode around Sylvester, who ends up on a cloud in a real angel outfit.

HARE TONIC
Bugs Bunny, Elmer Fudd; Nov 10; LT; Directed by Charles M. Jones; Story by Tedd Pierce; Animation by Ben Washam, Lloyd Vaughn and Ken Harris; Layouts and Backgrounds by Earl Klein and Robert Gribbroek; Musical Direction by Carl Stalling.
Elmer Fudd heads home with a captive Bugs Bunny from the market, singing "Mammy's little baby loves wabbit stew." The rabbit has second thoughts about escaping. "I just can't leave. I gotta stay and heckle that character!" The rabbit goes behind the radio and imitates a news announcer and warns that "All rabbits sold within the last three days are infected with the dread disease Rabbititus." Elmer panics at the thought of being "Twapped with a cwazy contaminated wabbit!" He tells Bugs he is free to scamper away, "far, far away!" Pretending to be puzzled, Bugs sniffs himself. "Don't tell me I offend?" The front door is posted with a warning "Quarantined for Rabbititus." Bugs tries to calm Fudd by proving he's not contagious. He displays spots before his eyes, a coated tongue (with a suit jacket), and throws fits. Bugs chases Elmer around the house, then comes to the door as "Dr. Killpatient." The doctor tests Elmer's "rabbit inclinations," which has Fudd screaming in horror, "I'm a wabbit!" Elmer gets wise and chases the rabbit out of the house. Bugs scares Fudd into

thinking the audience has Ribbititus. Fudd runs back indoors. Bugs reassures us that if we had Rabbititus we'd see colored spots (which we do), they would swirl, and everything would go black (which it does!).

NASTY QUACKS
Daffy Duck; Dec 1; MM; Directed by Frank Tashlin; Story by Warren Foster; Animation by Art Davis, I. Ellis, and Richard Bickenbach; Backgrounds by Richard H. Thomas; Voice Characterization by Mel Blanc; Musical Direction by Carl Stalling.
In still pictures we're told that "Once upon a time there was a doting father who gave his cute little daughter a cute little duckling. Then, as most pets do, the little duckling became like one of the family." Except that Daffy Duck has now grown up into an obnoxious house guest, slowly driving "Daddy" crazy. Papa tries to get rid of Daffy, but little Agnes forbids him to lay a hand on her pet.

The father puts Mickey Finn pills in Daffy's drink, then proposes a toast. Daffy switches glasses, causing Papa to run out, holding his mouth. Daddy next uses a mating call to lure Daffy, then chases the duck with an axe. Daffy takes the hint and packs his bags, but quickly returns to the door, remembering, "the government doesn't want us to do any nonessential traveling!"

Papa brings Agnes a new baby duckling. The girl forgets about Daffy completely, and Dad throws the screwball out. That night, Daffy intends to murder the duckling, but first feeds it Vitamin B1 to make it grow. It does, growing into a sexy girl duck. The next morning, Papa happily comes to the breakfast table. Daffy is there with his new wife and their brood of wacky, obnoxious ducklings!

1946

BOOK REVUE

Daffy Duck; Jan 5; LT; Directed by Robert Clampett; Story by Warren Foster; Animation by Robert McKimson, Rod Scribner, Manny Gould, and C. Melendez; Layouts and Backgrounds by Thomas McKimson, and Cornett Wood; Voice Characterization by: Mel Blanc; Musical Direction by Carl Stalling.

This is the ultimate cartoon of the books-come-to life genre. Midnight in a bookshop: *Young Man With a Horn* (Harry James) gives out with a trumpet solo; *The Whistler* and *The Sea Wolf* ogle *Cherokee Strip; The Complete Works of Shakespeare* pop a spring; *Henry the Eighth* runs home to *The Aldrich Family; The Voice in the Wilderness* (Frank Sinatra) drives the *The Little Women* crazy; *Freckles, Girls' Dormitory, Lady in the Dark,* Whistler's Mother (on the cover of the *Famous Painting*) and *Mother Goose* fall to his charms.

A jam session ensues with *Brass* (Tommy Dorsey), *Drums Along the Mohawk* (Gene Krupa), *The Pie-Eyed Piper* (Benny Goodman), and the *Arkansas Traveler.* Daffy Duck steps off the cover of *Looney Tunes Merrie Melodies Comics* to protest the swing music. He dons a zoot suit and wig from the *Saratoga Trunk* and, stepping in front of *Danny Boy,* imitates Danny Kaye singing "Carolina in the Morning" in a Russian accent. In a wild skat song, Daffy warns *Little Red Riding Hood* of the wolf. The wolf chases Daffy on pogo sticks in *Hopalong Cassidy,* to *Uncle Tom's Cabin* in black face, and into *The Petrified Forest. The Police Gazette* calls *The Long Arm of the Law* to bring the wolf to the *Judge.* The wolf is sentenced to *Life,* but makes an *Escape.* He trips on Durante's *So Big* nose, slides on *Skid Row* into *Dante's Inferno.* The book characters jitterbug in celebration! The wolf shouts to "Stop that dancing up there— you sillies!"

BASEBALL BUGS

Bugs Bunny; Feb 2; LT; Directed by I. Freleng; Story by Michael Maltese; Animation by Manuel Perez, Ken Champin, Virgil Ross, and Gerry Chiniquy; Layouts and Backgrounds by Hawley Pratt and Paul Julian; Voice Characterization by Mel Blanc; Musical Direction by Carl Stalling.

At the polo grounds, a baseball game between the Gas House Gorillas (a tough group of loud-mouthed, over-weight "Brooklyn Bums") and the Tea Totalers (old-timers, including one who boasts "I'm only 93½ years old!"). Bugs Bunny is watching from his hole in right field and heckles the Gorillas. They decide to teach him a lesson and take him up on his offer to take them on "all by himself."

The rest of the film is a series of gags around the baseball diamond, with Bugs playing all positions. Highlights include Bugs pitching one slow ball that strikes out three Gorillas, a Gorilla dressed up as an umpire call Bugs "out," but the rabbit tricks him into calling him safe, and Bugs distracting the player at home plate with a sexy pin-up, enabling the bunny to score.

The Gorillas need a home-run to tie in the last inning, and a player bats one with a tree trunk out of the park. Bugs takes a bus to a skyscraper, climbs the flagpole on the roof and throws his catcher's mitt, catching the ball for an out. When the Gorillas protest the call, the Statue of Liberty joins in, "That's what the man said, you heard what he said, he said that ..."

HOLIDAY FOR SHOESTRINGS

Feb 23; MM; Direction: I. Freleng;
Story by Michael Maltese, Tedd Pierce;
Animation by Gerry Chiniquy, Manuel
Perez, Ken Champin, and Virgil Ross;
Layouts and Backgrounds Paul Julian,
Hawley Pratt; Musical Direction by Carl
Stalling.

Signs all over town announce Help
Wanted at Jake's Shoe Repair. In this
takeoff on the old "shoemaker and the
elves" fable, little Fudd-like elves visit
Jake's shop and construct shoes in a
series of gags reused from *Rhapsody in
Rivets* (1941) and *Lights Fantastic*
(1942). Laurel and Hardy elves paint
shoe tongues red; an ice-skating elf
creates insoles; an Indian snake
charmer elf ties snakelike laces; and
Russian elves do a Cossack dance in
boots. Eventually, Jake wakes up, realizes what's going on, and tries to sneak
out for golf. The elves nail him to his
bed, with one taking his golf hat and
clubs for a reward.

QUENTIN QUAIL

*Mar 2; MM; Directed by Charles M.
Jones; Story by Tedd Pierce; Animation
by Ben Washam, Ken Harris, Basil
Davidovich, and Lloyd Vaugh;
Backgrounds by Robert Gribbroeck;
Musical Direction by Carl W. Stalling.*

Quentin Quail is looking for a worm for
his baby Toots' supper. Chasing a
worm, he gets socked into the ground,
"plunged" through the sky, and his
hand smashed. In a fit of frustration he
asks Toots, "Why don't you catch
him!" The baby brings the worm right
back then lets it go. A crow claims it,
starting a fight between the two birds
for the food. Toots eventually gets the
worm, but can't eat it because "he
looks like Frank Sinatra!"

A take-off on Fanny Brice's "Baby
Snooks" radio program. Another nice
combination of realistic and stylized
backgrounds.

BABY BOTTLENECK

*Porky Pig, Daffy Duck; Mar 16; LT;
Directed by Robert Clampett; Story by
Warren Foster; Animation by Rod
Scribner, Manny Gould, Robert
McKimson, and J.C. Melendez; Layouts*

*and Backgrounds by Thomas McKimson
and Cornett Wood; Voice
Characterizations by Mel Blanc; Musical
Direction by Carl W. Stalling.*

A postwar baby-boom cartoon begins
with a headline that reads: "Unprece-
dented Demand For Babies Overworks
Stork." Inside the Stork Club, the over-
worked stork gets drunk (a la Durante
"I do all the work, and the fathers get
all the credit!"). More headlines:
"Inexperienced Help Being Used To
Make Emergency Deliveries," "Some
Slight Mistakes Made." One example is
a baby skunk being delivered to
Mother Goose. Another, a baby kitten
to a mother duck and a baby gorilla to
Mrs. Kangaroo. A baby hippo is sent to
Scotty Dog, a baby cat to Mrs. Mouse,
and, the most painful, a baby alligator
to Mrs. Pig!

A new headline: "Porky Pig To Handle All Stork Problems With Daffy
Duck Assistant Traffic Manager." Cut
to "Pig and Duck, Nip and Tuck Delivery Service." Daffy is handling the
phone orders, sending orders parcel
post, and taking complaints from Bing
Crosby and Eddie Cantor. In the front
office, Porky is approached by a dog
inventor whose latest idea is "a lu-lu!"
His rocket pack explodes and "it's back
to the drawing board!" A conveyor belt
system, in which the babies are dia-
pered, fed, and burped, is used. Porky
finds an egg without an address and
forces Daffy to sit on it. Daffy runs off,
but Porky grabs his leg, stretching it all
over the factory. Porky chases Daffy
into the conveyor belt system, and they
both are caught and packaged as a
baby (one baby, that is, with Daffy on
top and Porky's feet out the bottom).
They are shipped to Africa and delivered to Mrs. Gorilla. She begins to
change baby's diaper and sees Porky.
She calls "Mr. Anthony" for advice!

HARE REMOVER

*Bugs Bunny, Elmer Fudd; Mar 23; MM;
Directed by Frank Tashlin; Story by
Warren Foster; Animation by Richard
Bickenbach, Art Davis, Cal Dalton, and
I. Ellis; Backgrounds by Richard H.
Thomas; Voice Characterization by Mel*

Blanc; Effects Animation by A.C. Gamer; Musical Direction by Carl W. Stalling.

In his laboratory, Elmer Fudd is trying to make a formula that will turn a normal character into a fiend. He tries it out on his dog, Rover, forcing him to drink it. Rover goes wild, breaks his bonds and runs outside to eat grass. Elmer needs to trap a rabbit for more experiments. He sets an old-fashioned rabbit trap. Bugs Bunny takes the carrot and goes along with the gag, pretending to be captured.

In the lab, Bugs gets suspicious. ("This guy's tryin' to slip me a mickey!") Elmer forces him to drink, and the rabbit has fits, cold spells, and spins around. Elmer anticipates a gruesome monster, but "No soap, Doc!" Elmer cries over being a lousy scientist. Bugs, to cheer him up, gives him the potion to drink. Elmer goes into fits and imitates a gorilla, while Bugs holds up picture cards indicating that Fudd is a "Screw Ball," a "Crack pot," a "Drip," and has "Bats in his Belfry." Elmer runs outside to join Rover eating grass.

A bear wearing Elmer's hat wanders into the lab, and Bugs thinks he's Fudd. Bugs tries to help, but the bear throws the potion at the rabbit. Bugs runs, and the bear picks up his carrot. Elmer returns and thinks the bear is Bugs Bunny. Seeing the real rabbit in the window, Elmer plays dead and the bear walks away. Bugs climbs on top of Fudd, imitating the bear, growling in Elmer's face. The bear is watching on the sidelines, holding up the "Screwball," "Crackpot," "Drip" picture cards.

DAFFY DOODLES

Daffy Duck, Porky Pig; Apr 16; LT; Directed by Robert McKimson; Story by Warren Foster; Musical Direction by Carl W. Stalling.

In a large eastern city a demon is loose. Daffy Duck is a mustache maniac who draws whiskers on all the ads, his life calling to put "a mustache on every lip!" Meanwhile, Policeman Porky Pig has stationed himself in a trash can, holding a picture frame, as a decoy. Daffy paints the pig, then runs into the subway to smear the train passengers.

Porky tracks Daffy to a theater where all the movie advertising has been vandalized (including a picture of Bugs Bunny). Daffy is painting his masterpiece on a giant billboard. Porky races to the roof. Daffy threatens to jump, and does—to the ledge. Porky chases him around the building. Porky almost falls, but Daffy grabs him and boasts, "Mighty sporting of the little black duck!" Daffy now chases Porky along the ledge on a motorcycle.

After a chase inside the building, Porky brings Daffy to trial. The duck is found not guilty by a jury of Jerry Colonnas!

The first cartoon directed by Robert McKimson. McKimson produced quite a few outstanding cartoons in the late forties, before settling into a squarer style in the 1950s.

HOLLYWOOD CANINE CANTEEN

Apr 20; MM; Directed by Robert McKimson; Story by Warren Foster; Animation by Cal Dalton, Don Williams, and Richard Bickenbach; Backgrounds by Richard H. Thomas; Musical Direction by Carl W. Stalling.

A fast-paced collection of spot gags at the USO Canteen for the pets of Hollywood stars, all drawn as dogs. Bing Crosby welcomes the servicemen. Inside, we watch Carmen Miranda, Abbott and Costello, Jerry Colonna, Blondie and Dagwood (drawn in Chic Young style), Laurel and Hardy, Edward G. Robinson, and Ed Wynn enjoy the sounds of Leopold Bowowski and his orchestra. Bing and Frankie serenade Dorothy Lamour, Kaynine Kyser, and Ishcapoodle. A jam session includes "Hairy" James, Tommy "Dorgy," Lionel "Hambone," "Boney" Goodman, and "Schnauser" Durante.

A running gag has a serviceman waiting to make a call, and finally getting his chance at a megaphone to call home.

HUSH MY MOUSE

Sniffles; May 4; LT; Directed by Charles M. Jones; Story by Tedd Pierce; Animation by Ken Harris, Ben Washam, Lloyd Vaughn, and Basil Davidovich; Layouts and Backgrounds, Earl Klein, and Robert Gribbroek; Voice Characterization by Mel Blanc; Musical Direction by Carl W. Stalling.

At Tuffy's Tavern, tough guy Edward G. Robincat comes in for today's special, Mouse Knuckles. Tavern keeper Art sends his moronic flunky Filligan to catch the over-talkative little Sniffles Mouse. After a few chase gags, Sniffles turns the tables by putting his little hat on a bulldog's bone. Filligan brings the bone to the tavern, where the bulldog retrieves his bone by beating up Robincat and Art. Filligan tells Tuffy over the phone, "No, he doesn't need mouse knuckles, but he can sure use some *brass* knuckles."

A take-off on the popular "Duffy's Tavern" radio program, this cartoon was Sniffles's last appearance.

HAIR-RAISING HARE

Bug Bunny; May 25; LT; Directed by Charles M. Jones; Story by Tedd Pierce; Animation by Ben Washam, Ken Harris, Basil Davidovich, and Lloyd Vaughan; Layouts and Backgrounds by Robert Gribbroek and Earl Klein; Voice Characterization by Mel Blanc; Musical Direction by Carl W. Stalling.

Bugs Bunny is about to go to bed. He has the feeling he's being watched, and he is, via television in the laboratory of an evil scientist (caricature of Peter Lorre). To feed his monster, Lorre sends a sexy robot rabbit to lure the bunny to his castle ("You don't need to lock that door, Mac. I don't want to leave!"). Bugs kisses the robot, but she falls apart. Bugs is anxious to meet Lorre's other friend, but it's a hairy, orange sneaker-wearing monster. Bugs packs his bags and tries to leave ("Don't think it hasn't been a little slice of heaven—cause it hasn't!"). Bugs

asks the monster to help him open the door. Seeing the creature, he goes into panic poses (with a "Yipe!" sign). The monster is so scary, he frightens his own mirror image away. The monster stalks Bugs all over the castle. Chase gags include Bugs disguised as a lamp (with lit bulbs in his ears), Bugs as a beauty shop manicurist ("Now let's dip our patties in the water"), a chase behind a series of bogus wall paintings, the rabbit jousting the monster with a lance, turning his suit of armor into "Canned Monster," and finally scaring the monster by pointing out the people in the audience. The sexy, mechanical rabbit walks by and gives Bugs a kiss. He follows her off: "So it's mechanical!"

KITTY KORNERED

Porky Pig, Sylvester; June 8; LT; Directed by Robert Clampett; Animation by Manny Gould, Rod Scribner, and C. Melendez; Layouts and Backgrounds by Thomas McKimson and Dorcy Howard; Voice Characterization by Mel Blanc; Musical Direction by Carl W. Stalling.

It's 9:00 p.m., "the witching hour, when everybody winds the clock and puts out the cat." At Porky Pig's house, the ritual is somewhat different: the cats throw *him* out. When Porky beats on the door, the cats answer in unison, "Milkman, keep those bottles quiet!" Inside, the four pussycats are drinking "Arsenic and Old Grapes" and singing "Auld Lang Syne." Porky makes a startling appearance at the window, and the cats scram. One squeezes into a little ceramic Scotsman, another into the fishbowl, another behind an alarm clock. The last tries to get into a mouse hole, and when Porky pulls it out, the cat pokes the pig's eye, causing cat and mouse to roll around the floor like balls on a pool table. Porky pulls another cat from a hanging moose head, extracting the moose himself from the wall!

Porky threatens the cats with his dog Lassie (Porky using hand-shadows). This sends three of the cats out the front door and one down the kitchen drain! One of the cats, Sylvester, gives them a speech. "Brother pussycats! We've been skidded out, scooted out, backed out, and booted out! It's un-catstitutional!" They concoct a plan and dress as Martians (the traditional Clampett "Gremlin" garb, including the lightbulb headpiece). They awaken Porky with a frantic news report about "Men from Mars landing on Earth." Porky panics when he sees Martians around his bed and runs for the musket he keeps "in case of invasion From mars." The cats charge Porky a la Teddy Roosevelt's Rough Riders. Porky lands in the snow, and asks, "does anyone in the audience know somebody who has a house to rent?"

HOLLYWOOD DAFFY

Daffy Duck; June 22; MM; Directed by I. Freleng; Story by Michael Maltese; Animation by Ken Champin, Virgil Ross, Gerry Chiniquy, and Manuel Perez; Layouts and Backgrounds by Hawley Pratt and Paul Julian; Voice Characterization by Mel Blanc; Musical Direction by Carl W. Stalling.

Daffy Duck gets off the bus in Holly-wood and kisses the sidewalk. He marches into Warmer Bros. studio, but a studio guard (looking like a Keystone Kop) throws him out. The guard greets Bette Davis and Johnny Weissmuller, and Daffy tries to get past by imitating Charlie Chaplin, Jimmy Durante, Bing Crosby, and finally as a gold Oscar statue! The studio guard presses a button "for gate crashers posing as the Academy Oscar." A mechanical arm kicks the duck out. The guard chases Daffy through the studio. Posing as a tour guide, Daffy forces the guard on the bus and points out the dressing rooms of Abbott and Costello (one fat, one tall), Ann Sheridan (surrounded by bear traps and barbed wire), and Jimmy Durante (with a trap on his foot!). Daffy abuses the guard and runs off. Daffy disguises himself as a direc-tor and flatters the cop into thinking he's an actor. Daffy covers the cop with a ton of make-up and "directs" him to jump over a wall. After the fall, the cop chases Daffy around the sets and back-drops and finally grabs him. Daffy demands to "See stars. And, I'm not leaving till I see them!" The guard obliges by beating him on the head and tossing him in the trash can. Daffy sees stars at last, imagining one of them is Ann Sheridan!

ACROBATTY BUNNY

Bugs Bunny; June 29; LT; Directed by Robert McKimson; Story by Warren Foster; Animation by Arthur Davis, Cal Dalton, and Richard Bickenbach; Layouts and Backgrounds by Cornett Wood and Richard H. Thomas; Voice Characterization by Mel Blanc; Musical Direction by Carl W. Stalling.

While Bugs Bunny sleeps in his fur-nished rabbit hole, the circus comes to town, and the lion's cage is put directly atop his home. The cage's occupant, hungry Nero Lion, sniffs the hole for breakfast. Bugs decides to go up and fix "the wise guy fanagling around up there." Leaving his hole, Bugs scans the huge interior of the lion's mouth and calls for "Pinocchio!" Sizing up the situation, Bugs runs from the cage that restrains the lion and teases the beast by running a paddle along the iron bars. Unfortunately for Bugs, the door is open, and the lion jumps out. Bugs jumps into the cage and locks the door. The lion recruits an elephant to help break open the cage, but Bugs uses a wind-up mouse to scare the pachy-derm, who in turn uses the lion as a weapon to beat the mouse. Nero uses his strength to open the bars and chases Bugs around the circus to a dressing room, from which the bunny emerges as a clown, singing, "Laugh, Clown, Laugh." He then mallets the big cat. Nero chases Bugs onto the trapeze, where Bugs lets the lion fall with no net. The bunny bounces into a cannon, and the lion follows, getting stuck in the barrel. Bugs fires the gun, leaving a dazed Nero as the dancing partner of a new musical act: "Bugs Bunny and His Hula Hula Lion."

THE EAGER BEAVER

July 13; MM; Directed by Chuck Jones; Story by Tedd Pierce.

"A never ending source of wonderment is the engineering skill exhibited by our friends, the beavers ..." So begins a series of fast-paced spot gags about our buck-toothed pals. To protect their homes, the beavers dam the river ("blankety blank blank" curse words appear); the beavers change their axe blades like razor blades, birds parachute out of falling trees shouting, "Geronimo!" A running gag shows a beaver foreman guiding a log, "Just a little further, just a little more to the right ..."

Eager Beaver is a goofy, ski-capped chap who is so eager he chops down phone poles. He gets the assignment to bring down the giant tree on the mountaintop and races for it to the tune of the "William Tell Overture." Meanwhile, a crow warns the beavers, "There's a flood coming! Get a move on, Stupid!" Eager Beaver finally cuts the tree with the aid of a termite and races the flood with the giant tree in his hands—getting it into the dam at the last moment and saving the day. The cartoon ends as the foreman, who has been precisely guiding one log through the whole film, tells them to "let 'er go!" It pounds him into the ground.

A fun little one-shot from Jones, who may have been trying to develop a new character here. Lots of fast moving "smear" animation, characters zipping from one pose to another.

THE GREAT PIGGY BANK ROBBERY

Daffy Duck; July 20; LT; Directed by Robert Clampett; Story by Warren Foster; Animation by Rod Scribner, Manny Gould, C. Melendez and I. Ellis; Layouts and Backgrounds by Thomas McKimson and Philip DeGuard; Voice Characterization by Mel Blanc; Musical Direction by Carl W. Stalling.

An absolutely classic Clampett Looney Tune.

One morning, in the barnyard, comic-book maniac Daffy Duck has just received his latest issue from the mailbox ("I can hardly wait to see what happens to Dick Tracy! I love that man!!"). Fancying himself to be like his hero, Daffy accidentally knocks himself out and dreams he's "Duck Twacy."

As Twacy, Daffy receives phone calls about stolen piggy banks ("It looks like a piggy bank crime wave!"); he finds his is missing as well. Going out to look for clues with his magnifying glass, Daffy bumps into a detective from Scotland Yard ("Scram Sherlock! I'm workin' this side of the street!"). He takes a street car (Porky Pig cameo as conductor) to the Gangster's Hideout (labeled with large signs and banners— including a lit neon one). Falling through a trap door, Daffy follows footprints that walk along the ceiling ("Nothing's impossible to Duck Twacy!") back to a mouse hole where he meets Mouse Man. Daffy runs into a plethora of colorful Chester Gouldesque vilains, including: "Snake Eyes, 88 Teeth, Hammer Head, Pussycat Puss, Bat Man, Double Header, Pickle Puss, Pumpkin Head, Neon Noodle, Juke Box Jaw, and Wolf Man." Rubber Head, a pencil-necked villain with an eraser head, tries to "rub" Daffy out. Daffy throws a grenade at Pumpkin Head, leaving a stack of pumpkin pies (35 cents each!). The duck then gets tangled up with Neon Noodle and twists him into "Eat At Joe's." Daffy mows them all down with a machine gun and finds the piggy banks, including his own. Kissing his piggy bank, the duck wakes up back on the farm, kissing a sow in the muddy pig sty. Says the pig, "I love that duck!"

BACALL TO ARMS

Aug 3; MM; Directed by Robert Clampett (uncredited); Animation by Manny Gould, Don Williams, Rod Scribner and I. Ellis; Layouts and Backgrounds by Thomas McKimson and Philip DeGuard; Musical Direction by Carl W. Stalling.

A wolf (the Hollywood variety) goes to the movies. On screen, the "Warmer News" newsreel shows how radar finds a useful place in the American home, in warning husbands of impending visits by their mothers-in-law. The wolf follows a sexy usherette to the lobby and gets slapped.

The feature attraction has Bogey Gocart and Laurie Becool in "To Have ... To Have ... To Have." A fat hippo makes his way down the aisle. Bogey, on screen, tells him, "Hey, fat boy! Sit down!" The wolf naps until Bacall comes on the screen. He goes wild at the sight of her and when Bogey and Bacall kiss, falls through his chair, then kisses the patron in front of him. When Bacall tosses her cigarette off the screen, the wolf races to get it. Bogart shoots the wolf, grabs the butt, and begins puffing. It explodes, leaving Bogey in blackface, saying, a la Rochester, "My, oh my! I can work for Mr. Benny now!"

OF THEE I STING

Aug 17; LT; Directed by I. Freleng; Story by Michael Maltese.

A battalion of mosquitoes is shown training for their mission, an attack on a succulent, fat farmer armed to the teeth with DDT, fly swatters, and an impenetrable fortress of wire screens. At Anopleles Field, the bugs train

through an obstacle course of swatters, Limburger cheese, and flypaper and crawl under bug spray foggers. They study a chart of their target, a human map with a close-up of the farmer's backside. They take off from a sardine can aircraft carrier, each mosquito with its insignia: Gravel Gertie, Mrs. Kalabash, Bugs Bunny. They attack, conquer, and return to base, but crash into the water due to a cross-eyed member of the ground crew.

A majority of this film is reused animation from the Private Snafu cartoon TARGET: SNAFU, in which the mosquitoes were malaria carriers.

WALKY TALKY HAWKY ACADEMY AWARD NOMINEE

Foghorn Leghorn, Henery Hawk; Aug 31; MM; Directed by Robert McKimson; Story by Warren Foster; Animation by Richard Bickenbach, Cal Dalton and Don Williams; Voice Characterization by Mel Blanc; Musical Direction by Carl W. Stalling.

High up in his tree-top home, young Henery Hawk is having a talk with his Pop. "The trouble's in my tummy. I crave something, but I don't know what it is." His father begins a classic speech about how "your mother and I are outcasts, hated and hunted, because of what we are, chicken hawks!"

Henery goes out to fulfill his destiny, hunting chickens. Meanwhile, in the barnyard, a dog smashes a watermelon over the rooster's head (Foghorn Leghorn, in his first appearance). Foghorn gets even by picking up the sleeping dog's tail and wacking his behind. Henery meets Foghorn, who introduces himself as a horse. Foggy points the dog out as a chicken. Henery takes a closer look at the dog and goes into a yiddish, "Oy, that's the biggest chicken I ever did see!" The dog chases Henery as far as his leash allows. Henery picks up the doghouse with the dog in it, until the dog gets wise. Foghorn concocts a plan by which they knock the dog onto a pair of rollerskates so that Henery can wheel him home. The dog and Foghorn argue over who's a chicken. Henery unscrews the dog's leash. The hound chases Foggy into the barn. Henery goes in and pulls out the dog, Foghorn, and a horse. "One of these things, I say, one of these things has got to be a chicken!"

RACKETEER RABBIT

Bugs Bunny; Sept 14; LT; Directed by I. Freleng; Story by Michael Maltese; Animation by Gerry Chiniquy, Manriy Perez, Ken Champin and Virgil Ross; Layouts and Backgrounds by Hawley Pratt and Paul Julian; Voice Characterization by Mel Blanc; Musical Direction by Carl W. Stalling.

On a rainy night Bugs Bunny finds an abandoned house and makes himself at home by drilling a rabbit hole in the floor. Meanwhile, the police trail two gangsters, Rocky (a caricature of Edward G. Robinson) and Hugo (a caricature of Peter Lorre), to the same house.

The gangsters are busy dividing their loot. Bugs sleepily asks, "What's up, Doc?" Rocky puts a dollar in the rabbit's hand, and Bugs thinks fast. Disguising himself as a henchman he asks, "How 'bout me, boss?" "And me, Boss?" Rocky gets wise and asks for his money back, giving Bugs the third degree under a spotlight (for which Bugs dons a bathing suit and sun glasses). Getting nowhere fast, Rocky orders Hugo to take Bugs for a ride (for Bugs that means another costume change into horseless carriage garb). Bugs returns from the "ride" and Rocky pulls a gun on the bunny. Bugs makes a cake and splatters him with it. Bugs, as "Mugsy" a thug who threatens, "It's curtains for you," then hands Rocky a set of window draperies. Bugs pretends the cops are at the door. The gangsters do the "hide me" gag. Finally, Rocky is stashed in a trunk. Bugs enacts a confrontation with police that includes, "would I do this if my dear old pal were in there?" and sticks a sword through the trunk! Bugs then drags the trunk up and down the stairs and hands Rocky a bomb that explodes while Bugs pretends to fight with the cops. Rocky staggers out of the trunk and chases down the street, yelling, "Help! Police! Don't leave me with that crazy rabbit!"

FAIR AND WORM-ER

Sept 28; MM; Directed by Charles M. Jones; Story by Tedd Pierce, Michael Maltese; Animation by Ben Washam, Ken Harris, Basil Davidovich and Lloyd Vaughn; Layouts and Backgrounds by Richard Morley and Peter Brown; Musical Direction by Carl W. Stalling.

An attempt to create the ultimate chase cartoon. A worm is chased by a crow, who is chased by a cat, who is chased by a dog, who is pursued by a dog catcher, who is threatened by his wife (armed with a rolling pin), who is chased by a mouse! Got that?

The worm is actually pursuing an apple, and, at one point, the crow disguises his hand as the fruit only to have it flattened by a mallet. The dog chases the cat up a tree, and the cat places banana peels on the bark so the dog will fall into the waiting catcher's net below. The crow, witnessing this, thinks, "A. Dog chases cat. B. Cat chases bird. C. I'm a bird, therefore, D. I gotta help dog!" So, bird scissors the net and dog falls through like a basketball. Cat dribbles dog back into the net, but bird kicks dog catcher in the shins, and the chase is on again. A "Pepe LePew"-like skunk chases them all into a lumber yard, where each sneaks among the wooden planks. The worm eventually gets his apple as the narrator asks: "Do you always have to go through that to get something to eat?" The worm's punchline: "Eat it, nothin'! This is the last furnished apartment in town!"

THE BIG SNOOZE

Bugs Bunny, Elmer Fudd; Oct 5; LT; Directed by Robert Clampett; Animation by Rod Scribner, I. Ellis, Manny Gould, and J.C. Melendez; Layouts and Backgrounds by Thomas McKimson, Philip DeGuard; Voice Characterization by Mel Blanc; Musical Direction by Carl W. Stalling.

Bob Clampett's last cartoon for Warners, and he ends, literally, with a bang! Elmer Fudd is chasing Bugs Bunny all over the countryside to the tune of the William Tell Overture. Elmer chases Bugs through a hollow log which Bugs maneuvers so that

Elmer exits in mid-air (re-used animation from Avery's *All This and Rabbit Stew*).

Elmer is fed up. He rips up his contract with Mr. Warner, goes fishing, "and no more wabbits!" Bugs begs him to reconsider. "Think what we've been to each other. Why we've been like Rabbit and Costello, Damon and Runyon, Stan and Laurel!! You don't want to break up the act?"

Elmer just walks away. While he takes a nap, Bugs looks into his heavenly dream (full of nice pink clouds) and disturbs his sleep with "Nightmare Paint," creating a surreal fantasy in which Elmer is nude (except for his hat and a ring of leaves around his waist), overrun by millions of abstract rabbits created by Bugs who is "multiplying" them with an adding machine. Next, the bunny ties Fudd to a railroad track as dozens of mini wabbits run over him. Bugs dresses Fudd in drag, high heels, wig, lipstick and an evening gown, and Elmer is chases by the zoot-suited wolves on Hollywood and Vine ("Have any of you girls ever had an experience like this?"). Bugs tells Fudd to "Run this way," a mixed-up run which includes the Russian kick dance. They leap off a cliff, but Bugs takes Hare Tonic, which "Stops falling hare." Elmer crashes and awakens, pastes his contract back together, and resumes the chase with Bugs.

THE MOUSE-MERIZED CAT
Babbit and Catsello; Oct 19; MM; Directed by Robert McKimson; Story by Warren Foster; Animation by Arthur Davis, Don Williams, Richard Bickenbach, and Cal Dalton; Layouts and Backgrounds by Richard H. Thomas and Cornett Wood; Effects Animation by A.C. Gamer; Voice Characterization: Mel Blanc; Musical Direction by Carl W. Stalling.
The film begins with the camera's point of view slowly trucking toward Earth in space, toward the United States, into "Mousachewsetts," to Fluger's Delicatessen, on to a mouse hole where Catsello, the mouse, has been waiting for us. "Hey, Babbit! The people are here!" His partner, Babbit, has other ideas on his mind. He plans to hypnotize Catsello to face the cat and bring back some food. Catsello resists, but eventually his personality is transformed into Bing Crosby, singing, "You Must Have Been a Beautiful Baby," then Frankie, singing, "Trade Winds," Jimmy Durante, strutting "The Lullaby of Broadway," and Rochester, taking a phone call from "Mr. Benny." Babbit convinces Catsello he's a chicken, then a vicious dog. Catsello frightens the feline, but the cat de-hypnotizes the mouse, and a battle of Catsello's will ensues. The mouse goes back and forth, hypnotized, de-hypnotized. Catsello turns the tables on his partner and the cat, using hypnosis to make the cat believe he is a horse and Babbit a cowboy. Alone with the delicatessen full of food, Catsello, stuffing his face, laments, "I'm a Baaad Boy!"

MOUSE MENACE
Porky Pig; Nov 2; LT; Directed by Arthur Davis; Story by George Hill.
Porky is having trouble getting rid of one wise-guy mouse. The cartoon opens on a pan shot of his empty mouse traps, with notes left by the clever rodent: "I just adore cheddar," "You know I don't like swiss!," and, in a cage filled with Limburger, "Are you kiddin'?"

Porky tries with a cat, which is rocketed from the house, a mountain lion, which is quickly stuffed and mounted, and a mobster cat (with violin case filled with brass knuckles, TNT, axes, etc.), who is simply conked out with a bowling ball. Porky builds a mechanical cat with all the proper push buttons, marked "Purr," "Scratch," "Kill

Mouse." The rodent gains some ground by giving the robot an electric shock, replacing his head with a toaster, and filling a robot mouse with explosives. When the robot cat pounces upon the robot rodent, Porky's house explodes. Porky shrugs the disaster off, thinking he has finally gotten rid of the mouse, with a smaller house to live in. But Porky's problem remains. The mouse reappears and asks, "Should I tell him?"

This was Art Davis's first cartoon for Warners as director, and it's clear from the outset that he has his own style. One of his first decisions was to give Porky a huge bowtie. Stories like this, a hep-talking, wise-guy rascal versus a hapless hero, are a Davis trait.

RHAPSODY RABBIT

Bugs Bunny; Nov 9; MM; Directed by I. Freleng; Story by Tedd Pierce and Michael Maltese; Animation by Manuel Perez, Ken Champin, Virgil Ross, and Gerry Chinquy; Layouts and Backgrounds by Hawley Pratt and Terry Lind; Voice Characterization by Mel Blanc; Musical Direction by Carl W. Stalling.

Bugs Bunny, in tuxedo, takes the stage to perform a piano solo. After shooting a man coughing in the audience, the bunny attempts to play Liszt's "Second Hungarian Rhapsody," but is foiled by a little mouse.

The gags are based on the music, including Bugs having a sexy pin-up in his sheet music, the mouse changing the tempo to boogie-woogie jazz, Bugs playing the piano as though a typewriter (having to return the keyboard after each musical sentence) and, finally, the mouse stealing the spotlight, out-playing Bugs on a miniature piano.

ROUGHLY SQUEAKING

Nov 23; LT; Directed by Chuck Jones; Story by Michael Maltese and Tedd Pierce.

Two mice, Hubie and Bertie, are trying to make away with some cheese when they encounter a goofy cat who is so dumb they convince him he's a lion. They shave his hair, put a mop on his head for a mane, and set him afire to make him roar. They convince him to eat moose instead of mice. They then put antlers on the dog. Running gag: a bird witnessing the mixed-up pets checks his temperature, takes medicine, etc. The mice convince the dog he is a gazelle. After the canine sees through their scheme, the mice tell him he's a pelican. "If I was a pelican, I'd have a fish in my mouth." The dog opens wide and there is a fish. The observing bird flips out and flies past, shouting, "And I'm a Thanksgiving Turkey!"—an appropriate serving dish is strapped to his body.

Jones seemed to like having Hubie and Bertie play head tricks on their adversaries. Their future psychological adventures get even more bizarre. See *The Hypochondri-cat* (1950).

1947

ONE MEAT BRAWL

Porky Pig; Jan 18; MM; Directed by Robert McKimson; Story by Warren Foster.

Grover Groundhog celebrates Groundhog Day by singing "A Groundhog and His Shadow." The radio announces that the press is anticipating the groundhog will see his shadow, but when Grover steps outside to greet his public, he is bombarded by hunter's bullets. Porky Pig and his dog, Mandrake, are hunting too. Porky gives Mandrake the scent, but the dog returns with an old shoe. When Mandrake corners Grover in a bush, the goundhog gives a classic sob story that wins the dog to *his* side. Porky puts earmuffs on Mandrake, but the groundhog transmits his sob story via radio.

The groundhog leaves a trap for Mandrake: "Free Food—Take One Only," leaving a bone and Grover as choices. The dog naturally picks the bone. Porky arrives on the scene, and thinks Mandrake has eaten the groundhog. He scolds Mandrake, with the help of Grover whispering in his ear, reminding him of the groundhog's "seventy-two kids, no polo ponies, his wife with no nylons." When Porky comes to his senses, he and Mandrake chase Grover into his home. A fight ensues, but it's only shadow boxing—"This way no one gets hurt."

THE GOOFY GOPHERS
Goofy Gophers; Jan 25; LT; Directed by Arthur Davis; Animation by Don Williams, Manny Gould, J.C. Melendez, and Cal Dalton.

A watchdog guarding a vegetable patch spots the Goofy Gophers stocking up on food. Using "Commando Tactics," he sneaks up on them camouflaged. The gophers offer him a pumpkin (on the head), some iron (a shovel, also to the head), and give him a hot foot. They continue to haul vegetables (to a conga beat) into their underground chambers. The watchdog disguises himself as a scarecrow and gets pulled under. The gophers shove him back outside with a telegram attached. "We're vegetarians, you screwball." They then steamroll the dog into the ground.

The dog disguises his paw as a female gopher, inviting the others to dance. They dance with his paw, but pull the disguise off and lead the paw into a mousetrap. The dog tries putting explosives into a carrot. The gophers fake the explosion, and the watchdog, feeling his job is done, takes a nap. While he is sleeping the gophers load the dog in a rocket launcher and blast him to the moon. The gophers remove the "Beware of Dog" sign and rejoice, "Now we have the garden all to ourselves!" Bugs Bunny reminds them, "Well, I wouldn't say that!"

THE GAY ANTIES
Feb. 15; MM; Directed by I. Freleng; Story by Tedd Pierce and Michael Maltese; Animation by Ken Chapin, Virgil Ross, Gerry Chiniquy, and Manuel Perez; Musical Direction by Carl W. Stalling.

Set in the 1890s. While a romantic couple cuddle in the park, their picnic lunch is being taken by a colony of black ants. Ants-taking-food gags include a string of hot-dogs moving like a train, the ants constructing a vehicle that uses donuts for wheels and a banana for a body. Black Russian ants eat up a Russian rye bread, an ant on skis braves the ice for a cherry atop a sundae; ants play pool with peas on a sardine can; female ants make fancy dresses out of flowers and olives (for a bustle), then do a parasol dance. Using a sardine can for a piano, an ant accompanies a female singer (with a highly speeded-up voice) singing "Time Waits For No One."

A running gag involves an ant constructing a sandwich (with the "Hold the Onion" joke). Each time the sandwich is done, it's grabbed by a romantic gentleman to give to his love. The sandwich chef gets even by placing the woman's hand between the bread, topped with mustard. The man bites the sandwich, causing his love to scream. The insects dance back to their ant hole with their loot, including one small fry with a giant watermelon.

BIRTH OF A NOTION
Daffy Duck; Apr 12; LT; Directed by Robert McKimson; Story by Warren Foster.

While the others fly south, Daffy has a scheme that will get him a home for the winter. He tricks a gullible dog, Leopold, into letting him stay at his house. Meanwhile, Leopold's master, Peter Lorre, needs a duck's wishbone for his experiments. Daffy tries to get Leopold to help kill his master, but the duck is found out, and a chase around the house ensues. When the duck escapes, Lorre ponders using a dog's wishbone instead. Daffy tries another house, but a Joe-Besser-like goose kicks Daffy into the air. "I'm going south for the winter, jet propelled!" Iris out as Leopold joins him.

TWEETIE PIE ^{ACADEMY AWARD WINNER}
Tweety, Sylvester; May 3; MM; Directed by I. Freleng.

Warner Bros. first Oscar-winning cartoon, and the first pairing of Tweety and Sylvester. Tweety is warming himself in the snow near a cigar butt, when Sylvester (called Thomas in this picture) sneaks up on the bird and makes a grab for him. The cat grabs the cigar butt, burning his paw. Sylvester's master yells for him, asking what is in his hand. She finds Tweety wrapped in his tail, and takes the bird inside, puts it in a birdcage, and warns Thomas not to try any tricks while she sleeps. She doesn't know him very well, do she?

First, Sylvester tries piling up the furniture to reach the bird cage, but Tweety saws a chair leg, causing a crash. Next, the cat tries metal furniture, but Tweety uses a blowtorch. Sylvester uses an electric fan to fly to the cage, but Tweety pulls the plug. Sylvester's fishing-rod pulley doesn't work. The cat gets Tweety under a glass, but a pin point causes Sylvester to scream. Tweety makes a noise to bring the lady. She throws the cat out. Sylvester tries to sneak back inside via the chimney, but Tweety starts a fire. Sylvester builds a "Rube Goldberg" bird trap that promptly crowns the cat with a bowling ball. He saws a hole in the ceiling around the birdcage, and the attic drops into the living room. In the end, Sylvester gets hit with a shovel by his new master, Tweety!

SCENT-IMENTAL OVER YOU
Pepe LePew; May 8; LT; Directed by Charles M. Jones; Story by Tedd Pierce and Michael Maltese.
On Park Avenue and 86th Street, all the fancy dogs except a little female Mexican hairless are sporting new coats. She tries on the furs of her owners, finally glueing on one that fits—a skunk fur. She tries to join the other dogs, but they all run from her. Crying, she attracts the attention of Pepe LePew, who chases her all over the city. Pepe sighs, "Ahh, zee moon, ahh, zee June ... " She wants no part of that. Eventually, she tires of the chase, and Pepe brings her to his tree home (mailbox reads "Stinky"). She reveals that she is just a little dog. Pepe is delighted, "I too am zee canine!" As they embrace, Pepe reveals to *us* that he's really a skunk after all.

RABBIT TRANSIT
Bugs Bunny; May 10; MM; Directed by I. Freleng; Story by Michael Maltese and Tedd Pierce; Animation by Manuel Perez, Ken Champin, Virgil Ross, and Gerry Chiniquy; Layouts by Hawley Pratt; Backgrounds by Philip DeGuard;
Effects Animation by A.C. Gamer; Voice Characterization by Mel Blanc; Musical Direction by Carl W. Stalling.
Bugs Bunny is taking a steam bath in the national park hot springs, reading the fable of the tortoise and the hare. Bugs is incensed by the outcome of the race, and Cecil Turtle, relaxing in the sauna as well, says he will race the rabbit. They agree not to cheat, but their accord doesn't last too long. Bugs speeds from the starting line, but the turtle confides to us, "Confidentially, it's in the ag-bay!" He shows us his rocket- powered shell. The turtle zips past the rabbit and sends Bugs a Christmas card from Chicago. Bugs decides to send him something—himself, special delivery! The turtle zooms after Bugs, but Bugs grabs the jet-propelled shell and uses it himself. The turtle finds Bugs up the road, trying to fix the engine. Cecil fixes it and zooms off, Bugs on top roasting weenies. Like any good camper, Bugs puts out the fire, drenching the rocket engine with water. Bugs paints the road's white line toward a tree trunk, and paints an opening in it. The turtle rides through it; when Bugs tries, he knocks himself out. Bugs races to the finish and beats the turtle. The turtle asks how fast he was going, and Bugs brags, "100 easy." Cecil brings the police, who arrest the rabbit for speeding. The turtle asks, "Ain't I a stinker?"

HOBO BOBO
Bobo; May 17; MM; Dircted by Robert McKimson; Story by Warren Foster.
In India, while all the adult elephants are hard at work carrying logs, little Bobo is dreaming of life in the circus. The little elephant decides to leave the jungle, but his attempts to get aboard ship all fail. He tries walking up a docking rope, but falls into the sea; then hides in a crate, but is discovered. Bobo next skis off a roof and lands

smashed on the deck. The minah bird (from Jones's Inki cartoons) tells Bobo to paint himself pink—no one will admit to seeing a pink elephant. Bobo walks on and has free reign of the ship. Soon he has arrived at "The Land of the Free, the Home of the Braves, the Dodgers, etc...." Everyone tries to ignore this pink elephant. A street cleaning truck washes away Bobo's pink paint, and he is arrested and put in chains. The judge gives him a life sentence—to be in the circus! He's then made a bat boy for the big top baseball team, but complains "Bat Boy, Shmat Boy! I'm still carrying logs!"

A HARE GROWS IN MANHATTAN

Bugs Bunny; May 22; MM; Directed by I. Freleng; Story by Michael Maltese, and Tedd Pierce; Animation by Virgil Ross, Gerry Chiniquy, Manuel Perez, and Ken Champin; Layouts by Hawley Pratt; Backgrounds by Philip DeGuard; Voice Characterization by Mel Blanc; Musical Direction by Carl Stalling.
Gossip columnist Lola Beverly takes us on a tour of the estate of Hollywood star Bugs Bunny. Bugs has a pool, statuary, and formal garden, but lives in a rabbit hole. Bugs tells "Lolly" of his humble beginnings, growing up on the East Side of New York. As a student in a Little Lord Fontleroy suit, Bugs dances home singing "She's the Daughter Of Rosie O'Grady." A gang of tough dogs picks on the bunny. "What is it? Maybe it's a gi-raffe!" They "dog-pile" on the rabbit, but Bugs gets on top, jumping up and down on the tough guy leader. The big dog chases Bugs into a sewer, and gets his head flattened with the manhole lid. The dog chases Bugs through the Stork Club, then to the Automat, where the dog gets a piece of cherry pie in the face! The chase goes on via elevator to the roof, where Bugs hides in an Egyptian cigarette advertising sign. Bugs asks the dog to "fetch the stick." He does and jumps off the roof. Bugs plays, "This little piggy" with the dog's fingers, dropping the big pooch into baby clothes, then into a baby carriage. Bugs continues home,

but makes a wrong turn into a newsstand and is surrounded by dogs. Grabbing a book for a weapon, he raises it above his head. The dogs read the cover and run. Bugs walks home reading the book, *A Tree Grows in Brooklyn*.

ALONG COME DAFFY

Daffy Duck, Yosemite Sam; June 4; LT; Directed by I. Freleng; Story by Tedd Pierce and Michael Maltese.
Two Yosemite Sam brothers (one with a red beard, the other black) are starving in a desolate, snow-bound cabin. They are beginning to imagine each other as food when cookbook salesman Daffy Duck knocks on the door. Daffy reads from the book, describing various delicious dinners. The brothers are interested only in the duck recipes. They chase him around the house so desperately that black beard accidentally grabs his brother and sticks him in the oven. Daffy hides in a roomful of Daffy Duck decoys, seven of them hopping around shouting "Hoo-Hoo!" Black beard shoots them all. Only the real Daffy remains. Black beard shoots him, leaving only a "bra and panties" of feathers. The two brothers finally get Daffy in the oven. Daffy offers a free turkey dinner from his company, the Classy Cut Knish Catering Company. Their eyes bug out at the thought, but mice stream out of the wall and eat all the food before the Sams have a chance. Daffy returns to their door offering after-dinner mints. As they pull him inside, the duck realizes, "Here we go again!"

INKI AT THE CIRCUS

Inki; June 21; MM; Directed by Charles M. Jones; Story by Michael Maltese and Tedd Pierce; Animation by Ken Harris, Phil Monroe, Lloyd Vaughn, and Ben Washam; Layouts and

Backgrounds by Robert Gribbroek. The African wild man of the circus turns out to be the jungle boy, Inki. A brown dog grabs the bone in Inki's hair and buries it in the ground, leaving Inki helplessly upside down. Another dog, gray with a red hair on his head, digs up the bone. Before the two dogs can fight over it, a large crate marked "Danger" rattles and shakes, the steel safe inside opens, and the mysterious minah bird pops out. The dogs follow him to a hole, they stick their noses in to sniff, and are tied together. The grateful Inki gets his top-knot bone spun like a propeller by the bird.

The dogs chase Inki into the Big Top, and onto the high wire. They try to get off the wire, but when the Minah bird walks on it, the wire snaps, Inki bounces, and his top knot gets stuck on the high wire's landing board. The dogs reach Inki via the trapeze swings. Eventually they all fall on aerial bicycles and go loop-de-loop into a water bucket. Each thinks he has the bone. The minah bird emerges from the bucket with it in his top-knot.

EASTER YEGGS

Bugs Bunny, Elmer Fudd; June 28; LT; Directed by Robert McKimson; Story by Warren Foster; Animation by Charles McKimson, Richard Bickerbach, and I. Ellis; Layouts by Cornett Wood; Backgrounds by Richard H. Thomas; Voice Characterization by Mel Blanc; Musical Direction by Carl W. Stalling.
As Bugs Bunny reads a book on "How to Multiply," he is interrupted by a crying Easter bunny who complains of sore feet. Bugs volunteers, "I'll deliver the technicolor hen fruit for ya!" Reminded to "keep smiling," Bugs sings a gooney song, "I'm the Easter Rabbit, Hooray." His first stop is a mean little kid who chants, "I Wanna Easter Egg, I Wanna Easter Egg ... " heckling the hare.

Returning, Bugs is goaded by the rabbit into one more try. This time, Bugs is greeted by banners and posters welcoming the Easter Bunny. It's the home of Elmer Fudd, who is hungry for "Easter wabbit stew." Elmer is disguised as a baby, but Bugs is suspicious. The bunny smashes an egg in Elmer's hand and takes off. Elmer ambushes Bugs. "I can't miss with my Dick Twacy hat!" The trap sends Elmer and Bugs through a Tunnel of Love. Bugs performs a magic trick that destroys Elmer's pocket watch. Fudd gets his gun and chases Bugs. The Easter Bunny puts up a rope to stop Bugs. In a daze, Bugs returns and manages to paint Elmer's head like an Easter egg for the mean little kid to pound with his hammer. Bugs takes care of the Easter Bunny by lighting a fuse on an explosive egg. Bugs reminds the Easter Bunny, "keep smiling!"

CROWING PAINS

Foghorn Leghorn, Sylvester, Henery Hawk; July 12; LT; Directed by Robert McKimson; Story by Warren Foster; Animation by John Carey, I. Ellis, Charles McKimson, and Manny Gould; Layout and Cornett Wood; Backgrounds by Richard H. Thomas; Voice Characterization by Mel Blanc; Musical Direction by Carl W. Stalling.
A bush moves around the barnyard. It's Sylvester trying to steal the bone from the barnyard dog. The dog chases the cat, but his rope restrains him, choking him. Sylvester swings an axe at the helpless dog. Foghorn Leghorn grabs the weapon, ordering the cat to "bury the hatchet!" Meanwhile, Henery Hawk grabs Foghorn and drags him away. Foggy laughs at Henery for thinking he's a chicken. He instructs Henery that a chicken has black fur like Sylvester's. Foghorn puts Henery in a trick egg and places it underneath the cat. At first Sylvester is proud to be a mother, but decides to get rid of the hen fruit. Henery, inside the egg, tries to stick with Sylvester and chases him around the barnyard. Sylvester tries to tell Henery he's not a chicken, but that Foghorn is. They argue and soon the dog joins in. Henery decides to wait till dawn to see who crows. At dawn, the crowing emanates from Sylvester, and Henery drags him away. Foghorn, with a ventriloquism manual in hand, advises, "I say you gotta keep on your toes."

THE UP-STANDING SITTER

Daffy Duck; July 13; LT; Directed by Robert KcKimson; Story by Warren Foster; Animation by Phil DeLara, Manny Gould, John Carey, and Charles McKimson; Layouts by Cornett Wood; Backgrounds by Richard H. Thomas; Voice Characterization by Mel Blanc; Musical Direction by Carl Stalling. In Cinecolor.

The Acme Baby Sitter Service sends its star sitter, Daffy Duck, to a hen house to mind an egg. On his way to the job, he sings a little rhyme: "Life is bitter, for I'm a sitter/and put little kiddies to bed./While I tuck the sheet around their feet,/They're busy slappin' my head!"

The little chick hatches and, afraid of strangers, runs from Daffy, who must chase the hatchling all over the barnyard. The chick hides in the mouth of Spike the bulldog. Spike backs Daffy onto the henhouse roof and makes him fall. The chick hides in a nest under a chicken. Daffy hides in a barrel and reaches for the hatchling. The chicken hides a dynamite stick under a feather duster and Daffy gets blasted.

The chick sits on a high wire. Daffy tries to reach him by pole vaulting and crashes into the dog's house; he then uses an umbrella to balance with, but the chick blows him into a pig sty; an elastic band propels him flat against the wall; a tree used as a catapult crushes Spike's house again; and a sky rocket destroys the dog's house. Spike spanks Daffy with a plank of wood. The duck calls in to the Acme Agency: "Your star sitter will have to do all his sitting *standing up!*"

A PEST IN THE HOUSE

Daffy Duck, Elmer Fudd; Aug 3; MM; Directed by Charles M. Jones; Story by Tedd Pierce and Michael Maltese; Layouts and Backgrounds by Richard Morley; Voice Characterization by Mel Blanc; Musical Direction by Carl Stalling.

"Once upon a time there was a labor shortage. It became so bad that employers would hire anybody, or *anything ...*"

A tired businessman (Arthur Q. Bryan using his real voice!), needing sleep, asks hotel manager Elmer Fudd for a room with peace and quiet. "If I'm disturbed at any time, I'm gonna bust you right in the nose!" Loudmouthed bellhop Daffy Duck makes him carry his own bags and screams along the way about "IF THERE'S ANYTHING WE'VE GOT PLENTY OF, IT'S PEACE AND QUIET." Daffy tips the guest and takes over his room. The businessman reenters the room to find Daffy trying on his hat. Too tired to hit the duck, the man goes to bed, but is soon awakened by Daffy hammering a "Do Not Disturb" sign on his door.

With each disturbance, the guest punches Elmer. Daffy decides the room is stuffy and opens the window to the city noise and traffic sounds. A drunk next door makes a racket and Daffy volunteers to take care of it. Soon he joins in singing, "How Dry I Am." Daffy then cleans the guest's window, singing, "Time Waits For No One" and making scratchy noises on the glass. Daffy comes back into the room laughing, waking up the guest. He tells him a joke about a traveling salesman. Halfway through, the guest goes down to sock Elmer and returns to the room. Daffy is still there, finishing the story and forgetting the punchline! Elmer catches Daffy trying to fix the steam pipes and covers them to prevent the pipes from banging. A whistle wakes up the guest. Daffy barges in screaming that this guest needs peace and quiet and blaming the disturbance on Fudd. Elmer tries promoting Daffy to manager to avoid getting punched again, but Fudd still gets hit. Daffy remarks, "Noisey little character, isn't he?"

THE FOXY DUCKLING

Aug 23; MM; Directed by Arthur Davis; Animation by J.C. Melendez, Manny Gould, and Don Williams; Layouts by Thomas McKimson; Backgrounds by Phil DeGuard.

In the forest an insomniac fox is trying to sleep. He uses clips but his giant bloodshot eyes won't close. Consulting his cure book he discovers that his pillow should be filled with duck down. He shakes his pillow empty. It's been loaded with all manner of metal appliances.

The fox pursues a yellow duck. He tries a decoy and duck call, but is blasted by other hunters. He tries to chase the duck in the water, but the duck points his diving board toward dry land. He tries to catch the duck up in the air by building extensions, hammering board after board until the weight of one duck feather is enough to make the construction fall. Finally, the fox can *Rest in Peace*, his angelic spirit continuing the chase in the sky.

LITTLE ORPHAN AIREDALE

Porky Pig, Charlie Dog; Oct 4; LT; Directed by Charles M. Jones; Story by Tedd Pierce and Michael Maltese; Animation by Lloyd Vaughan, Ben Washam, Ken Harris, and Phil Monroe; Voice Characterization by Mel Blanc; Musical Direction by Carl W. Stalling.

A color remake of *Porky's Pooch* (1941). A dog, Rags McMutt, breaks out of the city pound and encounters his old friend Charlie Dog. Charlie explains, in flashback, how he got his master. He had been hanging out on a busy city street, giving the big, soulful eyes routine, facially imitating everyone walking down the street (including one geek with an overbite, stammering "Duh, Duh, Duh ..."). Spotting a potential sucker in Porky Pig, Charlie follows the pig up to his apartment and proposes the idea of them being dog and master. He tells of his pedigree "Half collie, half airedale, half Pekinese, half St. Bernard, with just a pinch of spitz!" Porky throws him out. Charlie returns and to prove his affection; he chases cats only to get beaten up by them. He does tricks, including "play dead." Porky throws him out again. Charlie gives Porky a sob story, goes home "to mother," but returns instantly. "Mother wasn't home." Porky is tricked into thinking the dog is pregnant, but when he finds out the dog's name is Charlie, he boots him out again. Says the dog, "Well, there actually was such a case in Venezuela!"

Charlie pretends to be freezing outside (in the apartment hallway), and Porky lets the dog in and gives him a doghouse. Once the dog is inside, Porky ships the crate to Australia. Returning home, Porky finds Charlie in his bush hat greeting him, "Ello there, Nipper!" He shows how kangaroos hop, with Porky in his pouch.

Back to the present, Porky returns to his car and throws both dogs out. Charlie chases the car down the street, while the other pooch runs back to the dog pound.

SLICK HARE

Bugs Bunny, Elmer Fudd; Nov 1; MM; Directed by I. Freleng; Story by Tedd Pierce, and Michael Maltese; Animation by Virgil Ross, Gerry Chiniquy, Manuel Perez, and Ken Champin; Layouts by Hawley Praat; Backgrounds by Paul Julian; Voice Characterization by Mel Blanc; Musical Direction by Carl W. Stalling.

A night at the "Mocrumbo" restaurant, where dinner is "$600. Small Down Payment, No co-signers necessary." Inside, Humphrey Bogart orders fried rabbit from waiter Elmer Fudd and gives him twenty minutes to serve it. In a panic, Fudd searches the kitchen and finds Bugs Bunny among his carrot supply. Fudd explains that Mr. Bogart would like to have Bugs for dinner. Bugs replies, "If he wants me, all he has to do is whistle." Bugs turns on a whistling kettle and emerges in a tuxedo. Bugs, wise to Fudd's invitation, runs out into the club. The bunny is disguised as Groucho Marx. Fudd follows him as Harpo. Bugs hides on Carmen Miranda's fruity hat while she performs. Bugs is chased on stage and does a dance routine, which draws applause. Elmer chases Bugs into the kitchen, where the bunny pretends to be a waiter and orders pies to hit Fudd with. Elmer throws the next pastry at the fast thinking rabbit, Bugs ducks, and it hits Bogart, who asks Fudd, "Why did you hit me in the face with a coconut custard pie?" When Fudd fails to produce fried rabbit, Bogart hopes, "Baby" [Bacall] will settle for a ham sandwich. Bugs hears about "Baby" and jumps on the serving platter and makes "wolf" howls at the sexy star.

BUGS BUNNY in "SLICK HARE"

Merrie Melodie CARTOON in TECHNICOLOR

DOGGONE CATS

Sylvester; Oct 25; MM; Directed by Arthur Davis; Story by Lloyd Turner and Bill Scott; Animation by Basil Davidovich, J.C. Melendez, Don Williams, and Emery Hawkins; Layouts by Don Smith; Backgrounds by Philip DeGuard.

A goofy Sylvester and his orange feline friend are chased by Wellington the bulldog. The dog is given strict orders by his lady master to deliver a package to Uncle Louie, "And don't let go of it or else!" This gives the two cats a chance to pester the dog all along the way. The orange cat picks a fight with the dog while Sylvester smashes an egg in his face. Sylvester hooks the package from the dog's paws. The dog chases the cat, getting his head caught in a fence, then smashed by a garbage can. The cats march down the street with the package, but Wellington meets them and retrieves it. Sylvester forces the dog to dance, while his partner jabs the package out of his mouth, sending the parcel to the railroad track. The cats imitate a train and scoop it up, while Wellington is run over by the real train.

Wellington chases the cats, who disguise a weight as the parcel and toss the phony package off the bridge. Wellington goes after it in a boat that smashes and sinks with the weight of the phony package. Wellington next gets run over by a steamroller to protect the package. Battered and beat,

Wellington finally delivers the parcel to Uncle Louie. It contains dinner for the two cats! For being such a jack-ass, Wellington hits his head with the mailbox and crowns himself with the garbage can lid.

MEXICAN JOYRIDE

Daffy Duck; Nov 29; LT; Directed by Arthur Davis; Story by Dave Monahan; Animation by Don Williams, Basil Davidovich, J.C. Melendez, and Herman Cohen; Layouts by Thomas McKimson; Backgrounds by Philip DeGuard; Voice Characterization by Mel Blanc; Musical Direction by Carl W. Stalling.

Daffy Duck, singing "Gaucho Serenade," drives down to Mexico for a vacation. After a burning experience with Mexican food, Daffy takes in the bullfights. As if at a baseball game, Daffy heckles the bull. ("He's blind as a bat! Throw the phoney out!") The bull chases the duck around the arena. Daffy tries the "Good Neighbor Policy," offering the bull a "Cigarette? Sparkling champagne? A little gin rummy perhaps?" Daffy pulls a hat trick, betting the bull to guess which sombrero he's hiding under. When the bull guesses wrong, he cries over losing his money. Daffy volunteers weapons to help him commit suicide. The bull chases the duck with a machine gun into town, where the duck packs his bags and drives home, unaware the bull is in the back seat!

CATCH AS CATS CAN

Sylvester; Dec 6; MM; Directed by Arthur Davis; Story by Dave Monahan; Animation by J.C. Melendez, Basil Davidovich, Don Williams, and Herman Cohen; Layouts by Don Smith; Backgrounds by Philip DeGuard; Effects Animation by A.C. Gamer; Voice Characterization by Mel Blanc; Musical Direction by Carl W. Stalling.

A jealous Crosby parrot conspires with a hungry Sylvester (with a retarded voice) to kill a Sinatra canary. One of their schemes is Crosby giving Sylvester a bar of soap and knife that he carves into a beautiful girl canary decoy. It is placed near a greased kitchen counter. The canary sends the soap decoy sliding into the cat's mouth. Next, Sylvester puts buckshot in the canary's vitamin dish, then puts a magnet in his mouth. This attracts the birdcage and every sharp object in the house. Finally, Sylvester dresses as a maid and vacuums the bird, then tries to eat him from the vacuum bag. The canary turns the tables when he ties the cat's tail to the vacuum handle, his mouth to the pipe. The cat proceeds to suck up everything in the house, including the hot coals in the fire place.

In the end, Sylvester has eaten the parrot and has now assumed the Crosby mannerisms with pipe and hat!

1948

GORILLA MY DREAMS
Bugs Bunny; Jan 3; LT; Directed by Robert McKimson; Story by Warren Foster; Animation by Charles McKimson, Manny Gould, and John Carey; Layouts by Cornett Wood; Backgrounds by Richard H. Thomas; Voice Characterization by Mel Blanc; Musical Direction by Carl W. Stalling.
Bugs Bunny is adrift at sea in a barrel, reading Esquire and singing "Trade Winds." Meanwhile, in "Bingzi-Bangzi, Land Of Ferocious Apes," Mrs. Gorilla wonders why the stork hasn't visited. Crying by the river, she finds this bunny in a barrel and takes it to her tree top home. Bugs tries to tell her he's a rabbit ("technically known as a rabbitus rodentus!"). When she starts crying, Bugs gives in. Dressed in a baby bonnet and diapers, Bugs follows her to meet Mr. Gruesome Gorilla. Bugs goes ape, imitating a chimp jumping all over the house. "Daddy" hates kids and takes junior "for a little walk." He plays "upsy-daisy" and throws Bugs high into the sky and doesn't catch him. Bugs recommends, "Shall we try it again, my way?" His way is a shovel bashed to the head. Bugs does a conga dance, which brings a strategically placed coconut crashing on Gruesome's noggin. The gorilla chases the rabbit all over the jungle to the tune of Raymond Scott's "Dinner Music for a Pack of Hungry Canni-

bals." Chased to the edge of a cliff, Bugs throws himself on Gruesome's "tender mercies." He gets beaten and stomped on, until the ape is so tired that Bugs can blow him over. "Ha! I wore him out!"

A FEATHER IN HIS HARE
Bug Bunny; Feb 7; LT; Directed by Charles M. Jones; Story by Michael Maltese and Tedd Pierce; Animation by Ken Harris, Phil Monroe, Ben Washam, and Lloyd Vaughan; Layouts by Robert Gribbroek; Backgrounds by Peter Alvarado; Voice Characterization by Mel Blanc.
A dopey Indian goes hunting for Bugs Bunny. Bugs directs him to a rabbit hole marked by a dozen signs ("Rabbit" "In There," etc.). His wacky gags quickly backfire and the rabbit finds himself tied to a stake. Bugs manages to hop free and the chase is on! The bunny pelts the Indian with a snowball (in July, because it gets too cold to make them in the winter). The Indian tries to give Bugs a "Hare Cut and Scalp Treatment," but the tables are turned when Bugs bops the Indian with a stone razor.

Bugs takes advantage of a mud bank to practice his pottery skills molding, baking, and painting a vase to smash over the Indian's head. When the Indian reveals that he is the last Mohican, Bugs points skyward. Above, storks are bringing more Mohicans and hundreds of Bugs Bunnies, "Ehh, what's up, Pop?"

A good, but routine, cartoon from Jones. Most notable aspect is funny dialogue.

WHAT MAKES DAFFY DUCK?

Daffy Duck, Elmer Fudd; Feb 14; LT;
Directed by Arthur Davis; Story by
William Scott and Lloyd Turner;
Animation by Basil Davidovich, J.C.
Melendez, Don Williams and Emery
Hawkins; Layouts by Don Smith;
Backgrounds by Philip DeGuard; Voice
Characterization by Mel Blanc; Musical
Direction by Carl Stalling. In Cinecolor.
Duck season is open and Daffy is run-
ning scared. Taking time out for a
shower, he is grabbed by hunter Elmer
Fudd, and his rival, a hungry fox. The
duck proposes a race to determine who
gets him. While Elmer runs, the fox
makes off with Daffy. Daffy calls to
Elmer, "I'm your duck, Elmer! A tasty
morsel fit for a king!" while greasing
the mountain side causing the fox to
slide backward into a tree. Now in
Elmer's hands, the duck gives the
hunter a classic sob story ("Guns!
Guns! They're everywhere!") and runs
off. Daffy is seen admiring himself in a
mirror. Elmer has decided to disguise
himself as a female duck. Daffy falls in
love with the phony female. Daffy
catches on to the scheme and plays
along. "Let me take you away from all
this. Let us flee to glamorous Hollywood! I can get you a screen test with
Warner Bros." Daffy invites the disguised Elmer up to his apartment to
see his etchings. Daffy revives the fox
who mistakes Fudd for a female duck.
Elmer holds the fox at gunpoint and
grabs Daffy once and for all. Daffy
now goads the fox into reclaiming "his
duck." Elmer and the fox have a fist
fight. A park ranger posts a "Fox Season" sign. Elmer chases the fox into the
distance, as Daffy removes his ranger
disguise: "Obviously, I am dealing with
inferior mentalities!"

WHAT'S BRUIN' BRUIN?

Three Bears; Feb 28; LT; Directed by
Charles M. Jones; Story by Tedd Pierce
and Michael Maltese; Animation by Phil
Monroe, Ken Harris, Lloyd Vaughn, and
Ben Washam; Layouts by Robert
Gribbroek; Backgrounds by Peter
Alvarado; Effects Animation by A.C.
Gamer; Musical Direction by Carl W.
Stalling.
Papa Bear Henry decides it's time for
the three bears to hibernate in order to
have a good winter's nap. Unfortunately,
everything works against him; mama
snores and Junior's rocking cradle
squeaks. Junior is having a bad dream
and breaks his bed. He crawls in with
dad and things get worse. First, Junior
rolls over on papa, flattening him, then
Henry feels something wet in the bed.
It's a leak from the cave roof. Papa
moves the bed and has Junior stick his
finger in the leak; then stuffs a pair of
longjohns in the opening. With each
move the water damage gets worse.
Next, papa argues with mama about
keeping the window closed and nails it
shut. She opens it, he cements it with
bricks, she opens it. Snow covers papa,
and Junior thinks he's a snowman.
Henry sneezes, and the moose head
falls on him, causing mama to fire the
shotgun. Junior starts the chase with a
mallet, which reveals papa to the guilty
parties. Fade out. Fade in, the dripping
hole is plugged, the alarm clock is pad-
ded, the window is shut, Junior gagged
and bound to his bed. Outside, flowers
are blooming, ice is melting, birds are
chirping. Henry, with blood-red eyes
yells, "Quiet!" Springtime retracts, and
quiet winter returns.

DAFFY DUCK SLEPT HERE

Porky Pig, Daffy Duck; Mar 6; MM;
Directed by Robert McKimson; Story by
Warren Foster; Animation by Manny
Gould, Charles McKimson, and I. Ellis;
Layouts by Cornett Wood; Backgrounds
by Richard H. Thomas; Voice
Characterization by Mel Blanc; Musical
Direction by Carl W. Stalling.
Porky Pig is visiting the city. Every
hotel room in town is booked. Even a
10,000-room hotel under construction
has a line of people waiting around the

block. Porky lucks out, but has to share his room with Daffy Duck! As soon as Porky gets settled in bed, Daffy comes in singing "I'm Just Wild About Hymie." Hymie is Daffy's friend, a six-foot invisible kangaroo. Porky insists he must be pixillated. Daffy proves it by hopping around in his pouch.

Daffy disturbs Porky all night: Daffy adjusts the bed, gets hiccups, wets the bed (with water), and pulls up the covers. When Daffy's cold feet touch his back, Porky throws the duck out the window. Daffy returns and tricks Porky into thinking it's morning. He rushes Porky into getting dressed and onto the train (actually the window). Daffy peeks behind the window shade to watch Porky fall. Instead, he sees Porky on the caboose of the train wave goodbye! "Say, that's silly!" says Daffy. "I should have bought him some magazines to read on the trip!"

BACK ALLEY OPROAR

Elmer Fudd; Sylvester; Mar 27; MM; Directed by I. Freleng; Story by Michael Maltese and Tedd Pierce; Animation by Gerry Chiniquy, Manuel Perez, Ken Champin, and Virgil Ross; Layouts by Hawley Pratt; Backgrounds by Paul Julian; Voice Characterization by Mel Blanc; Musical Direction by Carl W. Stalling.

A color remake of *Notes to You* (1941). Elmer Fudd is sleepy. Just as he gets in bed, Sylvester sets up his music stand on the backyard fence. Sylvester sings "Figaro," causing Elmer to throw a pair of old shoes at the cat. Sylvester uses the shoes to stomp out the "Second Hungarian Rhapsody" up the porch steps. Singing "Some Sunday Morning," Elmer throws a book ("The Thin Man"), which the cat throws back (as "Return of the Thin Man"). Elmer runs outside to chase the cat. Sylvester has lined the steps with grease and tacks. The cat sings "You. Never Know Where You're Going Till You Get There," sees Elmer coming, and hands his sheet music to a big dumb orange cat, who goes into a soprano opera solo until Elmer crowns him. Elmer corners Sylvester, but the pussycat lulls Fudd to sleep by singing "Go to Sleep." Get-

ting Fudd back into bed, Sylvester wakes him again by becoming a one-man band. Sylvester rows past Elmer's window singing "Moonlight Bay." Fudd offers the cat some alum-laced milk, which shrinks his voice and head. Sylvester strikes back by performing "Angel In Disguise" a la Spike Jones (with lots of noisy sound effects). Elmer lights a box of dynamite, which explodes, sending him to peaceful heaven to be joined by Sylvester's musical nine lives!

I TAW A PUTTY TAT

Tweety, Sylvester; Apr 2; MM; Directed by I. Freleng; Story by Tedd Pierce; Animation by Virgil Ross, Gerry Chiniquy, Manuel Perez and Ken Chapin; Layouts by Hawley Pratt; Backgrounds by Paul Julian; Voice Characterization by Mel Blanc; Musical Direction by Carl W. Stalling. In Cinecolor.

A semi-remake of Tashlin's *Puss N' Booty* (1943), right down to the same street address, 1605 Maple Drive, starring Tweety and Sylvester in the leading Cat and Canary roles. Sylvester awaits the arrival of a new canary, Tweety. Sylvester asks the bird to stand still, and, when he does, he puts him in his mouth. Tweety lights a match to see what's going on, and in the smoke he flies out. The bird mallets the cat's foot to retrieve his "widdle hat." They play tag, and Sylvester reaches for the bird on the pantry shelf. Tweety accidently has eaten some alum and Sylvester is able to suck him into his mouth via a straw. Tweety works out, using the cat's tonsils as a punching bag.

Sylvester imitates a Swedish maid, cleans the birdcage, grabbing the object within—a stick of dynamite that explodes, turning the cat into Rochester. While playing hide and seek, Sylvester hits a vicious "puddy dog" with a mallet, causing the dog to chase the cat. Tweety brings both pets together in his birdcage. In the end, the lady of the house calls the pet shop to order a new cat.

RABBIT PUNCH

Bugs Bunny; Apr 10; MM; Directed by Charles M. Jones; Story by Tedd Pierce and Michael Maltese; Animation by Phil Monroe, Ken Harris, Lloyd Vaughan and Ben Washam; Layouts by Robert Gribbroek; Backgrounds by Peter Alvarado; Voice Characterization by Mel Blanc; Musical Direction by Carl W. Stalling.

At the World Champion fight, spectator Bugs Bunny heckles the champ. "The champ's a dirty fake. P.U.! Boo! Throw him out! Why don't you pick on somebody your own size?"

"Like, you?" asks the champ, throwing the ʀabbit into the ring. Bugs does his best against the champ; he fakes fainting. When the champ looks closer Bugs punches him; then rests in his corner (furnished with a lamp and radio), and sits in a soft easy chair, feet up, reading a book. The champ constructs a brick wall on his glove and socks Bugs with it. Bugs takes the announcer's microphone and uses psychology to beat the champ. ("The champ is confused; Bugs lands a beauty to the solar plexus; the champ is groggy; the champ is down!") Bugs tries to lift the champ, but his weight flattens the rabbit. Bugs tries to break his leg, and, disguised as a doctor, wraps him in bandages and punches him. In round 37, Bugs asks the champ to hold a giant sling-shot, and beans him with a boulder. In round 98, the champ fires from a cannon, Bugs shoots from an archer's bow, and they bash heads. In round 110, the champ ties Bugs to railroad tracks and engineers a train. The film breaks. Bugs apologizes for the interruption, but admits, "Confidentially, that film didn't exactly break!"

HOP LOOK AND LISTEN

Sylvester, Hippity Hopper; Apr 17; LT; Directed by Robert McKimson; Story by Warren Foster; Animation by Charles McKimson, Manny Gould, and I. Ellis; Layouts by Cornett Wood; Backgrounds by Richard Thomas; Voice Characterization by Mel Blanc;

At the zoo, a baby kangaroo, Hippity Hopper, hops out of his cage and explores the neighborhood, In one home, he spots housecat Sylvester practicing a "fishing for mice" technique by using a fishing rod with cheese as bait. He catches a mouse, but throws it back—it's too small. Hippity goes into the basement, and soon Sylvester is pulling him through the mouse hole, thinking he is a giant mouse.

Sylvester runs away and encounters a bulldog, who berates him for being afraid of a mouse. Sylvester tries again to catch Hippity and rides him like a bucking bronco. Landing outside beside the dog, he is sent back in with an axe. Sylvester chases Hippity around the house and tries boxing with the marsupial. A blow crash lands him on the doghouse. The dog decides to take care of matters himself, and encounters Hippity's mother, who has come to reclaim her baby. The bulldog and Sylvester hit the water wagon leaving town.

The first in a long running series of McKimson cartoons using the same plot.

NOTHING BUT THE TOOTH

Porky Pig; May 1; MM; Directed by Arthur Davis; Story by Dave Monahan; Animation by J.C. Melendez, Don Williams, John Carey, and Basil Davidovich; Layouts by Don Smith; Backgrounds by Philip DeGuard; Voice Characterization by Mel Blanc; Musical Direction by Carl W. Stalling.

The Gold Rush is on. Porky Pig decides to join in with his covered wagon (and an outhouse wagon) and heads West. Entering Indian Territory he is warned via road signs to "Keep your hat on—or do you want to wear a wig?" Porky gets ready to fight the redskins. "Get down, old pal, I'll use you as a shield." he tells his horse, but the steed isn't gonna take it: he'll use

Porky as *his* shield. "I bet Gene Autry's horse doesn't do that." The horse responds, "Listen, bub, Autry's horse makes more money!" They are attacked by a little Mohican with glasses and bulbous nose who wants to remove Porky's cap to scalp him. Porky can't take him seriously, telling him to "run along to your tee-pee, Pee Wee!" The Indian tries a few tricks: he hides in a street light, but Porky rides right past; he introduces his squaw so Porky will remove his cap, but the pig quickly dons a metal helmet; he gives Porky an Indian headdress as a gift, and attempts to ambush him from within it; dresses as a sexy squaw. Then he chases the pig with an axe, chopping a tree into a totem pole; and chases Porky into the river, where he and the Indian imitate salmon swimming upstream. The Indian gets caught and canned. In California, at last, Porky strikes gold, the Indian's gold tooth, in his mouth! "You were expecting maybe Humphrey Bogart?"

BUCCANEER BUNNY

Bugs Bunny, Yosemite Sam; May 8; LT; Directed by I. Freleng; Story by Michael Maltese and Tedd Pierce; Animation by Manuel Perez, Ken Chapin, Virgil Ross, and Gerry Chiniquy; Layouts by Hawley Pratt; Backgrounds by Paul Julian; Voice Characterization by Mel Blanc; Musical Direction by Carl W. Stalling.

On a deserted island, Pirate Sam is burying his treasure chest, singing "Yo-Ho-Ho and a bottle of ma's old-fashioned cider." The chest soars back to the beach, and Bugs emerges from the ditch wearing jewels and treasure. Sam points a pistol at the bunny, telling him, "Dead rabbits tell no tales." Bugs corrects him, "Dead *men* tell no tales." Sam almost shoots himself before he chases Bugs to his pirate ship. On board, Bugs, disguised as Captain Bligh, orders Sam to do all the chores. Sam chases Bugs and behind every port hole and gets blasted with a cannon. Next, the rabbit leads Sam through the "Freleng Door Gag"—running in and out of various doors on the ship.

Bugs stands over the gun powder hold, throwing lit matches down into it, Sam running down to blow them out. Sam decides to call the rabbit's bluff by acting nonchalant (playing jacks, etc.), but at the last second gives in. Too late, the ship explodes, blowing Bugs and Sam back to the island. Sam chases Bugs to a rabbit hole. Sam sticks his head in and gets blasted. The hole is really an underground cannon. The bunny declares, "I have not even begun to fight!"

BONE SWEET BONE

May 22; MM; Directed by Arthur Davis; Animation by Don Williams, Emery Hawkins, Basil Davidovich, and J.C. Melendez; Story by William Scott and Lloyd Turner; Layouts by Don Smith; Backgrounds by Philip DeGuard; Voice Characterization by Mel Blanc. In Cinecolor.

In the Museum of Natural History, an archaeology professor scolds his small, silent dog, Shep, for burying dinosaur bones. They go to the spot where Shep has placed a new one and discover that a big bulldog has just dug it up. The professor threatens to put Shep's bones in the canine section if he doesn't retrieve the rare specimen. Shep speeds away to get his bone, just as the professor realizes he has the real dinosaur bone after all.

Shep tries sneak the bone away from the sleeping bulldog but he awakens and football punts the small dog into orbit. Next, Shep tries an underground route to retrieve the object, but the bulldog uses a shovel to stop him and to swat the dog (in baseball fashion) out of his area. Shep tries an attack from the sky, via a high-wire that lands him in the doghouse. The bulldog dribbles Shep like a basketball into a waiting cement mixer. Shep's attempt to trade the bulldog with a bone filled with explosives only angers the canine who chases Shep around the fence.

Shep eventually returns to the professor with the bone, recounting his efforts in pantomime. When Shep finds out his is only a soup bone, he says, "If you think this little incident is going to upset me, you are *absolutely* right!" and goes into a series of wacky poses.

BUGS BUNNY RIDES AGAIN

Bugs Bunny, Yosemite Sam; June 12; MM; Directed by I. Freleng; Story by Tedd Pierce and Michael Maltese; Animation by Ken Champin, Virgil Ross, Gerry Chiniquy, and Manuel Perez; Backgrounds by Paul Julian; Layouts by Hawley Pratt; Voice Characterization by Mel Blanc; Musical Direction by Carl W. Stalling.

Into a rough western town, where the bullets fly so fast and thick they have to obey traffic lights to avoid hitting one another, comes Yosemite Sam, "the roughest, toughest he-man hombre that's ever crossed the Rio Grande—and I don't mean Mahatma Ghandi!" (reissue prints of this film have that last line re-dubbed "And I ain't no namby pamby!").

Sam is looking for any varmint who dares to tame him. He finds Bugs Bunny up to the task. They walk toward each other, gunfighter style. Says Bugs,"Just like Gary Cooper." Sam declares. "This town isn't big enough for the two of us!" Bugs takes a hammer and saw and builds a modern city with skyscrapers. Sam pulls a six shooter on Bugs, but the rabbit tops him with a seven shooter, a nine shooter, and a pea shooter. Sam makes Bugs do a tap dance, and Bugs turns it over to Sam, who uncontrollably dances into a mine shaft. Bugs dares Sam to "step over this line," maneuvering the bandit to step off a cliff. Bugs brings a mattress to the bottom of the cliff. "You know, sometimes me conscience kinda bothers me—but NOT this time!" as he pulls the mattress away.

Sam chases Bugs on horseback, but Bugs suggests they play cards "like the western pictures. And the loser leaves town." Bugs immediately wins and forces Sam out of town. When Bugs looks into the railroad car, he sees it's a "Miami Special" loaded with bathing beauties and leaves Sam behind. "So long, Sammy, see you in Miami!"

THE RATTLED ROOSTER

June 26; LT; Directed by Arthur Davis; Animation by Don Williams, John Carey, Basil Davidovich, and J.C. Melendez; Story by Dave Monahan; Layouts by Don Smith; Backgrounds by Philip DeGuard; Voice Characterization by Mel Blanc; Musical Direction by Carl W. Stalling.

"The Early Bird Gets the Worm" is the motto of a certain rooster who tries each morning to sneak out before his friends in the henhouse. Unfortunately, the others always zip out and return well fed before our rooster can get out the door! He tries to locate a worm via an electronic sonar radar device. A little sailor-capped, turtleneck wise-guy worm turns the tables at every turn. The worm hoses the rooster; fools the rooster by painting a self-portrait on the bird's finger, causing the frustrated fowl to mallet his own hand; shoots toothpaste into the rooster's mouth and brushes his hen's tooth; and, after inflating the rooster, causing him to fall into a lake, the wise guy worm rescues the bird with an electric wire. Chasing the worm, the rooster gets caught in a pipe. The worm sticks matches on the bird's feet, causing him to shoot out of the pipe like a bazooka. Next, the worm pretends to be a rattlesnake, attracting the attention of a momma rattlesnake who showers the worm with affection! Alerted, the momma snake chases the worm and rooster. Together, they trap the rattler in a fence knot hole. The rooster continues his chase of the worm, but gets trapped in the fence in the same way.

THE SHELL SHOCKED EGG

July 10; LT; Directed by Robert McKimson; Story by Warren Foster; Animation by Manny Gould, Charles McKinmson, I. Ellis; Layouts by Cornett Wood; Backgrounds by Richard H. Thompson; Voice Characterization by Mel Blanc; Musical Direction by Carl W. Stalling.

Nature note: turtles put their eggs in the sand so that the hot sun will hatch them. A turtle mom buries her eggs, naming them Tom, Dick, Harry, and Clem. While mom goes away to get a sun lamp, one egg, Clem, hatches out his legs and begins to roam the countryside. Wandering into a barnyard, Clem tries to get completely hatched by warming up to a cow. The cow "golfs" Clem into the barn, where a dog thinks he's just laid the egg. Meanwhile Tom, Dick, Harry, and their mom dig up the beach looking for the lost turtle.

The pooch, seeking fame and fortune as the first dog to lay an egg, chases Clem around the farm. Trying to retrieve his egg, the hound tussles with a chicken and a "Foghorn-like" rooster. In the end, the mother turtle finds her offspring and hatches the egg. Clem complains, "Wouldn't you know it, I'm still in a gone dang shell!"

HAREDEVIL HARE
Bugs Bunny, Marvin Martian; July 24; LT; Directed by Charles M. Jones; Story by Michael Maltese; Animation by Ben Washam, Lloyd Vaugan, Ken Harris, and Phil Monroe; Layouts by Robert Gribbroek; Backgrounds by Peter Alvarado; Effects Animation by A.C. Gamer; Voice Characterization: Mel Blanc; Musical Direction by Carl W. Stalling.
The newspapers announce that the first test rabbit is to be blasted into space. Bugs doesn't wants to go, but when he sees a payload of carrots being put aboard, he changes his mind.

Bugs crash lands on the moon, the thought of which causes him to do a series of wacky expressions. A "Mars-to-Moon Expedition" lands nearby, and Marvin Martian (known in this film as Commander X-2) surveys the Earth, preparing to blow up the planet. Bugs snuffs out his firecracker explosive (the Aludium Q36 Explosive Space Modulator). Bugs tries to radio Earth for help, but gets only a commercial jingle. X-2 calls out his reserve, K-9, a green Martian dog. Bugs, disguised as a delivery boy, gives X-2 some man-made dynamite. It blows the moon into a crescent shape, with Bugs, X-2, and K-9 hanging on, shouting into a radio transmitter, "Get me outa here!"

YOU WERE NEVER DUCKIER
Daffy Duck, Henery Hawk; Aug 7; MM; Directed by Charles M. Jones;

Story by Tedd Pierce; Animation by Ken Harris, Phil Monroe, Ben Washam, and Lloyd Vaughan; Layouts by Robert Gribbroek; Backgrounds by Peter Alvarado; Voice Characterization by Mel Blanc; Musical Direction by Carl W. Stalling.
At the National Poultry Show, the prize for Best Duck is only $5.00, while the prize for Best Rooster is $5000.00. Daffy Duck decides to don a rubber glove top-knot, plucks a real rooster for tail feathers, and enters the show as a "Rhode Island Red Buff" rooster.

Meanwhile, George K. Chickenhawk is showing off his knowledge of chicken species to his son Henery. Henery decides to impress his dad by sneaking out to the Poultry show and bringing home a prize chicken. He grabs a sleeping Daffy. When Daffy asks where the little fellow is taking him, Henery replies "To my old man, the greatest *judge* of chicken flesh in the world!" Daffy goes along, and shows off his fine points, then tries to escape when he realizes he's talking to a hungry chickenhawk. The elder chickenhawk grabs Daffy and prepares dinner as Daffy frantically tries to explain he's a duck. In a wild chase, Henery accidentally mallets his dad.

Back at the Poultry Show, Daffy loses the $5000 prize to George Chickenhawk disguised as a rooster, and the $5.00 prize goes to little Henery disguised as a duck.

DOUGH RAY ME-OW
Aug 14; MM; Directed by Arthur Davis; Story by Lloyd Turner; Animation by Basil Davidovich, J.C. Melendez, Don Williams, and Emery Hawkins; Layouts by Don Smith; Backgrounds by Philip DeGuard; Voice Characterization by Mel Blanc; Musical Direction by Carl W. Stalling.
Louie the parrot, reading "Rooster's Millions," is interrupted by Heathcliff, a big dumb housecat who has been caught in a mousetrap. Louie removes the trap, but Heathcliff is so dumb, the parrot must also remind him to breathe! Heathcliff asks his pal to read a piece of paper he found. It's a "Last Will and Testament" of their owner, who is about to leave $1 million dollars

to Heathcliff. If the cat disappears, the parrot will receive the money. Louie sends Heathcliff on a vacation, but the homesick cat comes back. The parrot pays a bulldog to beat up Heathcliff, but the cat pummels the dog. The parrot finds the cat cracking walnuts by holding the nut in his teeth, then using the nutcracker on his head. The parrot has Heathcliff play "radio" by putting wires in his ears, and then plugging them into the wall socket. When the cat receives a broadcast, Louie tries it, but lights up "Eat At Joe's." They play train; Louie sending him running along the train tracks. Heathcliff crashes and destroys the real train; the parrot gives the cat his birthday cake with dynamite candles. The cat finally dies and his spirit bids the parrot goodbye. Louie tells of the million bucks to be inherited, and Heathcliff decides to live. "If I can't take it with me, I'm not going!"

HOT CROSS BUNNY

Bugs Bunny; Aug 21; MM; Directed by Robert McKimson; Story by Warren Foster; Animation by Manny Gould, Charles McKimson, and Phil DeLara; Layouts by Cornett Wood; Backgrounds by Richard H. Thomas; Voice Characterization by Mel Blanc; Musical Direction by Carl W. Stalling.
Inside the Eureka Experimental Hospital, Paul Revere Foundation ("Hardly A Man Is Still Alive!"), a doctor is going to put the brains of a chicken into experimental rabbit No. 46, a.k.a. Bugs Bunny.

Bugs has been treated like a king, and, after passing a final examination (Bugs has a "coated tongue. And two pair of pants!") he is wheeled into the lab auditorium. Seeing an audience, Bugs decides to perform. "I'll ad-lib something!" First he mimics Lionel Barymore's Dr. Gillespie from the Dr. Kildare films, then does magic tricks, a soft-shoe dance, and, finally, a Danny Kaye scat routine. The doctor knocks him out, but Bugs zips back on his feet, selling hot dogs to the audience. A chase ensues. The rabbit hides in a closet with a skeleton in it (which "freaks" him out). He is chased around

a lab table of test tubes and chemicals. Bugs makes a chocolate malt, and, disguised as a boy scout, cooks weenies outside an oxygen tent. The chase goes on through a series of hospital doors. The doctor sprays him with laughing gas and pins the rabbit to the operating table. Bugs switches the wires and the doc and chicken exchange brains. Bugs declares the doctor, "A victim of fowl play!"

THE PEST THAT CAME TO DINNER

Porky Pig; Sept 11; LT; Directed by Arthur Davis; Story by George Hill; Animation by John Carey, Basil Davidovich, J.C. Melendez, and Don Williams; Layouts by Don Smith; Backgrounds by Philip DeGuard; Voice Characterization by Mel Blanc; Musical Direction by Carl W. Stalling.
Porky Pig is tired, but each chair he sits in falls apart. His home has been invaded by Pierre, the biggest and hungriest termite there is. Pierre demonstrates his appetite by eating the pig's dining room furniture. Porky tries to club the insect, but he eats the weapon.

Porky enlists the aid of Sureshot Exterminators. Sureshot, an ever-smiling dog who always says, "I'm here to help ya, son!" gives Porky a variety of arms with which to combat the pest. First, an insect spray guaranteed to send the bug to "Termite Heaven." Instead, Pierre sends Porky. Next, Porky tries to suck the insect out with a vacuum cleaner. The insect handcuffs Porky and destroys the basement and bathroom. Sureshot gives Porky his ultimate weapon, a lit stick of dynamite that destroys what's left of the house.

Fed up, Porky goes to Sureshot's office and begins to eat his furniture, then sets up a storefront with Pierre, selling termite-carved antique furniture!

HARE SPLITTER

Bugs Bunny; Sept 25; MM; Directed by I. Freleng; Story by Tedd Pierce; Animation by Gerry Chiniquy, Manuel Perez, Ken Champin, and Virgil Ross; Backgrounds by Paul Julian; Layouts by Hawley Pratt; Voice Characterization by

Mel Blanc; Musical Direction by Carl W. Stalling.

Spring is in the air, and Bugs Bunny is sprucing up for a date with his girl, Daisy Lou. Meanwhile, in the rabbit hole next door, a large dopey rabbit named "Casbah" is planning the same thing. Both rabbits emerge from the ground at the same time. Bugs notices his rival's bouquet is larger, so he goes back down and brings up a box of candy instead. Both compete for the best gift, with Casbah getting a heart-shaped box of bon-bons and Bugs a diamond ring. Casbah produces a pearl necklace; Bugs, nylons. Casbah has a mink stole; Bugs, boxes of perfume. Bugs emerges with an anvil and bashes the dumb bunny.

Bugs hops over to Daisy's, but finds she has gone shopping. This gives him a chance to dress up in her clothes to fool his rival, Casbah, who tries to make-out with "Daisy Lou." "She" offers him a carrot, an explosive, which blows out his teeth. Casbah wants to "pitch some woo," so Bugs complies with a kiss, using a suction cup and a mallet. Bugs disguises a dynamite ball as Daisy Lou's head. Casbah kisses it, it explodes, and he thinks she's a great kisser. Bugs disguises himself as Cupid and gets Casbah to bend over to receive his arrow. Casbah catches on and is going to sock Bugs, who asks, "You wouldn't hit a guy with glasses, would you?" He would! Casbah chases Bugs around the house, just as Daisy Lou returns home. Thinking she is Bugs in disguise, Casbah ambushes her. She screams and throws him out. Later, alone with Bugs, she allows him to get romantic. ("Your teeth are like pearls, real ones, no dime store phonies!") Daisy tries a carrot (an explosive one), they kiss, and both get turned on by the explosion in their kiss!

ODOR OF THE DAY

Pepe LePew; Oct 2; LT; Directed by Arthur Davis; Animation by J.C. Melendez, Don Williams, Emery Hawkins, and Basil Davidovich; Story by Lloyd Turner; Layouts by Don Smith; Backgrounds by Philip DeGuard; Musical Direction by Carl W. Stalling. In Cinecolor.

It's snowing and a homeless dog is looking for a place to sleep. He rests in a doghouse, but the bulldog who lives there punches him out. After being thrown out of an eagle's nest and a turtle's shell, the dog finds a house with a real bed. Pepe LePew walks in and climbs under the covers to sleep. The dog smells something, sees the skunk, holds his nose, and throws the stinker out. When he returns to bed, Pepe is there again. The dog puts a clothespin on his nose and attacks the skunk, fighting with him under the bed. They chase each other outside. The dog falls into frozen water, Pepe chops him out of the ice, and now the dog has a cold and can't smell. He locks Pepe out and returns to his sleep. Pepe throws a brick through the window with a note. "Colds can be fatal, get help now!" The dog calls for a doctor, and Pepe arrives in disguise. He puts the pooch in a washing machine, and hangs him out to dry. It actually cures the cold! Smelling the skunk, the dog runs from the house, lands in the lake, and catches cold again. The dog sprays Pepe with perfume, causing Pepe to run from the house. He falls in the lake, catches a cold as well. Unable to smell each other, they give up and sleep together.

There is no dialogue in this film, except for a mutual "Gesundtheit" at the end.

HOUSE-HUNTING MICE

Hubie and Bertie; Oct 7; MM; Directed by Charles M. Jones; Animation by Phil Monroe, Ben Washam, Lloyd Vaughan, and Ken Harris; Story by Michael Maltese; Layouts by Robert Gribbroek; Backgrounds by Peter Avarado; Voice Characterization by Mel Blanc; Musical Direction by Carl W. Stalling. In Cinecolor.

Two mice, Hubie and Bertie, decide to inspect a "House Of Tommorrow." Confronted with a large array of buttons on a master control panel, they first test the automatic record player, which pitches records to a robotic catcher's mitt. Next, an automatic sweeper sweeps cigar ashes. When they press the "Laundry" control, Hubie gets picked up, folded and starched. They try to tackle the cheese dispenser, but the automatic sweeper prevents them from having their snack. They throw a vase out the window, and the sweeper goes after it, coming back to chase the mice. The two drive the sweeper crazy by breaking records and lighting fire-crackers, and causing the robotic house-keeper to put on his hat and coat and quit! Bert pushes the spring cleaning button, which unleashes an army of sweepers, and the mice are hung like carpets and beaten by the mechanical sweepers.

THE FOGHORN LEGHORN

Foghorn Leghorn, Henery Hawk; Oct 9; MM; Directed by Robert McKimson; Story by Warren Foster; Animation by Charles McKimson, Manny Gould, Phil DeLara, John Carey, and Pete Burness; Layouts by Cornett Wood; Backgrounds by Richard H. Thomas; Voice Characterization by Mel Blanc; Musical Direction by Carl W. Stalling.
Although he's never seen one, and against the warnings of an old chicken-hawk, Henery Hawk is determined to hunt chickens. When the old-timer gets caught stealing two chickens by Fog-horn Leghorn, he is kicked out of the barnyard. Henery asks the elder chick-enhawk if Foghorn is a chicken and he replies that he is a "loudmouthed Schnook!"

Foggy gives Henery one of his long-winded speeches about keeping his eye on the ball ("Eye, Ball ... *Eyeball*! That's a joke, son!"), but Henery deter-mines that "Schnooks are sure noisy things!" Henery thinks the barnyard dog is a chicken, but Foggy tries to set him straight. They debate over his being a chicken and not a "loud-mouthed Schnook." Foghorn tries to prove that he is a chicken by crowing at sunrise, showing a photo of a cooked chicken dinner, then lying down in a pan; and, finally, just talking Henery into believing. Henery carries Foghorn home for dinner as Foghorn laments, "I'm just a loudmouthed Schnook!"

DAFFY DILLY

Daffy Duck; Oct 21; MM; Directed by Charles M. Jones; Story by Michael Maltese; Animation by Ben Washam, Lloyd Vaughan, Ken Harris, and Phil Monroe; Layouts by Robert Gribbroek; Backgrounds by Peter Alvarado; Voice Characterization by Mel Blanc; Musical Direction by Carl W. Stalling.
Daffy Duck is a huckster, selling joke books and gag novelties on a city street corner. When he overhears a radio broadcast that J. P. Cubish, the ailing "buzz-saw baron," will give a million bucks for one good laugh, he packs his bags and visits the Cubish mansion.

The droll butler does his best to keep Daffy out. He leads Daffy to a second story door that lands the duck in the garden fountain. Daffy throws a rope with a hook up to the bedroom window, pulling out the butler's false teeth. Daffy swings into the window, but the butler cuts the rope. Daffy tries to sneak down the chimney, but the butler is holding the flue shut.

Daffy sneaks into the house dis-guised as a bottle of champagne and is chased up and down the dumbwaiter. Taking out a cigarette, he imitates Bogart grilling a suspect, accusing the butler of "removing from the premises the only person capable" of restoring his master's health. Finally getting into the Cubish bedroom, Daffy trips and falls into the dessert tray, getting cake all over him. Cubish laughs and gives Daffy a well-paying job, receiving con-tinuous pelts from a laughing, pie-throwing Cubish.

A-LAD-IN HIS LAMP

Bugs Bunny; Oct 23; LT; Directed by Robert McKimson; Story by Warren Foster; Animation by Phil DeLara, Manny Gould, John Carey, and Charles McKimson; Layouts by Cornett Wood; Backgrounds by Richard H. Thomas; Effects Animation by A.C. Gamer; Voice Characterization by Mel Blanc; Musical Direction by Carl W. Stalling.
Digging a new rabbit hole, Bugs Bunny finds Aladdin's lamp. He shines it up, and out pops an arm-flailing genie, nicknamed Smokey (voiced by Jim Backus). The genie proves himself to Bugs by granting him his wish for two carrots! Bugs decides to go with the genie to Bagdad. The genie flies them

190

there via "Hare plane." After scanning the sights—the Brown Turban, Mad Man Hassan's Used Flying Carpet lot—Bugs literally drops in on the Royal Palace of Caliph Hassan Pheffer (built on G.I. Loans). Bugs asks the caliph, "What's up, Beaver Puss?" The caliph wants his lamp, but the rabbit intends to keep it. A chase ensues.

Bugs needs help from the genie, but each time he rubs the lamp, Smokey is busy—taking a bath, or about to kiss his girl. The genie warns him not to do it again. Bugs escapes the caliph by taking a flying carpet, which crashes at the palace. The Caliph grabs the lamp and rubs it, disturbing Smokey again. The genie beats Hassan Pheffer to a pulp and grants his "little buck-toothed pal" another wish. Suddenly surrounded by a harem of sexy hares, Bugs ponders, "I wonder what the poor rabbits are doing this season?"

KIT FOR CAT

Sylvester, Elmer Fudd; Nov 6; LT; Directed by I. Freleng; Story by Michael Maltese and Tedd Pierce; Animation by Virgil Ross, Gerry Chiniquy, Manuel Perez, and Ken Chapin; Layouts by Hawley Pratt; Backgrounds by Paul Julian; Voice Characterization by Mel Blanc; Musical Direction by Carl W. Stalling.

Homeless alley cat Sylvester and an orange kitten vie for leftovers in the trash cans. As the weather gets colder, Sylvester collapses on the doorstep of Elmer Fudd's house and is welcomed inside by Fudd. The orange kitten also appears and is brought inside for warmth. Showing preference for kittens, Elmer says he would like to keep one of the cats, but not two. Thus, Sylvester plans to do in his kitten companion.

While Fudd sleeps on it, Sylvester tries to frame the little feline by breaking milk bottles and a dozen dishes in the kitchen and hypnotizing the kitten to bat Fudd over the head. Each plan gets Sylvester in more trouble. Fudd warns him if he hears "just one more peep, it's out you go!" With this, the kitten makes plenty of noise and ruckus, shooting a gun, playing the radio, ringing bells, beating a cooking pan with a spoon, etc. An angry Fudd wakes up and makes up his mind. His landlord decides for him and evicts Fudd!

Back in the alley, Sylvester, the orange kitten, and Fudd search the trash cans for leftovers.

RIFF RAFFY DAFFY

Daffy Duck, Porky Pig; Nov 7; LT; Directed by Arthur Davis; Animation by Don Williams, Emery Hawkins, Basil Davidovich, and J.C. Melendez; Story by William Scott and Lloyd Turner; Layouts by Don Smith; Backgrounds by Philip DeGuard; Voice Characterization by Mel Blanc; Musical Direction by Carl W. Stalling. In Cinecolor.

Porky the policeman asks Daffy, the park vagrant, to move along. Later he finds Daffy sleeping in a trash can, then in a tree, and later in a gopher hole. He throws Daffy out of the park into the snow. Daffy finds a comfortable home setting in a department store window. Porky chases Daffy through the store, taking advantage of the items in the sporting goods department. He employs bows and arrows, axes, guns, and a duck call. Daffy tries a sob story on Porky, introducing his kids, Alphonse and Rodrigo (wind-up toys). Porky lets them remain in the front window. "I know how it is to be a father," he explains, leading his own wind-up children down the street.

THE STUPOR SALESMAN

Daffy Duck; Nov 20; LT; Directed by Arthur Davis; Story by Lloyd Turner, William Scott; Animation by J.C. Melendez, Don Williams, Emery Hawkins, and Basil Davidovich; Layouts by Don Smith; Backgrounds by Philip DeGuard; Voice Characterization by Mel Blanc; Musical Direction by Carl W. Stalling.

Slug McSlug, the notorious bank robber, escapes the police dragnet and hides out in an abandoned country house. He is visited by Daffy Duck, a salesman from the Excelsior Appliance Company, determined to sell something. Daffy sticks his foot in the door, and McSlug mallets it, but it's a fake foot. Daffy then shakes McSlug's hand with his "Sure-Shot Buzzer." The criminal puts Daffy against the wall, a gun pointed at his chest. Daffy polishes the gun with "Sure-Shine Shootin' Iron Polish," making it so shiny it melts! Daffy is thrown out, but keeps trying, returning via helicopter and elevator. "I'm not leaving till I sell you something!" McSlug asks for brass knuckles, which Daffy provides. "Gee, I'd hate to be socked with those babies!" McSlug demonstrates, but Daffy protects himself with an iron. McSlug chases Daffy into a closet and pumps a ton of bullets into the door. He runs out of bullets and Daffy offers him more from his sales trunk. He shoots the duck point blank. As the bullets bounce off, Daffy recommends his double-breasted, bullet-proof vest. "Guaranteed to get your money back if it fails to work!" Daffy turns on the gas oven to demonstrate his "Sure-Shot" lighter. McSlug throws him out again and tries the lighter himself, blowing the house to bits. Daffy finally knows what to sell him: "A house to go with his door-knob!"

A HORSE FLY FLEAS

Dec. 13; LT; Directed by Robert McKimson; Story by Warren Foster; Animation by Charles McKimson, Phil DeLara, Manny Gould, and John Carey; Layouts by Cornett Wood; Backgrounds by Richard H. Thomas; Effects Animation by A.C. Gamer; Voice Characterization by Mel Blanc; Musical Direction by Carl W. Stalling. In Cinecolor.

A little blue-skinned flea with a coonskin cap (last seen in 1943's *An Itch in Time*) hops to a house and finds a homeless horsefly. They gallop inside the house to make their home and find a dog. Wandering the canine's hairy body, the fleas walk into "Indian Flea Territory: Paleface fleas keep out!" They cut down some "trees" (giant dog hairs) and build a log cabin. Digging for a well with a pick axe makes the dog howl. The Indian fleas attack our hero. The dog sees smoke signals coming from his fur. The flea holds back the Indian fleas with his six-shooter. Running out of bullets, the flea flees on horse-*fly*-back. The dog uses flea pow-

der, but that just creates a snowy chase scene. The Indians pursue the flea and fly over the dog's body and face. Catching the flea, the Indians tie him to a stake and start a fire. The dog jumps into the garden fountain, and the flea escapes via canoe. While the dog rests by the fireplace, a flea circus heads toward their winter quarters, the dog. The Indians chase the flea and fly back to the dog, and they run into the circus. With a magnifying glass, and cotton candy, the dog enjoys the circus. The flea is happy, "As long as they're gonna chase me, I might as well be paid for it!"

MY BUNNY LIES OVER THE SEA

Bugs Bunny; Dec 14; MM; Directed by Charles M. Jones; Story by Michael Maltese; Animation by Ken Harris, Phil Monroe, Ben Washam, and Lloyd Vaughan; Layouts by Robert Gribbroek; Backgrounds by Peter Alvarado; Voice Characterization by Mel Blanc; Musical Direction by Carl W. Stalling.

Tunneling to Los Angeles, Bugs Bunny tries to find the La Brea Tar Pits. Taking a wrong turn, he finds himself in Scotland and immediately comes to the rescue of a poor old lady being attacked by a monster: the monster turns out to be a bagpipe, and the lady is McCrory, a kilt wearing Scotsman. Bugs greets him with "What's up, McDoc?" as the Scotsman pulls a rifle, takes aim, and fires at the hare. Bugs disguises himself as a Scot, and McCrory challenges him to a game of golf.

This leads to a round of golf gags with funny putting poses; Bugs digging a giant pit around the first hole, assuring a hole in one; the bunny shooting the golf ball as in billiards; Bugs holding an auction to get his high score down. At the 18th hole McCrory does get a hole in one, and, through creative digging, so does Bugs. McCrory claims Bugs was cheating and challenges him at the pipes—Bagpipes, that is! Bugs tops him by playing the pipes as part of a one-man-band ensemble.

SCAREDY CAT

*Porky Pig, Sylvester; Dec 18; MM;
Directed by Charles M. Jones; Story by
Michael Maltese; Animation by Lloyd
Vaughan, Ken Harris, Phil Monroe, and
Ben Washam; Layouts by Robert
Gribbroek; Backgrounds by Peter
Alvarado; Voice Characterization by Mel
Blanc; Musical Direction by Carl W.
Stalling.*

On a dark night, Porky Pig brings
Sylvester to their new
home, a gothic mansion. Sylvester is
scared out of his wits, clinging to Porky
at every moment. Porky orders the cat
into the kitchen as he goes up to bed,
but Sylvester sticks to Porky so close
that the pig puts his bed clothes on
around the cat. Porky throws the coward out. Downstairs, Sylvester sees a
death march, black-hooded mice
wheeling a cat to execution. Sylvester
runs back to Porky, but the pig orders
him out. Sylvester grabs a gun and
threatens to kill himself. With that,
Porky lets him stay.

Sylvester has a night of horror, while
the only thing disturbing Porky is the
cat's cowardice. The mice throw Porky's bed out the window; drop an anvil
on the pig; attempt to kill both with
knives, trapdoors, arrows, bowling
balls, etc. Only Sylvester is aware of
what's happening. Porky drags the
pussycat to the kitchen to prove what
"a yellow dog of a cowardly cat" he is.
In the kitchen, Porky is bound and
gagged and wheeled off to execution,
with a sign, "You were right, Sylvester!" The cat runs from the house, but
his conscience reminds him of how
Porky raised him. The cat grabs a tree
trunk and beats off the mice, saving
Porky and earning his respect once
again.

A HICK, A SLICK, AND A CHICK

*Dec 27; MM; Directed by Arthur Davis;
Animation by J.C. Melendez, Don
Williams, Emery Hawkins, and Basil
Davidovich; Story by Lloyd Turner and
William Scott; Layouts by Don Smith;
Backgrounds by Philip DeGuard; Voice
Characterization by Mel Blanc; Musical
Direction by Carl W. Stalling.*

Elmo (the Hick) gets all slickered up
and arrives, via hub cap, at his girlfriend's house. He catches Blackie (the
Slick) kissing Daisy Lou (the Chick).
He and Blackie compete for Daisy
Lou's affection. Elmo's flowers seem to
shrink to seeds next to Blackie's entire
flowershop. Elmo's jew's harp is no
match for the rhapsody Blackie plays
on the grand piano. Blackie's muscles
punch Elmo across the street.

Blackie presents Daisy Lou with a
mink, but Elmo promises to bring back
ermine, not knowing what ermine is.
He falls into some champagne bottles
and gets drunk. He spots a "Sylvester-
like" cat named Herman and tries to
fight the cat. Through sheer stupidity
he knocks the cat out and brings Daisy
Lou her new coat. As they leave,
Blackie asks aloud, "I wonder where he
got that ermine coat?" Herman, in
Durante's voice, responds, "Don't get
nosey, junior!" A coat shape cut-out on
his rear end answers the question (and
a coat-shaped Iris-out ends the
cartoon).

TWO GOPHERS FROM TEXAS

*Goofy Gophers; Dec 27; MM; Directed
by Arthur Davis; Animation by Emery
Hawkins, Basil Davidovich, J.C.
Melendez, and Don Williams; Story by
Lloyd Turner and William Scott;
Layouts by Don Smith; Backgrounds by
Philip DeGuard; Voice Characterization
by Mel Blanc; Musical Direction by Carl
W. Stalling. In Cinecolor.*

A theatrical dog hears the call of the
wild and decides to commune with
nature. Using a book, *Life in the
Woods,* he hunts for his own food and
quickly encounters the overly polite
Goofy Gophers. They argue over who
goes down their gopher hole first as the
dog speeds toward them. Their decision at the last second leaves the dog
hanging from a cliff.

Consulting his book, the dog tries
"Four ways to get a gopher." First, playing upon their curiosity, he leaves a
"Do Not Open Till Xmas" trunk, but
the dog gets hit with his own spring-
release boxing glove. Next, he tries
vegetables as bait, attaching a radish to
a boulder. The dog gets crushed!
Third, he plays upon their sentimental

feelings by disguising himself as Little Snookie, a baby (with guns, grenades, and brass knuckles). The Gophers take him on a ride and throw him down the mountain side; "If all else fails—and it has—Gophers love music!" The dog becomes a one-man band playing dixieland swing. This causes the gophers to dance, but they turn it around, trap the dog in the piano, tie hammers to the inside keys, and play hard for a musical finale.

1949

WISE QUACKERS
Daffy Duck, Elmer Fudd; Jan 1; LT; Directed by I. Freleng; Story by Tedd Pierce; Animation by Manuel Perez, Pete Burness, Ken Champin, Virgil Ross, and Gerry Chiniquy; Layouts by Hawley Pratt; Backgrounds by Paul Julian; Voice Characterization by Mel Blanc; Musical Direction by Carl W. Stalling.

Too tired to fly south for the winter, Daffy Duck makes a three-point landing (on a pitch fork) near hunter Elmer Fudd. Daffy begs Elmer not to shoot him, offering to be his slave, a la Uncle Tom's Cabin. Elmer likes the idea and agrees.

Daffy shaves his new master, resulting in numerous facial cuts. A hot towel only manages to turn Elmer's head topsy turvey. Daffy prepares a meal for Elmer and offers to sample it for poison. After consuming the entire meal, he imitates being poisoned, but doesn't fool Elmer, who chases Daffy with his gun. Daffy insists on chopping firewood: a tree crashes into the home of Fudd's next door neighbor. After being pummeled by his neighbor, Elmer observes, "My slave's escaped!" Elmer's hounds retrieve the duck, but Daffy hands Elmer a whip and begins screaming, "Don't beat me, massa! Don't whip this poor old body!" Daffy returns as President Lincoln and scolds Fudd, "What's this I hear about you whipping slaves!" and walks off to freedom.

HARE DO
Bugs Bunny; Jan 15; MM; Directed by I. Freleng; Story by Tedd Pierce; Animation by Ken Champin, Virgil Ross, Gerry Chiniquy, and Manuel Perez; Backgrounds by Paul Julian; Layouts by Hawley Pratt; Voice Characterization by Mel Blanc; Musical Direction by Carl W. Stalling.

Elmer Fudd is hunting with an army surplus "wabbit detector." Bugs Bunny gives him verbal directions, "You're gettin' warmer, Doc, warmer ...," and leads the hunter off a cliff! Seeing Fudd and his equipment smash at the bottom of the mountain, Bugs asks, "What's up, Doc?" The answer is a gunshot and a chase.

Bugs hitch-hikes and gets a lift into the city, boasting, "You gotta get up early in the morning to outsmart this rabbit!" "I got up at a quarter to five," responds the driver, Elmer Fudd. Bugs jumps out, right in front of a theater. Elmer chases Bugs to the balcony, where Bugs enters a full row. ("Excuse me, pardon me, excuse me ... ") After going back and forth, Bugs disguises himself as an old lady and scolds Fudd, "I'm sick of this ... " Elmer catches on and wrestles the disguised wabbit. The old lady calls the usher to throw this masher out. Elmer sneaks back in and chases Bugs into the men's room. The rabbit puts a Ladies room sign on the door and calls the ushers. Bugs controls the intermission sign, causing Fudd to be pummeled by the crowded audience. Bugs, disguised as an usher, leads Fudd to a prime seat: a unicycle on a tightrope, heading into the mouth of a lion.

HOLIDAY FOR DRUMSTICKS
Daffy Duck; Jan 22; MM; Directed by Arthur Davis; Animation by Emery Hawkings, Basil Davidovich, J.C. Melendez, and Don Williams; Story by Lloyd Turner; Backgrounds by Philip DeGuard; Voice Characterization by Mel Blanc; Musical Direction by Carl W. Stalling. In Cinecolor.

In the Ozarks a hillbilly brings home a turkey for Thanksgiving dinner. Daffy Duck, a resident of the farm, complains about "another mouth to feed." The turkey is given a ton of food to eat, but Daffy stops him, warning the turkey that this is part of a plot to stuff him for dinner. Daffy puts the turkey on a scale and reads his fortune: "You will be surrounded by friends and cranberries." While coaching Tom Turkey on an exercise program, Daffy watches and stuffs his own face. As the days go by, the turkey becomes as thin as a rail, while Daffy has grown into a fat slob.

At Thanksgiving, the hillbilly looks over the two birds and decides to have duck this year. Daffy goes on a crash diet and exercise program, which, in a matter of minutes, returns him to normal weight. Still in a panic, Daffy asks Tom Turk to hide him. The turkey sends Daffy to Rio, via the oven disguised as an ocean liner. Later that evening Paw asks Maw if dinner's ready, Maw, surrounded by thousands of matchsticks, replies, "I keep lightin' them and he keeps blowin' them out!"

AWFUL ORPHAN

Porky Pig, Charlie Dog; Jan 29; MM; Directed by Charles M. Jones; Story by Michael Maltese; Animation by Phil Monroe, Ben Washam, Lloyd Vaughan, and Ken Harris; Layouts by Robert Gribbroek; Backgrounds by Peter Alvarado; Voice Characterization by Mel Blanc; Musical Direction by Carl W. Stalling.

A crowd has gathered to watch street vendor Charlie Dog sell himself (with signs asking, "What is the greatest boon to mankind? Answer: Me!"). Garnering no takers, the dog spots a delivery man from a pet store and stows away in the canary cage being delivered to Porky Pig. Porky tries to complain, but Charlie on his phone imitates a pet shop employee and tries to convince Porky to keep him. When Charlie does his "pointer" bit, Porky throws him out. Charlie returns and forces the pig into the perfect dog-master situation. He seats Porky in his comfortable chair with a pipe, bathrobe, slippers, a good book, and fez, Charlie lying

peacefully at his feet. Again Porky throws him out. Next, Porky finds a baby (Charlie) at his doorstep. Porky kicks the baby basket away. Charlie tries as a lady, beating the pig with an umbrella, exclaiming "You brute!". He fakes a suicide from Porky's window and is served to Porky as his lunch! Porky ships the dog to Siberia, he returns as a dancing Russian. Charlie then gets Porky punched out by his upstairs neighbor, and the pig finally gives in just as Charlie decides *he* doesn't want to live with him. Porky flips out and forces Charlie to sit in *his* chair, with book, pipe, and fez, while Porky rests at *his* feet!

PORKY CHOPS

Porky Pig; Feb 12; LT; Directed by Arthur Davis; Story by William Scott and Lloyd Turner; Animation by Don Williams, Emery Hawkins, Basil Davidovich, and J.C. Melendez; Layouts by Don Smith; Backgrounds by Philip DeGuard; Voice Characterization by Mel Blanc; Musical Direction by Carl W. Stalling.

Vacationing in the northwoods, a Brooklyn-esque hipster squirrel (with zoot-suit and swinging a large key chain) is relaxing in the only standing tree at the lumber camp. Porky Pig is the "lumber-jackson" who is trying to chop down that tree. Unfortunately, Porky's chopping is disturbing the squirrel's rest. A battle of wits ensues.

The squirrel unzips an opening in the tree and removes Porky's axe blade. The pig responds, "Gee, you don't have to fly off the handle like that!" Porky fills a golf bag full of axes, but the squirrel lines the tree's bark with steel, destroying each of the pig's blades. The squirrel asks Porky to stop. "Cease the chop-chop, chubby! Blow, Joe—Scram, Ham!" and he pokes the pig in the eye! The squirrel goes back to bed. Porky gets a large saw, which the squirrel uses to launch Porky into the lake. Porky gets his gun and chases the squirrel up the tree and through a hollow log. Porky decides to destroy the tree by loading it with dynamite, which the squirrel puts into the hollow log. When it explodes a huge grizzly bear who was sleeping inside the log chases the two zanies. In the end, the bear claims the tree, the squirrel's pajamas, his bed, and his racing form.

MISSISSIPPI HARE
Bugs Bunny; Feb 26; LT; Directed by Charles M. Jones; Story by Michael Maltese; Animation by Ben Washam, Lloyd Vaughan, Ken Harris, and Phil Monroe; Layouts by Robert Gribbroek and Peter Alvarado; Effects Animation by A.C. Gamer; Voice Characterization by Mel Blanc; Musical Direction by Carl W. Stalling.

Cotton pickers singing "Dixie" accidentally pick Bugs Bunny out of the field and throw him in with the cotton being shipped via riverboat, "The Southern Star." The captain calls all aboard to Memphis, Vicksburg, Baton Rouge, New Orleans, and KUK-KAMONGA! Seeing how they treat stowaways, Bugs immediately disguises himself as a Southern gentleman. The rabbit meets Colonel Shuffle, a hot-tempered river gambler who challenges anyone to a game of poker. Bugs takes him on and beats the colonel's hand of five aces with six aces! Shuffle challenges the rabbit to a duel, which backfires into an exploding cigar in the colonel's face. His black face sends Bugs into a soft-shoe rendition of "Camptown Ladies." Shuffle gets his gun and returns to find the bunny selling tickets to "Uncle Tom's Cabinet." They chase around the boat until Bugs dresses up as a Southern belle, and beats the colonel with a parasol. The colonel gets wise to the rabbit and retaliates. A big Southern beau rescues the "damsel" in distress. Bugs continues his female disguise with the gentleman, but he sees "her" tail and goes wacky. Bugs laments, "Oh, well, we almost had a romantic ending!"

PAYING THE PIPER
Porky Pig; Mar 12; LT; Directed by Robert McKimson; Story by Warren Foster; Animation by Manny Gould, John Carey, Charles McKimson, and Phil DeLara; Layouts by Cornett Wood; Backgrounds by Richard H. Thomas; Voice Characterization by Mel Blanc; Musical Direction by Carl W. Stalling.

Porky, the "Pied Piper," rids the city of all the rats. The cats, now out of work, complain to their leader, the "Supreme Cat." He disguises himself as a giant rat and shows up in the mayor's office just as Porky is about to receive his reward money. The mayor refuses to pay Porky unless the giant rat is gone. Porky proceeds to chase the wise-guy rat all over town. He soon captures the rat's costume, but the Supreme Cat now steals Porky's prize money. After more chase gags, Porky eventually fools the feline by pretending to bring all the rats back, playing a record "Rat Stampede" to fool the cats on the other side of the fence. Porky trips the cat, takes his money, and gets the last line, "Eh, your sister drives a pickle wagon!"

One of the film's running gags has the cat-rat insulting Porky with lines like "Eh, your brother eats jelly beans!' or "Eh, your sister smokes corn silk." Porky replies, "No she doesn't. She works in a butcher shop and smokes *hams*!" Another repeat gag happens whenever Porky's back is turned. The rat flogs the pig's backside with his whiplike tail.

DAFFY DUCK HUNT
Daffy Duck, Porky Pig; Mar 26; LT; Directed by Robert McKimson; Story by Warren Foster; Animation by John Carey, Charles McKimson, Phil DeLara, and Manny Gould; Layouts by Cornett Wood; Backgrounds by Richard H. Thomas; Voice Characterization by Mel Blanc; Musical Direction by Carl W. Stalling.

Porky and his dog go hunting and encounter a completely wacky Daffy Duck (emitting tons of spit with every word he speaks). Daffy empties Porky's rifle of its shells then pops out of a giant decoy in a French can-can dress, singing "The Latin Quarter." Porky shoots and Daffy fakes a dramatic death. "I'm a-going—bye, now!" Porky's dog chases Daffy and gives him a sob story, "If I don't bring back a duck, he'll torture me!" Daffy lets the dog bring him home. He is put in a freezer to keep him fresh. The dog's devil and angel conscience fight over the right thing to do. The dog lets Daffy thaw, but won't let him leave. Daffy begins making loud noises, and, in a series of chase gags, begins to strain the relationship between Porky and his dog. They decide to kill Daffy with an axe but the duck has "Do Not Open Until Xmas" written on his stomach. Says Daffy, "By that time I'll figure a way out of this mess!"

REBEL RABBIT

Bugs Bunny; Apr 9; MM; Directed by Robert McKimson; Story by Warren Foster; Animation by Charles McKimson, Phil DeLara, Manny Gould, and John Carey; Layouts by Cornett Wood; Backgrounds by Richard H. Thomas; Voice Characterization by Mel Blanc; Musical Direction by Carl W. Stalling.

Walking through the woods, Bugs Bunny notices the bounty signs for his fellow wooodland creatures: $50 for a fox, $75 for a bear, and only 2c for a rabbit. Insulted, he mails himself to Washington to see the game commissioner ("I'm game, count me in!"). The game commissioner explains the bounty. "Rabbits are sweet and furry little creatures, perfectly harmless!" "He don't know me very well!" replies Bugs, who becomes determined to prove a rabbit can be more obnoxious than anybody.

The rabbit causes major damage to the Washington Monument; shuts off Niagara Falls; gives Manhattan back to the Indians ("They wouldn't take it unless I threw in a set of dishes!"); cuts loose Florida ("South America, take it away!"); swipes the locks off the Panama Canal; fills up the Grand Canyon; and ties up the railroad in a bow! Back

in Washington, a "Senator Claghorn" demands "that hare should die!" Bugs pops out of his desk, shouting, "Hare ... die ... Hair dye! That's a joke, son!" The armed forces chase Bugs Bunny (via live action stock footage), now with a million dollar bounty on his head. "Could it be that I carried this thing too far?" asks Bugs as bombs explode on him. In Alcatraz prison, the rabbit decides, "Hmm ... Could be!"

MOUSE WRECKERS ACADEMY AWARD NOMINEE

Hubie and Bertie, Claude Cat; Apr 23; MM; Directed by Charles M. Jones; Story by Michael Maltese; Animation by Lloyd Vaughan, Ken Harris, Phil Monroe, and Ben Washam; Layouts by Robert Gribbroek; Backgrounds by Peter Alvarado; Voice Characterization by Mel Blanc; Musical Direction by Carl W. Stalling.

Hubie and Bertie, hobo mice, are about to enter a new home but notice it's inhabited by a champion mouser, Claude Cat. They use various techniques to drive Claude crazy. They lower Bert by fishing line down the chimney; he swats the cat and is then pulled back up fast. They pump Claude full of air, sending him zooming around the room (causing the feline to swear off catnip) they lower a vicious bulldog to pummel him (cat checks tongue and takes a teaspoon of medicine). They put dynamite in the cat's pillow (cat drinks whole bottle of medicine); they tie the cat to a rope and drag him through ladder rungs, drain pipes, dishes, etc. Consulting his psychology book, Claude tries to laugh this nightmare off. The mice put earmuffs on the cat and reconstruct the living room upside down. The cat tries to hang onto the floor (actually the ceiling), while the mice put sideways paintings of the landscape out the window, driving the cat completely nuts. The film ends with the cat shivering nervously in a tree while the mice enjoy toasting marshmallows in the fireplace.

HIGH DIVING HARE

Bugs Bunny, Yosemite Sam; Apr 30; LT; Directed by I. Freleng; Story by Tedd Pierce; Animation by Gerry Chiniquy, Manuel Perez, Ken Champin,

Virgil Ross, and Pete Burness;
Backgrounds by Paul Julian; Layouts by
Hawley Pratt; Voice Characterization by
Mel Blanc; Musical Direction by Carl W.
Stalling.

Bugs Bunny is a carnival barker who
tells the people of an old western town
about the 15 sensational acts in the
sideshow. Fearless Freep, the high
diver, has no greater fan than Yosemite
Sam ("That's my boy!") who buys a
whole roll of tickets ("I'm a-splurgin'").
As the show begins, Bugs is informed
that Freep cannot arrive until the next
day. An angry Sam forces Bugs at gunpoint to perform the high-diving act he
loves so much to watch. Afraid of
heights, the bunny cleverly tricks Sam
into jumping. First, he makes Sam turn
around while he puts on his bathing
suit, giving Bugs a chance to spin the
diving board, causing Sam to fall off
into a tank of water. Bugs jumps on the
board so hard ("One for the money, two
for the show ... ") that he catapults Sam
off. He has forgotten to refill the tank,
so he sends the water racing Sam to the
bottom; the water makes it into the
tank, Sam smashes into the stage. Bugs
pulls a gravity gag ("I'm not upside
down, you are!"); he dares Sam "To
cross this line" at the edge of the
board. Bugs constructs a door, which
Sam is obliged to smash open. Finally,
Sam ties the rabbit to the edge of the
board and saws it off. Sam's part of the
platform crashes, while Bugs's defies
the law of gravity, "But I never studied
law," says the tricky rabbit.

THE BEE-DEVILED BRUIN

The Three Bears; May 14; MM;
Directed by Charles M. Jones; Story by
Michael Maltese; Animation by Ken
Harris, Phil Monroe, Ben Washam, and
Lloyd Vaughan; Layouts by Robert
Gribbroek; Backgrounds by Peter
Alvarado; Effects Animation by A.C.
Gamer; Musical Direction by Carl W.
Stalling.

The Three Bears are having breakfast.
Henry notices Junior's using all the
honey and decides to get more, despite
warnings from Maw.

To get to the beehive, Henry and
Junior try a fireman's ladder and crash

land. Next, Henry, holding a spoon and
honey jar, balances on a stick held by
Junior close to a beehive. When a bee
lands on Henry's nose, he can only
hum, "Rock-a-bye Baby" in an attempt
to put the insect to sleep. Junior helps
by bashing Henry's face with a shovel.

Henry walks an electric wire to the
hive. Junior decides to push the electric
switch, which turns Pa into a light fixture. Henry tries using spikes to climb
the tree where the hive is hanging. The
plan works too well. He is chased home
by a horde of bees, who have stung his
face into a swollen mound.

That night, in bandages, Henry asks
for ketchup. Ma opens the cabinet,
revealing shelves full of honey. "But,
Henry, I tried to tell you ...."

CURTAIN RAZOR

Porky Pig; May 21; LT; Directed by I.
Freleng; Story by Tedd Pierce;
Animation by Manuel Perez, Ken
Chapin, Virgil Ross, and Pete Burness;
Layouts by Hawley Pratt; Backgrounds
by Paul Julian; Voice Characterization
by Mel Blanc; Musical Direction by Carl
W. Stalling.

Porky Pig, the talent scout at the
"Goode and Korny Talent Agency," is
auditioning acts. Among them are a
grasshopper with an operatic voice
("We killed 'em in Ku-Kamonga!"); a
clucking Hen who literally lays an egg
(Tweety cameo in egg); a turtle who is
a "man of a thousand voices": Porky
counts to 999; Bingo, Frankie, and Al
(Jolson, that is), who sing a chorus of
"April Showers"; J. Finnan Hattie, who
dives into a glass of water, Crawford
Coo and his trained pigeons who fly
out the window at their first opportunity; and Itch & Scratch, the world
famous flea circus. Porky gets excited
when a two-headed man walks in, but
he's only the janitor. A running gag
involves a fox who claims to have the
greatest act of the century, and in the
end, performs it. Dressing in a Devil
costume, he consumes Atomic Powder,
TNT, gasoline, then lights a match and
explodes. Porky admits it's a great act,
but the fox's ghost explains he can do
it only once!

BOWERY BUGS

Bugs Bunny; June 4; MM; Directed by Arthur Davis; Story by William Scott, Lloyd Turner; Animation by Emery Hawkins, Basil Davidovich, J.C. Melendez, and Don Williams; Layouts by Don Smith; Backgrounds by Philip DeGuard; Voice Characterization by Mel Blanc; Musical Direction by Carl W. Stalling.

On a street corner in New York, Bugs Bunny tells an old-timer the story of Steve Brody, the man who jumped off the Brooklyn Bridge in 1886. Brody had a "terrific run of luck—all bad." Needing a rabbit's foot, Brody travels back to the woods, "to the forest prime-val—to Flatbush!" Brody points his gun at Bugs, who recommends Swami Rabbitima, who "Knows all, tells all!" Brody sees the mystic (Bugs in disguise), and has his palm "red," gets the bumps on his head, and his cards read. They reveal that a man wearing a carnation is his good luck mascot. Brody finds such a man (Bugs in disguise again). The mascot loses all of Brody's money (he actually gets three lemons from a slot machine). A gorilla bouncer throws Brody out of the gambling hall. Brody returns to the swami, who now tells him he'll be lucky in love. The first woman Brody approaches is Bugs (in ladies' disguise) who calls the police ("You masher! You Brute!"). Brody tells the swami he wants "some dough," so Bugs sends him to the address of "Grandma's Happy Home Bakery," where Brody gets baked in a pie. Brody catches on and revisits each person he met that day. Each of them is Bugs Bunny saying, "What's up, Doc?" Brody flips out and jumps off the bridge. This story convinces the old-timer to buy the bridge from the bunny.

MOUSE MAZURKA

Sylvester; June 11; MM; Directed by I. Freleng; Story by Tedd Pierce; Animation by Gery Chiniquy, Ken Champin, Virgil Ross, and Manuel Perez; Backgrounds by Paul Julian; Layouts by Hawley Pratt; Voice Characterization by Mel Blanc; Musical Direction by Carl W. Stalling.

In the Slobovian Mountains, Boris

Borscht, the Bagel Baron, has his home, and in it lives a mouse with a red village hat who polka-dances while he steals food. Enter Sylvester, with a green village hat, who intends to catch the mouse. While the mouse is out of his hole, Sylvester changes the lock on his door. The mouse mallets the cat, and the key is ejected on his tongue. Next, Sylvester disguises his hand as a slobovian village girl. The mouse dances with the girl and then brings her into his mouse hole and disguises the "girl" as a mouse. Sylvester mallets his own fingers. Sylvester chases the mouse behind some bottles, and the mouse pretends to be tossing a vial of nitro glycerine. The mouse accidentally (and unknowingly) drinks some real nitro and tortures Sylvester as he jumps off the cabinet, smokes, and dives off the rafters, confident that Sylvester will catch him. Sylvester takes the whole weight of a falling safe on his shoulders. The mouse does a violent jig, but his jig is up! He explodes and floats to heaven. The narrator laughs at Sylvester saying, "Now you'll never catch that mouse." Sylvester responds, "That's what you think!" He drinks some nitro, explodes, and chases the mouse into heavenly clouds.

LONG-HAIRED HARE

Bugs Bunny; June 25; LT; Directed by Charles M. Jones; Story by Michael Maltese; Animation by Phil Monroe, Ben Washam, Lloyd Vaughan, and Ken Harris; Layouts by Robert Gribbroek; Backgrounds by Peter Alvarado; Voice Characterization by Mel Blanc; Musical Direction by Carl W. Stalling.

Bugs Bunny is sitting outside his rabbit hole, strumming a tune on his banjo ("What Do They Do on a Rainy Night in Georgia"). Meanwhile, a few feet away is the opera singer, Giovanni Jones, practicing for tonight's concert. Unable to concentrate because of the rabbit's singing, Jones goes to the bunny and breaks his banjo. Later, the rabbit plays a lovely tune using a harp. Jones smashes that also. When the opera baritone interrupts Bugs's tuba solo and ties the rabbit's ears to a tree branch, Bugs allows as how "Of course, you realize this means war!"

That night, Bugs disrupts the singer's performance by bopping the band shell, causing such reverberations that Jones lands head first in the horn section. Bugs takes the shaken singer backstage and fixes him up with some liquid alum that shrinks his head! Next, Bugs dresses as a bobbysoxer asking for an autograph ("Frankie and Perry just aren't in it. You're my dreamboat") and hands him a dynamite writing pen. Bugs then enters the orchestra pit as "Leopold" the conductor. He forces Jones to hold a note so long he can mail for earmuffs, turn the singer's face purple, and crash the band shell completely over his head. Having evened the score, Bugs strums "Good Evening Friends" on his banjo.

HEN HOUSE HENERY
Foghorn Leghorn; Henery Hawk; July 2; LT; Directed by Robert McKimson; Story by Warren Foster; Animation by Manny Gould, John Carey, Charles McKimson, Pete Burness, and Phil DeLara; Layouts by Cornett Wood; Backgrounds by Richard H. Thomas; Voice Characterization by Mel Blanc; Musical Direction by Carl W. Stalling.
"I'm gonna get me a chicken today, or my name ain't Henery Hawk!" says the pint-sized chickenhawk. Meanwhile, Foghorn Leghorn, singing "Camptown Races," heckles his usual foe, the barnyard dog, with a fire escape trick that leaves the pooch with a beach ball in his mouth. Henery hits Foggy with his hammer, and the rooster demands to know, "What's it all about, boy?" Henery claims Foghorn as his victim, but the rooster tells him to "Start small and work up." Henery goes after some

ducks and almost drowns. Then he chases a turtle, ending up trapped in ts shell.

Meanwhile, Foghorn continues to harass the dog by painting his tongue green. In an artist's smock, he paints a false open gate in the fence for the dog to smash in. The dog gets free of his rope, but Leghorn has chopped down a tree and carved a baseball bat with which to slug the pooch. The dog and Henery team up to thwart Foghorn. They set a chicken trap, but Foggy gives Henery a speech about how "A smart chicken wouldn't step in it." Foghorn demonstrates and gets caught. The dog gets the last laugh, as Henery walks off with Foggy. "I don't want a smart chicken, I want him!"

KNIGHTS MUST FALL
Bugs Bunny; July 16; MM; Directed by I. Freleng; Story by Tedd Pierce; Animation by Ken Champin, Virgil Ross, Manuel Perez, and Gerry Chiniquy; Layouts by Hawley Pratt; Backgrounds by Paul Julian; Voice Characterization by Mel Blanc; Musical Direction by Carl W. Stalling.
In medieval times, for the horrendous act of tossing a half- eaten carrot into a suit of armor, Bugs Bunny is challenged to a duel by Sir Pantsalot of Drop Seat Manor.

What follows is a series of jousting tournament gags: The jousting arena is like a football stadium, complete with radio announcers and program vendors. Bugs puts a little "english" (pool room chalk) on his lance. The knight uses a mace and chain, which Bugs repels with a spring. The knight chops at Bugs's armor with an axe, but Bugs creates his own super armor, and they charge each other head on.

Bugs wins, and in the end sets up his own used armor dealership, dumping his carrot remains into Pantsalot's crushed armor.

BAD OL' PUTTY TAT
Tweety, Sylvester; July 23; MM; Directed by I. Freleng; Story by Tedd Pierce; Animation by Gerry Chiniquy, Manuel Perez, Ken Champin, and Virgil Ross; Backgrounds by Paul Julian;

Layouts by Hawley Pratt; Voice Characterization by Mel Blanc; Musical Direction by Carl W. Stalling.

The film begins with a pan downward on Tweety's barb-wired birdhouse, with a ruffled Sylvester below, plotting his next move. The cat uses a girdle to bounce up to the bird house, but each time he jumps up Tweety pushes something into Sylvester's face. Finally, the little bird shoves a stick of dynamite in the cat's diving helmet. Tweety escapes the birdhouse by sliding down a clothes wire. The wire is attached to the cat's tooth and Tweety attaches his end of the wire to a sky-rocket, which blasts the cat's teeth out of his head. Sylvester disguises his finger as a girl canary in a nest. As Tweety comes to her, Sylvester catches Tweety with his hand. Tweety switches his hat for "her" bonnet, and the cat bites his own finger. Tweety hides near a badminton game, becoming the "bird." Sylvester joins the game, intending to catch Tweety with his mouth. Tweety drops a lit stick of dynamite instead. Trying to flush out the fuse, the cat winds up inside the watercooler. In an act of desperation, Sylvester disguises his head to look like Tweety's birdhouse. Tweety enters, but takes control of the cat, imitating a railroad locomotive. Tweety, with an appropriate engineer's cap, steers the putty tat into a brick wall. "You know, I lose more putty tats dat way!"

THE GREY HOUNDED HARE

Bugs Bunny; Aug. 6; LT; Directed by Robert McKimson; Story by Warren Foster; Animation by John Carey, Charles McKimson, Phil DeLara, and Manny Gould; Layouts by Cornett Wood; Backgrounds by Richard Thomas; Voice Characterization by Mel Blanc; Musical Direction by Carl W. Stalling.

Tunneling into a dog track, Bugs Bunny decides to hang out and give the dogs "the once-over." The first pooch he encounters "looks a little undernourished, a little inny-skay in the elly-bay." The others are a bit flabby. Bugs likes Gnawbone, No. 7 ("Me lucky number!"). Checking his teeth, the rabbit observes, "a little shadow on that bicuspidor, you better see your dentist!" The race begins, and the dogs are identified. Bill's Bunion "looks like a little sore"; Pneumatic Tire "has run into shape"; Father's Mustache "looks a little droopy"; Motorman's Glove "will have a hand in it"; Bride's Biskit "is hard as a rock"; and Grandpa's Folly "is being scratched."

The dogs chase a mechanical bunny, with which Bugs falls in love. Bugs chases the dogs and beats them off in order to protect the bunny. Bugs lures the dogs off the track and into a taxicab he orders driven to the dog pound. Only No. 7 continues to chase the electric rabbit. Bugs gets his attention by ordering him to "Fetch the stick"—a stick of dynamite! No. 7 charges at Bugs "like a bull." Bugs waves a red cape, and the dog crashes into it, knocking himself out on the fire hydrant behind it. Bugs kisses his "dreamboat," and gets a tremendous electric shock.

OFTEN AN ORPHAN

Porky Pig, Charlie Dog; Aug 13; LT; Directed by Charles M. Jones; Story by Michael Maltese; Animation by Lloyd Vaughan, Ken Harris, Phil Monroe, and Ben Washam; Layouts by Robert Gribbroek; Backgrounds by Peter Alvarado.

Dumped by his previous owner, Charlie Dog tries to recruit a new master by using the large soulful eyes routine. Spotting farmer Porky Pig, Charlie makes him a "prepasition": "You can be my master, and I can be your dog!" Porky refuses, but Charlie plays up his pedigree, 50 percent pointer, pointing "Dere it is, Dere it is … "; 50 percent Boxer; 50 percent Setter; then, putting a pipe in his mouth, "Irish Setter"; 50 percent Spitz, and lobs one into a spittoon. 50 percent Doberman Pincher, and 100 percent Labrador Retriever. He adds, "If you doubt my word, get me a labrador and I'll retrieve it." Porky kicks him out, but it's not as easy as that. Returning with a pig under one arm and a chicken under the other, Charlie asks, "What do you say we have some ham and eggs?" Charlie gives Porky a classic sob story about how he's dreamed of "wholesome farm living," and needing "fresh leafy vegetables," how life in the city is an urban nightmare where he can't breathe and trucks "Honk, Honk. You can't think! Look out for that taxi! The towers are falling!" Porky lets him sleep in a sleeping bag, which he ships to Scotland. Charlie returns in kilts playing a bagpipe. Porky gives up, and takes the dog on a picnic. When Porky leaves the car, Charlie drives off. Porky flips out and does the "large soulful eyes" routine, getting picked up by the dog pound truck.

THE WINDBLOWN HARE
Bugs Bunny; Aug 27; LT; Directed by Robert McKimson; Story by Warren Foster; Animation by Charles McKimson, Phil Delara, Manny Gould, and John Carey; Layouts by Cornett Wood; Backgrounds by Richard H. Thomas; Voice Characterization by Mel Blanc; Musical Direction by Carl W. Stalling.

After reading the story of "The Three Little Pigs," three real little pigs, fearful of the wolf, decide to sell their houses of straw and sticks and live in the brick house. Bugs Bunny comes along and, deciding to buy, is sold the straw house for $10. The wolf comes along and blows the house down. Bugs next buys the stick house, which the wolf also blows over. Muttering, "This means war," Bugs disguises himself as Red Riding Hood and gives the wolf a copy of the popular fairy tale. The wolf hurries over to Grandma's house, takes her place, and waits for Red Riding Hood. Doing the "what big eyes you got" routine, Bugs abuses the wolf. They chase around the house, doing the staircase gag, turning the lights on and off, then chasing on bicycles out into the woods. Bugs and the wolf decide to team up and get even with the pigs. The wolf miraculously blows the brick house down with the help of Bugs Bunny and his detonator.

DOUGH FOR THE DO-DO
Porky Pig; Sept 2; MM; Musical Direction by Carl W. Stalling; Voice Characterization by Mel Blanc. No other credits on screen.

Porky Pig hunts the rare Dodo bird in Darkest Africa. A remake of Bob Clampett's *Porky in Wackyland* (1939), with new music, redubbed voices, color backgrounds. and much of the original animation painted in color. Friz Freleng's unit provided the new bits of animation. The Dodo is bright green with a yellow face and red hair and shoes.

New animation includes Porky's reaction shots when he first arrives in Wackyland, Porky falling, actually floating in front of a treadmill background being turned by the Dodo; the Dodo dropping one more brick on Porky from a cloud; and the last scene, as Porky dresses as a Dodo bird and claims to be the last. The real Dodo handcuffs himself to Porky, and Porky takes the bird to claim six trillion dollars. A group of Dodo birds gathers and mocks the pig: "Yes, sir! He's got the last Dodo!"

FAST AND FURRY-OUS
Roadrunner; Sept 16; LT; Directed by Charles M. Jones; Story by Michael Maltese; Animation by Ken Harris, Phil Monroe, Ben Washam, and Lloyd Vaughan; Layouts by Robert Gribbroek; Backgrounds by Peter Alvardo; Effects Animation by A.C. Gamer; Musical Direction by Carl W. Stalling.

In an American desert, a Roadrunner (Accelerati Incredibulis) is chased by a Coyote (Carnivarious Vulgaris). Clearly unable to outrun the bird, the Coyote uses 11 various methods to try to stop the roadrunner, (1) A pot lid that the Roadrunner uses to smash the Coyote. (2) "One Genuine Boomerang guaranteed to return." (3) A school crossing and Coyote disguised as a little girl. The bird hits the Coyote and runs. Then the Coyote holds a sign saying, "Roadrunners can't read!" (4) He launches himself via rocket to the mountain ledge and (5) rolls a boulder, which thunders down to smash the Coyote. (6) He paints a tunnel on a flat mountainside, which the Roadrunner can travel through but the Coyote cannot. (7) He tries to use dynamite, but the Coyote's detonator explodes it. (8)

He buys an Acme Super Outfit that doesn't work. (9) Employs a refrigerator, an electric motor, a meat grinder, and a pair of skis to create a high-speed ski chase, ending off a cliff with the Coyote wishing everyone a "Merry Xmas." (10) With "Fleet Foot Jet Propelled Tennis Shoes" the Coyote *is* just as fast as the Roadrunner. They chase all around the cloverleaf highways until the Coyote runs out of fuel. (11) Finally, the Coyote takes a short cut, getting ahead of the Roadrunner. Hearing his "Beep, Beep!" the Coyote lifts his axe and is run over by a truck.

EACH DAWN I CROW

Elmer Fudd; Sept 23; MM; Directed by I. Freleng; Story by Tedd Pierce; Animation by Virgil Ross, Gerry Chiniquy, Manuel Perez, and Ken Chapin; Layouts by Hawley Pratt; Backgrounds by Paul Julian; Musical Direction by Carl W. Stalling.
One morning on the farm, the narrator warns John Rooster that farmer Elmer Fudd is sharpening his axe, preparing for a chicken dinner. Rooster is worried and tries to hide. The narrator laughs and taunts the poor bird. John gets the axe and buries it, while the narrator teases, "You've got a good head on your shoulders, too bad you *can't* keep it there!" Elmer waters a plant, and it sprouts the axe! John Rooster starts chain smoking. The narrator goads the rooster into "Getting him before he gets you!" John sends Elmer out duck hunting. He attaches a duck decoy to Elmer's hat. When the rooster blows the duck decoy, he gets blasted by other hunters! John paints a grenade to look like an egg, but Elmer makes the rooster sit on it till it hatches (and explodes). Elmer takes his axe to do the "disagreeable job"—chopping down a tree. But, with John's luck, the tree falls on him! In the end, Elmer is inviting friends over for an "unexpected chicken dinner." John Rooster is in the oven, basting himself!

FRIGID HARE

Bugs Bunny; Oct 7; MM; Directed by Charles M. Jones; Story by Michael Maltese; Animation by Phil Monroe, Ben Washam, Lloyd Vaughan, and Ken
Harris; Layouts by Robert Gribbroek; Backgrounds by Peter Alvarado; Voice Characterization by Mel Blanc; Musical Direction by Carl W. Stalling.
On a two-week vacation from Warner Bros., Bugs Bunny is burrowing to Miami Beach. Taking that proverbial "wrong turn" he arrives instead at the South Pole, where he is knocked over by a cute little penguin and a big dumb Eskimo chasing it. Bugs is determined to leave; the penguin wants to go with him. Bugs pretends to stay, then kicks the bird into the Eskimo's sack.

Feeling guilty, Bugs returns to rescue the penguin by pretending to be a female Eskimo. Bugs accepts the penguin as a gift, but the Eskimo gets wise and chases the rabbit. The Eskimo catches the bunny on an ice ledge that is about to give way. The Eskimo sneezes, and they fall. The penguin saves Bugs by forming an ice bridge.

Bugs wonders what he's going to do with only four days of vacation left. The penguin tells him that the days here are 4 months long, meaning Bugs "won't have to be back at work until July 1953!" Bugs dons a tuxedo and marches off with the penguin to have a "formal vacation."

SWALLOW THE LEADER

Oct 14; LT; Directed by Robert McKimson; Story by Warren Foster; Animation by Phil DeLara, Pete Burness, John Carey, and Charles McKimson; Layouts by Cornett Wood; Backgrounds by Richard H. Thomas; Effects Animation by A.C. Gamer; Voice Characterization by Mel Blanc; Musical Direction by Carl W. Stalling.
On March 19 each year, the swallows return to the mission at San Juan Capistrano. And, as a narrator points out, "There is always a lover of birds waiting to greet them." Waiting to "greet" the birds is a hungry cat, with a radar scope and his mouth and head and as a nest for the first swallow.

Luckily, the advance scout for the birds is a clever fellow. He puts a jack-in-the-box in the bird nest, making the cat's neck bounce. The bird then paints a statue of a swallow. When the cat eats the metal bird, he becomes a slave to the magnet that the bird has. The magnet pulls the cat through pipes and up rough ladder prongs. The cat tries to fly with two wooden "wings," then dresses as Superman, but both tricks crash land. The cat finally nails the swallow on a sheet of flypaper. The bird is rescued by his companions, as thousands of swallows dive bomb to Capistrano, dropping light bulbs and thumb tacks, and then picking the cat up into the sky and dropping him.

The cat gives up and gets drunk at "Sloppy Joes, the best *swallow* in town!"

BYE, BYE BLUEBEARD

Porky Pig; Oct 21; MM; Directed by Arthur Davis; Story by Sid Marcus; Animation by Basil Davidovich, J.C. Melendez, Don Williams, and Emery Hawkins; Layouts by Don Smith; Backgrounds by Philip DeGuard; Voice Characterization by Mel Blanc; Musical Direction by Carl W. Stalling.

Porky, eating in unison with the 1-2-3-4 routine of a radio exercise show, is pestered by a mouse. A news bulletin reports that the killer Bluebeard is at large. Porky bolts all the windows and doors. The menacing shadow of Bluebeard appears (it's a mouse in disguise). Porky is so scared his head opens up and his ghost flies out. When the radio describes the killer as weighing 350 pounds and standing six feet eleven inches tall, Porky puts his ruler next to the rodent pretending to be Bluebeard. Porky chases the mouse with an axe. When he pulls an indigo beard from under his table, he encounters the real Bluebeard.

Bluebeard ties Porky to a rocket and sits back to enjoy some steak. The mouse competes with the killer for Porky's food, but gets chased around the kitchen table for his trouble. Bluebeard builds a guillotine, and puts Porky on it. The mouse serves up dinner—a tray full of bombs! After a terrific explosion that destroys Bluebeard, Porky resumes his original meal, sharing it with the mouse!

After this film Arthur Davis's unit disbanded. Davis remained with Warners as an animator for Freleng's unit, returning as a director in the 1960s.

FOR SCENT-IMENTAL REASONS

Pepe LePew; Nov 12; LT; Directed by Charles M. Jones; Story by Michael Maltese; Animation by Ben Washam, Lloyd Vaughan, Ken Harris, and Phil Monroe; Layouts by Robert Gribbroek; Backgrounds by Peter Alvarado; Voice Characterization by Mel Blanc; Musical Direction by Carl W. Stalling.

Pepe LePew is in a perfume shop sniffing the various scents. The shopkeeper runs in horror and recruits a female cat to lure the skunk out of the shop. She tosses the cat inside, and a bottle of dye falls over, painting a white stripe down the cat's back. Pepe pursues the cat, intent on making love.

The frightened cat hides in a glass case. Pepe pretends to shoot himself. The cat runs out, concerned. Pepe peers over the transom, boasting, "I am zee locksmith of love!" and chases the cat out the window. She falls into a water bucket, and he plops into a can of blue paint. The paint blocks his smell, and, thinking Pepe is a fellow feline, the cat falls in love with Pepe and chases the skunk. Running in horror, Pepe declares, "You know, it is possible to be too attractive!"

HIPPETY HOPPER

Sylvester, Hippety Hopper; Nov 19; MM; Directed by Robert McKimson; Story by Warren Foster; Animation by Pete Burness, John Carey, Charles McKimson, and Phil DeLara; Layouts by Cornett Wood; Backgrounds by Richard H. Thomas; Voice Characterization by Mel Blanc; Musical Direction by Carl W. Stalling.

At the waterfront, a mouse about to commit suicide is saved by a kangaroo, Hippety Hopper, awaiting delivery to the city zoo. The mouse enlists Hippety's aid in getting even with the cat, Sylvester, who had driven the rodent to sad desperation.

The mouse tells Sylvester that he will "take vitamins and grow as big as you are!" Sylvester laughs, until he sees Hippety, who boxes him into the wall and tosses him out of the house. The bulldog tells the cat, "We all gotta job to do," and sends the confused cat back in. Hippety punches him out again. Sylvester tells the dog that the mouse is a giant. The dog puts a pair of glasses on the cat (causing the cat to see abstract images of the bulldog) and assures him, "Nobody hits a guy with glasses. Of course, I could be wrong!" After Sylvester comes crashing out again, the bulldog goes inside and dares the mouse to kick him out. Hippety kicks, the mouse bites, and the dog goes running. The mouse threatens to pin the dog's ears back. The dog replies, "Any time a mouse can pin my ears back, I'll take ballet lessons!" Needless to say, the film ends with Sylvester and the Bulldog pirouetting into the sunset.

WHICH IS WITCH?

Bugs Bunny; Dec 3; LT; Directed by I. Freleng; Story by Tedd Pierce; Animation by Ken Chapin, Virgil Ross, Arthur Davis, and Gerry Chiniquy; Layouts by Hawley Pratt; Backgrounds by Paul Julian; Effects Animation by A.C. Gamer; Voice Characterization by Mel Blanc; Musical Direction by Carl W. Stalling.

A native witch doctor, Dr. I. C. Spots, is preparing a potion and needs a rabbit to complete it. Strolling through the jungle, Bugs Bunny encounters the Doc and immediately starts heckling him. First, Bugs presumes he's Dr. Livingston and takes his picture; then he smashes his spear. The witch doctor chases Bugs into his hut, where he has prepared a hot bath for the bunny. When Bugs settles in, the Doc locks him into the kettle. The rabbit escapes through a steam outlet. Bugs disguises himself as a Zulu native, stretching his face with plates in his mouth and putting a dozen rings around his neck. The witch doctor chases Bugs to the river, where Bugs swims for a riverboat. The Doc pursues, but an alligator eats him. Bugs battles the gator as well, turning the croc into an alligator bag, the Witch doctor inside wearing alligator shoes.

BEAR FEAT

The Three Bears; Dec 10; LT; Directed by Charles M. Jones; Story by Michael

Maltese; Animation by Ben Washam, Lloyd Vaughan, Ken Harris, and Phil Monroe; Layouts by Robert Gribbroek; Backgrounds by Peter Alvarado; Musical Direction by Carl W. Stalling.

As the Three Bears eat breakfast, Papa spots an ad, "WANTED: Trick Bear Act. Apply Mingling Bros. Circus." The family practices the old routines, and in each case, by virtue of his weight or stupidity, Junior ruins the rehearsal. In practicing a high-wire act, Junior's weight brings the tightrope to the ground. When Pa tells him to get off, he is propelled into space. When Pa does a high dive, Junior's thirst consumes the entire bucket of water. Pa tries the motorcycle in the barrel stunt, which goes fine until Junior throws in a banana peel. Other acts include trapeze, roller skating through a hoop, and various acrobatics.

When Henry rereads the newspaper ad and sees it is from April 1928, he tries to commit suicide by jumping off the mountain top. Junior save him with a full bucket of water, but gets socked for his trouble. "What'd I do? What'd I do?"

A HAM IN A ROLE

Goofy Gophers; Dec 13; LT; Directed by Robert McKimson; Story by Sid Marcus; Animation by Charles McKimson, Phil DeLara, J.C. Melendez, and Emery Hawkins; Layouts by Cornett Wood; Backgrounds by Richard H. Thomas; Voice Characterization by Mel Blanc; Musical Direction by Carl W. Stalling.

One of McKimson's best. A Shakespearian dog is tired of getting pies in the face for mere "Looney Tunes." He writes a resignation letter to Mr. Warner, quits his contract, and goes home to study the bard. He discovers the Goofy Gophers sleeping in his copy of *Hamlet.* They heckle the thespian, relating each gag to a quote from Shakespeare. When he reads a line about "tormenting flames," they give him a hot foot. From, *Romeo and Juliet,* he asks to "drink the joy of life," and recieves a bathtub of water on his head. When "A rose by any other name would smell as sweet," he is plopped with Limburger cheese. Reading from *Hamlet,* "Alas, poor Eurich," the gophers dress as a skeleton and taunt the actor. Wearing armor to recite from "St. George and the Dragon," the dog is dragged by a magnet across ceiling rafters. Reading from *Richard the Third,* he asks "My kingdom for a horse" and a mule kicks him through the air to the Warner Bros. studio. Back on stage, he performs "To be or not to be" and gets hit with a pie, ending the cartoon exactly as it began!

RABBIT HOOD

Bugs Bunny; Dec 24; MM; Directed by Charles M. Jones; Story by Michael Maltese; Animation by Ken Harris, Phil Monroe, Ben Washam, and Lloyd Vaughan; Layouts by Robert Gribbroek; Backgrounds by Peter Alvarado; Voice Characterization by Mel Blanc; Musical Direction by Carl W. Stalling.
Sherwood Forest is studded with "No Poaching" signs, "Not even an egg!" Bugs Bunny tries to swipe a carrot from the king's carrot patch, but is caught crimson fisted by the sheriff of Nottingham. Just then, a goofy Little John announces, "Don't you worry, never fear, Robin Hood will soon be here!" Robin doesn't appear (the film's running gag), so the bunny announces "Lo, the king approacheth!" As the sheriff bows for the king, Bugs bops him and runs. The sheriff chases the bunny to the king's Royal Ground, where the rabbit imitates a real-estate salesman and sells the sheriff the land. The flim-flam works so well, the sherrif is building the second story of a house before he finally gets wise. The sheriff corners the rabbit, who comically introduces Little John to him.

Next, Bugs pretends the king is coming and this time disguises himself as his highness and bestows knighthood on the sheriff. Bopping him with his staff with each word, Bugs declares the sheriff "Sir Loin of Beef, Earl of Cloves, Baron of Munchausen, Milk of Magnesia, Quarter of Ten." The groggy sheriff sings "London Bridge" as he falls into a freshly baked layer cake. Little John finally introduces Robin Hood—a live-action shot of Errol Flynn, causing an astonished Bunny to shrug, "Eh, it *couldn't* be him!"

1950

HOME TWEET HOME

Tweety, Sylvester; Jan 14; MM; Directed by I. Freleng; Story by Tedd Piece; Animation by Virgil Ross, Arthur Davis, Gerry Chiniquy, and Ken Champin; Layouts by Hawley Pratt; Backgrounds by Phil DeLara; Voice Characterization by Mel Blanc; Musical Direction by Carl W. Stalling.
Tweety is taking a bath in the park birdbath. Sylvester sneaks closer, pretending to read the paper on the park bench. The cat gets so close that Tweety uses his tongue as a towel to dry off. As the cat chases the bird around a park statue, a nanny comes to Tweety's rescue, beating the cat away. ("You coward, you bully, you shmoe!") Sylvester disguises himself as the nanny's charge, complaining, "Baby wants a pretty birdie!" The nanny gives him Tweety, which he puts right in his mouth. The nanny spanks him. ("How many times do I have to tell you not to put birds in your mouth!") Tweety hides on top of Sylvester's head ("He'll never find me here!"). He escapes to a window ledge. Sylvester follows, using bubblegum to float upward. Tweety pops his gum and hands him an anvil (then "saves" the cat with an anvil-stuffed pillow!). Sylvester disguises himself as a tree with a nest in his branch. Tweety rests in the nest. A bulldog also thinks he's a tree and sniffs him, chasing him down the street. Tweety calls the pet shop to order another putty tat. "I'm fwesh out!"

HURDY GURDY HARE

Bugs Bunny; Jan 21; MM; Directed by Robert McKimson; Story by Warren Foster; Animation by J.C. Melendez, Emery Hawkins, Charles McKimson, John Carey, and Phil DeLara; Layouts by Cornett Wood; Backgrounds by Phil DeGuard; Voice Characterization by Mel Blanc; Musical Direction by Carl W. Stalling.

Bugs, the entreprenurial bunny, reads a classified ad for a hurdy gurdy and monkey and decides to go into the music business. ("Ah! The old masters! Beet-hoven ... Batch!"). Bugs' monkey collects the coins all right, but "pockets" the take in his cap, leaving Bugs to can the chiseling chimp and make like a monkey himself. Using a ladder, he climbs the outside of swank apartments on Fifth Avenue. The little monkey sicks a pal on Bugs, a gruesome gorilla ("Obviously a barbell boy") in the Central Park Zoo. The big ape means to thrash Bugs on one of the building ledges, but the wiley rabbit continually gets the jump. He tells the gorilla to stop breathing into his cup, and isn't fazed when the gorilla switches the ladder he's on so that Bugs runs toward him instead of away from him. ("I've seen you before, I never forget a face. But in your case I'll make an exception!") Bugs builds a brick wall around his head (with an explosive cigar). He finally calms the savage beast with his violin and uses him as a big monkey to collect big money instead of coins! "I sure hope Petrillo [head of the American Federation of Musicians] doesn't hear about this!"

BOOBS IN THE WOODS

Porky Pig, Daffy Duck; Jan 28; LT; Directed by Robert McKimson; Story by Warren Foster; Animation by Phil DeLara, J.C. Melendez, Emery Hawkins, Charles McKimson, and Pete Burness; Layouts by Cornett Wood; Backgrounds by Richard H. Thomas; Voice Characterization by Mel Blanc; Musical Direction by Carl W. Stalling.

Daffy Duck walks through the woods singing a "Looney-Toony" song, while amateur artist Porky Pig sets up his canvas to do some still-life painting.

Daffy "gets into" his picture by posing against the scenery, but the pig tells him to get out ("There ought to be a law against crazy ducks!"). Daffy heckles the portly painter by claiming the lake is his and he doesn't want it painted. Disguised as "the old man of the mountains" Daffy doesn't want them painted either! Porky gets wise and grabs his rifle, but Daffy counters as the sheriff who nails the pig for "hunting ducks out of season," and calls for the "executioner" to chop his head off. Daffy then dresses as "Pocahontas" to save him.

Porky tries to fish, using a string and a bell. Daffy asks the pig if he has a fishing license—he does. A dog license? He does! No marriage license though, so the duck nuzzles up to him ("Whaddaya say you and me go steady?"). Porky decides to leave, but his car engine won't start. Daffy gets under the hood and pretends to be the motor. Porky ties Daffy to his motor permanently, showing his "Permit to use Daffy Duck as a motor."

MUTINY ON THE BUNNY

Bugs Bunny, Yosemite Sam; Feb 11; LT; Directed by I. Freleng; Story by Tedd Pierce; Animation by Gerry Chiniquy, Ken Champin, Virgil Ross, and Arthur Davis; Backgrounds by Paul Julian; Layouts by Hawley Pratt; Voice Characterization by Mel Blanc; Musical Direction by Carl W. Stalling.

Shanghi Sam, the cruel captain of "The Sad Sack" (formerly "The Bounty"), needs to recruit a new crew (his previous "crew" has escaped, saying, "I was a human being once!"). Sam offers, carnival barker style, a free cruise around the world. Bugs Bunny takes him up on the offer, but soon finds himself rowing the ship by himself! The rabbit complains, but the captain will not hear of it. He orders Bugs to swab the deck ("Oh no I'm not!" "Oh, yes you are!"). The bunny puts graffiti on the bulkheads ("The Captain's wife wears army boots," "The Captain loves Gravel Gertie," "The Captain is a Schnook!"). Bugs declares a disaster, but refuses to let Sam leave ("The Captain goes down with his ship!"). Sam makes Bugs the captain. It's women and children first, so Sam dresses as a woman! Bugs makes Sam catch his "baby" (an anchor in blankets), sinking his lifeboat. Sam goes after the rabbit. Bugs is digging for treasure, but Sam takes his map and starts chopping through the hull. The ship sinks. After repairing the craft, Sam fires the cannon at Bugs, but the cannon ball breaks the hull, sinking the ship again! In the end, Sam is rowing the lifeboat, with Bugs in tow, on their way to Rio de "Jan-ario."

THE LION'S BUSY

Beaky Buzzard; Feb 18; LT; Directed by I. Freleng; Story by Tedd Pierce; Animation by Arthur Davis, Gerry Chiniquy, Ken Champin, and Virgil Ross; Layouts by Hawley Pratt; Backgrounds by Paul Julian; Voice Characterization by Mel Blanc; Musical Direction by Carl W. Stalling.
In the jungle, Leo the Lion is having his tenth birthday party and receives a present from Beaky Buzzard. It's a book that says that "Lions rarely live beyond the age of ten years!" Thus begins a chase around the jungle: the lion accidentally falls off a cliff, and Beaky starts making a sandwich of his tail. The lion takes it out and screams into the sky. Beaky catches him in a frying pan, but Leo attacks him with a baseball bat! Beaky hides up a tree, and the lion climbs it, but slides off: Beaky has greased the bark. The lion uses spikes to climb the tree, but at the top he reveals a fear of heights! Beaky offers to get him down—with an axe! The lion takes a skyrocket to the moon to escape the hungry buzzard. The buzzard is there waiting! The lion hides in a cave, and comes out a few months later, but Beaky's *still* there! The lion comes out in 1957, now an old-timer, and confronts the patient buzzard. "It's no use! You might as well eat me now and be done with it!" But Beaky is just as old: "Sorry, Leo, can't eat nothing anymore but marshmallows!"

THE SCARLET PUMPERNICKEL

Daffy Duck and a cast of thousands;

Mar 4; LT; Directed by Charles M. Jones; Story by Michael Maltese; Animation by Phil Monroe, Ben Washam, Lloyd Vaughan, and Ken Harris; Layouts by Robert Gribbroek; Backgrounds by Peter Alvarado; Voice Characterization by Mel Blanc; Musical Direction by Carl W. Stalling.
"You're killing me," screams Daffy "I'm telling ya, J. L., you're typecasting me to death. Comedy, always comedy." Pleading for a dramatic part with the studio bigwig, Daffy has the very script they've been looking for, by one Daffy Dumas Duck. It's about a swashbuckler paying homage to the classic Michael Curtiz/Errol Flynn costumers of the '30s as well as Leslie Howard's *Scarlet Pimpernel*. "Once upon a time (great opening, huh?) in Merry Olde England there was a daring young highwayman [Daffy himself as Errol Flynn, and also the narrator]. The Lord High Chamberlain [Porky Pig as Claude Rains] was simply furious, but Milady Melissa, the Pumpernickel's Maid Marian, (after Olivia De Havilland), was simply delighted." To set a trap for "That masked stinker," the Chamberlain announces the betrothal of Melissa to the Grand Duke (Sylvester as Basil Rathbone). The Pumpernickel stops at the King's Nostril Inn, run by Elmer Fudd (Blanc not Bryan), masquerading as a foppish gentleman, his disguise fooling the Chamberlain and the Duke. After a few slapstick pratfalls, Daffy crashes the wedding (literally) and rescues his lady love from the very threshold of the altar (actually she carries him off! "So what's to save?") and takes her back to the inn. There, unfortunately, she's

spotted by the Duke, and the whole thing climaxes in a swordfight, that, as the studio boss begs for the finish, is the first of a series of climaxes that includes the cavalry, bursting dams, erupting volcanos, and skyrocketing prices of kosher food.

HOMELESS HARE

Bugs Bunny; Mar 11; MM; Directed by Charles M. Jones; Story by Michael Maltese; Animation by Ken Harris, Phil Monroe, Ben Washam, and Lloyd Vaughan; Layouts by Robert Gribbroek; Backgrounds by Peter Alvarado; Voice Characterization by Mel Blanc; Musical Direction by Carl W. Stalling.

A roughneck, musclebound construction worker upearths Bugs's rabbit hole with a steam shovel, ignoring Bugs's plea to restore it because of "the sanctity of the American home." "Okay, Hercules, you asked for it," Bugs informs the brute via a message on a brick dropped from a few dozen stories up, followed with a steel beam. The laborer takes the elevator after Bugs, who throws the control switch up and down so the roughneck gets flattened against the floor and ceiling of the car, and then flies out the top. He waves to a pigeon and falls into a trough of cement being mixed (a smaller and meeker construction worker appropriates his cigar). Bugs then impersonates a strict foreman, barking orders ("Tote that barge, lift that bale") at the roughneck to finish a very high wall, on top of which Bugs tricks him into trying to balance on a very tipsy plank (he throws off his clothes to save weight). "Maybe that'll teach that big baboon some manners," says Bugs. Instead, the big palooka slams a girder into Bugs, causing him to dizzily "dream walk" across the partially constructed building, narrowly avoiding disaster. Finally, he falls into a barrel of water ("It ain't Saturday night!"). Bugs ultimately plots the course of a red-hot rivet to have it burn through a rope holding up an enormous steel casing. It drops directly on the lunch-mooching lug. The building finally goes up around the rabbit hole. "After all, a man's home is his castle!"

Theme: "Don't Sweetheart Me."

STRIFE WITH FATHER

Beaky Buzzard; Apr 1: MM; Directed by Robert McKimson; Story by Warren Foster; Animation by Emery Hawkins, Charles McKimson, Phil DeLara, Rod Scribner, and J.C. Melendez; Layouts by Cornett Wood; Backgrounds by Richard H. Thomas; Voice Characterization by Mel Blanc; Musical Direction by Carl W. Stalling.

On the doorstep of the tree-house home of English birds Monte and Evelyn Sparrow, a mysterious figure leaves an egg. They take it and raise the hatchling, an ugly bird, into Beaky Buzzard!

Father Monte introduces Beaky to the facts of life. First, he tries to teach him to fly by sawing the branch he's standing on ("Flying sure hurts a fella's head!"). Father then tries to teach him to catch a chicken, but the buzzard hits his dad with the mallet. Father uses a grenade to catch a chicken, but Beaky thinks it's an egg, chasing Monte around the yard trying to give it to him. Beaky brings the grenade to Mama, who throws it out the window, where it explodes near Monte. Father comes back in shambles. "If I were king ...." Beaky retorts, "That's no king, that's Monte!"

THE HYPO-CONDRI-CAT

Hubie and Bertie; Claude Cat; Apr 15; MM; Directed by Charles M. Jones; Story by Michael Maltese; Animation by Ben Washam, Lloyd Vaughan, Ken Harris, and Phil Monroe; Layouts by Robert Gribbroek; Backgrounds by Phil DeLara; Voice Characterization by Mel Blanc; Musical Direction by Carl W. Stalling.

One rainy night, the mice Hubie and Bertie enter a new home and warm themselves by the fireplace, filling themselves with cheese until they are chased by the house cat, Claude. They learn that Claude is a hypochondriac, afraid of catching cold, who takes pills and bundles up. They use the power of suggestion to make Claude feel worse. "Look at him, Bert, he's turnin' green!" He is: also purple and plaid. The cat begs the mice to stay and help him.

The mice operate on the cat by preparing eggbeaters, saws, and axes while the cat shakes under the covers. They take a slice of cheese, but the cat passes out and goes into a surrealistic nightmare. When Claude awakens, the mice pretend the cat has died. They cry over his grave, while the cat begs to be be seen (they've attached golden wings to his back with safety pins). "See, here I am! Ta-daaa." The mice "see" Claude as a ghost, and the cat begs again for help. Hubie and Bertie lead him to "cat heaven" (a sign posted at the edge of a cliff) and tell him to "take off." Claude cries, "But I can't fly!" The mice push him and wave goodbye as he floats upward via a helium balloon. Claude, now filled with an inner peace, bids them, "Farewell, you poor earthly creatures."

BIG HOUSE BUNNY

Bugs Bunny, Yosemite Sam; Apr 22; LT; Directed by I. Freleng; Story by Tedd Pierce; Animation by Virgil Ross, Arthur Davis, Gerry Chiniquy, and Ken Chapin; Layouts by Hawley Pratt; Backgrounds by Phil DeGuard; Voice Characterization by Mel Blanc; Musical Direction by Carl W. Stalling.
It's "Open Season for Rabbits," and Bugs Bunny is running from hunters. He hops in a rabbit hole and comes up in Sing Song Prison ("No Hanging Around"). Mistaken for a convict by the prison guard (Yosemite) Sam Shultz, he spends the rest of the film trying to get out of the pen. Bugs tricks Sam into firing the ball he's chained to, via cannon, over the wall. Bringing him back, Sam is next tricked into thinking he's in a cell and Bugs is free ("Gee I don't get it, Doc! How come you locked me outside?"). The irate Sam intends to give Bugs solitary for 99 years, so Bugs tricks Sam into changing uniforms. Sam is thrown in a cell, and Bugs, as a guard, gives him tools and helps him escape! Sam tunnels out, coming up in a jungle that is actually the plants in the warden's office. The warden scolds Sam, who gets even by chasing Bugs to a noose. Once again, Bugs turns the tables and hangs Sam! Disguised as the warden, Bugs sits Sam in the electric chair. Sam gets wise and chases Bugs, accidentally hitting the real warden! Sam decides the only way to get the bunny is to let him out, but the warden has had enough and puts Sam on the rock pile. Sam asks, "I'd like to know what dirty stool pigeon squealed on me?" Bugs gets on a stool and imitates that particular bird!

THE LEGHORN BLOWS AT MIDNIGHT

Foghorn Leghorn; May 6; LT; Directed by Robert McKimson; Story by Warren Foster; Animation by Charles McKimson, Phil DeLara, Rod Scribner, J.C. Melendez, and Emery Hawkins; Layouts by Cornett Wood; Backgrounds by Richard H. Thomas; Voice Characterization by Mel Blanc; Musical Direction by Carl W. Stalling.
Foghorn Leghorn is playing solitaire in the barnyard when his foe, the dog, bashes his head with a pair of cymbals. Foggy gets a cream pie from the farmer's window and mashes it in the dog's face. The dog chases the rooster, who painfully scalds the dog with hot water. Henery Hawk enters the scene, thinking the dog is a chicken. The hound points him in another direction, to Foghorn. Foggy helps Henery with his pumpkin trap and gets the pumpkin on his head! Henery explains he's a chickenhawk and is taking him home. Foggy gives him a sob story and recommends "pheasant"—the dog! Foggy puts vanishing cream on Henery and pretends he's invisible. The dog chases Henery away, but Foggy tells him not to give up and reminds him of the great chickenhawks in history (shown in stick figures). The dog and Foghorn have a fist fight, in front of Henery's cooking pot. Says the chickenhawk, "I don't care who wins. I'll fricasee the loser!"

HIS BITTER HALF

Daffy Duck; May 20; MM; Directed by I. Freleng; Story by Tedd Pierce; Animation by Ken Champin, Virgil Ross, Arthur Davis, and Gerry Chiniquy; Layouts by Hawley Pratt; Backgrounds by Paul Julian; Voice Characterization by Mel Blanc; Musical Direction by Carl W. Stalling.

Daffy Duck is reading the want ads in his swamp dwelling. "WANTED: Man with herd of cattle wishes to meet woman with frying pan. Object: Hamburger!" "Refined wealthy lady duck with home and income wishes to meet refined single gentleman duck. Object: Matrimony." This catches Daffy's attention. He dons hat and jacket, buys chocolates at the 5 & 10; and, the next thing you know, he has married the lady duck. When they get home, she lays down the law (or she'll wipe the smile off his face—literally!). Daffy is forced to do all the chores. He cleans, sweeps, and dusts all at once. He's exhausted, but must attend to the little yellow duck, "Wentworth," her "cute-like-a-stomach-pump" son.

After a swift kick in the tail-feathers, Daffy is forced to play "Indian." While his wife eats chocolates and reads, Daffy is getting scalped! Next, they attend an amusement park, where Daffy shows Wentworth how to work the rifle in a shooting gallery. The little duck keeps hitting the back of the barker's head. This gets Daffy socked. Daffy helps Wentworth shoot fireworks, but gets blasted himself. Wentworth disguises himself as a firecracker. Daffy mistakes a real firecracker for Wentworth and spanks it until it explodes. Despite his wife's threat to "pluck every feather off your scrawny carcass," Daffy refuses to take Wentworth to the zoo. He packs his bags and leaves, with all his rear feathers removed!

AN EGG SCRAMBLE

Porky Pig; May 27; MM; Directed by Robert McKimson; Story by Warren Foster; Animation by Phil DeLara, Rod Scribner, J.C. Melendez, Emery Hawkins, and Charles McKimson; Layouts by Cornett Wood; Backgrounds by Richard H. Thomas; Voice Characterization by Mel Blanc; Musical Direction by Carl W. Stalling.

On Porky's Pig's farm ("home of the world famous Hammond Eggs"), Porky picks up the daily eggs from his hens—Miss Prissy, embarrassed to even try, is the exception. Porky warns her to lay or else. Prissy tries (while reading "The Egg and I"). Another in the henhouse helps her out by putting one of hers, marked "Prissy," in her nest. Porky is pleased and puts it in the truck for market. Prissy wants it back and follows the truck into town.

Prissy follows the egg from a general store (where she is caught smashing eggs) to a housewife about to boil it. Prissy grabs her egg and runs through the back alleys of the city. Meanwhile, Porky goes to the police to find Prissy, but they're more concerned with capturing Pretty Boy Bagel, the escaped criminal. They have him cornered at 13 13th St., the exact spot where Prissy is hiding; she thinks the crook is trying to protect her and her egg. The police open fire and throw tear gas. Prissy comes out, and Porky brings her home. Porky still wants her egg, but she insists it is hers. The hens reveal that Agnes laid it, the egg hatches, and a Prissy chick pops out, proving it was really Miss Prissy's egg after all!

WHAT'S UP, DOC?

Bugs Bunny, Elmer Fudd; June 17; LT; Directed by Robert McKimson; Story by Warren Foster; Animation by J.C. Melendez, Charles McKimson, Phil DeLara, and Wilson Burness; Layouts by Cornett Wood; Backgrounds by Richard H. Thomas; Voice Characterization by Mel Blanc; Musical Direction Carl W. Stalling.

Bugs Bunny gets a call from "Disassociated Press" asking for his life story. In flashback, we learn that Bugs is "a rabbit in a human world!" Bugs played piano at an early age, studied dance at "Moray's Dance School," and became a chorus boy in such Broadway hits as "Girl of the Golden Vest," "Wearing of the Grin," and "Rosie's Cheeks" ("Oh, we're the boys of the chorus/We hope you'll like our show/We know your roo-

tin' for us/but now we have to go!'").
One night, the star is sick, and Bugs
fills in. Despite giving his all, he hears
only crickets after his performance.
Times are hard: Bugs is shown sharing
a park bench with Al Jolson, Jack
Benny, Eddie Cantor, and Bing Crosby.
Jolson spots Elmer Fudd, the big Vaudeville star. "I hear he's looking for a
partner for his act." The others audition
as he walks by, but when Fudd spots
the rabbit he exclaims, "Bugs Bunny!
Why are you hanging around with
these guys? They'll never amount to
anything!" Fudd goes on, "I need you
in my act! You're great! You're wonderful!" They open in Peoria, where Bugs
is the patsy for Elmer's jokes. Bugs
decides to do the punchlines and grab
some laughs for himself. Fudd gets
angry and confronts the bunny with his
rifle on stage. When Bugs asks, "Eh,
What's up, Doc?" the crowd roars with
laughter. They're a hit! Soon offers
pour in from around the country, then
comes Hollywood and Warner Bros.,
where their film career is launched. On
the sound stage, Bugs and Elmer perform the song, "What's Up, Doc?"
Bugs begins his first picture, a part
written especially for him. He is doing
the same chorus-boy song from his
Broadway days!

ALL A-BIR-R-R-D

*Tweety, Sylvester; June 24; LT;
Directed by I. Freleng; Story by Tedd
Pierce; Animation by Ken Champin,
Virgil Ross, Arthur Davis, Emery
Hawkins, and Gerry Chiniquy;
Backgrounds by Paul Julian; Layouts by
Hawley Pratt; Voice Characterization by
Mel Blanc; Musical Direction by Carl W.
Stalling.*
"Mommy" (voiced by Bea Benederet)
puts Tweety alone on a train bound for
Gower Gulch. Tweety sings his litle
song ("I'm a Tweet little bird in a
gilded cage/Tweety's my name, but I
don't know my age ... "), attracting that
hungry putty tat, Sylvester. The con-
ductor warns the cat off, and puts
Tweety's cage on a higher perch. That
doesn't stop the cat from trying.
Sylvester stacks baggage and climbs for
the bird. Tweety pulls the emergency

cord and sends the cat into the furnace!
Sylvester angers a large bulldog, also
riding in the car. Sylvester cuts the
emergency cord and tries again;
Tweety pulls it, stopping the train
again! Sylvester grabs Tweety, but the
conductor comes by, so the cat stashes
the bird in the mail sack, hanging it on
the mail hook. Sylvester runs to
retrieve his dinner, opens the mail
sack, and is surprised by the dog. The
dog chases the cat atop the train, and
Sylvester falls off. At the Gower Gulch
station, a lady (Sylvester in disguise)
picks up Tweety, but gets the dog
instead, who pummels the puss!

8 BALL BUNNY

*Bugs Bunny; July 8; LT; Directed by
Charles M. Jones; Story by Michael
Maltese; Animation by Phil Monroe,
Ben Washam, Lloyd Vaughan, Ken
Harris, and Emery Hawkins; Layouts
and Backgrounds by Peter Alvarado;
Voice Characterization by Mel Blanc;
Musical Direction by Carl W. Stalling.*
A little, top-hatted performing penguin
misses his ride after the Brooklyn Ice
Palace show closes. Chasing after the
car, he falls down Bugs Bunny's rabbit
hole, and the rabbit tries to pacify the
"boid in a tuxedo" by consenting to
take him home. On learning from a
book that penguins come from the
South Pole, it's "Ooh! I'm dyin'!"
Heading south as stowaways on a
freight train, they're accosted by a
hungry hobo whom Bugs disposes of.
In New Orleans Bugs puts the boid
aboard the "S.S. Admiral Byrd," learns
the ship is bound for Brooklyn, and,
swimming aboard, finds that the bird
has ended up "on the menu." In Marti-
nique, Bugs strums calypso style and
offers some change to panhandler
Humphrey Bogart ("a fellow American
who's down on his luck"). The penguin
carves out a canoe, which leaves the
two of them adrift for ten days without
food (Bugs suppressing the recurring
voice of the hobo, "penguins is practically chickens"). They're saved when
they sight land. Bugs decides to save
two bits for the Panama Canal and
walks through the jungle. They're both
about to be eaten by natives ("you and

your short cuts") until a "bwana" frightens the natives away. He turns out to be Bogart again! They finally make it past alligators, over mountains, and across the sea to the South Pole, where the penguin reveals that he's actually "The only Hoboken-born penguin in captivity." When Bogie turns up one last time, Bugs asks him if he can help out a fellow American down on his luck, and hands Bogie the penguin! "Ooh! I'm dyin' again!"

Theme: "Don't Sweetheart Me."

IT'S HUMMER TIME
July 22; LT; Directed by Robert McKimson; Story by Warren Foster; Animation by Rod Scribner, J.C. Melendez, Charles McKimson, Phil DeLara, and John Carey; Layouts by Cornett Wood; Backgrounds by Richard H. Thomas; Effects Animation by Harry Love; Voice Characterization by Mel Blanc; Musical Direction by Carl W. Stalling.

A hummingbird lands on a birdbath statue that actually is a disguised cat. The cat accidentally grabs a bulldog, who punishes the feline in unique ways. First, the cat begs "Not the fence," but the dog pulls the cat through a knothole in the fence by his tail. Each time the cat tries for the bird, he ends up disturbing the dog, who exacts his punishment. "No, not Happy Birthday!" has the dog setting the cat up with a birthday party and a cake with dynamite candles! "Not the rain-pipe," has the dog tying the cat with rope and forcing him down the drain-pipe. "Not the Thinker!" has the dog putting the cat in a cement mixer, the feline coming out a statue!

Finally, "Not the works! Don't do it, in the name of humanity!" has a rope pulling the cat by the tail through all the obstacles in the house, the drain pipes, and into the cement mixer. The hummingbird ties the dog's tail and he goes through it too, both the dog and cat coming out in the shape of a birdbath, which the feathered fellow uses to swim in!

GOLDEN YEGGS
Daffy Duck, Porky Pig; Aug 5; MM; Directed by I. Freleng; Story by Tedd

Pierce; Animation by Arthur Davis, Gerry Chiniquy, Ken Champin, Virgil Ross, and Emery Hawkins; Layouts by Hawley Pratt; Backgrounds by Paul Julian; Voice Characterization by Mel Blanc; Musical Direction by Carl W. Stalling.*

On the Egg and Rye Ranch farmer Porky Pig hears a ruckus in the henhouse. A 24-karat golden egg has been laid, and Porky wants to know who did it. The "golden goose" tells Porky that Daffy Duck did it. The next thing you know, Daffy is front-page news on the *Daily Blurp* and *Life* magazine. Big city ganster Rocky decides "We're going in the poultry business." They take Daffy from Porky and at gunpoint force the duck to lay another egg. ("All right duck, make wit da golden egg!") Daffy stalls them by saying he needs atmosphere. Courtesy of the gangsters, Daffy spends the next day lounging in a swimming pool with a drink in his hand!

Rocky gives the duck five minutes to lay an egg. Daffy asks for privacy ("I never lay eggs in public!"), and tries to sneak out, but behind the door is Rocky, reminding him: "Four minutes." Daffy escapes with the laundry, but comes back folded and starched. Rocky reminds, "Three minutes." At the two-minute mark, Daffy ties sheets together and climbs out the window, meeting Rocky hanging on the sheets! Daffy sweats out the remaining time. The gansters enter his room and blow his top-knot off. Suddenly, a 24K gold egg is in his basket. "It just goes to show, you don't know what you can do until you have a gun pointed to your head!" Daffy begins to leave, but the gangsters show him to a room filled with dozens of empty egg crates. Rocky orders "Fill 'em up!"

HILLBILLY HARE
Bugs Bunny; Aug 12; MM; Directed by Robert McKimson; Story by Tedd Pierce; Animation by Rod Scribner, Phil DeLara, John Carey, Emery Hawkins, and Charles McKimson; Layouts by Cornett Wood; Backgrounds by Richard H. Thomas; Voice Characterization by Mel Blanc; Musical Direction by Carl W. Stalling.

Bugs Bunny happily sings "I Like Mountain Music" while vacationing in the Ozarks until he encounters Curt Martin pointing a rifle in his face. "Be ya'all a Martin or be ya'all a Coy rabbit?" Bugs replies, "My friends say I'm very coy!" Bugs gives the hillbilly a sob story, then ties his rifle barrel into a bow. He then meets brother Pumpkinhead, who also points his gun at him. The mountainmen chase the rabbit into a powder house full of explosives. Bugs offers them a lighter to help them see. The shack is blown to bits!

Bugs disguises himself as a hillbilly girl, with whom both hillbillies fall in love. They square dance, and Bugs grabs the fiddle forcing the two hillbillies into a series of violent routines. ("Grab a fence post, hold it tight, whomp your partner with all your might ... Whomp him low and whomp him high, stick your finger in his eye!"). They pull beards, wallow in the pig pen, fall into the river, get "squared" in the hay baler, and run off the cliff!

DOG GONE SOUTH

Charlie Dog; Aug 26; MM; Directed by Charles M. Jones; Story by Michael Maltese; Animation by Ben Washam, Lloyd Vaughan, Ken Harris, Phil Monroe, and Emery Hawkins; Layouts by Robert Gribbroek; Backgrounds by Phil DeGuard; Voice Characterization by Mel Blanc; Musical Direction by Carl W. Stalling.

Kicked off a freight train for being a tramp, Charlie Dog lands in the deep south ("Platt Falls," to be exact). Charlie comes across a Southern colonel on his plantation and tries to endear himself by singing, "Yankee Doodle." This enrages the colonel, who orders the dog off the plantation. Charlie proposes a dog-master relationship, but the colonel calls his own bulldog, "Belvedere" to get rid of this pest. Charlie puts a "Yankee" hat on the bulldog and flag reading "The North Forever" in his mouth. The colonel wearing his Confederate gray, charges his dog. Charlie pretends to be a wounded veteran. It almost works until he asks for some "Yankee pie." The colonel calls for Bel-

vedere, whom Charlie has now dressed in a New York Yankees baseball uniform. The bulldog accidentally beats up the colonel, who dismisses Belvedere and accepts Charlie as his dog. Suddenly a red-bearded colonel comes by and offers to take the dog. Charlie goes off with his new master who promptly kicks him onto a freight train. The red-bearded master is Belvedere in disguise. He walks off with the colonel singing "Dixie."

THE DUCKSTERS

Porky Pig, Daffy Duck; Sept 2; LT; Directed by Charles M. Jones; Story by Michael Maltese; Animation by Lloyd Vaughan, Ken Harris, Phil Monroe, and Ben Washam; Layouts by Robert Gribbroek; Backgrounds by Peter Alvarado; Voice Characterization by Mel Blanc; Musical Direction by Carl W. Stalling.

"Aren't we gruesome?" Porky Pig is on a radio quiz program, "Truth or AAAAGGGHH! Brought to you by the Eagle Hand Laundry (If your eagle's hands are dirty ...)" with Daffy Duck playing a sadistic emcee who shouts, "Times up," before Porky can say, "George Washington." Porky wants to leave with his prizes, the Rocky Mountains and the La Brea Tar Pits, but Daffy promises, "The next question's a snap," giving him an impossibly difficult question about Cleopatra's aunt ("maternal or paternal," asks Porky). The outrageous penalty is naming all 48 states before the TNT shoved in his mouth explodes, then giving the name of the referee at the New Zealand Heavyweight Fight in 1726. Daffy refuses to award Porky his jackpot because it's a real pot and Porky's name ain't Jack. Instead, Porky gets another penalty. He has to push one of two buzzers, one of which brings a safe down on top of him, while the other gives him a prize, the Rock of Gibraltar and 600 gallons of genuine Niagara Falls on his head! After failing to identify a "passage" (one single note!) from *Rigoletto* and to recognize "Miss Shush" (a gorilla), Porky is allowed to have the $26,000,000.03 pay-off. Porky uses the money to buy the station and subject Daffy to his own boulders, waterfalls, and buzzsaws.

BUNKER HILL BUNNY

Bugs Bunny, Yosemite Sam; Sept 23; MM; Directed by I. Freleng; Story by Tedd Pierce; Animation by Gerry Chiniquy, Ken Champin, Virgil Ross, and Arthur Davis; Layouts by Hawley Pratt; Backgrounds by Paul Julian; Voice Characterization by Mel Blanc; Musical Direction by Carl W. Stalling.
The historic Revolutionary War battle of Bagel Heights is fought when Bugs Bunny defends his fort against (Yosemite) Sam Von Schamm, the Hessian. Bugs dares Sam to "try and take" his native soil. Sam tries, yelling "Charge!" The Hessian takes Bugs's fort, and Bugs captures Sam's fort! Each returns to his own fort, but Sam attacks again, running into Bugs's cannon.

Sam pitches a dynamite ball to Bugs, Bugs bats it back to Sam, who imitates an outfielder ("I got it, I got it!"), catching it as it explodes! Sam fires a cannon ball to Bugs, who catches it in his cannon and blasts it back. The ball goes back and forth, exploding on Sam. The Hessian next tries tunneling under the ground, coming up in Bugs's gunpowder house, which explodes! Sam puts a barrel of gunpowder at Bugs's front door, but has spilled some into his pants, leaving a trail of powder that Bugs ignites! Blasted once more, Sam gives up! "If you can't beat 'em, join 'em!" Bugs teams with Sam on fife and drum walking off to "Yankee Doodle."

A FRACTURED LEGHORN

Foghorn Leghorn; Sept 16; MM; Directed by Robert McKimson; Story by Warren Foster; Animation by Rod Scribner, Phil DeLara, J.C. Melendez, and Charles McKimson; Layouts by Cornett Wood; Backgrounds by Phil DeGuard; Voice Characterization by Mel Blanc; Musical Direction by Carl W. Stalling.
Here we have yakety-yak-yaking Mr. Foghorn Leghorn, who can't even shut up shuttin' up, versus a silent cat (the same as in (*It's Hummer Time)* on the subject of a worm. The chicken

wants to eat it, the cat wants to use it as bait to catch a fish (at the start of the film, he gets a note, "Dear Dope—you can't catch us fish without a worm on the hook. Signed, The Fish."). When the worm (read: killer jowls) sees the two of them coming, he gets them to crash into each other around a corner. Foggy constantly berates the pussy with his jabbering ("What's the big idea, chasin' my worm? ... I don't go 'round chasin' mice!"). The cat traps Foggy's head in front of a rotating wheel that smacks the Leghorn in the kisser with a paint brush. When Foggy uses an air pump to force out the worm, the cat grabs it. When the cat forces the worm, at gunpoint, into the water, Foggy takes it ("What kept ya, son? I can't hold my breath forever!"). Foggy tells the cat they'll dee-vide the worm, one part going to Foggy, the other to the cat. The worm avoids the axe by scrunching all up to one side, ("Well, barbecue my hammocks, your half is gone"). Thanks to Foggy's blustering, the worm gets away, leaving the cat to say his only line, "Aw, shut up!" Foggy agrees, but proceeds to hold the iris out back so he can keep blabbering!

CANARY ROW

Tweety, Sylvester; Oct 7; LT; Directed by I. Freleng; Story by Tedd Pierce; Animation by Virgil Ross, Arthur Davis, Emery Hawkings, Gerry Chiniquy, and Ken Champin; Layouts by Hawley Pratt; Backgrounds by Paul Julian; Voice Characterization by Mel Blanc; Musical Direction by Carl W. Stalling.
Sylvester, in the headquarters of the Bird Watcher's Society, through his bincoculars spies Tweety in the window of the Broken Arms Hotel. Dogs and cats are not allowed in the place, so Sylvester is summarily bounced from the lobby, and, on climing up the drainpipe, is heaved out the window (down a couple of stories) by Granny. He next goes up the inside of the drainpipe, to be thwarted by Tweety's bowling ball. He rolls down the street and into a bowling alley with the ball inside his belly! He takes the place of an organ grinder's monkey, which fools Granny

until he takes off his cap ("I was hep to ya all the time!"). Granny calls down to the desk clerk for a boy to carry her bags. Sylvester comes and successfully sneaks out with the cage only to find Granny waiting for him with an umbrella. He tries catapulting with a plank and a 500 lb. weight, but gets his puss pushed in, and, on swinging between the two buildings, slams straight into the bricks. Lastly, he tight-rope walks atop the cable car wires and ends up fleeing electrocution from a trolley that turns out to be engineered by Tweety and Granny ("You did see a puddy tat!").

In addition to singing over the titles, his 1950-51 theme "Tweet Little Bird," (as introduced by Tweety on his Capitol Record, "Tweety's Good Deed"), Tweety also treats us to a chorus of "When Irish Eyes Are Smiling."

STOOGE FOR A MOUSE
Sylvester; Oct 21; MM; Directed by I. Freleng; Animation by Arthur Davis, Gerry Chiniquy, Emery Hawkins, Ken Chapin, and Virgil Ross; Layouts by Hawley Pratt; Backgrounds by Paul Julian; Voice Characterization by Mel Blanc; Musical Direction by Carl W. Stalling.

Sylvester is resting comfortably on his friend Mike the bulldog. A mouse sneaks out of his hole and tries to get some cheese, but Sylvester traps him in his mouth. The mouse escapes back to his hole, saws a hole in the ceiling, and lowers a telephone toward the dog's ear. He tells the dog, "All the dogs in the alley are talking about you. They say you are a sissy, that you like cats. How come?" The mouse plants a knife in Sylvester's hand and tells Mike, "He's gonna cut your throat!" The dog wakes the confused cat and orders him to the other side of the room.

The mouse mallets the bulldog and puts the weapon in Sylvester's hand. The dog punches the puzzled pussycat. The rodent then puts an exploding cigar in the sleeping dog's mouth with an "April Fool" sign in Sylvester's paw. The blasted bulldog puts the cat in shackles: "Our friendship is over!" The mouse tries other tricks, including a

magnetic boxing glove on the cat's paw that slams into the dog's jaw. A battle ensues between the cat and dog. They wreck the house and knock themselves out. The mouse now walks out to get his cheese. As he passes the pummeled pets, the magnet attracts one more metallic object, an overhead light fixture, which conks the mouse atop the dog and cat.

POP 'EM POP!
Sylvester, Hippety Hopper; Oct 28; LT; Directed by Robert McKimson; Story by Warren Foster; Animation by Charles McKimson, Rod Scribner, Phil DeLara, Manuel Perez, and J.C. Melendez; Layouts by Cornett Wood; Backgrounds by Richard H. Thomas; Voice Characterization by Mel Blanc; Musical Direction by Carl W. Stalling.

At the circus, the carnival barker introduces Gracie, the Fighting Kangaroo, and her son, Hippety Hopper, who bounces out of the circus and down the street ruining a cement worker's freshly laid sidewalk (this is a running gag). Meanwhile, Sylvester is telling his son tall tales about catching a giant mouse. When Hippety comes behind him, Junior goads his dad into fighting the giant rodent. "C'mon, Pop! Go get the mouse like you said you could, unless you want to destroy a child's faith in his father!" Sylvester boxes with the kangaroo in the yard, getting beaten to a pulp. Sylvester chases the "giant mouse" down the street into the fresh cement and into the circus tent. Sylvester boasts to his son about beating the mouse, "Why, I wish he was twice as big, with two heads and four arms ... " just as Gracie, with Hippety in her pouch, emerges from the circus tent, scaring the cats away.

BUSHY HARE
Bugs Bunny; Nov 11; LT; Directed by Robert McKimson; Story by Warren Foster; Animation by Phil DeLara, J.C. Melendez, Charles McKimson, Rod Scribner, and John Carey; Layouts by Cornett Wood; Backgrounds by Richard H. Thomas; Voice Characterization by Mel Blanc; Musical Direction by Carl W. Stalling.

The adventures of "Crocadile Bunnee." Bugs Bunny arrives in the outback by two accidents; one being carried aloft by an Italian balloon-vendor's merchandise, two, bumping into the stork, none-too-alert even when sober, who mixes him up with a baby kangaroo. The stork binds and delivers him to an expectant Momma kangaroo. Bugs gives in to her cryin' and calls her "Mother," and the maternal marsupial threatens to kill Bugs with kindness by way of a roller-coasterlike ride in her pouch. The next Australian Bugs encounters, an abrasive aborigine whom Bugs calls "Nature Boy" (after the Nat Cole hit), wants to kill him! First, he throws a deadly boomerang at them (Bugs thinks "Mother" threw it and responds, "Next time you wanna chastise me, try psychology"), then challenges Bugs to an "Unga Bunga" competition. Nature jabs his javelin into what he thinks is Bugs (who responds by tickling him). Bugs escapes in a canoe that has Nature in it. The cave they ride into becomes a "Tunnel of Love" ("Gosh, Nature, I didn't know you cared!"). After the two fight wildly *inside* her pouch, Mother kicks the interloper off a cliff, and the two are joined by the real baby kangaroo, descending with the balloons. Attaching an outboard motor to her tail, Mother and baby prepare to give Bugs a ride home, 7,400 miles back to the U.S.A. Bugs is properly grateful. It would have been an "awful long swim."

CAVEMAN INKI

Inki; Nov 25; LT; Directed by Charles M. Jones; Story by Michael Maltese; Animation by Lloyd Vaughan, Ken Harris, Phil Monroe and Ben Washam; Layouts by Robert Gribbroek; Backgrounds by Philip DeGuard; Musical Direction by Carl W. Stallings. Orchestrations: Milt Franklyn.

In prehistoric times, Inki and his little dinosaur go hunting for food. They upset a bee who chases them. The mountain splits open to reveal the minah bird. Inki follows the bird, while a sabre-toothed lion pursues Inki for his top-knot. The lion smashes into a caveman who is wearing an animal skin while making stew (this is a running gag).

The lion and Inki stalk each other through the prehistoric terrain. They hop on to cliffsides, tree branches, and on the back of, and inside, a dinosaur. The dinosaur chases the minah bird, but the bird ties him up. The caveman catches Inki and the lion in his snare trap and prepares to enjoy hot stew, only to find that the minah bird has eaten it and flown off with his animal skin!

THE RABBIT OF SEVILLE

Bugs Bunny, Elmer Fudd; Dec 16; LT; Directed by Charles M. Jones; Story by Michael Maltese; Animation by Phil Monroe, Ben Washam, Lloyd Vaughan, Ken Harris, and Emery Hawkins; Layouts by Robert Gribbroek; Backgrounds by Philip DeGuard; Voice Characterization by Mel Blanc; Musical Direction by Carl W. Stalling.

The Hollywood Bowl Orchestra is tuning up for *The Barber of Seville* when the perennial rabbit hunt lands Elmer Fudd and Bugs Bunny on stage. The raised curtain gives Bugs the chance to shave Elmer within an inch of his life to the opera's famous overture. Razor flying, Bugs hacks away at Fudd's face (which looks like it "might have gone through a machine") covered with a frothy milkshake of shaving cream. Next, in Italianate drag, Bugs announces himself as a senyereeter (rhymes with "sweetah") who exposes Fudd's flowery drawers and ties his gun barrel in knots, so when he fires the recoil puts him back in the barber chair. Barber Bugs, deadpan, massages Fudd's bald scalp and tosses a fruit salad atop it, warding off Fuddy's retaliation with an electric shaver he snake charms. Bugs flees upward on a hydraulically ascending barber chair. A chase ends with Fudd getting sandbagged. For his third and final chair session, Bugs shoe-shines Fudd's cranium and gives him a severe pedicure, grows and mows a beard on Fudd's face, gives him a cement mud-pack, and with "Figaro Fertilizer" coaxes hairs on Fudd's head that blossom into flowers. Incensed, Fudd tears after Bugs, and the two confront each other with increasingly large axes and guns until Bugs appears with flowers and a ring. This scene escalates to his "marrying" Fudd in a bridal gown and dropping him from the theater rafters into a cake from "Il Nozze De Figaro." Calls Bugs at the end, "Next!"

TWO'S A CROWD

Claude Cat, Frisky Puppy; Dec 30; LT; Directed by Charles M. Jones; Story by Michael Maltese; Animation by Ken Harris, Phil Monroe, Ben Washam, Lloyd Vaughan, and Emery Hawkins; Layouts and Backgrounds by Peter Alvarado; Voice Characterization by Mel Blanc; Musical Direction by Carl W. Stalling.

Enjoying some catnip bon bons, Claude Cat is leading a contented life until his master brings home a new pet for his wife's birthday, a little puppy with long floppy ears: Frisky Puppy! Whenever Frisky barks, it send a nervous Claude jumping to the ceiling. Claude has to get along with the puppy or he goes. That night, while the masters are out at the theater, Claude tries to get even, but each scheme backfires. He lays a "puppy biskit" trail to the washing machine in which Claude gets trapped, emerging as a giant "puff." He attaches dynamite sticks to a string of sausages. They blow up the furnace and ruin the house.

Claude gets kicked out, but gets even. He sneaks back in, creeps up to Frisky, and barks from behind. The dog jumps to the ceiling!

1951

HARE WE GO

Bugs Bunny; Jan 6; MM; Directed by Robert McKimson; Story by Warren Foster; Animation by Phil DeLara, Charles McKimson, John Carey, Rod Scribner, and J.C. Melendez; Layouts by Cornett Wood; Backgrounds by Richard H. Thomas; Voice Characterization by Mel Blanc; Musical Direction by Carl W. Stalling.

Christopher Columbus is sure that the world is as round as his head. The king insists that it's as flat as Columbus' head (which he flattens). Bugs helps Columbus demonstrate the planet's roundness by tossing a baseball, which comes back from the other direction, covered with travel stickers (making better use of the sole good gag in *Kristopher Kolumbus, Jr.*, 1939).

Ship's Log: "April 7, 1492, today we set sail from Spain—Bugs Bunny on board as mascot for luck." The crew immediately suspects that a rabbit on a ship is a jinx, and by June, Chris writes, "No land in sight. Crew grumbling, blame mascot." Weeks later they're ready to throw Bugs overboard, but Bugs tricks them into jumping overboard with a picture of a beach scene. By October, "Mascot now cook. May have to cook mascot." Bugs has only one bean to serve, so Chris imagines the rabbit as a roast chicken and chases him about the ship. Just then, the ship grounds on shore, and Bugs agrees to let Chris have all the credit. "No use changin' the history books just for little old me."

Very funny pidgin-Italo-American diaglogue (all of Chris's swear words are various pastas). The Spanish king sounds like Speedy Gonzales.

A FOX IN A FIX

Jan 20; MM; Directed by Robert McKimson; Story by Tedd Pierce; Animation by Rod Scribner, Phil DeLara, Charles McKimson, Emery

Hawkins, John Carey, and J.C. Melendez; Layouts by Cornett Wood; Backgrounds by Richard H. Thomas; Voice Characterization by Mel Blanc; Musical Direction by Carl W. Stalling. "As the last light went out," the fox narrates, "I knew my chance had come to get at those chickens!" The *It's Hummertime* (1950) bulldog, guarding the place, catches the fox red handed and tosses him out of the farmyard. "Foiled, but I was determined to succeed. All that night, my scheming, crafty brain searched for a way to get those chickens. Suddenly, like a sledgehammer, an idea hit me." He disguises himself as a dog! It doesn't work for so much as a single frame. He has to give a big sob story, and the dog agrees to let him stay. Fox sweats bullets when he has to wait out the day, resisting the urge to consume chickens and other foxlike activities. The bulldog offers to teach him the lessons of watchdoggery, including "fetching the stick," which naturally turns out to be TNT. That night, when they go to bed, the fox sneaks out of the room and grabs a few pullets, making like a sleepwalker when the dog catches him. He is about to sleepwalk away when he discovers the biggest chicken of them all. Naturally, it's the bulldog in disguise, who tells him lesson five is "Don't be greedy." The bulldog is about to share lesson six when the fox thumbs a ride on a truck. It turns out that this last lesson is never hitch rides with strangers. The truck belongs to a fox furrier company.

CANNED FEUD

Sylvester; Feb 3; LT; Directed by I. Freleng; Story by Warren Foster and Cal Howard; Animation by Ken Champin, Virgil Ross, Arthur Davis, Manuel Perez, and John Carey; Backgrounds by

Paul Julian; Layouts by Hawley Pratt; Voice Characterization by Mel Blanc; Musical Direction by Carl W. Stalling. Freleng's masterpiece of timing, pantomime acting, and the lost art of building and releasing tension. Instead of having Sylvester's angst slowly gather momentum, it *begins* with the cat totally freaking out when he realizes his people have gone to California on a vacation and forgotten to put him out. The hysteria sustains throughout. The house becomes an obstacle course strewn with pratfalls in which Sylvester, convinced he'll starve, frantically runs huggermugger, continually stumbling over mislaid furniture. Sylvester discovers a pantry full of canned goods, the only can-opener to be found is in the hands of a wise guy mouse. Not only won't he hand it over, he uses it to taunt the out-of-control cat into smashing at walls, electrocuting himself, and dropping a piano on his own head. This frustration, real enough to make you sweat yet cartoony enough to make you laugh, reaches a climax when Sylvester raises an axe to try chopping open one of the cans and the blade goes flying backward out the front door mail slot. The mouse fixes Sylvester's vacuum to suck him into its bag, then sends a fireplace of burning coals after him. After blowing up half the house, Sylvester finally gets the can opener, but learns there's now a lock on the pantry, and the mouse has the key. Rather than throw another fit, Sylvester just plain passes out!

RABBIT EVERY MONDAY

Bugs Bunny, Yosemite Sam; Feb 10; LT; Directed by I. Freleng; Animation by Manuel Perez, Ken Champin, Virgil Ross, and Arthur Davis; Layouts by Hawley Pratt; Backgrounds by Paul Julian; Voice Characterization by Mel Blanc; Musical Direction by Carl W. Stalling.

A most unusual cartoon for 1951, for by then they'd stopped making screwball hunting pictures (which had never used Sam anyway). Yosemite Sam stalks Bugs "Sarah Vaughn" Bunny (singing "It's Magic" to his carrots) to his hole, threatening to shoot a fella in the audience he suspects is trying to leave and warn the rabbit. Not that the rabbit needs any help; his screwy antics keep short-tempered Sam befudd-led, especially when he takes refuge *in* Sam's rifle ("I just love the smell of gunpowder"), and then messes up gun and owner with bubblegum. Sam apprehends the carrot-chewin' coyote by diggin' up his entire hole. Even when taken home and prepared to be roasted, the fur-bearin' critter doesn't stop with the wacky antics, such as throwing Sam's hat on the fire and letting him replace it with a burning log. Forced into the oven ("Now quit stallin' and start roastin'!") Bugs takes along a fan and ice water ("Hot in dere!") to keep cool. On his reappearance, he requests a bottle-opener, cracked ice, and an extra chair. The sound of crowd noises and hot jazz circa 1925 convince Sam that there's a party goin' on inside his oven. Bugs gets Sam to step inside, but his conscience gets to him ("I couldn't do that to the little nimrod"), and he's about to let him know it's a gag when he sees a live action party really is taking place. He joins in! "I don't ask questions, I just have fun."

PUDDY TAT TWOUBLE

Tweety, Sylvester; Feb 24; LT; Directed by I. Freleng; Story by Warren Foster; Animation by Arthur Davis, Manuel Perez, Ken Champin, and Virgil Ross; Layouts by Hawley Pratt; Backgrounds by Paul Julian; Voice Characterization by Mel Blanc; Musical Direction by Carl W. Stalling.

"This is what I get for dweaming of a white Chwistmas," says Tweety, shoveling snow out of his wittle nest atop a pole. He's been spotted by Sylvester on one side and a big orange tabby cat on the other. "Hey! I'm suwwounded by puddy tats!" Both chase after the bird, which entails beating up on each other (but no dialogue, as both cats are silent, and all the lines go to Tweety), grabbing the bird, and zipping back and forth between their two buildings until Sylvester falls down the steps into the cellar. There, Tweety chances upon a toy "dunking bird" and mistakes it for a real bird ("What's a matter? Puddy tat got your tongue?"). The orange cat

does the same and swallows the dunker, thinking it's Tweety and is compelled to go through the dunking motion. When Tweety hides in Sylvester's mouth, the orange cat snatches him out and runs back upstairs as Sylvester hurls heavy objects at him and misses. Orange sticks his tongue out at Sylvester and gets kayoed by an iron and slides down the stairs holding Tweety ("Let's do dat again, dat was fun!"). After Tweety's dodging into a section of pipe leads to more mutual cat clouting with ashtray and rifle, Tweety runs back outside into the snow and tricks the cats into running over a frozen lake where he ice-picks out a hole around them. We end on both puddies trying to recover from colds in their respective domiciles. "Da poor puddy tats."

CORN PLASTERED

Mar 3; MM; Directed by Robert McKimson; Story by Warren Foster; Animation by Charles McKimson, Rod Scribner, Phil DeLara, J.C. Melendez, and John Carey; Layouts by Cornett Wood; Backgrounds by Richard H. Thomas; Voice Characterization by Mel Blanc; Musical Direction by Carl W. Stalling.

It looks like a test film for a new series: strangely timed, unfamiliar characters, one with a really off-center non-Blanc voice. Only Stalling's "stings" remind one that this is a Warner's cartoon. A bearded, old curmudgeon farmer is at war with a wacky, double-propellered, beany-cap-wearing crow. While singing "You Can't Scare a Crow with a Scarecrow," the crow eats his way through the farmer's cornfield. The farmer blasts him inside a stump, but he pops out, saying,"You didn't exactly miss me ... but I wasn't exactly standing where you shot." He empties the farmer's bag of feed and then follows him into the chicken yard. The farmer chases him with an axe and chops down the tree he's in. Too late, he tries to get his car out of the way. They next make a big to-do about the light in the refrigerator, the farmer proving his theory that it goes out when the crow locks him in. Next, the farmer's reading of a book called "How to Kill Crows" gets interrupted by the crow's boogie-woogie piano solo. The crow proceeds to rig the instrument to collapse. The crow then switchs the TNT onto the farmer's explosive corn so he blows his durn old self up. The crow turns the old geezer's cannon around so that the ball hurls him into a boat thay starts to sink. "At least there's no crows where I'm goin'!" says the sinking farmer. "Not yet, but there will be," sayeth the crow.

BUNNY HUGGED

Bugs Bunny; Mar 10; MM; Directed by Charles M. Jones; Story by Michael Maltese; Animation by Ken Harris, Phil Monroe, Ben Washam, and Lloyd Vaughan; Layouts by Peter Alvarado; Backgrounds by Philip DeGuard; Voice Characterization by Mel Blanc; Musical Direction by Carl W. Stalling.
Rabbit Punch (1948) had Jones, Maltese, and Bugs taking on boxing; this slightly lesser follow-up has them trying to parody the world of pro wrestling, with its slurry announcers and good guy/bad guy theatrics. Though no cartoon could out-cartoon the ludicrousness of real-life wrestling (it's sort of like trying to spoof a Spike Jones record), this is pretty funny stuff. Bugs is the mascot of good guy "Ravishing Ronald" (a take-off on Gorgeous George), who steps in as "The Terror" for his boss when the bad guy, "The Crusher," is about to pulverize him and ruin Bugs's bread and butter. These gags will more than do: Bugs getting a headlock on his titanic foe and the Crusher merely yawning and using him as a straw hat for a "Shuffle Off to Buffalo" dance; the Crusher winding up Bugs's ears and making him into a model plane; Bugs making the Crusher think he's ripped his pants and reappearing as "Stychen Tyme, tailor: Mending done while u wait" and getting a chance to needle his enemy. Bugs ultimately manages to pin the Crusher's shoulders to the floor (literally) after slamming his body into a safe door and rendering him slap happy. After Bugs is pronounced winner and new world's champion, the Crusher snaps out of it, but when he tries to bite Bug's arm during a supposedly friendly handshake, Bugs one-ups him as usual by subbing a TNT stick.

SCENT-IMENTAL ROMEO

Pepe Le Pew; Mar 24; MM; Directed by Charles M. Jones; Story by Michael Maltese; Animation by Ben Washam, Lloyd Vaughan, Ken Harris, Phil Monroe, and John Carey; Layouts by Robert Gribbroek; Backgrounds by Peter Alvarado; Voice Characterization by Mel Blanc; Musical Direction by Carl W. Stalling.
"Ah ze l'amour! Ah ze toujour! Ah ze grande illusion!" Mam'selle kitty, in order to get in on feeding time at the zoo, paints a white stripe down her back, and before you can say "Django Reinhardt," Pepe Le Pew is whispering sweet nothings and sweet somethings in her ear. Pulling down theatre-set walls from nowhere, he turns his cage in the zoo into a hotel room for a rendezvous. By the time he's opened the champagne, she's fled, and he becomes ze lovair chaser, pursuing her all over the park and zoo ("Where are you, my stutz-bearcat of love?"). When she climbs a wall, Pepe is there to do an impression of Chevalier singing, "Baby Face." When she dashes down an alley, he engages her in an Apache dance. When the keeper drags Pepe back to his zoo, he waves a sad farewell. "Sweeting is such part sorrow!"

The last "generic" Pepe. Future entries mixed in other elements (usually settings) This doesn't make much use of the zoo or the park background except for a good bit in the tunnel of love, and could use a stronger ending. All one can say is "Viva L'amour!"

Theme: "April in Paris." More music: "Strolling Through Le Park" (sung by Pepe), "Latin Quarter," "Kiss Me Again."

A BONE FOR A BONE

Goofy Gophers; Apr 7; LT; Directed by I. Freleng; Story by J.B. Hardaway; Animation by Virgil Ross, Arthur Davis, Manuel Perez, and Ken Champin; Layouts by Hawley Pratt; Backgrounds by Paul Julian; Animation by Harry Love; Voice Characterization by Mel

Blanc; Musical Direction by Carl W. Stalling.

For Freleng's first gopher toon (mainly notable as a precursor to his best, *I Gopher You*) he stresses their gentility over their goofiness. The Gophers (voiced by Mel Blanc and Stan Freberg), attack only when provoked, their eruditeness offset by the blustering bullying-type dopey dog, determined to bury his bone in their underground living room and interrupting their card game ("Do you mind if I have gin?"). The dog grabs one gopher, who yells for help (first receiving permissions) the other climbs up the dog's back and inquires, "Shall I you-know-what?" he asks. "Yes, I think you should." The gopher then produces a mallet with which he pounds the pooch's head down into his dog collar. The gophers mess with his head by rigging a piece of hose with a glove to make him think they're stretching his arm across the street and befuddle him further with a trick card that contains a picture of a TNT stick that explodes on him, using his own gunpowder, and lighting it with his own matches. He follows them down their gopher hole, tip toes through their tunnel and into a piece of pipe labeled, "They went in there." He lights a match to see where he is. Boom!He staggers out of an oven! As he grabs his coat, suitcases. and hat (to "Shuffle off to Buffalo"), the gophers return to their hole arm in arm.

THE FAIR HAIRED HARE

Bugs Bunny, Yosemite Sam; Apr 14; LT; Directed by I. Freleng; Story by Warren Foster; Animation by Ken Champin, Virgil Ross, Arthur Davis, Manuel Perz, and John Carey; Layouts by Hawley Pratt; Backgrounds by Paul Julian; Voice Characterization by Mel Blanc; Musical Direction by Carl W. Stalling.

"Great horny-toads!" Bugs Bunny's underground home on the range is covered over by a newly erected ranch-style house, into which moves Yosemite Sam. Bugs climbs up through the floorboards to investigate, coming out through a bearskin rug, making it look like the bear's attacking the rabbit ("playin' possum fer 20 years!"). Bugs wants Sam to move his home away from what Bugs considers his property. Sam wants Bugs to haul his "flea bitten carcass off'n my real estate!" Bugs takes the case to the "highest court in the country" (in terms of elevation, if not judicial wisdom), where the judge rules that they "both share this property under the same roof, and in the event that one of you should pass on, the other shall inherit the entire property," a clause that immediately has Sam chuckling fiendishly. That night, as they bed down in twin bunks, Sam comes after Bugs with a big hammer. When Bugs turns on the light he explains that the "carpet keeps rollin' up." In the morning, he spikes Bugs's breakfast carrot juice with a permanent Mickey Finn, but Bugs out-wises him by spinning the table around. Finally, he shoves a few tons of explosives down Bugs's rabbit hole, unaware that Bugs has detoured under Sam's foundation. When Sam lights it, the whole house heads toward the heavens as in *the Wizard of Oz*. "Well, whaddya know! I got a cabin in the sky!"

A HOUND FOR TROUBLE

Charlie Dog; Apr 28; LT; Directed by Charles M. Jones; Story by Michael Maltese; Animation by Lloyd Vaughan, Ken Harris, Phil Monroe, Ben Washam, and John Carey; Layouts by Robert Gribbroek; Backgrounds by Philip DeGuard; Voice Characterization by Mel Blanc; Musical Direction by Carl W. Stalling.

Charlie Dog is in Mother Italy, but he can't get a master until he finds someone who'll capeesh-a da English. He spies "Pasquale's Palazzia de Spaghettini" and reasons, "What could be more logical than a restaurant owner for a master?" But Pasquale doesn't see the logic and insists on remaining senza dog (translation: he's-a no good-a pooch). He kicks Charlie out with a pot of pasta on his head, but the dog returns after Pasquale leaves for 15 minootsa and decides to endear himself by "serving" a customer who orders a long, complicated-sounding dish (and Charlie silently razzes us for being surprised he can understand it). He serves the spaghet (on a fishing reel) okesy-dokesy, but geev-a da customer da heartburn when he serves "wine" he makes on the spot by dancing on grapes. Pasquale returns annoyed ("What for you chase-a my customer away?"). Charlie tries to placate him by demonstrating his floorshow act, a jolly Neapolitan number, mainly concerned with pastas ("Attsamattah-foyou?"), causing the restaurateur to relent. He promises to adopt Charlie and give him his own piazza, but it's part of a ruse to rid himself of the dog by telling him that the leaning tower is about "to fall on our leetle house" and running off "for help," leaving Charlie to hold it up!

EARLY TO BET

May 12; MM; Directed by Robert McKimson; Story by Tedd Pierce; Animation by Phil DeLara, Emery Hawkins, Charles McKimson, and Rod Scrinber; Layouts by Cornett Wood; Backgrounds by Richard H. Thomas; Voice Characterization by Mel Blanc; Musical Direction by Carl W. Stalling.
"Not *The Post*! No, not *The Post*!" 1950's *It's Hummertime* rethought and improved and this time the "penalties" make more sense because they're the punishment the cat must accept from the bulldog when he loses a game of cards and has to keep playing games of chance with the bulldog because the Gambling Bug (voiced by Stan Freberg and introduced by scenes containing examples of his work) keeps biting him. Each time he loses he's got to spin the penalty wheel (to the tune of "Blues in the Night"), getting subjected to a deadly mixture of bubble gum and sneezing powder, "William Tell," getting a plunger shot in his face, "Roll Out the Barrel," pushing a wheelbarrow full of gunpowder and trying to outrun a lit trail of the stuff. "You're too unlucky," the dog finally tells the cat, "I'm quittin' before ya kills yaself." The Gambling Bug himself offers to play and, when *he* loses, it's his turn to be subjected to a sadistic penalty— "the *Post*," being swatted at with a rolled copy of the *Saturday Evening Post*.

RABBIT FIRE

Bugs Bunny, Daffy Duck, Elmer Fudd; May 19; LT; Directed by Charles M. Jones; Story by Michael Maltese; Animation by Lloyd Vaughan, Ken Harris, Phil Monroe, and Ben Washam; Layouts by Robert Gribbroek; Backgrounds by Philip DeGuard; Voice Characterization by Mel Blanc; Musical Direction by Carl W. Stalling.
Bugs and Daffy each try to use hunting regulations to induce Elmer to shoot the other, arguing endlessly whether it's really rabbit season or duck season. Daffy usually gets the worst of it, emerging from each confrontation with the knowledge of new directions in which his beak can be blasted. The first round goes mainly to fall-on-the-floor funny dialogue, as in "Hey, laughing boy! One bullet left!" Things get more visual when Daffy and Bugs crudely disguise themselves as each other (brilliant work from Blanc: Bugs lisping and Daffy asking, "What's up, Doc?"). Next they try to whet Elmer's appetite by reading recipes aloud from books containing a thousand ways to cook a rabbit or a duck, the juiciest being "Rabbits au gratin du jour under tubed leather, drool, drool." This doesn't work as Elmer tells them he's a vegetarian! Bugs points out to Elmer he's using an elephant gun and advises him to shoot an elephant. He calls in an elephant doing Joe Besser's act to pound him, warning, "You do and I'll give you such a pinch!" After a variation on the drag bit, with Bugs as a stacked huntress and Daffy as her/his "naughty bow-wow," the two start pulling "season" signs off a tree, first rabbit, then duck, then rabbit. Finally, they come to one with a shot of Fudd labeled "Elmer season." The last shot (pun!) has Bugs and Daffy in Fudd-hunting outfits, speaking a reversal of Fudd's trademark line and laugh, "Be wewy, wewy quiet, we're hunting Elmers."

ROOM AND BIRD

Tweety, Sylvester; June 2; MM; Directed by I. Freleng; Story by Tedd Pierce, Warren Foster; Animation by Virgil Ross, Arthur Davis, Manuel Perez, and Ken Champin; Layouts by Hawley Pratt; Backgrounds by Paul Julian; Voice Characterization by Mel Blanc; Musical Direction by Eugene Poddany; Orchestrations by Milt Franklyn.

The setting is the Spinsters Arms Hotel (subtitled, "Baby, It's Cold Inside"). A tough-looking dick is on hand to enforce the no-pets-allowed rule. Nonetheless, Tweety and Sylvester are snuck in by their old lady mistresses (who aren't heard from again). Hearing Tweety sing ("I'm a tweet wittle bird ... "), Sylvester officially opens the round with a phony letter, "I'm just mad about your singing. Come over and we'll make beautiful music together." The familiar cat and bird and, later, dog antics are periodically interrupted by the suspicious detective, meaning they have to take special care to whoosh quietly by him. Sylvester tries climbing furniture, then taking the place of an elevator, which Tweety unwittingly descends. Sylvester learns rather late in the next scene that he's been walking on a bulldog's head. Bird, cat, and dog turn up running out of every door but the one the detective is facing. Ultimately, he broadcasts, "Attention everyone, someone has pets in this house and I want them out of here immediately." At once he's caught in the middle of a stampede of domestic and wild animals, about which the cop can only utter his own, "I tawt I taw" line, to which Tweety adds, "You did see a puddy tat, a moo-moo cow, a big gorilla, a diddyap horsie, and a wittle monkey."

CHOW HOUND

June 16; LT; Directed by Charles M. Jones; Story by Michael Maltese; Animation by Phil Monroe, Ben Washam, Lloyd Vaughan, and Ken Harris; Layouts by Peter Alvarado; Backgrounds by Philip DeGuard; Voice Characterization by Mel Blanc (Bea Bernaderet); Musical Direction by Carl W. Stalling.

What a racket! This con-man canine, this flim-flam fido, this despicable doggy! His scam is to plant his unwilling patsy, a frightened cat, into different houses and to pose as the pet of various masters. The cat poses as a turtlenecked "Butch," a ribboned and purring "Harold," and, at the zoo, in prehistoric disguise, as a "Saber Toothed Alley Catus." He gathers dinner from each, which he's forced to fork over to the dog, who continually badgers him with, "What, no gravy!" The dog accelerates his activities: he withholds the cat from its assorted owners until they get antsy enough to post rewards. By means of a cat bed with a trick bottom, dog returns the pussy to each and collects the reward. The big pay-off comes when he returns the "Saber Tooth" to the local zoo. Now, he'll be "set for life! I'll never be hungry again!" Cut to a "sold" sign on the door of a butcher shop ("Acres and acres of meat, and they're mine, all mine!"). Cut again to the Dog and Cat hospital where the overstuffed, bloated mutt lies helpless as veterinarians discuss pumping his stomach. The cat and another ex-stooge, a mouse, come in and announce, "This time we didn't forget the gravy!" as they pour it down his throat.

FRENCH RAREBIT

Bugs Bunny; June 30; MM; Directed by Robert McKimson; Story by Tedd Pierce; Animation by Rod Scribner, Phil DeLara, Charles McKimson, and Emery Hawkins; Layouts by Cornett Wood; Backgrounds by Richard H. Thomas; Voice Characterization by Mel Blanc. Musical Direction by Eugene Poddany; Orchestrations by Milt Franklyn.

A crate of carrots (from the U.S.A.) falls off a truck in Gay Paree, and out comes Bugs Bunny, who decides to take a "stroll down the bullyvard and look over the monsewers and the madamoyzels." Two chefs, Francois and Louie, who have restaurants on opposite sides of the street, insist on having thees rabbit for ze dinner menu! Bugs plays the two against each other, provoking "a display of temper" that begins with the tweaking of noses. Francois wins and is about to cook Bugs. The rabbit drops a mention of "Louisiana Bayou Backbay Bunny Borderlay, a la Antoine" ("Of New Orleans?" "I don't mean Antoine of Flatbush!"). The chef implores Mssr. Rarebit to "show" him the recipe. For this the chef must act the part of the rabbit, with rubber glove and suger cubes thoughtfully applied. First he is immersed thoroughly in wine, pickled, then shaken, stuffed with volcanic hot herbs, dipped liberally in flower, rolled with a rolling pin, kneaded gently (brutally!), and covered with various veggies ("Hold la onions!") ... and just a dash of eau-de-cologne. Louie enters and, mistaking Bugs for Francois ("You were expecting maybe "Umphrey Bogart?"), demands he too be shown the recipe. Bugs repeats the process for chef number two and shoves both into la oven ("Don't they look yummy-yummy?") and adds some TNT. The goofy Gauls emerge, singing a jaunty chorus of "Alouette." Viva a la carte!

THE WEARING OF THE GRIN

Porky Pig; July 14; LT; Directed by Charles M. Jones; Story by Michael Maltese; Animation by Lloyd Vaughan, Ben Washam, Ken Harris, and Phil Monroe; Layouts by Robert Gribbroek; Backgrounds by Philip DeGuard; Voice Characterization by Mel Blanc; Musical Direction by Eugene Poddany; Orchestrations by Milt Franklyn.

A wee bit of a Porky Gothic horror story that goes into exotic and quaint fantasy. "Sure, and it's still twelve miles to Dublin town," a sign tells weary traveler Porky Pig, whose only refuge on this dark and stormy night is a foreboding castle. One Shamus O'Toole introduces himself as the caretaker, and even though O'Toole warns him that, "there's never a livin' thing here ... but the leprechauns," Porky thinks it's a crock o'blarney he's handing him and insists on a room for the night. "Now you take my bags up to my room, you picturesque peasant caretaker of the Olde Sod, you!" When Porky is knocked out, O'Toole splits into two leprechauns with different personalities: Pat, hysterically worried

that the pig has come after their pot o'gold, and Mike, calmer, with more practical ideas on how to deal with the intruder. When Porky wakes up, the reunited O'Toole takes him to his room, and, before long, shows him a "sight enough to set the heart crossways in yer" by revealing his upper and lower halves. Porky dives into the bed, which carries him down a shaft into a courtroom where the two leprechauns put him on trial for trying to steal their gold. Finding him as guilty as the day is long, they sentence him to the wearing of the green shoes. These leave their wearer unable to stop dancing an Irish jig and carry him through a comic-nightmarish wackyland of gooniness with harps, lyres, gold pieces, and four-leaf clovers consorting against him over an abstract green landscape. Waking from his "dream," Porky runs out of the castle. O'Toole's shaking hands with himself leaves us wondering whether it was a dream after all.

LEGHORN SWOGGLED

Foghorn Leghorn, Henery Hawk; July 28; MM; Directed by Robert McKimson; Story by Warren Foster; Animation by Charles McKimson, Rod Scribner, Phil DeLara, and Emery Hawkins; Layouts by Cornett Wood; Backgrounds by Richard H. Thomas; Voice Characterization by Mel Blanc; Musical Direction by Eugene Poddany; Orchestrations by Milt Franklyn.

We open on an exciting story-in-progress note, the barnyard dog getting Foggy to look at a "total eclipse, free" and slamming a pumpkin on his head ("now you just know I'm gonna do somethin' about this!"), then into seven minutes of rather complicated inter-scheming, all of which revolves around Foghorn, but in which he doesn't participate, functioning as a kind of Greek chorus. Henery is a rootin' tootin' western chicken hawk who lassoes Foggy (in the middle of "Some Sunday Morning"). Foggy sends him packing. Br'er Dog offers to help him catch the chicken if he'll supply a bone for him. In quick succession, a cat offers to show Henery a bone in exchange for a fish, and a mouse to give him fishing tips for "a little piece of cheese." Foggy alternates between his back-and-forth with the dog, building a model railroad for the sole purpose of hitting him with a pie, trapping him by the neck over a pole (swinging back and forth with his behind atop a paint brush), and "helping" to procure said piece of cheese, fish, and bone. When he sees li'l hawk dispense presents to everyone but him, he demands what's coming to him, at which point the barnyard dog clouts him with the bone and puts him down on the model train, on which Henery rides off, doing an imitation of Foggy, "I may be little, ah say, I may be little, but ah sho' caught me a big chicken!"

HIS HARE RAISING TALE
Bugs Bunny; Aug 11; LT; Directed by I. Freleng; Story by Warren Foster; Animation by Virgil Ross, Manuel Perez, Ken Champin, and Arthur Davis; Layouts by Paul Julian; Backgrounds by Hawley Pratt; Voice Characterization by Mel Blanc; Musical Direction by Carl W. Stalling.
Bugs tells tall tales to his little nephew, Clyde Rabbit, illustrated by a photo album containing clips from old cartoons. As a ballplayer (*Baseball Bugs*), he was called in to save the day at a World Series game against the Boston Argyle Socks, but since the clip contains the Gas House Gorilla's hit without Bugs's spectacular catch, he has to end the anecdote with, "After I got back from the Foreign Legion, I went into vaudeville ..." as in *Stage Door Cartoon*. But since his partner (Fudd) insisted on equal billing he broke up the act. He tells Clyde, "Besides, there was more money in boxing anyway," as he demonstrates with a *Rabbit Punch*. The fight might never have ended, but along came the war and Bugs took on "the most dangerous job I could think of," a test pilot (*Falling Hare*, sans Gremlin). "Gee, Uncle Bugs, you've been every place, I guess except the moon." Bugs claims to have been there too. His footage from *Haredevil Hare* and newspaper clippings supports this. By the time Bugs ends the story ("It took 'em 22 years to build a ladder long enough to ... "), Clyde is skeptical.

"Why, if everything I've told you isn't true, I hope I'm run over by a streetcar!" After said vehicle comes straight through the living room, Bugs comments, "I suppose you don't believe I was run over by a streetcar."

CHEESE CHASERS
Hubie and Bertie, Claude Cat; Aug 28; MM; Directed by Charles M. Jones; Story by Michael Maltese; Animation by Ben Washam, Lloyd Vaughan, Phil Monroe, and Ken Harris; Layouts by Robert Grobbroek; Backgrounds by Philip DeGuard; Voice Characterization by Mel Blanc; Musical Direction by Carl W. Stalling.
Hubie and Bertie (voiced by Blanc and Stan Freberg) have broken into a cheese factory and overdone it: they estimate they've consumed enough of cheese to last the average mouse 2,000 years! Not being able to touch the stuff again ("there's nothin' left to live for") they decide that it's goodbye cruel world, and they're off into the mouth of sleeping Claude Cat. Claude, who wakes up suspicious that there's something rotten in Denmark (his thoughts illustrated with a map), refuses to eat the mice despite their pleading, and when they refuse a piece of cheese, he looks up a page in a book on mental health, folds it into a Napoleonic hat, and constructs a ship in a bottle (he's in the bottle, not the ship!). The mice try to force him into eating them, and he runs, figuring, "I'll never be able to eat another mouse again, so what is there left to live for?" Leaving a suicide note—"Goodbye Cruel World—P.S. (No P.S.)"—Claude throws himself at the equally suspicious bulldog, who does a perfect Oliver Hardy take when Claude requests, "I want you to massacre me. Go ahead, chew me up!" The dog tries to make the facts make sense on his adding machine: cat doesn't want to eat mice, mice don't want to eat cheese, cat wants dog to massacre him, et al, but "It just don't add up," and *he* in turn runs off, entreating the dog catcher to "Wait for baby!" the cat and the mice not far behind!

LOVELORN LEGHORN
Foghorn Leghorn; Sept 8; LT; Directed

by Robert McKimson; Story by Tedd
Pierce; Animation by Rod Scribner, Phil
DeLara, Charles McKimson, Emery
Hawkins, John Carey, and J.C.
Melendez; Layouts by Cornett Wood;
Backgrounds by Richard H. Thomas;
Voice Characterization by Mel Blanc;
Musical Direction by Carl W. Stalling.
"Happy husband-huntin', dearie," the
old biddy hens cackle to Miss Prissy.
"Did you take somethin' with you to
clunk him on the head with?" At this
she shows them her rolling pin. She
shows it to Foghorn Leghorn also, in
the midst of his receiving an unwanted
attack on his person from the dog. He
treats her as he would Henery Hawk,
telling her that the dog "Is a rooster all
right, he just wears that dog suit to
keep the lovesick hens away from
him!" He instructs her to tempt the
pooch with a casaba melon, and she
does an alluring dance while waving
the melon in front of his face. When he
runs after it, Foggy appears and turns
the situation into a football match that
ends in his kicking the mutt's melon-
covered head for a field goal. When
Prissy tries to remove his doggy skin,
it's Br'er Dog's turn to give her advice
on rooster-snaring. Foggy, unable to let
a lady do a man's work, helps her load
a bowling ball into a sluice that leads to
a long, involved Rube Goldberg (there
certainly were enough of these in '50s
Warner toons!) doodad. The purpose is
to drop the bowling ball on Foggy's
own head. The cackling hens see
Prissy returning with a large market
basket and ask, sarcastically, if she's got
a husband in there, the cue for Foggy
to stick his head out and do his impression of Prissy's trademark line, "Yes!"
Theme: "Fiddle De-Di."

TWEETY'S S.O.S.
Tweety, Sylvester; Sept 22; MM;
Directed by I. Freleng; Story by Warren
Foster; Animation by Arthur Davis,
Manuel Perez, Ken Champin, and Virgil
Ross; Layouts by Hawley Pratt;
Backgrounds by Paul Julian; Voice
Characterization by Mel Blanc; Musical
Direction by Carl W. Stalling.
Starving Sylvester, despondent on a
dockside, spies Tweety through an

ocean liner porthole and purrs, "Hello,
breakfast!" Near-sighted Granny is
also on board, and she'll teach him "to
molest helpless little birdies." Her
glasses are a prime element here. If
Sylvester can keep them away from
Granny, he can get at the bird.
Tweety's restoring them to Granny's
face is a way to keep Sylvester away.
The cat paints crude Tweety images on
both lenses, so they form a cel and
background Tweety when she looks at
his cage. Now he chases the bird over a
vibrating wire. When Tweety spies the
cat turning green, he offers him a "nice
fat juicy piece of talt pork." Sylvester
downs some seasick remedy and gives
chase once again (dashing into the furnace by mistake). Tweety rekindles his
seasickness by rocking a picture of a
boat. This time Sylvester swallows
nitroglycerine, which, as usual, gives
him the desirable cartoon power of
explosive expectorations. Granny clobbers him with her umbrella and sends
him into orbit, landing him on the captain (who taut he taw a puddy tat).
Granny and Tweety at the steering
wheel confirm in unison, "You did, you
did see a puddy tat!"

BALLOT BOX BUNNY
Bugs Bunny, Yosemite Sam; Oct 6; MM;
Directed by I. Freleng; Story by Warren
Foster; Animation by Ken Champin,
Virgil Ross, Arthur Davis, and Manuel
Perez; Layouts by Hawley Pratt;
Backgrounds by Paul Julian; Voice
Characterization by Mel Blanc; Musical
Direction by Carl W. Stalling.
One of the cornerstone films of the
Bugs-Sam series, using political rheto-
ric to modulate into irreverence and
then to adult black humor. Bugs hears
candidate Sam campaigning on a plat-
form that includes rabbit genocide. He
fights fire with fire by running against
Sam himself. Bugs advocates Teddy
Roosevelt's "Speak softly and carry a
big stick" policy while Sam preaches,
"Speak loud and carry a bigger stick!"
and kisses a load of unwilling tykes
until Bugs in baby get-up makes trouble for him with a load of handbag-
packin' mommas. Sam swipes Bugs's
cigars, unaware that Bugs has slipped

him the exploding variety, then tries to sabotage Bugs's picnic with an ant colony. Bugs booby traps a water melon heading back to Sam on the back of an ant. Sam rigs a cannon outside the rabbit's campaign headquarters, and doctors a piano to explode on a certain note in "Those Endearing Young Charms." The ending is a humdinger: Sam and Bugs both losing the race to a "dark horse," "the New Mare," then deciding to end it all with Russian roulette. Don't worry: Sam doesn't get a bullet and Bugs misses.

Theme: "What's Up, Doc."

A BEAR FOR PUNISHMENT

The Three Bears; Oct 20; MM; Directed by Charles M. Jones; Story by Michael Maltese; Animation by Ken Harris, Phil Monroe, Lloyd Vaughan, and Ben Washam; Layouts by Robert Gribbroek; Backgrounds by Philip DeGuard; Uncredited Voices: Billy Bletcher, Bea Bernederet, Stan Freberg; Musical Direction by Carl W. Stalling.

"At last, the great day has come at last!" Ma and Junior should know by now that Paw isn't the type to get all mushy over Father's Day, but their lame-brained attempts at honoring him on "his day" make for one of the funniest cartoons of this series.

"But I don't wanna have breakfast in bed!" especially when Junior trips and spills it all over him. "A good old shave for good old Paw on good old Father's Day." Paw especially reluctant as Junior's straight razor has a broken edge. A few scenes later, the dope is afraid he's manslaughtered his old man and Maw pulls the covers over the Father's Day cake. Finally, the bears stage a family musicale that opens with Junior reciting a ludicrously over-mushy Father's Day poem (Ken Harris's depiction of the big lug's moronic cuteness may be the greatest piece of animation ever), as Paw cringes. He gets shell-shocked even beyond cringing as Maw does a Palace theater buck and wing to "I'm Just Wild About Harry," rewritten as an inane fete to father, and even more so when Junior and Maw go into a patriotic march-time pro-Paw number

that ends in a *tableau vivant idiotic* with the family as Washington, Lady Liberty, and Lincoln.

SLEEPY TIME POSSUM

Nov 3; MM; Directed by Robert McKimson; Story by Tedd Pierce; Animation by Charles McKimson, Rod Scribner, Phil DeLara, Emery Hawkins, and John Carey; Layouts by Cornett Wood; Backgrounds by Richard H. Thomas; Voice Characterization by Mel Blanc; Musical Direction by Carl W. Stalling.

Maw Possum cain't get junior possum to peel the 'taters like he's s'posed ter, on account he insists on sleeping every time you turn your back on him, authentic possum fashion, upside-down. "But I got an idea how to git some life into him," says Paw. "Good thing I saved this huntin' dog outfit. I'll scare him so he won't never sleep in the daytime no more!" The first effect the dog suit has is to scare the daylights outta Maw. Paw then hangs by his tail next to Junior and wakes him up with his gun. The following chase is certainly one of the most off-center in Warner toonology, what with the "dog" constantly pulling back his fake head to talk to the audience and the little possum unceasingly sleeping upside down whenever he can find something to wrap his tail around. Rather than the usual chase-and-fight, it's more properly described as a chase-and-*sleep*! When Paw/Dog chops down the tree in which Junior's sleepin', Junior sleeps on the handle of the saw. He uses a rock to bend down a tree so he can climb up. It turns into a catapult. Returning home, Paw, after scaring Maw into another wild, dish-dropping take, announces that he's found a way to get Junior to peel the taters: suspending him right side up from a balloon so he can't fall asleep.

DRIPALONG DAFFY

Daffy Duck, Porky Pig; Nov 17; MM; Directed by Charles M. Jones; Story by Michael Maltese; Animation by Phil Monroe, Lloyd Vaughan, Ben Washam, and Ken Harris; Layouts by Robert Gribbroek; Backgrounds by Philip DeGuard; Voice Characterization by

ORIGINAL RELEASE CARTOON
COLOR BY TECHNICOLOR

DRIP-ALONG DAFFY

featuring

DAFFY DUCK and PORKY PIG

Mel Blanc; Musical Direction by Carl W. Stalling.

A western parody with gags galore in which Dripalong Daffy and his sidekick, Porky, are accurately identified by subtitles as "Western-Type Hero" and "Comedy Relief." Snake Bite Center, the "Lawless western town" that they're a-hankering to bring law and order to, is inadequately described by its subtitle. The place is nothing but a series of nonstop overlapping shoot 'em ups, in which everybody that isn't shooting at or robbing someone is being shot at or being robbed, even the horses. Dripalong vows, "I'm gonna clean up this one-horse town! Hi-yo, Tinfoil!" and kicks open the swinging doors of the town saloon wanting to make a grand entrance with his guns drawn. Instead, he pulls off his trousers by mistake, failing to attract anyone's attention. A bullet goes through his glass, fired by the villain Nasty Cansta (standing in front of a wanted poster that identifies him as rustler, bandit, and square dance caller). Nasty makes Daffy and Porky drink his "usual" superdeadly concoction, which has both reciting "Mary Had a Little Lamb." Daffy challenges N. C. to a thrilling shoot out, "photographed" from outlandish *High Noon* angles. It's Porky who brings down the bad guy with a toy soldier. The cheering crowd appoints the pig sheriff. He reserves the job of street cleaner for Dripalong, still vowing to "Clean up this one-horse town." Porky observes, "Lucky for him it is a one-horse town."

DOG COLLARED

Porky Pig; Dec 2; MM; Directed by Robert McKimson; Story by Tedd Pierce; Animation by Charles McKimson; Rod Scribner, Phil DeLara, and J.C. Melendez; Layouts by Cornett Wood; Backgrounds by Richard H. Thomas; Voice Characterization by Mel Blanc; Musical Direction by Carl W. Stalling.

Learning of "Be-Kind-to-Animals Week," Porky makes the mistake of befriending an overaffectionate, horse-sized pooch. The dog's tremendous slobbers immediately overpower Porky, who now devotes his time to getting rid of the dog. He tries calling him a mongrel, then feels like a first-class heel and takes it all back. He throws a stick and runs in the opposite direction. The dog grabs the leg off a fruit stand and wrecks it, then appears in the back seat of Porky's car and lovingly bear hugs the pig so he can't drive straight. Porky narrowly misses a gouty old geezer and doesn't miss crashing in a dead end street. Porky then resorts to public transportation to get away from the mutt, switching from bus to trolley to subway in a bewildering variety of disguises, ending as a Chinese, only to find the dog behind him. Porky locks the dog out, but has a change of heart when the TV informs him that this dog belongs to a rich family offering a $5,000 reward. He finds the dog about to jump off a bridge. The dog sees where Porky is taking him and subs a toy dog by the time the door is opened. The butler tells Porky that the dog they're after is a talking dog. The real dog tells Porky, "Well, fat boy, you got yourself a dog."

BIG TOP BUNNY

Bugs Bunny; Dec 12; MM; Directed by Robert McKimson; Story by Tedd Pierce; Animation by Charles KcKimson, Rod Scribner, Phil DeLara, and Bob Wickersham; Layouts by Peter Alvarado; Backgrounds by Richard H. Thomas; Voice Characterization by Mel Blanc; Musical Direction by Carl W. Stalling.

Bugs vies with Bruno, an egotistical Russian acrobatic bear, jealous of his coveted spot as the star of Colonel Korney's World Famous Circus. Bruno sabotages Bugs's acrobatic act by leaving anvils in inconvenient places and not catching Bugs as he's supposed to. On the next trapeze routine, Bruno hands Bugs a phoney set of handlebars instead of arms, but Bugs converts them into unattached "air" bike handles, to the amazement of the audience. From there, the two proceed into the toon's best bit, each trying to outdo the other in a high dive (Bugs setting him up, 'natch). It begins with 200 feet into a tank of water, grows to 300 feet into a bucket, then 500 feet into a damp sponge, and finally to 5000 feet into a block of cement ("on my head, yet!") with the bear going first. Bugs then puts the dazed bear through a series of remarkably dangerous-looking circus stunts, ending with the bear getting fired clear out of the big top from a cannon. Says Bugs, "Well, that's one way to wind this up with a bang!"

Soundtrack includes "Acrobat's Daughter" and other familiar circus themes.

TWEET TWEET TWEETY

Tweety, Sylvester; Dec 15; LT; Directed by I. Freleng; Story by Warren Foster; Animation by Manuel Perez, Ken Champin, Virgil Ross, and Arthur Davis; Layouts by Hawley Pratt; Backgrounds by Paul Julian; Effects Animation by Harry Love; Voice Characterization by Mel Blanc; Musical Direction by Carl W. Stalling.

Sylvester's people camp in a national forest, and the cat immediately makes for a nest he has spied atop a tree, despite the game warden's warning that hunting and fishing are not permitted in this game refuge. He finds an egg in the nest, and it hatches, giving birth to Tweety, who says, "Get that catty carcass off me" and does with the aid of a pin. Sylvester tries pumping Tweety out of the tree with an air pump, then tries chopping the enormous tree down and swinging up to him (too close to a piledriver). Both times he gets flattened. When Tweety poses proudly in front of a bunch of amateur wildlife photographers, Sylvester sneaks up on him with a phony tripod. The warden makes him spit the bird out. Tweety next tricks him into going into the geyser Old Faithful just as it's about to erupt. Lastly, Sylvester, in a rowboat, chases Tweety down a river that he doesn't see leads to a waterfall until he's rowed most of the way down it. His frantic attempts to row back up are thwarted by Tweety ("Keep wowing, puddy tat,

I'll save you!"). Tweety turns a dial that blocks off the water. "You know, that puddy tat gonna hurt himself if he not more careful!"

THE PRIZE PEST

Porky Pig, Daffy Duck; Dec 22; MM; Directed by Robert McKimson; Story by Tedd Pierce; Animation by Rod Scribner, Phil DeLara, Emery Hawkins, and Charles McKimson; Layouts by Peter Alvarado; Backgrounds by Richard H. Thomas; Voice Characterization by Mel Blanc; Musical Direction by Carl W. Stalling.

"The 'What's the name of your name' "radio quiz show comes to Porky Pig's home to award the Grand Prize, he opens the box, wondering what it could be, and out pops Daffy like a girl coming out of a cake! "It's a duck, fat stuff. A genuine live duck," Daffy endears himself to Porky by trying to redecorate his dump by getting rid of some of this trash (including Porky and then demanding to know if he has a duck coop, preferably a convertible coop since he's a convertible duck. When Porky throws him out, Daffy goes into his Jekyll-and-Hyde bit in which he's nice when Porky butters him up but "when some wise guy starts pushing me around," he becomes a gruesome, fanged monster—the only problem with the routine being that Daffy's too grotesque-looking and his personality too thoroughly disturbing to be funny. He gives Porky a good spooking, especially when the Pig tries to call the authorities to let them know there's a lunatic loose in his house and Daffy subs for the phone, doing all the voices. When Porky gets wise, he retaliates by putting on an even more frightening Halloween suit, and they do the "mirror" bit, until Daffy realizes this new creep is even more hideous than him and does a really far out "falling apart" take (the first in a series in McKimson cartoons), then jumps back in the box and hightails it. "Gosh, what a scaredy cat," says Porky, "Anyone who'd be scared of a masquerade costume is a craven little coward." But then he gets a load of himself and heads for the chandelier. "So I'm a craven little coward.

1952

WHO'S KITTEN WHO

Jan 5; LT; Directed by Robert McKimson; Story by Tedd Pierce; Animation by Phil DeLara, Emery Hawkins, Charles McKimson, and Rod Scribner; Layouts by Peter Alvarado; Backgrounds by Richard H. Thomas; Voice Characterization by Mel Blanc; Musical Direction by Carl W. Stalling.
Hippety Hopper, inside a crate headed for the zoo, hops off (the sight causes one sober citizen to dispense with his bottle) and enters the basement of a house just as Sylvester is lecturing his wee one as to "The mysteries of life," i.e., mouse-catching, boasting, "I'm just the cat who can show you all the tricks of the trade. They don't come tricky enough or big enough for your father." Or do they? Hippety Hopper repeatedly bounces Sylvester out of the room to the shame of his boy. "Wherever I go," Junior laments, "people will point at me and say, 'There goes the kid whose father was thrown out by a mouse!'" Some good bits: Sylvester sticking his head out from behind a door to describe the battle as if it were going his way, though obviously he is getting pummeled ("I've got him right where he wants me"); Sylvester trying to mimic the mammoth mouse with springs on his feet; trying to tell Junior about "the giant, king-sized mouse," and the unsympathetic kid putting a bag over his head ("I'm ashamed to show my face in public"); Junior going after the mouse with a sheet of flypaper, the kangaroo falling on him, sandwiching the kitten and leading Sylvester to observe, "Now people will point at me and say, "There goes the cat whose only son was eaten by a mouse!'" Oh the shame of it."
Theme: "Meow."

OPERATION: RABBIT

Bugs Bunny, Wile E. Coyote; Jan 19; LT; Directed by Charles M. Jones; Story by Michael Maltese; Animation by Lloyd Vaughan, Ben Washam, Ken Harris, and Phil Monroe; Layouts by Robert Gribbroek; Backgrounds by Philip DeGuard; Voice Characterization by Mel Blanc; Musical Direction by Carl W. Stalling.
"Allow me to introduce myself. My name is Wile E. Coyote, genius." Actually, we were introduced to Wile E. in 1949's *Fast and Furry-out*. In the intervening three years he's acquired a voice, a first name and middle initial, and a new target for his attempts to satisfy both his craving for food and mental craving for the thrill of capturing some helpless desert animal with an elaborate scientific contraption. He first presents himself to Bugs as a supergenius and offers to let Bugs give himself up easily, but, as he says to himself, "They always want to do it the hard way." His plans consist of 1) a pressure cooker placed over Bugs's hole (Bugs tricks him into looking under) 2) a cannon that fires into a pipe directly leading into the hole, with Bugs sending it back at him through an extra section of pipe (Bugs then makes his own attempt on Wile E. with a doubly booby-trapped fountain pen; 3) an explosive decoy of a good looking robot rabbit chick, with Bugs beating him to the punch with a coyote counterpart exploding on Wile E.; 4) a flying saucer programmed to blast a rabbit, which Bugs confounds with a chicken mask, sending it back to Wile E. and blasting his whole cave to oblivion; 5) carrots filled with nitroglycerine, but which go off on him as Bugs uses a tractor to haul Wile E.'s shed in front of an oncoming train. "Allow me to introduce myself, my name is mud."
Theme: "What's Up, Doc."

FEED THE KITTY

Feb 2; MM; Directed by Charles M. Jones; Story by Michael Maltese; Animation by Robert Gribbroek; Backgrounds by Philip DeGuard; Musical Direction by Carl W. Stalling.
The adorable little kitten, Pussyfoot (whose theme is "Ain't She Sweet"), encounters Marc Antony, a ferocious bellowing bulldog. Not knowing to be afraid, the kitty's affectionate purring quickly reduces the hulk to a mere Mister Softie. Intending to adopt the kitten he brings it home in time to hear the lady of the house (Bea Bernaderet

as Blanche Morton) warning not to "Bring one more thing into this house … not one single solitary thing." So, he must hide Pussyfoot from the mistress, by pretending the cat is a wind-up toy or a powder puff. The emotions of both bulldog and audience go through the ringer when the dog thinks the cat has fallen into the flour that the mistress is baking for cookies. As the dog bawls, the audience does the same, the irony of having seen Pussyfoot climb out of the mix unharmed beforehand only taking the slightest edge off this harrowing, funny/serious scene. After the cookies are baked, the extremely long-faced doggy receives a kitten-shaped cookie, which he sadly plops on his back in place of the real Pussyfoot. Soon, both truths come to light: Marc Antony learns that Pussyfoot wasn't blended into cat biscuits, and the mistress discovers that her dog has a pet cat. All works out well: she permits the dog to keep his pal.

14 CARROT RABBIT

Bugs Bunny, Yosemite Sam; Feb 16; LT; Directed by I. Freleng; Story by Warren Foster; Animation by Manuel Perez, Ken Champin, Virgil Ross, and Arthur Davis; Layouts by Hawley Pratt; Backgrounds by Irv Wyner; Voice Characterization by Mel Blanc; Musical Direction by Carl W. Stalling.

In the "Klondike, where men are men, and women are women (a darn good arrangement)," prospectors are terrified of "Chilico Sam, the roughest, toughest, rootin'est, shootin'est claim jumper that ever jumped a claim." Sam, after getting only a few dollars for a dishonest day's work, meets Bugs turning in a huge gold boulder for some carrots in the Next to Last Chance saloon. "They say when he is near

gold," Piere the barkeep explains, "a funny feeling comes over heem!" After seeing the funny feeling help the rabbit (singing "Fiddle De-De-Di") find a gold collar button, Sam proposes, "Say, I like you, you're a good Joe! I like you so much I'm-a gonna make ya my partner! All ya have to do is find the gold, and we'll share it fifty-fifty. ("Honest and for true?" asks Bugs, sarcastically.) The partnership lasts long enough for Bugs to get Sam started in a dig, but not long enough for him to tell Sam he's heading through the bottom of a cliff. Sam's next dig is in the back of a dump truck, which Bugs deposits off a cliff. (Sam thinks, "I musta dug clear through to Chinee!") Sam vows to chase Bugs through every state in the union, which is what happens since Bugs has got his running pants on (great shots of the two running across a map). In Kentucky, Bugs gets the funny feeling once more. Sam doesn't want to fall for that trick again, but can't take any chances. He starts digging and gets hauled off by the MPs for breaking into Fort Knox. Bugs tells them he's waiting for a streetcar. An ocean liner arrives. "In a spot like, this a boat will do!" Bugs says in farewell.

GIFT WRAPPED

Tweety, Sylvester; Feb 16; LT; Directed by I. Freleng; Story by Warren Foster; Animation by Arthur Davis, Manuel Perez, Ken Champin, and Virgil Ross; Layouts by Hawley Pratt; Backgrounds by Irv Wyner; Voice Characterization by Mel Blanc; Musical Direction by Carl W. Stalling.

Sylvester is upset over the lack of mice on the night before Christmas ("not a creature was stirring, not even—). He gets excited when morning comes: "Oh, goody! Goody! Santa Claus came for real! Oh, I've been a good pussycat!" He's disappointed when he gets only a rubber mouse instead of a real one and shows more interest in Granny's present: Tweety in a cage. He switches the gift labels. Granny's a little surprised to receive a rubber mouse, but by the time she realizes they've been "accidentally mislabeled," Sylvester has already swallowed Tweety. Granny makes him spit Tweety out, but has a hard time giving the little birdie a Christmas kiss. As soon as Granny has gone, he's at the bird again, briefly distracted by a big unopened box under the tree. This contains a huge bulldog who swallows the cat whole! Sylvester later uses a toy steam shovel to get at the bird, and then tries sawing through the ceiling. Next they play Western, Sylvester as an Indian, Tweety as Hopawong Cassidy. Granny stops him before Tweety becomes shishkabob ("Ya didn't count on Pocahontas, did ya, Geronimo?"). Granny's had enough when Sylvester reroutes the model railroad car carrying Tweety into his mouth, and the dog subsequently devours Sylvester (dogs *eat* cats?). "This is the limit! I'm going to show you two there's to be peace in this house once and for all!" Last shot: Granny and the animals singing "Hark the Herald Angels," Sylvester and doggy finding it difficult with Christmas seals plastered over their mouths.

FOXY BY PROXY

Bugs Bunny; Feb 23; MM; Directed by I. Freleng; Story by Warren Foster; Animation by Virgil Ross, Arthur Davis, Manuel Perez, and Ken Chapin; Layouts by Hawley Pratt; Backgrounds by Irv Wyner; Voice Characterization by Mel Blanc; Musical Direction by Carl W. Stalling.
This is 1941's *Of Fox and Hounds* refitted for Bugs, an adaption of an adaption considering the original source was *Of Mice and Men.* A pack of hunting dogs are after a fox, their intention to cut his tail off. One dopey Lenny-type (replacing the original Willoughby) runs into Bugs Bunny (replacing the original George the Fox). The rabbit puts on a very phony-looking fox suit and gets the pack to chase him, but while it takes a smidgin of his brain to avoid them, he's got to do the opposite with Lenny, keeping "on" him until he realizes what Bugs is supposed to be (and insisting on talking to him at whatever angle Bugs holds his phony fox mask). Bugs also stamps phony fox tracks in the ground that lead to train

tracks. This gives him ammunition to convince the mutt he really is after a train. It's the other dogs who strart to keep Bugs busy. Bugs takes a circuitous route to avoid them. This doesn't work; when Bugs removes his fox suit they decide they're after rabbit! He gets rid of most of them with the ever-reliable log-over-the-edge-of-a-cliff routine. As he watches them fall, he brags, "Those dogs might be able to get a fox's tail, but they'd never get a rabbit's tail." While Bugs is saying this, Lenny has snipped and made off with Bugs's backside cotton puff. "Oh, well," says Bugs, displaying his shaved behind for the camera, "just call me stubby."

THUMB FUN

Porky Pig, Daffy Duck; Mar 1; LT; Directed by Robert KcKimson; Story by Tedd Pierce; Animation by Rod Scribner, Phil DeLara, Charles McKimson, and Bob Wickersham; Layouts by Peter Alvarado; Backgrounds by Richard H. Thomas; Voice Characterization by Mel Blanc; Musical Direction by Carl W. Stalling.
"Ya don't catch *this* little black duck flapping his way to Miami," says Daffy Duck, boasting of a cushier way to travel south for the winter. "I'm thumbin' it this season." When two cars go out of their way not to pick him up, Daffy resorts to the desperate measure of painting a phony Grand Canyon on the road and forcing himself on motorist Porky "Miami or Bust" Pig. From there on it's an expansion of the old vaudeville routine "Pay the Two Dollars" (done by Victor Moore and Edward Arnold in *Ziegfield Follies*), in which Porky prides himself on being a safe, speed-limit conscious driver while the obnoxious Daffy puts his foot in Porky's mouth. Daffy gets the pig into trouble with a tiny midget car that contains an irate driver so enormous that the sight of him causes Daffy to bark like a dog. He raises his fist in McKimsonian moving-perspective. Now there is an Irish highway cop whom Daffy stymies with a trunk so overcrowded with suitcases it explodes, and then a judge before whom Daffy can't let Porky get away with just pay-

ing the fine of two dollars. Finally, Porky presents Daffy with a wrapped gift "In appreciation for all you've done for me." Daffy's present turns out to be an "ACME Hitch-Hiker Thumb."

LITTLE BEAU PEPE
Pepe Le Pew Mar 29; MM; Directed by Charles M. Jones; Story by Michael Maltese; Animation by Lloyd Vaughan, Ben Washam, Ken Harris, and Phil Monroe; Layouts by Robert Gribbroek. Backgrounds by Philip DeGuard; Voice Characterization by Mel Blanc; Musical Direction by Carl W. Stalling.
The Foreign Legionnaires are attending to business as usual, drilling and marching, when who should arrive but "ze disillusioned" Pepe Le Pew. "I weesh to eenlist in ze Foreign Legion so I may forget." On getting a whiff of the new applicant, not only does the recruiting officer scram-ez vous, so does the entire company! Pepe deduces this is because they have already appointed him to their highest post of honor: left to defend the fort! But even honor can wait when Pepe casts his eyes on la belle femme skunk fatale (actually, a pussycat who passed under a freshly-painted ladder). With "La Vie En Rose" in the background, Pepe smothers his little demi-monde with kisses, but of course she wishes to "put on her face before we continue with ze wooing (such dainty rabbits these ladies!)". La Belle flees around the upper wall (seeing Pepe in Napoleon costume) and into a barrel ("Like shooting fish in a barrel, is it not?") and dashes out of the fort, he taking the dunes in his stride. By the time they make it to an oasis she has passed out. Dressed as a Valentino-style sheik, he carries the prostrate pussy into a tent. Wondering how she can rest with him so near he "decides to restoke the furnace of love" with a mixture of Aromas Arabienne that function as an aphrodisiac. The haunting primitive love song he strums for her overstrokes the furnace, and she chases him: "Le rowr-rowr!"

KIDDIN' THE KITTEN
Apr 5; MM; Directed by Robert McKimson; Story by Tedd Pierce; Animation by Phil DeLara, Charles McKimson, and Rod Scribner; Layouts by Peter Alvarado; Backgrounds by Richard H. Thomas; Musical Direction by Carl W. Stalling.
Dodsworth, a fat, lazy, and utterly unappealing cat gets the warning from the lady of the house, "If you don't get busy and get rid of those mice, out you go!" No Dodsworth has worked for generations, the word "busy" being just as revolting as the word "out." He devises a solution that involves posting a sign advertising a mouse-catching school. His first pupil is a little empty-headed white kitten. Telling him experience is the best teacher, Dodsworth puts the kitten to work. A fishing line is tied to his collar, which he tugs when he lights on a mouse. He catches a whole bunch with metallized cheese and a magnet. Though it was the kid who rounded up the rodents, Dodsworth presents them to the mistress as his own work for which he's to be rewarded with a can of sardines. The kitten overhears and extracts his revenge. He sets the mice loose. They tie and bind old Doddsy so he's helpless (not that he isn't generally) and then kick Dodsworth and the kitten out. In the wind-up, the kid has grown as lazy and shiftless as Dodsworth was at the start, letting the mice have free run and telling us, "One of these days, I'm gonna have to buy me a mouse trap."

WATER, WATER EVERY HARE
Bugs Bunny; Apr 19; LT; Directed by Charles M. Jones; Story by Michael Maltese; Animation by Ben Washam, Ken Harris, Phil Monroe, and Lloyd Vaughan; Layouts by Robert Gribbroek; Backgrounds by Philip DeGuard; Effects Animation by Harry Love; Voice

Characterization by Mel Blanc; Musical Direction by Carl W. Stalling.
Jones's surreal extension of *Hair-Raising Hare* has fewer big gags and more of a mesmerizing quality. Flooding carries Bugs and mattress off the bed and out of the rabbit hole, down river past the castle of an evil scientist (adorned with neon signs calling attention to its owner). In need of a brain for his mechanical monster, the scientist pulls in the sleeping Bugs from a waterfall. The shrieking rabbit wakes up surrounded by mummies and monsters. The doc sends the scariest of these, the hairy orange hump-headed humanoid in sneakers, after the rabbit, but Bugs thinks fast and makes like a gabby hairdresser ("My stars! Where did you ever get that awful hairdo?") chattering incessantly ("If an interesting monster can't have an interesting hairdo, then I don't know what things are coming to!"). He gives the orange-furred creature a permanent with dynamite rollers. Bugs disposes of the monster with two of the doc's potions, vanishing fluid for himself and reducing oil for the monster, who then takes up residence in a mouse hole. It's the scientist's turn to demand Bugs's brain ("Sorry, Doc, but I need what little I've got."). He axeidentally opens a bottle of ether which makes both characters move in slow motion until they fall asleep. Bugs awakens in his flooded abode, thinking, "It must have been a nightmare," but all at once the miniature monster rows by responding, "Oh yeah, That's what you think!"

LITTLE RED RODENT HOOD

Sylvester; May 3; MM; Directed by I. Freleng. Story by Warren Foster; Animation by Ken Champin, Virgil Ross, Arthur Davis, and Manuel Perez; Layouts by Hawley Pratt; Backgrounds by Irv Wyner; Voice Characterization by Mel Blanc; Musical Direction by Carl W. Stalling.
Sweet little Timmy mouse visualizes the story of Red Riding Hood in cat-and-mouse terms, with Granny, already having been mousified, telling him said story. One of the few cartoons that effectively juxtaposes '30s-style, wide-

eyed enchantment with 50s gags and explosions. In this version, Timmy is wearing the Red Riding Hood as he trips through wildflowers (house carpet patterns) and the forest of chair and table legs, past the big bad wolf (Sylvester), who, in gran'ma drag, ejects three other similarly clad would-be bad pussycats who want to get into the act (plus, as in *Little Red Riding Rabbit*, a little one under the pillow). Timmy goes through the familiar dialogue with Sylvester. "My, Granny, what big bags you have under your big bloodshot eyes!" After the "cue line" about the teeth, Sylvester chases the mouse down the banister, some well-placed butter sending him out the door where he threatens to huff and puff the place down, instead getting into trouble with a bulldog and dynamite. Sylvester poses as the li'l tyke's "Fairy Godmother," complete with electric cattle-prod magic wand that the dog tricks him into using on himself. After blowing Sylvester up with a toy tank, Timmy holes up. End of story, almost. Says Granny. "Luckily, Little Red Riding Hood found a large firecracker left over from the Fourth of July ..." Says the mouse, "I bet that blew him all up." Says Sylvester, "You're not just whistling "Dixie," brother."

SOCK-A-DOODLE DOO

Foghorn Leghorn; May 10; LT; Directed by Robert McKimson; Story by Tedd Pierce; Animation by Charles McKimson, Rod Scribner, and Phil DeLara; Layouts by Peter Alvarado; Backgrounds by Richard H. Thomas; Voice Characterization by Mel Blanc; Musical Direction by Carl W. Stalling.
"Kid Banty, World's Champion Fighting Rooster— Pinfeatherweight Champ," a punch-drunk pug about as sharp as a bowling ball, is so groggy he starts throwing punches whenever he hears a bell (he kayoes a cow this way: "Anyone for buttermilk?"). Banty falls off his special truck and heads for the familiar farm just as Foghorn Leghorn and the barnyard dog are in the midst of their ongoing feud, the dog duping Foggy with a phony flying saucer attraction. Foggy's alarm clock pro-

vokes Banty into bashing him in the bazooka, and the Leghorn immediately strarts thinking up schemes to use Banty against ol' Br'er Dog. Telling Banty he needs a good workout, Foggy sends him to the doghouse to ask for a punching bág. Just at the right moment, the dog is on the receiving end of one of Banty's blows. The dog sends back a "punching bag" with Banty in a gift-wrapped box. Foggy opens it to find a clock with a bell ("I was right, it was a booby trap!"). Foggy next sets up the dog as the rooster's sparring partner, giving his head lumps so he can reach the minimum height and blowing him up with an exploding cigar before Banty can have a crack at him. The dog tells Banty he needs someone his own size. He traps Foggy in a phony burlesque house, the Hulie-Hulie Hut, getting him to stick his head through a peep hole. Banty then lets him have it!

Theme: "Ain't We Got Fun?"

BEEP, BEEP

The Coyote (Carnivorous Vulgais) and the Road Runner (Accelarti Incredibius); May 24; MM; Directed by Charles M. Jones; Story by Michael Maltese; Animation by Ben Washam, Ken Harris, Lloyd Vaughan, and Phil Monroe; Layouts by Robert Gribbroek; Backgrounds by Philip DeGuard; Musical Direction by Carl W. Stalling.
It's still early in the game: in the second Road Runner picture, the Coyote still acts as though he . has a chance of catching his prey and actually carries napkins and silverware. After a boxing glove sprung from a boulder fails, the Coyote blueprints his plans as he did in *Operation: Rabbit*, beginning with an anvil he intends to drop from a high wire suspended between two peaks. He then rigs up a "last glass of water" with an explosive booby-trap, which the bird simply ignores, explaining with a sign: "Road Runners can't read and don't drink," whereupon Coyote chases the Road Runner into a series of tunnels and mine shafts, the two being shown mainly on a maplike cross section (which looks like one of those modern "You are here" deals). The two are vis-

ible mainly from the lights on their miner's helmets. This sequence ends with the Coyote lighting a match to see where he *is:* It turns out he's is in a store-room of explosives. Outside, a small catapult hurls him into the ground and a rocket zooms straight up with him (becoming fireworks that advertise "Eat at Joe's") before running out of fuel in mid-air. The exasperated Coyote then crawls over to a glass of water, not realizing it's the explosive drink he rigged up a few scenes earlier. Finally, a phony railroad crossing not only fails to halt the Road Runner, but leads to the Coyote's getting smashed by a real locomotive, with the Road Runner waving from the caboose!

THE HASTY HARE

Bugs Bunny, Marvin Martian; June 7; LT; Directed by Charles M. Jones; Story by Michael Maltese; Animation by Ken Harris, Lloyd Vaughan, and Ben Washam; Layouts by Robert Gribbroek; Backgrounds by Philip DeGuard; Voice Characterization by Mel Blanc; Musical Direction by Carl W. Stalling.
Marvin Martian, whose official title here is Commander Flying Saucer X-2, and his canine Lieutenant, K-9, are assigned "to bring back one (1) Earth creature." They choose Bugs Bunny.When their weaponry convinces Bugs (still singing "Fiddle-De-Di") that they're not costumed trick-or-treaters, he out-smarts them by doing Blanc's classic railroad station announcer bit and then by implicating K-9 in a mutiny. Finally taking him on the ship with the help of an "Acme Straightjacket-Ejecting Bazooka," Bugs coerces the martian Mutt into letting him have a jacket that's more his size and slips the original on the dog, then gets one on Marvin on the pretense that they've "struck an iceboig! ... Get into this life presoiver." Bugs's amateurish attempt at turning the saucer around to head for "little old oith" accidentally hooks a constellation of half-moons, ringed planets, and stars onto the ship. One "I. Firsby," at the Shalomar observatory, spots all this and resigns: "When I start seeing things like this, it's time to take up turkey farming."

AIN'T SHE TWEET

Tweety, Sylvester; June 21; LT; Directed by I. Freleng; Story by Warren Foster; Animation by Virgil Foster, Arthur Davis, Manuel Perez, and Ken Champin; Layouts by Hawley Pratt; Backgrounds by Irv Wyner; Voice Characterization by Mel Blanc; Musical Direction by Carl W. Stalling.

Sylvester and Tweety (singing "Fiddle-De-Di") encounter each other on opposite sides of a pet shop window, Tweety sharing his discovery with a mouse and Sylvester being prevented by a cop from breaking the window with a brick. A delivery truck takes Tweety off, delivered to Granny, the daffy old dame who's wild about pets and, Sylvester is not too thrilled to learn, keeps a yard full of frisky bulldogs ("they're so cute and active"). Sylvester tries to get through to the house and up to the second story window where Tweety is encaged. First he walks across a branch which Tweety saws off (observing "that puddy tat's got a pink skin under his fur coat"). Next he uses a pair of stilts with Tweety supplying a toolbox for the dogs to work with ("Here, puddy dogs, could you use dese?"). Sylvester employs a rocket, which he builds from a blueprint, setting his fur afire. He waits until the doggies have left the yard but finds them in the house (an old man, thinking he's doing Sylvester a favor, shoves him back over the fence!). He hides in a package he thinks is intended for Granny, but which actually contains dog food. Lastly, he tip-toes through the sleeping mutts in the middle of the night. They're rudely awakened by an alarm clock, as Tweety inquires innocently, "Now who do you suppose would want to disturb those doggies so early in the morning?"

THE TURN-TALE WOLF

June 28; MM; Directed by Robert McKimson; Story by Tedd Pierce; Animation by Phil DeLara, Charles McKimson, Herman Cohen, and Rod Scribner; Layouts by Peter Alvarado; Backgrounds by Richard H. Thomas; Voice Characterization by Mel Blanc; Musical Direction by Carl W. Stalling.

The Big Bad Wolf's very proper little nephew (a combination of Sylvester, Jr. and Bugs's nephew Clyde) complains, "To think that my own uncle is that fiendish big bad wolf who huffed and puffed and blew the little pigs houses down!" Uncle protests, "I never done nothin' of the kind, that was a bum rap!" He tells *his* side of the story, in which he was "just an innocent, nature-lovin' kind" and "da three pigs was da mugs." in his flashback, he's an effeminate type (better, a rough mug trying to act light and deliberately overdoing it), who communes with the bees and the trees, but dreads passing the houses of the three mean pigs (from *Wind-Blown Hare*). "Oh, drat, you three little pigs! Why must you always torment me?" The three little hoodlums invite him to "play" with them, "games" which are far from the "ginger-peachy" pastimes the wolf imagines. "Slingshot"is one in which the pigs rubber-band a boulder right into his puss, and in "swat the fly" he wears play wings and they wallop him with big placard-like swatters. The play gets even rougher when they learn of a $50 bounty for a wolf's tail and contrive to cut it off by making him their king and sitting him on a guillotine chair. They then chase him to *his* house and huff and puff it down! When the nephew doesn't believe it, Uncle offers the stump of his tail as evidence (confiding in us that he lost it in a swingin' door!).

CRACKED QUACK

Daffy Duck, Porky Pig; July 5; MM; Directed by I. Freleng; Story by Warren Foster; Animation by Arthur Davis, Manuel Perez, Ken Champin, and Virgil Ross; Layouts by Hawley Pratt; Backgrounds by Irv Wyner; Voice Characterization by Mel Blanc; Musical Direction by Carl W. Stalling.

Daffy Duck, again desirous of an alternative to autumnal migration (as in *Daffy's Southern Exposure* and *Birth of a Notion*) smashes into Porky Pig's house and spies a stuffed duck on the mantle. "Well, there's one of our boys that's got this flying south business licked." His first idea is to offer the stuffed duck companionship for the long winter evenings, but, after knocking the stuffings out of him, decides to take his place. "This is where this ingenious little black duck gets himself some free room and board." He heads for the fridge ("and the goodies therein"), not having to worry about Porky, who's busy figuring out his taxes. His suspicious dog is another matter ("I can see where this moron is going to give me trouble"). Dropping a vase on the dog doesn't help. Porky demonstrates to Rover that the duck is stuffed by wacking his head on the ground. Daffy temporarily gets rid of the dog with the "catch the stick" routine but setting him up to attack the original stuffed duck backfires, as Porky restuffs the live Daffy with a box of cotton. We cut to a flock of ducks flying overhead, spotting the overstuffed Daffy on the mantle. They decide *this* is a good way to beat that flying south routine. Porky: "This darn income tax would come out all right if I only had a few dependants." Daffy: "Did you say dependants?" Showing him a room full of party-hearty ducks playing cards and loafing, he remarks, "Brother, you got 'em!"

OILY HARE
Bugs Bunny; July 26; MM; Directed by Robert McKimson; Story by Tedd Pierce; Animation by Rod Scribner, Phil DeLara, Charles McKimson, and Herman Cohen; Layouts by Peter Alvarado; Backgrounds by Richard H. Thomas; Voice Characterization by Mel Blanc; Musical Direction by Carl W. Stalling.
Bugs is a happy-go-lucky western rabbit, living in Deepinahola, Texas (nearby to Deepinaharta). His rabbit hole attracts the attention of a million-

aire Texas oilman (sort of Yosemite Sam with a haircut and more of an accent), who drives in a car so large that he not only has to telephone the driver, he has to call him long distance! Anyhow, he wants to do something about the "hole out there in mah property that ain't a-gushin' oil." He and his sidekick, Maverick, a silent fellow whose over-large clothes hang from his body and cover his face, hastily construct an oil derrick on top of the rabbit hole. Bugs is not about to be evicted and sends all the oilman's weaponry right back at him, beginning with a load of dynamite returned to his adversary as "candles" on a birthday cake, and a bunch of bullets that bounce back through a piece of piping. After Bugs gets into Maverick's duds, the oilman himself then goes down the hole and decides to blast "the critter" out, failing to notice that there's a Maverick both inside and outside. He has the place stuffed with explosives until the ground literally bulges with dynamite (Bugs somehow doesn't mind this demolishing of his domicile!). The oilman flicks on a cigarette lighter to take a look around, and immediately there is an enormous explosion. Boss and crony aren't harmed, but are carried to the top of a "gusher" of carrots that shoots up out of the ground. "Yeah, I know, I know," Bugs says to the audience, "Anything can happen in Texas."

HOPPY GO LUCKY
Sylvester, Hippety Hopper; Aug 9; LT; Directed by Robert McKimson; Story by Tedd Pierce; Animation by Charles McKimson, Herman Cohen, Rod Scribner, and Phil DeLara; Layouts by Robert Givens; Backgrounds by Richard H. Thomas; Voice Characterization by Mel Blanc; Musical Direction by Carl W. Stalling.
Sylvester's latest baby kangaroo-sure-looks-like-a-giant mouse fiasco, this time with a dopey lug named Benny as his companion instead of his son. Sylvester (repeatedly called George so you don't miss the *Mice and Men* reference) is interested in getting a meal, while Benny seeks companionship ("To have one for my very own, to love him

and pet him, to hug him and hug him, pet him and pet him"). When Sylvester encounters the "giant mouse" in a dockside warehouse, Benny doesn't believe him any more than Junior did. Each time he goes in the warehouse, Hoppy boots him out, and each time Hoppy shoves him out, Sylvester throws him back in. Sylvester finally goes in for a look of his own, and lights a "candle to see where I am going at." He throws away the candle when it makes too much noise, not realizing it's noisy because it's a lit stick of TNT. Sylvester catches it in a bag thinking it's the mouse making breathing noises. Sylvester then sees Hoppy dragging Benny down the dock and realizes that he's left holding the bag and gets an explosion in his face.

Benny's theme music is one we haven't heard for a while: "Woodenhead, Puddin' Head Jones."

GOING! GOING! GOSH!

The Road Runner (Accelerati Incredibus),the Coyote (Carnivorous Vulgaris); Aug 23; MM; Directed by Charles M. Jones; Story by Michael Maltese; Animation by Lloyd Vaughan, Ben Washam, and Ken Harris; Layouts by Robert Gribbroek; Backgrounds by Philip DeGuard; Voice Characterization by Mel Blanc; Musical Direction by Carl W. Stalling; Orchestrations by Milt Franklyn.
The Coyote fires an arrow from a bow, but the explosive arrow stays. He tries to fire himself with a giant slingshot, but it snaps out of the ground and goes backward into him. He covers the road with quick-drying cement, which is splattered over him by the Road Runner. A boulder rolls on top of the manhole cover before he can throw the grenade. The Road Runner won't fall for his Southern belle disguise because he's "already got a date." The Road Runner runs through the trick painting of a bridge where the bridge is really out. A truck comes out of it, but it tears like canvas when the Road Runner tries it. The earth-shattering boulder Coyote rolls on the bird instead travels the circuitous mountain ledges back to him. The anvil he drops from his

makeshift balloon (holding a street-cleaner's wagon) causes the craft to jerk upward and lose its gas. On hurling a javelin at the bird, he goes straight into a beep-beeping truck with the Road Runner at the wheel.

BIRD IN A GUILTY CAGE

Tweety, Sylvester; Aug 30; LT; Directed by I. Freleng; Story by Warren Foster; Animation by Manuel Perez, Ken Champin, Virgil Ross, and Arthur Davis; Layouts by Hawley Pratt; Backgrounds by Irv Wyner; Voice Characterization by Mel Blanc; Musical Direction by Carl W. Stalling.
A department store, after closing time, supplies the backdrop for Sylvester's latest Tweety hunt. After he spots the bird through a half-closed window, he enters through a mail slot. He wolf whistles at mannequins modeling French bathing suits and introduces the bird ("How naive can you get?") to a game called "sandwich." The bird hides on a lighting fixture, so Sylvester constructs a rather surreal ladder of mannequin body parts to reach him. Somehow the bird gets roller skates underneath the ladder, sending him down the stairs. He comes racing up in a strange mixture of lingerie and mannequin anatomy. When Tweety hides in a pile of ladies hats, Sylvester tries a few on while making funny faces (to the tune of "Oh You Beautiful Doll"). When our bird hides in a hole in the wall, Sylvester opens fire and hits his own rear. Tweety leaps into a mail tube, and Sylvester waits open-mouthed for him, but gets a TNT stick instead. Leaving the store and turning the corner (to "Tip Toe Through the Tulips"), Sylvester gets the offscreen explosion. "Well, birds are off my [diet] list. That one sort of upset my stomach."

MOUSE WARMING

Claude Cat; Sept 8; LT; Directed by Charles M. Jones; Story by Michael Maltese; Animation by Ben Washam, Lloyd Vaughan, and Ken Harris; Layouts by; Robert Gribbroek; Backgrounds by Philip DeGuard; Voice Characterization by Mel Blanc; Musical Direction by Carl W. Stalling; Orchestrations by Milt Franklyn.

The cuteness of a boy-girl flirtation effectively interlaced with the cartoony violence of a cat-and-mouse chase. A family of mice with an adorable teen-aged (and she's got the boby sox to prove it) girl moves in across the room from a bow-tied boy mouse. As he tries to get to her, Claude tries to catch him. Failing to do so with conventional cartoon-mouse-chase methods, Claude exploits the boy's heart-wrenching crush on his new neighbor. He sends a phony note to the boy in which the girl describes herself as being "deemed not unattractive by my friends." He baits the trap with a hand puppet girl mouse, then stirs up trouble by sending a hate letter from the boy to the girl's father ("Get out because I'm moving in!") and posting a "boarder wanted" sign on their door. Finally, the mouse decides he can write notes too, and sends a letter of friendship from the bulldog to Claude that ends with an invitation to a game of canasta. Claude doesn't realize somethin' ain't right until after he's set up the card table and drinks. Back in the kitchen, boy mouse and girl mouse share a soft drink through two straws.

Theme: "Three Blind Mice." Soundtrack: "Sweethearts," "My Buddy," "Quarter to Nine," "My Lucky Day."

RABBIT SEASONING

Bugs Bunny, Daffy Duck, Elmer Fudd; Sept 20; MM; Directed by Charles M. Jones; Story by Michael Maltese; Animation by Ben Washam, Lloyd Vaughan, and Ken Harris; Layouts by Maurice Noble; Backgrounds by Philip DeGuard; Voice Characterization by Mel Blanc; Musical Direction by Carl W. Stalling.

Bugs: "Would you like to shoot me now or wait till you get home?" Daffy: "Shoot him now!" Bugs: "You keep out of this, he doesn't have to shoot *you* now!" Daffy: "He does so have to shoot me now! I demand that you shoot me now!" The hunting routine established in *A Wild Hare* gets extended to its extremes here to emphasize verbal one-upmanship, which translates directly into shots in the head, inevitably directed at Daffy and blowing his beak into a sequence of unpredictable positions. First, Bugs gets Elmer to give it to Daffy instead of him (in the midst of what they think is rabbit season) with the above quoted "pronoun trouble," Daffy's discovery of which fails to prevent him from giving Elmer another cue to shoot him, as does his attempt to explain the deal ("If I was a rabbit what would you do?"). Bugs and Daffy hide in Bugs's hole, Daffy peeking out only to be shot by Elmer "Still lurking about," Bugs suggests a new plan, and Daffy responds, "No more for me, thanks, I'm driving." Bugs emerges in a Lana Turner sweater and killer pumps to seduce Elmer into reblasting the duck. Uncovered, Bugs returns to the pronoun trouble of the beginning, varying it once more so that Elmer doesn't shoot Daffy now, he waits till they get home. After which Daffy adjusts his beak once more and tells Bugs, "You're despicable."

Theme: "What's Up, Doc?"

THE *EGG-CITED* ROOSTER

Foghorn Leghorn, Henery Hawk; Oct 4; MM; Directed by Robert McKimson; Story by Tedd Pierce; Animation by Rod Scribner, Phil DeLara, Charles McKimson, Herman Cohen; Layouts by Robert Givens; Backgrounds by Richard H. Thomas; Voice Characterization by Mel Blanc; Musical Direction by Carl W. Stalling.

Mrs. Leghorn warns her husband, "If you dare leave that egg uncovered for so much as one minute, I'll put more lumps on that fat head of yours than there are in a bride's mashed potatoes!" As we all know, sitting on eggs is out! Especially when the barnyard dog comes by and takes a poke at hubby, hits him with a melon, and verbally abuses him by calling him a "mutha." If I could get someone to mind this egg for a spell," figures Foggy, "I'd go over and pay that dog a little social call!" As if on cue, enter Henery Hawk, playing Indian as the last of the Mo-Hawk-ans and identifying Foghorn as "the biggest chicken ever I seen!" The big rooster dupes Henery into sitting on the egg on the pretext that he wants "a tender chicken. All ya gotta do is sit on it a while and thaw it out." Although the mini-hawk covers only about as much as a flapper's skirt in a high wind, it gives Foggy the chance to traipse over to the doghouse and convert its occupant into a flashing electric sign. Returning, he prevents Henery's hammering open the egg by giving him a "hen grenade" and instructions to plant it under the "nice warm dog." After the explosion, the dog and Henery conspire to swipe the egg and tattle to wifey, but Foggy re-swipes the egg and there's a three-way back and forth with it until she catches him and lets him have it with a rolling pin. This is topped by Henery's making good his threat to scalp him!

Theme: "Camptown Ladies."

TREE FOR TWO
Sylvester; Oct 4; MM; Directed by I. Freleng; Story by Warren Foster; Animation by Ken Chapin, Virgil Ross, Arthur Davis, and Manuel Perez; Layouts by Hawley Pratt; Backgrounds by Irv Wyner; Voice Characterization by Mel Blanc; Musical Direction by Carl W. Stalling.
Headline: "Black Panther Escapes Zoo." The beast is shown stalking through the city, eventually stopping in a pile of ash cans in an alley. Along come two dogs, the tough, nasty lunkhead Spike (in turtleneck and bowler hat, a la *A Hare Grows in Manhattan*) and his eager little hero-worshipping lacky, Chester (voiced by Stan Freberg), who constantly babbles out doggy activities to amuse his idol. ("You wanna play ball, huh, Spike? You wanna chase cars?"). Spike shows no interest until Chester reveals he knows where there is a cat that he can beat up on for a few yocks, leading him to Sylvester. Spike interrupts the cat's jaunty "Charleston," chasing him into

an alley behind a fence. Spike follows, leaving Chester outside. Instead of the pussy cat, the bulldog runs into the panther. He is repeatedly thrashed and thinks it's by Sylvester. Spike turns white with fear and gets tossed out. To the astonished disbelief of Spike, Chester grabs the real Sylvester and whirls him around. Spike heads into the alley, daring Sylvester and gets clawed into slices by the panther. By this time Chester is demanding that the terrified bulldog face Sylvester for his own good, and tosses the cat into the ash-can again. The next shot shows that the tables have turned, and it's now Spike who's babbling: "You and me is pals, ain't we, Chester? Chester, yoose my hero 'cause you's so strong!"

THE SUPER SNOOPER
Daffy Duck; Nov 11; LT; Directed by Robert McKimson; Story by Tedd Pierce; Animation by Herman Cohen, Rod Scribner, Phil DeLara, and Charles McKinson; Layouts by Robert Givens; Backgrounds by Richard H. Thomas; Voice Characterization by Mel Blanc; Musical Direction by Carl W. Stalling.
Pierce always loved writing genre takeoffs, and this (his first with McKimson) is one of his best. Here we have a private eye movie parody, narrated in real hard-boiled *noir* fashion by the protagonist, Detective Duck Drake (Private Eye, Ear, Nose, and Throat). While disposing of his latest case (of empty bottles), the phone rings, and he's summoned to the J. Cleaver Axehandle Estate in plush Beveridge Hills, where he counts off the whodunit flick elements. First, a suspicious acting butler who tells him to "walk this way" (an old gag made more effective by underscoring it with the Alfred Hitchcock show theme). Enter the inevitable amorous babe, who's just crazy about you gumshoes (not to mention that she is built like a brick wall). She assumes, understandingly so, that Daffy means her when he asks to see "the body." Duck Drake begins to put together a complicated murder plot in his head, theorizing that the Body offed her hubby by rerouting a train through their living room. He's all wrong, however, as he's

got the wrong mansion! That doesn't stop the amorous babe from making goo-goo eyes at D. D., eyes that have the old ball and chain look in them. Daffy beats it out of there while he's still single, with the Body not far behind.

RABBIT'S KIN

Bugs Bunny; Nov 15; MM; Directed by Robert McKimson; Story by Tedd Pierce; Animation by Charles McKimson, Herman Cohen, Rod Scribner, and Phil DeLara; Layouts by Robert Givens; Backgrounds by Richard H. Thomas; Voice Characterization by Mel Blanc; Musical Direction by Carl W. Stalling.

Imagine the cutest little bunny you ever did see, with great big eyes, floppy ears and feet, and a totally unintelligible speeded-up voice. Bugs saves him from the hungry slob Pete Puma (voiced by Stan Freberg) and shows him a few pointers in the fine art of cartoon heckling, one of them a recurring gag in which Bugs serves the Puma tea, asks how many lumps he wants, and raps his head that many times. When the Puma appears in the ludicrous guise of the rabbit's mother, thinking he's outsmarted Bugs by requesting coffee instead of tea, he gets his head lumps just the same. When the little Bunny wants to get in the act, Bugs lets Pete abduct him to his cave where he's surprised to find Bugs in an even more ludicrous Puma suit, passing himself off as Pete's second cousin Paul Puma. Ostensibly helping with the oven, "Paul" asks Pete how many lumps (ostensibly of coal) he wants, and Pete asks for "a whole lotta lumps." Instead of letting Bugs wallop him, this time Pete insists on helping himself. The two rabbits walk off, Bugs saying sarcastically,"C'mon, shorty, we better get out of here, he's much too smart for us."

TERRIER STRICKEN

Claude Cat; Nov 29; MM; Directed by Charles M. Jones; Story by Michael Maltese; Animation by Ken Harris, Lloyd Vaughan, and Ben Washam; Layouts by Robert Gribboeck;

Backgrounds by Philip DeGuard; Voice Characterization by Mel Blanc; Musical Direction by Carl W. Stalling.

Claude Cat versus Frisky Puppy, round two. Claude, no longer the dupe of Hubie and Bertie, has feline cunning and deviousness on his side. The puppy-pup has only canine naivete and spontaneous barking spasms that send the nervous Claude flying. After playing with a ball and a flea (a triumph of semi-naturalistic animation), Frisky needs a bath. One of his spasms has the gloating Claude flying into the tub, another puts him against the ceiling with a wet bucket around him. After more attempts land him in a watering can and a fish bowl, he resorts to chasing the pup with an axe. This initiates the first of two harrowing rides: a Frisky bark sends Claude up to the ceiling, coming back on the banister down the stairs, onto a roller skate, out of the house, onto a wagon, over a wall, into the second story of the next house, back out again into a rain barrel, up in the air (another bark), into the chimney, atop a bunch of fireplace logs, down the basement and inside a water cooler. Wild ride number two starts with Claude following the pup up the stairs by a thread from a sweater he's wearing from a drycleaning truck. Claude reaches the end of the thread and doesn't let go before the truck has pulled him through stair supports, in and out of two mouse holes, the handles on a vase, faucets in the kitchen sink, a tea kettle, out the door and onto a diving board and the waterless pool below, where he dopily pantomimes the act of swimming.

FOOL COVERAGE

Daffy Duck, Porky Pig; Dec 13; LT; Directed by Robert McKimson; Story by Tedd Pierce; Animation by Phil DeLara, Charles McKimson, Herman Cohen, and Rod Scribner; Layouts by Robert Givens; Backgrounds by Carlos Manriquez; Voice Characterization by Mel Blanc. Musical Directions: Carl W. Stalling.

What's the quickest way to make Daffy even more despicable? Make him an insurance salesman! In trying to unload a policy on homeowner Porky, Daffy, representing the Hot Foot Casualty Underwriter's Insurance Company, follows Porky through his chores to demonstrate how prevelant accidents are in the home. Of course, he has to arrange a few accidents, a dangerously overstuffed hall closet (Porky doesn't own a sidesaddle), a rigged rocking chair tilted in front of a hole he's sawed in the floor, and a candle in the basement that's really a white TNT stick whose explosion creates several levels of Daffy Duck silhouette holes in ceilings. But then the retaliation "After witnessing your unfortunate mishaps about the house," says Porky, "I'm ready to sign on the dotted line!" Daffy has previously mentioned a policy that pays a million dollars for a black eye, but spared Porky the minor provisions: "Provided the accident occurs as a result of a stampede of wild elephants in your own home, between 3:55 and 4:00 PM on the Fourth of July during a hail storm!" No sooner does Porky say, "I knew there'd be a catch to it!" than we hear the roar of elephants coming through the door. Daffy checks and, one by one, all the provisions are met, even one he has just added, that the elephant herd must be followed by a baby zebra!

HARE LIFT
Bugs Bunny, Yosemite Sam; Dec 20; LT; Directed by I. Freleng; Story by Warren Foster; Animation by Manuel Perez, Ken Champin, Virgil Ross, and Arthur Davis; Layouts by Hawley Pratt; Backgrounds by Irv Wyner; Voice Characterization by Mel Blanc; Musical Direction by Carl W. Stalling.
When the world's largest airplane parks on top of Bugs's rabbit hole, the curious rabbit wanders through it taking the 50-cent tour. Meanwhile, bank-robber Sam, making a getaway ("and keep reachin' fer the ceilin' till ya reach it"), speeds to the airport and enters the plane. Finding Bugs fooling around in the cockpit, Sam assumes he is the pilot, and before Bugs can convince him that he ain't, Sam has got a gun in his face and is barking orders to get going. Bugs first takes them to the

proximity of the moon. As they turn back and terra firma gets closer, Sam comes across Bugs calmly reading "Learn to Fly." What's worse, Bugs refuses "To look up any more reference because you talked mean to me." Before Bugs will make a move to prevent crashing, Sam has got to say he's sorry, with sugar on it, yet! Sam, sweating like a pig, tries to appear nonchalant (with a yoyo and jacks, even!), before he gives in. Bugs next tricks Sam in and out of both doors of the plane and the bomb bay. When Sam demands the wheel, Bugs uproots it and tosses it out the window. Certain they're going to crash, both try the automatic pilot, which turns out to be a robot who absconds with one of the plane's two parachutes. Sam grabs the second and plunges into a waiting police car below, while Bugs manages to land the plane. "Lucky for me this thing has air brakes."

1953

DON'T GIVE UP THE SHEEP
Ralph Wolf, Sam Sheepdog; Jan 3; LT; Directed by Charles M. Jones; Story by Michael Maltese; Animation by Ken Harris, Ben Washam, Lloyd Vaughan; Layouts by Robert Gribbroek; Backgrounds by Carlos Manriquez; Voice Characterization by Mel Blanc; Musical Direction by Carl W. Stalling.
Sam Sheepdog punches in for work (relieving the night dog, Fred) counts the sheep, and sets about his job of watching them. Ralph Wolf's first attempt at getting at the flock consists of speeding the time clock so that Sam has lunch and goes home at 9:00! Ralph next carries off a lamb to a bush, but gets followed and clobbered by Sam. Inspired by a book of Greek myths, Ralph, his legs hairier in this first appearance, makes like the ancient Pan to lull the shepherd to sleep but gets immediately walloped. He tunnels underground and yanks the sheep through holes, mistakenly pulling Sam through one as well, then a wildcat who goes straight for him. He swings Tarzan style from a tree hang-

ing over a cliff, grabbing Sam instead. He tries sawing off the branch holding the rope, but Sam saws off his branch. Sam chops down the tree, but when Ralph pick-axes through the cliff, the mountain falls down instead! When Ralph snorkles underwater, Sam drops a TNT stick in his breathing-tube pipe, and Ralph sinks! Lastly, Sam detects Ralph's flawless disguise. The night sheepdog, Fred, resumes paddling Ralph.

SNOW BUSINESS

Tweety, Sylvester; Jan 17; LT; Directed by I. Freleng; Story by Warren Foster; Animation by Virgil Ross, Arthur Davis, Manuel Perez, Ken Champin; Layouts by Hawley Pratt; Backgrounds by Carlos Manriquez; Voice Characterization by Mel Blanc; Musical Direction by Carl W. Stalling.
Another neat-o Tweety picture crammed to the brim with fast-moving plot and way-out gags. A blizzard has blocked all the roads to Granny's cabin so she can't drive through. Her "bird and cat are up there ... they'll starve." Correction: Tweety won't starve. Realization of their snow-bound situation has them looking around for food and coming up with closet after closet filled with birdseed. And neither will Sylvester, as he and his pal Tweety (who never does get wise in this one) put on their thinking caps and Sylvester does in fact think of something that "puddies wike to eat." Sylvester lures Tweety atop the broiler with games like sailing on a paper boat in a big tureen and skating on grease in the frying pan. Complicating matters is a starving, delirious mouse. "I gotta have food, I forgot what food looks like." On seeing Sylvester, he yells "Food!" Sylvester's chase after the unsuspecting bird keeps being interrupted by the mouse's turnabout-is-fair-play efforts to eat the pussycat, whether gnawing at his furry head, sticking his tail in a toaster, pushing him into the same pot in which he is trying to cook Tweety, or dragging him by the foot into his mouse hole and roasting his leg over sterno canned heat! When Granny finally makes it on snow shoes with a pack of food, she learns she's brought only more bird seed! Making the best of it, Tweety asks Sylvester how he likes it just at the moment the mouse bites into Sylvester's tail, The cat yowls in pain, Tweety says,"It can't be dat bad."

A MOUSE DIVIDED

Sylvester; Jan 31; MM; Directed by I. Freleng; Story by Warren Foster; Animation by Art Davis, Manuel Perez, Ken Champin, and Virgil Ross; Layouts by Hawley Pratt; Backgrounds by Irv Wyner; Voice Characterization by Mel Blanc; Musical Direction by Carl W. Stalling.
"A fine thing," says Sylvester. "I've become the father of a breakfast!" The eternally inebriated stork, too sloshed to locate the proper parents of the bundle he's bearing, drops it off at the residence of Mr. and Mrs. Sylvester Cat. Coincidentally, the missus has just been handing her sourpuss husband that old etcetera about the pitter-patter of little feet around the house. The parental thrills of both turn to astonishment when they open the bundle and find a Gerber's baby mouse. Mrs. S. is instantly won over. Sylvester's first impulse is more carnivoral than paternal. He's about to satisfy that urge when wifey leaves, diapering the little lad in pepper and salad oil. Sylvester too gives in when the toddler calls him daddy. The other cats on the block don't share his fatherly affection, however, and when Da-Da takes baby for a stroll, the entire house is surrounded by marauding felines. Sylvester, on the winning end of these quick blackout-type bits for a change, outwits the catty cut-ups who pose first as a vacuum cleaner salesman and a babysitter. He thrusts TNT sticks on those who would swipe the crib from a hole sawed through the floor and sends more up the chimney to ho-ho-ho a pseudo-Santa Claus. When the stork returns to correct his mistake, his fishing rod catches Sylvester instead. The last shot shows a rather peeved Sylvester in baby get-up and carriage pushed by a mouse couple. "Nothing like this ever happened on my side of the family."

FORWARD MARCH HARE

Bugs Bunny; Feb 4; LT; Directed by Charles M. Jones; Story by Michael Maltese; Animation by Ben Washam, Lloyd Vaughan, and Ken Harris; Layouts by Maurice Noble; Backgrounds by Philip DeGuard; Voice Characterization by Mel Blanc; Musical Direction by Carl W. Stalling; Orchestrations by Milt Franklyn.

Who drafted Bugs Bunny? "So they're inducting rabbits." B. Bunny gets a "Greetings" notice intended for his neighbor, B. Bonny, and most of the laughs come from the reactions of straight-laced military types to the presence of a cartoon animal in this man's army. It begins with Bugs getting a physical where, among other things, he reads an eye chart with sharp rabbit vision, right down to the microscopic "Reg. U.S. Pat. Off." (The soundtrack plays "I Only Have Eyes for You.") Most of Bugs's time goes toward unintentionally causing catastrophic frustration for his sergeant (a more sympathetic role for the construction bully in *Homeless Hare*). First, he trips his line of men with his big rabbit feet, then the colonel. Both sergeant and private are forced to drill all night as punishment. Bugs is awakened five minutes later by reveille and murders the bugler. Next day, he gets in more hot water (literally) by bathing in the colonel's helmet, "cleans and dresses" a bunch of chickens for dinner in top hats and tuxes like funny animals, and nearly kills half the camp when he hangs up a pin-up with a bomb attached. Finally, the Sergeant, having been demoted to corporal, then back to private, thanks to Bugs, asks what the bandaged bunny has against him. At last he realizes they've inducted a rabbit. Bugs pleads with the general to be assigned a patriotic service, and ends up testing bombs on an assembly line. "And just think, in thirty years I can retire."

KISS ME CAT

Marc Antony, Pussyfoot; Feb 21; LT; Directed by Charles M. Jones; Story by Michael Maltese; Animation by Lloyd Vaughan, Ken Harris, and Ben Washam; Layouts by Maurice Noble; Backgrounds by Philip DeGuard; Voice Characterization by Mel Blanc (Bea Bernaderet); Musical Direction by Carl W. Stalling.

Hearing that Pussyfoot has "got to do his job and catch mice or we'll just have to get another cat," Marc Antony, the bulldog, takes it upon himself to educate the kitten in the fundamentals of mouse-catching. First, he acts out strategy, then with cartooney drawings on a blackboard, only to learn that a mouse has co-opted the witless kitten as a beast of burden for his food-swiping missions! The bulldog shocks the mouse unconscious (with a jack-in-the-box) and plants the paralyzed rodent in the kitten's mouth. By the time Marc has dragged in the master to show how good the kitten is, the mouse has reharnessed Pussyfoot. As a distraction, the kitten does a ballet dance with a lampshade. "Very touching!" says the irate master, walloping him. To distract him again, he plays "guess who" with the master, who guesses he's Grandma Esmarelda come all the way from Duluth! Things get even tougher when the master catches Antony stuffing cheese into the mousehole, not knowing that the dog is paying ransom for the kit-napped Pussyfoot. After the cat's puss, made frightening by a magnifying mirror, scares the mouse and his whole family out, the master beams, "I always knew that cat had the makings of a champion mouser."

DUCK AMUCK

Daffy Duck; Feb. 28; MM; Dircted by Charles M. Jones; Story by Michael Maltese; Animation by Ben Washam, Ken Harris and Lloyd Vaughan; Layouts by Maurice Noble; Backgrounds by Philip DeGuard; Voice Characterization by Mel Blanc; Musical Direction by Carl W. Stalling.

"Stand back, musketeers!" swordsman Daffy cries, surrounded by Dumas-ian scenery, credits, and music. "They shall sample my blade," but within a few thrusts and touches, Daffy notices that the background behind has ended. "Hey, psst, whoever's in charge here, the scenery, where's the scenery?" A paintbrush comes across the screen and puts down a farmyard setting. Daffy leaps back into his musketeer garb, realizes it's inappropriate, and returns with overalls and hoe, then notices that the scenery has changed into a North Pole setting. "Would it be too much to ask if we could make up our minds, hmmm?"

And so it goes. After changing the setting from the Antarctic to Hawaii, a pencil comes in from off screen and redraws the shrugging Duck as a cowboy, and he tries to play his guitar but discovers there's no sound then gets the wrong sound effects. His demand for some scenery is answered by a childish empty-outline background, and he gets yellow, green, and red patterns slapped all over him when he asks the "slop-artist" for color. Daffy is erased again, then the off-screen animator re-re-draws him as a nonsensical creature with the ducks's face on a flower-headed, webfooted quadruped. "You know better than that!" Daffy yells, and this time comes back as a sailor. When the animator draws the ocean around him, Daffy splashes in, climbing out on an island in the distant background where his cries for a close-up ("A close-up, ya jerk!") result in the entire screen being blacked out except for the tiny portion around his face.

"The End" title card appears just when he cries, "Let's get this picture started." The worst is yet to come. The gate on the projector starts rolling so the screen is split in two, with a bottom Daffy and a top Daffy, who immediately start arguing with each other and are about to come to blows when the pencil erases one of them and draws a pilot's helmet and fighter plane. There is just time to register this in our brains before it crashes into a mountain. The same holds for Daffy's parachute, which is almost immediately redrawn as an anvil. Daffy, still dutifully going through the routine each background suggests, starts groggily reciting "The Village Smithy," while hammering said anvil, which itself gets redrawn into a bomb. After an explosion, Daffy yells, "All right! Enough is enough! This is the final, this is the very, very last

straw! Who's responsible for this! I demand that you show yourself! Who are you!" Pull back to reveal Bugs Bunny, seated by a live action animator's light table, admitting to the audience, "Gee, ain't I a stinker?"

A brilliant parody of virtually every cartoon convention, not only breaking the "fourth wall," but the fifth and sixth as well.

UPSWEPT HARE
Bugs Bunny, Elmer Fudd; Mar 14; MM; Directed by Robert McKimson; Story by Tedd Pierce; Animation by Charles McKimson, Herman Cohen, Rod Scribner, and Phil DeLara; Layouts by Robert Givens; Backgrounds by Richard H. Thomas; Voice Characterization by Mel Blanc; Musical Direction by Carl W. Stalling.

"What's a wabbit doing in my bathwoom?" Bugs is unwittingly transported to a plush New York penthouse when Elmer brings home a rare plant specimen, uprooting all the dirt around it, said soil containing Bugs's hole. Next morning, Bugs discovers this is not, in fact, his home and decides, because of the decor of Fudd's domicile, that this is all, in fact, a mirage. When Elmer (in beret and dressing gown) discovers this trespassing wabbit is real, he produces his rifle and fires on Bugs only to blow holes through the bottom of his pool/tub, sending the water onto an angry man-mountain of a neighbor below. Cut to Bugs amusing himself on the penthouse patio with some ballet moves. When Fudd fires on him, the wabbit makes the following sporting proposition: "If you can prove you're better than me, I'll leave." Bugs has in mind an anything-you-can-do-I-can-do-better series of contests of skills. Each thing Elmer tries gets him in trouble. Weight lifting pushes him through the floor onto his guy downstairs again, doing a William Tell has Elmer not noticing that Bugs has not only missed the apple, he's darn near killed him. A high-jump competition has Elmer plummeting off the skyscraper and onto a peanut wagon below. In the end, Bugs agrees to leave since Fudd has "proved" himself the better man, "but only because I'm a rabbit."

A PECK O' TROUBLE

Mar 28; LT; Directed by Robert McKimson; Story by Tedd Pierce; Animation by Herman Cohen, Rod Scribner, Phil DeLara, Charles McKimson; Layouts by Robert Givens; Backgrounds by Richard H. Thomas; Musical Direction by Carl W. Stalling.
Dodsworth, that pudgy pussy who so capably kidded the kitten in the previous season (sounding not unlike comic Sheldon Leonard), tries to procure a woodpecker for breakfast (close to the one in 1945's *Peck Up Your Troubles*) without stooping to physical effort. The kitten comes meowing along and Dodsworth offers to learn him "the art of boid catchin' under the tutelege of a past master of the noble art." "Your first lesson," says Dodsworth with professor's cap and school bell, "you grab that red-headed squab in that tree up there and bring him down to me." The quick succession of gags begins with the kitten falling on Dodsworth's head, pushing it into his shoulders so that his small head sits on top of his bulbous body. He flies up on a kite and brings down a stick of dynamite. A folding-and-unrolling fireman's ladder removes Dodsy's fur and crushes him. A long pole is used but the woodpecker places a convenient bottle of nitro on it. As he's about to fire the kitten on a crossbow, he warns him, "If ya don't bring him back this time, I'm gettin' me a new pupil." After sounds of a fight in the tree quiet down, he suspects the kitten has consumed his breakfast." It is just the opposite. The little one has taken his mother's advice, "If you can't beat 'em, join 'em," and with a strap-on

bill and rubber- glove comb, he joins the woodpecker in pecking out "Gnats to cats" on the side of the tree.

FOWL WEATHER

Tweety, Sylvester; Apr 4; MM; Directed by I. Freleng; Story by Warren Foster; Animation by Ken Champin, Virgil Ross, Arthur Davis, and Manuel Perez; Layouts by Hawley Pratt; Backgrounds by Irv Wyner; Voice Characterization by Mel Blanc; Musical Direction by Carl W. Stalling.
F-f-fast and f-f-funny Sylvester episode, with extra doses of charm and audacity. Farm-owner Granny, who has more than a few boards loose in her barn, warns her bulldog, Hector, "Don't let anything happen to Tweety or …" and mimics machine-gun fire with her little old lady's umbrella. The dog foils Sylvester's first attempt (dialogueless this time), which involves sneaking up on Tweety (singing "Kiss Me, Sweet") in a scarecrow disguise. Tweety says, "as long as I'm outa my cage, I might as well look around a bit," and greets the various farm animals, the moo moo cow, the dirty pig, instantly identifying a goat as the puddy in a mask. When the bird hides beneath a mother hen in the chicken coop, Sylvester gets them all to stand and salute with a patriotic theme, but when he grabs Tweety, the hens and roosters protect him like one of their own. So Sylvester tries the same thing, disguising himself as a chicken, but the tough customer head rooster ("I like you, baby! You're different!") calls his bluff and demands he lay an egg. Failing that, he's forced to "hatch" a hand grenade.

Cut to the bulldog: "Jumpin' jupiter! Da boid's gone!" Hector hears Granny's buggy approaching and visualizes Granny shooting him. Since Sylvester doesn't know where Tweety is, the dog splashes yellow paint on him, sticks him in the cage, and yells, "Sing, you buzzard!" It fools the pixilated Granny, and Tweety remarks, "If he's a birdie, dat makes me a puddy tat!"

MUSCLE TUSSLE

Daffy Duck; Apr 18; MM; Directed by Robert McKimson; Story by Tedd Pierce; Animation by Rod

Scribner, Phil De Lara, Charles McKimson, and Herman Cohen; Layouts by Robert Givens; Backgrounds by Carlos Manrique; Voice Characterization by Mel Blanc; Musical Direction by Carl W. Stalling.

On the beach, Daffy and his girlfriend are muscled-in on by a Chattanooga Charles Atlas, a hulk of a hunk from Tennessee. When Daffy is too much the scrawny, nine-pound weakling (actually, a ten-pound weakling) to fight back, the girlfriend goes off with br'er beefcake. There just happens to be a medicine show barker on this beach, and he gives Daffy, absolutely free for five dollars, a shot of Atomcol, a concoction of 10% pure tap water and 90% hot mustard which he claims will instantly build up muscles. It's a load of hooey all right, but when he gets Daffy to lift a phony 5,000 pound weight, it gives Daffy the confidence to think himself a "virile, red-blooded he-duck!" He challenges the beefy bully to a contest of strength. Every feat the big guy does Daffy tries to mimic with disastrous results, including chewing up a piece of chain, which the bully spits out as links while Daffy spits out his own shattered teeth. When the bully balances on a bottle with one finger, Daffy falls in. Finally, Daffy shows off with the "5,000-pound" barbell, the Chattanoogan tries it and hurls himself skyward, landing in such a way that he becomes a deformed dwarf. He tells Daffy and his girl, "you-all can call me Shorty!" Says the fickle female, "C'mon Daffy, I only like 'em if they're tall, dark, and gruesome, like you."

SOUTHERN FRIED RABBIT

Bugs Bunny, Yosemite Sam; May 2; MM; Directed by I. Freleng; Story by Warren Foster; Animation by Art Davis, Manuel Perez, Ken Champin, and Virgil Ross; Layouts by Hawley Pratt; Backgrounds by Irv Wyner; Voice Characterization by Mel Blanc; Musical Direction by Carl W. Stalling.

"Well, call me corn-pone, if it ain't the li'l ol' South!" The shriveled-up carrots of the north and news of a record carrot crop in Alabama have prompted Bugs to announce he's "Alabama bound." It's a long, discouraging hike ("I wonder why they put the South so far south") but once he reaches that dear old Mason-Dixon line, the land immediately becomes the lush, fertile South. But, the line is being defended by Colonel Sam of the Confederate Army, who has been ordered by General Lee not to let any Yankee cross it (when Bugs points out that the Civil War ended 90 years ago, Sam exclaims, "I'm no clock watcher!"). Sam chases the "fur bearin' carpet bagger" all around th' ol' plantation, while Bugs adds a twist of mint julep to his familiar deviltry. He disguises himself as Gen'l Brickwall Jackson and marches Sam into a deep well ("Fall in!"), cross-dresses as a Southern belle who feigns guarding the Yankee in a closet containing a cannon, then rides up to the house as one of our boys, a shell-shocked messenger bearin' the bad tidings that the Yankees are in Chattanooga. Sam rides off, and the final shot has him holding the entire N.Y. ball team at gunpoint, threatening, "The first dang Yankee what steps out of that dugout gets his haid blasted off!"

Main title theme: "Are You From Dixie?"

ANT PASTED

Elmer Fudd; May 9; LT; Directed by I. Freleng; Story by Warren Foster; Animation by Virgil Ross, Art Davis, Manuel Perez, and Ken Champin; Layouts by Hawley Pratt; Backgrounds by Irv Wyner; Effects Animation by Harry Love; Voice Characterization by Mel Blanc; Musical Direction by Carl W. Stalling.

"Oh boy, this is an ideal spot for a Fourth of July picnic!" says Elmer Fudd. "I can hardly wait to shoot off my firecwackers and wockets and woman candles!" He gets a kick out of upsetting first one little ant, then an entire colony with his firecrackers. The ants answer, "Of course, you know this means war!" The ants, all speaking in highspeed voices, prepare for World War II. Ant President Harry Truman (!) gets the ant congress to officially declare it: ants pick names out of a fish bowl; drafted ants go to ant boot camp.

248

As Elmer snoozes, the ants make off with a box of explosives and commence hurling them at Fudd. "Okay, ants," he declares, "if it's war you want, it's war you'll get!" They fire explosives with mousetraps, deposit them in his pot-helmet, and slip him a big one that he holds at arm's length, shattering his wristwatch. He drops explosives straight into the anthill, into their peri-scopes, and straight into their head-quarters through a pipe. They rubber band a bomb back into his throat. Trying to swallow enough water to extinguish it (he's got a water cooler in the middle of the woods) he explodes himself into the tank! The ants' bar-rage of missiles is hurled by suitcases and flying ants (some from *Target Snafu* and *Fighting 69 1/2*) prove too much for Elmer. He shoves his remain-ing fireworks into a wheelbarrow and runs, screaming, "You'll never take me alive!"

MUCH ADO ABOUT NUTTING

May 23; MM;. Directed by Charles M. Jones; Story by Michael Maltese; Animation by Lloyd Vaughan, Ken Harris, and Ben Washam; Layouts by Maurice Noble; Backgrounds by Philip DeGuard; Voice Characterization by Mel Blanc; Musical Direction by Carl W. Stalling; Orchestrations by Milt Franklyn.

A squirrel attempts to open a bowling-ball-sized nut he finds at a street stand and brings it home with him to his tree in the park. The little feller's methods grow increasingly elaborate as time goes on. When he can't bite into it, he tries hitting it with rocks, slamming it onto the ground, and then easing up a tree until he gets it high enough to drop it. It only sinks into the earth. He gets some tools from a nearby shed, then saws, axes, and even pneumatic drills the thing. TNT sends it into the air, but doesn't penetrate the shell. He finally goes to an impossible extreme, pushing the heavy nut up all eight zillion steps one by one of an Empire State Build-ing-sized skyscraper, and pushes it off. It lands with such force that the cars on the street bounce up and down. It remains undamaged. At the end, he

does get the thing open, but how he does it and what he finds inside is quite a surprise.

HARE TRIMMED

Bugs Bunny, Yosemite Sam; June 20; MM; Directed by I. Freleng; Story by Warren Foster; Animation by Manuel Perez, Ken Chapin, Virgil Ross, and Arthur Davis; Layouts by Hawley Pratt; Backgrounds by Irv Wyner; Voice Characterization by Mel Blanc; Musical Direction by Carl W. Stalling.

Here's an odd-ball romantic triangle, even by toon standards. Bugs and Sam are fighting each other over Granny. Neither really has purely amorous motives. Sam is interested only because he's heard that Granny has inherited 50 million dollars ("When I get my hands on that money I'll have the orphan's home torn down and I'll get rid of the police department!"). Bugs is a self-declared boy scout, anx-ious to protect Granny from snake-in-the-grass Sam, doing his good deed for the day.

Each bursts in on Granny, making verbal love to her in his own manner. Sam, brashly screams, "I want you, baby! Your eyes! Your lips! Come with me to the Casbah! We'll make beauti-ful music together!" and produces a trumpet to play a few brassy bars of "Sweet Georgia Brown." Bugs next appears at the door, duded up like a bedroom-eyed Frenchman. "Aha! I find you, my little romantic pigeon! Fly with me to ze Casbah!" and does a few laps with Granny. Bugs and Sam immediately decide to duel, Bugs stretching out the requisite ten paces so that Sam paces out into traffic. When Sam returns, Bugs fixes his wagon by disguising himself as Granny and seri-ously messing with his head. What makes it so effective is that Bugs's Granny is only a hair (make that a "hare") screwier than the genuine arti-cle, so his/her pushing pianos and the like on top of Sam seems perfectly believeable. Ultimately Bugs/Granny suggests they elope, and after taking a few things along ("everything but the kitchen sink," Sam correctly observes), we cut to the church for the last scene:

Bugs-in-drag and Sam walking up the aisle together, the wedding dress catching and revealing Bugs's rabbit legs and cotton tail and Sam running away hysterically. "Boo-hoo," sighs Bugs, "Always a bridesmaid."

THERE AUTO BE A LAW
June 6; LT; Directed by Robert McKimson; Story by Tedd Pierce; Animation by Phil DeLara, Charles McKimson, Herman Cohen, and Rod Scribner; Layouts by Robert Givens; Backgrounds by Richard H. Thomas; Voice Characterization by Mel Blanc; Musical Direction by Carl W. Stalling.
A spot-gag cartoon about cars. Automotive gags include a "horseless carriage" being whipped like a horse, a massive traffic back-up caused by a lady putting on her make-up, a hot rod beaten in a speed race by a horseless carriage, a man syphons gas and becomes revved up, and a running gag about a motorist asking a cook at a hamburger stand for directions off a cloverleaf highway. In the end, we find that the fast-food proprietor has also become lost getting off this freeway and had to open the hamburger stand to keep from starving. The motorist opens his own stand, selling mustard and pickles!

TOM TOM TOMCAT
Tweety, Sylvester; June 27; MM; Directed by I. Freleng; Story by Warren Foster; Animation by Ken Champin, Virgil Ross, Arthur Davis, and Manuel Perez; Layouts by Hawley Pratt; Backgrounds by Irv Wyner; Effects Animation by Harry Love; Voice Characterization by Mel Blanc; Musical Direction by Carl W. Stalling.
As *Little Red Rodenthood* transformed the Riding Hood routine into cat-and-mouse terms, here the Indians attacking the covered wagon and fort motif gets infused with Sylvester and Tweety albeit without the rationalization of a dream pretense. Granny and Tweety playing pioneers, singing their way across the prairie, are sighted by a tribe of Indian cats (all Sylvesters or Sylvester variants) who go into a war dance before attacking the wagon. The Sylvesters ride other cats as horses ("I taw lots of puddy tats!"). When Tweety

and Granny make it to the fort, Granny observes, "The place is deserted, we'll have to go it alone!" The odds are evened with Tweety and Granny using guns and explosives while the puddy tribe has to make do with more primitive weaponry, such as battering rams (straight into Granny's cannon) and arrows that catch a TNT stick instead of Tweety, whose accidental shot knocks a half-dozen puddies out of a tree. Chief Rain-in-the-P-P-Puss commands one Sylvester to "scalp-um old lady squaw." The cat comes out scalped himself ("Ya got any more bright ideas"?). Granny finally disguises herself as Sitting Bull to lure the cats through a tunnel into the powder room and, at their request, provides them with a match so's they can see where they are. For an appropriately imaginative ending, Tweety opens an umbrella as injun cats fall from the skies. "It's waining puddy tats!"

WILD OVER YOU
Pepe Le Pew; July 11; MM; Directed by Charles M. Jones; Story by Michael Maltese; Animation by Ken Harris, Ben Washam, and Lloyd Vaughan; Layouts by Maurice Noble; Backgrounds by Philip DeGuard; Voice Characterization by Mel Blanc; Musical Direction by Carl W. Stalling; Orchestrations by Milt Franklyn.
"All is love in fair and war." A female wildcat escapes from the zoo at the Paris Exposition of 1900, providing Pepe Le Pew not only with something a little out of the ordinary to chase (she gets a white stripe down her back, self-applied to scare off a zoo keeper and dog), but a witty setting to chase through. He thinks she is a "Keeng-sized belle femme skunk fatale." Each time Pepe gets close to her he makes with the sweet nothings and the kisses ("You are ze corned beef to me, I am ze cabbage to you"). Their embrace becomes a dizzying blur of flying claws, after which Pepe emerges not the least bit discouraged, saying, "I like eet." The amorous pursuit takes them through a fortune-teller's tent ("You are going to meet a small dark male who weel bring romance into your drab

existence"), around various wax works (she as Marie Antoinette's stole, he as Daniel Boone's coonskin) and other exhibits (suits of armor for amour and Madame Pompadour's coach). The wildcat thinks she's gotten away when she leaves the earth in a balloon, but guess who's in the basket with her? As they ascend skyward out of sight, she starts clawing again, and he tells us, "If you have not tried eet, do not knock eet!"

DUCK DODGERS IN THE 24 1/2TH CENTURY

Daffy Duck, Porky Pig, Marvin Martian; July 25, MM; Directed by Charles M. Jones; Story by Michael Maltese; Animation by Lloyd Vaughan, Ken Harris, and Ben Washam; Layouts by Maurice Noble; Backgrounds by Philip DeGuard; Effects Animation by Harry Love; Voice Characterization by Mel Blanc; Musical Direct. n by Carl W. Stalling.

"I have sent for you, Dodgers, because we are facing a crisis. The world's supply of aludium fozdex, the 'shaving cream' atom, is alarmingly low. We have reason to believe that the only remaining source is on Planet X." Can (Daffy) Duck Dodgers find Planet X? Indubitably. "Because there's no one who knows his way around outer space like DUCK DODGERS IN THE 24 1/2TH CENTURY!" After takeoff, eager space cadet Porky suggests they find Planet X by following the alphabet of Planets A, B, C. "Gad! How do *I* do it!" exclaims Daffy. No sooner does Daffy claim Planet X in the name of Earth than along comes Marvin Martian, who claims it for Mars. On the terrain of the planet, Earthling and Martian make war, delivering one heavy blow after another against the other side. Porky presents the Martian with a booby-trapped package, telling him, "Happy b-b-birthday, you thing from another world, you." In the end, both sides have bombed the planet to cantalope size. Daffy's success in claiming it causes Porky to comment, "B-b-big deal!"

An ace parody of serial, radio, and movie space operas, with Daffy announcing his full name (and the cartoon's title) in resonant boldface as with the opening of a TV show (a la *Captain Video*).

BULLY FOR BUGS

Bugs Bunny; Aug 8; LT; Directed by Charles M. Jones; Story by Michael Maltese; Animation by Ben Washam, Lloyd Vaughan, and Ken Harris; Layouts by Maurice Noble; Backgrounds by Philip DeGuard; Voice Characterization by Mel Blanc; Musical Direction by Carl W. Stalling.

Before we encounter Bugs, we get an eyeful of a magnificent bull in action as he makes short work of a matador. Bugs, looking for a carrot festival (that left turn at Albuquerque again) tunnels into the middle of the arena. Bugs becomes hostile when the bull's breath steams up his tail, and then bops him high into the air. He utters his deathly declaration, "Of course, you realize this means war" and steps back into the arena in full toreador costume, directing the bull headfirst into an anvil with his red cape, then doing a show-stopping dance (to "La Cucaracha") with the now slap-happy bull. Another bit of choreography, follows a few short gags later, this one set to the Mexican hat dance and employing as its central idea that Bugs has to walk right up to this behemoth of an animal and slap him repeatedly in the face— in tempo! Next, Bugs booby-traps his cape with a rifle, the bull accidently swallowing it, enabling him to fire bullets out of his horns. That is, until he abuses the privilege by trying explosive-headed bullets! Bugs then sends the bull out of the stadium, and, by the time he returns, Bugs has arranged for his defeat with a Rube Goldberg-routine that sets off a powder keg just as the bull flies over it. This heads the bull straight into the side of the arena.

251

Over his battered backside Bugs displays a banner that reads, "The End."

PLOP GOES THE WEASEL

Foghorn Leghorn; Aug 22; LT; Directed by Robert McKimson; Story by Tedd Pierce; Animation by Herman Cohen, Rod Scribner, Phil DeLara, and Charles McKimson; Layouts by Robert Givens; Backgrounds by Carlos Manriquez; Voice Characterization by Mel Blanc; Musical Direction by Carl W. Stalling.

"That dog is strictly G.I.—gibberin' idiot, that is!" Foghorn Leghorn hates the dog so much he's willing to sacrifice his people, the other chickens, to the weasel. "The slovenly, slippery, slobbering parasite!" is giving Foggy a hard time. Similarly, Br'er Dog doesn't hesitate to put his job in jeopardy by encouraging the weasel to bump off Foggy. Foggy gets his licks in first, lifting the chicken wire so one, two, then a whole mess o' little chicks can get out to lead the dog on a merry chase (in restoring them, he accidentally lets the weasel hold them for a second). Then, it's the dog's turn when Foghorn makes a stink about being on the wrong side of the fence. The barnyard dog stuffs him back in through a knot hole! Foggy tells the weasel of a nice juicy "red Island Rhode," which is the dog, feathers stuck on with syrup and a rubber-glove comb. The weasel drags the dog to his lair, where the creep starts peeling off his fur! The dog says, "I know where there's a big fat loudmouthed slob of a rooster, and I'll tell yez how we'll get 'em." They conspire to clobber Foggy and make him suffer the indignity of a drunk test ("I'm a teatotaller—I never touch the stuff.") All dopey from the blow, he is made to walk a straight line, right into the weasel's home. As Foggy shrieks, the dog looks as though he's about to have second thoughts. "I can't stand to hear the big shnook sufferin' like that … " He puts on earmuffs! "Ah, that's better."

CAT-TAILS FOR TWO

Speedy Gonzales; Aug 29; MM; Directed by Robert McKimson; Story by Tedd Pierce; Animation by Rod Scribner, Phil DeLara, Charles

McKimson, *and Herman Cohen; Layouts by Robert Givens; Backgrounds by Richard H. Thomas; Voice Characterization by Mel Blanc; Musical Direction by Carl W. Stalling.*

"Will ya, George, will ya, huh? Will ya let me catch mice with ya, huh, George? Will ya, huh, George?" "Awwright awwright, but ya gotta promise not to do stupid things like yer always doin'." McKimson's use of the *Mice and Men* concept, in which waterfront cats George and Benny go to board the good ship *Pancho Cucaracha* in search of Mexican food ("It gives me the heartburn and I love it"), which is to say mice. On board they discover Senor Speedy Gonzales. In his premiere appearance filmo, the golden, buck-toothed, wide-eyed leetle mouse and the fact of his being (as his calling card announces) the "fastest mouse in all Mexico" take a back seat to the cats' antics. In between tricking Benny into dropping a crate of anvils on his partner and setting up George so that he slides into a series of exploding dynamite sticks (Benny tries to cool him off with a bucket of water, but "petrol" is "a funny way to spell water"!), he's constantly commenting, "I like those fellows, all the time having foon!" George next tries rigging up a phony casino front attached to a pipe, only discovering a new way for Benny to clobber him on the head. Their final attempt consists of cramming his hole full of TNT through a pipe, not noticing that Speedy has redirected the pipe toward them. The resultant explosion sends them sailing through the smoke stack and into the drink ("I kinda lost my appetite for Mexican food!"). Speedy calls out from a porthole, "I love those fellows, they're so seely!"

A STREET CAT NAMED SYLVESTER

Tweety, Sylvester; Sept 5; LT; Directed by I. Freleng; Story by Warren Foster; Animation by Virgil Ross, Arthur Davis, Manuel Perez, and Ken Champin; Layouts by Hawley Pratt; Backgrounds by Irv Wyner; Voice Characterization by Music: Carl W. Stalling.

"Baby, it's cold outside," says the fweezing Tweety, warming himself on a cigar butt. "I gotta find a sanctuary or fweeze my wittle tail feathers off." He comes into the home of Sylvester and Granny, and now it's Sylvester who says, "I tawt I taw a Tweety Bird!" Sylvester keeps the fact of Tweety's existence from Granny, so she doesn't interfere with his chase, but Hector the bulldog protects the bird from the puddy in spite of a broken leg and Granny coming in every time he makes a noise to fill his face with putrid doggy medicine.

Sylvester conceals Tweety in a vase, and after several bits with Granny and the dog finally returns to it, reaches in, and pulls out not the bird but a dynamite stick. He hides Tweety in Hector's mouth, and when Granny shoves in the medicine, Tweety winds up swallowing it. Tweety hides in Granny's knitting box, and the cat goes in after him. When Granny resumes her knitting, Tweety begins to pull off Sylvester's fur. When the cat reknits his fur back on his catty body, he gains a multicolord patchwork lower half ("Stigmatism," says Granny, wiping her glasses). On dropping a refrigerator on Hector, Sylvester winds up with a broken leg himself, and Granny dutifully pumps the medicine into his mouth; he turns green. One factor in this is Tweety's having mixed some other chemicals into the stuff, "Dat puddy's gonna be in an awful pwedicament when that medicine starts to work."

ZIPPING ALONG

Road Runner (Velocitus Tremendus), The Coyote (Road Runner Digestus); Directed by Charles M. Jones; Story by Michael Maltese; Animation by Ken Harris, Ben Washam, and Lloyd Vaughan; Layouts by Maurice Noble; Backgrounds by Philip DeGuard; Voice Characterization by Mel Blanc; Musical Direction by Carl W. Stalling; Orchestrations by Milt Franklyn.

This is a different kind of opening, the Road Runner outpacing a speeding locomotive and then repeatedly running over and knocking down the Coyote at an intersection. Then it's the usual hysterical round of back-firing explosive devices and misdirected boulders. When using a hand grenade, the Coyote learns that it's wisest to throw the grenade and hold onto the pin, instead of the other way around. A million mousetraps go flying onto him when the bird breezes by (as they do on Sylvester in *Speedy Gonzales*. When his plan is to drop a bomb on the bird from a kite, instead of soaring he merely plummets. He chops a tree, which turns out to be a telephone pole that pulls another pole on his head. When booby-trapping with free bird seed and trying to catch the Road Runner with a magnet, he snares instead a huge TNT container. In hypnotically inducing the Road Runner to jump off a cliff (it works on a fly!), the bird's mirror makes it work in reverse. A boulder intended to catpault him up lands smack on his head. A row of rifles all turn and fire on him. Cutting the ropes on a bridge causes the mountain, not the bridge to fall. The cannon goes whooshing backward. The wrecking ball swings in a 360- degree angle back onto him. He rigs an ingenious booby-trapped door on a "house" promising free bird seed, but has to use it himself when a truck comes.

DUCK! RABBIT! DUCK!

Daffy Duck, Elmer Fudd; Oct 3; MM; Directed by Charles M. Jones; Story by Michael Maltese; Animation by Ken Harris, Ben Washam, Lloyd Vaughan, Richard Thomson, and Abe Levitow; Layouts by Maurice Noble; Backgrounds by Philip DeGuard; Voice Characterization by Mel Blanc; Musical Direction by Carl W. Stalling.

This is the talkiest of the Elmer-Bugs-Daffy hunting trilogies (after 1951's *Rabbit Fire* and 1952's *Rabbit Seasoning*). It also is one of the funniest. There's much hysterical dialogue. Bugs and Daffy try to one-up both Elmer and each other on technicalities: (a) they're operating under the assumption that it's rabbit season and (b) that Elmer having a license to hunt rabbits is hardly specific enough, Bugs insisting he needs a "fricaseeing rabbit" license. Daffy hastily prepares one, asking Bugs to spell that word, Bugs spells out "fricaseeing duck" instead. Daffy is now the one to get shot! From there, Bugs and Daffy banter about a bunch of animal names ("I guess I'm the goat ... I'm a dirty skunk ... Am I a pigeon?") each followed by a sign reading "———season open." Daffy gets shot, and his beak gets blown in yet another direction. Other bits: Bugs making Fudd think he's an angel, then disguising as a duck ("Shoot the duck!" Daffy yells). Ultimately, Elmer runs into the "Game Warden" (Bugs in another obvious disguise) who sets the record straight. It's really baseball season! As Elmer, gone loco from this news, goes off shooting a baseball, Daffy confides, "Everybody knows it's really duck season." After several dozen hunters appear and blast him, he crawls up to Bugs and tells him, "You're despicable."

EASY PECKINS

Oct 17; LT; Directed by Robert McKimson; Story by Tedd Pierce; Animation by Charles McKimson, Herman Cohen, Rod Scribner, and Phil DeLara; Layouts by Robert Givens; Backgrounds by Richard H. Thomas; Voice Characterization by Mel Blanc; Musical Direction by Carl W. Stalling.

A fox's efforts to get past the fence surrounding a poultry farm are constantly foiled by a big, tough rooster, presented in bang! bang! bang! blackout gags. It opens with the fox getting home with a bag of chicken and finding the rough rooster instead. There is a now-you-see-him-now-you-don't routine played behind a series of Dutch doors. The fox plays Paul Revere to the rooster's Redcoat. Unknowingly, he cooks a phony chicken stuffed with gun powder. The rooster scientifically breeds an explosive egg. The one extended gag is the last, wherein the fox plays up to a romance-starved (as opposed to his own "just plain starving") hen, whom he sweet talks with butchered *Romeo and Juliet* quotes ("Come On-a My House") into thinking he's a chicken equivalent of Pepe Le Pew, bouncing up and down on springs as shown from inside her window. He offers to give her precious

jewels and expensive cars ("and heavy too!"), and she falls for it. "Just give me time to pack my bag, lover boy!" The big chicken intervenes, clobbering the carnivorous Cassanova, telling the horny hen, "Clara, act your age!" He gives her a fox fur jacket anyhow. "You shouldn't have done it, George." The dopey, naked fox concurs.

CATTY CORNERED

Tweety, Sylvester; Oct 31; MM; Directed by I. Freleng; Story by Warren Foster; Animation by Arthur Davis, Manuel Perez, Ken Champin, and Virgil Ross; Layouts by Hawley Pratt; Backgrounds by Irv Wyner; Voice Characterization by Mel Blanc; Musical Direction by Carl W. Stalling.

"Tweety Bird Missing! Rare Bird Feared Kidnapped! Police authorities believe that Tweety Bird is being held for ransom by the notorious Rocky and his gang. And if you are listening, Rocky, don't hoit the boid!" Sylvester, about to dig into his usual trash meal hears about Tweety and starts after him, his concern being more carnivorous than civic. The gangsters, Rocky and Nick (not Mugsy), deliver the trademark lines, "Hey, boss, we tawt we taw a puddy tat." They send Sylvester falling into an alley. When Tweety gets into a hallway, Sylvester nobly offers to let him hide in his mouth and then in a can. Nick searches the pussy cat, and Rocky lets him think he's getting away with something ("Get your package and scram"). He's really switched a TNT stick for the boid. Next, Sylvester uses the construction site next door, but the beam that hoists him up subsequently lands on his head. Sylvester infiltrates the gang's hideout in the dumb waiter as the police arrive. The cops and reporters assume he's a hero cat. He makes the front page and is about to be decorated at City Hall by the mayor when he tries to take a bite out of Tweety instead of kissing the little birdie!

OF RICE AND HEN

Foghorn Leghorn; Nov 14; LT; Directed by Robert McKimson; Story by Warren Foster; Animation by Herman Cohen, Rod Scribner, Phil DeLara, and Charles

McKimson; Layouts by Robert Givens. Backgrounds by Richard H. Thomas; Voice Characterization by Mel Blanc; Musical Direction by Carl W. Stalling. One of the wittiest of the entire run of Foggies. The snobby barnyard hens sneer down their noses at old maid Miss Prissy (crueler than in *An Egg Scramble* or *Lovelorn Leghorn*). They won't let her touch one of their children and don't even wait before her back is turned to call her too much of a D-R-I-P to land a husband. She tries to commit suicide by leaping off a barn, but Foghorn Leghorn catches her and she immediately sets her sights on him although he has a lifelong membership in Bachelor's Anonymous, his greater passion being to roust the old hound dog while singing a lively calypso (!) number. Prissy throws herself at Foggy, dolling up in a gaucho suit (very Fredericks) and doing a seductive flamenco dance to "Lady of Spain," then trying to travel through his stomach to his heart though he insists there's a detour sign. The dog gives her the tip-off, to play hard to get (humming "Frankie and Johnny"). Her ignoring Foghorn gets him interested, and then when he sees her with another rooster (the dog in a chicken suit) he's ready to fight for her! He clobbers the interloper for beating his time and rushes Prissy off to the poultry parson, and they're pronounced "rooster and hen." Says Foggy, "I won, I won!" When it all sinks in, "Hey, there must've been some way I coulda lost!"

CAT'S AWEIGH

Sylvester, Junior, Hippety Hopper; Nov 28; MM; Directed by Robert McKimson; Story by Tedd Pierce; Animation by Phil DeLara, Charles McKimson, Herman Cohen, and Rod Scribner; Layouts by Robert Givens; Backgrounds by Richard H. Thomas; Voice Characterization by Mel Blanc; Musical Direction by Carl W. Stalling.
Sylvester the freeloader and Junior, as ship's cats. Sylvester trying to goof off on the pretence that "You're a little cat so you take care of the little mice. I'm a big cat, so I take care of big ones, if any come along. Fair enough?" In the hold, a little mouse runs into a cage marked, "Baby Kangaroo," and Junior unknowingly releases Hippety Hopper, who looks like a "great giant mouse," and we're off to the races again. Sylvester tries rushing the kangaroo with Harpo Marx-style fisticuffs, but gets tossed out so he can exchange some witty repartee with Junior ("Did you give him his just desserts, Father?" "No. He doesn't like desserts!"). Then Sylvester changes his tune: "Look, Son, there's a whole mess of little mice, and only one big one. So, it's only fair for me to round up the little ones and you take care of the big one." Junior enters the hold cautiously and realizes Hippety is mimicking his actions. He tricks Hippety back into his cage. As he promised ("If I gotta, I gotta") Sylvester pursues a little mouse, telling Junior "No matter what you hear, don't open this door!" Upon running into a ferocious creature in the next room, Sylvester screams for Junior to open the door. As the beast throws Sylvester into the steel walls and makes Sylvester imprints thereupon, Junior observes, "That's what makes me proud of my Pop. Wherever he goes, he always makes a good impression."

ROBOT RABBIT

Bugs Bunny, Elmer Fudd; Dec 12; LT; Directed by I. Freleng; Story by Warren Foster; Animation by Virgil Ross, Arthur Avis, Manuel Perez, and Ken Champin; Layouts by Hawley Pratt; Backgrounds by Irv Wyner; Voice Characterization by Mel Blanc; Musical Direction by Carl W. Stalling.
Farmer Fudd, peeved at carrot-thief Bugs, who not only has the temerity to loot his carrot patch but intrudes on his vocalizing, becomes more incensed when the business-as-usual Bunny fools him into thinking he's kicked the bucket. "This is the wast stwaw, wabbit!" Fudd says, phoning the ACME Pest Control service for their "ewectwonic pest contwoller with a wobot bwain," which Fudd programs with an illustration of the pest in question, commanding it, "Go get that wong-eared wascal, Mr. Wobot!" When Bugs realizes the "fugitive from a Stanley

Steamer" is going to cause him "no end of trouble" (it actually lands a mechanical punch on the rabbit and extracts him from his underground sanctuary), Bugs gets the "cigarette machine" to rust by chasing it under Fudd's rotating water sprinkler. He then unveils his latest drag variation, an antique stove, with lipstick and bucket-head turning him into a robotess, exciting the male of the species, who presents him with a box of assorted nuts (metal ones) whilst Bugs throws a monkey wrench into his machinery. Finally, Bugs gets "old tin pants" to chase him through a piled-river on a construction site. Fudd wonders aloud how his robot is making out and Bugs answers his question with a bucket of bolts. "You know, someday these scientists are gonna invent something that will outsmart a rabbit."

PUNCH TRUNK
Dec 19; LT; Directed by Charles M. Jones; Story by Michael Maltese; Animation by Lloyd Vaughan, Ken Harris, and Ben Washam; Layouts by Maurice Noble; Backgrounds by Philip DeGuard; Voice Characterization by Mel Blanc; Musical Direction by Carl W. Stalling.
"The whole incredible thing started on a fine spring morning at the foot of Canal Street. The S. S. *Michael Maltese* was unloading a cargo of tropical fruit at Pier 38, when suddenly, out of a stalk of bananas, *it* came, a bull elephant only five inches tall." Rather than gags per se, most of the humor derives from the funny faces of people reacting to the sight of the puny elephant in the silliest places. For instance, in a bird bath. When the owner calls the police they haul him off as a kook; a woman is hanging her laundry when he dives in her washing machine; a guy who's just bought new glasses (to the accompaniment of "I Only Have Eyes for You") sees him a little girl and her mother encounter the elephant in their doll house, a drunk spots him and isn't fazed but complains that he's late; full-sized circus elephants do a take and react as if he were a mouse; a psychiatrist lies on his own couch and tells his own life story; a

crowd of people flee to the top of a flagpole on a skyscraper. Headlines announce, "Mass Hallucination Grips City," "Hundreds Claim to Have Seen Tiny Elephant," "Picayune Pachyderm Panics Populace." A noted scientist goes on TV to explain the "mythical elephant is simply a product of our troubled times," and the beastette makes off with his microphone! Says the announcer, "The opinions of this speaker do not necessarily reflect those of this station."

1954

DOG POUNDED
Tweety, Sylvester; Jan 2; LT; Directed by I. Freleng; Story by Warren Foster; Animation by Manuel Perez, Ken Champin, and Arthur Davis; Layouts by Hawley Pratt; Backgrounds by Irv Wyner; Voice Characterization by Mel Blanc; Musical Direction by Carl W. Stalling.
A very funny series of blackout gags with Tweety in a nest in the middle of the city dog pound where hundreds of vicious bulldog Tweetie-protectors are just waiting for Sylvester to try and cross their yard so they can make mince-meat out of him. Freleng and Foster cram in more gag sequences. A few highlights are Sylvester's walk across a tight rope holding an umbrella for balance, the dogs collectively blowing a wind of doggie-breath at him; disguising himself in a dog suit, the dog catcher putting him right back in the pound (Blanc voicing Sylvester as a dog is terrific: like Jimmy Stewart imitating John Wayne). Sylvester gets the idea of mass hypnotism to knock out the pooches, but Tweety tricks him into blurting out the secret of how to restore them to normal. Tip-toeing through the apparently empty yard, and climbing Tweety's tree. Sylvester discovers the bulldogs all sitting on various branches. Trying to swing through the pound Sylvester has all the dogs jumping on the swing with him (uninvited). Sylvester manages at last to scare them all away with a phoney skunk stripe painted down his back, but just as he is grabbing Tweety, Pepe Le Pew, out of

nowhere, arrives to make love to him.

I GOPHER YOU

Goofy Gophers; Jan 30; MM; Directed by I. Freleng; Story by Warren Foster; Animation by Ken Champin, Virgil Ross, Arthur Davis, and Manuel Perez; Layouts by Hawley Pratt; Backgrounds by Irv Wyner; Voice Characterization by Mel Blanc; Musical Direction by Milt Franklyn.

The Goofy Gophers (in their best 50s flick), voiced by Blanc and Stan Freberg, are about to harvest their ripe-looking vegetables when vandals confiscate the produce and truck it off to a food-processing plant. Following, they find the factory a "veritable paradise" for veggie lovers. They look high and low for their missing goods, intercut with some very good machinery gags, one machine dabbing talcum on some hen fruit and labeling the results "powdered" eggs, mushrooms being pushed off steaks and into little cans. One gopher gets accidentally bottle-capped, and, in trying to toss tomatoes off a conveyor belt, gets canned so his colleague has to open about a thousand cans before he finds him ("I was in the first can, you started from the wrong end!"). Working independently, one gopher walks into a pickle vat and gets soused, thereafter blundering through a succession of dangerous machines with blades and piledrivers and the like. A conveyor belt carries him into the dehydration unit, packing him up with various foodstuffs, an apple in his mouth as part of a just-add-water dinner for six. The gophers decide to take home their vegetables dehydrated, and stuff their tunnels full of the little packages. "If we had a little water we could have dinner," says one. "Allow me to get the water," says the other. Unfortunately, a whole stream of the stuff gushes into the tunnel and soon the field explodes with produce. "You know, we're going to have a terrible time getting all this food back into the packages."

FELINE FRAME-UP

Marc Antony, Pussyfoot, Claude Cat; Feb 13; LT; Directed by Charles M. Jones; Story by Michael Maltese; Animation by Richard Thompson and Abe Levitow; Layouts by Maurice Noble; Backgrounds by Phil DeGuard; Voice Characterization by Mel Blanc; Musical Direction by Carl W. Stalling.*

Marc Antony again risks embarrassment to his bulldog masculinity to protect his dear, helpless baby kitten Pussyfoot from his genuinely evil adversary, Claude Cat. Claude is a rival for the master's attention (and the soft pillows), so Claude frames the big lug, making it look like Marc has consumed the kitten. Marc is thrown out. Claude then taunts the exiled Marc with images of kitten abuse, the bulldog finding a way to get at him from the porch by tossing a small but effective lasso from the mail slot (and whacking Claude's back against the door) and slamming down on an outside floorboard which continues under Claude inside. Some schemes backfire: a miscalculation on the spot to saw through the floorboard brings down the master (whose face is on-screen for once) instead of Claude, as does luring Claude to the window with phony snow (in July). Claude next sees a balloon inflating under the door, which rises and lifts the latch, Marc rushing in and pummeling him till the cat signs a confession. After Claude restores Pussyfoot to the pillow, he gets kicked out in front of an oncoming streetcar. "Just one of those days, I guess," concludes the clobbered Claude.

CAPTAIN HAREBLOWER

Bugs Bunny, Yosemite Sam; Feb 16; LT; Directed by I. Freleng; Story by Warren Foster; Animation by Manuel Perez, Ken Champin, Virgil Ross, and Art Davis; Layouts by Hawley Pratt; Backgrounds by Irv Wyner; Voice Characterization by Mel Blanc; Musical Direction by Carl W. Stalling.

Pirate Sam, terror of the Main, has reputation enough to frighten the entire crew of an "unprotected" ship, save Bugs Bunny. "Surrender, rabbit!" commands Sam, "I've got ya out-numbered one to one!" But Bugs has "never hoid of the woid! So you'll have to try to take this ship!" We're talking *lots* of explosions in the face here, in rapid-fire succession. Sam gets blown up real good. Bugs's ship slowly inches toward Sam's, coming alongside Sam's price-lessly expressive face and letting him have it. Sam yells, "Two can play that game," and gets another cannon! Sam swings himself onto Bugs's ship and goes straight into a big cannon. Sam sends over a powderkeg on a tiny sail, which Bugs blows back with an electric fan. Sam swims over with a bomb (that stays lit underwater) and gets chewed by a huge fish. Sam chases Bugs off the mast and Bugs lands in the sea, Sam on a rock. We close with a nonchalance bit (*Bugs Bunny Rides Again, Hare Lift*) whereby Bugs calmly tosses lit matches into Sam's powder room and Sam sweats like a pig to out-wait his unflappable foe. Bugs doesn't mind when Sam does the same to his ship because he thinks the only powder in his powder room is talcum. When it goes kablooey, he comments, "I could be wrong, ya know!"

WILD WIFE
Feb 20; MM; Directed by Robert McKimson; Story by Tedd Pierce; Animation by Rod Scribner, Phil DeLara, Charles McKimson, and Herman Cohen; Layouts by Robert Givens; Backgrounds by Richard H. Thomas; Voice Characterization by Mel Blanc; Musical Direction by Carl W. Stalling.
"Oh, you women, with all the time in the world on your hands you never find time to get anything done!" An unli-berated housewife (Bernaderet) tries to explain her problems to her male chau-vinist pig husband (Blanc), by describ-ing her long, hard day. After frantically making breakfast for her unapprecia-tive family (yowling, awful kids, hus-band ignoring her) at six a.m., she tries to clean with a counterproductive vac-uum he bought her for their anniver-sary. Hubby has given her checks to deposit at the bank, but she gets stuck behind not one but two old ladies mak-ing enormous deposits entirely in pen-nies. She then donates a pint at the Red Cross Blood bank (behind one Casper J. Fragile, who's trying to make

a withdrawal!). She buys a pair of socks for her better half at Lacy's ("and a few little things for myself"—boxes and boxes!) and navigates her packages to a lunch counter where she guzzles gallons of chocolate malt. At the beauty parlor, she has to run out in curlers and mudpack to refeed the parking meter. What's worse, public works installs a fire hydrant next to her car! "And that's all you did with your time all day?" the unsympathetic husband demands? "No dear, as a matter of fact, I bought you a little present!" It is a rolling pin with which she summarily kayoes him.
Theme: "Can't We Talk It Over."

NO BARKING
Feb 27; MM; Directed By Charles M. Jones; Story by Michael Maltese; Animation by Ken Harris; Layouts by Maurice Noble; Backgrounds by Philip DeGuard; Voice Characterization by Mel Blanc; Musical Direction by Carl W. Stalling. Orchestrations by Milt Franklyn.
The climax of the Frisky puppy trio and one of Jones's mini-masterpieces: nervous Claude Cat looking for some-thing to eat, is perpetually interrupted and annoyed by Frisky's inopportune barking spasms, which send him head-ing skyward. With no people around to supply framing dialogue, Jones relies exclusively on the studio's great anima-tor, Ken Harris, to do the whole car-toon. Claude's a junkyard alley cat forced by other birds who drop a brick on his head, to give up a bird that he swallowed. He can't shake Frisky, who sends him leaping when he tries to dig up the pup's coveted bone. The pup plays with a shoe that, naturally, flies into Claude's face, A chase through a tunnel ends in the cat flying out of a manhole. The next yelp sends Claude into an oncoming elevated train. Frisky does a precocious pantomime perform-ance with a mirror, a flea, and a rope. They then chase each other through a lumberyard. Claude starts to ease up a tree toward a nest, but a Frisky bark sends him flying past its resident, Tweety Bird, who says, "I tawt I taw a puddy tat." Finally, Claude catches the

pup and silences his barks with a gag, but a huge bulldog charges, and his bark sends the cat straight up to the bottom of a plane flying off into the horizon. Says Tweety, "I did, I did taw a puddy tat."

Theme: "Little Dog Gone."

BUGS AND THUGS

Bugs Bunny; Mar 2; LT; Directed by I. Freleng; Story by Warren Foster; Animation by Manuel Perez, Ken Champin, Virgil Ross and Art Davis; Layouts by Hawley Pratt; Backgrounds by Irv Wyner; Voice Characterization by Mel Blanc; Musical Direction by Milt Franklyn.

Sophisticated urbanite Bugs, remarking on how much safer he is in the city than the country during hunting season, withdraws a few carrots from his bank and then calls a cab that he doesn't realize is actually the getaway vehicle for bank robbers Rocky and Mugsy. They take him for a ride because he "knows too much" (among other things, that Carson City is the capitol of Nevada). When Rocky orders the chatty rabbit to shut up, he soon alters that order to "Shut up shuttin' up!" The ride to the hangout includes a stop at a gas station, where Bugs phones the cops and pulls one through the phone system when Mugsy heaves him away. Next is an episode in which Bugs directs the car into an oncoming train, and, in punishment, is forced to serve as the vehicle's fourth wheel. At the hideout, Bugs convinces Mugsy that when Rocky said to "let him have it," he meant to *give* him the gun. Bugs makes noises like cops approaching and shoves the hoods in the oven, proceeding to demonstrate what he would never do to the stove if his pal Rocky were in there (like turning on the gas and lighting it!). Rocky and Mugsy soon beg the real cops to arrest them, and the final shot has Bugs in Sherlock Holmes suit answering the phone: "Bugs Bunny, private eyeball, thugs thwarted, arsonists arrested, bandits booked, forgers found, conterfeiters caught, and chiselers chiseled!"

CAT'S BAH

Pepe Le Pew; Mar 20; LT; Directed by

Charles M. Jones; Story by Michael Maltese; Animation by Ken Harris, Ben Washam, Abe Levitow, Richard Thompson, and Lloyd Vaughan; Layouts by Maurice Noble; Backgrounds by Philip DeGuard; Voice Characterization Mel Blanc; Musical Direction by Carl W. Stalling.

The fourth Le Moko epic (after *Pepe le Moko, Algiers* and *Casbah*), and Le Pew's most direct homage to Boyer in the film that inspired his name. "You are here to interview me about ze greatest love of my life, yes?" says Pepe to the camera. "Come with me to the Casbah, a very long time ago, when I had set up Bachelor's Quarters and was putting the finishing touches to my toilette before setting forth in search of amorous adventure."

The object of said search is a "belle americaine touriste femme skunk," actually the victim of dripping white paint, whom he "liberates" from her lady owner. "Just theenk, radiant flower, you do not have to come weeth me to ze Casbah, we are already here!" She hides in one of a hundred ceramic jugs placed on the seat of a camel built for two (who has learned to put up with everything). Out of a nearby basket comes Pepe, making like a snake ("and you have charmed me"), into Omar Tent's (where Pepe misquotes the *Rubiyat*). Funniest of all, into a Rick's-inspired cafe that affords Pepe the opportunity to spoonerize "As Time Goes By" in his phony French. After the flashback, the cartoon ends on a kinky note: "Now we are inseparable," says Pepe, meaning literally ball and chain. "Are we not, darling?" She nods in agreement, but immediately gets to work on the chain with a hacksaw!

DESIGN FOR LEAVING

Daffy Duck, Elmer Fudd; Mar 27; LT; Directed by Robert McKimson; Story by Tedd Pierce; Animation by Phil DeLara, Charles McKimson, Herman Cohen, and Rod Scribner; Layouts by Robert Givens; Backgrounds by Richard H. Thomas; Voice Characterization by Mel Blanc; Musical Direction by Carl W. Stalling.

Daffy's again selling something, or,

rather, giving it away, he claims. It is a complete line of supermodern household appliances (for ten days free trial). Barging in on Fudd, who is on his way to work, Daffy tells him all about his line and about having the place technologically renovated with one work-saving doodad after another. For instance, the relaxing chair that shakes him up, the automatic robot fireman that extinguishes his cigar the instant he lights it, a garbage disposal under the sink is a sloppy hog, the automatic wall cleaner that at first washes the wallpaper pattern off (and then the actual walls), and, to save him the trouble of looking at dirty windows, a robot that comes out and lays a brick wall in front of them. Most imaginative, what replaces the old-fashioned stairs isn't an elevator but the whole second story being pulled down, bringing "the upstairs downstairs" and thereby crushing the funiture and possessions on that level. In the wind-up, the thoroughly disgruntled Fudd pushes the buttons on the big panel of controls, choosing two devices Daffy would rather wish he didn't, the first being a "pushbutton salesman ejector" robot, which gets rid of Daffy, the other a red button he was warned again and again not to touch. It's the "In Case of Tidal Wave" button, and it lifts the entire house high into the air, where Daffy (in a helicopter) offers to sell him the blue button that'll fix everything.

BELL HOPPY

Sylvester, Hippety Hopper; Apr 17; MM; Directed by Robert McKimson; Story by Tedd Pierce; Animation by Charles McKimson, Herman Cohen, Rod Scribner, and Phil DeLara; Layouts by Robert Givens; Backgrounds by Richard H. Thomas; Voice Characterization by Mel Blanc; Musical Direction by Carl W. Stalling.
No Junior in this one, but here's a whole gang of alley cats trying to make a chump out of Sylvester with Hippety hopping into the middle of it. The gang is the "Loyal Order of Alley Cats Mouse and Chowder Club" (a *Honeymooners*-type lodge), and Sylvester does so want to be a member but keeps

getting the black ball. To give Sylvester a hard time, the gang offers to initiate him into the club if he can catch a big mouse and put a cowbell around its neck (there's a switch!). The Grand Poo-Bah instructs the lodge members, "When yez hear the bell, we'll gang up on the monster." As it happens, Hippety has just hopped away from a city zoo truck and runs smack into Sylvester as he's looking for "some really tremendous mouse." Hoppy is less than eager to be belled, but what happens is that Sylvester's bell keeps ringing and the gang keeps jumping him. Sylvester gets an idea: "I can't seem to overcome him with my muscles, so I'll have to resort to a little ch-ch-chicanery." With a mirror trick, he gets Hoppy to slip the bell on, and announces this to the gang. In the meantime, Hoppy has been caught by the zoo-keeper, and the cats unwittingly "jump" an oncoming truck!

NO PARKING HARE

Bugs Bunny; May 1; LT; Directed by Robert McKimson; Story by Sid Marcus; Animation by Herman Cohen, Rod Scribner, Phil DeLara, and Charles McKimson; Layouts by Robert Givens; Backgrounds by Richard H. Thomas; Voice Characterization by Mel Blanc; Musical Direction by Carl W. Stalling.
The Bugs versus construction worker theme of HOMELESS HARE revived, with the big cruel lummox trying to blast Bugs out of his rabbit hole so that he can build a freeway, the rabbit refusing to move because, "A man's house is his castle!" The big bruiser begins by circling the hole with explosives and setting them off, leaving a long tubular patch of earth with Bugs's hole perfectly preserved ("I hear ya knockin', but ya can't come in"). From that point on he tries to penetrate and demolish Bugs's home. When he climbs a ladder, Bugs saws it in two, and he lands in wet cement. When he tries to crush it with a 60-ton weight, Bugs poses as a foreman who gives him directions, turning the weight directly above the crewman's crane. When he tries sawing through, Bugs (reading "The Raven") steers it

into an electrical wire, giving him an explosive shock. Lastly, he tries dumping cement, which helps Bugs to insure that nothing will destroy his hole. A newspaper announces, "City Compromises with Rabbit. Freeway Goes Thru." The last shot shows a modern freeway *around* Bugs's hole, the rabbit beaming. "The sanctity of the American home must be presoived."

DR. JERKYL'S HIDE

Sylvester, Spike and Chester; May 8; LT; Directed by I. Freleng; Story by Warren Foster; Animation by Arthur Davis, Manuel Perez, Ken Champin, and Virgil Ross; Layouts by Hawley Pratt; Backgrounds by Irv Wyner; Voice Characterization by Mel Blanc; Musical Direction by Carl W. Stalling.

"I say, we're jolly chums, aren't we, Alfie, ol' boy, through thick and thin and all that sort of rot." Spike and Chester as cockney canines and Sylvester really turning into the terror. Here, "Alfie" acts even more cruelly with his adoring sidekick than he did as "Spike" in the previous film, until Chester suggests, "We'll have a jolly time thrashing [a] cat, eh wot, gov'nor?"

They wake the slumbering Sylvester, and he flees into the lab of one Dr. Jerkyl. There, thirsty and out of breath, the cat consumes some of the infamous Hyde formula. Alfie goes in to the lab thinking he'll have an easy time pulverizing the puddy, Instead, he shakes white with fear at the sight of the Sylvester/Hyde monster. When the other dog looks all he sees is the retransformed Sylvester ("You're spoofing, Alf!"). Again, as the monster, the cat scratches Alf to little pieces, then

turns back to Sylvester before the little dog sees him. Chester pushes Alf back in for his own good. When Alf sees Sylvester bolting out the window he thinks he can win back his reputation with phony fight noises. A fly gets a drop of the Hyde juice and turns into a behemoth that pummels Alf. The last scene has Alf sucking up to the little dog. "Chester's me hero cuz he's so brave and strong."

CLAWS FOR ALARM

Porky Pig, Sylvester; May 22; MM; Directed by Charles M. Jones; Story by Michael Maltese; Animation by Lloyd Vaughan, Ken Harris, Ben Washam, Abe Levitow, and Richard Thompson; Layouts by Maurice Noble; Backgrounds by Philip DeGuard; Voice Characterization by Mel Blanc; Musical Direction by Carl W. Stalling.

"This looks like a perfectly splendid place to spend the night, doesn't it, Sylvester?" asks Porky. "It's so quaint and picturesque." The naive pig attributes the lack of people on the streets and in the lobby to everyone's being asleep. The frightened feline realizes that this is a haunted hotel in the middle of a ghost town! Even as the two walk up the steps, murderous mice eyes are upon them, and strange things begin to happen at once. Porky signs the register and a noose issues from a moose, lowering slowly from a mounted head, which then follows Porky along the ground with a rifle. The pig attributes the commotion to Sylvester's terrified tomfoolery ("You psychopathic old pussycat, you!"). Another rope is lowered around his neck, Sylvester cuts it, and Porky comes to only to find the cat holding the noose in one hand and a razor in the other! A killer mouse swings on a rope Tarzan-style, holding a knife, while others gang up to make like a sheeted ghost. More fire a rifle through a hole in the wall. Porky merely inquires if there's any insanity in Sylvester's family (never getting wise as he did in *Scaredy Cat*). The bloodshot-eyed Sylvester has to guard Porky with a rifle all night, and when the rested pig wakes up announcing that they may stay for a week the petrified pussycat clobbers him, and the two drive away (with little killer eyes appearing behind the dashboard).

LITTLE BOY BOO
Foghorn Leghorn; June 5; LT; Directed by Robert KcKimson; Story by Tedd Pierce; Animation by Herman Cohen, Rod Scribner, Phil DeLara, and Charles McKimson; Layouts by Robert Givens; Backgrounds by Richard H. Thomas; Voice Characterization by Mel Blanc; Musical Direction by Carl W. Stalling.
Foghorn Leghorn, fearful of spending another winter in his chilly shack, spies the Widow Hen's "cozy little roost" and decides, "Maybe I've been a bachelor too long." Winning over the man-hungry widow takes only a two-second candy-and-flowers courtship and telling her, "I need your love to keep me warm." Her one stipulation is that he prove he'd make a good father to her son Junior (another one of those McKimson characters with an enormous head and a teeny-weeny body). Foghorn learns that Junior is the silent, intellectual type, who prefers ponderous tomes like "Splitting the Fourth Dimension" to kid stuff. The big chicken shows him a bevy of peanut-gallery games the boy has never even seen before, and this expressionless Einstein effortlessy masters them all. They fold paper airplanes, and the kid origamis one that not only flies better, it shoots Foggy's plane down! The wildest bit is a game of hide and seek, where the Leghorn hides in a feedbox and the kid uses a slide rule to find him. Finally, the big dumb cluck messes with the kiddie's chemicals, blows himself up, and tells the widow that the deal's off. Now he's got his bandages to keep himself warm.

DEVIL MAY HARE
Bugs Bunny, Tasmanian Devil; June 19; LT; Directed by Robert McKimson; Story by Sid Marcus; Animation by Herman Cohen, Rod Scribner, Phil DeLara, and Charles McKimson; Layouts by Robert Givens; Backgrounds by Richard H. Thomas; Voice Characterization by Mel Blanc; Musical Direction by Carl W. Stalling.
A stampede of animals fleeing from the Tasmanian Devil runs past Bugs's hole. While Bugs looks up the beast in his encyclopedia, it enters his home and makes ready to devour our hero. Bugs stalls by offering to help find a menagerie of creatures to consume. First, they dig for groundhogs. Bugs gets him covered with dirt. It does no good as he instantly reappears and growls, "What for you bury me in the cold, cold ground?" Bugs constructs a chicken for the Devil out of bubble gum and bicarbonate of soda (so he hiccups a huge bubble), then a little pig out of a life raft (which inflates within the devil). Bugs phones in a personal ad to the *Tasmanian Post Dispatch*: "Lonely Tasmanian Devil would like to meet lonely lady Devil. Object: Matrimony." A plane instantly lands carrying a she-devil in a bridal veil. And Rabbi Bugs marries them with a ceremony of Devil snarl gibberish. "All the world loves a lover," says Bugs after the newlyweds fly off. "But in this case we'll make an exception."

MUZZLE TOUGH
Tweety, Sylvester; June 26; MM; Directed by I. Freleng; Story by Warren Foster; Animation by Ken Champin, Virgil Ross, Arthur Davis, and Manuel Perez; Layouts by Hawley Pratt; Backgrounds by Irv Wyner; Voice Characterization by Mel Blanc; Musical Direction by Carl W. Stalling.
The activity of Granny moving into a city brownstone with her pets Tweety and the bulldog supplies the backdrop for this Tweety chase, with Sylvester scarcely believing his eyes when he sees the movers carrying in the birdcage. Sylvester tries sneaking in disguising himself as a lamp, and then as one of the moving men. Tweety directs him as he carries a piano up the stairs ("My but you're stwong") and out the attic window, leaving him with piano keyboard teeth ("that last step was a wuwu"). Next the cat puts on a bear-skin rug, which Tweety digs ("Oh, wook! A cute wittle teddy-bear coming to pway wiff me!") and Granny shoots. To get past the dog, the cat dons a female dog costume, swiveling his hips

to "It Had to Be You." Before he can mallet the real dog, he's netted by the dogcatcher and carried off. Sylvester takes off his suit to show the catcher he's really a cat. This gets an immediate rise of the other dogs in the van!

THE OILY AMERICAN

July 10; MM; Directed by Robert McKimson; Story by Sid Marcus; Animation by Phil DeLara, Charles McKimson, Herman Cohen, and Rod Scribner; Layouts by Robert Givens; Backgrounds by Richard H. Thomas; Voice Characterization by Mel Blanc; Musical Direction by Carl W. Stalling.
There's no particular pleasure in watching the chump get it in the end or in the basic premise of a wealthy Indian, but there is imagination in this and it certainly is different. The oil-rich Moe Hican and his erudite English valet/caddy are in the mansion, ready to go hunting. The mansion is elaborately rigged with a combination Euro-American uppercrust and Hollywood Indian incongraphy. It has a stream up which they travel in a canoe through the indoor "forest room" and under the grand piano. Today's prey is a moose, and though he looks like a big buck of a beast, when they let him loose he's a mere midget moose. However, he's quite capable of fending for himself. When the Injun sounds a moose call, the moose answers with an Indian love call horn that gets the Injun's heart pounding. The midget then sets fire to the Indian's behind. The moose also causes most of the Injun's weapons to backfire on the butler, who keeps returning them, saying something along the lines of "Your arrow, sir" and "Your Thomas-Hawk [formal for tommyhawk] Sir," and finally handing in his resignation. Moe ultimately chases the moose outside, accidentally downing the butler's helicopter and getting a good spanking.

BEWITCHED BUNNY

Bugs Bunny; July 24; LT; Directed by Charles M. Jones; Story by Michael Maltese; Animation by Lloyd Vaughan, Ken Harris, and Ben Washam; Layouts by Maurice Noble; Backgrounds by Philip DeGuard; Voice Characterization by Mel Blanc; Musical Direction by Carl W. Stalling.
"This looks like a job for the Masked Avenger," says Bugs, "but since he ain't around, I guess I'll have to take care of it meself!" The job is rescuing the Teutonic Toddlers, Gretel and Hansel, from wicked Witch Hazel (June Foray), whose motherly impulses, strong as they are, do not cancel with her cannibalistic (and carnivorous) cravings. Bugs infiltrates the witch's cottage disguised as a bespectacled truant officer. He alerts the chubby cherubs that she is indeed a witch who means to eat them for her supper. They bolt, but the witch doesn't let Bugs get away so easily, chasing him all over her bizarre bungalow (dig the crazy fish-skeleton motif). She dopes a carrot with sleeping potion, and the two parody a mother-child relationship. The rabbit is awakened by the prince-hero looking for Snow White, having intruded on the story of "Hansel and Gretel" by accident. Trapped in a dead-end hallway, Bugs hurls a magic powder he finds in a case marked, "In case of emergency, break glass." Hazel is transformed into an inviting femme bunny. "Going my way?" inquires make-out man Bugs, and the two stroll off goo-goo-eyed to "It had to be you."

SATAN'S WAITIN'

Tweety, Sylvester; Aug 7; LT; Directed by I. Freleng; Story by Warren Foster; Animation by Virgil Ross, Arthur Davis, Manuel Perez, and Ken Champin; Layouts by Hawley Pratt; Backgrounds by Irv Wyner; Voice Characterization by Mel Blanc; Musical Direction by Carl W. Stalling.
In the course of chasing Tweety all over the city's telephone wires and rooftops, Sylvester falls off a building—and *dies*! His ghostly spirit goes to Hades and awaits his other eight lives. A satanic bulldog goads Sylvester into losing his other lives, encouraging him to chase the canary into the most violent situations.

Chasing Tweety through a road construction site, Sylvester loses life #2 getting flattened by a steamroller. Chasing the bird into an amusement park, the cat is scared to death in the "Fun House." Running through a shooting gallery causes the cat to lose four more lives. Sylvester loses life #8 on a roller coaster.

Sylvester decides to be more careful, stops chasing Tweety, and tries to protect his last life by camping out in a bank vault. That night, two crooks use nitroglycerin to blow the vault open, killing themselves and Sylvester!

STOP, LOOK AND HASTEN
The Coyote (Eatibus Anythingus) and the Road Runner (Hot Roddicus Supersonicus); Directed by Charles M. Jones; Story by Michael Maltese; Animation by Abe Levitow, and Richard Thompson. Effects Animation by Harry Love; Layouts by Maurice Noble; Backgrounds by Philip DeGuard; Musical Direction by Carl W. Stalling.
Reduced to eating flies and licking tin cans, the Coyote gets tramped on by the Road Runner and automatically envisions him as a running roast. He employs a series of devices to capture the Road Runner: The boulder with a string attached falls on him; the noose on the road snares a passing truck; the Burmese tiger trap catches a Burmese tiger ("Surprisibus! Surprisibus!"); the steel wall set to spring up into the Road Runner just doesn't work; when he chases the bird across a series of train tunnels he runs up against the inevitable train (which fails to "Stop! In the name of humanity"); a powderkeg he intends to place under the road goes off while he's still laying it; a motorcycle goes right into a telephone pole (which happens so quickly the camera doesn't even follow it); he saws off the part of a bridge that the bird is standing on, and the whole thing falls except that little circle; a family-sized box of ACME Triple Strength Fortified Leg Muscle Vitamins give him brawny legs and speed to burn up the road (literally), but he rush right back into the steel wall! Clever ending: the Road Runner's smoke spells out, "That's all Folks," which fades to the end title.

YANKEE DOODLE BUGS
Bugs Bunny; Aug 28; LT; Directed by I.

Freleng; Story by Warren Foster; Animation by Art Davis, Manuel Perez, and Virgil Ross; Layouts by Hawley Pratt; Backgrounds by Irv Wyner; Voice Characterization by Mel Blanc; Musical Direction by Milt Franklyn.*
"Know American history? Why, we rabbits have *made* American history!" Bugs gives his little nephew Clyde pointers on early Americana, back when the Statue of Liberty was just a little goil and the Dutch bought Manhattan from the Indians for a song (pun) to the Revolutionary War. Bugs writes himself into about half of the events: helping Ben Franklyn to discover electricty, a blow on the head resulting in stars that inspire Betsy Ross, and running the outboard for George Washington's Delaware crossing. Other bits include George Washington getting drafted and telling his wife, Martha, she has to run the candy store while he's off to fight, and the frost-bitten troops of Valley Forge blasting their Good Humor man. One real ringer stands out, the looney king of England happily spreading tacks on the colonists' tea (told they are carpet tacks, he chortles, "Well, they're tea tax now!"). Later, when Bugs asks Clyde how he made out in history class at school, the little rabbit takes out a dunce cap and asks, "Does this answer your question?"

GONE BATTY
Bobo; Sept 4; LT; Directed by Robert McKimson; Story by Sid Marcus, Ben Washam; Animation by Charles McKimson, Herman Cohen, Rod Scribner, and Phil DeLara; Layouts by Robert Givens; Backgrounds by Richard H. Thomas; Voice Characterization by Mel Blanc; Musical Direction by Carl W. Stalling.
A newspaper informs us: "Championship Baseball Today," with the Greenville Goons, a rough, nasty-looking bunch of bullies, versus the Sweetwater Shnooks, turn-of-the-century-style ballplayers ("Do ya get a banjo with that outfit?"). Through a series of dirty tricks and "fowl" plays, the Goons eliminate the Shnooks' pitchers one by one. "Well, folks, it

looks like they'll have to give up," the announcer announces, "Jumpin' jehosephat! They're putting the mascot [Bobo the Elephant] into the game! He's going to pitch for the Shnooks!" With the aid of a pin in his pachydermy posterior, Bobo shoots the ball so fast it burns the Goons' bats or travels so slow it strikes three Goons out at once. Bobo proves no less effective as a batter, managing on his first play to hit one right through three Goon gloves. He slides home with such force that he burrows underground. Subsequent plays have Bobo wisely letting a booby-trapped ball get past him, and hitting all the balls fired from a pitching bazooka so that he scores 167 runs in his first inning ("Not bad for a beginner"). However, one more run is needed to win. The Goons' last dirty trick is tying Bobo's leg to the plate, so when he makes the hit he's unable to run around the bases. He foils the Goons by stretching his trunk, the two "fingers" on its end acting as little legs to make the run and win! Bobo's sure a great ball player, all agree. "And he works for peanuts!"

GOO GOO GOLIATH

Sept 18; MM; Directed by I. Freleng; Story by Warren Foster; Animation by Art Davis, Manuel Perez, Ken Champin, and Virgil Ross; Layouts by Hawley Pratt; Backgrounds by Irv Wyner; Musical Direction by Carl W. Stalling.
The steadfastly-stinko stork is too pooped to deliver a *big* baby to Mrs. Giant at the top of the beanstalk, so he drops it at the nearest house. "Never saw a house yet that a baby wasn't welcome." The narrator tells us, "These people were overjoyed that the baby had a healthy appetite," meaning gallons and gallons of milk. It's not long before little giant outgrows his bassinet and even a full-sized bed. He requires cement mixers full of pablum, the swimming pool for a tub, and an auto tire as a teething ring. Baby's first steps are treacherous, but "Junior" is helpful in getting the car started. Babies often take advantage of open gates and wander away: a 42-foot baby wearing the Brown Derby restaurant

hat isn't too hard to miss, even for skeptical policemen. The stork returns to correct his dropoff and finds the titanic toddler in the arms of the Statue of Liberty. Stork returns him to the giant, to swap for the normal sized baby the giant is currently using a jeweler's glass to help him diaper. "Thank goodness, things are straightened out at last," hiccups the stork. "To each his own, I always say." The last shot reveals he's left the normal human baby in the pouch of a kangaroo!

BY WORD OF MOUSE

Sylvester; Oct 2; LT; Directed by I. Freleng; Story by Warren Foster; Animation by Gerry Chiniquy, Art Davis, Ben Washam, and Ted Bonnicksen; Layouts by Hawley Pratt; Backgrounds by Irv Wyner; Voice Characterization by Mel Blanc; Musical Direction by Milt Franklyn.
The first of three annual pro-American-economic-system cartoons sponsored by the right wing philanthropic Sloane Foundation. Warner's profit on the arrangement exemplifying the very capitalistic message the films illustrate. Warners not only keeps the films for their backlog but comes out ahead to begin with (having been paid $25,000 per entry for films that cost $22,000 to make).

In der little town of Knockwurst on der Rye, Hans tells his family of his trip to America. He was met by his cousin Willie at the docks and shown the nexus of all Americanism, a department store. Hans gets confused by all the "lamps, clamps, postage stamps, roasters, coasters, electric toasters" el al. Willie isn't quite up to explaining the secrets of mass production and consumption and takes him to a friend who is an economics professor mouse at Putnell University (Old P.U.). The prof expounds the American mass market phenomenon in between rounds of being chased by Sylvester, the cat seeking to eliminate the middle stages of American retail in favor of a more direct connection with his food chain, "mouse consumption." When they see him coming, Hans yells, "I tawt I taw a puddy tat" in German and the mice continue their lecture in various out-of-the-way spots. At one point they hide in a file cabinet where Sylvester finds them under "M." Wind-up gag: Willie asking his wife if she understands mass production, and she, indicating dozens of mice, answers, "I'm a victim of it."

FROM A TO Z-Z-Z-Z ACADEMY AWARD NOMINEE

Oct 16; LT; Directed by Charles M. Jones; Story by Michael Maltese; Animation by Ken Harris, Ben Washam, and Lloyd Vaughan; Layouts by Maurice Noble; Backgrounds by Philip DeGuard; Musical Direction by Carl W. Stalling.

"Well, Mr. Phillips, daydreaming again?" Yet another Jones highwater mark, in which the imagination of the director, the animators, writer, and designer is out-done only by that of the protagonist, little boy Ralph Phillips (voiced by Dick Beals), who uses every day school room events as jumping-off points for elaborate fantasies, from which he is rudely awakened each time by the teacher (voiced by Bea Benederet). Staring idly at a bird outside the window, the boy dreams he can fly. Forced to answer a math problem, he believes the numbers are laughing at him so he becomes a white-on-black chalkboard figure and fights with the doodle-figures, improvising letters as weapons. Sent outside to mail a letter, he becomes a western Pony Express rider trying to escape Injuns and a storm of arrows. A fish tank becomes the scenario for a deep-sea diving adventure in which he swims 700 fathoms down, without a diving suit, past a saber toothed-tiger shark (whom he slices in two) carrying a submarine containing his teacher, (cast as the heroine of these adventures) back to the surface. Forced to stand in the corner, he imagines it's the corner ropes of a boxing ring where he lets an enormous bruiser have it right in the kisser. The bell he hears turns out to be the school bell. Teacher sends him home, but on leaving he becomes Douglas MacArthur, vowing, "I shall return!"

QUACK SHOT

Daffy Duck, Elmer Fudd; Oct 30; MM; Directed by Robert McKimson; Story by Phil DeLara; Animation by Rod Scribner, Phil DeLara, Charles McKimson, and Herman Cohen; Layouts by Robert Givens; Backgrounds by Richard H. Thomas; Voice Characterization by Mel Blanc; Musical Direction by Carl W. Stalling.

Daffy, regaining a smidgen of his 30s hoo-hoo-hoo hysteria as well as a moral sense, tries to prevent Elmer Fudd from shooting ducks as much on general principle as on saving his own skin. "Stop right where you are!" Daffy demands, bandaging Elmer's first victim and setting him free. He threatens, "If you shoot one more duck, you'll be in big trouble!" BANG! "Now you're in trouble! Prepare to defend yourself!" Most of his anti-Elmer schemes backfire, such as those involving scuba gear and drills, bulletless guns ("Go ahead, shoot me, see if I give a moon and sixpence"), balloons, phoney fog dispensers, booby-trapped decoys ("Nothing more serious than a few minor concussions and some broken bones"). He does get in a couple of zingers: an explosive toy boat that piques Elmer's curiosity, and really cooking Elmer's goose after Fudd ties him to a boatfull of explosives, wiggling off before the boat hits the dock and Fudd. Cut to a bandaged Elmer on his boat, having decided duck hunting is too strenuous. He'll fish instead. Along comes a giant, angry fish. "Stop right where you are! Now you listen to me, Buster! If you catch one more fish, just one more fish, you'll be in trouble!" Daffy pops out of Fudd's hat to comment, "Strong union" and hops off wackily.

LUMBERJACK RABBIT

Bugs Bunny; Nov 13; LT; Directed by Charles M. Jones; Story by Michael Maltese; Animation by Ben Washam, Lloyd Vaughan, Richard Thompson, Abe Levitow, and Ken Harris; Layouts by Maurice Noble; Backgrounds by Philip DeGuard; Voice Characterization by Mel Blanc; Musical Direction by Carl W. Stalling.

"Most everyone has heard of Paul Bunyan, the giant lumberjack, but some people still doubt that old Paul really existed. If you're one of those doubters, you might ask the opinion of a certain rabbit, who happened one day to wander into Paul Bunyan country." Bugs doesn't notice that he's surrounded by giant vegetables until he discovers a "carrot mine," which old Paul has instructed his 124-foot, 4,600-ton frisky puppy, Smidgen to guard from intruders. The big bow-wow chases Bugs into a worm hole (scaring out a foot-long inchworm). Bugs tickles his nose until the dog sneezes him into Bunyan's giant-sized cabin. His landing in a moose horn provokes the dog to blowing it, summoning à normal-sized moose who runs away yelping at the sight of the big dog. Bugs next lands in a gun, so large the bullet looks like a torpedo. Smidgen fires into an apple and eats it. Bugs escapes on a toothpick and then swings around from the dog's ears to his back. He wins the dog over by scratching his back, but the pooch is more of a pest when he's friendly. His affectionate slobbers threaten to wipe Bugs out. Bugs at last gets to return to his carrots by directing the dog toward a giant redwood tree, as Bugs winks slyly at the camera.

Warner's only cartoon produced in 3-D made absolutely no creative use of the possibilities except for a gag with the opening "W-B" shield crashing forward and bouncing back to its usual position at the front of the film.

MY LITTLE DUCKAROO
Daffy Duck, Porky Pig; Nov 27; MM; Directed by Charles M. Jones; Story by Michael Maltese; Animation by Ken Harris, Ben Washam, Abe Levitow, Richard Thompson and Lloyd Vaughan; Layouts by Maurice Noble;

Backgrounds by Philip DeGuard; Voice Characterization by Mel Blanc; Musical Direction by Milt Franklyn.
A disappointing sequel to the classic *Dripalong Daffy*. It starts out promisingly with Daffy as western hero "The Masked Avenger" ("Hi-Yo-Tinfoil"). Porky reappears as "comedy relief," again out to catch the rustler Nasty Canasta (whose crimes include "gag stealing" and "square dancing in a round house") for the $10,000 reward. "It isn't the principle, it's the money." The satire soon gets bogged down in Daffy's grandstanding look-at-me attempts to get Canasta's attention once he invades the crook's clearly-marked cabin (shouting his name like *Duck Dodger in the 24 1/2 Century*) and reappearing as other kinds of heroes, the whip-wielding Freesco Kid ("You don't have to come quietly, you can make a little noise") and as the caped and underweared "Super Guy." Only a "Gravedigger's Joke Book" gets any rise out of Canasta. After the climactic off-screen fight, during which comedy relief Porky whittles as the house shakes, the defeated Daffy shows us how he's made good his claim to fix the bad guy's little red wagon.

SHEEP AHOY
Ralph Wolf, Sam Sheepdog; Dec 11; MM; Directed by Charles M. Jones; Story by Michael Maltese; Animation by Richard Thompson and Abe Levitow; Layouts by Maurice Noble; Backgrounds by Phil DeGuard; Voice Characterization by Mel Blanc; Musical Direction by Carl W. Stalling.
Comes the dawn (set to the appropriate movement from "William Tell"), Ralph Wolf waits for that brief interlude of watchdogs between the night shift (Fred) and the day shift (Sam, still identified as Ralph) before making off with a sheep. Sam's first act on duty thus is to gently kick a boulder off the cliff onto Ralph's head. Ralph's attempt at pole vaulting gets thwarted by Sam's robbing the pole and thrashing him. An ACME Smoke Screen bomb creates a fog around him that Sam changes from white to black by dropping an explosive into the cloud.

Next, it's another fine ACME product, an artificial rock, the official copy on which reads, "Have fun! Be popular! Be a rock!" which almost gets by Sam until he sledge hammers the "rock," which falls into little pieces that scamper off. Swinging from a balloon, he accidentally punctures it with his fishing rod, is then himself duped by a powderkeg with phony lamb legs. Ralph's bicycle- powered submarine then is detoured by Sam down a waterfall. Lastly, a catapult-lever set succeeds only in bringing the big sheepdog right to him. The sheepdog/wolf thrashing gets interrupted by the change in shifts, Sam (Ralph) to Fred Sheepdog, and Ralph (Sam) to George Wolf (the night wolf), but the beating continues.

BABY BUGGY BUNNY

Bugs Bunny; Dec 18; MM; Directed by Charles M. Jones; Story by Michael Maltese; Animation by Abe Levitow, Lloyd Vaughan, Ken Harris, and Ben Washam; Layouts by Ernest Nordli; Backgrounds by Philip DeGuard; Voice Characterization by Mel Blanc; Musical Direction by Milt Franklyn.

The midget gangster, Baby Faced Finster, in a long trenchcoat that conceals his stilts, pulls a bank job. He disguises himself as a baby in a buggy (where he's stashed the booty) so the police go right by him. The carriage accidentally rolls down Bugs's rabbit hole, and to reclaim it, he fixes himself up with a note. "Dear Kind Rabbit, Please take care of my little baby. His name is Finster. Thank you, oh thank you, (signed) a mother (broken-hearted)." Once inside, the gangster/pseudo-baby tries to make off with the bag of stolen bills and then to kayo Bugs with a baseball bat as he puts him to bed and turns out the light. Bugs wises up when static from "Baby" Finster's electric shaver causes interference on his TV set just as the news describes the wanted criminal. Then, what was funny before becomes knee-slappingly hilarious as Bugs takes the little larcenite through a viciously-sarcastic parody of the overprotective parent: tidying

him up in the washing machine, tossing him in the air so he slams both on the ceiling and the ground (Bugs: "Oh dear, I do believe I've forgotten my fudge!"), and spanking him when he draws a knife and when he curses upon accidentally stabbing his own behind ("This hurts you more than it does me"). Police find the little terror-tyke tied up in the same foundling waif baby basket, and we end on the incarcerated infant in a prison playpen.

1955

PIZZICATO PUSSYCAT

Jan 1; MM; Directed by I. Freleng; Story by Warren Foster; Animation by Virgil Ross, Manuel Perez; Layouts by Hawley Pratt; Backgrounds by Richard H. Thomas; Voice Characterization by Mel Blanc; Musical Direction by Milt Franklyn.

"A story about an ordinary cat, and an extraordinary mouse (who) lived in an ordinary house occupied by an ordinary couple." The mouse, a polite English rodent leaves his hole to swipe some sheet music (rather than cheese), and gets caught by the cat when his glasses fall off. The mouse pleads, "Please Mr. Cat, you'll be making a terrible mistake. I'm no ordinary mouse, I'm considered to be a very fine pianist." The laughing cat (This I gotta see!") demands a demonstration, and gets it, but just about 30 seconds into "The Minute Waltz" Mr. and Mrs. Jones (she wondering about strange piano sounds at night) burst in. The cat shoves the mouse and his toy piano inside the grand piano and pantomimes playing it. The Jones instantly call the press and soon reporters and photographers besiege the place, and the cat paw-prints numerous contracts for engagements. Critics are in attendence when Cat makes his concert debut at Carnegie. Mr. and Mrs. Jones beam from the balcony, everything goes fine for about eight bars until one of the hammers accidentally hits the mouse in the face and smashes his spectacles. Unable to read the music, the mouse produces frightening Cecil Taylor-like thumps which cause press and public alike to reject the miracle cat as a fraud (the squares). In a postscript, the cat chases the mouse across a trap drum set and learns he has a true talent for percussion! We end with the two jamming on a piano/drums duet of "Crazy Rhythm."

FEATHER DUSTED

Foghorn Leghorn; Jan 15; MM; Directed by Robert McKimson; Story by Charles McKimson and Sid Marcus. Animation by Rod Scribner, Phil DeLara, Charles McKimson, and Herman Cohen; Layouts by Robert Givens; Backgrounds by Richard H. Thomas; Voice Characterization by Mel Blanc (and Bea Bernaderet); Music by Milt Franklyn.

"Mothers's little man, humph! She's making a pantywaist out of that poor kid! I think I'll just mosey over there and help that little bookworn turn." It looks like leftover gags from the previous season's *Little Boy Boo*, though the material is almost as good. The games that deadpan Junior embarrasses Foggy at are: croquet ("chicken, that is"), whereby he works out a formula to make the ball go through every wicket on one shot; cops and robbers, in which play-bankrobber Foggy gets caught by the real cops off screen, escaping through the ground; cowboys and Indians, in which Injun Foggy pulls the li'l cowboy's cork and gets a facial explosion; pirates ("some red-blooded adventure!"), in which Foggy's insistence on firing the cannon against Junior's formula results in the cannon balls bouncing back into his mouth, turning him into a tenpin; and swimming, where you can predict what happens when the bathing-suited Foggy makes the mistake of saying "Look boy, I'm a battleship, let's see you sink me!" Widow Prissy returns and scolds Junior, wet after saving Foggy from sinking, then berates the Leghorn, "Mark my words, some of these days some of your childish pranks are going to backfire on you!" Foggy answers, standing up to reveal water pouring out of his body like a sieve, "Ma'am, you are so right!"

PEST FOR GUESTS

Goofy Gophers, Elmer Fudd; Jan. 29; MM; Directed by I. Freleng; Story by Warren Foster; Animation by Virgil Ross, Art Davis, Manuel Perez, and Ken Champin; Layouts by Hawley Pratt; Backgrounds by Irv Wyner; Voice Characterization by Mel Blanc; Music by Milt Franklyn.

"Anytime those two little nutcrackers think they can outsmart Elmer Fudd, they got another think coming!" The gophers (voiced by Blanc and Stan Freberg) switch from using a tree as a nut-stashing device (since when do gophers have a need for nuts?) to using an old-fashioned chest of drawers; their "impeccable taste" and genteel sensibilities are thrilled when Elmer Fudd (blushing at the word "drawers") buys said furniture and installs it in his home. Fudd doesn't share their enthusiasm though, and finds them out after they've rigged his drainpipe to catch acorns and guide them into the chest. Finding "the wascals that are wesponsible" Fudd decides to fix their wittle wed wagon and bwast them with his twusty wepeating wifle, which, coming from a drawer stuffed with nuts, first shoots acorns into their hands ("Isn't this nice of the gentleman?"). He chases them around the house ("He isn't really nice at all, is he?" "Not at all. I think he means to do us bodily harm"), sending a TNT stick on a balloon which the gophers take their time about popping with a pin they happen to have. Fudd then slips on his nut-covered floor, dragging his water cooler downstairs to the basement with him (water coolers are de rigeur for Fudd toons). When he traps them under a "primitive" box, unexplained car-crash sound effects provoke him into lifting it. The gophers run up his patio tree, and the vibrations of his chopping shake an ocean of acorns into his living room washing Fudd away when he opens the door. "Ah nuts!"

Theme: "So Early in the Morning."

BEANSTALK BUNNY

Bugs Bunny, Daffy Duck, Elmer Fudd; Feb 12; MM; Directed by Charles M. Jones; Story by Michael Maltese;

Animation by Ken Harris, Richard Thompson, Abe Levitow, and Keith Darling. Layouts by Robert Givens; Backgrounds by Richard H. Thomas; Voice Characterization by Mel Blanc; Musical Direction by Carl Stalling.
"Odds my bodkins!" Daffy, as Jack, is at first upset at having traded a "perfectly good grade-A homogenized Holstein cow" for three stupid beans ("Jack, you're a jerk") until the beanstalk starts sprouting out of a rabbit hole. Jack climbs it eagerly, anticipating﹕ finding some "solid gold goodies" at the top. Bugs gets involved because his bed has been carried upwards by the beanstalk. Elmer, imaginatively cast as the Giant, obviously enjoys a rare opportunity to play a genuine threat, notwithstanding his lisp and harmless manner. There's the post *Rabbit Seasoning* word play we've grown accustomed to, specifically a very funny running gag about Daffy trying to convince Elmer that Bugs is really Jack, so that a confused Elmer announces that he'll use to "open up with a pair of Jacks". The distinguishing gags here are the visual ones: one-inch high Bugs and Daffy riding on popped champagne corks, hiding in Elmer's snuff box, running around on the inside of his head (when he smokes them out, they try to sneak out through the cigarette), climaxing in the teeny-tiny Bugs tripping the colossal Elmer just by sticking out a microscopic rabbit foot. Bugs knows it's time to be going, but Daffy won't leave without the treasure he came for, "On account of I am greedy." Bugs does get his reward, a field of giant carrots to eat himself silly in. The last scene has a captive Daffy recruited as a living cartoon-character watch.

ALL FOWLED UP
Foghorn Leghorn, Henery Hawk; Feb 19; LT; Directed by Robert McKimson; Story by Charles McKimson and Sid Marcus; Animation by Phil DeLara, Richard Thompson and Keith Darling; Layouts by Robert Givens; Backgrounds by Richard H. Thomas; Voice Characterization by Mel Blanc; Musical Direction by Carl Stalling.

The barnyard battle opens with Foghorn wacking the dog on the butt and tricking him down a well, doghouse and all, the pooch retaliating by slapping a silver platter cover over him. Foghorn prepares to re-retaliate, first exercising his out-of-shape muscles back into shape. In the middle of a push-up, he comes across Henery Hawk trying to carry off a hen and dispenses with the pint-sized chicken hawk on an ad-hoc flying saucer, causing the dog to worry about men from Mars. The dog gives Henery the scoop that the big, ugly shnook is an overstuffed, fat, flabby snob of a chicken. "In you that big fella would look real good." As Foghorn does chin-ups, he discovers that the Hawk is jacking a pot under him ("Jack ... pot ... I made a funny son, and you're not laughin'"!). Foghorn knows "that marble-headed mongrel is in back of all this!" He's about to blow a TNT stick through a pipe (to "cause more confusion than a mouse at a burlesque show") but the dog blows another back at him first ("fortunately I keep my feathers numbered for just such an emergency"). Foghorn plans to pour wet cement on the doghouse, but the stuff gets all over him and hardens him into a statue which Henery carries off. "Of all the kinds of chicken in the world, I have to catch me a Plymouth rock!"
Theme: "De Camptown Ladies."

STORK NAKED
Daffy Duck; Feb 26; MM; Directed by I. Freleng; Story by Warren Foster; Animation by Arthur Davis, Virgil Ross, and Manuel Perez; Layouts by Hawley Pratt; Backgrounds by Irv Wyner; Voice Characterization by Mel Blanc; Music by Milt Franklyn.
The stork has a busy day: First he delivers to Mr. and Mrs. Pierce. He joins in a toast, making the bird a little tipsy. In Paris, his delivery is greeted with champagne, the bird a trifle pixilated. On an Indian Reservation, they celebrate with "fire water" and the bird is completely blotto!
Meanwhile, the object of his last delivery, an egg to Mr. and Mrs. Daffy and Daphne Duck, is being anticipated

by the man of the house. Daffy is determined to keep the stork away, and has set up artillery cannons and anti-aircraft guns atop their roof. The duck reviews his checklist: Bear trap in the bushes, trampoline in the fireplace, guillotine in the doorway, and alligators in the basement. Daffy checks his radar just as the stork walks in! The drunken stork misses the alligator trap, but Daffy, throwing the stork out, does not! The stork tries the windows but is blasted by a cannon. Daffy puts an elastic band on the back door, causing the running stork to bounce backward, knocking Daffy out the front door. Daffy chases the stork up a pole with an axe. The stork walks across a wire, but Daffy chops, causing the pole to fall backward, landing the duck in the basement with the alligators. The egg is about to hatch, but Daffy scares the stork away with his gun. The egg (now with two legs extended) runs into the house. Daffy chases it, narrowly missing the doorway guillotine. Daffy grabs the egg, just as it hatches. It is a baby stork! Daffy flies the baby stork to its daddy. "For once, the stork will get a dose of his own medicine!"

LIGHTHOUSE MOUSE

Sylvester, Hippetty Hopper; Mar 12; MM; Directed by Robert McKimson; Story by Sid Marcus; Animation by Phil DeLara, Charles McKinson, Herman Cohen, and Rod Scribner; Layouts by Robert Givens; Backgrounds by Richard H. Thomas; Voice Characterization by Mel Blanc; Music by Milt Franklyn.
Sylvester mistakes Hippetty Hopper for a giant mouse. This film is supplemented by plenty of plot pegs to keep things going. The setting is a lighthouse, whose light disturbs a little rodent trying to sleep. When the mouse unplugs it, the Scotch lighthouse keeper is alerted by his wiseguy parrot, but not before a ship has brushed against the island, accidentally dropping some of its cargo, including a crate containing Hippetty Hopper. The Scotsman threatens his cat Sylvester, ordering him to catch the crazy "moose that loose in the hoose." Sylvester swears he'll catch the mouse in a "mat-

ter of seconds ... just count the seconds and I'll show ya." Up in the lamp room, Sylvester's mouse trap catches not the "pipsqueak of a rodent" but king-sized Hippetty! Sylvester does one of those self-fragmenting takes and runs (past the seconds-counting Polly) into the bathroom where he checks his eyes and douses himself in vitamins. More back-and-forth follows, Sylvester trying to keep the light on, Hippetty and the mouse trying to cut the wire and finally blowing it up, the Scotsman threatening to thrash Sylvester. In one funny bit, doors open and close, alternately revealing Sylvester beating up on the wee mouse and the "big mouse" trouncing Sylvester. For the last shot, Sylvester has taken the place of the lamp, rotating with a car battery rigged so that searchlight beams emit from his eyes.

Theme: "I Cover the Waterfront."

SAHARA HARE

Bug Bunny, Yosemite Sam; Mar 26; LT; Directed by I. Freleng; Story by Warren Foster; Animation by Gerry Chiniquy, Ted Bonnicksen, and Arthur Davis; Layouts by Hawley Pratt. Backgrounds by Irv Wyner; Voice Characterization by Mel Blanc; Music by Milt Franklyn.
"Miami Beach at last! Hooray!" shouts bathing-suited Bugs as he pops out of his tunnel and runs across the sand, missing the signs reading "Sahara Desert" and "Keep off the Grass" ("Dig this crazy beach") When it doesn't lead to water, Bugs realizes his faux-pas, though at first he mistakes a tiny puddle for the Atlantic Ocean (which he always pictured as being "so much bigger"). By getting footprints all over the desert, he arouses the ire of Riff Raff Sam, bedsheeted bandit (riding an un-whoa-ble bump-backed camel, the first of a series of such beasts of burden as in *Knighty Knight Bugs* and *Prince Violent*). Sam also doesn't appreciate Bugs' conversion of Sam's Arab headdress into a towel dispenser. The sneaky sheik chases Bugs into a nearby Foreign Legion outpost. Sam tries to enter the fortress by pole vaulting over the top, by chiseling out one of the blocks, by approaching it on

stilts, and then by breaking down the door with an elephant that Bugs renders harmless with a wind-up mouse. Bugs's giant rubber bands hurl Sam into two trees, his shimmying up a board results in his getting split in two along with the board. After rigging up an endless series of doors to a bomb, Bugs wonders aloud if Sam is stubborn enough to open them all, and the explosion informs him, "Yup, he's stubborn enough!" Just as Bugs walks away, he's passed by Daffy Duck in a bathing suit, excited about Miami Beach. Bugs starts to tell him but decides, "Let him find out for himself."

SANDY CLAWS   <small>ACADEMY AWARD NOMINEE</small>
Tweety, Sylvester; Apr 2; LT; Directed by I. Freleng; Story by Arthur Davis and Warren Foster; Animation by Art Davis, Manuel Perez, and Virgil Ross. Layouts by Hawley Pratt; Backgrounds by Irv Wyner; Voice Characterization by Mel Blanc; Music by Carl Stalling.
Business as usual, at a very high level. At the beach, Granny leaves Tweety's cage on top of a rock while she goes to change into her new "bikini bathing suit" (an all-covering 1890's outfit). Meanwhile, Sylvester, frustrated with the worm and fishing routine ("There must be an easier way for a pussycat to get sustenance!"), spies Tweety and starts after the sunglass-wearing bird. Before he can get to Tweety, the tide comes in with enormous waves that all but drown him and trap Tweety out in the middle of the sea on the rock. Sylvester tries to "save him" (for himself, 'natch), with the added difficulty of having to avoid the water, not only out of respect for feline tradition but because this is one of those beaches where the waters are full of sharks. Sylvester tries lowering himself with a fishing reel, driving a motorboat out, and powering himself with an outboard motor atop a pair of waterskis and water wings which aren't sharkproof. Granny returns and summons help from Sylvester in a life guard uniform ("Look at that wonderful brave cat trying to save my little bird"). He is no more successful with his surfboard. He then goes after Tweety in a diving suit

while Granny mans the air supply. Tweety rows himself ashore, and the cat's suit expands like a blimp. He escapes just as Granny remarks that the "heroic pussycat ... deserves a just reward." He finds that his parachute has lowered him into the city dog pound!

THE HOLE IDEA
Apr 16; LT; Directed by Robert McKimson; Story by Sid Marcus; Animation by Robert McKimson; Layouts and Backgrounds by Richard H. Thomas; Voice Characterization by Mel Blanc (June Foray); Music by Milt Franklyn.
McKimson's "auteur" film is one of his proudest moments. It is not an insult to observe that he was a better animator than director. "This is the story of science and invention," beginning with the caveman's use of tools (for obtaining mates), to the modern city and highway, to our unsung genius, Professor Calvin Q. Calculus, whose invention of the portable hole goes unappreciated by his nagging wife. Not so by the world. Papers headline his discovery as a movie newsreel (in black and white) demonstrates various uses for the floppy circles. It shows them used by chore-avoiders, bone-burrying doggies, golfers, and a baby locked in a safe. Upon receiving a scientific award, the Professor expresses the hope that his invention will never be used for evil purposes. But that's what happens when a sneaky-looking crook filches the briefcase of holes becoming a "holey terror" responsible for a portable, hole-crime wave that the cops are unable to stop. Crook easily enters banks, jewelry store windows, and even Fort Knox! He tries to carry a blond babe out of a burlesque show, the police right on his tail. When he tries to escape through a hole he put in the side of a mountain a train comes roaring out. Running in another direction, he comes up against a whole yard-full of cops. Turning down a dead end, he "escapes" through a wall, into the state prison! Back home, the Professor's wife is busting his chops again, so he drops a handy hole and sends her to the devil who sends her back!

READY, SET, ZOOM!

*Road Runner (Speedibux Rex) and
Coyote (Famishus Famishus); Apr 30;
LT; Directed by Chuck Jones; Story by
Michael Maltese; Animation by Ben
Washam, Abe Levitow, Richard
Thompson, and Lloyd Vaughan.*
Just gags. The glue the Coyote covers
the road with prevents him from running from an oncoming truck, and then
affixes a lit dynamite stick to him; the
Coyote detours the Road Runner through
a log hanging over a cliff, which falls
when he enters it; a 10,000-pound
weight jams when the Road Runner
passes under it, then falls when the
Coyote does (squishing him into a
poker chip); the bird takes a detour of
his own, leaving the Coyote's lasso with
TNT sticks to go off in his furry face; a
giant rubber band sends the Coyote
into a truck when the Road Runner
distracts him; a combination Acme outboard motor, jim-dandy wagon, wash-
tub and roller skates propels him right
to the middle of a chasm where the
bridge is out; riding on a rocket carries
him straight through the highway and
out an old mine which blows up; a
female roadrunner suit ("It Had To Be
You") attracts not the desired bird but
dozens of other hungry coyotes. The
Road Runner's sign informs us that it's
"The End."

HARE BRUSH

*Bugs Bunny; May 7; LT; Directed by I.
Freleng; Story by Warren Foster;
Animation by Ted Bonnicksen, Art
Davis and Gerry Chiniquy; Layouts by
Hawley Pratt; Backgrounds by Irv
Wyner; Voice Characterization by Mel
Blanc; Music by Milt Franklyn.*
"I am Elmer J. Fudd, millionaire. I
own a mansion and a yacht." Holy
reversal, Batman! Friz and Foster
really put on their thinking caps to
work out this little gem: tycoon Elmer
thinking he's a rabbit, a fact which
worries his corporate board no end.
They send him to a sanitarium where,
far from being cured, he gets to indulge
his delusion further. Bugs happens to
be passing by and, not knowing what's
going on, agrees to trade places with
Elmer. The shrink assigned to Elmer
mistakes Bugs for Fudd saying this is
the worst case of "rabbitschenia" he's
ever seen. Through a combination of
pills and *Clockwork Orange*-style
psychic programming, Bugs leaves the
hospital, wisping and waffing, convinced he's Fudd. He immediately goes
hunting for west and wewaxation.
Hunting gags follow which would be
funny even if they didn't have Bugs/
Elmer drawing a gun on Elmer/Bugs,
Elmer/Bugs subbing for Bugs' gun and
sicking a bear on him that pushes the
playing-dead hunter off a cliff. Freleng
also has the tact not to push these
reverse-hunting bits further than
they'll stretch. Ending the cartoon on a
left-field punchline: Bugs/Elmer being
dragged off to prison for the money he
owes in back taxes, Elmer/Bugs telling
the audience , "I may be screwy, but
I'm not going to Alcatraz."

PAST PERFUMANCE

*Pepe Le Pew; May 21; MM; Directed
by Charles M. Jones; Story by Michael
Maltese; Animation by Ken Harris,
Richard Thompson, Lloyd Vaughan;
Layouts by Robert Givens; Backgrounds
by Phil DeGuard; Voice
Characterization by Mel Blanc; Music
by Milt Franklyn.*
Paris, 1913: the casting director for
animals (Arthur Q. Bryan) at Super
Magnifique Productiones (Studios de
Le Picteurs Motion) has procured all
the creatures necessary for M'sieu Le
Directeur's new motion picture (including "Chimps Elysees"), except for one
odorless skunk, a female cat with a
white stripe on her back. Pepe enters
the studio and frightens everyone off
the set, including the animal trainer
who leaves the female pseudo-skunk
directly to Pepe!
   Pepe chases his latest love interest
all over the studio. They run across the
set for Julio and Romiet, wherein Pepe,
looking adorable in pantaloops, calls

her his "little much ado about something." In the midst of a Dumasian action scene, he finds that the other two musketeers are less than anxious to have Pepe as their third ("Le yipe"). After removing her from a film magazine, he finds his "pink rabbeet" next in a room de projection, his aroma causing a black and white silent sheik on the screen to exclaim, "Un pole cat de pew es en le audience! Take it vous on le lam!" The pair run past sets for Uncle Tom, Tarzan, the "Daring Young Flea on the Manly Trapeze" and the "Pearls de Pauline." When the white stripe washes off the cat, Pepe continues the chase, painting over his own stripe. "If you can not beat them, join them! Wait for baby!"

TWEETY'S CIRCUS
Tweety, Sylvester; June 4; MM; Directed by I. Freleng; Story by Warren Foster; Animation by Arthur Davis, Gerry Chiniquy, and Ted Bonnicksen. Layouts by Hawley Pratt; Backgrounds by Irv Wyner; Voice Characterization by Mel Blanc; Music by Milt Franklyn.
Sylvester opens this one by singing "Meow," Stalling's perennial cat theme. It is the only time the lyrics made it into a Warner toon, which is only appropriate as this Tweety-chase through the circus hinges on Sylvester's feline pride. He razzes a lion, in the first scene for having the audacity to be billed as "The King of the Cats." To Sylvester's delight, the circus includes a Tweety Bird with the tigers, elephants, and camels. He chases the canary into the big top, where, to his dismay, the lion he angered is waiting for him. He also gets an elephant ticked off when Tweety hides in his trunk, mistaking it for a hose, slamming it painfully on the ground! The elephant slams the cat in turn, throwing him back to the lion's cage where the big cat claws him into little chunks. In further trying to catch Tweety and avoid the lion, Sylvester exploits his abilities as a high-diver (by the time he lands in the tank Tweety has fed its contents to Mr. Elephant), fire-eater, and high-wire walker. Just when he thinks his lion problem is solved, he realizes he's

locked himself in a cage full of the big cats! Outside the tent, Tweety, with straw hat and cane, barks, "Huwwy! Huwwy! Huwwy! Da gweatest show on earth, 50 wions and one puddy tat!" After a ferocious roar emerges from the tent, the spiel becomes, "Step wight up! 50 wions, count 'em, 50 wions!"

RABBIT RAMPAGE
Bugs Bunny; June 11; LT; Directed by Charles M. Jones; Story by Michael Maltese. Animation by Ben Washam; Layouts by Ernest Nordli; Backgrounds by Philip DeGuard; Voice Characterization by Mel Blanc; Music by Milt Franklyn.
Scene 1: A woodland scene, rabbit hole in foreground. Buggs Bunny comes through hole. *Bugs:* "Eh, What's Up, Doc?"

Thus reads the script on an animator's desk. The artist takes a brush and paints this first scene, making a drastic change. He draws Bugs' rabbbit hole in the sky. Bugs crawls out of his hole and crashes to the earth! Bugs is upset with the animator and tells him he won't stand for it. Bugs tries to dive back into his hole, but the animator has erased it! The animator paints Bugs' back yellow; draws picket signs ("I Won't Work!" "I Refuse To Live Up To My Contract!"); and draws a variety of outlandish headgear (bonnets, oversized hats, tube socks, a judge's wig, a diving helmet, a huge top hat) on Bugs' head. Bugs walks away, but the animator has drawn the background upside down. Bugs tries to climb up into his rabbit hole, but falls on a concrete highway. Stumbling off the background (to a field of pure white) Bugs grumbles over his predicament. The animator erases the rabbit's head and draws a pumpkin head in its place. Bugs demands a rabbit head (as it states in his contract), and the animator draws a tiny head on his body. The artist draws his head the correct size, sans ears! When Bugs demands them, the animator puts human ears on his head! He then draws extra-long rabbit ears. The animator draws Bugs as a child-like stick figure, then draws extra rabbits. Bugs has had enough and refuses to move until he can see the boss. The artist puts a train track background behind him, and sends a train barrelling through. "There's one way out" says Bugs, pulling a "The End" title from above. The camera reveals the artist to be Elmer Fudd, who is delighted with his work. "I finally got even with that screwy rabbit!"

LUMBER JERKS

Goofy Gophers; June 25; LT; Directed by I. Freleng; Story by Warren Foster; Animation by Art Davis, Virgil Ross, and Manuel Perez; Layouts by Hawley Pratt; Backgrounds by Richard H. Thomas; Voice Characterization by Mel Blanc (and Stan Freburg); Musical Direction by Milt Franklyn.

The Gophers (by now more considerate and complimentary than goofy), having just moved into their new tree, commence storing their nuts for winter. They discover that their home has been uprooted. Taking definite steps to regain their property, they trail the tree to a nearby river where it and other trunks of raw wood await processing at the local sawmill. They manage to row their tree back up-river, despite the precarious predicament of a waterfall. The tree trunk nevertheless is consumed by the sawmill, our heroes waking just in time to miss being sliced in two. The gophers view the machinery, which impresses them as being bent on the destruction of our forests (real logs are ground up and reconstructed as fireplace logs; trees are pencil-sharpened into toothpicks). Their tree is manufactured into furniture, but the gophers sabotage the delivery truck, reposess the stuff and haul it back to their stump. There they reconstruct their home out of dressers, chairs and tables. Being urbane gophers, they prefer this to the old tree, especially as they now have television which they admit will be better when they get electricity.

Goofiest moment: A gopher gets wood-shavings on his head which form a blonde wig, prompting him to sing,

"There was a little girl / Who had a little curl ... " then apologizing for acting so silly.

THIS IS A LIFE?

Bugs Bunny, Daffy Duck, Elmer Fudd, Yosemite Sam; July 9; MM; Directed by I. Freleng; Story by Warren Foster; Animation by Ted Bonnicksen and Arthur Davis; Layouts by Hawley Pratt; Backgrounds by Irv Wyner; Voice Characterization by Mel Blanc; Music by Milt Franklyn.

The ever-unruffled Bugs Bunny at the center of a lot of pressure. He's been unexpectedly put at the center of "America's most talked about program" by the show's emcee, Elmer (Ralph Edwards) Fudd. Bugs is called up to entertain everyone in television with anecdotes from early in his illustrious career. Bugs also has to worry about Daffy Duck, who, from the moment Fudd starts describing the surprise guest ("thoughtful of others, a sparkling personality, genewous, chawitable, self-effacing") is convinced that he was meant to be the guest on the show. Daffy continues trying to hog the spotlight from Bugs, (and literally bellyaching when the rabbit acts humble. Bugs: "Oh I'm so unimportant." Daffy: "Easy, stomach don't turn over"). Elmer tries to get Bugs to talk about his life. He obliges and begins at the dawn of time, then again at his birth (from *Hare Grows In Manhattan*) finally settling for the "first time" he and Elmer met (from *Hare Do*). Bugs fails to recognize the voice from his (recent) past, Yosemite Sam, who recalls an episode from *Buccaneer Bunny*. Both episodes end with Bugs's pursuers getting the worst of it. Bugs continues to add insult to injury. "And then, there was the time you was down in the powder magazine and I threw a match down in it, and the time you found eels in your bed, and I dumped that truck load of cement on ya ... " Bugs's sparring partners conspire to unload a booby-trapped present on him, but, Daffy, greedy as he is naive, winds up taking their explosion!

DOUBLE OR MUTTON

Ralph Wolf, Sam Sheepdog; July 13;

LT; Directed by Charles M. Jones; Story by Michael Maltese; Animation by Richard Thompson, Abe Levitow, Keith Darling and Ken Harris; Layouts and Backgrounds by Pihlip DeGuard; Voice Characterization by Mel Blanc; Music by Milt Franklyn.

Ralph and Sam punch in to work, exchanging "Good mornings." Ralph waits for the whistle before tunneling right next to Sam! He lassoes one sheep while on a high wire, but finds Sam on both ends of said wire. A well-aimed rocket then carries Sam off, but not as far as Ralph has hoped. A Bo Peep disguise gets Ralph into Sam's cave, but, just as Bo Peep is really Ralph in disguise so the sheep is really Sam! Sam yanks Ralph's helicopter right out of the sky (he uses the parachute only after crashing), rolls Ralph into a bowling ball (after his catapult hurls him straight into a tree) and then flips Ralph's cannon back at him. Lastly, Ralph causes hair to grow in front of Sam's eyes so he can't see the wolf dancing in front of him, but he grabs Ralph immediately when he makes for a sheep! Luckily for Ralph, in the middle of being beaten up by Sam, the five o'clock quitting whistle goes off and the two wish each other good night.

JUMPIN' JUPITER

Porky Pig, Sylvester; Aug 6; MM; Directed by Charles M. Jones; Story by Michael Maltese; Animation by Ken Harris, Keith Darling, Abe Levitow and Richard Thompson. Effects Animation by Harry Love; Layouts by Robert Givens; Backgrounds by Philip DeGuard; Voice Characterization by Mel Blanc; Music by Carl Stalling.

You know the take where the character sees something and reacts half a beat later? This whole cartoon is like that, except that the strange things Porky sees never sink in, whereas Sylvester is *all* reaction shots.

"Isn't this wonderful, Sylvester, camping way out here in the middle of nowhere?" It's the western desert, and Sylvester's fear of coyotes and such establishes him as a yellow dog of a cowardly cat even before the funny

stuff starts. After Porky retires to his tent, a buzzard from the planet Jupiter lands his flying saucer, his mission to obtain examples of earthling animal life. He achieves this by boring underneath the campsite and mounting the whole patch of land to the top of his saucer, then carrying it through space. Porky makes an art of not noticing things. Sylvester shows him the alien, but Porky dismisses him with, "You'll just have to return to your wigwam, we'll look at your rugs and trinkets in the morning." The lack of gravity in outer space doesn't strike Porky as anything strange. Perhaps it's catching. The Jupiterian doesn't notice when tent and car drift off his ship. In the morning, Porky merely stretches and says, "Things sure look different after a good night's sleep." They drive off for home. Porky doesn't realize he is no longer on Earth.

A KIDDIE'S KITTY

Sylvester; Aug 20; MM; Directed by I. Freleng; Story by Warren Foster; Animation by Arthur Davis, Gerry Chiniquy and Ted Bonnicksen; Layouts by Hawley Pratt; Backgrounds by Irv Wyner; Music by Milt Franklyn.

Suzanne, a little girl who abuses her toys, wants a real cat to play with. Meanwhile Sylvester has been chased into her yard by a vicious bulldog. Suzanne "adopts" Sylvester, who goes along with the little girl to escape the dog. She "hugs" (chokes) him, then drags him down into the cellar by his tail and shoves him in the washing machine. Sylvester emerges from the drier as a floating fuzzball.

Suzanne feeds him milk, but when Mom comes by, she throws Sylvester into the freezer. The little girl thaws the cat from the tray of ice with an electric blanket which fries him. The dog is still waiting outside, so Sylvester puts up with the little girl a little longer. She force feeds him liver and sardines, made of mud! When Suzanne puts the cat on the swing, she pushes him up into the trees where the dog beats him up. Suzanne plays nurse and bandages the cat from head to toe. While watching "Captain Electronic" on TV, she dresses the cat as a spaceman and blasts him via skyrocket into the sky.

When Suzanne's mom finds out about the cat, she allows her to keep Sylvester. This causes Sylvester to run out of the house to find the dog, who chases him down the street.

HYDE AND HARE

Bugs Bunny: Aug 27; LT; Directed by I. Freleng; Story by Warren Foster; Animation by Gerry Chiniquy, Virgil Ross, Art Davis and Ted Bonnicksen; Layouts by Hawley Pratt; Backgrounds by Irv Wyner; Voice Characterization by Mel Blanc; Music by Carl Stalling.
Bugs, playing the timid woodland creature, gets himself adopted as a pet by a kindly soul who has been feeding him carrots every day. As he carries the coy rabbit home, Bugs's friend remarks, "It's strange that you should call me Doc, I happen to be a doctor." The camera pans upwards to reveal the name on his shingle: "Dr. Jekyll." While Bugs bangs out the "Minute Waltz" on the Doc's piano, Dr. Jekyll gives in to the temptation to drink his evil potion. Bugs realizes this is a mental case, but never does figure out that the monster is his friend transformed. Every time he hides himself and the Doc from the maniac, the Doc undergoes his metamorphosis and Bugs finds he has locked himself in with an axe-wielding alter-ego. The most stunningly-directed of these transformations takes place entirely in the dark, revealed only by the change in eyes. In the end, Doc suspects that the rabbit has consumed the last of his potions. The sensitive rabbit takes this as an affront to his integrity. He returns to the park and is transformed into a monstrous rabbit Hyde (albeit keeping his Bugs' dispostion). He has no idea why he's scaring everyone away. "You'd thing they'd never seen a rabbit before."

DIME TO RETIRE

Sept 3; LT; Directed by Robert McKimson; Story by Charles McKimson, Sid Marcus; Animation by Robert McKimson and Keith Darling; Layouts by Robert Givens; Backgrounds by Richard H. Thomas; Voice

Characterization by Mel Blanc; Music by Milt Franklyn.
Weary traveller Porky Pig is delighted to find a vacant hotel room, especially with a charge of only ten cents a night. Manager/bellhop Daffy shows him to the "super duper deluxe special" suite. Here's the catch: as Porky tries to sleep, Daffy infests his room with a succession of rest-disturbing pests, each of which costs Porky a bundle to get rid of. First a mouse noisily munches on a celery stalk at midnight and is removed for a "pussycat fee" of five bucks. But the cat won't get out of Porky's bed, until he forks over ten bucks for a boxer dog "cat eliminator," who, in turn, gets chased out by a lion for $26, who is then scared out by an elephant "lion eradicator" for $72. It costs Porky $666 to get rid of the elephant scared out with the original mouse. "That's the last straw," says Porky, bags packed, "I'm gettin' outa this hotel." He refuses to pay the original ten cents, so Daffy withholds his baggage, not realizing that they're leaking explosive samples from the Acme Powder Company, which are set off by Porky's backfiring car. After the place explodes, Daffy asks for "a little traveling music please" and runs out with his tail feathers ablaze.

SPEEDY GONZALES   ACADEMY AWARD WINNER

Speedy Gonzales, Sylvester; Sept 17; MM; Directed by I. Freleng; Story by Warren Foster; Animation by Gerry Chiniquy, Ted Bonnicksen and Art Davis; Layouts by Hawley Pratt; Backgrounds by Irv Wyner; Voice Characterization by Mel Blanc; Music by Carl Stalling.
Where *Cat-Tails for Two* constituted the "pilot" film for the character, this constitutes the real debut of the series. They've homogenized Speedy considerably and turned him over to the senior director. They've give him quite an entrance: hungry Mexican mice are being kept out of a cheese factory by Sylvester (the mouse who draws the shortest straw has to try, and, when the cat gets him, his empty sombrero is tossed onto a big pile of empty sombreros). We find Speedy Gonzales, "a

friend of everybody's seester," in a shooting gallery where people pay for shots at him. Speedy gets past Sylvester quite easily, as the cheering mice watch from an egg stand converted into bleachers. All the bits are funny (this might be the best in the series), and four deserve singling out: Sylvester laying a load of mouse traps on the ground, all of which fall on him when Speedy goes whooshing by; Speedy smuggling himself in inside a baseball; Sylvester getting caught in the middle of a field of landmines he planted, then gently tip toe-ing out, and as soon as he thinks he's safe, BOOM!; Speedy running through Sylvester's mouth and out his tail. In the end, Sylvester tries to prevent them from getting the cheese by blowing up the factory, scattering the cheese all over them. Says Speedy, "I like theese poosycats fellow, he's seely."

KNIGHT-MARE HARE
Bugs Bunny; Oct 1; MM; Directed by Chuck Jones; Story by Tedd Pierce; Animation by Ken Harris, Ben Washam, Abe Levitow, and Richard Thompson; Layouts by Ernie Nordli; Backgrounds by Philip DeGuard; Voice Characterization by Mel Blanc; Music by Milt Franklyn.
Bugs's episodic treatment of "A Connecticut Yankee in King Arthur's Court," both the Twain original and the Bing Crosby version (using the latter's wrap-up parallel of past and present). An apple falls on Bugs' hairdryer ("Just washed my ears and I can't do a thing with 'em"), sending him back to medieval England. There, he instantly asks for trouble with a big angry knight in his cast-iron tuxedo who hasn't heard of Bugs' royal friends, the Duke of Ellington, the Count of Basie, the Earl of Hines, the Cab of Calloway, and the Satchmo of Armstrong. Though he's unable to lift his enorumous sword, he trips the knight and sends him flying into a nearby castle. "Putting that 8-ball in the side pocket is all very well," says Bugs, "but it still don't explain what I'm doing in this booby-hatchery, or how I'm getting out." Bugs then gets rid of a fire-breathing dragon with a lit-

tle fire-extinguishing seltzer and wanders into a castle where he meets the beany-capped Merlin the sorcerer. Bugs pleads with him to "sorce" something. When Merlin turns the rabbit into a pig, Bugs simply finds the zipper and removes the pig skin. He then spurts Merlin with magic powder turning him into a donkey. Merlin unzips dozens of donkey skins, each time finding another donkey underneath. ("Well, that gives him a hobby.") After returning to the present by re-striking his head with an apple, he's shocked to discover a donkey in a beanie cap named Merlin.

TWO SCENT'S WORTH
Pepe Le Pew; Oct 15; MM; Directed by Charles M. Jones; Story by Charles M. Jones; Animation by Keith Darling, Abe Levitow, Richard Thompson, and Ken Harris; Layouts by Robert Gribbroek; Backgrounds by Philip DeGuard; Voice Characterization by Mel Blanc; Music by Milt Franklyn.
"It is not just a case of physical attraction, I admire her mind too!" In a little village nestled in the French Alps, a nogoodnik Apache-type hoodlum buys a fish, uses it as bait to catch a cat, and, with the aid of white paint, transforms it into a skunk that he lowers into a bank. When everybody beats it, he cleans the place out. Meeting Pepe outside, the crook voluntarily locks himself in the nearest jail, leaving his unwilling accomplice, the pseudoskunk, even less willing to take part in Pepe's amorous activities ("Permit me to introduce myself, I am Pepe Le Pew, your lover"). She starts up the Alps in a ski-lift car, and runs to the top. This builds to a first-class chase sequence: Jones uses the idea of a snow-chase so effectively you wish he'd devised a Road Runner-type series with a winter

backdrop. Riding down the ski ramp, the girl cat/skunk on one ski and Pepe on two, Pepe makes like a World War II pilot ("I pierce you with the ack-ack of love, flower pot"). Crashing into a tree fails to stop him—he swings through the branches like Tarzan and makes it back on to his skis. When she heads towards the end of the slope and backpedals furiously, managing to stop the ski just at the edge, it is time for Pepe to whoosh by. As he flies through the air, she grabs on to him for dear life. "She is no longer timid" Pepe notes as he releases his parachute.

RED RIDING HOODWINKED

Tweety, Sylvester; Oct 29; LT; Directed by I. Freleng; Story by Warren Foster; Animation by Arthur Davis, Gerry Chiniquy, and Ted Bonnicksen; Layouts by Hawley Pratt; Backgrounds by Irv Wyner; Voice Characterization by Mel Blanc; Music by Milt Franklyn.

You're never sure if Sylvester and Tweety are guests in the story of Little Red Riding Hood, or if Red Riding Hood and the wolf are intruding on a Tweety-Sylvester chase. Both stories share a common Granny and the spirit of Jackie Gleason looms largest of them all. The Riding Hood story has been modernized, city girl Red taking public transportation to visit her Grandma in the country, her gift of Tweety bird in hand attracting the interest of Sylvester. Like all modern mass-transit, the bus lets her off so far away from her destination that she has still to hike though the woods, attracting the attention of the big bad wolf, as forgetful as he is hungry, who constantly has to be reminded (by signs that come from out of nowhere) of what his name is and what he's supposed to be doing.

When Red Riding Hood and Tweety make it to the cottage, they find two funny animals in Granny costumes, the Big Bad Wolf and the Big Bad Puddy-tat. They go through the famous dialogue in duplicate. After getting in each other's way in slapstick antics both inside (Sylvester slamming a door on the wolf) and outside the house (Sylvester accidentally rubber banding a boulder into the wolf's stomach), little girl

and little bird flee and flag down a bus. When the wolf and Sylvester try to board this bus, they're instantly thrown off, by Granny in the diguise of Bus-driver Ralph Kramden. "I told 'em, one of these days . . ." she says, and Red and Tweety finish the line in unison, "Pow! right in the kisser!"

ROMAN LEGION HARE

Bugs Bunny, Yosemite Sam; Nov 12; LT; Directed by Friz Freleng; Story by Warren Foster; Animation by Virgil Ross, Art Davis, and Gerry Chiniquy; Layouts by Hawley Pratt; Backgrounds by Irv Wyner; Voice Characterization by Mel Blanc; Music by Milt Franklyn.

The scene is Rome, 54 A.D., and the feeding of "victims" to the lions in the colosseum is a sport treated with same fanfare as is football today. The Charles Laughton-like Emperor Nero has consented to throw out the first victim. However, when informed that they're out of victims, he sends for the Captain of his Guards, Sam, and threatens, "Get me a victim right away, or it will be you." Sam selects Bugs Bunny, who has followed them because it had looked like a parade. When they charge after him, he trips the troops with one foot. Sam chases after Bugs and passes him due to an un-whoa-able chariot horse, pursuing him through the back of the colosseum, where they spend most of the rest of the film, both trying to avoid the lions and sicking them on each other. Bugs finds the lever to open one lion's cage *after* Sam has already annoyed the beast. He then pulls Sam under a door on a throw rug and slides his battered body back out again. When Sam and Bugs have to tiptoe through a room of sleeping lions, Bugs lowers an alarm clock while Sam is in the middle of the room. "How Now, Brown Cow?" Bugs asks from the other side of a pit of lions, which Sam attempts to cross with stilts until Bugs tosses stilt-sawing tools to the cats. Trying to get out, Bugs accidently runs out into the middle of the arena. When the lions are released, they run straight past Bugs and head for Sam and Nero. As the killer cats chop down the column the two are standing on, the

Emperor produces his violin and plays "Taps."

HEIR CONDITIONED

Elmer Fudd, Sylvester; Nov 26; LT; Directed by Friz Freleng; Story by Warren Foster; Animation by Art Davis, Gerry Chiniquy, and Virgil Ross; Layouts by Hawley Pratt; Backgrounds by Irv Wyner; Voice Characterization by Mel Blanc; Music by Milt Franklyn.

A cat in an alley comes across a newspaper and reads, "Pet Cat Inherits Fortune." Spreading the good word Tweety says, "Ooh, twee million dowwars!" In the cartoon, the serious ideas put forth are even zanier than the comedy. On the fun level, it's Sylvester and his alley cat cronies trying to sneak a satchel of loot past Elmer Fudd so they can have a high old time, re-using the hole in the floor and the something-or-other cleaner company bits from *A Mouse Divided*. On the sponsor (Sloane Foundation)'s message, serious level, Fudd pweaches how Sylvester's investing of the "idle cash" he's inherited from his late owner will lead to new pwoducts, new industwies, and a higher standard of living. Fudd's takes out a projector to show on film how savings lead to capital investment that have helped everyone (sort of anticipating the same scene in Kurt Vonnegut's *Player Piano*) and converts the alleycat. When Sylvester gets the money to them, they scold him, "What you tryin' to do, upset our whole economic structure? PUT IT BACK!" Sylvester finally agrees to invest it, snarling at a shot of the old lady, "Sakes! You'd'a saved me a lotta trouble if you'd'a figured out a way to take it with ya!"

GUIDED MUSCLE

Coyote (Eatibus Almost Anythingus), and Road Runner (Velocitus Delectibus); Dec 10; LT; Directed by Charles M. Jones; Story by Michael Maltese; Animation by Richard Thompson, Ken Harris, Ben Washam, and Abe Levitow; Layouts by Philip DeGuard; Backgrounds by Richard H. Thomas; Voice Characterization by Mel Blanc; Music by Carl Stalling.

This one begins with the Coyote cooking a tin can and the Road Runner zooming by persuading him to try again for his feathered friend. The Coyote fires himself with an arrow head on his nose out of the big bow, has another one of those enormous slingshots that doesn't sling; his cannon propels missiles backwards, a wrecking ball misses the bird and brings down stuff on him, as does a big medicine ball, covering the road with grease. Then he's unable to run away from a truck. He swings from one cliff to another, landing flat on a third cliff right below his own. He lowers a TNT stick to the Road Runner on a fishing rod. It doesn't go off; the length of rope and the Coyote's body turn into a big fuse, igniting the rest of his explosives. A book on "How to Tar and Feather a Road Runner" inspires the Coyote to invent a tarring and feathering machine which turns on him; his running over a bomb he's planted is perfectly timed to the length of his fuse; at this point he displays a sign: "Wanted: One Gullible Coyote, Apply to Manager of This Theater," then pulls out the "That's all Folks."

PAPPY'S PUPPY

Sylvester; Dec 17; MM; Directed by Friz Freleng; Story by Warren Foster: Animation by Gerry Chiniquy; Layouts by Hawley Pratt; Backgrounds by Irv Wyner; Voice Characterization by Mel Blanc; Music by Carl Stalling.

In a dog and cat hospital, Butch J. Bulldog nervously awaits the arrival of his son. He takes his puppy home and teaches him to walk with a "mean look," and to attack cats. The puppy plays with a ball, which rolls toward Sylvester. At first, the puppy runs from the feline, but, realizing it's a cat, the puppy comes back to attack. Sylvester takes care of the little pest by putting him in a tin can. Butch rescues his son and hammers the cat into same can. Sylvester walks across the yard, passing Butch, with the little puppy playing with his tail. When the cat goes behind the fence, the cat swats the puppy away. Butch runs after Sylvester and slaps him.

Sylvester throws a stick and the puppy fetches it. He then throws the stick into the street traffic, but the puppy returns it. Butch throws the stick back into the busy street and forces Sylvester to get it. The cat narrowly misses getting hit but is run over by a scooter on the sidewalk. Sylvester nails the pesky puppy in Butch's dog house with a dynamite stick but Butch replaces his son with Sylvester. Sylvester rigs a rifle trigger to a bone but just as the puppy grabs the bone, Butch walks by. Sylvester grabs the rifle, puts his finger in it, and gets blasted. The stork comes to the front gate looking for Butch with an addition to his family, a basket of bulldog puppies!

ONE FROGGY EVENING

Dec 31; MM; Directed by Charles M. Jones; Story by Michael Maltese; Animation by Abe Levitow, Richard Thompson, Ken Harris, and Ben Washam; Layouts by Robert Gribbroek; Backgrounds by Philip DeGuard; Music by Milt Franklyn.

Picture, if you will, a member of a wrecking crew demolishing an 1892 building and opening the cornerstone to see a frog entering stage left, doing a song-and-dance, singing "Hello, My Ragtime Gal." The finder's mind races with the possibilities of getting rich by exploiting this singing frog. But the frog will not sing if anyone is present. At a talent agency, the finder gets an agent to look at the frog (today called "Michigan J. Frog"). Investing his mattress of life savings in renting a theater, the finder lures a crowd in with the promise of "Free Beer." The frog does his stuff atop a high wire, finishing just as the entrepeneur manages to lift the jammed curtain. Months later, a policeman hears someone singing (*Barber of Seville*) in the park and when our friend points to the frog, the film dissolves to a shot of him in a psycopathic hospital, the frog leaning on a window bar crooning "Please Don't Talk About Me When I'm Gone." Years later, a broken and desolate man, he finally dumps the frog in the cornerstone of a building about to be constructed. A hundred years pass, and rayguns disintergrate the old building. Some things never change, as the discoverer of *this* cornerstone is also convinced he can make a fortune with the singing frog.

One of the most celebrated films in animation history, and justly a masterpiece of concept, timing and nuance.

1956

BUGS BONNETS

Bugs Bunny, Elmer Fudd; Jan 14; MM; Directed by Chuck Jones; Story by Tedd Pierce; Animation by Ben Washam, Abe Levitow, Richard Thompson and Ken Harris. Layouts by Robert Gribbroek; Backgrounds by Richard H. Thomas; Voice Characterization by Mel Blanc; Music by Milt Franklyn.

"It is a known psychological fact that people's behavior is strongly affected by the way they dress," the narrator explains, "even a change of hats will usually bring certain changes. Let's have this mild-mannered man (Fudd) put a hunter's cap on his head and see what happens." A truck of headwear from the Acme Theatrical Hat Co. spills its cargo across the forest as death-hungry Fudd ("Wet me see the color of your spurting blood!") is after woodland creature Bugs Bunny. A sergeant's helmet lands on the rabbit, who immediately barks orders at Fudd to forward march into the lake. Fudd returns as Douglas MacArthur and starts firing on the helmet but is busted by Bugs as game warden for "shooting sergeants out of season." As a pilgrim, Elmer explains he was shooting Thanksgiving turkeys. Bugs becomes an Indian who chases him, then a boy scout helping old lady Fudd across the street. Next, Bugs comes out flipping a coin like a gangster. Elmer becomes a cop who doesn't accept a bribe but gets sent up for 45 years by Judge Bugs anyway. Lastly, Elmer proposes in a bridal veil and Bugs accepts in a topper, and we end with the "groom" about to carry the "bride" over the threshold, Bugs saying, "You know, I think it always helps a picture to have a romantic ending."

TOO HOP TO HANDLE

Sylvester, Hippetty Hopper; Jan 28; LT; Directed by Robert McKimson; Story by Warren Foster; Animation by Robert McKimson and Keith Darling; Layouts and Backgrounds by Richard H. Thomas. Film Editor: Treg Brown; Voice Characterization by Mel Blanc; Music by Milt Franklyn.

Zoo superintendent: "What's that? The baby kangaroo got out again?" The formula: Sylvester and Junior mistake Hippetty Hopper, the escaped baby kangaroo, for a giant mouse. The background: Sylvester claims he can't show Junior how to catch mice because there are no mice around, so Junior tries to round up some mice by carving a windpipe like the one used by the Pied Piper. The trick is figuring how many holes in the wood pipe will attract the mice. Thematic variations: For once Junior sees the mouse a scene before his Pop, and has to convince him that something fishy is happening. Also, Sylvester and Junior both see Hippetty being hauled back to the zoo at the end and realize he's really a kangaroo. The series will never be the same again. Reasons for watching: The plot does have a little more blood than usual and there's a good ruckus as Hoppy sends Sylvester for a wild ride on the back of a pig, but McKimson proves he's got

the old pepper by animating a beautiful establishing scene between Sylvester and Junior ("And just how, pray tell, could a cat attract a mouse?").Wind-up gag: Junior proves that four holes in the pipe attract a swine, five a cow, six a "giant mouse," so Sylvester tries breaking it in half to attract little mice and, instead, is beset by a dozen bruiser bulldogs (Junior: "I wonder if anyone would be interested in adopting a fatherless kitten?").

WEASEL STOP

Foghorn Leghorn; Feb 11; MM; Directed by Robert McKimson; Story by Ted Pierce; Animation by Keith Darling, Ted Bonnicksen, and Russ Dyson; Layouts and Backgrounds by Richard H. Thomas; Voice Characterization by Mel Blanc; Music by Milt Franklyn.

On one of those quiet summer days when "you can hear a caterpillar sneaking across a moss bed in tennis shoes—sneakers that is," Foghorn fools a guard dog into running around crazy-like by yelling "weasel!" When the real weasel comes, the dog doesn't believe Foghorn and so doesn't lift a finger to help. Foghorn gets revenge by teaming up with the thief, telling him, "I like a sneaky li'l ol' underhanded weasel like you." Foghorn sets up various methods for the weasel to get rid of the dog, all of which backfire on both weasel and rascally rooster. This includes drifting over the dog on a balloon with a dynamite stick and sneaking up to the dog with various implements of destruction concealed by piles of hay. For punishment, the dog puts both through a hay machine, which removes Foghorn's feathers and bales them.

It's not the usual barnyard dog (the one identified as Mandrake in *One Meat Brawl*) here, but a lethargic middle-southern hick who caint stop mumbling stupid sayin's and whittlin' somethin' to hit the weasel with.

THE HIGH AND THE FLIGHTY

Foghorn Leghorn, Daffy Duck; Feb 18; LT; Directed by Robert McKimson; Story by Tedd Pierce; Animation by Ted Bonnicksen, Russ Dyson, and Keith Darling; Layouts by Robert Gribbroek;

Backgrounds by Richard H. Thomas. Film Editor: Treg Brown; Voice Characterization by Mel Blanc; Music by Carl Stalling.

Daffy Duck, the travelling salesman (like most in Warner toons, from Walla Walla, Washington), comes across Foghorn Leghorn and the barnyard Dog up to their old tricks. Foghorn gets the dog to strangle himself on the rope and popping a beach ball in his mouth; the dog hurls a watermelon in Foghorn's face from a few stories up. Daffy tells us, "Brother! What a golden opportunity for a go-gettin' salesman in my line of merchandise— Ace Novelty Co.: Practical Jokes for Every Occasion. Daffy adds fuel to the feud, supplying both sides with prepackaged dirty tricks at a reasonable markup for himself. Foghorn buys a "spring bone" that opens inside the dog who comes back at Foghorn with an electrified cob of corn. The tricks sometimes backfire. Foghorn tries a phoney choo-choo facade which the dog sidesteps while Foghorn goes careening into a real train. Finally, Foghorn and the dog discover each other setting up the Ace Novelty Pipe Full o' Fun Kit Number Seven and realize "We have been flim-flammed!" The two conspire against the interloper and trap him in his own pipe full o' fun, a rubber band which snaps him into a pipe funneling him into a jar. Foghorn has his own capital-istic idea. "You know, there might, I say there just might, be a market for bottled duck."

BROOM-STICK BUNNY

Bugs Bunny; Feb 25; LT; Directed by Chuck Jones; Story by Tedd Pierce; Animation by Richard Thompson, Ken Harris, Ben Washam and Abe Levitow; Layouts by Ernie Nordli. Film Editor: Treg Brown; Backgrounds by Philip DeGuard; Voice Characterization by Mel Blanc; Music by Milt Franklyn.
All the gags from 60s monster sitcoms are done here first and better, using Witch Hazel (June Foray, from *Bewitched Bunny*) who is as vain about her ugliness as most women are about their beauty. She even has a Magic Mirror on her wall (like witch queen did in Disney's *Snow White*), which she asks, "Who is the ugliest one of all?"; she's deathly afraid of getting pretty as she grows older. Her claim to the title of the ugliest is threatend by Bugs, trick or treating as a creepy hal-loween witch. Bugs wants to worm her ugly secrets out of her with "Who undoes your hair? It's absolutely hide-ous!" Bugs removes his mask not know-ing she needs a rabbit's clavicle for her brew. She chases him around her house meaning to do Bugs "serious hoits." After reeling him in with a carrot, she's about to chop into him with a blade "sharp enough to split a hare" (laughs!), when he makes with the soul-ful eyes routine, reminding her of "Paul ... my pet tarantula," causing her to blubber hysterically. Bugs tries to soothe her sobs with a spot of tea, which she forgets has all sorts of beau-tifying potions in it. She is transformed into a ravishing sex symbol. The magic mirror genie gets a gander, does a Bob Hope "rowr-rowr," and flies after her, she on her broomstick, he on his magic carpet. "Hello, air-raid headquarters?" Bugs winds up, "you're not gonna belive this, but I just saw a genie with light brown hair chasin' a flying sorceress!"

ROCKET SQUAD

Porky Pig, Daffy Duck; Mar 10; MM; Directed by Chuck Jones; Story by Tedd Pierce; Animation by Ken Harris, Ben Washam, Abe Levitow and Richard Thompson; Layouts by Ernie Nordli; Film Editor: Treg Brown; Backgrounds by Philip DeGuard; Voice Characterization by Mel Blanc; Music by Milt Franklyn.
A lame spoof of *Dragnet*, set in outer space. "Ladies and Gentlemen: the story you are about to see is true. The drawings have been changed to protect the innocent." Daffy: "This is the milky way, a nice galaxy. 875 billion trillion people live here, a nice place to live. It's my job to keep it that way. I'm a space cop. My name's Monday. My partner's name is Tuesday. He always follows me." That's the best line in the film. Now it is the super-deadpans of Porky and Daffy in gumshoe suits,

relentlessly puffing cigarettes, Daffy constantly naming the time and Porky correcting him. They're in search of kids who've blown the ring of Saturn ("When will parents learn to keep uranium out of their children's reach?"). When the pair are summoned back to headquarters, they go through mail-chute like tubes and are sent out in search of the "Flying Saucer Bandit." They process clues gathered by crime robots through computers (a player piano) and come up with the name of George "Mother" Machre, a crook so devious he's never been suspected of anything. They use their criminal detecto set (which also tells you where to find Jones, Pierce and Blanc) to find him at a space drivein. After a chase they arrest him and, as a result of the trial, the two arresting officers are sentenced to 20 years for false arrest.

TWEET AND SOUR

Tweety, Sylvester; Mar 24; LT; Directed by Friz Freleng; Story by Warren Foster; Animation by Virgil Ross, Art Davis, and Gerry Chiniquy; Layouts by Hawley Pratt; Backgrounds by Irv Wyner; Voice Characterization by Mel Blanc (June Foray); Music by Milt Franklyn.

"Let me warn you, Sylvester," Granny threatens, "if there's one little feather, just one little feather, harmed on this bird, I'm going to sell you to the violin string factory!" With that, she mimes and mimics fiddling Chopin's "Funeral March." After Granny leaves, Tweety "plays" the air-fiddle to remind the cat of Granny's threat. Said threat encompasses other felines who are hungry for Tweety, and Sylvester has to rescue Tweety from a scroungy, one-eyed orange alleycat. "Listen, cat," Sylvester yells, "lay offa this bird! You want me to be made into violin strings?" What follows is grab-the-bird-and-run back and forth between the two putty tats, each armed with an endless arsenal of mallets and anvils (not explosives). Sylvester does not intend to eat Tweety but to save his own skin. When Sylvester gropes in a hen house for the canary, a rooster gets ready to pound down on his hand when the other cat butts in and puts *his* paw under the rooster's hammer! When Sylvester gets the bird back in the house, Tweety compliments him, "Say, you're weally a *nice* puddy tat!" Sylvester counters, "I just don't relish the idea of having p-p-pizzicatos played on me in some string section!" He finally gets rid of the rival cat with a few balloons carrying dynamite. Granny returns just as he's putting Tweety back *in* the cage, "Ah, what's the use," he sobs, playing the "March" and falling back in a violin case, "She'll never believe me!"

HEAVEN SCENT

Pepe Le Pew; Mar 31; MM; Directed by Chuck Jones; Story by Chuck Jones; Animation by Abe Levitow, Richard Thompson, Ken Harris, and Ben Washam; Layouts by Erni Nordli. Backgrounds by Philip DeGuard; Voice Characterization by Mel Blanc; Music by Milt Franklyn.

This basic Pepe routine would be without any distinguishing characteristics were it not so funny. The femme cat applies the stripe to get past a bunch of relentless dogs who separate her from a basket of fish at the waterfront, and does it by rubbing her back against a freshly-painted flagpole. Pepe chases her through the park (that he sings about "strolling through") where she hides in a basket of grapes ready to be made into wine, then up a tree, where Pepe appears and says "marry me." Resolved to play "not quite so easy to get," he runs ahead of her saying, "Marriage, I don't know ... " He heads her off at the pass and chases her through the mountains where he combines single echoes into the phrase "I love you" and advises, "all you need is a little occupational therapy, like making love." Pepe hangs from a cliff by his toes ("security isn't everything"), she runs into a tunnel. Pepe sees the sign, "No entre—Le tunnel is blocked." Before he goes in "for the kill," he quotes, "as a distinguished colleague of mine once noted, there is very little difference between men and women," but, Pepe concludes, "Viva la difference!"

MIXED MASTER

Apr 14; LT; Directed by Robert McKimson; Story by Tedd Pierce; Animation by Russ Dyson, Keith Darling, Ted Bonnicksen, and George Grandpre; Layouts by Robert Gribbroek; Backgrounds by Richard H. Thomas. Film Editor: Treg Brown; Voice Characterization by Mel Blanc; Music by Milt Franklyn.

Like owner, like dog: Harry brings home Robert, a shaggy puppy dog, but his slightly snooty wife Alice is worried that her very snooty thoroughbred pekinese Chang won't like the newcomer and he doesn't. Things get worse when the overaffectionate, sloppy mutt overnight grows to the size of a small horse (although "the man assured me he wouldn't get any bigger"). "I'm sorry, but if they don't get along, Robert's just got to go back," Alice threatens. The big dog overhears from outside. "It would be different if he were a throughbred." Harry insists Robert might be pedigreed, and looks though a book containing names and pictures to find out what. An important phone call comes in from his boss, and, while Harry tries to concentrate on a big deal, the dopey dog keeps interrupting, trying to demonstrate that he's various kinds of pedigreed pooches: a bird dog (he plummets from a tree), a boxer (by putting on gym shorts and boxing gloves), a Doberman Pinscher (he goes around pinching Harry, and, unfortunately, Alice), an Irish setter (he does a jig to a loud "Irish Washerwoman") and a sheep dog (as Harry is about to leave for an emergency business trip, Robert brings home a flock of sheep). Three weeks later, when Harry returns, Alice announces she's discovered what "Roberta" is, a mother with a whole litter full of little pooches all of whom look like their mom, except one that's the spitting image of Chang, who winks slyly for the camera.

RABBITSON CRUSOE

Bugs Bunny, Yosemite Sam; Apr 28; LT; Directed by Friz Freleng; Story by Warren Foster; Aninmation by Gerry Chiniquy, Virgil Ross, and Art Davis; Layouts by Hawley Pratt; Backgrounds by Irv Wyner; Voice Characterization by Mel Blanc; Music by Milt Franklyn.

This typically side-splitting Freleng Bugs cartoon, like the year's other such entry *Napoleon Bunny-Part*, uses a historio-literary background for the critter's doin's. Sam plays Crusoe, whose desert island seting is divided into three areas, the main part in the middle, a smaller island containing the coconut tree (his sole source of sustenance lo these 20 years), and his wrecked ship, containing supplies such as matches (were he to logically gather all this onto one island there'd be no fun!). The man-eating shark, Dopey Dick, very creatively designed, yelps like a dog and has no qualms about following his prey onto dry land, preventing Sam's movement between the islands. There are funny goings on enough even before Bugs (singing "Trade Winds") washes ashore on cue. Sam is getting fed up with coconuts (having prepared them as imaginatively as "New England Boiled Coconut"). Bugs is dunked into Sam's caldron just as he's celebrating being on dry land again. Bugs douses the flame, and when Sam returns from the ship with another match, it's the no-good, bushwackin' barracuda that leaps out of the pot at him. Now Bugs is on the ship (singing Doris Day's hit "Secret Love") and Sam's got to get past the shark to get at him; he tries a surfboard, then a balloon. As soon as Sam restores the rabbit in the pot, a tidal wave obliterates the place and Bugs, floating in the pot, agrees to save Sam from the no fin-flappin' flounder only if they make a deal that Sam paddle the entire trip home to San Francisco!

GEE WHIZ-Z-Z

The Coyote ("Eatius Birdius"), the Road Runner ("Delcius Delicius") May 5; LT; Directed by Charles M. Jones; Story by Michael Maltese; Animation by Ben Washam, Abe Levitow, Richard Thompson, and Ken Harris; Layouts by Ernie Nordli; Backgrounds by Philip DeGuard; Music by Milt Franklyn.

Here is an abundance of riches: most of the greatest Road Runner/Coyote gags are in this one. There is the flustered bullet that can't outrace the Road Runner, exploding in the Coyote's face and the "Acme Triple Strength Armor Plate." There's also the TNT stick on the fishing rod, the giant rubber band to hurl the anvil downward, the dynamite on the doodad (some cartoon props resist verbal description), the phony bridge-out painting which doesn't stop the Road Runner but which causes the Coyote to go flying off a cliff as if there were a real bridge out, the TNT handle that stalls, the Acme jet motor and handlebars that function like a rocket sled, leaving our anti-hero plummeting once again, asking whosoever is in charge of these things (via signs), "How about ending this carton before I hit?" and "Thank You" when the iris out starts to close. The biggest howl is the infamous Acme Batman outfit (re-used in *Adventures of the Road Runner*) which enables the Coyote to fly though it doesn't occur to him to look where he's going.

TREE CORNERED TWEETY

Tweety, Sylvester; May 19; MM; Directed by Friz Freleng; Story by Warren Foster; Animation by Arthur Davis, Gerry Chiniquy, and Virgil Ross. Layouts by Hawley Pratt; Backgrounds by Irv Wyner; Voice Characterization by Mel Blanc; Music by Milt Franklyn.
"This is the city. Three million people. Three hundred thousand puddy tats. That's where I come in. I'm a little bird. I live in a cage. My name is Tweety." Kudos to Blanc here for making Tweety do an admirably ludicrous Jack Webb impression. "I looked out the window, I tawt I taw a puddy tat. I checked, I did, I did tee a puddy tat! A bwack puddy tat, wed nose,

white chest, name: Sylvester." The "meat" is basically standard-type gags: Sylvester trying to nail a bridge of boards from his window to Tweety's; swinging from one building to the other; buying a "pilot ejector seat" which doesn't stop for phone wires; "Monday, 10:15 A.M., I was feeding with the pigeons in fwont of the pubwic wibwary," Sylvester chasing Tweety in the automat and locating him in the pie section (only five cents for a slice of Tweety Pie); "December 14th, 2:15 P.M., the day after the big blizzard," Sylvester, on skiis, chasing Tweety, using spoons for snowshoes, "March 26th, 10:22 A.M., I finally found refuge, I knew dat bad puddy tat couldn't get me here," Tweety in a tree in the middle of a minefield!); Sylvester trying to tiptoe across with a mine-detector, Tweety handling him a magnet which pulls all the explosives toward him; "May 22nd, 11:20 A.M., Colorado seemed like a place where dat puddy tat couldn't find me, but I was wrong," Sylvester chasing Tweety under a wooden bridge, sawing through and landing in the boat of a fishing tourist who tawt he taw a puddy tat.

THE UNEXPECTED PEST

Sylvester; June 2; MM; Directed by Robert McKimson; Story by Warren Foster; Animation by Keith Darling, Ted Bonnicksen, George Grandpre, and Russ Dyson; Layouts by Robert Gribbroek. Backgrounds by Richard H. Thomas. Film Editor: Treg Brown; Voice Characterization by Mel Blanc; Musical Direction by Carl Stalling.
"Hey, Marsha, why do we have to put up with that dirty old cat, scratchin' up the furniture and makin' a mess outa the house?" "Well, John, we got him to get rid of the mice, remember?" "Yeah, but there hasn't been a mouse around the house for months." "That's right, I'll call the society tomorrow and get rid of him." Hearing this, Sylvester realizes, "I've gotta get a mouse to keep my happy home!" Unable to find a mouse in the house, he locates one outside who faints dead away at the sight of him. Sylvester brings the rodent inside, forcing the mouse to do

as he's told or else "down the hatch." His chores consist of scaring the lady good and letting Sylvester catch and clobber him. "Oh John, we'll have to keep the cat, he just caught a great big mouse, and there might be others around!" Or, says Sylvester, "the same one lots of times." Days pass, and finally one day Sylvester takes out the mouse who says, "Just a minute, cat, I've been doing some thinking. It looks like you need me. From now on, it makes *me* boss around here." The mouse then frolics through a series of dangerous stunts, knowing that Sylvester has to protect him from whatever happens. He takes it too far when he sits on a TNT stick. Sylvester tosses it in the next room, where it exploes on the master. The next shot has the band-aged cat watching as the mouse fakes suicide. "After all he's been through, I thought he deserved a happy ending."

NAPOLEON BUNNY-PART

Bugs Bunny; June 16; MM; Directed by Friz Freleng; Story by Warren Foster; Animation by Gerry Chiniquy, Virgil Ross, and Art Davis; Layouts by Hawley Pratt; Backgrounds by Irv Wyner; Voice Characterization by Mel Blanc; Musical Direction by Milt Franklyn.

Bugs Bunny tunnels into the "head-quarters du Napoleon" (apparently wrong turns "off the Hollywood free-way" mislead him through time as well as geography) and assumes the lush palace is a theater lobby (those were the days). Finding Napoleon planning a battle strategy, Bugs annoys the hot-headed emperor by dropping poker-faced hints, reverse psychology, and sneezing. "Nappy," as Bugs calls him, tries to have the rabbit arrested as a spy, summoning his lummox guard (Mugsy sans Rocky) to his aid, though he serves largely to bayonet Napoleon's

behind. When Napoleon slides into the next room, he gets a gander of Bugs dressed in drag as Josephine. She/he suggests they dance to a tune from a jukebox that includes "St. Louis XIV Blues" by the Count Du Basie, "Bas-tille Boogie" by Duc D'Ellington and "I Ain't Got Nobody" by the Guilloti-ners, the jig being up when Nappy sees Josie's cottontail. Bugs even finds wacky antics to pull on the guillotine, shaving the shreiking emperor's behind and switching places with the execu-tioner. At this point, two keepers from the *Maison D'Idiot* carry him off. "Imagine that guy thinking he's Napo-leon," says Bugs, donning the familiar *chapeau*, "when *I* really am!"

TUGBOAT GRANNY

Tweety, Sylvester; June 23; MM; Directed by Friz Freleng; Story by Warren Foster; Animation by Virgil Ross, Art Davis, and Gerry Chiniquy; Layouts by Hawley Pratt; Backgrounds by Irv Wyner; Film Editor: Treg Brown; Voice Characterization by Mel Blanc; Musical Direction by Milt Franklyn.

"Oh dat bad ol' puddy tat, he never give up!" Though Granny, for the only time, gets her name in the title (a play on *Tugboat Annie*), she only appears in the opening scene, a precocious kiddie-song duet with her baby bird about tug-boat life. For the rest of the toon, it's strictly Sylvester's attempts to board the li'l tug as it chugs past. The first boat he uses is sunk by Tweety's anchor; his second, an inflatable raft, by a dart Tweety makes a present of to Sylvester. Number one attempt at jumping off a bridge onto the tug lands Sylvester down the smokestack and into the flaming furnace. Number two finds him with a parachute that only opens underwater. When he tries mov-ing underwater with a snorkle, a sea-gull insists on sitting on the pipe and blocking his air (and depositing an egg in the cat's mouth). A motorboat takes him over a waterfall, and when, he tries lassoing Tweety, he latches on to a speedboat. Now he waterskis until he smashes into a pole, causing a fish to gurgle, "I tawt I taw a puddy tat."

STUPOR DUCK

Daffy Duck; July 17; LT; Directed by Robert McKimson; Story by Tedd Pierce; Animation by Ted Bonnicksen, George Grandpre, Russ Dyson, and Keith Darling; Layouts by Robert Gribbroek; Backgrounds by Richard H. Thomas; Effects Animation by Harry Love; Voice Characterization by Mel Blanc; Musical Direction by Carl Stalling.

A TV parody highlighted by broad, loose-limbed animation: "Possessing extra-ordinary powers, this strange being from another planet is faster than a bullet (as in a pop gun), more powerful than a speeding locomotive (an ancient put-put choo choo), able to leap the tallest building (and get himself stuck on the flagpole)." In his day job as Cluck Trent, mild-mannered reporter on a metroplitan newspaper, Daffy Duck/Cluck Trent/Stupor Duck overhears a Russian voice in the editor's office, threatening to "blow up everything, buildings, bridges; power plants, trains ... everwhere ruin and destruction, then *I, Aardvark Ratnik* will be supreme!"

Daffy suspects "Ratnik" might be in league with the forces of evil, and, not knowing the voice was only from a "corny soap opera," heads for the broom closet to change into Stupor Duck. His search for the nonexistent villain begins by smashing through a window and into a building across the street ("Sakes! Wouldn't ya think they could find some other place to put a building?"). Other backfiring, non-existent examples of Ratnik's work: a falling building is only "being wrecked to make way for a new city hall," a ship sinking is a submarine, "planting dynamite at the base of that railroad trestle! The work of that rat Ratnik or I don't know my rats!" is only a stunt for a Warners movie, and a rocket he somehow concludes is one of Ratnik's missiles takes him straight to the moon.

"STUPOR DUCK"
a Looney Tune
– CARTOON –
color by
TECHNICOLOR

BARBARY COAST BUNNY

Bugs Bunny; July 21; LT; Directed by Chuck Jones; Story by Tedd Pierce; Animation by Abe Levitow, Richard Thompson, and Ken Harris; Layouts by Robert Gribbroek; Film Editor: Treg Brown; Backgrounds by Philip DeGuard; Musical Direction by Carl Stalling.

Tunnelling through the ground en route to his Cousin Hoiman in San Francisco, Bugs doesn't make a wrong turn at "Albacoikee," but bumps into a solid gold boulder and goes through a Daffy Duck-style greed fit ("I'm rich! I'm rich! I'm fabulously wealthy! I'm independent beyond the realm of sheer avarice!"). He is overheard by the villain Nasty Canasta (more comical and less frightening than in *Drip-a-Long Daffy*), who uses a phony bank and achieves the impossible by duping the rabbit out of his gold. Bugs doesn't even have to tell us, "You realize that this is not going to go unchallenged." Six months later, Bugs, clad like a clod from Hicktown, shows up at Canasta's Casino (presumably built with Bugs's booty) and using his rube act, proceeds to empty the place and Canasta of his money. He treats a slot machine like a "tellerphone" with which he calls home for money, making like the jackpot pay-off is from his Mom. After cleaning him out at roulette ("Marbles—Frisco style"), draw poker (pun) where he has a bigger hand (pun, pun), and even winning a jackpot from Canasta's six shooter, he leaves Canasta and us with, "The moral of this story is don't try to steal no 18 carrots from no rabbit."

ROCKET-BYE BABY

Aug 4; MM; Directed by Chuck Jones; Story by Tedd Pierce; Animation by Ken Harris, Abe Levitow, and Ben Washam; Layouts by Ernie Nordli; Backgrounds by Philip DeGuard; Effects Animation by Harry Love; Film Editor: Treg Brown; Musical Direction by Milt Franklyn.

"This is the planet Mars. In the summer of 1954, this planet passed extremely close to Earth, so close that a cosmic force was disturbed and a baby intended for the Earth was delivered to

Mars, while a Martian baby went by mistake to Earth." Imagine Mr. Wilbur (Daws Butler)'s surprise when his baby is born green and with antennae, and imagine his reluctance to take baby for a stroll when the kid frightens old ladies. When Mr. Wilbur comes home from work one day, his wife (June Foray) tells him, "I'm so worried about baby. He's doing your income tax! And that isn't all." It seems he's spelled out the Einstein theory with his building blocks and has constructed molecules out of tinker toys! In an effort to get little "Mot" to play more, they sit him down in front of the Captain Schimdeo TV program. Based on one that the Cap holds up on TV, he constructs a working flying saucer. That night they're visited by a rocket with a message from Sir U. Tan of Mars, telling them to guard the Martian baby Mot and they'll soon be able to exchange him for their own child, "Yob" (spell it backwards!). Mot however, has taken off in his own little saucer, and Mr. Wilbur has to chase him into a hall where an authority happens to be lecturing on the phoniness of the flying saucer scare. Mr. Wilbur wakes up in the hospital, the whole Mot-Yob affair a dream. One surprise: the earthling baby's wrist-tag reads "Yob!"

HALF FARE HARE
Bugs Bunny; Aug 18; MM; Directed by Robert McKimson; Story by Tedd Pierce; Animation by George Grandpre, Russ Dyson, Keith Darling, and Ted Bonnicksen; Layouts by Robert Gribbroek and Richard H. Thomas; Voice Characterization by Mel Blanc; Musical Direction by Carl W. Stalling.
One of the lost episodes of *The Honey-*

mooners. Up in the cold north, Bugs reads a headline telling him of a local carrot crop freeze and conversely about a bumper crop in Tennesse. "Rabbits leaving (this) state in droves." "But I don't have a drove," says Bugs, "I'll just have to hop a choo choo for Chattanooga." It so happens that the Chattanooga Choo Choo has other stowaways, two deadbeat bums, Cramden and Norton, who are so hungry their stomachs think their throats have been cut, and have started consuming their feet. When Bugs boards, they yell "food." The seemingly naive rabbit doesn't make like he catches on, asking them what they're having for dinner and being told it's a surprise. When the lights go out, Norton pushes Cramden into the pot instead of Bugs, who beats it. The bums chase him over the top of the train, where he uses a curtain of smoke ("We must be going through Los Angeles") to fool them into a tank load of alligators heading for Florida (standard equipment on south-bound trains). Bugs then gets them to duck into another car, which he washes out with water ("drinks on the house"). All three get knocked off by low train tunnels. The ending has Bugs, not getting to Chattanooga, but getting his "bumper crop" with really grotesque lumps on his head.

RAW! RAW! ROOSTER
Foghorn Leghorn; Aug 25; LT; Directed by Robert McKimson; Story by Tedd Pierce; Animation by Russ Dyson, Ted Bonnicksen, George Grandpre, and Keith Darling; Layouts and Backgrounds by Richard H. Thomas; Film Editor: Treg Brown; Voice Characterization by Mel Blanc; Musical Direction by Carl W. Stalling.
"This is living," says Foghorn Leghorn, surrounded by his adoring harem of hens. "I wonder what the poor chickens are doing." But news from a telegram threatens his bliss, "Put out the red carpet for your old college chum, Rhode Island Red." Foggy, who "had enough of that bird-brained loudmouth in college," decides to barricade the door (complete with signs such as "Foggy doesn't live here anymore")

against his arrival. It is no good, since the Jackie Gleason-inspired Wisenheimer has already infiltrated the barnyard in the guise of the telegram boy! In no time the hardy-har-har'ing overgrown collegiate has driven his buddy slap happy with joy buzzers and squirting flowers ("same old Foggy ... anything for a laugh!"). Foghorn decides he's got to "get rid of this cornball before he palsy-walsies me to death!" As Red sings "Freddie the Freshman," Foghorn tries a trick chair with a boxing-glove camera, and makes other unsuccessful attempts on R.I. Red's person, including booby-trapping his football (after Red promises the adoring hens to show them the "star of Chicken Tech in action") and his golf balls. Finally, Foghorn puts on Red's telegram boy disguise and serves him with a phony telegram ("Contact me at once regarding an inheritance, signed A. Shyster, Lawyer"). Before Red leaves, Foghorn presents him with a time bomb he passes off as an electric bowling ball and clock ("Tells you when it's time to bowl!"). After the explosion, says Red, "With a friend like you, I'll never need an enemy!"

THE SLAP-HOPPY MOUSE

Sylvester, Hippety Hopper; Sept 1; MM; Directed by Robert McKimson; Story by Tedd Pierce; Animation by Ted Bonnicksen, George Grandpre, Keith Darling, and Russ Dyson; Layouts by Robert Gribbroek; Backgrounds by Richard H. Thomas; Film Editor: Treg Brown; Voice Characterization by Mel Blanc; Musical Direction by Carl Stalling.

For once Sylvester and Junior have it soft, as pets in a plush mansion, they have "nothin' to do all day but purr and meow and eat and sleep!" However, local cat gossip has is that Sylvester senior, a once-great mouser, is a has-been! The shame of it is more for Junior than "One of my tender years can take!" To prove that what they're saying isn't so, Sylvester takes his son mouse-catching. As they're among the landed gentry these days, Sylvester approaches the hunt as if it were a mouse safari. In proper hunting gear, the two scout a "big old run down mouse-infested house" (the for-sale sign in front advertises it as such). There Sylvester prepares to demonstrate his incomparable stalking technique. Unbeknownst to him, Hippetty Hopper has fallen off the circus train on the nearby railroad tracks and coincidentally, has wandered into the same house that Sylvester and Junior are mouse-hunting in. For once, Sylvester doesn't have to convince Junior of the giant mouse's existence as Junior sees him right off the bat. That doesn't make him any less adamant about making Pops catch the mouse, because after all, "He's only a mouse, Father, and cats aren't afraid of mice." Each attempt to lunge at Hoppy results in Sylvester geting tossed out. In the wind-up, Sylvester gets accidently glued to the floor and Junior saws out the wood around him. "Oh the shame of it all, carrying my father home again, stiff as a board!"

A STAR IS BORED

Bugs Bunny, Daffy Duck, Elmer Fudd, Yosemite Sam; Sept 15; LT; Directed by Friz Freleng; Story by Warren Foster; Animation by Arthur Davis, Gerry Chiniquy, and Virgil Ross; Layouts by Hawley Pratt; Backgrounds by Irv Wyner; Film Editor: Treg Brown; Voice Characterization by Mel Blanc; Musical Direction by Milt Franklyn.

"Why would anyone wanna read about little old me?" Movie star Bugs Bunny gushes to his favorite columnist, Lolly, while, outside, Daffy the janitor seethes, "Whadda job for someone with my talent, while others with absolutely no talent get all the breaks!" Daffy storms into the front office demanding to be put into a picture as they look for a stunt double on the current Bugs Bunny flick. They haven't found anyone dumb enough to do it. Daffy gets the job and reports to the set in a rabbit suit, swearing "I could be sent to prison for the scenes I'm gonna steal." The German director only sends him in to get blasted by Yosemite Sam. When Elmer Fudd is about to saw into a branch Bugs is sitting on, Daffy clouts him and takes his place and saws all the way through, causing the tree to fall instead of the branch. The next scene involves just sitting on the dock and fishing. Daffy immediately is eaten by a giant fish. When Daffy horns in on one of the old gun bits, he gets blasted. Lastly, Daffy gets off on the sight of Bugs's jet about to crash, and then stonefacedly learns he's going to have to sub for Bugs in the crash. Complaining again, Daffy demands his own picture; they just happen to have a script ready called *The Duck*. Just when he thinks things have changed, he learns that this part also calls for him to be repeatedly blasted!

DEDUCE, YOU SAY

Daffy Duck as "Dorlock Homes" and Porky Pig as "Watkins"; Sept 29; LT; Directed by Chuck Jones; Story by Michael Maltese; Animation by Abe Levitow, Richard Thompson, Ken Harris, and Ben Washam; Layouts by Maurice Noble; Backgrounds by Philip DeGuard; Voice Characterization by Mel Blanc; Musical Direction by Milt Franklyn.

A thoughtful "Sherlock Holmes" parody, ribbing the movies and Conan Doyle stories down to Watkins's narration. Exceedingly clever verbal gags (Daffy's mispronunciations of cockney slang), combine with intricately beautiful visuals. As Holmes and Watkins trail the "Shorepshire Slasher" to a tough pub, Daffy tries to play the calm, know-it-all Holmes, but he's too eager to collect fingerprints from everyone who crosses his path and to gather cigarette ashes and heads from beer glasses as clues (even from Watkins), and to look as if he knows what he's doing even as he falls on his face ("I may be down, but the jig is up!"). When a giant knife misses Daffy by a few inches, that too constitutes "a clue!" and Porky says, "Really, Holmes, you never cease to amaze me!" When the Slasher himself appears, Daffy disrobes and tries to tackle the man-mountain with turn-of-the-century wrestling techniques, while Porky calmly "interrogates" him

(Name? Shropshire Slasher. Occupation? Shropshire Slasher.). He wants to give himself up, and everything would be a bit of all right if only Daffy didn't bust the chops of a little old cockney flower woman ("Hawking dandelions without a license, eh? I'm gonna run you in!"). He knows he is in for it when the Slasher identifies her as "Mother!" Ultimately, Slasher and Mum depart, leaving our two heroes to do the old one about the school in which Holmes learned to be a detective: "Elementary, my dear Watkins, elementary."

YANKEE DOOD IT

Sylvester, Elmer Fudd; Oct 13; MM; Directed by Friz Freleng; Story by Warren Foster; Animation by Gerry Chiniquy, Virgil Ross, and Art Davis; Layouts by Hawley Pratt; Backgrounds by Irv Wyner; Film Editor: Treg Brown; Musical Direction by Milt Franklyn.

The King of the Elves (or "*El*ver Fudd, if you will) summons one of his subjects to fetch back the group of elves who've been helping the shoemaker lo these last 150 years. The shoemaker bellyaches that he won't be able to stay in business without the little people doing the work for him (sound familiar?). Meanwhile, the messenger elf comes closer and closer to being turned into a mouse each time the Shoemaker says the magic word, "Jehosophat," much to the delight of ever-hungry Sylvester. At this point the King arrives and explains the fundamentals of capitalist theory to the shoemaker, telling him how investments lead to new machinery that will "pwoduce a gweater pwoduct for evewy one and gweater pwofits" and so and and so forth, blah, blah, blah. Months pass, and the King returns to find that the shoemaker is a businessman supreme, with 500 people working for him. His new product is to be called "the Jehosphat boot." The word turns the King into a mouse, but he too can't remember the mouse-to-elf word, and runs down the street trying various Rumpel-combinations with Sylvester in hot pursuit.

What kind of cartoons do they watch in Russia? Comrade Cat and Bolshevik

Bunny explaining to Webster Wombat why the workers should control the means of production?

WIDEO WABBIT

Bugs Bunny, Elmer Fudd; Oct 27; MM; Directed by Robert McKimson; Story by Tedd Pierce; Animation by George Grandpre, Ted Bonnicksen, Keith Darling, and Russ Dyson; Layouts by Robert Gribbroek; Backgrounds by Richard H. Thomas; Film Editor: Irvin Jay; Voice Characterization by Mel Blanc; Musical Direction by Carl W. Stalling.

Bugs Bunny answers a want ad offering a career in television and learns that this career is predestined to be short-lived. Elmer Fudd, host of "The Sportsman's Hour," and his gushy producer (Frank Nelson) want him to help demonstrate the "pwoper pwocedure for twacking down, fwushing out, and bwasting to smitheweens a weal, wive wabbit!" Bugs has other ideas, and, instead of being a voluntary victim to mass-medium murder, visits the sets of other TV programs in appropriate costumes as Fudd pursues. Bugs does Groucho on the quiz show "You Beat Your Wife," turns "You Asked For It" into "You're Asking For It" so he can give the hunter a pie in the puss. As piano-toothed "Liverace," Bugs assigns Fudd as "Brother George" to deliver a TNT candelabra to their mother ("Because I want my program to go over with a bang"), then detours him through "You Were There"'s recreation of Custer's Last Stand (after which he has to go to "The Medic"). As an effeminate producer, Bugs ushers him into the "Masquerade Party" dressing room, costuming him as a rabbit so they can reverse roles on the "Sportsman's Hour" rabbit-blasting scenario. Fudd gets steamed, but Bugs as Art Carney turns him into the Marx Brother and goes, "Sheesh! What a grouch-o!"

THERE THEY GO-GO-GO

Road Runner; Nov 10; LT; Directed by Chuck Jones; Story by Michael Maltese; Animation by Richard Thompson, Ken Harris, Abe Levitow, and Ben Washam; Layouts and Backgrounds by Philip DeGuard; Effects Animation by Harry Love; Film Editor: Treg Brown; Musical Direction by Carl W. Stalling.

The Coyote is about to eat a clay chicken he has sculpted and fired, but he tosses it in a clay wastebasket. The Road Runner runs by, burning up the road so that the Coyote's feet (and other parts) catch on fire. C. uses a diving rod to locate underground water with which to put out his tail fire. The Coyote then tries to harpoon the Road Runner while swinging a rope. A pistol he has rigged up to spring at the bird instead goes into his own face. A tree-type catapult thrashes him against the ground and a spinning wheel of maces flies after him. Stupidly he uses a ladder he had tampered with as a booby trap for the Road Runner; he attaches dynamite to the spokes of a wheel that rolls off firing a rocket straight out the back; releases a load of rocks on himself and holds up a sign "In heaven's name, what am I *doing*?" Too late, from underneath the pile of rubble and coyote fragments another banner arises, bearing the device "The End."

TWO CROWS FROM TACOS

Nov 24; MM; Directed by Friz Freleng; Story by Tedd Pierce; Animation by Virgil Ross and Art Davis; Layouts by Hawley Pratt; Backgrounds by Irv Wyner; Film Editor: Treg Brown; Musical Direction by Milt Franklyn.

Cartoon rules: you're allowed to clobber your partner if the pint-sized creature the two of you are chasing (a grasshopper in this case) lands on his head. If, when one of you grabs said object and the two of you fight over it, you look in your hand and find a TNT stick, you *have* to give it to your partner because he still thinks it's the grasshopper.

Two Mexicali crows, prototypes of the 1959 gatos shmoes in name (Jose and Manuel) and personality, are after a Speedy Gonzales-like grasshopper. They begin reclining on a branch, their lethargic serenade interrupted only by a suddenly energetic "release," after which they return half asleep to the branch. After spotting the grasshopper from high up, they zoom towards the insect divebomber style and end up crashing into each other. Jose asks the silent bug, "Why you no come out and play weeth me? I'm a grasshopper too, a big grasshopper," and starts into an inane song of the sort he imagines will attract grasshoppers, "Hoppy Hoppy Grasshopper," which gets him an immediate clubbing from his el stupido partner ("Hey, Jose, we gonna eat a big grasshopper"). When he holes up in a tree, they "fool" him by saying loudly, "He's too smart for us. We go to Guadalahara where ees stupid grasshoppers." After coming out, the grasshopper fools them into attacking a creature made of cactus. We end as lazily as we began, the two crows singing screechily in their tree.

THE HONEY-MOUSERS

Dec 8; LT; Directed by Robert McKimson; Story by Ted Pierce; Animation by Ted Bonnicksen, George Grandpre, Keith Darling, and Russ Dyson; Layouts by Robert Gribbroek; Backgrounds by Richard H. Thomas; Film Editor: Irvin Jay; Musical Direction by Milt Franklyn.

"Morton, *you* are a mental case!" Mice Ralph Crumden and his wife Alice (June Foray), starving in their mousehole since the last people moved out, nearly resort to belting each other before their pal, Ned Morton (Daws Butler) enters with joyous tidings: "Hey, Ralphie Boy! New people movin' in! You oughta see what they're movin' in, like havin' Greenblatt's delicatessen right next door to us!" The only thing to prevent them from getting at it is the cat, but Crumden and Morton use the old cranium to concoct no end of unsuccessful cat-passing techniques, among them a tomato can that Ned covers Ralph in for armor, provoking Alice's comment, "Don't tell me there's a market for canned slob." Converting a barrel into a "trojan dog," the mice ride tank-like up to the fridge and start piling in the goodies (sardines, ice cream, "fish a la mode," olives, a pimento as a

memento, pickles, and rice). When they climb back in their tank, they've got the cat for company ("sheesh, what a grouch!")! Alice makes the obvious suggestion, "Get rid of this cat," and carries it out herself, walking stright up to the puss and belting him one. In front of Morton, Ralph acts angry at her, but when Ned leaves it's, "Alice, you're the greatest!"

TO HARE IS HUMAN

Bugs Bunny, Wile E. Coyote; Dec 15; MM; Directed by Chuck Jones; Story by Michael Maltese; Animation by Ken Harris, Abe Levitow, Richard Thompson, and Ben Washam; Layouts by Maurice Noble; Backgrounds by Philip DeGuard; Film Editor: Treg Brown; Voice Characterization by Mel Blanc; Musical Direction by Milt Franklyn.

An expansion on *Operation Rabbit* with the Coyote relying even more heavily on complicated technology (instead of a door, he goes down Bugs's hole in a portable elevator). Bugs is less ruffled and sure of his common sense, talking his way out of a sack (a la *Hare Tonic*) and be-bopping back to his hole to "Sweet Georgia Brown." By the second scene, Wile E. has constructed a "Univac Electronic Brain (Do it Yourself)" which supplies him with the answers when he punches in questions i.e., "rabbit. in hole. combination lock." It advises burglary methods, supplying him with the combination. He gets into the hole all right, but once there, Bugs has placed a banana peel so that Wile E. goes flying right out the Coyote disposal. The Univac's other solutions result in similar disasters: hand grenades placed in Bugs's toaster spring back at him, a plunger pulls him in, Bugs empties the vacuum bag he's slipped the TNT stick into in the same trash pail Wile E. is hiding in, the booby trapped carrot patch has the Coyote asking the Univac, "Rock falling. What'll I do" and the machine answers flatly, "go back and take your medicine." He does, and then we cut to the computer's screen sliding open revealing Bugs beneath: "Of course, the real beauty of this machine is that it has only one moving part."

1957

THREE LITTLE BOPS

Jan 5; LT; Directed by Friz Freleng; Story by Warren Foster; Animation by Gerry Chiniquy and Bob Matz; Layouts by Hawley Pratt; Backgrounds by Irv Wyner; Film Editor: Treg Brown; Narrator: Stan Freberg; Musical Direction by Shorty Rogers.
"The Three Little Pigs are still around/ But they're playin' music with a modern sound!" Man! This is a cartoon to dig like the most! Done entirely in music, with a heavy incessant beat throughout and Freberg's hip rhythmic spieling. The three gigging pigs are an in-the-groove (and post-King Cole) trio, whose set at the House of Straw club goes smoothly until a trumpet-toting wolf demands to sit in. This cat is bad and that ain't good! They forcibly eject him, but he counters "They stopped me before I could go to town, so I'll huff and puff and blow their house down." "The House of Straw was blown away/The Pigs had to find another place to play/The Dew Drop Inn, The House of Sticks/The Three Little Pigs were giving out licks!" The wolf shows up again, and when his bum blasting causes the crowd to shout, "Stop the music! Throw the square out!" he obliterates this joint. In the wreckage, the pigs vow, "So we won't be bothered by his windy tricks, the next place we play in must be made of bricks." "Sturdy place this house of bricks/Built in 1776/High class place with a high-class crowd/Sign on the door "No Wolves Allowed." Unable to blow this place up with his horn, or to fool them with his even cornier disguises, he tries blowing it up with explosives and blows himself straight to "the other place." But in death, his ghostly silhouette visits the pigs, and what a difference: "The big bad wolf/ He learned the rule. You gotta get hot to play real cool!"

TECHNICOLOR®

TWEET ZOO

Tweety, Sylvester; Jan 12; MM; Directed by Friz Freleng; Story by Warren Foster; Animation by Art Davis, Virgil Ross, and Gerry Chiniquy; Layouts by Hawley Pratt; Backgrounds by Irv Wyner; Film Editor: Treg Brown; Voice Characterization by Mel Blanc; Musical Direction by Milt Franklyn.
The guided tour of the zoo includes rhinos, tigers, and skunks, but the puddytat member of the tour group is interested only in the single known specimen of the tame and lovable Tweety Bird. He enters the cage, Tweety exits, and the chase is on. Tweety's ploy (oh he's a clever little bird!) is to take refuge in the cages of various dangerous animals, under the accurate impression that Sylvester will do something to annoy them and get clouted. In trying to net Tweety, Sylvester accidentally beans a bear, then hides in a wagon that contains steaks for the Bengal tigers who talk like Bengal lancers and don't watch what they eat. Tweety's bag of peanuts is consumed by an elephant ("Oh, you're a glutton, Mr. Elephant!") who stands over a hole concealing Tweety. With a toy mouse, Sylvester gets him to move. The petrified pachyderm pounces on the pussycat in fear! Our cat then trespasses into the crocodile pond, which isn't something you'd want to do twice even in a boat. A lion angered by Sylvester sinks the boat and himself. For revenge, he dips Sylvester back in said croc pond, then tosses him into the bear pit for good measure. You'd think Sylvester would know better than to try polevaulting past the greedy gators and carnivorous crocs. Leaving the zoo, he decides to remove birds from his diet, the cue for a flock of feathered friends to follow him!

SCRAMBLED ACHES

Road Runner; Jan 26; LT; Directed by Chuck Jones; Story by Michael Maltese; Animation by Abe Levitow, Richard Thompson, Ken Harris, and Ben Washam; Layouts by Maurice Noble; Backgrounds by Philip DeGuard; Film Editor: Treg Brown; Musical Direction by Carl W. Stalling and Milt Franklyn. Tastyus Supersonicus (the Road Runner) makes a sharp left turn which sends Eternalii Famishiis (The Coyote) sliding into the desert and off a cliff. The following nine attempts fail to catch the speedy bird: 1) The Coyote tries to trip the Road Runner with a false foot which the bird causes to spin out of control; 2) a dynamite stick on a lasso; 3) the Coyote attempts his chase on roller skates, using a wind-sail strapped to his back, propelled by an electric fan; 4) a large sky-rocket which blasts off with him; 5) using a lever to propel himself only causes a large boulder to smash the Coyote; 6) dropping an anvil from a helium balloon, which smashes through a bridge, bounces upwards on electric wires and destroys the ledge the Coyote is on; 7) a giant coil spring; 8)"Dehydrated Boulders" which crush him; 9) a "Junior Size Outboard Steam Roller" which chases the bird to a detour, into an "escape tunnel," (a disguised cannon which doesn't explode until the Coyote looks into it). The film ends as the Road Runner waves goodby to the blasted Coyote who gets run over by the out-of-control steamroller (He holds up a sign "This is The End").

ALI BABA BUNNY

Bugs Bunny, Daffy Duck; Feb 9; MM; Directed by Chuck Jones; Story by Michael Maltese; Animation by Richard Thompson, Ken Haris, Abe Levitow, and Ben Washam; Effects Animation by Harry Love; Layouts by Maurice Noble; Backgrounds by Philip DeGuard; Film Editor: Treg Brown; Voice Characterization by Mel Blanc; Musical Direction by Carl Stalling and Milt Franklyn.

In search of Pismo Beach ("and all the clams we can eat!") Bugs and Daffy, having goofed up the customary "left turn at Albakoikee," tunnel to ancient Bagdad, right underneath a giant ogre of a guard named "Hassan" and into an Arabian treasure cave. Upon discovering the jewels and coins therein, "greedy slob" Daffy O.D.'s on sheer avarice. "It's mine! Mine! Mine! ... I'm

rich! I'm wealthy! I'm comfortably well-off!" Meanwhile, outside, Hassan, who has been warned, "Guard well this treasure or the jackals shall grow fat on thy carcass!" gropes for the magic word to open the cave door (it ain't saddle-soap or septegenarian). Upon finding it, he bursts in on Daffy in the middle of looting the place. Blind in his greed, Daffy mistakes the brutish guard for a red cap. Bugs remains cool as a cucumber, however, and pretends to be a genie in a lamp. "Magically" he grants Hassan a wish by a chant-dance ("ickety-ackety-oop-ah-ah") that will give him, Bugs says, all this treasure for his very own. This doesn't keep Daffy out of trouble very long, so Bugs has to get rid of Hassan by a rope trick. Even Bugs can't help when Daffy "desecrates the spirit of the lamp" and a real genie makes Daffy suffer the consequences. Cut to Bugs on the beach, some time later, wondering "how that crazy duck ever made out with the genie." All of a sudden, the one-inch Daffy attacks a pearl Bugs finds. "It's mine! Mine! Mine! ... I'm a happy miser!"

GO FLY A KIT

Feb 23; LT; Directed by Chuck Jones; Story by Michael Maltese; Animation by Ken Harris, Abe Levitow, Richard Thompson; Layouts by Maurice Noble; Backgrounds by Philip DeGuard; Film Editor: Treg Brown; Musical Direction by Milt Franklyn.

The tale of a flying cat, literally! Most of the film goes to describing his fight with a rough, tough bulldog who catches our cat chasing a girl cat he's fallen instantly in love with. But that's getting ahead of our story, which is a flashback to begin with, narrated by two gents at an airport (Blanc and Daws Butler) as an explanation for why a girl cat happens to be waiting at the airport. Seems this kitten "was adopted by an old lady eagle with an overdeveloped mother instinct." She taught him everything she could about being a bird. When he accidentally plunges off a cliff, he's somehow able to teach himself to fly. When the time comes for him to leave the nest, he spooks three birds sitting on a phone wire (great three-way, head-banging take). He spots the bulldog below chasing his girl friend-to-be and she watches nervously as the two fight. She needn't worry, her boyfriend soon has the dog tearing at his own foot (his face, as he realizes, is a howl) and clubbing himself on the head. When he tries trapping the bird/cat in an overturned ashcan, the cat deposits both dog and can on a skyscraper antenna. "That was the beginning of a beautiful friendship. Every fall he flies south for the winter and each spring she waits for him to return." By now, they've a litter of airborne kittens as well!

BEDEVILLED RABBIT

Bugs Bunny, Tasmanian Devil; Apr 13: MM; Directed by Robert McKimson; Story by Tedd Pierce; Animation by George Grandpre, Ted Bonnicksen, and Keith Darling; Layouts by Robert Gribbroek; Backgrounds by Richard H. Thomas; Film Editor: Treg Brown; Voice Characterization by Mel Blanc; Musical Direction by Milt Franklyn.

A crateful of carrots parachutes down to Tasmania. It contains Bugs. "Take a little nap in a carrot patch and next thing I know I'm here." He witnesses a stampede of animals running from the Tasmanian Devil. A crocodile (who out of fear has converted himself into a handbag) shows Bugs a guide book that describes the Devil as "a vicious, ravenous brute with powerful jaws like a steel trap"; his menu takes up a whole page, ending with "and especially rabbits!" Bugs escapes by making like a monkey, perhaps the one item not on the list. The Devil gets wise and asks, "How come you say you monkey when you got little powder puff tail like rabbit?" The bound Bugs spies Tazzy tossing a mean salad (about a bathtub full), "Any real gourmet knows you don't serve a tossed salad with rabbit, ya soiv it with *wild turkey surprise.*" The Devil has to have this, so he unties the rabbit, who dons his chef's hat and his mock-Italian accent (left over from *Hare Ribbin'*) and serves the Devil a powderkeg

with ruffled decorations. The final course has Bugs adapting his drag bit, adding a bear trap mouth to the usual dress, wig and lipstick. This causes the she-devil (you'll recall they were married at the end of *Devil May Care*) to use her rolling pin on him and Bugs to go, "She's a niiice lady."

BOYHOOD DAZE

Ralph Phillips; Sept 20; MM; Directed by Chuck Jones; Story by Michael Maltese; Animation by Abe Levitow, Richard Thompson, and Ken Harris; Effects Animation by Harry Love; Layouts by Maurice Noble; Backgrounds by Philip DeGuard; Film Editor: Treg Brown; Musical Direction by Milt Franklyn.

Sent to his room for breaking a window, that starry-eyed daydreamer Ralph Phillips (Dick Beals) starts fantasizing again. This isn't quite as funny as having him dissolve in and out of a pipe-dream in the middle of class, as in the original *From A to Z-Z-Z-Z*, but it's still delightful. The juiciest of his adventures begins when he tosses a paper plane into the air. It becomes a jet in which ace pilot Phillips engages in aerial combat with a dozen nasty-looking planes piloted by unfriendly Martians who all got A in arithmetic. The Martians knock him for a loop, but he comes roaring back, arm in a sling, a giant cannon emerging from his ship which provokes one Martian to hold up a sign, "It's Ralph Phillips and his Secret Weapon." The cannon fires a lasso that snares all the ships by the tail. Ralph delivers his "routine" report, "Martians captured, world safe." Cut to a statue of Ralph being unveiled by the President, in front of cheering crowds and proud parents, fantasy dissolving back to his room, which in turn, becomes a prison cell. As the prison door opens, we fade back to reality and his father, telling him he's going to have to pay for the window out of his allowance. He's permitted to go out and play, but the sight of a cherry tree and an axe summons a vision of young George Washington ...

CHEESE IT, THE CAT

The Honeymousers; May 4; LT; Directed by Robert McKimson; Story by Tedd Pierce; Animation by Ted Bonnicksen, Keith Darling, and George Grandpre; Layouts by Robert Gribbroek; Backgrounds by Bob Majors; Film Editor: Treg Brown; Musical Direction by Carl W. Stalling and Milt Franklyn.

Well va-va-voom! Those wacky, and highly original Honeymousers are at it again! Ralph to Ned: "I'm startin' over to the refrigerator to get the cake for the party tonight, see? And when I open the door I'm nearly torn to shreds by a cat. Is he mean!" Ned to Ralph: "Okay Ralphie-Boy, the cat's gotta go, and I got just the cat destroyer to do the job." Not surprisingly, the getting-past-the-cat schemes of these mice go goofy: a wind-up toy tank, covering Ned with invisible ink which Ralph uses, hoping to make the cat think he's invisible (which impresses the cat with its sheer chutzpah). They also try to fly over on a champagne cork. When they finally get the cake and throw the surprise party, Ned has stupidly used dynamite sticks (itty-bitty ones) instead of candles. They avoid casualties by tossing the cake outside the hole at the cat. "No casualties?" says the cat sitting in the lighting fixture, "Hoo! Hoo! Hoo!"

FOX TERROR

Foghorn Leghorn; May 11; MM; Directed by Robert McKimson; Story by Michael Maltese; Animation by Keith Darling, George Grandpre, and Ted Bonnicksen; Layouts by Robert Gribbroek; Backgrounds by Bob Majors; Film Editor: Treg Brown; Voice Characterization by Mel Blanc; Musical Direction by Carl Stalling, Milt Franklyn.

Foggy versus Doggy, again with a third character trying to use their feud to his advantage. Here the newcomer is a wiley fox who keeps trying to distract the dog while he invades the chicken house. He appears in different disguises and makes various suggestions for Foghorn that never cease to make trouble. Attired like a peddler of hot watches, the fox beckons Foghorn with "Hey Bud, c'mere" and insists the big chicken go hunting instead of fishing. This means Foghorn has to recruit the dog as a pointer and drag him away from the coop at an inopportune time. He does this by making the naive Foghorn think he's on a TV game show where the challenge is to push a button that sets off a stick of TNT in the dog's mouth. Then the fox dresses as a Swami who sells Foghorn a lucky charm that turns out to be the dog folded up (ya really gotta see this one!). Finally, Foghorn and doggy get wise ("Hold it, dog! How come ya do me like you do-do-do?") that someone's trying to keep dog from guarding the chickens, and they pull a switcheroo on the fox. Dressed up like two slightly seedy drug pushers, they approach the fox with a "Hey, bud, c'mere!" They then do another quick change and appear as duelists who draw their muskets on the fox and fire. The last change has them dressed as English fox hunter and horse.

TWEETY AND THE BEANSTALK

Tweety, Sylvester; May 16; MM; Directed by Friz Freleng; Story by Warren Foster; Animation by Virgil Ross, Gerry Chiniquy, and Art Davis; Layouts by Hawley Pratt; Film Editor: Treg Brown; Voice Characterization by Mel Blanc. (Uncredited: June Foray); Musical Direction by Milt Franklyn.

As 1955's *Beanstalk Bunny* meshed Jones Bugs-Daffy-Elmer with "Jack & Beanstalk" elements, Freleng's foray up the beanstalk gives an added kick to the usual Sylvester and Tweety shenanigans by having Sylvester go through his old tricks but in a giant world against a giant Tweety ("acres and acres of Tweety bird!") and a giant bulldog. Sylvester has arrived there thanks to Jack's mother having discarded the magic beans under his bed He wakes up in giant country. The big guy hangs Tweety's cage from a rafter in the center of the big room, and Sylvester tries reaching him with a casting rod (tying one end to his tail and reeling himself up, ending in a giant mousehole meeting a giant mouse). He unscrews the bottom of the bird's giant cage with a screwdriver on a stick, then pops up there on a flying champagne cork. After getting caught between the giant bulldog's deathly percussive games, he manages to grab the bird, thanks to a makeshift catapult that backfires. Anyway, the giant returns ("Fee fo fi fat—I tawt I taw a puddy tat.") and chases Sylvester down the beanstalk. The cat chops it so the giant plummets, landing right on Sylvester, pushing him straight through the ground to China, where he is observed by a coolie-Tweety, who tawt he "taw honolable puddy tat."

PIKER'S PEAK
Bugs Bunny, Yosemite Sam; May 25; LT; Directed by Friz Freleng; Story by Warren Foster; Animation by Gerry Chiniquy, Art Davis, and Virgil Ross; Layouts by Hawley Pratt; Film Editor: Treg Brown; Voice Characterization by Mel Blanc; Musical Direction by Carl W. Stalling and Milt Franklyn. (Theme: "When I Yoo Hoo").
"The big event of this festival day is the climbing of the Schmatterhorn for a prize of 50,000 cronkites." Sam is the only contestant for the pay-off, until he passes Bugs en route to the mountain. Bugs reasons that "50,000 cronkites would buy a lot of carrots" and decides to give it a go. From that point on, Sam isn't only trying to climb the mountain, he's determined to reach the top before Bugs and to throw Bugs off. One after another of his dirty tricks—mainly boulders rolled from different angles or with ropes tied around them and noise-sensitive avalanches—backfire and drag him back to the village at the bottom. Each time he disgustedly passes through, the crowd cheers and the band plays an oompah theme. Along the way, Sam also has trouble with a Swiss army knife that flicks open everything but the cutting blade he needs, and a St. Bernard dog who mixes himself a martini. Finally, Sam makes it to the peak, but the camera

pulls back to reveal him on the top of the Eiffel Tower. "Well," says Bugs, "If he's happy, why tell him?"

STEAL WOOL
Ralph Wolf, Sam Sheepdog; June 8; LT; Directed by Chuck Jones; Story by Michael Maltese; Animation by Richard Thompson, Ken Harris, and Abe Levitow; Effects Animation by Harry Love; Layouts by Maurice Noble; Backgrounds by Philip DeGuard; Film Editor: Treg Brown; Voice Characterization by Mel Blanc; Musical Direction by Milt Franklyn.
Pals and neighbors Ralph Wolf and Sam Sheepdog walk to work and punch in together. At work, it's Ralph's job to try and swipe the sheep and Sam's to watch over them; the off-the-job friendship of the two has no influence on Sam's professional pulverizing of Ralph whenever he catches him red-handed. Ralph's attempts begin with a simple hoisting of a sheep, tip-toeing off (ending in Sam transforming his nose into an accordion). They then grow increasingly complex. Next, Ralph fires a lasso, guided by a periscope, from an underground vantage point (his whole body is turned into an accordion). He then flees with a sheep on a bridge of TNT sticks, lighting them so Sam can't follow. Sam appears on the other side anyhow, and lights the other end of the bridge. Next, neither jumping on a lever wedged under Sam's backside nor rolling an enormous cannon up the hill behind him work. The most elaborate is one of Jones's domino-effect giant rubber bands. Intended to hurl a boulder at Sam from between two rocks, the band instead pulls Ralph backwards through a mountain pass and onto a tree, all objects ultimately smashing him against the side of a cliff. At five o'clock quitting time, Sam advises his

banged-up pal, "You've been working too hard, Ralph, Why don't you take tomorrow off? I can handle both jobs." Says Ralph, "Gee, thanks Sam. You're a buddy."

BOSTON QUACKIE

Daffy Duck, Porky Pig; June 22; LT; Directed by Robert McKimson; Story by Tedd Pierce; Animation by George Gradpre, Ted Bonnickson, Keith Darling, and Russ Dyson; Layouts by Robert Gribbroek; Backgrounds by Bob Majors; Film Editor: Treg Brown; Voice Characterization by Mel Blanc; Musical Direction by Milt Franklyn.

"Boston Quackie, friend to those who need no friends, enemy to those who have no enemies." Where *The Super Snooper* effectively introduced McKimson's Daffy to the trench coat crowd (no fair comparing it to *The Great Piggy Bank Robbery!*) his other two Daffy detective flicks quickly ran the idea into the ground, their being dated (being specific TV program parodies) far less of a crime than unfunniness. Daffy as Boston Quackie is trying to enjoy a vacation in Paris with his girl friend Mary when his boss, Inspector Faraway (Porky in glasses) assigns him to deliver a priceless attache case to the consul in West Slobovia. Quackie assures Porky that it couldn't be in safer hands. It's instantly stolen by a spy known as the "Man in the Green Hat." Daffy chases him into the train depot and onto the "Cloak and Dagger express," a train whose whistle screeches like a murder victim and whose bells play a funeral march. There is much running through different cars in a search of the agent (taking time to do the old "lumps" with tea bit) and a tangling with the "lively bunch of felons" on the train. Green Hat is then apprehended, not by Quackie, who's got himself caught in a mailsack, but by Mary. Daffy delivers the briefcase to the ambassador, the pay-off gag including a jar of "instant girl" to provide him with a va-va-voom escort for the embassy ball. Says Daffy, "There just might a market for this!"

WHAT'S OPERA, DOC?

Bugs Bunny, Elmer Fudd; July 6; MM; Directed by Chuck Jones; Story by Michael Maltese; Animation by Ken Harris, Richard Thompson, and Abe Levitow; Effects Animation by Harry Love; Layouts by Maurice Noble; Backgrounds by Philip DeGuard; Film Editor: Treg Brown; Voice Characterization by Mel Blanc; Musical Direction by Milt Franklyn. Song "Return My Love" Lyrics by Michael Maltese.

Wabbiterdamerung, translated from the German, meaning "Twilight of the Wabbits." Whereas *Tristan* was considered the ne-plus-ultra of Wagner, *What's Opera, Doc?* expresses the apex of Jones at his most brilliant, the ribbing of Wagner's "Ring" Cycle being secondary to the self-parody of the elements of Bugs Bunny/Warner house style. Jones elaborates on the standard post-*A Wild Hare*: Elmer asks us to be "vewy quiet" as he's hunting wabbits. He has a conversation with the nervy bunny before he realizes "that was the wabbit." Bugs fools him twice, first by going in drag, then by pretending to be dead. The basic story idea has been thoroughly dressed up visually with more angles/shots than any other cartoon, each scene with a beautifully realized arty layout, using clouds, lightning etc. as stage props; and musically by adding ludicrously banal lyrics to the most majestic of Wagner's leitmotifs. Also "The Pilgrim's Chorus" from *Tannheuser* becomes the pseudo Tin Pan Alley "Return my Love" duet. There is matching and mis-matching of Wagner to Warners. Elmer is the hunter as the demigod Siegfried, Bugs in drag and blonde wig as the Valkyrie Brunhilde atop an obese horse. Their ritualistic courtship climaxes in a pinkish ballet as well as duet (sung beautifully by Blanc and Bryan). Elmer then slays Bugs with his "spear and magic helmet" and carries the carcass up to the burial pyre, as in the third act of *Valkyrie*. "Well, what did ya expect in an opera? A happy ending?"

TABASCO ROAD
ACADEMY AWARD NOMINEE

Speedy Gonzales, Sylvester; July 20; MM; Directed by Robert McKimson; Story by Tedd Pierce; Animation by Ted Bonnicksen, and George Grandpre; Layouts by Robert Gribbroek; Backgrounds by Bill Butler; Film Editor: Treg Brown; Voices Characterization by Mel Blanc; Musical Direction by Carl Stalling and Milt Franklin.

One of the more interesting McKimson Speedy flicks, it offsets the nondescript main character with two more personalized cohorts, Pablo and Fernanado, two mice who have too much tequila at a cantinita throwing a "Celebration para Speedy Gonzales." They start for home, but as soon as they get out into the alley they pick a fight with a tough, hungry pussygatos, from whom Speedy has to continually rescue them. He gets Fernando home while hiding Pablo in an empty sardine can, but Fernando immediately gets back into trouble and the cat uncans Pablo. Speedy next subs a TNT stick for Pablo in the cat's mouth, telling the audience, "Excusa, ees too mucho rapido for the eyes to follow ... " and shows us the whole bit again in "slow motiano." After inserting yet another bomb in the cat's puss, he beats it past the "ceety leemits," just as Pablo and Fernando are looking for trouble with a whole alley-load of cats!

A superior script, with in-house ribbing of the Tweety trademark lines ("You deed! You deed see a poosy-gato!"), very funny lyrics for their inebriated serenade and overall spindled Spanish nearly as clever as Pepe Le Pew's fractured French.

BIRDS ANONYMOUS
ACADEMY AWARD WINNER

Tweety, Sylvester; Aug 10; MM; Directed by Friz Freleng; Story by Warren Foster; Animation by Art Davis, Virgil Ross, Gerry Chiniquy; Layouts by Hawley Pratt; Backgrounds by Boris Gorelick. Film Editor: Treg Brown; Voice Characterization by Mel Blanc; Musical Direction by Milt Franklyn.

A great idea: "Birds Anonymous" is the pussycat's equivalent of Alchololics Anonymous, with cats testifying to addictions and supporting each other in their goals to "kick the bird habit." It is carried out beautifully with Freleng (as usual) really getting under the skin of Sylvester, who for the only time is devoting all his energy and brainpower towards *not* eating Tweety, going "cold turkey" or rather "cold Tweety." Nothing helps. To get birds off his mind, he turns on the TV and finds a cooking program describing the delights of roast birds (as his stomach roars) and the radio is playing songs like "Bye Bye Blackbird" and "When the Red Red Robin ... " He tries chaining himself to the radiator so he "won't be able to get the bird," but Tweety's confused query, "Oh Mr. Puddy-Tat, don't you wike me anymore?" drives him wild enough to heave the entire radiator from the wall! Fortunately, his comrade from "B. A." fires a plunger into his face. That night, Sylvester tosses and turns, his eyes red with bird desire, "Just one little bird, no one'll know the difference ... Then I'll quit." Again the B. A. cat (later identified as "Sam") helps him stop. By this point, he's a craven, blubbering addict. "I gotta have a bird! I'm weak but I don't care! I can't help it! After all, I am a pussy cat." The B. A. cat's demonstration of how birds and cats can live together in peace involves his kissing Tweety and getting a taste of bird, and soon wanting more ... You can imagine the rest. "Once a bad ol' puddy tat, always a bad old puddy tat."

DUCKING THE DEVIL

Daffy Duck, The Tasmanian Devil; Aug 17; MM; Directed by Robert McKimson; Story by Tedd Pierce; Animation by George Grandpre and Ted Bonnicksen; Layouts by Robert Gribbroek; Backgrounds by Bill Butler; Voice Characterization by Mel Blanc; Musical Direction by Milt Franklyn.

A good premise: Daffy tries to snare the Tasmanian Devil for a $5,000 reward. He has one weapon against the duck-devouring brute: as the radio says, the Devil "becomes docile when exposed to music." McKimson and Pierce set the scene so that Daffy is ten miles from the zoo, and has to keep coming up with music to lure the Devil there. First he tries a radio, which is no good as the cord gives out, then he purchases a trombone from one of those cartoon mail order firms that delivers a few moments after the order is dropped in the mailbox. The slide goes shooting away from Daffy too quickly (Jack Teagarden or Albert Manglesdorf could handle this!). So, he starts singing, beginning with "Tourjours, Lamour," then "I'm Looking Over a Four-Leaf Clover," and "Carolina in the Morning," but ten miles is a long time to keep singing and walking. By the time they're only a mile away, Daffy's hoarse voice can barely croak "When Irish Eyes are Smiling." Finally approaching the Devil's cage at the zoo, Daffy's voice gives out on "Moonlight Bay." He revives it with an atomizer just long enough to slam the door on the beast.

BUGSY AND MUGSY

Bugs Bunny, Rocky and Mugsy; Aug 31; LT; Directed by Friz Freleng; Story by Warren Foster; Animation by Virgil Ross, Gerry Chiniquy and Art Davis; Layouts by Hawley Pratt; Backgrounds by Boris Gorelick; Film Editor: Treg Brown; Voice Characterization by Mel Blanc; Musical Direction by Carl Stalling and Milt Franklyn.

Bugs at his meanest, stirring up trouble between two pals (inspired by *Stooge for a Mouse*) so that they virtually kill each other, his behavior justified since they're gangsters on the lam from a bank job. Bugs feels that, "Someone oughta show them that crime doesn't pay, and it looks like that someone's gotta be me." Bugs has left his rabbit hole for drier quarters (rain) and the house he has chosen, we soon learn, is where Rocky and Mugsy are hiding out from the cops. Because he's a no-good dirty crook, Rocky is almost too eager to believe the voice (Bugs) that comes to him in his sleep telling him that his pal Mugsy is "gettin' ideas" and to believe the worst when he sees him sleeping with an axe that Bugs has planted on him. Before long, Rocky

feels he has to tie Mugsy's arms and legs and lock him in the other room. Some one saws through the floor around his chair and he screams at the still-bound Mugsy, "I don't know how youse done but I know youse done it!" Bugs's piece-de-resistance is clapping roller skates on Mugsy and manipulating his movements from the basement with a magnet, starting a big fight between them by slamming him into Rocky. Eventually the police, presumably attracted by the noise, show up and haul them in, and Bugs displays a neon sign he's just built for a nightclub called "Rocky's Hideaway."

ZOOM AND BORED

Wile E. Coyote (Famishus Vulgaris) and the Road Runner (Birdibus Zippibus); Sept 14; LT; Directed by Chuck Jones; Story by Michael Maltese; Animation by Abe Levitow, Richard Thompson, and Ken Harris; Effects Animation by Harry Love; Layouts by Maurice Noble; Backgrounds by Philip DeGuard; Film Editor: Treg Brown; Musical Direction by Carl W. Stalling and Milt Franklyn.

From the Coyote's running into a patch of dust that covers up the fact of his having run off a cliff to his being carried by a harpoon through an unending series of tunnels and other sticky places, this remains a highlight. In between, we establish that the Coyote has to nervously leap whenever the bird sneaks up on him and beep-beeps. A pneumatic drill for digging holes (suggested to him by a book on roadrunner trapping) gives him a bad case of the shakes. He builds a brick wall across the road that leads to his dynamiting his own backside. A jar of ACME bumble bees goes straight for him rather than the Road Runner; an anvil he had intended to drop on the bird carries him straight through the plank off which he wanted to drop it; a long panning shot up an elaborate sluice device he must've spent months building goes for naught as the TNT simply goes off in his face; and a catapult drops its boulder on him (a precurser to *To Beep or Not*). For the climax, there is a harpoon gun which carries the Coyote through a drain pipe, through a truck, into a train tunnel and to the top of a cliff. Just when we think the bird is going to beep-beep the pathetic creature, he flashes a sign, "I just don't have the heart."

GREEDY FOR TWEETY

Tweety, Sylvester; Sept 28; LT; Directed by Friz Freleng; Story by Warren Foster; Animation by Gerry Chiniquy, Art Davis, and Virgil Ross; Layouts by Hawley Pratt; Backgrounds by Boris Gorelick; Film Editor: Treg Brown; Voice Characterization by Mel Blanc; Musical Direction by Milt Franklyn.

The three-way chase of Tweety, Sylvester, and the bulldog lands them in the animal hospital. It becomes a four-corner plot with the addition of Nurse Granny. Our friends are determined to keep chasing each other despite their cumbersome casts, and have no conscience at all when it comes to slamming one another's broken limbs with the biggest objects to be found. Very good bits: after Sylvester cuts the rope holding the doggy's leg, Granny gives him a tranquilizer and we get Sylvester's eye-view of the dog coming toward him as he loses his fight to stay awake. Granny finds Tweety missing and Sylvester burping yellow feathers. She X-rays the cat and we next see him with a patch on his stomach! A mouse hammers both their legs, and Granny decides to strap cat and dog into their beds so they can't hurt each other. Sylvester's bed-ridden "hobby" becomes constructing a mechanical device that drills a hole in the dog's cast and inserts a stick of dynamite. The dog, however, switches casts with Sylvester just before the stuff goes off.

Granny picks this moment to announce that they're being released from the hospital. When she looks out the window and sees that the dog, cat, and canary are running back into traffic, all she has to say is, "Que sera sera."

TOUCHE AND GO

Pepe LePew; Oct 12; MM; Directed by Chuck Jones; Story by Michael Maltese; Animation by Richard Thompson, Ken Harris, and Abe Levitow; Layouts by Maurice Noble. Backgrounds by Philip DeGuard; Film Editor: Treg Brown; Voice Characterization by Mel Blanc; Musical Direction by Milt Franklyn.

Even underwater, Pepe Le Pew can sense the presence of a female skunk and makes a beeline for her. Well, she's not really a skunk but a cat who has been chased by a dog down a highway just as a painter is applying a white stripe to the road. Embracing her, Pepe starts singing his amorous air, "Ze arms of Pepe are upon you." When she runs from his side, he reasons, "Zere are pleenty of othair feesh in ze ocean … zat ees, eef you like feesh. Personally, I prefer a rock." He appears out of the drink offering to get her a glass of water. She's gone by the two seconds he takes to fetch it from the shore, so he pours the water onto the rock explaining how he never touches the stuff himself. Hiding on a yacht, she encounters Pepe in a Captain's cap. "I am ze captain and you are ze first mate, promotions will follow quickly!" The chase continues under water (Pepe needing no oxygen mask since a skunk can hold its breath for a long time). His aromatic strength drives off a shark who swallows her and sends him yelping onto the beach like a dog. He searches for her in the sea. "Where are you, my leetle she-anemone?" She thinks she's safe when, hours later, she swims ashore on a desert island, but Pepe is waiting for her in Crusoe costume. "Friday? Monday? Right now?" The chase goes on. "One nice thing is, the game of love is never called on account of darkness." The camera pulls back to display the island's heart shape.

SHOW BIZ BUGS

Bugs Bunny, Daffy Duck; Nov 2; LT; Directed by Friz Freleng; Story by Warren Foster; Animation by Gerry Chiniquy, Art Davis, and Virgil Ross; Layouts by Hawley Pratt; Backgrounds by Boris Gorelick; Film Editor: Treg Brown; Voice Characterization by Mel Blanc; Musical Direction by Milt Franklyn.

Vaudevillian Daffy, dismayed to find Bugs's billing larger than his own, is told that this is according to drawing power. He resolves to prove that the rabbit "couldn't draw flies if he was covered with syrup." However, Bugs's basic charisma charms the audiences no matter what he does, while Daffy's despicableness instantly turns viewers off. Example: the two perform 32 bars of breathtaking hoofing, moving gracefully and elegantly (kudos to Freleng and Ross for that) to "Four Leaf Clover" and "Tea For Two." Though the dance is in perfect unison, Bugs gets the applause while Daffy gets zip. The crowd then goes simply wild over Bugs's two-second "shave and a haircut" totally ignoring Daffy's backbreaking routine of "Jeepers Creepers." Daffy's trained pigeon act goes bust (the birds head straight out the window) as does his attempt to expose Bugs's "fake" sawing a person in half routine. And his rigging up the rabbit's xylophone to explode when he strikes a certain note on "Endearing Young Charms." Daffy's final attempt to win the audience's approval, wearing a devil suit, swallowing numerous explosives and blowing himself up, brings down the house. The catch is he can only do this once!

MOUSE-TAKEN IDENTITY

Sylvester, Junion, Hippetty Hopper; Nov 16; MM; Directed by Robert McKimson; Story by Tedd Pierce; Animation by George Grandpre and Ted Bonnicksen; Layouts by Robert Gribbroek; Backgrounds by Bill Butler; Film Editor: Treg Brown; Voice Characterization by Mel Blanc; Musical Direction by Carl W. Stalling and Milt Franklyn.

Junior: "Oh father, I'm so excited about going along with you on your mouse-catching job! Why I've never even seen a mouse. You've never taken me mouse catching before. You're being a real pal to your little son!" Sylvester: "Aw, knock it off, will ya, son?" What they don't know, as Sylvester punches in for work at the County Museum, is that Hippetty Hopper has escaped from a nearby zoo and has taken refuge in a stuffed kangaroo's pouch. When Junior is ashamed to learn that the mice who've been giving his Pop such a hard time over the years are such tiny things. Sylvester gives him the old snow job by telling him, "You see son, mice come in assorted sizes. Little runties, like the ones around here, and king-sized mice like I used to hunt." On hearing this, Junior points out that the big stuffed kangaroo must be an example of the latter when Hippetty emerges from the pouch and now Sylvester's got to make good his boasting. The ensuing chase around the museum has Sylvester repeatedly tossed out of a cave in a prehistoric exhibit, acquiring a stowaway when he tries attacking in a giant turtle shell, getting bludgeoned and shot by his well-meaning son who tries to "save" him from a mounted lion head, and being scalped in an American Indian exhibit. In the windup, Sylvester crossbows himself into an Egyptian display. Junior gushes, "Oh father, now you can be my daddy and my mummy too!"

GONZALES' TAMALES

Sylvester; Nov 30; MM; Directed by Friz Freleng; Story by Warren Foster; Animation by Art Davis, Virgil Ross, and Gerry Chiniquy; Layouts by Hawley

Pratt; Backgrounds by Boris Gorelick; Film Editor: Treg Brown; Voice Characterization by Mel Blanc; Musical Direction by Carl Stalling and Milt Franklyn.

Pedro and Manuel and all the other mice are fed up with Speedy Gonzales, who has made all the pretty girls in the village fall in love with him; "All the rest are chihuahas." Speedy has intercepted a kiss from a pretty senorita that she's about to plant on her boy friend (after he's been courting her for six years) and a flower from the outstretched arms of one would-be serenader. The male mice "get an idea," to clout Sylvester with a rock and forged note, "Gringo Pussycat—eef I see you, I weel pool your tail out by eets *roots*. Signed, Speedy Gonzales." Sylvester pays a call on Speedy, who immediately carries out the note's threat. Sylvester's failed attempts at revenge include Speedy dis-assembling Sylvester's rifle one piece at a time, a grenade going back and forth after the pin has been yanked, and a wind-up senorita doll that lures Speedy out. He hides in a stand of hot peppers, and Sylvester vows to eat every one of them to find him. He's able to do this by guzzling cool water in between peppers, until Speedy substitutes hot tabasco sauce! We close as we opened, with Pedro and Manuel discussing the airborne Sylvester. "That theeng in the sky, ees eet a bird? A plane? No, eet ees the gringo pussycat."

Freleng's Speedies are much funnier than McKimson's and almost justify the character's longevity.

RABBIT ROMEO

Bugs Bunny, Elmer Fudd; Dec 14: MM; Directed by Robert McKimson; Story by Michael Maltese; Animation by Ted Bonnicksen and George Grandpre; Layouts by Robert Gribbroek; Backgrounds by Bill Butler; Film Editor: Treg Brown; Voice Characterization by Mel Blanc; Musical Direction by Milt Franklyn.

The Acme Animal Delivery Service drops off a package to Elmer Fudd from his Uncle Judd. It contains Millicent (voiced by June Foray), a fat, ugly, lovesick Slobovian rabbit. It immediately wrecks Elmer's guest room and cries. Uncle Judd will give Elmer $500 to take care of the rabbit. Elmer goes out looking for a mate to keep the homely hare happy.

Bugs Bunny is freezing in the winter cold. "I've eaten so many icicles I'm 20 degrees cooler inside!" The bunny accepts Elmer's carrot bait and goes home with him. Millicent is happy to see Bugs and wants a kiss! The bunny rubs a goldfish on her lips (the goldfish goes back into his bowl to kill himself). When she closes her eyes for another kiss, Bugs runs and hides. She looks for him, using her great strength to pull a locked closet (containing the hiding Bugs) out of the wall. Millie then gives Bugs a strangling bunny-hug and wants marriage now. Bugs jumps out the window.

Elmer brings Bugs back at gunpoint. Millie dresses Bugs in Slobovian garb and they do a courtship dance. When she wants another kiss, Bugs shoves an electric fan in her face. He proposes they elope and drops her out the window. As Millicent bangs on the front door, Bugs tells Fudd his Uncle Judd is here, and tricks him into a rabbit costume. When Elmer answers the door, Millicent falls in love with Fudd, and chases him off into the sunset.

1958

DON'T AXE ME

Daffy Duck, Elmer Fudd; Jan 4; MM; Directed by Robert McKimson; Story by Tedd Pierce; Animation by Ted Bonnicksen, George Grandpre, and Tom Ray. Layouts by Robert Gribbroek; Backgrounds by Bill Butler; Film Editor: Treg Brown; Voice Characterization by: Mel Blanc; Music Direction by Milt Franklyn.

Two of Farmer Elmer Fudd's animals, Daffy Duck and the barnyard dog (called Mandrake by Porky Pig, Br'er Dog by Foghorn Leghorn, and "Wover,") have a food fight, over food not with it. It begins with Daffy, pig that he admits to be, swiping the dog's hambone, and the dog getting even when he overhears Fudd's middle-aged wife wondering what to cook. Dog tries to drop a hint by imitating a duck (with swim fins). Finally, he tells her outright. She importunes hubby to chop off the black duck's head with his axe, but Daffy flatters him out of it, telling him he's just written a letter naming Fudd for the "outstandingly-kind-to-animals award." Daffy tries to get rid of Fudd's axe, but the dog keeps returning it to Elmer, who decides to do it without letting Daffy know. "This wazor will be easier to conceal than an axe." When Daffy sees the razor, he volunteers to shave Fudd (who should know better by now.) Fudd, Daffy, and doggy engage in a three-way grab-it-and-run bit, ending with Daffy's giving up and requesting to be decapitated by a sharp axe, then grinding the blade to nothingness. The dog fetches Fudd's gun, but it's all for naught—their guest is a vegetarian.

TORTILLA FLAPS

Speedy Gonzales; Jan 18; LT; Directed by Robert McKimson; Story by Ted Pierce; Animation by George Grandpre, Ted Bonnicksen; Layouts by Robert Gribbroek; Backgrounds by Richard H. Thomas; Film Editor: Treg Brown; Voice Characterization by Mel Blanc; Musical Direction by Milt Franklyn.
When a hungry bandito bird interrupts the Mexican mouse community's fiesta, along with Speedy Gonzales's game of exhibition "peeng pong" against himself, it's up to the fastest mouse in all Mexico who volunteers to "take care of Senor Vulturo, but good!" When the big, dopey crow is about to swoop down on one of their number, Speedy quickly hides a TNT stick under the little mouse's sombrero. The bird chases Speedy out into the countryside, road-runner-style. This is not coordinated quite well enough to stop in time to avoid an oncoming locomotive when Speedy runs across the tracks. When the bird next aims a cannon at Speedy, one well-timed "yea-hah!" startles him so he leaps in the air and lands on the

wrong side of the big gun. Speedy then offers to lead him to "one leetle mouse" he can "catch real easy-mente." When they run back into town, all the Bird gets at the mousehole he crashes into is Speedy's voice going, "Nobody in here but us chickens." The bird tries booby-trapping Speedy with an explosive ball-and-cup game (with a phony note, "From your own Lupe"; Speedy wonders which of "his own Lupes" it is) and feels obligated to demonstrate for Speedy. After the featherless wreck of a bird waves the white flag, he learns that his punishment is to be the object of two shooting gallery-like attractions, baseballs at his head, and darts which hurt his pride.

HARE-LESS WOLF

Bugs Bunny; Feb 1; MM; Directed by Friz Freleng; Story by Warren Foster; Animation by Gerry Chiniquy, Art Davis and Virgil Ross; Layouts by Hawley Pratt; Backgrounds by Boris Gorelick; Film Editor: Treg Brown; Voice Characterization by Mel Blanc (Uncredited: June Foray); Musical Direction by Milt Franklyn.
Now let's see, who's chasing Bugs this time? A hunter? A dog? It's this *Red Riding Hoodwinked* wolf whose shrewish wife makes him "get out there and shoot a rabbit" for dinner. When he runs into Bugs, he has to be reminded what he is hunting for (A woodchuck? No. A porcupine?). Bugs seems to be pulling his punches because his pursuer is so addle-brained. Bugs checks out the wolf's gun for him ("You're too good a shot to miss at such close range.") Results: The wolf gets blasted.

305

Bugs even provides the wolf with a hand grenade, complete with instructions informing him rather too late that he has only ten seconds in which to perform the entire operation. When the Wolf chases Bugs into a train tunnel, Bugs psyches him out with a train whistle and flashlight, then gets clobbered by the next thing that comes out of the tunnel, a *real* train ("Now why was I tryin' to catch a train?"). The wolf then stupidly follows a lit fuse all the way back to his powder keg. We end with the Wolf once more ferretting what he wants, trying to remember ("A hippopotomous?") late into the night.

A PIZZA TWEETY PIE

Tweety, Sylvester; Feb 22; LT; Directed by Fritz Freleng; Story by Warren Foster; Animation by Virgil Ross, Gerry Cheinquy, and Art Davis; Layouts by Hawley Pratt; Backgrounds by Tom O'Loughlin; Film Editor: Treg Brown; Voice Characterization by Mel Blanc; Musical Direction by Milt Franklyn.
Granny (June Foray) welcomes Tweety to romantic Italy. "Here we are at last in Venice, with all its Venetian blinds!" Granny leaves Tweety on the terrace to ·sing "Santa Lucia," attracting the attention of an Italian Sylvester ("Sooferin' a-Soocatasha"). Trying for a Tweety sandwich, the cat employs various methods to get across the canal to grab the canary. Sylvester cuts loose a gondola and it sinks. He tries a rubber raft, but Tweety bursts it, shrinking it tightly around the cat's rear-end. Sylvester swings across on a rope, but plunges underwater, into a shark's mouth! The cat floats by in a helium balloon, but Tweey shoots a tack into it.

The cat finally makes it to the hotel window, just as Granny takes Tweety out for a gondola cruise. Sylvester tries using a fishing pole to catch the canary, but gets his line caught in a motor boat which causes him to "water ski" into a bridge (with a sign that reads "Ducka you head, Lowla Bridgeada"). The cat tries one more time, using a strand of spaghetti as a lasso. He gets bopped in his noodle by a mallet Granny places in the pasta, causing the cat to see birds who twirl around his head saying "I tawt I taw a puddy tat!"

ROBIN HOOD DAFFY

Daffy Duck, Porky Pig, Mar 8; MM; Directed by Chuck Jones; Story by Michael Maltese; Animation by Abe Levitow, Richard Thompson, and Ken Harris; Layouts by Maurice Noble; Backgrounds by Philip De Guard; Film Editor: Treg Brown; Voice Characterization by Mel Blanc; Musical Direction by Milt Franklyn.
A classic Jones comedy, "which is to laugh!" Wanted posters scattered across Sherwood Forest tell us that Daffy Duck is Robin Hood, but Porky Pig, as fat friar Tuck who would fain join up with Robin Hood and his band of jolly outlaws, isn't so easily convinced, He first sees Daffy playing a tune on his lute that includes the line, "trip along merrily," the cue for him to splash into a lake, getting in over his head. Friar Porky decides Daffy is only a travelling clown. To prove he really is Robin to the excessively jolly Porky, Daffy offers to rob a rich traveller of his gold and "give it to some poor unworthy slob." Daffy's backfiring attempts at getting the gold aren't as funny as Porky's sarcastic comments. When Daffy fires himself from his bow by mistake and ends up wearing a tree, Porky wise-cracks, "I·don't know how I could've doubted you. Shall we spend the gold in one place?" When Daffy swings from one tree he slams into a series of other trees, shouting "Yoicks and away," each time. He then gets flattened by his own wrecking ball a la Wile E. Coyote. Going from bad to worse, he fires a spear at his intended victim which helps the victim cross a chasm. In trying to stop him from crossing a drawbridge, Daffy gets flattened by it. "I'm sorry," says Porky, "I

can't join you, I'm convinced you're just not Robin Hood." "Never mind joining me, I'll join you," says Daffy, in monk's robes, "shake hands with Friar Duck."

HARE-WAY TO THE STARS
Bugs Bunny, Marvin Martian; Mar 29; LT; Directed by Chuck Jones; Story by Michael Maltese; Animation by Richard Thompson, Ken Harris, and Abe Levitow; Layouts by Maurice Noble; Backgrounds by Philip De Guard; Effects Animation by Harry Love; Film Editor: Treg Brown; Voice Characterization by Mel Blanc; Musical Direction by Milt Franklyn.

Bugs Bunny, groggy from a rabbit hangover, climbs out of his hole and into a rocket ship parked directly above and thinks he's still in his rabbit hole. He reaches the top and is carried off by a satellite onto a futuristic landscape of panels suspended in outer space. He tries to rent a U-Drive flying saucer from a local character wearing a spittoon—Marvin Martian in his Roman hairbrush helmet. Marvin advises not to bother as "The Earth will be gone in just a few seconds ... I'm going to blow it up, it obstructs my view of Venus." To save the planet, Bugs makes off with the Aludim Q-36 Explosive Space Modulator the Martian has built. The Commander orders four buzzard-headed *Jumpin'-Jupiter*-style "Instant Martians" ("Just Add Water") after Bugs. Bugs sends them plummeting through space with variants on traditional Warner toon bits, the "mirror" routine taking care of the first, and Freleng's "door" bit eliminating the others. Before the commander can send more Martians, Bugs swipes a flying saucer ("This Martian hot rod better get at least a million miles to the gallon, the earth ain't just across the street!"), but on zooming back to home, he accidentally switches the modulator for the instant Martian gum ball machine, and the gum-balls spill out into a sewer. "Run for the hills, folks!" warns Bugs, as their top knots start cracking through the pavement, "Or you'll be up to you arm pits in Martians!"

WHOA BE-GONE!
Road Runner; Apr 12; MM; Directed by Chuck Jones; Story by Michael Maltese; Animation by Ken Harris, Abe Levitow, and Richard Thompson; Layouts by Maurice Noble; Backgrounds by Philip De Guard; Effects Animation by Harry Love; Film Editor: Treg Brown; Musical Direction by Milt Franklyn.

The Coyote, riding a miniature rocket, is just about to grab the Road Runner with his knife and fork when he slams into the top of a tunnel. The rocket goes on through but gets turned around, giving him more trouble. After two or three falls off a cliff, the Coyote realizes that he keeps falling on the same spot and decides it might be a good idea to put a trampoline there, but instead of bouncing he smashes right through it. He then gets the idea of tripping the Road Runner with a giant rubber band. The band simply sends the two boulders crashing towards him. His next device, a barrel lined with TNT sticks and suspended over the highway, covers him rather than the Road Runner, and when he booby-traps the bridge, the Road Runner simply stops before crossing and the displaced concrete lands directly on the Coyote. Then it's "One ACME Do-It Yourself Tornado Kit, seed your own tornadoes,": the idea is to squirt the instant tornado pellets with water as the bird goes by. Instead, the water drips onto the whole can of pellets right next to him, and he gets caught up in a miniature tornado that carries him straight into a nearby army minefield!

The funniest gag is the one that most obviously could never work in a million years: the Coyote riding down a wire on his head via a helmet with a roller skate on it!

A WAGGILY TALE
Apr 26; LT; Directed by Friz Freleng; Animation by Art Davis, Virgil Ross, and Gerry Chiniquy; Layouts by Hawley Pratt; Backgrounds by Boris Gorelick; Film Editor: Treg Brown; Musical Direction by Milt Franklyn.

Junior, a little boy with glasses (voiced

by Daws Butler), forces his dog to play with him and mistreats the mutt. His mother sends him to his room, telling him, "You wouldn't want to be treated that way if you were a dog!" Junior dreams he *is* a dog and wakes up in a pet shop window. At first he is delighted ("No more baths, no more school!") with his new dog life, but is soon bought by a cute little girl. The girl has a tug of war for the dog with Melvin, a little boy who wants to carry him. Then he gets beat up by Melvin's dog, and the girl bandages the pooch from head to toe. Next, she readies him for a bath in the washer-dryer. He emerges as a floating puff! Finally she brushes his teeth with shaving cream. Junior runs out, foaming at the mouth. Thinking he's a mad dog, the authorities put him in solitary in the city pound.

Junior wakes up and tells his dog, Elvis, he's going to treat him better. The dog confides to us: "That's okay with me, 'cause I'm not really a dog, I'm another little boy having a dream!'"

FEATHER BLUSTER
Foghorn Leghorn; May 10; MM; Directed by Robert McKimson; Story by Tedd Piere; Animation by Ted Bonnicksen, Tom Ray, George Grandpre, andWarren Batchelder; Layouts by Robert Gribbroek; Backgrounds by Bill Butler; Film Editor: Treg Brown; Voice Characterization by Mel Blanc. Musical Direction by Milt Franklyn and Carl Stalling.
Believe it or not, Foghorn Leghorn and the barnyard dog have managed to avoid annihilating each other and have actually grown to senior citizen senility. In fact, these two old geezers have become checker-playing pals, and it takes the sight of their two grandsons scrapping in the barnyard to remind them that they ever had any beef with each other. Watching Foggy III wallop the behind of Br'er Dog III brings back memories of the days when the original Foghorn used to do the same to the dog. "Like the time ya took up art,"

leads to a flashback in which artist Foggy gets the dog to crash into the painting of an open fence, then, in a sawmill, to carve a tree into a bat so he can have something to wallop him with. As the two grandsons listen, Foggy's next anecdote recalls, "I'll always cherish the memory of my superb coup-de-grace that left such a bad taste in your mouth," referring to when he got the dog to chase him to the end of his rope limit, and painted his yelping tongue bright green. In the wind-up, their worries that the kiddies might've picked up on some of their violent habits become confirmed when Little Foggy paints the little doggie's tongue chartreuse.

NOW HARE THIS
Bugs Bunny; May 31; LT; Directed by Robert McKimson; Story by Tedd Pierce; Animation by Tom Ray, George Grandpre, Ted Bonnicksen, and Warren Batchelder; Layouts by Robert Gribbroek; Backgrounds by Bill Butler; Film Editor: Treg Brown; Voices Characterization by Mel Blanc; Musical Direction by Milt Franklyn.
"Look Mac, when a rabbit holes up in his own digging's, ya can't just reach in and grab him, ya gotta out-clever him, get 'em out in the open. Better start scheming." That's Bugs's advice to the hungry, boulder-hatted Big Bad Wolf who would join the list of the valiant who've pursued Bugs. This creep is dumber than most and far less sympathetic. "I just wanna see if he's got any moxie," Bugs tells us, "otherwise I won't bother with him." He doesn't and Bugs shouldn't. Bugs reacts to virtually every scheme he tries like he's been through it a dozen times before (in fact he has, about 144 times), and his boredom communicates itself to the audience. The wolf tries getting his saccharine-sweet li'l nephew ("that'd be peachy keeno, Uncle Big Bad") to pose as various fairy tale heroines (Red Riding Hood, Goldilocks's Baby Bear) each of which Bugs, going along with the gag, "feels sorry for" and takes the place of, outwitting the wolf in the middle of the trap rather than avoiding it.

The running gag is equally predictable: Bugs repeatedly trying to tell the wolf there's only one way to have a rabbit for dinner: as a guest. "Like I say," concludes Bugs at the wolves' table, "If ya can't eat 'em, join 'em!"

TO ITCH HIS OWN

June 28; MM; Directed by Chuck Jones; Story by Michael Maltese; Animation by Abe Levitow, R. L. Thompson, Ken Harris, and Ben Washam; Layouts by Maurice Noble; Backgrounds by Phil DeGuard; Film Editor: Treg Brown; Musical Direction by Carl W. Stalling.
The Mighty Angelo, the very strong strongman at the flea circus, has "been working too hard," he says in a note, "so I'm gong to take a rest on some nice quiet dog in the country." Angelo, top heavy with big handlebar mustache and "Italian" T-shirt, finds what he's after in a peaceful pooch happily snoozing on an estate. We begin to realize how strong the strong man is when, in response to the dog's foolish attempt to scratch, he causes veritable canine earthquakes with the mere stamp of his feet. More trouble comes from the mean bulldog next door, who kicks Angelo's dog and swipes his pillow. Angelo puts the pillow as well as a bone back in his dog's mouth, getting the bull angry. Though neither dog can see our miniscule muscleman, he is to loom large in their destinies. First, Angelo drags the bully bulldog through a knothole in the fence and then comes at him with a sledgehammer. All the while he is wondering what hit him, throwing away his bottle of "Old Dog Nip," and taking "the Oath" of sobriety. The bully's last ploy is placing Angelo's pooch in front of the dog catcher, but Angelo wacks the dog catcher on the rump and puts the paddle in the bulldog's paw, so he's the one who gets hauled off to the pound. We end with the Mighty Angelo relaxing, watching "Glassie" on his teeny-weeny TV set.

DOG TALES

July 26; LT; Directed by Robert McKimson; Story by Tedd Pierce; Animation by George Grandpre, Ted Bonnicksen, Warren Batchelder, and

Tom Ray; Layouts by Robert Gribbroek; Backgrounds by Richard H. Thomas. Film Editor: Treg Brown; Voice Characterizations by Mel Blanc; Musical Direction by Milt Franklyn.
Blackout bits concerning canines: a dog setting and pointing confuses the narrator into wondering whether to describe him as a setter pointing or a pointer setting (which leads to a shot of a pointsettia! Gnong! Gnong! Gnong!), romantic French poodles make like Pepe Le Pew; a Doberman Pinscher who pinches Doberman (from *Sgt. Bilko*), an Elvis dog from the South wriggles his hips suggestively while telling us he's nothing but a hound dog. A dog show includes the Great Dane, who does an impression of Victor Borge (labeled "Victor Barky" in case you missed it) and ends when a cat gets loose and the entire show of bow-wows goes chasing it. The last routine describes a dog who ran all the way across the country to join his family and dig up his bone. And those are the *good* gags!

Old Friends Dept.: Charlie Dog's "50% Pointer" monologue from *Often an Orphan*, the St. Bernard who drinks his own cocktails from *Piker's Peak*, the barking mass of mutts from *Foxy by Proxy*.

KNIGHTY-KNIGHT BUGS _{ACADEMY AWARD WINNER}

Bugs Bunny, Yosemite Sam, Aug 23, LT; Directed by Friz Freleng; Story by Warren Foster; Animation by Virgil Ross, Gerry Chiniquy, and Art Davis; Layouts by Hawley Pratt; Backgrounds by Tom O'Laughlin; Film Editor: Treg Brown; Voice Characterizaton by Mel Blanc; Musical Direction by Milt Franklyn.
Bugs Bunny is the hapless court jester who sets himself up for disaster by joking that "Only a fool would go after the Singing Sword" after King Arthur has declared that the Knights of the Round Table are chicken for not having the gumption to rescue the Sword from its kidnapper, the Black Knight. Bugs sneaks into the villain's castle while Black Knight Sam and his firebreathing, cold-ridden dragon (another one

of Sam's beasts of burden who won't "whoa" on cue) snooze. Why, Bugs wonders out loud, is it called the Singing Sword? It starts to hum (via a musical saw) "Cuddle Up a Little Closer." The rabbit makes off with the sword, Sam chasing after him, and Bugs holes up in Sam's castle. The Black Knight tries to get back in, threatening, "Okay, Rabbit, ya forced me to use force." "Force" means a catapult that flattens his face onto the side of the castle and a rope he tries to shimmy across on. The Black Knight and his fire-sneezing big lizard get inside when Bugs tries to tiptoe out. They accidentally end up in the explosives storeroom; the dragon's final sneeze converts the entire turret of the castle in a rocket heading straight for the moon. Bugs wishes them "Farewell to Thee" as the sword begins to sing, "Aloha."

WEASEL WHILE YOU WORK
Foghorn Leghorn; Aug 6; MM; Directed by Robert McKimson; Story by Michael Maltese; Animation by Warren Batchelder, Tom Ray, George Grandpre, and Ted Bonnicksen; Layouts and Backgrounds by Robert Gribbroek; Film Editor: Treg Brown; Voice Characterization by Mel Blanc; Musical Direction by John Seely.
"The snow is so deep," says Foghorn Leghorn, "the farmers have to jack up the cows so they can milk 'em! But I like winter!" The snow-covered countryside provides the setting and props for this season's Foggy-doggy battle. The Weasel, by now such a regular he needs no explanation, is the interested third party. Foggy begins by rolling Br'er Dog into a snowman ("There is but one course for me to follow, I'll moider da bum!"). The dog retaliates by over-sharpening Foggy's ice-skates. Then Foggy sends a giant snowball down after the mutt. It rolls back on his own person. When the "little old lint-pickin' weasel" appears, Foggy plays up the pooch as "delicious venison," putting a wild and crazy pair of antlers on the dog's head. The dog then sends the weasel back after some "Chicken-seye Frozen Chicken," obligingly trap-

ping the tobagganing Foghorn in a solid block of ice. When the weasel has Foggy in his pot, he makes him into a 60-foot Foghorn Leghorn statue of ice. "Now I won't have anything to worry about until the Fourth of July!" On grabbing the dog's tail from his doghouse, he gets a string attached to a rocket instead! Sayeth the dog, "The fourth of July came a little early this year."

That canned music hurts, but this snappy one-liner helps: "Pay attention, boy, I'm cuttin' but you ain't bleedin'"

A BIRD IN A BONNET
Tweety, Sylvester; Sept 27; MM; Directed by Friz Freleng; Story by Warren Foster; Animation by Gerry Chiniquy, Art Davis, and Virgil Ross; Layouts by Hawley Pratt; Backgrounds by Tom O'Loughlin; Film Editor: Treg Brown; Voice Characterization by Mel Blanc; Musical Direction by John Seely.
"Oh boy, this is fun, widing awound on a hat!" Sylvester has chased Tweety into a millinery shop just as Granny is picking out a new hat, choosing a darling one with what she and the salesgirl think is a stuffed yellow bird. Sylvester follows Granny all over New York, trying not to let her know what he's up to. It doesn't generally work out that way. Sylvester approaches her hidden in the top hat of a master who makes a fresh remark, Granny clouts the both of them with her umbrella. In Lacy's department store, he makes it into the elevator just in time to have his tail stretched a few stories, and in J. D. Denny's, he absconds with her chapeau on the the window ledge, leaping to safety with a balloon. All is hunky-dory until Tweety bursts the balloon, causing Sylvester to plummet into an open manhole (landing on an Art Carney impersonator who goes, "Va-va-voom, hey look at this, Ralph, a pussy cat!"). He blows the hat off with a bellows and has to bring it to safety out of dangerous traffic, only to be run over by a motor scooter when he gets into a "safe" alley. His most elaborate hat-grabbing effort uses a fishing rod when a taxi in which he is riding pulls him

all over the city un'til he manages to reel himself to the top. Just as he succeeds in opening a skylight and grabbing the bird, he runs smack into the rim of the Holland Tunnel. Tweety: "You know, I wose more puddy tats dat way."

HOOK, LINE AND STINKER

The Road Runner (Burnius-Roadibus) and the Coyote (Femishius-Famishius); Oct 11; LT; Directed by Chuck Jones; Story by Michael Maltese; Animation by Richard Thompson, Ken Harris, and Ben Washam; Layouts and Backgrounds by Philip DeGuard; Film Editor: Treg Brown; Musical Direction by John Seely.
From traps as simple as catching the Road Runner in a pan or clobbering him with a mallet to schemes as complicated as swinging after him with a harpoon while suspended from a balloon or one of Jones's longest and most involved Rube Goldberg this-hits-that devices designed to drop a cannon ball on his prey, the best-laid plans of the Coyote go aft-a-gley. So do such evil-minded ideas as placing bird seed on the train tracks and dropping a grand piano. Even simple wires, the kind that connect dynamite sticks to their control boxes, conspire against the Coyote, rolling backward so that the TNT follows him.

Even the inferior entries in this series never fail to entertain, although this one suffers from the lack of any major gags and lifeless canned music.

PRE-HYSTERICAL HARE

Bugs Bunny, Elmer Fudd; Nov 1; LT; Directed by Robert McKimson; Story by Tedd Pierce; Animation by Ted Bonnicksen, Warren Batchelder, Tom Ray, and George Grandpre; Layouts by Robert Gribbroek; Backgrounds by William Butler; Film Editor: Treg Brown; Voice Characterization by Mel Blanc; Musical Direction by John Seely.
"Someday they'll outlaw this annual madness known as rabbit season," pants Bugs Bunny, on the lam as usual from Elmer Fudd. He's about to find out how old that annual madness is as he falls into an ancient cave and opens a huge powderhorn containing a reel of motion picture film ("It must've been a real

stinkeroo to bury it out here in the woods"). Running it on his home projector, it turns out to be "A Micronesian Film Documentary in Cromagnoscope, Color by Neanderthal Color." It takes place in the year 10,000 B.C., narrated by Blanc (who also does Elmer's voice, unfortunately), opening with the dinosaurs from *Caveman Inki,* and going on to hunting gags involving Elmer Fuddstone (a hairy Fudd in caveman digs) and the sabertoothed rabbit (Bugs with extended buck choppers). The rabbit pulls Fudd down from a tree by a trick noose and reverses his poison dart (as in *Bushy Hare*), and, when Fudd pulls the old sob story, Bugs feels like an awful slob and helps Fuddstone catch him. "One of these days some smart apple's going to invent gunpowder and the gun will follow." Naturally, Fudd's subsequent invention of gunpowder inspires Bugs to invent the gun. Both go off in Fudd's face. "Twas ever thus, those smart hunters are never no match for us dumb rabbits," says the twentieth-century Bugs, the twentieth-century Fudd behind him with a drawn gun saying, "That's what you think, wabbit." The gun explodes, suprise!, on Fudd. "That's what I think!"

GOPHER BROKE

Goofy Gophers; Nov 15; LT; Directed by Robert McKimson; Story by Tedd Pierce; Animation by Warren Batchelder, Tom Ray, George Grandpre, and Ted Bonnickson; Layouts by Roert Gribbroek; Backgrounds by William Butler; Film Editor: Treg Brown; Voice Characterization by Mel Blanc; Musical Direction by John Seely.
The gophers' vegetables get harvested by the farmer just as the rodents are ready to pluck them, and are stored in the barn guarded by the sleeping barnyard dog (Foghorn Leghorn series). Two gophers get past the mutt, using the exact same "psychological wearing down process" used in *Mouse Wreckers* on same dog. We begin with nerve-shattering metal banging around the dog, leaving him to stumble across a floor covered with banana peels. Then the gophers tie a rope around his tail

311

and drop him down a well. For help he does as *The significance of Dreams by Sigmund Fraud* advises and convinces himself it never really happened. Phase number three is the gophers tying the snoozing pooch to a balloon and sending him floating away. They restore the veggies to their underground domicile via a metal tube, as the dog awakens atop a telephone pole. Not only does Br'er Dog flip his lid and fly after a crow ("Hey, wait for baby!"), so does a deadpan pig who has been witnessing each of his mental mishaps. The last bit has the pig on the couch of Dr. Cy Kosis, who's trying to explain to him that dogs don't fly. They then see the corsetted canine flap past his window and lie down next to the pig!

Seely's canned "score" functions as part and parcel of the lame antics.

HIP HIP—HURRY
Road Runner (Digoutius-Unbelieveus) and Coyote (Eatius-Slobbius); Dec 6; MM; Directed by Chuck Jones; Story by Michael Maltese; Animation by Ken Harris, Ben Washam, Abe Levitow, Richard Thompson, and Keith Darling; Layouts by: Maurice Noble; Backgrounds by Philip De Guard; Effects Animation by Harry Love; Film Editor: Treg Brown; Musical Direction by John Seely.
Great shot of the Coyote *just* about to catch the Road Runner when the bird puts on extra speed and causes the highway paving to whip, pulling telephone poles behind him, and burning a hole right through a bridge, which the Coyote proceeds to fall through. Next the Coyote drops a grenade on the bird. It bounces back on a phone wire and explodes before he can restore the pin. He then tries to swing trapeze-style after the Road Runner but goes into the side of a cliff and falls in front of an Acme truck. He fires a dynamite stick wih a slingshot which goes off on his face. Leaving TNT on the road, the matches explode on him and then the bird (More agressive than usual) gets him near the stick. Before he can roll a boulder off a cliff, the whole precipice falls off, and both rocks catapult and

sandwich him. He's made it around one waterfall in his speed boat but unexpectedly goes off another. His ACME High-Speed tonic works on a mouse, so he consumes a whole jar of the stuff, but is unable to control the superspeed it gives him and the bird merely trips him into the dynamite room of a construction site—sending him skyward like a rocket.

CAT FEUD
Pussyfoot and Marc Antony; Dec 20; MM; Directed by Chuck Jones; Story by Michael Maltese; Animation by Ken Harris, Ben Washam, Abe Levitow, and Richard Thompson; Layouts by Maurice Noble; Backgrounds by Philip DeGuard; Film Editor: Treg Brown; Voice Characterization by Mel Blanc; Musical Direction by Milt Franklyn.
Marc Antony is a ferocious guard dog at a construction site whose sentimental, fatherly side is brought out by Pussyfoot, a cuddly, little kitty he discovers left for dead in a paper sack. He puts Pussyfoot to bed on a beam, making him a present of a big juicy sausage. Enter a hungry alley cat (a sort of scraggly, Grinch-ish version of Claude Cat), determined to swipe Pussyfoot's sausage. From here on it's Marc Antony versus "Claude" Cat, involving various high-tech construction paraphernalia, as well as the old-fashioned hurling of steel beams into each other's faces. The innocent Pussyfoot wanders across the building lot in complete ignorance of the danger he's in (the idea from the Fleischer Popeye landmark *A Dream Walking*). Marc is forever swinging beams or sending elevators to arrive right under his feet just when he's about to unknowingly step off. By a few minutes into the film, you'd think that hydraulic cranes had no purpose other than being there for cats and dogs to bang each other's heads with steel beams and that superstrong electromagnets were conceived for the express purpose of giving cartoon characters more ammunition to fight each other with.

1959

BATON BUNNY

Bugs Bunny; Jan 10; LT; Directed by Chuck Jones and Abe Levitow; Story by Michael Maltese; Animation by Ken Harris, Richard Thompson, and Ben Washam; Layouts by Maurice Noble; Backgrounds by Tom O'Laughlin; Film Editor: Treg Brown; Voice Characterization by Mel Blanc; Orchestrations by Milt Franklyn.

The Warner Bros. Symphony, "Morning, Noon, and Night in Vienna," by Franz Von Suppe. Guest Conductor: Bugs Bunny. Where *What's Opera Doc?* resounds as the forte finale to the Warners (specifically Jones and Freleng) European art music cycle, this unpretentious little charmer scores a perfectly appropriate pianissimo encore. As a conductor/pantomimist, Bugs milks the score for full dramatic effect, alternating between slow stretches executed with agonizing deliberateness and fast ones zing-zing-zing. He wavers between quiet subtle passages conducted by tiny finger wiggles and big waves of melody, cued by exaggerated gestures as though by Stokowski or Kenton. An annoying fly gets in his way, and the challenge becomes finding shared movements in the actions of fly-swatting and conducting. He then has the same problem with a pair of travelling cufflinks. For a climax, Bugs singlehandedly acts out an entire cowboy and Indian chase, using both sides of the podium to separate the good guys from bad guys, harps serving as bows and horns becoming muskets. Bugs's ears take the shape of cowboy hats and Indian headdresses, the climax is the cavalry's ride to the rescue with tuba/cannons and a dramatic death scene. Lastly, Bugs chases the fly through the orchestra, tramping on most of the instruments. He is about to swat with two cymbals when the piece ends. Taking his bows, he discovers the hall is empty, so he bows to the fly.

MOUSE-PLACED KITTEN

Jan. 24; LT; Directed by Robert McKimson. Story by Tedd Pierce; Animation by Ted Bonnicksen, Warren Batchelder, Tom Ray, and George Granpre; Layouts by Robert Gribbroek; Backgrounds by William Butler; Film Editor: Treg Brown; Voice Characterization by Mel Blanc; Musical Direction by Milt Franklyn.

A kindly mouse couple, Matilda and Clyde, adopts a left-for-dead baby kitten, Gradually they conclude that he should be with people and so leave him with the folks in the main house. Some time later, they get the urge to visit Junior on his birthday. The cat risks getting in trouble with the lady of the house (Foray) to spend time with them. He offers to treat them to some rare imported cheese, but the boss lady catches him in the middle of raiding the fridge and shoos them out. Clyde tries to get the cheese himself, climbing on a bottle of hard cider. He accidentally falls in, and Junior has to rescue his pie-eyed pappy from various potential mishaps such as mouse traps, and vacuum cleaners. Finally the boss threatens, "Junior, one more boo-boo and out you go, permanently." Luckily, Ma and Pa (with an ice cube on his head) are just leaving. Sometime later, another baby is abandoned on their doorstep. Pa describes him as "a cute little stinker" and out comes an infant skunk. Pa puts a clothespin on his nose and says, "Here we go again."

CHINA JONES

Daffy Duck, Porky Pig; Feb 14; LT; Directed by Robert McKimson; Story by Tedd Pierce; Animation by Tom Ray, George Grandpre, Ted Bonnicksen, and Warren Batchelder; Layouts by Robert Gribbroek; Backgrounds byWilliam Butler; Film Editor: Treg Brown; Voice Characterization by Mel Blanc; Musical Direction by Milt Franklyn.

"This is Hong Kong, the melting pot of the Orient, where every man and his brother is out for a quick buck, and I'm not above making a fast buck meself. They call me China Jones." The speaker is Daffy, with a brogue adorning his for-once-lispless voice, as an Irish private eye in the Far East. Finding a call for help in a fortune cookie

("I'm being held prisoner ..."), he heads off for Limey Louie's in search of a clue. First he is badgered by Porky Pig as stuttering Charlie Chung who keeps appearing at odd intervals to bring up the matter of money. It is Limey Louie who has set up the whole bit to get revenge on China Jones for sending him to jail. Limey, in drag as his own wife, roughly acts out with Daffy what he thinks the police may be doing to his/her "husband." Daffy get a hot tip to head for Wong Way. There he meets the "Dragon Lady," not quite straight out of the pages of Milt Caniff. She explains her name by breathing fire at him. Back at L.L.'s he gets another tip and is sabotaged on a junk. The third time Louie reveals himself and tells Daffy that the whole thing has been a set-up. Daffy again encounters Porky/Charlie Chung, who explains he's not the detective but a laundryman. He is after Daffy to pay his bill. Daffy quotes Confucious about not being able to get blood from a turnip, and Porky quotes the ancient one: "Better to press shirts than luck." We end with Daffy ironing like mad, "Help I'm being held prisoner in a chinese laundry," he calls out.

HARE-ABIAN NIGHTS
Bugs Bunny, Yosemite Sam; Feb 28; MM; Directed by Ken Harris; Story by Michael Maltese; Animation by Ben Washam, and Ken Harris; Layouts by Samuel Armstrong; Backgrounds by Philip DeGuard; Film Editor: Treg Brown; Voice Characterization by Mel Blanc; Musical Direction by Milt Franklyn.
A Dixieland band, the Timbuk Two + 2, grinding out "Sweet Georgia Brown," fails to entertain the Sultan, and neither does "El-viz Pretzel" singing "Hound-Camel." Along comes Bugs tunneling under the floor panels looking for Perth Amboy, having made a wrong turn in Des Moines. Bugs is forced to perform as a "Teller of Tales." "Make your story-telling entertaining to the sultan, oh long-eared one, or it's

the croc pit for you!" Bugs begins with the tale of *Bully for Bugs*. He sees the sultan reach for the croc-pit button and "soon I was on my way again and ... found myself in the Sarara desert, where I met the stupidest character of them all, Yosemite Sam." You'd think Bugs would hesitate to tell a story illustrating Sam's stupidity and then say, "That Yosemite Sam, what a character, what a maroon, what a chicken-pickin' cotton-plucking' guy." Sam turns out to be the Sultan, but the clever rabbit has already turned off the electricity on Sultan Sam's button. Trying to open the door, the Sultan falls in the pit himself. The crocs chase Sam off and Bugs assumes his jeweled turban and throne. "Not a bad act, but don't call us, we'll call you and I can think of a few thing I'd like to call him!"

THE MOUSE THAT JACK BUILT
Apr. 4; MM; Directed by Robert McKimson; Story by Tedd Pierce; Animation by George Grandpre, Ted Bonnicksen, and Warren Batchelder; Layouts by Robert Gribbroek; Background by Robert Singer; Film Editor: Treg Brown; Voices Performed by Jack Benny, Mary Livingston, Rochester, Don Wilson, and Mel Blanc; Musical Direction by Milt Franklyn.
Here is the culminaton of the Warner toon studio's twenty-plus year love affair with Jack Benny (and Rochester). Little mice live in the house of Jack Benny ("Star of Stage-Screen-Radio-Television. Also Cartoons"). Jack and his valet, Rochester, are getting ready for his girlfriend Mary's birthday. First Jack gets Rochester to return the new jacket he rented from him, then he counts the cheese in the vault (protected by a myriad of alarms, booby-traps, and somebody named Ed Blanc who wonders if we've won the war yet and what they'll do with the Kaiser). Upstairs, Mary arrives, as does Chubby Don, who starts to read a commercial. Jack reminds Don that this is a movie. Jack receives a phony leaflet from a hungry cat from something called "The Kit Kat Club—Cheapest Nightclub in Town— Entertainers

Admitted Free" and they're off in the Maxwell, Mary reminding Jack he's promised her a bottle of champagne and Jack suggesting a good "mouse-katell." The club looks just like a cat, inside and outside, down to its red carpet tongue. There's no one in the place, although Jack tries to liven things up by playing "Tea for Two" on his violin. By the time they are certain where they are, the cat's mouth has already closed. Now dissolve to the real Jack Benny in live action waking up. "Gee, what a crazy dream. Imagine! Mary and me as mice." He hears a scratchy "Rockabye Baby" from his own cat, asleep, and sees two litle mice climbing out of its mouth! Benny then gives the camera one of those all-telling, indescribable *looks*.

TRICK OR TWEET

Tweety, Sylvester; Mar 21; MM; Directed by Friz Freleng; Story by Warren Foster; Animation by Art Davis, Virgil Ross, and Gerry Chiniquy; Layouts by Hawley Pratt; Backgrounds by Tom O'Loughlin; Film Editor: Treg Brown; Voice Characterization by Mel Blanc; Musical Direction by Milt Franklyn.
"I tawt I taw a puddy tat," says Tweety, meaning Sylvester. "I tawt I taw another puddy tat," says Tweety, meaning Sam, Sylvester's orange pal after they scaled the top of a long pole to get at Tweety's nest. After they slap each other around a bit, Sylvester pleads, "Hold it, Sam! Isn't it silly to jeopardize our neighborly relations over this scrawny little bird? He's not even a mouthful for either of us." ("You see," says Tweety, "I've been sick.") They decide to leave him alone, both volunteering to be the one to put him back and neither eager to leave the yard first. Both keep after Tweety, trying to keep this fact from the other (they each get the bright idea of climbing the pole in a garbage can). Eventually, they return to an out-and-out rout, as Tweety says, "I may be wrong but I just don't twust puddy-tat's honor." How true. Seconds after Tweety installs barbed wire on the pole, we

hear Sylvester yelling and picking clumps of black fur off said wire, Sam trying to trampoline up on a stretched corset. Then there's Sylvester high-wire walking. When he tries a flying "Batman costume," he crashes into Sam wearing the same. Sylvester stows away on Sam's balloon, pops it so Sam can't use it again, and, as they crash, Tweety observes, "I never wealized just bein' a little bird could be so complicated."

APES OF WRATH

Bugs Bunny; Apr 18; MM; Directed by Friz Freleng; Story by Warren Foster; Animation by Art Davis, Virgil Ross, and Gerry Chiniquy; Layouts by Hawley Pratt; Backgrounds by Tom O'Laughlin; Film Editor: Treg Brown; Voice Characterization by Mel Blanc; Musical Direction by Milt Franklyn.
The stork, perpetually toasted by proud parents, is constantly getting sloshed and losing his cargo. Forced to come up with a baby for Mr. and Mrs. Gorilla, the stork clobbers an unsuspecting Bugs and delivers him to the Gorilla as their new baby. Papa Gorilla takes one look at Bugs in diapers and bonnet and wants to put him out of his misery. Bugs at first thinks he has a hangover on the morning after a costume party. Both sides then try to make the best of the situation. Bugs overdoes the baby bit to hilariously obnoxious extremes, while Elvis Gorilla (yes, that's his name) tries to kill Bugs with kindness, rocking his cradle too hard, drowning him when he bawls for a drink of water, and throwing him high in the air, not catching him. The baby-father relationship is taken to the point where baby gets to amuse himself by endlessy pounding

Daddy on the head with a baseball bat. The stork picks that moment to deliver the real baby! Realizing what this means, Bugs beats it, fleeing from the ferocious gorilla. Elvis accidentally drops a boulder on his wife. In the pay-off, the stork delivers a "substitute" bundle to Bugs, this one containing a similarly clobbered-and-diapered Daffy Duck!

HOT ROD AND REEL!

The Coyote (Famishus Famishus) and the Road Runner (Super Sonicus); May 9; LT; Directed by Chuck Jones; Story by Michael Maltese; Animation by Richard Thompson, Ben Washam, and Keith Darling; Layouts and Backgrounds by Philip DeGuard; Film Editor: Treg Brown; Orchestrations by Milt Franklyn.

Just the gags: the Coyote stepping from one cliff to another and the second one falling, landing on another cliff, which also falls (to the bottom of a river); the Coyote roller-skating down a hill after the Road Runner and leaping off the mountain to avoid being tripped; an explosive camera kit ("Fool your friends—be popular"), heralded by the sign "Free Snapshots—Road Runners Only," going off in his face; a try at bouncing off a trampoline at the bird resulting in enveloping him in a sack; his crossbow flying forward leaving the dynamite stick behind; the jet powered pogo stick going backwards off the nearest cliff; his phony railroad cross-ing bit (compete with a hi-fi record of railroad crossing sounds) bringing on a real train; his sluice of bombs heading down a mountain jams and all going off in his face as he ends up sliding down toward it; his ACME jet-propelled uni-cyle getting out of control and, as soon as he gets it upright, taking it past the Road Runner and off another cliff. This time the "The End" letters mater-ialize above a little puff of smoke.

A MUTT IN A RUT

Elmer Fudd; May 23; LT; Directed by Robert McKimson; Story by Tedd Pierce; Animation by George Grandpre, Ted Bonnicksen, Warren Batchelder, and Tom Ray; Layouts by Robert Gribbroek; Backgrounds by William Butler; Film Editor: Treg Brown; Voice Characterization by Mel Blanc; Musical Direction by Milt Franklyn.

"Two go out, but only one comes back." That's the warning Elmer Fudd's dog gets watching a TV show directed at dogs. The program denounces the evils of mean masters, who, after a lifetime of abuse, when said dog "is old and has worn out his usefulness, pick up their guns and, ... "Come on, Wover boy, let's go hunting!" Fudd says he knows something's obviously bothering Rover, but not that Rover suspects his master plans to kill him. When they start into the woods Rover goes from hostile hound to paranoid, petrified pooch. "It's him or me," thinks Rover, starting a bunch of back-firing attempts to bump off his innocent master. He shoots at Fudd and gets a bear by acci-dent, then buries dynamite underneath Elmer. All the while Fudd thinks he's saving him from all these catastrophes instead of initiating them. "Wover, you woyal, bwave, hewoic dog, I'll see that you get a medal for this!" In the end, the bandaged bow-wow watches TV and, seeing the same program, runs off. Fudd wonders where wover went, and sees him on the TV set attacking the commentator who caused all the commotion. "For obvious reasons, this program must be temporarily interrupted."

BACKWOODS BUNNY

Bugs Bunny; June 13; MM; Directed by Robert McKimson; Story by Tedd Pierce; Animation by Warren Batchelder, Tom Ray, George Grandpre, and Ted Bonnicksen; Layouts by Robert Gribbroek; Backgrounds by William Butler; Film Editor: Treg Brown; Voice Characterization by Mel Blanc; Musical Direction by Milt Franklyn.

Burrowing into the Ozarks, Bugs Bunny decides to spend his vacation there. Meanwhile, up in a tree house, two hillbilly buzzards, Pappy and Elvis (voiced by Daws Butler) spot the bunny and try to catch the hare for their stew.

There are many chase gags, includ-ing Bugs in drag as a hillbilly girl and

Bugs adding extension pipe to Elvis' gun barrel. By the time he counts to four the gun is long enough to shoot Pappy in the tree house. Every time someone says four: Elvis shoots Pappy. The film ends with Bugs in a leisure suit singing, "I'm looking over a *four* leaf clover ..."

REALLY SCENT

Pepe Le Pew; June 27; MM; Directed by Abe Levitow; Story by Michael Maltese; Animation by Ken Harris, Richard Thompson, and Ben Washam; Layouts by Samuel Armstrong; Backgrounds by Philip DeGuard; Film Editor: Treg Brown; Voice Characterization by Mel Blanc; Orchestrations by Milt Franklyn.

A breath of fresh air for a series that needs it. Here virtually all of the rules de Le Pew are reversed. June Foray narrates this tale set in old New Orleans, beginning on a momentous day in the lives of Pierre and Fifi Cat. This is the day their daughters are born, one little kitten, by a "calamity of birth" coming into the world with a white stripe down her back! It only matters to "Fabrette" the following spring. Her sister easily attracts an eager boy friend, but the local tomcats are frightened by her skunk-like stripe. As fate would have it, Fabrette's ship comes in—from France, and containing Pepe Le Pew! The two spot each other and instantly there are stars in their eyes. Their passionate embrace is disturbed only by her sad discovery that one whiff of her lover is enough to make her pass out! She tries to combat Pepe's pungency by holding her breath (turning all sorts of colors). Pepe mistakes her red face for blushing and sprays himself with perfume. Pepe decides to look up "what thees 'pew' means every time I appear." He declares, "For her I will make myself dainty" and heads into "Henri's Deodorizing Service," just as Fabrette, about to commit suicide, realizes, "If you can't lick them ..." and dashes into "Pierre's Limberger Chesse Co." The last scene has the foul-smelling female chasing after the now-sanitary Pepe.

MEXICALI SHMOES

Speedy Gonzales; July 4; LT; Directed by Friz Freleng; Story by Warren Foster; Animation by Virgil Ross, Gery Chiniquy, and Art Davis; Layouts by Hawley Pratt; Backgrounds by Tom O'Laughlin; Film Editor: Treg Brown; Voice Characterization by Mel Blanc; Musical Direction by Milt Franklyn.

You just don't expect a 1959 Speedy Gonzales cartoon to be this funny, or this well-directed or animated: a real sleeper. The Mexicali Shmoes, who are wisely allocated far more screen time than the bland Speedy, are two cats by the name of Jose, a chubby tabby who claims to have brains enough to catch Gonzales, and Manuel, a skinny kitty who wants to know where to get these brains. Although playing and singing their music is of paramount importance, the minute Speedy comes within reach they don't hesitate to use their guitars to pound him with, once they have lured him out of his hole on the pretense of having a fiesta. Jose tries fishing for Speedy using cheese for bait, having seen "the greengo Bugs Bunny" do it in a movie. Instead Speedy drags him out of town. Later, Jose returns, telling Manuel that his sister in Los Angeles says hello! They plant TNT in Speedy's hole and he makes them think it's gone off. They fight over the mouse until Jose realizes the stick is still lit and lets Manuel have it (literally!). They plant a mine field and get caught in the middle of it, Manuel offering to carry Jose out as he knows where them mines are. He gets to the end without hitting one, but as soon as he puts Jose down, instant kablooey! Giving up on Speedy, Manuel tells Jose of another rodent, Slowpoke Rodriguez, the slowest mouse in all Mehico. Jose is off before Manuel finishes talking and must learn the hard way that Slowpoke, "he packs a gun."

TWEET AND LOVELY

Tweety, Sylvester; July 18; MM; Directed by Friz Freleng; Story by Warren Foster; Animation by Art Davis, Gerry Chiniquy, and Virgil Ross; Layouts by Hawley Pratt; Backgrounds by Tom O'Laughlin; Film Editor: Treg Brown; Voice Characterization by Mel Blanc; Musical Direction by Milt Franklin.

Sylvester, in his flat, spies Tweety in his bird house in the middle of "Singin' in the Bathtub," and learns that only one thing stands between him and the bird—Spike, the bulldog. So, he designs Wile E. Coyote-like contraptions, among them a robot dog that instantly attacks him, a smoke bomb which fills the yard with smoke but doesn't prevent the dog from letting Sylvester have it ("What a sorehead!"), an artificial storm cloud which goes off (with lightning and thunder) inside Sylvester's apartment, invisible paint which allows Sylvester to carry off the befuddled Tweety ("I must be walking in my sleep, but I'm not walking and I'm not sleeping. They must've repealed the law of gravity"). Spike sprays yellow paint all over Sylvester to save him. Lastly, Sylvester puts the finishing touches on an implement of destruction about which he says, "There's no guesswork about it this time! This'll get rid of that dog for good!" He leaves the room and, after an off-camera explosion, comes back in as an angel, tearing up the blueprints and declaring, "It's a good thing pussy-cats have got nine lives!"

WILD AND WOOLY HARE

Bugs Bunny, Yosemite Sam; Aug 1; LT; Directed by Friz Freleng; Story by Warren Foster; Animation by Virgil Ross, Gerry Chiniquy, and Art Davis; Layouts by Hawley Pratt; Backgrounds by Tom O'Loughlin; Film Editor: Treg Brown; Voice Characterization by Mel Blanc; Musical Direction by Milt Franklin.

How long has it been since Yosemite Sam has been indentifed on-screen by his full, unmodified name? The last of the Bugs Bunny Westerns is a "Gunfight at the U.P.A. Coral," with very attractive stylized settings and some of the old Bugs-Sam vinegar. When the saloon crowd hears Yosemite Sam, the fastest and meanest shot in the west, is in town, some beat it. Another ("Injun

Joe," asking a local to hold his beer) tries his skill against Sam (off-camera). Only Bugs Bunny has nerve enough to insult Sam and try to outwit him. Wavering between Bunny batty and Gary Cooper cool, Bugs stays one jump ahead of Sam with shooting both fancy and plain and a gentlemanly (which is against Sam's principles) duel. Their fun is interrupted by Sam's having to catch and rob the 5:15 train which Bugs vows to save. He assumes the role of the engineer as Sam, on his "idjit" horse riding along the side of the tracks, crashes into poles, tunnels and down canyons, not paying attention to where he's going. Finally, Sam gets in another locomotive heading towards Bugs head on. They play a suspenseful game of "chicken," neither backing out but Bugs extending the "legs" on his locomotive so Sam's car passes underneath and off the end of the track. "So long, Screwy," yells Bugs, "see ya in St. Louie!" Sam: "I hate that rabbit."

CAT'S PAW

Sylvester, Junior; Aug 15; LT; Directed by Robert McKimson; Story by Tedd Pierce; Animation by George Granpre, Ted Bonnicksen, Warren Batchelder, Tom Ray; Layouts by Robert Gribbroek; Backgrounds by William Butler; Film Editor: Treg Brown; Voice Characterizaton by Mel Blanc; Musical Direction by Milt Franklin.

Father: "Sufferin' succcotash! With all the merit badges he could go after, my bright little son has to pick bird-stalking!" Son: "But Father, stalking birds is an important part of every pussycat's life. You must teach me sometime!" Now they are in the mountains, and when Junior points out a giant owl he'd like them to go after, Sylvester is too afraid to admit he's afraid and cops out, telling him, "Those big ones are no sport, they're too slow. For some real he-cat sport, it's the little ones you gotta go after. The smaller they are, the tougher and scrappier they turn out to be." That turns out to be a perfect description of the bird they run into: What looks like a helpless little chick is, unbeknownst to them, a very dangerous dwarf eagle. He beats Sylvester up and terrifies him with his piercing shriek, much to the shame of his embarrassed boy. "How can I ever face the fellows in troop 12?" In the end, Sylvester tells Junior he'll have to chase butterflies or nothing, and instantly gets thrashed by a killer butterfly.

HERE TODAY, GONE TAMALE

Speedy Gonzales, Sylvester; Aug 29; LT; Directed by Friz Freleng; Story by Michael Maltese; Animation by Gerry Chiniquy, Art Davis, and Virgil Ross; Layouts by Hawley Pratt; Backgrounds by Tom O'Loughlin; Film Editor: Treg Brown; Voice Characterization by Mel Blanc; Musical Direction by Milt Franklyn.

In the midst of a cheese famine, the waterfront Mexican mice are so hungry they've started *dreaming* about cheese. Imagine their frustration when a boat carrying a cargo full of the stuff comes into port, guarded by that gringo pus-scat, Sylvester, who chases them off yelling, "And stay off, ya miserable little sneakin' crooked cheese thieves!" One of the mice considers suicide (prompting another to inquire, "Can I have your sombrero after you're gone, Fernando?"). Speedy Gonzales immediately comes to their rescue, and piece by piece gets the cheese down the gangplank past Sylvester. Once again, the Freleng Speedy has the best bits: Speedy in Sylvester's net dragging him across the deck; Sylvester getting locked in the limburger storage room and turning bright blue; Sylvester pretending to offer some of the cheese to Speedy (and, for one of the only times, addressing him by name) intending to mallet him but flattening his own hand instead, then facing us and whimpering; Sylvester rigging up a guillotine on the edge of the gangplank which shaves his own backside. ("I forgot all about that silly thing!"). He ultimately decides to join 'em since he can't beat 'em, and, donning a pair of Mickey Mouse Club ears, leaps in the middle of the mice's flamenco dance.

BONANZA BUNNY

Bugs Bunny; Sept 5; MM; Directed by Robert McKimson; Story by Tedd Pierce; Animation by Tom Ray, George Granpre, Ted Bonnicksen, and Warren Batchelder; Layouts by Robert Gribbroek; Backgrounds by William Butler; Film Editor: Treg Brown; Voice Characterization by Mel Blanc; Musical Direction by Milt Franklyn.

In 1896, into a saloon in Dawson, Alaska, a lawless, gold-mad boom town, walks Bugs, carrying a bagful of rocks and complaining to the bar keep, "I goofed. Everybody talkin' about carrots around here, diggin' like crazy, and all I get are shovels full of these little yellow rocks." A shot breaking his glass signifies the first round of give and take between Bugs and his new sparring partner, Black Jacque Shellaque, the French-Canadian answer to Yosemite Sam. Unfortunately, it's a pretty uninspired rehash of gags from *Bunker Hill Bunny, Bugs Bunny Rides Again* and *Dripalong Daffy* (footage from this one too), treated as though they expected the strength of the great new character to be enough to pull it off. The most interesting new gag has Bugs and "B. J." gambling at "21" with Bugs drawing one 21 card. Bugs's closing line: "The fun you can have with a bunch of old rocks and a can of yellow paint."

A BROKEN LEGHORN

Foghorn Leghorn; Sept 26; LT; Directed by Robert McKimson; Story by Warren Foster; Animation by Ted Bonnicksen, Warren Batchelder, Tom Ray, and George Grandpre; Layouts by Robert Gribbroek; Backgrounds by William Butler; Film Editor: Treg Brown; Voice Characterization by Mel Blanc; Musical Direction by Milt Franklyn.

Foghorn Leghorn does a good deed and look what he gets in return! He overhears a bunch of cackling old biddy hens making disparaging remarks about childless old Prissy Hen, forever trying to lay an egg. Foggy arranges "a surprise for those old busy bodies" by slipping another egg into the nest of "old square-britches." To their astonishment, Prissy's egg immediately hatches into a little baby rooster whom the flock of hens immediately covet. The first thing the kid says to Foggy, (in his baritone Henery Hawk voice), "You must be that rooster whose job I'm takin' over!" So, Foggy reasons, "This kid's gotta go!" and tells the widder, "as senior rooster around here, it's my duty and my pleasure to instruct junior roosters in the ancient art of roostering." As you'd expect every roosterian activity he demonstrates is booby-trapped to annihilate the chick. They all go off, instead, in Foggy's face. The tricks are crossing the road (explaining why chickens are prone to this activity); learning patience waiting near a drainpipe where Foggy slides down a dynamite stick; attaching an ear of corn to a rifle; and the old "phony worm in the land mine" trick. At last, Foggy has it out with the boss, "It's gotta be that kid or me! One of us has gotta go!" The final shot has Foggy hauled away in a truck saying, "When ya gotta go, ya gotta go!"

WILD ABOUT HURRY

The Coyote (Hardheadipus Delirius) and the Road Runner (Baduouticus.) Directed by Chuck Jones; Story by Michael Maltese; Animation by Ken Haris, Abe Levitow, Richard Thompson, Keith Darling, and Ben Washam. Layouts and Backgrounds by Philip DeGuard; Effects Animation by Harry Love; Film Editor: Treg Brown; Orchestrations by Milt Franklyn.
Great credits: the film title on a boulder the Coyote is preparing to drop, Jones's name on a rocket underneath the Coyote. A giant slingshot hurls the Coyote straight into the ground. A flat rock refuses to fall until he starts jumping on it, and then he runs so fast to spin it, he burrows through the ground into a train tunnel. Only half of a roller skate he rigs is pulled by a magnet attracted by iron pellets he has planted in the bird's tummy. The half containing the hand grenade remains. A bowling ball dropped through a chute not only bounces back into his face, it pounds him into the pavement. The Coyote then brings out his piece-de-resistance, an ACME Indestructo Steel Ball which he gets inside and rolls after the Road Runner—but the thing detours onto another highway and into a lake, perching him on the edge of a Hoover-sized dam. From there he bounces off more boulders and into a river leading to a waterfall and then washes onto a train track. The locomotive knocks him into a minefield, the resultant chain of explosions sending him back to the top of the cliff where he started. It doesn't end there, he rolls down the original cliff once more, passing the Road Runner who produces a banner which says, "Here we go again."

A WITCH'S TANGLED HARE

Bugs Bunny, Witch Hazel; Oct 31; LT; Directed by Abe Levitow; Story by Michael Maltese; Animation by Richard Thompson, Ken Harris, Ben Washam, and Keith Darling; Layouts by Owen Fitzgerald; Backgrounds by Bob Singer; Film Editor: Treg Brown; Voice Characterization by Mel Blanc; Musical Direction by Milt Franklyn.
William Shakespeare, in search of poetic inspiration, comes across the castle of Macbeth and finds Witch Hazel chasing Bugs ("What's up, Zsa-Zsa") Bunny therein. The Bard jots down their dialogue as possibilities for dramatic situations. Chanting and mixing her brew, Hazel makes up "the most important ingredient," one fresh rabbit, who mistakes her caldron for a hot bath until he gets a gander at the ingredient list and dashes across the foggy moor. Hazel mounts her broom side-saddle ("modesty is one of my girlish qualities") and follows him to the castle courtyard where they have a

fiendish cackle contest. He causes her to crash with an anvil. (It's a rule: Bugs hands you an anvil, and you have to hold onto it.) When she appears from a balcony, Bugs, suddenly in wig and pantaloons, heaves a rock through yonder window and the two make like Romeo and Juliet, ending when he offers to catch her ("As you like it") and letting her crash. Running again, he comes across the prostrate poet, who isn't Shakespeare after all but a cockney named Sam Krubish, who turns out to be Witch Hazel's long lost boy friend. "Why didn't you show up that night to meet my folks?" she asks, and he insists he went to apartment No. 2B as she said. They wander off arguing as to what the apartment number really was. Says Bugs, "2B or not 2B, that is the question."

UNNATURAL HISTORY

Nov 14; MM; Directed by Abe Levitow; Story by Michael Maltese; Animation by Ben Washam, Richard Thompson, and Keith Darling; Layouts and Backgrounds by Bob Singer; Film Editor: Treg Brown; Voice Characterization by Mel Blanc; Musical Direction by Milt Franklyn.

"Animal lovers, we can learn a great deal from our little wild cousins, even the tiniest creatures have much to teach us." So begins a lecture by Professor Beest Lee entitled, "Are animals human or vice versa?"

Blackout gags on animal life include: A chicken showing off by laying a square egg; a test animal rabbit rocketed to Mars and returning with a female rabbit with antenna which address each other as "John" and "Martian"; porcupines kissing each other very carefully; a running gag about a dog waiting faithfully for three years for his master to return and then browbeating him when he does. Best

gag is the old one about the talking dog in the theatrical agent's office, who says "ruff," in answer to the questions about the top of a house (roof), the owner's name (Ralph) and the greatest ballplayer (Ruth). When they both are thrown out, the dog has second thoughts, "Maybe I should've said DiMaggio?"

TWEET DREAMS

Tweety, Sylvester; Dec 5; MM; Directed by Friz Freleng.

The year's second "Economy" cartoon, with Sylvester, gone neurotic after years of myopic fixation on the "little yellow bird." He goes to see a pyschiatrist to get the whole story off his chest. His father, he tells the note-taking head-shrinker, never taught him how to catch mice like all the other cats so he "was forced to find sustenance by other means." This includes fishing before he discovered his perfect good food source (*Sandy Claws*), the Tweety Bird, desirable but forever out of reach. He tried going to a circus to forget the yellow bird, but Tweety turns up there (*Tweety's Circus*), and he made up his mind to get rid of the bird once and for all (the knitting gag from *A Street Cat Named Sylvester*) and even taunts the puddy with his delicious little self on Christmas morning ("Oh puddy, you're a wreck!" from *Gift Wrapped*). "Frustration began to set in ..." By now the doctor is asleep, and, waking, he realizes the time and that he's got to fly to Detroit ("Call me for an appointment"). He flies by flapping his arms out the window, and Sylvester follows, "Wait! Wait!'

PEOPLE ARE BUNNY

Bugs Bunny, Daffy Duck; Dec 19; MM; Directed by Robert McKimson; Story by Tedd Pierce; Animation by Ted Bonnicksen, Warren Batchelder, Tom Ray, and George Grandpre; Layouts by Robert Gribbroek; Backgrounds by William Butler; Film Editor: Treg Brown; Voice Characterization by Mel Blanc; Musical Direction by Milt Franklyn.

This spoof on 1950s game shows can't compete with the ludicrousness of the real thing, but is a howl nonetheless. Daffy chases Bugs around a TV studio, his eyes on a thousand smackeroo pay-off for the first hunter who brings in a rabbit to the hunting program, "The Sportsman's Hour." Seeing successful contestants carry off prizes that include yachts and the key to Fort Knox, Daffy locks Bugs in a phone booth while he goes on *People are Phoney*, whose obnoxious host Art Lamplighter challenges him to tackle a combative little old lady who will *not* be helped across the street (shown on a TV monitor in black and white with a laugh track). In the booth, Bugs wins a jackpot from a phone-in show by virtue of his skill at multiplying, and then gives Daffy a chance to do the same but with a TNT stick subbed for the phone. Bugs, posing as an usher, next misdirects Daffy onto the set of *Were You There*, "Indian Massacre at Burton's Bend," which leaves him scalped. As a wardrobe man, Bugs lures Daffy onto *Costume Party*, dresses him up as a rabbit and then collects the prize himself. When Daffy protests, "Now just a darn minute, I'm not a rabbit, I's a duck!" the gushy host (Frank Nelson) comes back, "Ooh, that's nice because now it's duck season!" Daffy gets blasted. Bugs insists "they always shoot blanks on TV," to which Daffy responds, "Blanks, he says, have a handful o' blanks. Jeez!"

1960

FASTEST WITH THE MOSTEST
The Coyote (Carniverous Slobbius) and the Road Runner (Velocitus Incalculus); Jan 19; LT; Directed by Chuck Jones; Animation by Ken Harris, Richard

Thompson, Ben Washam, and Keith Darling; Layouts and Backgrounds by Philip DeGuard; Film Editor: Treg Brown; Musical Direction by Milt Franklyn.

Not one of the more frequently-revived Road Runners, but one which deserves more attention, as besides being especially funny, it utilizes a slightly different format: instead of being mainly quick blackout gags with one or two extended bits, *Fastest* consists entirely of three long scenes. Plan one involves dropping a rocket-bomb from a balloon, but as he tries to blow it up as the air goes the wrong way, so the Coyote inflates instead. He starts to float away, and tries to hold himself down by grabbing onto the rocket for support. Bad idea! He propels himself upward by letting the air out, but then there's nothing to hold him up, and he plummets to the ground with the rockets behind him. Miraculously, it doesn't explode on impact, and he oh-so-painstakingly tries to diffuse it, but ... The next bit has the Coyote trying a trap that involves hanging over the Road Runner who has stopped running to partake of the Coyote's advertised "tranquilizer bird seed," and when he falls the bird kindly places a spring underneath him (for which the Coyote holds up a sign reading "Thanks"). Last, the Coyote thinks he's got him, he even gets out his knife and fork and napkin yet, when he corners the Road Runner at the edge of a cliff. But his part gives way and he falls right through (his cutlery giving him a close shave), before he knows it, landing in a river which carries him through a series of tunnels and out a faucet. At the end of this ordeal, he gazes at the Road Runner standing calmly on the unconnected yet stable piece of precipice, and comments, via a sign, "I wouldn't mind, except that he defies the law of gravity." The Road Runner answers with a sign of his own, "Sure, but I never studied law."

WEST OF THE PESOS
Speedy Gonzales, Sylvester; Jan 23; MM; Directed by Robert McKimson;

Story by Tedd Pierce; Animation by Tom Ray, George Grandpre, Ted Boonnicksen, and Warren Batchelder; Layouts by Robert Givens; Backgrounds by William Butler; Film Editor: Treg Brown; Voice Characterization by Mel Blanc; Musical Direction by Milt Franklyn.

In an experimental lab, Mexican mice are guinea pigs awaiting their doom. In their hometown, a list of "Meesing Personas" is posted (including such names as "Rudy Zamora, Pablo Picasso, Sam Fernando," et al.). The mice send Speedy Gonzales to tackle the guard pussy-gato, Sylvester.

Speedy rescues the mice óne by one, with Sylvester trying to foil each attempt. The cat employs a snare which Speedy pulls, dragging Sylvester through a knot-hole, getting skinned. Sylvester holds a boulder, but Speedy "Yee-Ha's" causing the cat to toss the rock in the air. It lands on his head. Speedy get a group of mice out disguised as a daschundt; another group as a train. Sylvester gets wise and sets up his mouth as a tunnel for the train to travel into. It does,right through his body and out his tail! Speedy returns the "meesing" mice and receives his reward, a kiss from a senorita, which drives him wild!

HORSE HARE

Bugs Bunny, Yosemite Sam; Feb 13; LT; Directed by Friz Freleng; Story by Michael Maltese; Animation by Gerry Chiniquy, Virgil Ross, and Art Davis; Layouts by Hawley Pratt; Backgrounds by Tom O'Laughlin; Film Editor: Treg Brown; Voice Characterization by Mel Blanc; Musical Direction by Milt Franklyn.

In 1886, calvary solider Bugs Bunny is ordered to guard Fort Lariat while the troops are away. Taking advantage, Yosemite Sam leads his Indians in an attack on the fort. Gags include Bugs singing "Ten Little Indians" while shooting the braves; Geronimo ramming the gate with Sam in the middle getting flattened; Sam shooting at the fort, and with each shot, Bugs peashoots the Indian Chief, causing him to sock Sam.

In the end, the calvary returns and attacks the Indians, with Sam, caught in the middle, flattened again!

WILD WILD WORLD

Feb 27; MM; Directed by Robert McKimson; Story by Tedd Pierce; Animation by George Granpre, Ted Bonnicksen, Warren Batchelder, and Tom Ray; Layouts by Robert Gribbroek; Backgrounds by William Butler; Voice Characterization by Mel Blanc; Musical Direction by Milt Franklyn.

Flintstones-style spot gags depict caveman times as a rocks-and-dinosaurs replication of the modern world. For instance, there's a long sequence about a cro-magnon department store, with an elevator that works because of the weights of various rocks dumped into baskets. When a customer wants to go to the basement, the ropes are simply cut! The whole thing is framed, as in *Pre-Hysterical Hare,* by the claim that this is an actual movie from ancient times, narrated by soft-spoken "Cave Darroway." A semi-running gag concerns a trio of foolhardy hunters who blithely attack huge dinosaurs that merely flick them aside. Man discovers fire for such useful purposes as giving each other hot foots. Weapons such as the boomerang serve to restore errant wives to the caves, but not when she has a rolling pin. You get the idea. In the last gag, Garroway gets inside a "modern" elevator to go to the basement and *his* ropes are cut.

GOLDIMOUSE AND THE THREE CATS

Sylvester; Mar 15; LT; Directed by Friz Freleng; Story by Michael Maltese; Animation by Virgil Ross, Art Davis, and Gerry Chiniquy; Layouts by Hawley Pratt; Backgrounds by Tom O'Loughlin; Film Editor: Treg Brown; Voice Characterization by Mel Blanc; Musical Direction by Milt Franklyn.

Once upon a time, a father cat (Sylvester), a mother cat, and their "spoiled brat" decide to take a walk to let their porridge cool. When they do that a little mouse with blond hair named Goldimouse comes into their home, eats their porridge, and sleeps in their beds. Junior wants a mouse and goads his dad into chasing her, every scheme Sylvester tries ending in failure.

Sylvester tries an arrow, which pulls the cat into the mouse hole, mother and Junior rescue him with a bathroom plunger; then a dart in a blowpipe, which Goldimouse blows down Sylvester's throat and out his tail; also dynamite in a cheese trap, which Sylvester falls into; and a "better mouse trap" which catches a certain pussycat.

Mother and Junior move into their bomb shelter for Sylvester's next scheme, which isn't shown, but an explosion is heard off screen. A battered Sylvester comes over to his family and dumps a bowl of porridge on his spoiled brat's head!

PERSON TO BUNNY
Bugs Bunny, Daffy Duck, Elmer Fudd; Apr 1; MM; Directed by Friz Freleng; Story by Michael Maltese; Animation by Art Davis, Gerry Chiniquy, and Virgil Ross; Layouts by Hawley Pratt; Backgrounds by Tom O'Loughlin; Film Editor: Treg Brown; Voice Characterization by Mel Blanc; Musical Direction by Milt Franklyn.
This is a spoof of Edward R. Murrow's *Person to Person.* In his home, Bugs Bunny is being interviewed on a TV show when Daffy Duck walks in, becoming flustered. When "Edward Burrows" Asks Bugs about Elmer Fudd, the rabbit responds "His I.Q is P.U."

Fudd marches over to Bugs' rabbit hole and demands an apology. While Bugs deals with Elmer, Daffy auditions for Mr. Burrows doing his Ted Lewis imitation. Bugs tricks Daffy into get-

ting shot by Elmer. Elmer gets wise and chases Bugs, who pulls the log gag from *All This and Rabbit Stew* (1942). Meanwhile Daffy is doing his soft-shoe audition (reused animation from *Show Biz Bugs,* 1957). Bugs and Burrows agree to let Daffy perform for the cameras, but when they tell him 40 million people will be watching, the duck gets stage fright.

WHO SCENT YOU?
Pepe Le Pew; Apr 23; LT; Directed by Chuck Jones; Story by Michael Maltese; Animation by Richard Thompson, Ken Harris, Ben Washam, and Keith Darling; Layouts by Maurice Noble; Backgrounds by Philip DeGuard; Film Editor: Treg Brown; Voice Characterization by Mel Blanc; Musical Direction by Milt Franklyn.
A female feline studies a "Pleasure Cruise" travel poster and tries to board the ship. The cat sneaks under a freshly painted fence, and gets a white stripe on her black back. Pepe LePew spots the female from the shore and runs into the sea (running because he cannot swim) even the fish "smell" him! The captain abandons ship because of the female "skunk," leaving Pepe free to pursue his love. He uses great lines such as: "Your aloneness is almost over!" and "You are my peanut, I am your brittle!"

Pepe freshens up in the beauty salon, then chases the cat all over the abandoned ship. When the cat finally escapes in a life boat, Pepe is adrift with her. He hangs a sign, "This is the life" over the side.

HYDE AND TWEET
Tweety, Sylvester; May 14; MM; Directed Friz Freleng; Animation by Art Davis, Gerry Chiniquy, and Virgil Ross; Layouts by Hawley Pratt; Backgrounds by Tom O'Loughlin; Film Editor: Treg Brown; Voice Characterization by Mel Blanc; Musical Direction by Milt Franklyn.
Sylvester is sleeping on the ledge outside the office of Dr. Jekyll (whom we see in his office drinking the potion that turns him into a monster). Sylvester wakes up and chases the birds off

the ledge. Tweety flies by and Sylvester chases him into Jekyll's lab. Tweety hides in the Hyde formula and becomes a giant Tweety monster terrorizing Sylvester. When Tweety returns to normal, the cat resumes the chase, always being caught with Tweety in a tight situation when the little bird reverts to "Mr. Hyde" size.

At one point, the monster Tweety chases the cat out of the window. A giant bird grabs him in mid air, then reverts to tiny Tweety, dropping the cat some twelve stories. Sylvester returns to put Tweety in a sandwich. The Monster emerges from the two slices of bread and eats the cat! Sylvester jumps out of his big mouth and screams for help. ("Help! Open the door! I'm locked in with a killer!") then wakes up (it was all a dream) on the window ledge. When Tweety lands next to him, Sylvester runs through the brick wall, screaming for help!

RABBIT'S FEAT

Bugs Bunny; Wile E. Coyote; June 4; LT; Directed by Chuck Jones; Animation by Ken Harris and Richard Thompson; Layouts and Backgrounds by Philip DeGuard; Film Editor: Treg Brown; Voice Characterization by Mel Blanc; Musical Direction by Milt Franklyn.
Chuck Jones harkens back to an earlier wabbit persona, a "wacky" Bugs Bunny!

Wile E. Coyote introduces himself to us, telling us of his plan to capture and eat the rabbit. Bugs is sleeping (in a baby's crib), while the Coyote unpacks a picnic lunch outside his rabbit hole. Bugs climbs out and joins him, eating his food. When the rabbit asks, "What's cookin'?" the coyote responds, "You are!" scoops the bunny up in his picnic blanket and brings him to his stew pot. Bugs screams, "You're killing me!" but the coyote is wiser than that trick and confronts the rabbit making painful noises. When Bugs realizes the Coyote is on to him, he acts looney. "Daddy, you're back from Peru! Oh, Papa! We thought you'd been run over by an elevator!"

The Coyote ponders his next plan,

inadvertently consulting with Bugs. Coyote: "What if I lured him into a rock crusher?" Bugs: "Too complicated." Coyote: "What if I built a Burmese tiger trap?" Bugs: "Too much detail!" Finally Coyote has a plan to use a dynamite filled carrot. Bugs screams and tells him "That would hurt!" then flies out. (It should be noted that Bugs uses his ears in strange ways in this film, spinning them to fly, etc.) Wile E. comes after the rabbit with his rifle, but Bugs spins the barrel so the blasts hit the Coyote. The Coyote throws a grenade in the rabbit hole, but as usual, he gets blasted. Bugs reminds us, "Don't take life too seriously, you'll never get out of it alive!"

CROCKETT-DOODLE-DOO

Foghorn Leghorn; June 25; MM; Directed by Robert McKimson; Story by Tedd Pierce; Animation by Warren Batchelder, Tom Ray, George Grandpre, and Ted Bonnicksen; Layouts by Robert Givens; Backgrounds by Bob Singer; Effects Animation by Harry Love; Film Editor: Treg Brown; Voice Characterization by Mel Blanc; Musical Direction by Milt Franklyn.
Foghorn Leghorn (in a coonskin cap) is going camping, and decides to teach the little book worm, Egghead Jr. (seen reading "Basic Research in Physical Science"), all about the great outdoors. Everything Foggy tries to teach, Egghead does better, figuring it out scientifically.

Foghorn tries to start a fire, but gets his feathers burned. Foggy also fails with a duck call, and with smoke signals. The rooster fakes an Indian rain dance. Egghead Jr. puts dry ice in a paper airplane, creating a storm cloud over Foghorn, zapping him with lightning. Foggy shows him a simple box trap set-up, but Little Egghead has a rope trap which Foggy demonstrates won't work and gets trapped in it! Says Foghorn, caught in his snare, "Ya got anymore of them long-haired books?"

MOUSE AND GARDEN ^{ACADEMY AWARD NOMINEE}

Sylvester; July 15; LT; Directed By Friz Freleng; Animation by Gerry Chinquy, Virgil Ross, and Art Davis; Layouts by

Hawley Pratt; Backgrounds by Tom O'Loughlin; Film Editor: Treg Brown; Voice Characterization by Mel Blanc; Musical Direction by Milt Franklin. Sylvester and his gooney orange friend Sam (voiced by Daws Butler) share leftovers from the trash cans at the pier. When Sylvester finds a live mouse, however, he tries to keep it secret from his pal. Sam gets wise and replaces the mouse, under Sylvester's foot, with a dynamite stick. Sylvester puts the TNT in his mouth, where it explodes. They each claim the mouse, then decide to share it.

That night, they put the mouse in a jug, then hang the bottle under their house, which is on stilts perched over the sea, each one trying to get at it without the other knowing. Sylvester can't trust Sam, so he ties him to his bed. Sylvester tries for the mouse, but Sam mallets him (still tied to the bed, with the mallet in his mouth). Sam sneaks out, and goes underwater to reach for the mouse, using a pipe for breathing; Sylvester puts a dynamite stick in the pipe. Sylvester ties Sam's tail to a motor boat, but the orange cat pulls Sylvester (and the jug) with him, water-skiing, out into the ocean. The two cats end up on a rock in the middle of the sea, kicking each other as the mouse paddles back to shore in the jug.

READY WOOLEN AND ABLE

Sam Sheepdog, Ralph Wolf, July 30; MM; Directed by Chuck Jones; Story by Michael Maltese; Animation by Ken Harris, Richard Thompson, and Ben Washam; Layouts by Maurice Noble; Backgrounds by Philip DeGuard; Film Editor: Treg Brown; Voice Characterization by Mel Blanc; Musical Direction by Milt Franklin.
Sam the Sheepdog rattles to work in his Model-T, while Ralph Wolf speeds ahead of him in his hot rod. After punching time clocks, they get right into their tussle. Sam stops Ralph from getting sheep by placing a rake strategically under the wolf so he gets hit with it. Ralph places a lit dynamite stick at one end of a lever, while jumping on the other end: instead of becom-

ing propelled, the dynamite rolls toward the wolf and explodes! Ralph rolls a keg of gun powder, with a lit fuse, at the sheepdog, but the keg bounces over the dog, and blows a boulder back at the wolf.

The Wolf also tries two ACME bed springs which bounce Ralph toward his foe, and a trapeze to swing from one cliff to another. But he ends up seeing Sam everywhere he looks, including in the lake and underwater. Ralph swims away from the sheepdog into the mouth of a whale. Sam is in there as well. Getting back to the beach, Ralph encounters dozens of sheepdogs!

Sam drives home in his Model-T, but is passed by an ambulance with Ralph on back, in a straight jacket!

MICE FOLLIES

The Honey Mousers; Aug 20; LT; Directed by Robert McKimson; Story by Tedd Pierce; Animation by George Granpre, Ted Bonnicksen, Warren Batchelder, and Tom Ray; Layouts by Robert Gribbroek; Backgrounds by Bob Singer; Film Editor: Treg Brown; Musical Direction by Milt Franklin.
It's two o'clock in the morning, and Ralph and Ned Morton have promised to return home from their lodge meeting at 11! "If Alice catches me comin' home at this time in the mornin', she'll really chew me out." "Trixie's liable to kick me out too." "You oughta be on television, Morton, you're a riot! Har-har, de-hardy har-har!" and so on. On the way home, Morton ticks off a hungry cat who follows them, and tries to eat them as they're trying to sneak home without waking up their wives, and they don't even realize the cat is around. The cat enters their apartment as they do, the lights out, and assume that the cat (whose "meows" sound like "Ralph") thrashing them is their angry wives. The boys decide to spend the night in the park. The girls, coming home from a movie, make the same mistake (assuming the thrashing cat is their angry husbands) and also head for the park. It ends with the husbands and the wives sleeping peacefully, unknown to each other, on adjacent park benches.

FROM HARE TO HEIR

Bugs Bunny, Yosemite Sam; Sept 3; MM; Directed by Friz Freleng; Story by Friz Freleng; Animation by Art Davis, Gerry Chiniquy, and Virgil Ross; Layouts by Hawley Pratt; Backgrounds by Tom O'Loughlin; Film Editor: Treg Brown; Voice Characterization by Mel Blanc; Musical Direction by Milt Franklyn.

At Bedlam Manor, Sam (the Duke of Yosemite) is told he has no more money. Bugs Bunny comes to his door from a company which has selected Sam to recieve one million pounds as a "person of mild temperament." Any outburst of temper and Bugs has the right to deduct from the gift.

That night, Bugs makes Sam's life miserable. He plays the piano, and becomes a one-man band in the middle of the night. He hogs the bathroom. Sam rants and raves, and each time he does, Bugs deducts a sum from his monetary gift. By next morning, Sam shows Bugs, that he has his outbursts licked. His servants kick and bop him and he doesn't mind. Bugs confides to us, "I haven't got the heart to tell him he's used up all the money!"

THE DIXIE FRYER

Foghorn Leghorn; Sept 24; MM; Directed by Robert McKimson; Story by Tedd Pierce; Animation by Ted Bonnicksen, Warren Batchelder, Tom Ray, and George Granpre; Layouts by Robert Givens; Backgrounds by William Butler; Film Editor: Treg Brown; Voice Characterization by Mel Blanc; Musical Direction by Milt Franklyn.

Foghorn Leghorn flies South for the winter (via a basket attached to a flock of migrating ducks). Jumping out at a southern plantation, the rooster is spotted by two hungry hillbilly chicken hawks, Pappy and Elvis (both voiced by Daws Butler, last seen as buzzards in *Backwood Bunny*, 1958). The hawks grab Foghorn, and start plucking his feathers, dragging him to the chopping block. "I'm a rooster, not a roaster!" says Foggy, escaping the pair. They chase him around a tree, Elvis shooting Pappy. Foggy gets them to duel,

but, after three paces, they fire at the rooster, whose beak falls to the ground. ("That's the first time somebody else shot my mouth off!") Foghorn fakes a tornado coming, then one really does and strips the rooster (who uses ACME Instant Feathers to redress). Foggy hides in a gunpowder shed, and the two chicken hawks follow. Unable to see in the dark, Foghorn loans Pappy a match. The barn explodes, landing the birds in the tree top where they return to eating "black-eyed' peas.

HOPALONG CASUALTY

The Road Runner; Oct 8; MM; Directed by Chuck Jones; Story by Chuck Jones; Animation by Tom Ray, Ken Harris, Richard Thompson, and Bob Bransford; Layouts by Maurice Noble; Backgrounds by Philip DeGuard; Film Editor: Treg Brown; Musical Direction by Milt Franklyn.

The Road Runner (Speedipus Rex) runs toward us, pursued by the Coyote (Hard Hepipus Ravenus) who actually grabs the animal by the neck. So he thinks, but it is only a cloud of Road-Runner-shaped dust. In the first minute of this film, the Coyote is smashed by a telephone pole, run over by a truck and blown up by his own dynamite trap. The remaining screen time has the coyote getting the worst of the ACME Christmas packing machine ("makes neat small packages"), of a fishing rod with dynamite on the hook, and of the classic ACME earthquake pills ("Why wait! Make your own earthquakes! Loads of Fun"). The Coyote leaves a pile of pills as "Free bird seed," which the Road Runner promptly eats. When nothing happens to the bird, the Coyote tries one. Nothing happens either, and he's so hungry he downs the whole bottle. He spots a label warning, "Caution—Not effective on Road Runners." Suddenly his toe begins to shake, then the rest of his body. The vibrations of his body crush rocks, boulders, and move mountains. When the shaking stops, the Coyote is relieved that he survived without a scratch. He staggers off happy and walks off a cliff!

TRIP FOR TAT

Tweety, Sylvester; Oct 29; MM; Directed by Friz Freleng; Story by Michael Maltese; Animation by Gerry Chiniquy, Virgil Ross, and Tom Ray; Layouts by Hawley Pratt; Backgrounds by Tom O'Loughlin; Film Editor: Treg Brown; Voice Characterization by Mel Blanc; Musical Direction by Milt Franklyn.

Granny goes on a world tour with Tweety, Sylvester joining them as a stowaway. It becomes a chase of the little bird around the world.

While Granny is sleeping, Sylvester grabs Tweety from his cage, but Tweety pulls the "seasick gag," rocking a picture of the ocean making the cat turn green. Tweety tries to make the cat feel better by offering him a "a nice fat, juicy piece of pork!" In Paris, Granny is "finger painting" (that is, painting a picture of her thumb). Tweety also tries art, drawing a picture of the bad 'ol putty tat. When Sylvester sticks his face where Tweety's drawing has been, the bird erases the ugly face. The cat runs to a tattoo parlour to get a new face drawn on! In the Swiss Alps, Granny and Tweety go skiing (Tweety uses spoons on his feet). Sylvester follows and gets clobbered by a tree. In Japan, Sylvester chases Tweety, and gets caught by a fisherman. In Italy, he tries a swing to reach Tweety, but flies into a jackhammer and gets squashed. The cat finally dines at an Italian restaurant, crosses fowl off his diet menu, and digs into a big plate of spaghetti.

DOG GONE PEOPLE

Elmer Fudd; Nov 12; MM; Directed by Robert McKimson; Story by Tedd Pierce; Animation by Warren Batchelder, George Grandpre, Ted Bonnicksen, and Tom Ray; Layouts by Robert Gribbroek; Backgrounds by William Butler; Film Editor: Treg Brown; Voice Characterization by Mel Blanc; Musical Direction by Milt Franklyn.

Hoping for a promotion, Elmer Fudd (voiced by Hal Smith) is delighted to do his boss, Mr. Crabtree, a favor by babysitting his dog Rupert.

The dog thinks of himself as a human being, and is offended by Elmer setting him up in front of the TV to watch "Classie." The dog is about to leave, but Elmer pleads forgiveness and they shake on it. Elmer next tries to feed him dog food, but Rupert wants (and gets) real meat, with Fudd eating the dog food. Elmer tries to get the dog to sleep in the "Bow Wow" doggie bed, but the dog gets his way and sleeps in Fudd's bed.

The next morning, watching Elmer gargle, Rupert accidentally drinks bay rum and gets drunk. Elmer takes Rupert for a drive, but the dog takes the wheel, driving wildly through town. They are thrown in jail for drunk driving. The boss bails them out, telling Fudd he's "going to move up" in the company. In the end, Fudd is painting the roof-top flagpole, while Rupert is made Vice President!

HIGH NOTE ACADEMY AWARD NOMINEE

Dec 3; LT; Directed by Chuck Jones; Story by Michael Maltese; Animation by Richard Thompson and Ken Harris; Layouts by Maurice Noble; Backgrounds by Philip DeGuard and William Butler; Film Editor: Treg Brown; Musical Direction by Milt Franklyn.

This is an unusual musical cartoon from Warners, an attempt by Chuck Jones to combine graphic designs and stylized animation with story and personality. As with his 1965 Oscar winning M.G.M. cartoon *The Dot and the Line*, he suceeds quite nicely.

The characters are all musical symbols (notes, G clefs, sharps) which construct the sheet music for "The Blue Danube." A conductor-note begins to play the piece, but one note is missing, a drunken note (the "high" note) with a red head, straggling out of the sheet music of "Little Brown Jug." He plays tic-tac-toe with the sharp sign, and does tricks with his "dog-note." The conductor chases the high note, which gets trapped on a runaway bronco-note. The conductor lassos him, and places him back in his proper position on the staves. When the conductor begins the piece, High Note is missing again, along with all the others. They are all at the "Little Brown Jug." High Note is resting atop "How Dry I Am."

LIGHTER THAN HARE

Bugs Bunny, Yosemite Sam; Dec 17; MM; Directed by Friz Freleng; Story by Friz Freleng; Animation by Virgil Ross, Art Davis, and Gerry Chiniquy; Layouts by Hawley Pratt; Backgrounds by Tom O'Loughlin; Film Editor: Treg Brown; Voice Characterization by Mel Blanc; Musical Direction by Milt Franklyn
A spaceship lands and surveys the "City Dump" where Bugs Bunny lives. Inside the ship "Yosemite Sam of Outer Space" orders his robot ZX29-B to capture the earth creature, but Bugs uses the robot as a receptacle for his trash!

Sam sends out a demolition squad of three red robots, but Bugs destroys the spacemen. Sam goes after the rabbit himself in an "indestructable tank," but Bugs is ready for him with dynamite! Sam goes after Bugs in his space ship, and then in his "rocket suit," but the bunny escapes by twirling his ears to fly like a helicopter. Sam uses a robot ferret, but Bugs counters it with a robot wise-guy rabbit. Sam takes the robot rabbit back to his superiors. Bugs tunes in his radio, listening in as Sam presents the creature to his leader. It explodes ("Those earth creatures, always shooting off their mouths!"). Bugs flips the dial on the radio, wondering whether "Amos and Andy are on yet"!

1961

CANNERY WOE

Speedy Gonzales, Sylvester; Jan 7; LT; Directed by Robert McKimson; Story by Tedd Pierce; Animation by George Granpre, Ted Bonnicksen, Warren Batchelder, and Tom Ray; Layouts by Robert Gribbroek; Backgrounds by William Butler; Film Editor: Treg Brown; Effects Animation by Harry Love; Voice Characterization by Mel Blanc; Musical Direction by Milt Franklyn.
Near the local cannery, Two Mexican mice, Manuel and Jose, who live in a rundown sardine can, are hungry and wondering what they will do for food. They see a sign for a political rally, "Grand Cheese Fiesta! Re-Elect Mayor Raton. Free Cheese for all". The two mice run to the rally, but are kicked out of the festivities.

The "Cheese Committee" arrives at the gathering and reports, "No cheese, Senor Mayor. From the store we go to get cheese, but something new has been added!—a cat". The Mayor is outraged, but Jose and Manuel have a plan: they will recruit Speedy Gonzales in exchange for political favors. Speedy races to the cheese shop. Sylvester, underestimating the little rodent, plays along and lets him in the store. Speedy runs under the cat, tearing off his fur, leaving a message, "Speedy was here!" Sylvester runs out of the shop and Speedy rips his rear with the message, "Also Here!" Speedy presents four wedges of cheese to the Mayor and races back for more. Sylvester spreads tacks, uses a cannon, and sets a whole room full of mouse traps, to no avail.

Speedy receives a medal from the mayor, and Manuel and Jose get their wish, to be made "Official Cheese Inspectors." Speedy, to his delight, is appointed "Official Chick Inspector."

ZIP 'N' SNORT

The Road Runner; Jan 21; MM; Directed by Chuck Jones; Story by Chuck Jones; Animation by Richard Thompson, Bob Bransford, Tom Ray, and Ken Harris; Layouts by Maurice Noble; Backgrounds by Philip DeGuard; Film Editor: Treg Brown; Musical Direction by Milt Franklyn.
The Coyote (Evereadii-Eatibus) chasing the Road Runner (Digoutis-Hot-

Rodis) on the highway first must out-run a truck, and he does so by running off a cliff and splattering down a mountain side. His attempts against the speedy bird include a grenade in a model plane; some ACME iron pellets mixed with Ajax bird seed, his magnet on a fishing rod which attracts only electric wires; a giant cannon which falls from a cliff on top of the coyote; ACME axle grease that lets the Coyote slide across the desert and into cactus, down a mountain, over electric wires, to the railroad track, to be pursued by the express train (with the Road Runner as engineer!).

HOPPY DAZE

Sylvester, Hippety Hopper; Feb 11; LT; Directed by Robert McKimson; Story by Tedd Pierce; Animation by Ted Bonnicksen, Warren Batchelder, Tom Ray, and George Grandpre; Layouts by Robert Gribbroek; Backgrounds by Bob Singer; Effects Animation by Harry Love; Film Editor: Treg Brown; Voice Characterization by Mel Blanc; Musical Direction by Milt Franklyn.
On the waterfront, a tough guy cat (wearing a green turleneck sweater and derby) complains that he can't catch a mouse. Spotting Sylvester rummaging the trash cans, he convinces the lisping pussycat that he can be a "champeen mouser" with his training.

First they approach the ACME warehouse, and the trainer tells him to run in there and "tag your mouse." Sylvester chases a mouse into a crate which happens to contain Hippety Hopper, whom Sylvester mistakes for a giant mouse. The kangaroo decks Sylvester on the dock. Each time his coach sends him in, the "giant mouse" bounces him back. ("If it keeps up like this, the kid'll make a *vege-tanarian* outa me!") The tough mouse tells Sylvester to keep his "left" up. Sylvester springs after Hoppy on a bed spring hopping into a smoke stack (all the while keeping his left up). Hoppy passes the dazed cats on the dock and concludes this bout by doing a "Durante" Ach-cha-cha-cha-chu!

THE MOUSE ON 57th STREET

Feb 25; MM; Directed by Chuck Jones; Story by Michael Maltese; Animation by Ken Haris, Richard Thompson, and Bob Bransford; Layouts by Maurice Noble and Owen Fitzgerald; Backgrounds by Philip DeGuard; Film Editor: Treg Brown; Voice Characterization by Mel Blanc; Musical Direction by Milt Franklyn.
Across the street from Spiffany's, the world's largest jewelers, is Antonie's Bakery with a 100-proof rum cake in the window. A little brown mouse in a yellow hat climbs into the window and eats the cake, getting drunk and staggering down the street.

Waking up the next morning with a hangover, the mouse searches for some ice to put on his head. He climbs into Spiffany's window, takes the valuable "Sunflame Diamond" and ties it to his head. The police, a big dumb "Muldoon" and his red-mustachioed partner, chase the mouse into Lacy's department store where the mouse is mistaken for a novelty brooch. They chase the mouse into the subway, a train sending the cops and the mouse flying back to the street. The diamond lands on Muldoon's head. Thinking the mouse is still attached to the diamond, Muldoon beats his partner with his night stick. The mouse returns to the bakery window to have some more rum cake!

STRANGLED EGGS

Foghorn Leghorn, Henery Hawk; Mar 18; MM; Directed by Robert McKimson; Story by Tedd Pierce; Animation by George Grandpre, Ted Bonnicksen, Warren Batchelder, and Tom Ray; Layouts by Robert Gribborek; Backgrounds by Bob Singer; Film Editor: Treg Brown; Voice Characterization by Mel Blanc; Musical Direction by Milt Franklyn.
Foghorn Leghorn is out of food, his cupboard "as bare as a cooch dancer's midriff!" With no prospects for getting any food, he decides to court Miss Prissy in order to live comfortably in the winter.

A knock at the door reveals a baby

abandoned on Miss Prissy's door step. It's young Henery Hawk, whom Foghorn wants to eat and Prissy wants to keep. Foggy proposes to teach the little tyke to be like a chicken. First he shows Henery how to crow, but by now the chicken hawk has decided he wants to eat Foggy! Foghorn paints an army surplus hand grenade and teaches him how to hatch an egg. When he pulls the pin, via a string, the grenade flys at him. Next Foggy plants land mines and attempts to teach Henery how to scratch for food but Henery leads Foghorn on a chase through the minefield and the rooster gets blasted. Foggy pretends to be a chicken hawk and dives for Henery, but Prissy protects her "baby," slamming the door in Foghorn's face. A clobbered Leghorn remarks, "Like my pappy used to say, "Shoemaker, stick to your last" and this is my last!"

BIRDS OF A FATHER

Sylvester; Apr 1, LT; Directed by Robert McKinson; Story by Dave Detiege; Animation by Warren Batchelder, George Grandpre, and Ted Bonnicksen; Layouts by Robert Gribbroek; Backgrounds by William Butler; Film Editor: Treg Brown; Voice Characterization by Mel Blanc; Musical Direction by Milt Franklyn.

Sylvester is resting in his hammock, proudly watching his son chase a little bird, but soon the bird is chasing Junior! Sylvester is shocked to learn that his son is best friends with this blue bird named "Spike."

Sylvester decides to teach his son "the facts of life." He gives Junior a book on "Cat Psychology" which explains that "real" cats chase, catch, and eat birds ("Oh father, are we cannibals?" Sylvester, in a sly laugh replies "Yeah-heh-heh-heh!"). Junior tells his pal Spike that he must chase him, but the bird comes up with a plan. Junior chases the bird into the tool shed, and inside they pretend to fight. Sylvester stops his son from chopping the bird with an axe, deciding to show him how to catch a bird "like a true sportsman." They go hunting with a rifle; each

attempt ends in disaster. Sylvester shoots a badminton bird, and gets hit with the racquet. Sylvester shoots the bird off the hat of a lady who clobbers him with her umbrella ("She's about as helpless as a porcupine in a nudist colony!"). The lisping pussycat uses a radio-controlled jet plane, but the bird returns a full-sized bullet-spraying jet fighter back at the feline. In the end, Junior introduces a new friend to his dad, Spike in kitten disguise!

D'FIGHTIN' ONES

Sylvester; Apr 22; MM; Directed by Friz Freleng; Animation by Gerry Chiniquy, Virgil Ross, and Art Davis; Layouts by Hawley Pratt; Backgrounds by Tom O'Loughlin; Film Editor: Treg Brown; Voice Characterization by Mel Blanc; Musical Direction by Milt Franklyn.

In a spoof of a current hit film *The Defiant Ones*, Sylvester and a tough bulldog are handcuffed together and escape from a truck taking them to the city pound. First the dog drags Sylvester through the swamps and woods, and then Sylvester gets even by chasing a mouse and dragging the pooch.

They try to remove the cuffs, but each try leads to disaster. Finally they remove their chains by hanging on a precipice, letting a train cut their bonds. They fall into the city dump and cheer, but their freedom is short-lived. Both have their legs caught in a pipe!

THE ABOMINABLE SNOW RABBIT

Bugs Bunny, Daffy Duck; May 20; LT; Directed by Chuck Jones; Co-Directed by Maurice Noble; Story by Tedd Pierce; Animation by Ken Harris, Richard Thompson, Bob Bransford, and Tom Ray; Backgrounds by Philip DeGuard. Film Editor: Treg Brwon; Voice Characterization by Mel Blanc; Musical Direction by Milt Franklyn.

Tunneling underground to Palm Springs, Bugs Bunny and Daffy Duck arrive in the Himalayan Mountains ("I told you to turn west at East St. Louis!" quacks Daffy). Daffy heads back to Perth Amboy, but runs into the Abominable Snowman who thinks the duck is a bunny rabbit named "George." Daffy leads the Snowman to Bugs, but the rabbit turns the tables and convinces the dopey Snowman that Daffy is the bunny. The Snowman gets wise and follows Bugs to Palm springs, Daffy following. There, Bugs sips drinks at poolside with the melting Snowman. When Daffy pops up, Bugs secretly puts a pair of rabbit ears on him, causing the Snowman to grab him again! Bugs looks over to see Daffy in a pool of water, "Hey, He really was a snowman!" The drenched Duck replies, "Abominable, that is!"

LICKETY SPLAT

The Road Runner; June 3; LT; Written and Directed by Chuck Jones; Co-Directed by Abe Levitow; Animation by Richard Thompson, Bob Bransford, Tom Ray, and Ken Harris; Layouts by Maurice Noble; Assitant Layout: Corny Cole; Backgrounds by Philip DeGuard and Bob Singer; Effects Animation by Harry Love; Film Editor: Treg Brown; Musical Direction by Milt Franklin.

The Coyote ("Apetitis Giganticus") versus the Road Runner ("Fastius Tasty-us"), a bird so fast the highway curls up, bridges bunch up and cactus follows him flying! The Coyote tries roller skates on skis which work fine until he crashes into the mountainside; a giant bow, from which the Coyote tries to launch himself as an arrow; dynamite sticks attached to darts which he lets loose en masse from a hot air balloon, the only problem being that one dart pops his balloon while another rips his parachute.

The Coyote tries to hit the Road Runner with a jack hammer, and to shoot him with a rifle, but the darts show up and ruin everything. The Coyote falls off a cliff at the end, with two darts landing near his head, opening up to say "The End"!

A SCENT OF THE MATTERHORN

Pepe Le Pew; June 24; LT; Directeur et Story: M. Charl Jones; Animateurs: M. Tomme Ray, M. Cannes Harris, M. Dicque Thompson, M. Robaire Bransford; Lai-out: M. Maurice

Nobelle; Le Ground Bacque, M. Philipe De Guard; Effex Specialitie: M. Harre Amour; Film Editeur: Docteur Treg Brown; Voix Characterization: M. Mel Blanc; Musique: M. Milt Franklin. (The titles actually appear on screen this way)

In the French mountains a highway-white-stripe painting machine gets loose and rolls to a nearby farm where it paints everything, including a female cat whom Pepe Le Pew naturally mistakes for a girl skunk.

Pepe chases the feline with lines like, "Everyone should have a hobby—mine is making love!" and "You may call me Streetcar because of my desire for you!" Pepe chases her all over the mountain. Finally, the cat jumps off a cliff to escape and lands in Pepe's paws. They slide into an ice-cave, where the multiple reflections of the female drives Pepe wild. "Acres and acres of girls, and they're mine, all mine!"

REBEL WITHOUT CLAWS

Tweety, Sylvester; July 15; LT; Written and Directed by Friz Freleng; Animation by Virgil Ross, Art Davis, and Gerry Chiniquy; Layouts by Hawley Pratt; Backgrounds by Tom O'Loughlin; Film Editor: Treg Brown; Voice Characterization by Mel Blanc; Musical Direction by Milt Franklin.

In the Confederate Army all the carrier pigeons have been shot down, leaving only Tweety to get a message through to headquarters. The Yankees send out their secret messenger destroyer, Sylvester after the bird. The little bird says, "Tawt I taw a damn Yankee Tat!" and runs through the Civil War battlefield pursued by Sylvester who ends up full of holes!

Sylvester is blasted by a record number of cannons as he chases the yellow canary, including a re-do of the cannon gags in *Buccaneer Bunny*. Tweety gets through the enemy lines, but encounters Sylvester dressed as a Confederate general. Tweety is sent to a firing squad ("I regret I have only one life to give to my country"), but the inept Yankees shoot Sylvester! The cat remarks, "It's a good thing I have *nine* lives. With this kind of army, I'll need all of 'em!"

COMPRESSED HARE

Bugs Bunny, Wile E. Coyote; July 29; MM; Directed by Chuck Jones; Co-Director: Maurice Noble; Story by Dave Detiege; Animation by Ken Harris, Richard Thompson, Bob Bransford, and Tom Ray; Assistant Layout: Corny Cole; Backgrounds by Philip DeGuard and William Butler; Effects Animation by Harry Love; Film Editor: Treg Brown; Voice Characterization by Mel Blanc; Musical Direction by Milt Franklyn.

Wile E. Coyote sneaks upon Bugs Bunny's rabbit hole and leaves a telephone. Bugs, taking a bath, dries himself off and answers the phone call from Wile E. who introduces himself as his new neighbor, asking to borrow a cup of carrots. Approaching his new neighbor's cave dwelling, Bugs notices the name on mailbox, "Wile E. Coyote—Genius," and gives a sarcastic "look." He knocks on the door, asking "Are you in, genius? Are you in, capable? Are you in, describable?" The Coyote pulls the rabbit in and ties him to a stake. Bugs hops on the floor boards, popping a wine cork which ricochets around the room, releasing the bed-in-the-wall to crash the Coyote to the ground. Bugs hops, tied to the stake, back to his rabbit hole.

Other plans which don't work for the "genius" include using a vacuum cleaner to suck up the rabbit hole and getting a rabbit decoy made of dynamite sticks; a cannon shot into his rabbit hole unaware of Bugs's cannon ball-sized pipe which sends the explosive back to the Coyote; Quick Drying Cement which Bugs places so the Coyote walks into it and, finally, one 10,000,000,000 volt electric magnet "Do-It-Yourself kit" which attracts not only every metallic item in Bugs's hole, but barbed wire, knives, street lamps, busses, ocean liners, the Eiffel Tower, satellites, and rocket ships all hurled at Wile E.

THE PIED PIPER OF GUADALUPE

ACADEMY AWARD NOMINEE

Speedy Gonzales, Sylvester; Aug 19; LT; Directed by Friz Freleng; Co-Directed by Hawley Pratt; Story by John Dunn; Animation by Gerry Chiniquy, Virgil Ross, and Bob Matz; Backgrounds by Tom O'Loughlin; Film Editor: Treg Brown; Voice Characterization by Mel Blanc; Musical Direction by Milt Franklyn.

Sylvester, chasing mice in a Mexican town, gets no respect. The mice laugh in his face, hit him with boards carrying picket signs like "Loco El Gato!" and outrun him. Seeing a book on the "Pied Piper," Sylvester dresses up like one and hypnotizes the mice into dancing into his jug.

Speedy Gonzales resists and begins to rescue his friends, one by one. Sylvester tries to stop the racing rodent with dynamite, but Speedy turns a bulldog on the cat. Sylvester chases Speedy on a motorcycle, but the mouse leads the "gato" off a cliff. The cat comes out of the infirmary on stilts and bandaged, while Speedy heckles Sylvester by playing his flute.

PRINCE VIOLENT

Bugs Bunny, Yosemite Sam; Sept 2; LT; Directed by Friz Freleng; Co-Director: Hawley Pratt; Story by Dave Detiege; Animation by Gerry Chiniquy, Virgil Ross, Art Davis, and Bob Matz; Layouts by Willie Ito; Backgrounds by Tom O'Loughlin; Film Editor: Treg Brown; Voice Characterization by Mel Blanc; Musical Direction by Milt Franklyn.

Sam the Terrible, a Viking, terrorizes the kingdom except for Bugs Bunny who immediately kicks the intruder out of the castle. Sam uses a goofy Viking elephant to ram the castle, lobbing boulders with his trunk (until he sneezes). Sam tries to cross the drawbridge, but the weight of his elephant smashes the wooden bridge. Sam gets rid of the useless pachyderm and begins chopping through the castle, the castle crashing down on him. Sam tries a ton of TNT at the castle door, and although he is personally blown up, it does destroy the door and enters, to be chased off by his former elephant ("I'm on the good guy's side now!").

Re-titled *Prince Varmint* for network TV broadcast.

DAFFY'S INN TROUBLE

Daffy Duck, Porky Pig; Sept 23; LT; Directed by Robert KcKimson; Story by Dave Detiege; Animation by Ted Bonnicksen, Warren Batchelder, and George Grandpre; Layouts by Robert Gribbroek; Backgrounds by Willam Butler; Film Editor: Treg Brown; Voice Characterization by Mel Blanc; Musical Direction by Milt Franklyn.

Daffy Duck in the middle of the desert, is fed up with sweeping floors for Porky Pig's Bristol Inn, and decides to open his own inn across the street. Daffy competes with signs that say "Free TV! We Give Plaid Stamps!" Daffy hustles up his first customer. He turns out to be a crook who robs him. Daffy checks out a crowd in front of Porky's Inn staring at a live action shot of chorus girls. Daffy goes in drag, performing "The Latin Quarter" to gain customers and gets tomatoes instead! When Porky refuses to become partners with Daffy, the duck tries to crush Porky's place with a boulder, but crushes his own inn instead. Geting into drag once again, Daffy visits Porky's restaurant and plants dynamite. The TNT destroys Porky's building, but creates a gusher of oil under the property! Now rich, Porky offers Daffy an office in his new hotel. It's full of brooms!

WHAT'S MY LION?

Elmer Fudd; Oct 21; LT; Directed by Robert McKimson; Story by Dave Detiege; Animation by Keith Darling, George Grandpre, Ted Bonnicksen, and

Warren Batchelder; Layouts by Robert Gribbroek; Backgrounds by William Butler; Film Editor: Treg Brown; Voice Characterization by Mel Blanc, and Hal Smith; Musical Direction by Milt Franklyn.

In "Mountain Country," Rocky the mountain lion is the king of beasts who roars like thunder. Elmer Fudd posts a notice that says, "Hunting Season Opens Today." Immediately, guns blast and explosions are everywhere. Rocky runs to "Tourist Haven," a hunting lodge, using his claw as a glass cutter to get inside. He removes a stuffed animal head mounted on the wall and puts his head in its place.

Elmer comes into the room for a new rifle and aims it at Rocky for practice. Fudd then smokes his pipe, resting his rifle in the lion's mouth. His smoke causes Rocky to sneeze, causing the gun to go off, destroying Elmer's pipe! A pesky fly bothers Fudd and he swats it on the lion's head. When Elmer goes for lunch, Rocky tries to escape, but the hunters are still out there, so he goes back. Elmer's lunch is steak with tabasco sauce. When Fudd goes to the phone, Rocky eats the steak and is burning up because of the hot sauce. Fudd takes down the "hunting season" signs, Rocky reveals himself, shakes Fudd's hand, and leaves, as does the whole herd of mounted heads on the wall!

BEEP PREPARED ACADEMY AWARD NOMINEE

The Road Runner; Nov 11 MM; Directed by Chuck Jones; Co-Director: Maurice Noble; Story by John Dunn and Chuck Jones; Animation by Bob Bransford, Tom Ray, Ken Harris, and Richard Thompson; Backgrounds by Philip DeGuard; Effects Animation by Harry Love; Musical Direction by Milt Franklyn.

The Coyote (Hungrii Flea Bagius) chases the Road Runner (Tidbittius Velocitus) and the following gags occur:

The Coyote gets a severe flat foot from a truck rolling over it. After a mishap with an arrow, the Coyote gets caught between two boulders while falling from a cliff. The Road Runner uses a "portable hole" on a bridge for the Coyote to fall through. The Coyote dresses in an elaborate bat-wing/sky-rocket outfit which explodes. ACME Iron Bird Seed is left as a "Free Lunch" by the magnet-wielding, roller skating Coyote. The magnet drags the Coyote to train tracks and he is flattened by the "Super Chief." An elaborate, ejector-road device backfires and a trip-wire double machine gun ambush misfires. The ACME Little Giant Do-It-Yourself Rocket-Sled Kit, along with 30 miles of railroad track, blasts the Coyote into Space, creating a new Coyote constellation!

THE LAST HUNGRY CAT

Tweety, Sylvester; Dec 2; MM; Directed by Friz Freleng; Co-Director: Hawley Pratt; Story by John Dunn and Dave Detiege; Animation by Gerry Chiniquy, Virgil Ross, Bob Matz, Art Leonardi, and Lee Halpern; Backgrounds by Tom O'Loughlin; Film Editor: Treg Brown; Voice Characterization by Mel Blanc; Musical Direction by Milt Franklyn.

In a spoof of "Alfred Hitchcock Presents," a large figure of a bear in silhouette presents "tonight's story about a murder." While Tweety is sleeping in his birdcage, Sylvester sneaks up to grab the bird but trips and falls, and, fearing Granny, runs through the alley. The narrator speaks to the cat, "Sardines and milk weren't enough, *you* had to commit murder!" Sylvester sees a newspaper headline (Police hunt "the Cat") and runs in panic, heckled by the Hitchcock narrator accusing him of murdering Tweety. Sylvester turns on the radio and hears "Your local company will now present *gas chamber music,* I mean, your local gas company will present chamber music." His guilty conscience makes Sylvester wear a groove in the floor pacing, as he gulps down pots of coffee and smokes a pack of cigarettes. He can't sleep and downs a dozen sleeping pills, sobbing "Other cats have eaten birds!" The narrator suggests that Sylvester give himself up. Sylvester runs back to Granny and finds Tweety alive. He kisses the little canary, Granny hitting him with her

brooom. Sylvester gets even with "Hitchcock" by beaning him with a brick!

NELLY'S FOLLY ACADEMY AWARD NOMINEE

Dec 30; MM; Directed by Chuck Jones; Co-Directors: Maurice Noble and Abe Levitow; Story by Dave Detiege and Chuck Jones; Animation by Richard Thompson, Ben Washam, Tom Ray, and Ken Harris; Backgrounds by Philip DeGuard; Film Editor: Treg Brown; Voice Characterization by Mel Blanc, Gloria Wood; Musical Direction by Milt Franklyn.

In a dark brooding African jungle (an abstract-technicolor-stylized Maurice Noble African Jungle), Nelly the giraffe is singing to her friends. An explorer finds her and talks her into leaving the jungle to find fame and fortune in the city as the world's only singing giraffe.

In a recording studio, she sings commercial jingles to the tune of "Auld Lang Syne" and goes to Broadway, becoming a hit singing "I'm the Flower Of Gower Gulch." She becomes a sensation, inspiring fashions and trends, cutting albums like "Music To Neck By" and "Beat-Neck Nelly." Wandering into a zoo, she falls in love with a married giraffe. Her affair with the giraffe causes a scandal. Audiences disappear, her lover rejects her, and she leaves New York. Back in the jungle, Nelly sings to herself and a handsome giraffe appears. They sing together, their necks forming a heart-shape in silhouette.

No "That's all, Folks!" title. Just "MM;. A Warner Bros. Cartoon" with white letters on black background.

1962

WET HARE

Bugs Bunny; Jan 20; LT; Directed by Robert McKimson; Story by Dave

Detiege; Animation by George Grandpre, Ted Bonnicksen, Warren Batchelder, and Keith Darling; Layouts and Backgrounds by Robert Gribbroek; Film Editor: Treg Brown; Voice Characterization by Mel Blanc; Musical Direction by Milt Franklyn.

Under a waterfall, Bugs Bunny is singing "April Showers" when the water suddenly stops, Bugs goes up to see the beavers who may have put up a dam. Instead, he meets Black Jacque Shellac, the ruthless lumberjack, who wants all the water for himself. Bugs tricks him into removing one little strategic rock which dislodges the dam.

Bugs continues to shower, but again the water stops. Jacque is ready for another rabbit trick, and when he spots a shark fin, he assumes it's the bunny and dives in with his knife. It's a real shark, and Bugs "saves" Jacque by luring the shark to crash into the dam.

Jacque, sure the rabbit will pull another stunt, spots a small stick of dynamite floating toward his new wall. Jacque diverts it, but while his back is turned a huge barge full of explosives destroys his dam. Jacque gets his rifle and fires as he hears singing under the falls. It's only a record player. Jacque builds a dam of steel, but Bugs blocks "his" water with his own dam. Jacque destroys the rabbit's dam, but there is another behind it, and another behind that. Jacque destroys them all. Finally, he attempts to destroy the Grand Cooler Dam thinking it's the hare's. The federal autorities take him away. Bugs isn't fooled. "He'll be back, in like 20 years!"

A SHEEP IN THE DEEP

Ralph Wolf, Sam Sheepdog; Feb 10; MM; Written and Directed by Chuck Jones; Co-Director: Maurice Noble; Animation by Tom Ray, Ken Harris, Richard Thompson, and Bob Bransford; Assistant Layout: Corny Cole; Backgrounds by Philip DeGuard and William Butler; Film Editor: Treg Brown; Voice Characterization by Mel Blanc; Musical Direction by Milt Franklyn.

A Rube-Goldberg device, "The ACME Instant Awakener" gets Ralph the wolf up for another day of work. He arrives at the time clock just ahead of Sam, the sheepdog. Among the morning activities: Sam trips up Ralph's attempts to get sheep with a banana peel which skids him into a tree; Ralph tries balloons to fly over the sheep, but Sam uses a pea-shooter to prick the balloons. After lunch, Ralph tries a record, "Music To Put Sheep Dogs To Sleep By." Ralph manages to catch a sheep, but it's really Sam in disguise. Ralph takes off his "costume" to reveal that he also is sheep! They both remove endless "costumes" until the 5:00 o'clock whistle blows. They'll begin again tomorrow.

FISH AND SLIPS

Sylvester; Mar 10; LT; Directed by Robert McKimson; Story by Dave Detiege; Animation by Warren Batchelder, George Granpre, and Ted Bonnicksen; Layouts and Backgrounds by Robert Gribbroek; Film Editor: Treg Brown; Voice Characterization by Mel Blanc; Musical Direction by Milt Franklyn.

After seeing a television broadcast about a fisherman (Mr. Treg Brown), Sylvester boasts to his son about being a top cat fisherman. He takes Junior to the aquarium, and uses his tail as a fishing line. He puts his tail in the piranah tank, and gets it chewed. He goes into a tank with hammerhead and shovelnose fish and gets pounded into a hole!

Junior catches a small fish which Sylvester uses as bait for a larger fish. He dangles it over a huge tank and gets swallowed by a whale. The lisping pussycat makes a fire, and the whale spits him out. A pair of dolphin snares the cat and play catch with him. Sylvester gives it another try in a diving suit. Electric eels, lobsters, and an octopus attack him. Junior is distracted from pumping air to his father, almost choking him. Junior pumps faster to compensate, and blows up his father's diving suit. This lands the cat in the "dogfish" tank. "No matter what father tries to do, he always winds up going to the dogs!"

QUACKODILE TEARS

Daffy Duck; Mar 31; MM; Directed by Art Davis; Story by John Dunn and Carl Kohler; Animation by Gerry Chiniquy, Virgil Ross, Bob Matz, Lee Halpern, and Art Leonardi; Layouts by Robert Gribbroek; Backgrounds by Tom O'Loughlin; Film Editor: Treg Brown; Voice Characterization by Mel Blanc; Musical Direction by Milt Franklyn.

After 13 years, Arthur Davis returns to directing, for one cartoon (He would resume director duties for DePatie-Freleng later in the sixties).

Daffy Duck is a henpecked husband, whose wife (voiced by June Foray) orders him to sit on her egg. Daffy resists, until she gives him a swift kick in the rear! While he is making the nest more comfortable, the egg rolls downhill, landing in a pile of crocodile eggs. When Daffy takes an egg from the stack, the croc and his wife think he's stealing one of theirs! A battle for the egg goes back and forth between the duck and the reptile. Daffy paints a grenade to look like an egg, but the wife comes back and forces Daffy to sit on the exploding egg-grenade!

After Daffy has put out the fire on his tail feathers, the croc's wife again warns him against anything happening to that egg. "Or I'll slap your face clean off," which she does anyway! The egg hatches a baby crocodile, who bites Daffy's rear. Mrs. Duck loves her "ugly duckling" as does Mrs. Crocodile with her featherd hatchling.

CROW'S FEAT

Elmer Fudd, The Two Crows; Apr 21; MM; Directed by Friz Freleng; Co-Director: Hawley Pratt; Story by John Dunn; Animation by Gerry Chiniquy, Virgil Ross, Bob Matz, Lee Halpern, and Art Leonardi; Backgrounds by Tom O'Loughlin; Film Editor: Treg Brown; Voice Characterization by Mel Blanc; Musical Direction by Milt Franklyn.

Jose and Manuel, two crows going to Guadalajara, hitch a ride on the back of a jet. They hop off onto a corn field,

but are frightened by an Elmer-like scarecrow ("We see him in the drive-in, chasing the gringo Bugs Bunny!"). Jose steals the scarecrow's hat and jumps up and down shouting, "What's up, Doc?" Suddenly, Elmer Fudd shows up and starts shooting. The crows hide in the corn stalks, but Elmer pounds them. Elmer puts dynamite in the corn which explodes on the birds. They leave, hitching a ride on the Explorer 7 rocket ship. The film ends with the count down: "4 ... 3 ... 2 ... 1."

MEXICAN BOARDERS

Speedy Gonzales; Sylvester; May 12; LT; Directed by Friz Freleng; Co-Director: Hawley Pratt; Story by John Dunn; Animation by Gerry Chiniquy, Virgil Ross, Bob Matz, Art Leonardi, and Lee Halpern; Backgrounds by Tom O'Loughlin; Film Editor: Treg Brown; Voice Characterization by Mel Blanc; Musical Direction by Milt Franklyn.

"Sylvero Gato" (Sylvester) is pooped from chasing Speedy Gonzales. After following him up a staircase, the cat completely collapses. Sylvester answers a knock on his door and meets Speedy's cousin, Slowpoke Rodriquez, the opposite of Speedy. Speedy speeds him past Sylvester into his mouse hole and offers him food. Speedy races out and back with some cheese. Now Slowpoke wants Tabasco Sauce. Speedy races for it, but gets stuck in a glue trap. Sylvester then tries to eat the mouse, but Speedy pours the Tabasco Sauce in his mouth. Sylvester tries to catch Speedy with a wire net screen, but the mouse runs right through it. When Sylvester tries, he gets cut into cubes! That night, Slowpoke goes to the refrigerator for a midnight snack. Sylvester grabs him, but Slowpoke hypnotizes Sylvester into being a fan-waving slave for their late night meal.

BILL OF HARE

Bugs Bunny, Tasmanian Devil; June 9; MM; Directed by Robert McKimson; Story by John Dunn; Animation by Keith Darling, Ted Bonnicksen, Warren Batchelder, and George Grandpre;

Layouts and Backgrounds by Robert Grobbroek; Film Editor: Treg Brown; Voice Characterization by Mel Blanc; Musical Direction by Milt Franklyn.
The Tasmanian Devil breaks loose on a pier and encounters Bugs Bunny cooking dinner under the boardwalk. Taz immediately puts Bugs in his own stew pot.

When he takes a peek at his dinner, Bugs imitates a woman in the shower. Bugs then pretends he's drowning, and when Taz takes a closer look, the rabbit seals him in the kettle and shoves it into the ocean. Bugs resumes cooking his meal, but Taz returns and again starts to cook rabbit stew. Bugs tells Taz he should be eating moose, "The natural food of Tasmainian Devils all over the world!" They go hunting, with Bugs tricking the Devil into thinking the express train is a moose. Bugs next pretends to be the Maitre d' of a Hungarian restaurant, "Petruchka's Shishkabob Emporium," and offers up a serving of dynamite shishkabob. Bugs then tricks the dazed Devil into a cage.

Bugs visits Taz in the zoo, and offers him some food, but the Devil shakes his head and lowers a sign, "Please, don't feed the animals!"

ZOOM AT THE TOP
The Road Runner; June 30; MM; Written and Directed by Chuck Jones; Co-Director: Maurice Noble; Animation by Ken Harris, Richard Thompson, Bob Bransford, and Tom Ray; Backgrounds by Philip DeGuard; Film Editor: Treg Brown; Musical Direction by Milt Franklyn.
The chase continues between the Coyote (Overconfidentii Vulgaris) and the Road Runner (Disapperialis Quickius). The Coyote sets a sensitive bear trap, with "Free Bird Seed" piled on top, but the Road Runner eats the seed and jumps on the lever. Nothing happens until the Coyote puts a drop of oil on it. The trap snaps shut on the hungry animal (for you trivia buffs, the Coyote says "ouch"). He next tries the ACME Instant Icicle Maker ("Freeze your friends—loads of laughs!"). It freezes the Coyote. The Coyote then tries a glue-soaked boomerang which transports the Coyote through the air, his hands glued to his head!

THE SLICK CHICK
Foghorn Leghorn; July 21; LT; Directed by Robert McKinson; Story by Tedd Pierce; Animation by Ted Bonicksen, Warren Batchelder, George Grandpre, and Keith Darling; Layouts and Backgrounds by Robert Gribbroek; Film Editor: Treg Brown; Voice Characterization by Mel Blanc and Julie Bennett; Musical Direction by Milt Franklyn.
Widow Hen asks Mr. Cackle, an old-timer rooster, to babysit her Junior. He refuses, telling her he's a "bad boy." Foghorn Leghorn butts in, eager to prove. "there's no such thing as a bad boy!"

As Foggy takes a nap, Junior looks for something to destroy and creates a "false alarm" causing Foghorn to race out of bed, get dunked in cement, and harden into the "thinker" pose. Junior finds a weather balloon and attaches it to Foggy's hammock ("It looks like I'm gonna be the first to put a rooster in orbit!"). Junior helps Foghorn down by shooting an arrow into the balloon, and placing a land mine on his landing pad. Foggy recovers from the explsion, saying, "I still say he's not a bad boy, he's the worst. *Worst*, that is!"

LOUVRE COME BACK TO ME
Pepe Le Pew; Aug 18; LT; Directed by Chuck Jones; Co-Director: Maurice Noble; Story by John Dunn; Animation by Richard Thompson, Bob Bransford, Tom Ray, and Ken Harris; Backgrounds by Tom O'Loughlin and Philip DeGuard; Film Editor: Treg Brown; Voice Characterization by Mel Blanc; Musical Direction by Milt Franklyn.
It is Paris in spring and Pepe LePew, the lovesick skunk, is walking and singing in the park. Everything in his path melts or stiffens at his scent. The stink makes one female alley cat jump up a freshly-painted flagpole, painting a white stripe on her black fur back. Pepe pursues the feline through the Louvre Museum, where even the stat-

ues react to his smell. The girl's orange tomcat boy friend tries to chase after Pepe, but is done in by the smell. Pepe seeks out his love, asking, "Where are you, my little object d'art? I am going to collect you!" The tomcat catches up to Pepe (holding his breath with a clothespin on his nose). Pepe understands, and at great length, describes a duel they will have. The cat runs out for air.

Pepe continues to search for his love, and finds her in the air conditioning unit in the basement, spreading his scent throughout the museum, causing the great paintings to react. The watches in Dali's "The Persistance Of Vision" pop their main springs; the farm couple of "American Gothic" hide their heads; Millet's "The Gleaners" run away; the paint from a Degas ballet portrait fall off, revealing it was "paint-by-numbers"; and the "Mona Lisa" just grins. "I can tell you chaps one thing, It's not always easy to hold this smile!"

HONEY'S MONEY

Yosemite Sam; Sept 1; MM; Directed by Friz Freleng; Story by John Dunn; Animation by Gerry Chiniquy, Virgil Ross, Bob Matz, Lee Halpern, and Art Leonardi; Layouts by Hawley Pratt; Backgrounds by Tom O'Loughlin; Film Editor: Treg Brown; Voice Characterization by Mel Blanc, June Foray, and Billy Booth; Musical Direction by Milt Franklyn.

Yosemite Sam marries an ugly widow for her money. Shortly after the wedding ceremony, she forces him to do the housework and to entertain her big moronic son, Wentworth. After breaking his back playing "horsie," Sam tries to kill the kid off. They go to the playground where Sam tells the kid to chase a ball into traffic but mama makes Sam get the ball. He gets flattened! Sam takes Wentworth swim-

ming and gets the idea of loading alligators into the pool. Wentworth causes such a big splash the gators land on Sam.

In the end, Sam considers leaving, but stays. All this torture *is* worth a million bucks!

THE JET CAGE

Tweety, Sylvester; Sept 22; LT; Written and Directed by Friz Freleng; Animation by Gerry Chiniquy, Art Leonardi, Virgil Ross, Lee Halpern, and Bob Matz; Layouts by Hawley Pratt; Backgrounds by Tom O'Loughlin; Film Editor: Treg Brown; Voice Characterization by Mel Blanc, June Foray; Musical Direction by Milt Franklyn.

Tweety sits in his cage, forlorn over not being able to fly around free like other birds. Grannny orders a new-fangled flying bird cage, jet-powered and complete with crash helmet.

Tweety tries it out in the backyard, and heckles Sylvester. One crow, observing this, tells another, "And all this time I've been doing it the hard way!" Sylvester tries to capture the bird with a butterfly net, but gets dragged along the yard, crashing into a pole. Tweety lands to get more instructions and returns to his cage. Sylvester hides inside. Tweety takes off again, unaware of the pussycat behind him. Getting wise, the little canary ejects the cat through the bomb bay. Sylvester doesn't give up and tries a "Nike" rocket, which zooms out of control, exploding in his hiding place. Next, he employs a fishing rod with magnet which "hooks" the jet cage but drags the cat into street traffic where he gets hit by a truck. He tries two fans which permit the cat to fly, but, when he drops the fans to grab Tweety, he falls.

Sylvester, in bandages, reads an Air Force recruitment poster and joins up to learn to fly!

MOTHER WAS A ROOSTER

Foghorn Leghorn; Oct 20; MM; Directed by Robert McKimson; Story by Dave Detiege; Animation by George Grandpre, Keith Darling, Ted Bonniksen, and Warren Batchelder;

Layouts and Backgrounds by Robert Gribbroek; Film Editor: Treg Brown; Voice Characterization by Mel Blanc; Musical Direction by Milt Franklyn.
One night at the Cawstone Ostrich Farm, the barnyard dog steals an ostrich egg and puts it near the sleeping Foghorn Leghorn. The rooster wakes up the next day and claims his egg, and proud to be a "mother" sits on the egg.

The egg hatches and Foggy introduces the ostrich to the dog. The dog insults the bird ("He's the ugliest chicken I ever saw!"), who buries his head in shame. Foghorn tries to get revenge for the remark by tying an anvil to a bone. The anvil falls on Foggy's head. Foggy teaches his "son" to play football, but the dog puts dynamite in the pigskin. The dog insults the ostrich again, and Foggy challenges the hound to a boxing match. They smash into a water tower which buries their heads. The ostrich is confused, "They left me all alone! Where'd everybody go?"

GOOD NOOSE

Daffy Duck; Nov 10; LT; Directed by Robert Mckimson; Story by Dave Detiege; Animation by Warren Batchelder, George Grandpre, Keith Darling, and Ted Bonnicksen; Layouts and Backgrounds by Robert Gribbroek; Effects Animation by Harry Love; Film Editor: Treg Brown; Voice Characterization by Mel Blanc; Musical Direction by William Lava.
On a large ship at sea, a captain (a caricature of Charles Laughton) gives his first mate, a parrot named Mr. Tristan, the job of finding stowaways. The parrot immediately finds stowaway Daffy Duck in a life boat. The captain intends to hang the duck, but Daffy saves his neck by entertaining him with magic tricks. First Daffy pulls a fish out of his magic hat, but the parrot recommends, "Hang 'em, hang 'em, String him up!" Daffy attempts a card trick, but the parrot slips a dynamite stick in the deck! Daffy's next trick involves the Captain's pocket watch. The duck smashes it, grinds it up, and throws it overboard. The captain asks for a rope but Daffy takes the rope to do an escape trick. He ties himself up, gets into a sack, locks himself in a trunk, then struggles to get out. Ten days later, they let the duck out. The captain gives him one more chance, and Daffy uses it to try to get even with the heckling parrot. He places the squawking bird on a keg of gunpowder, blowing the ship to pieces. The Captain floats back to land in a barrel, with Daffy in tow, with a rope around his neck. The parrot is delighted. "What a trick! No one's ever made a whole ship disappear!" Daffy comments, "Yeah, but what do I do for an encore!"

SHISHKABUGS

Bugs Bunny, Yosemite Sam; Dec 8; LT; Directed by Friz Freleng; Story by John Dunn; Animation by Gerry Chiniquy, Virgil Ross, Bob Matz, Lee Halpern, and Art Leonardi; Layouts by Hawley Pratt; Backgrounds by Tom O'Loughlin; Film Editor: Treg Brown; Voice Characterization by Mel Blanc; Musical Direction by Bill Lava.
Sam is the cook for the king and tonight the king wants "Hassenpheffer." Meanwhile Bugs Bunny comes to the back door to borrow a cup of diced carrots. When Sam realizes that Hassenpheffer is a rabbit dish, he invites the bunny to dinner. Sam serves the rabbit raw and alive! The king scolds Sam and demands it be prepared right. Bugs escapes and leaves a surprise for the king, a spring-released pie-in-the-face! The king has Sam taken away, and Bugs becomes the new chef serving carrots! Bugs confides, in a cockney accent, "It just goes to show ya how a one-eyed jack (rabbit) can beat a king!"

MARTIAN THROUGH GEORGIA

Dec 29; LT; Directed by Chuck Jones and Abe Levitow; Co-Director: Maurice Noble; Story by Carl Kohler and Chuck Jones; Animation by Tom Ray, Ken Harris, Richard Thompson, and Bob Bransford; Backgrounds by Philip DeGuard; Film Editor: Treg Brown; Voice Characterization by Mel Blanc, Ed Prentise; Musical Direction by Bill' Lava.

Designer Maurice Noble goes wild!! Here is an over-stylized sci-fi cartoon that begins, "Once upon a time ... way way out in space ... on another world, there dwelt a very, very happy population." That is except for one small bored miserable citizen who was fed-up, for whom "the whole idea of thought projection became terribly dull." Sexy Martian girls were not of interest to him. He goes to see a psychiatrist and is advised to travel.

Going to Earth, he studies the culture. Regarded as a monster, he is captured and sent to prison. He escapes. Hearing of a monster on the loose (himself) he sets out to destroy the creature and be a hero. A little kid telld the Martian that he is the monster, showing him a comic book that explains "How to Recognize a monster: No nose!" The Martian considers suicide, but remembers someone who loves him, a sexy Martian girl friend, and returns to the red planet to find happiness.

1963

I WAS A TEENAGE THUMB
Jan 19; MM; Directed by Chuck Jones; Co-Director: Maurice Noble; Story by John Dunn and Chuck Jones; Animation by Bob Brnasford, Tom Ray, Ken Harris, and Richard Thompson; Layouts by Bob Givens; Backgrounds by Philip DeGuard; Film Editor: Treg Brown; Voice Characterization by Mel Blanc, Julie Bennet, Ben Frommer, and Richard Peel; Musical Direction by Bill Lava.
George Ebeneezer Thumb and his wife Prunehilda are at home. He is reading *Tyme* magazine, she's knitting dozens of little booties. The only pitter-patter of little feet are a dog, a cat, and a mouse wearing the booties. A magician by the name of Ralph K. Merlin, Jr. (who hiccups and turns into other objects like elephants, bathtubs, balloons, etc.) overhears Prunehilda wish for a baby no bigger than her thumb, and he grants her wish. A super cute Jones-designed baby is born to the couple, so small they take him for a walk in a wheeled thimble.

One night, the baby is snatched by a cat, grabbed by a bird, and falls into a fish's mouth. The fish is caught, and brought to the King for dinner. The king finds the child and makes the baby a knight who is soon slaying dragons and giants, and marries a princess. They have a child the size of his thumb!

But what of his parents, George and Prunehilda? She is shown knitting a giant bootie. He faints!

DEVIL'S FEUD CAKE
Yosemite Sam, Bugs Bunny; Feb 9; MM; Directed by Friz Freleng; Story by Friz Freleng and Warren Foster; Animation by Gerry Chiniquy, Virgil Ross, Bob Matz, Art Leonardi, and Lee Halpern; Layouts by Hawley Pratt; Backgrounds by Tom O'Loughlin and Irv Wyner; Film Editor: Treg Brown; Voice Characterization by Mel Blanc; Musical Directionn by Milt Franklyn.
The film opens with footage from *Hare Lift* (1952) redubbed and rescored. Bugs Bunny is inside an airplane which bankrobber Sam hijacks as a getaway vehicle. The plane is going to crash and Sam bails out but his parachute doesn't work. Sam dies, goes to Hades, and meets the Devil. Sam makes a deal. If he brings back Bugs, he'll be set free.

Sam goes to where Bugs is performing "Ben Hur" and, in stock footage from *Roman Legion* Hare (1955), they begin a chase. Sam crashes back to Hades, but the Devil gives him another chance, and pops him back into *Sahara Hare* (1955). After redoing those gags, Sam returns to the Devil, who'll give another chance. But Sam decides he'd rather stay in Hell than face that rabbit again.

FAST BUCK DUCK

Daffy Duck; Mar 9; MM; Directed by Robert McKimson; Co-Director: Ted Bonnicksen; Story by John Dunn; Animation by Keith Darling, Ted Bonnicksen, Warren Batchelder, and George Grandpre; Layouts and Backgrounds by Robert Gribbroek; Film Editor: Treg Brown; Voice Characterization by Mel Blanc; Musical Direction by Bill Lava.

Daffy Duck, broke and literally down in the dumps, reads in the paper that a millionaire has left his fortune to his butler. When he finds a want ad for another millionaire who wants, "A boon companion. Must be loyal, entertaining, and trustworthy," the duck jumps at the chance!

Applying for the job, Daffy spends most of his time trying to get past the giant bulldog standing guard. When Daffy offers it food, the dog chews his arm. Daffy burrows under the wall, but gets flattened. He tries to fly over the wall with a kite, but the dog cuts his string. Mallets, helium balloons, and sleeping powder do not work. Daffy makes the bulldog fetch a stick of dynamite, but the dog hands him the TNT at the front door.

Daffy finally gets in, is interviewed, and gets the job. It's not for the millionaire, it's for Percy, his bulldog!

THE MILLION HARE

Bugs Bunny, Daffy Duck; Apr 6; LT; Directed by Robert McKimson; Story by Dave Detiege; Animation by Ted Bonnicksen, Warren Batchelder, George Grandpre, and Keith Darling; Layouts and Backgrounds by Robert Gribbroek; Effects Animation by Harry Love; Film Editor: Treg Brown; Voice Characterization by Mel Blanc; Musical Direction by Bill Lava.

Outside Bugs Bunny's rabbit hole is a huge TV antenna. Underground, Daffy Duck is addicted to his favorite program, "Beat Your Buddy." On this show, two names are called. The first one to make it to the studio wins the big prize. The host calls Bugs and Daffy's names—and Daffy zips away!

Daffy takes a motor boat, but Bugs

sabotages it. Bugs hops ahead of Daffy with springs on his feet. Daffy later overtakes the rabbit by using a scooter, which goes off an unfinished bridge. Daffy uses a rocket belt to get to the top floor of the TV studio building. In trying to divert Bugs, Daffy and the bunny crash through all the floors of the building. Bugs and Daffy race to the top floor in wheelchairs—and Daffy wins! His prize is a "Million Box," which contains a million little boxes inside. With nothing to lose, Daffy shows off his "good nature" by giving his "buddy" Bugs the prize. The announcer than tell them that inside each little box is a crisp one dollar bill. Daffy's head turns into a jackass "Hee-Hawing" into the camera.

MEXICAN CAT DANCE

Speedy Gonzales, Sylvester; Apr 20; LT; Directed by Friz Freleng; Story by John Dunn; Animation by Gerry Chiniquy, Virgil Ross, Bob Matz, Lee Halpern, and Art Leonardi; Layouts by Hawley Pratt; Backgrounds by Tom O'Loughlin; Film Editor: Treg Brown; Voice Characterization by Mel Blanc; Musical Direction by Bill Lava.

In a Mexican bullfighting arena, the bull chases a bullfigher (stock footage from *Bully For Bugs*, 1953). Later, while everyone takes a siesta, the mice stage their own bull fight, Speedy Gonzales versus Sylvester, acting like a bull. Speedy uses hat pins, anvils, dynamite sticks, and glue to thwart "el gato." Sylvester fights back with rocket propelled jet skates which drill him into the ground, then blast him out of the arena!

WOOLEN UNDER WHERE

Ralph Wolf, Sam Sheepdog; May 11; MM; Directed by Phil Monroe and Richard Thompson; Animation by Richard Thompson, Bob Bransford, Tom Ray, and Ken Harris; Designed by Maurice Noble; Layouts by Alex Ignatiev; Backgrounds by Philip De Guard; Film Editor: Treg Brown; Voice Characterization by Mel Blanc; Musical Direction by Bill Lava.

Ralph Wolf and Sam Sheepdog are having breakfast. After they punch in and the whistle blows, they go at their work, Ralph trying to get some sheep, Sam preventing him from succeeding.

Ralph tries tunneling under the grass, wearing a suit of armor, firing a cannon mounted atop a unicycle, dynamiting the area around Sam, and a skin-diving suit in his efforts to get some sheep. Ralph sets up an arsenal of weapons surrounding the sheepdog (a dozen cannons, missiles, sharks, a guilllotine, etc.) just as the 5 o'clock whistle blows.

NOW HEAR THIS ACADEMY AWARD NOMINEE

Apr 27; LT; Directed by Chuck Jones; Co-Direction: Maurice Noble; Story by John Dunn, and Chuck Jones; Animation by Ben Washam, and Bob Bransford; Backgrounds by Philip DeGuard; Sound Effects Created by Treg Brown; Musical Direction by Bill Lava.

An official "Chuck Jones Artistic Masterpiece," this is the most abstract animated film produced by the studio, a film which introduced the "modern" new-graphic title sequence which unfortunately has become associated with the inferior films later produced by DePatie-Freleng, and the even later Bill Hendricks cartoons.

A very hard film to describe. It begins with an old Britisher throwing away his green megaphone hearing aid for a brand new red one he finds on the street. The man begins to hear everything incredibly magnified: insects sound like helicopters; strange sound effects pop in and out around the man, leading to a "Giantic Explosion" (with the words printed full screen). The man retrieves his old green hearing aid from the trash—and the Devil reclaims the red one, his horn!

Moral: The other fellow's trumpet always looks greener.

HARE-BREADTH HURRY

Bugs Bunny, Wile E. Coyote; June 8; LT; Directed by Chuck Jones; Co-Director: Maurice Noble; Story by John Dunn; Animation by Tom Ray, Ken Harris, Richard Thompson, and Bob Bransford; Backgrounds by William Butler; Effects Animation by Harry Love; Film Editor: Treg. Brown; Voice Characterization by Mel Blanc; Musical Direction by Bill Lava.

The Coyote chases a beeping cloud of dust along a desert highway, but it's not the Road Runner, it's Bugs Bunny, who explains that he's standing in for the Road Runner because he "sprained a giblet." Bugs really can't run this fast and he takes ACME Super Speed Vitamins. As long as he doesn't run out of pills, he'll be all right.

Among the gags: the Coyote tries to "fish" for Bugs using a carrot for bait, pulling in a giant fish instead!; Bugs adds an extension pipe to the Coyote's gun barrel causing the hungry character to shoot himself!

BANTY RAIDS

Foghorn Leghorn; June 29; MM; Directed by Robert McKimson; Story by Robert McKimson; Animation by George Grandpre, Keith Darling, Ted Bonnicksen, and Warren Batchelder; Layouts and Backgrounds by Robert Gribbroek; Film Editor: Treg Brown; Voice Characterization by Mel Blanc; Musical Direction by Bill Lava.

A beatnik rooster falls for some "chicks" in Foghorn Leghorn's barnyard. Disguised as an orphan, he leaves himself on Foghorn's doorstep, claiming Foggy as his "Daddy-O." Foggy teaches his son how to heckle the dog but, behind his back, the beatnik is kissing the girls and playing rock and roll music.

Foggy gets wise and hooks the beatnik to an electric detector which proves he's girl crazy. Meanwhile, the dog hooks up a mechanical contraption which takes Foghorn and dresses him in drag. The hipster rooster grabs Foggy and tells the dog to "link us!". The dog performs a marriage, Foggy trying to tell him, "I'm a rooster!" The beatnik replies, "We all can't be perfect!"

CHILI WEATHER

Speedy Gonzales, Sylvester; Aug 17; MM; Directed by Friz Freleng; Story by John Dunn; Animation by Gerry Chiniquy, Virgil Ross, Bob Matz, Lee Halpern, and Art Leonardi; Layouts by

Hawley Pratt; Backgrounds by Tom O'Loughlin; Film Editor: Lee Gunther; Voice Characterization by Mel Blanc; Musical Direction by Bill Lava.

The Guadalajara food processing factory is discovered by the local mice, They want in, but Sylvester is guarding the goods. Speedy Gonzales leads the cat on a chase through the factory, and onto the conveyor belts. Speedy narrowly misses being chopped, but Sylvester doesn't.

Speedy puts grease on the floor, causing the cat to slide into a vat of hot Tabasco sauce. Sylvester grabs Speedy on the bottle conveyor, but gets "bottle-capped." Sylvester chases Speedy, and blinded by the bottlecap, he runs into a dehydrator and shrinks! Sylvester sees Speedy, thinks he's a giant mouse (At last! A *real* giant mouse!), and runs off. Speedy thinks the loco cat should see a psychiatrist!

THE UNMENTIONABLES

Bugs Bunny, Rocky and Mugsy; Sept 7; MM; Directed by Friz Freleng; Story by John Dunn; Animation by Gerry Chiniquy, Virgil Ross, Bob Matz, Art Leonardi, and Lee Halpern; Layouts by Hawley Pratt; Backgrounds by Tom O'Loughlin; Film Editor: Treg Brown; Voice Characterization by Mel Blanc, Ralph James; Musical Direction by Bill Lava.

A clever spoof of the TV series *The Untouchables* with Bugs Bunny in the role of agent "Elegant Mess." The film begins with a 1920s montage drawn in the style of John Held Jr. The narrator tells of the crime wave, and how Mess (Bugs) tracked the criminals (Rocky and Mugsy) to their hideout. Inside, they put the rabbit's feet in cement and throw him in Lake Michigan.

Unknown to the criminals Bugs hops out. The gang members are having a party for Rocky's birthday (invited are "Legs" Rhinestone, Baby Face Half-Nelson, Pizza-Puss Lasanga, Pistol Nose Pringle, and "Teeth" Malloy). Bugs pops out of a birthday cake disguised in drag as a flapper. Rocky gets wise, but Bugs pulls his carrot on them

and shoots them with it. In darkness; they chase Bugs into the ACME Cereal warehouse. Bugs maneuvers the crooks into the packaging machine and they end up in their own breakfast cereal boxes. Bugs slaps the cuffs on Rocky and Mugsy, who are sent to prison for 20 years of hard labor.

AQUA DUCK

Daffy Duck; Sept 28; MM; Directed by Robert McKimson; Story by John Dunn; Animation by Keith Darling, Ted Bonnicksen, Warren Batchelder, and George Grandpre; Layouts and Backgrounds by Robert Gribbroek; Film Editor: Treg Brown; Voice Characterization by Mel Blanc; Musical Direction by Bill Lava.

Daffy Duck, wandering in the desert, is crazy with the heat and lost beyond hope. Desperate for water, he sees a mirage and starts to dig, finding a gold rock instead. He buries the nugget and intends to keep it secret, but a mouse steals it. Daffy at gun point makes the mouse give the rock back. He continues his thirsty trek with the rock in his arms.

Daffy finally breaks down and buys water from the mouse (in exchange for the gold rock). Just as he takes a sip, it starts to rain. The desert becomes flooded. ("One thing you gotta admit, when I buy water I sure get my money's worth!")

MAD AS A MARS HARE

Bugs Bunny, Marvin Martian; Oct 19; MM; Directed by Chuck Jones; Co-Director: Maurice Noble; Story by John Dunn; Animation by Ken Harris, Richard Thompson, Bob Bransford, and Tom Ray; Backgrounds by Bob Singer; Effects Animation by Harry Love; Film Editor: Treg Brown; Voice Characterization by Mel Blanc; Musical Direction by Bill Lava.

Marvin Martian is watching Earth from space, via his giant telescope. Observing a rocket launch, he admires the "fledgling leaving his nest." It soon crashes into his lab.

Astro rabbit Bugs Bunny (in an orange space suit and football helmet) is lured outside the spaceship (to plant the flag and claim the planet in the name of Earth) by a robotic arm with a carrot. Bugs contemplates why it is he loves carrots. ("There isn't much meat on 'em ... they're kinda dry, but I love 'em")When he bites the bait it turns out to be aluminum. It opens up, a brass band plays "Yankee Doodle" and hoists an American flag! The Martian points his gun at the rabbit, but the bunny takes his gun and distintegrates him. After reintegrating, the Martian uses his ACME Space Time Gun, planning to send Bugs into the future where the hare will be "a useful but harmless slave to me!" The gun turns him into a neanderthal rabbit ("I got the silly thing in reverse!"). The monster bunny confides to us, munching on the metal carrot, "When I get back to Earth, old Elmer Fudd and the rest of those hunters are due for a big surprise!"

CLAWS IN THE LEASE

Sylvester; Nov 9; MM; Directed by Robert McKimson; Story by John Dunn; Animation by Warren Batchelder, George Grandpre, and Ted Bonnicksen; Layouts by Robert Gribbroek; Backgrounds by Richard H. Thomas; Film Editor: Treg Brown; Voice Characterization by Mel Blanc, Nancy Wible; Musical Direction by Bill Lava.
Sylvester and son are rummaging through the trash dump for food. Junior is fed up with their poverty-stricken lifestyle and heads off to find a home for them.

Junior knocks on the door of a nice house, and the fat lady inside is taken with the kitten. While she goes to get a saucer of milk, Junior runs back to get his dad. When the lady sees Sylvester drinking the milk, she hits him with her broom, and takes Junior in. Sylvester sneaks in the house and takes a can of cat food. In sneaking out, he passes the TV as the lady is turning it on. Appearing on the screen, Sylvester imitates a commercial for "Pussykins Cat Food." She gets wise and throws him out.

Sylvester sneaks into Junior's room.

Hearing the lady coming, he hides in the shower. She unknowingly picks Sylvester up and uses him as a back scrubber. She again throws him out. Sylvester comes up with a plan to stuff her house with mice. When she screams he comes to the rescue as Super Puss (complete with red cape!). Instead, the mice throw him, Junior, and the lady all out of the house. In the end, the cats are back at the dump, looking for leftovers, now joined by the fat lady. One big happy family!

TRANSYLVANIA 6-5000

Bugs Bunny; Nov 30; MM; Directed by Chuck Jones; Co-Director: Maurice Noble; Story by John Dunn; Animation by Bob Bransford, Tom Ray, Ken Harris, and Richard Thompson; Layouts by Bob Givens; Backgrounds by Philip DeGuard; Film Editor: Treg Brown; Voice Characterization by Mel Blanc, Ben Frommer, and Julie Bennett; Musical Direction by Bill Lava.
Bugs Bunny is tunneling to Pittsburgh but comes up in Trannsylvania. He asks for directions at a mysterious castle. There he meets Count Bloodcount, who offers him a room to rest in. Bugs finds a book on magic words and phrases. It tells him that whenever he says, "Abracadbra" the Count will be transformed into a bat (which Bugs swats like a pesky insect). When Bugs says "Hocus Pocus," he turns him back. Luckily Bugs says each word just as the Count is about to attack.

The Count reveals himself to Bugs as a vampire. Bugs uses his magic word to turn him into an umpire! The Count turns into a bat, Bugs turns himself into a baseball bat and pummels the Count. Bugs fools around with words like "Walla Walla Washington" and "Newport News," turning the Count into a two-headed vulture, attracting a love-sick, two-headed female vulture perched outside. Bugs finds a phone at last, but fools with a magic word, turning his ears into bat wings which he uses to fly home.

TO BEEP OR NOT TO BEEP

The Road Runner; Dec 28; MM; Directed by Chuck Jones; Co-Director:

Maurice Noble; Story by John Dunn and Chuck Jones; Animation by Richard Thompson, Bob Bransford, Tom Ray, and Ken Harris; Backgrounds by Philip DeGuard; Effects Animation by Harry Love; Film Editor: Treg Brown; Musical Direction by Bill Lava.

When he finds a picture of baked Road Runner while skimming a book of "Western Cookery" the Coyote licks his chops. Determined to catch and eat the bird, the Coyote tries to snare him in a noose. Instead, he falls backward off a cliff. He tries to leap forward using a large coil spring attached to a boulder. The boulder becomes propelled, dragging the Coyote off a cliff.

The Coyote tries using a wrecking ball, but it rolls backwards toward the control cab. Then, the catapult! Its purpose is to hurl a boulder at the Road Runner. It manages to crush the Coyote, no matter where he stands. On his last try, the catapult stalls and the Coyote cautiously creeps out from his manhole hiding place to un-jam it. As you might predict, he gets tossed through the air riding the boulder as it goes through a mountain top before being bounced back, flattening the Coyote like a pancake. It seems the catapult was built by "The Road-Runner Manufacturing Co."

1964

DUMB PATROL
Bugs Bunny, Yosemite Sam, Porky Pig; Jan 18; LT; Directed by Gerry Chiniquy; Story by John Dunn; Animation by Virgil Ross, Bob Matz, Lee Halpern, and Art Leonardi; Layouts by Bob Givens; Backgrounds by

Tom O'Loughlin; Film Editor: Treg Brown; Voice Characterization by Mel Blanc; Musical Direction by Bill Lava.

1917, somewhere in France. Officers meet to determine who will rid the skies of Baron Sam Von Shamm (Yosemite Sam). Captain Smedley (Porky Pig) picks the longest straw, but hero Bugs Bunny drops a brick on Porky's head and takes his place. ("He's got a wife and six piglets!")

Meanwhile, Sam receives an Iron Cross, and wants a furlough "to make whoopie, with schnapps and beautiful frauleins!" Bugs heckles Sam from above, dropping him flowers and a note: "Roses are red, violets are blue, Leghorns are chicken, and so are you!" A bee inside the bouquet stings Sam on the nose. Sam takes off after Bugs and they battle in the sky, Bugs shooting down every plane Sam can get. Battle gags include Sam falling out of his bomb bay, and Sam's giant tri-plane.

Sam eventually gets blasted and is last seen floating upward in a devil suit to meet his maker. Bugs comments, "I've heard of Hell's Angels, but I Never thought I'd see one!"

A MESSAGE TO GRACIAS
Speedy Gonzales, Sylvester; Feb 8; LT; Directed by Robert McKimson; Story by John Dunn; Animation by George Grandpre, Ted Bonnicksen, and Warren Batchelder; Layouts and Backgrounds by Robert Gribbroek; Effects Animation by Harry Love; Film Editor: Treg Brown; Voice Characterization by Mel Blanc and Roger Green; Musical Direction by Bill Lava.

El Supremo, the leader of the Mexican mice, gives Manuel a message to deliver to General Gracias. Unfortunately, Manuel doesn't make it due to that pussy-gato, Sylvester. One of the mice recommends Speedy Gonzales. Speedy runs over Sylvester and zooms off. Sylvester follows the mouse in a drag racer. When Speedy stops for lunch, the cat puts on the brakes, but crashes. Sylvester tries a rope trap, but catches a wild beast instead, which proceeds to tear him to shreds! Sylvester also tries a motor boat and a lasso, to no avail.

Speedy delivers the message: Happy Birthday. Speedy is upset that he went through all that trouble for such a trivial message and sets Sylvester loose on the mice. Fade out as cat chases the general into the distance.

BARTHOLOMEW VERSUS THE WHEEL

*Feb. 29; MM; Directed by Robert McKimson; Story by John Dunn; Animation by George Grandpre, Ted Bonnicksen, Warren Batchelder; Layouts by: Bob Givens; Backgrounds by Robert Gribbroek; Film Editor: Treg Brown; Voice Characterization by Mel Blanc, Leslie Barrings; Musical Direction by Bill Lava. *features new graphic opening titles.*

Robert McKimson's stab at an "art film." Drawn in James Thurber style, this cute film might have rated some attention ten years earlier, but by 1964 it was old hat.

Narrated by a little boy, he tells the story of his dog, Bartholomew. One day, Bartholomew's tail is run over by a scooter wheel and that makes him mad. He begins to steal wheels, and as he grows older, he steals bigger wheels from cars and trucks. One day he tries to grab an airplane wheel.

The neighborhood kids look for him, but Bartholomew has landed with the plane in the Sahara Desert. After a series of misadventures, the dog grabs another plane. When Bartholomew returns, he stops hating wheels or anything, except what a dog is supposed to hate, cats!

FREUDY CAT

Sylvester, Hippety Hopper; Mar 14; LT; Directed by Robert McKimson; Story by Tedd Pierce; Animation by Ted Bonnicksen, Warren Batchelder, and George Grandpre; Layouts and Backgrounds by Robert Gribbroek; Film Editor: Treg Brown; Voice Characterization by Mel Blanc; Musical Direction by Robert McKimson.

A cheater cartoon mainly comprised of footage from earlier Sylvester/Hipetty Hopper epics. Sylvester runs home sweating and screaming, "Save me!

Save me from the giant mouse!" Junior takes his father to Dr. Freud E. Katt, cat psychiatrist. Junior explains to the doctor, in flashback via scenes from *The Slap Hoppy Mouse* (1950) and *Cat A-Weigh* (1953). In the end, Hippety jumps into the doctor's office, and all three cats hop out!

DR. DEVIL AND MR. HARE

Bugs Bunny, Tasmanian Devil; Mar 28; MM; Directed by Robert McKimson; Story by John Dunn; Animation by Ted Bonnicksen, Warren Batchelder, and George Grandpre; Layouts and Backgrounds by Robert Gribbroek; Film Editor: Treg Brown; Voice Characterization by Mel Blanc; Musical Direction by Bill Lava.

The Tasmanian Devil scares all the jungle animals except Bugs Bunny, who's taking a bubble bath in the river (singing "By A Waterfall"). Taz pours ketchup on the hare, who starts his "I'm bleedin'! Get a doctor!" bit. The Devil goes to a doctor's office and meets Bugs now disguised as a medic, who gives him all the old gags: painting his tongue green, putting glasses with spots before his eyes, etc. Bugs gives Taz a new wonder drug, nitroglycerine, which explodes the Devil.

Bugs next disguises himself as a German psychiatrist who treats the Devil. ("Tell me about your id, when you was a kid, yah!"). He mails Taz overseas for treatment and this really angers the beast. The Devil walks into Bugs' Maternity Ward ("eh … What's up, Pop!"), and is handed a baby, an exploding bomb in blankets. Taz washes up to assist Bugs in the operating room, helping to deliver "Frankie," a ten-foot monster, who has Bugs calling, "Is there a doctor in the house?"

NUTS AND VOLTS

Speedy Gonzales, Sylvester; Apr 25; LT; Directed by FrizFreleng; Story by John Dunn; Animation by Gerry Chiniquy, Virgil Ross, Bob Matz, Art Leonardi, and Lee Halpern; Layouts by Hawley Pratt; Backgrounds by Tom O'Loughlin; Film Editor: Treg Brown; Voice Characterization by Mel Blanc;

Musical Direction by Bill Lava.

Sylvester chases Speedy Gonzales all over the hacienda. Tired out, the pussycat decides to try "Automation," and tackle the rodent with a series of electronic gadgets.

First he sets up an electronic-eye beam outside his mouse hole that triggers Sylvester on a large coil spring. He smashes against the wall. Sylvester next tries a robot to chase the mouse but when Speedy shouts "Yee-Hah!" the robot jumps and smashes against the ceiling. The robot crashes into the control panel, destroying itself and blasting Sylvester. The cat rebuilds the machine and uses its extended arm to place a stick of dynamite into Speedy's hole. Speedy quickly places the dynamite behind Sylvester's back. Speedy gets into the technology, sending a robot dog after the lisping cat.

THE ICEMAN DUCKETH

Bugs Bunny, Daffy Duck; May 16; LT; Directed by Phil Monroe; Co-Directed by Maurice Noble; Story by John Dunn; Animation by Bob Bransford, Tom Ray, Ken Harris, Richard Thompson, Bob Matz, and Alex Inatiev; Layouts by Bob Givens; Backgrounds by William Butler; Effects Animation by Harry Love; Film Editor: Treg Brown; Voice Characterization by Mel Blanc; Musical Direction by Bill Lava.

At a trading post in the Klondike, Daffy Duck overhears that they are paying big bucks for furs. He heads north to trap Bugs Bunny and cash in. As Daffy hunts the rabbit, Bugs does everything he can to create avalanches to fall on the duck.

Daffy tries to smoke Bugs out of a tree, but he melts the snow just enough to create frozen rain, trapping the duck in ice. When Daffy continues the chase, Bugs throws water which instantly freezes. ("I saw a guy do this in a toothpaste ad once. 'Invisible shield,' ya know!"). The duck crashes into the ice. Daffy rolls a pebble down a hill, which turns into a snow boulder, eventually landing on the duck. Hibernating bears chase the duck up a tree. That night Bugs says "Good night" to the duck, feathers missing, shivering, with growling bears waiting below.

WAR AND PIECES

The Road Runner; June 6; LT; Directed by Chuck Jones; Co-Director: Maurice Noble; Story by John Dunn; Animation by Ken Harris, Richard Thompson, and Tom Ray; Layouts by Dave Rose; Backgrounds by Philip DeGuard; Film Editor: Treg Brown; Musical Direction by Bill Lava.

The Road Runner (Burn-em Upus Asphaltus) runs from the Coyote (Caninus Nevous Rex). The Coyote's bad luck continues as he throws a grenade which rebounds from a cactus, exploding in his face; tries to launch himself a la bow and arrow, ripping off his lower half and revealing polka-dot boxer shorts, hairy human legs, and socks; triggers an electric eye-beam that crushes him between two walls; tries ACME invisible paint, that has him hit by a truck and fall off a cliff; and disguises his double barrel shotgun as a peep show ("Secrets Of The Harem"), which the Road Runner fully enjoys!

The Coyote also tries a rope with a hook that accidentally snags a storm cloud, which sends a bolt to electrocute him! Finally he tries a rocket car, which smashes through the earth to China where a Chinese Road Runner uses a gong to smash the Coyote.

HAWAIIAN AYE AYE

Tweety, Sylvester; June 27; MM; Directed by Gerry Chiniquy; Story by Tedd Pierce and Bill Daunch; Animation by Virgil Ross, Bob Matz, Art Leonardi, and Lee Halpern; Layouts by Robert Gribbroek; Backgrounds by Tom O'Loughlin; Film Editor: Treg Brown; Voice Characterization by Mel Blanc, June Foray; Musical Direction by Bill Lava.

"Imagine me in Honolulu in a muumuu" says Granny, enjoying her Hawaiian Island vacation. She goes to a luau, leaving Tweety alone with "Sharkey" the pet shark (who lives in a dog house in the ocean), as protection. Meanwhile, Sylvester spots Tweety and rows toward the island. Tweety sends Sharkey to "sic 'em." The fish bites into Sylvester's rubber raft, inflating Sharkey and sinking the cat. Sylvester tries a wire-and-pulley lift to get himself over to the island while dreaming of his delicious "broiled swab" meal. He fails to notice that he's heading into Sharkey's house! Other tactics: Sylvester tries a rubber underwater suit, but Sharkey cuts his air line; wooden stilts which are cut by a legion of sawfish. Granny and Tweety say "Aloha" to the islands aboard their ocean liner taking them home, but Sylvester doesn't give up easy. He is seen rowing after them, as Sharkey follows the cat.

FALSE HARE

Bugs Bunny; July 16; LT; Directed by Robert McKimson; Story by John Dunn; Animation by Warren Batchelder, George Grandpre, and Ted Bonnicksen; Layouts by Bob Givens; Backgrounds by Robert Gribbroek; Film Editor: Treg Brown; Voice Characterization by Mel Blanc; Musical Direction by Bill Lava.
In an effort to catch a rabbit for dinner, the Big Bad Wolf and his nephew open the Club Del Conejo, a private club for rabbits. Bugs gets wise, but decides to play along. He signs up (an insurance form) and is asked to take the initiation tests. The wolf has a boulder rigged to fall when the bell is rung. The Big Bad Wolf demonstrates the correct way, and gets clobbered. Bugs is to stand for the club picture, in front of a spiked casket. Once again the wolf demonstrates and gets it.

The wolf asks Bugs to wait in a hollow tree for further instructions, while loading it with dynamite. Bugs crawls out the other side ("It's too dark in there!"). The tree explodes, falling on the club house and on the wolf. The frazzled Big Bad asks, "I wonder if anyone would like to join a chicken club?" Foghorn Leghorn makes a cameo. "Did somebody mention my name?"

A moment of silence for the last Bugs Bunny theatrical cartoon.

SENORELLA AND THE GLASS HUARACHE

Aug 1; LT; Directed by Hawley Pratt; Story by John Dunn; Animation by Gerry Chiniquy, Bob Matz, Virgil Ross, and Lee Halpern; Layouts by Hawley Pratt; Backgrounds by Tom O'Loughlin; Effects Animation by Harry Love; Film Editor: Treg Brown; Voice Characterization by Mel Blanc and Tom Holland; Musical Direction by Milt Franklyn. Features new graphic opening titles.
The last cartoon produced by the old Warner Bros. cartoon studio, this is a spoof of *Cinderella* as told by an old Mexican.

Senorella lives with her evil "strapmother and strapsisters" in a house full of cockaroaches. When the Prince (Don Jose Miguel) holds a fiesta, Senorella is left at home. Her fairy godmother transforms the roaches into mules, and Senorella into a sexy senorita. Jose falls in love with Senorella and they tango—until midnight.

Jose searches the town for the girl who fits the glass hurache. He and Senorella get "mucho married," but the old storyteller regrets the sad story. Sad? Because it was he who married the wicked "strapmother."

PANCHO'S HIDEAWAY

Speedy Gonzales; Oct 24; LT; Produced by DePatie-Freleng; Directed by Friz Freleng; Co-Directed by Hawley Pratt; Story by John Dunn; Animation by Bob Matz, Norm McCabe, and Don Williams; Backgrounds by Tom O'Loughlin; Film Editor: Lee Gunther; Voice Characterization by Mel Blanc and Ralph James; Musical Direction by Bill Lava.
The first of 37 cartoons produced for Warner by the newly formed DePatie-Freleng Enterprises (Producer David H. DePatie and Director Friz Freleng). The studio became best known for creating the Pink Panther.

Bandit Pancho Vanilla (a stylized Yosemite Sam with a black beard and a Mexican accent) rides into town and robs the bank. The townspeople complain to the mayor about their losses, overheard by Speedy Gonzales. Speedy goes to Vanilla's hideout to retrieve the money, one coin at a time.

Speedy races into his hideout for a coin, but Vanilla faces him "gunfighter style," shooting himself in the foot. Pancho puts up a wooden trap with only one entrance, his gun covering it. Speedy runs through the gun and gets another coin. Pancho sets up an electronic eye with a dozen guns rigged to shoot. Speedy tricks him into standing in its path.

Speedy returns all the money to the bank, but the frazzled Pancho Vanilla gets revenge. He sneaks up on Speedy, who's counting the money, and screams, making the rodent lose count.

ROAD TO ANDALY

Speedy Gonzales, Sylvester; Dec 26; MM; Directed by Friz Freleng; Co-Director: Hawley Pratt; Story by John Dunn; Animation by Norm McCabe, Don Williams, and Bob Matz; Assistant Layout: Homer Jones; Backgrounds by Tom O'Loughlin; Film Editor: Lee Gunther; Voice Characterization by Mel Blanc; Musical Direction by Bill Lava.
Speedy Gonzales leads the pussy-gato Sylvester on a chase into the desert, shouting "Yee-Hah," scaring the cat at every turn. Sylvester is desperate to find a way to get Speedy. He buys Malcom Falcon, a mean attack bird, to help catch the fast-paced rodent.

The bird chases Speedy, Sylvester attached to his claws, dragging him through cactus and boulders. Sylvester beats a lesson into him: "When I say 'Let Go,' I mean it!" Malcom goes after Speedy again, with Sylvester in tow, flying high into the sky. Sylvester yells "Let go," and the cat goes crashing back to earth! Malcom gets sucked into a jet engine, but returns to help Sylvester. Speedy tells the cat he has a "Secret under my sombrero." While the mouse takes a siesta, Sylvester orders the falcon to get what's under his hat. The bird brings Sylvester a lit stick of dynamite. Speedy restrains Malcom by putting salt on the falcon's tail, but when Sylvester puts salt on his own tail to prove nothing happens, his tail falls off. Malcom and Sylvester walk back to town to get some glue. Salt accidentally falls on Speedy's tail and he joins them on their trip into town.

1965

IT'S NICE TO HAVE A MOUSE AROUND THE HOUSE

Daffy Duck, Speedy Gonazales, Sylvester; Jan 16; LT; Directed by Friz Freleng; Co-Director: Hawley Pratt; Story by John Dunn; Animation by Don Williams, Bob Matz, and Norm McCabe; Layouts by Dick Ung; Backgrounds by Tom O'Loughlin; Film Editor: Lee Gunther; Voice Characterization by Mel Blanc, and George Pearson; Musical Direction by Bill Lava.
Sylvester, chasing Speedy Gonzales around the house lands in the pool. Concerned for her cat, Granny calls the Jet Age Pest Control—Daffy Duck. ("If you've got a pest in your nest, we remove it with zest!"). Daffy feels one mouse shouldn't be too difficult to remove. When he puts his stethoscope in the mouse hole, Speedy's trademark "Yee-Hah!" has Daffy jumping to the ceiling. Daffy sets a cheese trap, and nets Speedy but the mouse proceeds to drag the net and Daffy all over the house. Daffy tries glue outside his mouse hole, but another "Yee-Hah!" sends Daffy sticking to the ceiling! Daffy next tries a vacuum cleaner. Speedy runs to the pool. The vacuum cleaner sucks in all the water, explodes and lands Daffy on the cement bottom of the empty pool.

Daffy tries a robot mouse disposal but Speedy outsmarts the machine by programming a Daffy Duck comic book into it. The machine chases Daffy through the neighborhood!

CATS AND BRUISES

Sylvester, Speedy Gonzales; Jan 30; MM; Directed by Friz Freleng; Co-Director: Hawley Pratt; Story by John Dunn; Animation by Bob Matz, Norm McCabe, Don Williams, Manny Perez, Warren Batchelder, and Lee Halpern; Layouts by Dick Ung; Backgrounds by Tom O'Loughlin; Film Editor: Lee

Gunther; Voice Characterization by Mel Blanc; Musical Direction by Bill Lava. The Mexican mice are holding a fiesta on Cinco de mayo, while outside their gathering Sylvester plots to ambush them. The cat dons a pair of "Mickey Mouse" ears and joins them in dance. The mice immediately get wise and run, leaving Speedy behind to heckle the "pussy-gato."

Speedy leads Sylvester to a dog pound where his "Yee-Hah!" propels the cat into a snag of hungry dogs. Sylvester puts a rocket engine in his hot rod and chases Speedy. When the mouse stops, the cat forgets where the brakes are and crashes into the lake. Sylvester tries darts, boulders, rubber rafts, steel pipes, etc. to no avail.

THE WILD CHASE

The Road Runner, Speedy Gonzales, Sylvester; Feb 27; MM; Directed by Friz Freleng; Co-Directed by Hawley Pratt; Animation by Norman McCabe, Don Williams, Manny Perez, Warren Batchelder, and Laverne Harding; Layouts by Dick Ung; Backgrounds by Tom O'Loughlin; Film Editor: Lee Gunther; Voice Characterization by Mel Blanc; Musical Direction by Bill Lava.
This is essentially a Road Runner cartoon, reusing animation from earlier Chuck Jones films, with Speedy Gonzales and Sylvester drawn in as extras.

A big race is held to determine who is the fastest: Speedy Gonzales ("The Fastest Mouse in Mexico")—or the Road Runner ("The Texas Road Burner"). Meanwhile, the Coyote and Sylvester wait in the rocks with fork and knife. The cat and coyote try to propel boulders with a lever; with iron pellets in bird seed and cheese; and by dropping a huge flat rock off a mountain ledge. The two adversaries chase the speedy pair in a rocket car, which goes so fast they pass the mouse and bird and win the race!

MOBY DUCK

Daffy Duck, Speedy Gonzales; Mar 27; LT; Directed by Robert McKimson; Animation by Don Wiliams, Manny Perez, Warren Batchelder, Bob Matz, LaVerne Harding, and Norm McCabe;

Layouts by Dick Ung; Backgrounds by Tom O'Loughlin; Film Editors: Lee Gunther and Treg Brown; Voice Characterization by Mel Blanc; Musical Direction by Bill Lava.*
Speedy Gonzales and Daffy Duck are shipwrecked on a desert island. Daffy complains about having no food and being stuck with a useless partner. The greedy duck spots a box of canned food, and wants it all. "This is survival of the fittest, and I'm the fittest!" Daffy banishes Speedy to another part of the island, but Speedy has the can opener! Daffy is determined to open the cans without Speedy's help. When Daffy tries with an axe, the blade flies into the ocean. Daffy recruits a swordfish, but the fish attacks the duck's rear. Speedy gives Daffy the can opener but the crate has drifted out to sea.

Daffy cries over the food loss, just as Speedy and Robinson Crusoe go out to eat at "Friday's Restaurant." Daffy runs to the eatery, then gulps at the menu: "Today's special: Pressed Duck."

ASSAULT AND PEPPERED

Daffy Duck, Speedy Gonzales; Apr 24; MM; Directed by Robert McKimson; Story by John Dunn; Animation by Manny Perez, Warren Batchelder, Bob Matz, LaVerne Harding, Norm McCabe, and Don Williams; Layouts by Dick Ung; Backgrounds by Tom O'Loughlin; Film Editor: Lee Gunther; Voice Characterization by Mel Blanc; Musical Direction by Bill Lava.
Daffy Duck is the evil land baron of El Rancho Rio Daffy, who declares war on poverty by whipping poor mice ("I've told you peons a thousand times not to starve on my property. It lowers the value!"). Speedy Gonzales comes to their rescue.

Daffy challenges Speedy to a duel in the grand manner. Each positions himself in his fort, armed with cannons. Daffy's cannonball chases Speedy everywhere he goes, so the little mouse runs to Daffy's door to blast the duck. Speedy borrows a cannon ball from Daffy, but the duck chases the rodent back to his fort demanding it back. He gets it, blasted in his face. Daffy plants a mine field, but Speedy steals his map of the mine locations. Speedy offers to guide the duck back to his fort, leading him into every explosion. Speedy gives up and goes home to eat some supper. Daffy is so delighted with "his victory," he gives himself a 21 gun salute. All of the cannons fire, but blast the duck, Speedy happily counting each explosion.

WELL WORN DAFFY

Daffy Duck, Speedy Gonzaeles; May 22; LT; Directed by Robert McKimson; Story by David Detiege; Animation by Warren Batchelder, Bob Matz, LaVerne Harding, Norm McCabe, Don Williams, and Manny Perez; Layouts by Dick Ung; Backgrounds by Tom O'Loughlin; Film Editor: Lee Gunther; Voice Characterization by Mel Blanc; Musical Direction by Bill Lava.

In the hot desert, Speedy Gonzales and two Mexican mice companions are dying of thirst. They find an oasis, but are driven away from drinking some water by Daffy, the arab duck! Daffy is a water waster keeping his grass and his camel washed.

Speedy tries to help his two friends by luring Daffy away. When the duck chases Speedy, the other mice are surprised by a camel in the well. Speedy steals a dipper of water, but Daffy shoots holes in it. Daffy sits in the well barrel to keep Speedy away but the little mouse scares the duck with a "Yee Hah!" Speedy grabs a pail of water, but the camel trips him. Speedy grabs the hose and sucks the water until Daffy pops out of the hose and starts shooting. Daffy ties dynamite around the well, but the mouse ties it to the camel.

The mice take over the well and drink up. Daffy comes crawling back for water, and the mice spray him. "There's only one thing worse than a smart mouse, three smart mice!"

SUPPRESSED DUCK

Daffy Duck; June 26; MM; Directed by Robert McKimson; Story by Dave Detiege; Animation by Bob Matz,

Manny Perez, and Warren Batchelder; Layouts by Dick Ung; Backgrounds by Ron Dias; Film Editor: Lee Gunther; Voice Characterization by Mel Blanc; Musical Direction by Bill Lava.

In the woods, hunter Daffy Duck jumps out of his jeep excited about hunting season. The forest ranger announces a boundary line for hunters and bears, so Daffy must resort to trickery to catch his game.

He fries some bacon to atttract a bear. He shoots at a bruin, but the tough bear unloads Daffy's rifle and loads the bullets in the duck's mouth, causing Daffy to cough explosives! Daffy, trying to sweep away the boundary line, walks off a cliff. The duck hides in a tree stump, and crosses the boundary, but a bear sends out the alarm and the Forestry Patrol bombs the stump. Daffy digs a hole under the boundary line, but the bear puts an "explosive shed" over the spot where the duck emerges, blowing the duck's feathers off. Trying to paste all his feathers back on, Daffy finds the bear is wearing some of them. The ranger prevents the duck from crossing the boundary to retrieve them. Daffy, wearing a barrel, states, "You haven't seen the last of me," walks off into the distance—his featherless backside revealed to the camera.

CORN ON THE COP

Porky Pig, Daffy Duck; July 24; MM; Directed by Irv Spector; Story by Friz Freleng; Animation by Manny Perez, Warren Batchelder, and Bob Matz; Layouts by Dick Ung; Backgrounds by Tom O'Loughlin; Film Editor: Lee Gunther; Voice Characterization by Mel Blanc and Joan Gerber; Musical Direction by Bill Lava.

Granny, shopping on Halloween, is scared by the trick-or-treaters. Meanwhile, a crook disguised as "Granny" robs a supermarket. The shopkeeper reports the crime, and Policeman Porky Pig and Sgt. Daffy O'Duck pursue the thief. They chase Granny who thinks Daffy and Porky are costumed trick-or-treaters and hits them with her umbrella.

They follow Granny to her house where the real crook is hiding out. Between Granny and the crook, Porky and Daffy have a hard time entering the premises. They try lowering themselves from the roof on a rope, wooden planks nailed together, and a shaky ladder. Granny grabs the real crook, whom she also thinks is a trick-or-treater and hands him to the cop on the beat. She also grabs Porky and Daffy by the ear and takes them "home to their parents."

RUSHING ROULETTE

The Road Runner; July 31; MM; Directed by Robert McKimson; Story by David Detiege; Animation by Bob Matz, Manny Perez, Warren Batchelder, Norm McCabe, and Don Williams; Layouts by Dick Ung; Backgrounds by Tom O'Loughlin; Film Editor: Lee Gunther; Musical Direction by Bill Lava.
Well, here's something we thought, we'd never see—a Road Runner cartoon by Robert KcKimson!

The Coyote tries all sorts of methods to catch the speedy bird, including offering a "Free Photo" to the Road Runner. The cannon hidden in the camera only explodes in the Coyote's face. Next, he tries ACME spring boots ("put a spring in your step!") that bounce him off a cliff; then Ajax Stixall glue which only works on coyotes. During a battle on the railroad tracks in separate handcars, the Coyote uses a large mirror to direct a powerful beam of sunlight which the Road Runner diverts to destroy the rigging the Coyote is on. Lastly "Free piano lessons" using the "Those Endearing Young Charms" as an explosive key gag; and a helicopter pursuit, which ends with a crash.

RUN, RUN, SWEET ROAD RUNNER

The Road Runner; Aug 21; MM; Directed by Rudy Larriva; Story by Rudy Larriva; Animation by Hank Smith and Tom McDonald; Layouts by Erni Nordli; Backgrounds by Tony Rizzo; Film Editor: Lee Gunther; Musical Direction by Bill Lava.

The first of eleven Road Runner cartoons by Rudy Larriva farmed out to independent studio, Format Films.

In this film, the Coyote plays hopscotch with the Road Runner, which leads him to hop off a cliff. The Coyote hangs spikes over "Free Bird Seed," and through elaborate means (the suns rays reflect in the Coyote's binoculars and burn the rope) the Coyote gets spiked! The Coyote makes a female Road Runner decoy from a lightning rod, then beats a tom-tom drum, does a rain dance, and attempts to get the Road Runner to cuddle the decoy. Lightning strikes the Coyote instead!

TEASE FOR TWO

Daffy Duck, Goofy Gophers; Aug 28; LT; Directed by Robert McKimson Story by David Detiege; Animation by Warren Batchelder, Bob Matz, and Manny Perez; Layouts by Dick Ung; Backgrounds by Tom O'Loughlin; Film Editor: Lee Gunther; Voice Characterization by Mel Blanc; Musical Direction by Bill Lava.
Daffy Duck rides out to the woods looking for gold, but finds the Goofy Gophers instead. They are living on the spot his map says is a gold mine. Daffy orders them out, but they produce a deed to the gopher hole. Daffy tries various methods of getting out the gophers: bathroom plungers, vacuum cleaners, and rifles, with all his techniques ending in explosions. The duck tries a water hose, but the gophers tie it in knots, causing an explosion which sends Daffy into orbit, passing two Russian cosmonauts! The Gophers move the land marker, and the duck digs elsewhere. The Gophers cover the rocks with gold paint and throw them in the dig hole. Mac compliments Tosh, "Such talent! A regular Vincent Van Gopher!"

TIRED AND FEATHERD

The Road Runner; Sept 18; MM; Directed by Rudy Larriva; Story by Rudy Larriva; Animation by Hank Smith, Virgil Ross, and Bob Bransford; Layouts by Erni Nordli; Backgrounds by Anthony Rizzo; Film Editor: Lee Gunther. Musical Direction by Bill Lava.

The Coyote once again chases the Road Runner, this time grabbing two feathers from the bird as he falls off the cliff. He attempts to fly with the two feathers, to no avail.

Other gags include the Coyote painting a bullseye on the mountain side and rolling a heavy log up the mountain until the Road Runner beeps him, causing him to lose his grip and get crushed; The Coyote, having read how fast Road Runners go, straps a motor with a propeller to his back, ending up in a hole in the ground; lastly, the Coyote setting up a phony telephone made of dynamite and painting a huge billboard informing the Road Runner of "Free Phones." While setting up, the phone rings! The Coyote answers, the phone explodes, and the rest is history!

BOULDER WHAM

The Road Runner; Oct 9; MM; Directed by Rudy Larriva; Story by Len Janson; Animation by Virgil Ross, Bob Bransford, and Hank Smith; Layouts by Erni Nordli; Backgrounds by Anthony Rizzo; Film Editor: Lee Gunther; Musical Direction by Bill Lava.
The Coyote chases the Road Runner, but the road has collapsed. The following methods do not get the Coyote across the chasm: pole vaulting; a tight rope; an "ACME Deluxe High Bounce Trampoline"; and hypnotism. Attempting a karate leap, the Coyote finds himself in mid-air. He holds up a sign "That's all, Folks!"

CHILI CORN CORNY

Daffy Duck, Speedy Gonzales; Oct 23; LT; Directed by Robert McKimson; Story by David Detiege; Animation by Manny Perez, Warren Batchelder, and Bob Matz; Layouts by Dick Ung; Backgrounds by Tom O'Loughlin; Film Editor: Lee Gunther; Voice Characterization by Mel Blanc and Gonzales Gonzales; Musical Direction by Bill Lava.
A sign at Daffy Duck's cornfield says it all. "No Trespassing! Violators will be shot and towed away!" Speedy Gonzales meets up with an old amigo, Loco Crow, who sits at the fence afraid of the scarecrow. Speedy discovers that Daffy Duck is hiding inside the Scareceow with his rifle, and decides to heckle the mouse-hating duck.

Speedy knocks over the scarecrow, and Daffy chases the pair in his helicopter, which Speedy maneuvers into the thrashing machine. Daffy outsmarts the two with iron corn but a dentonator explodes in Daffy's face. Fed-up, Daffy offers the crow all the delicious corn if he will kill Speedy. The crow is about to do it, but can't. Daffy offers the bird the whole field if he lets him shoot Speedy. Speedy outruns the duck, and returns to his friend the crow who decides to be selfish with the corn. The crow throws Speedy back at Daffy, but all the other crows are feasting on his corn! Daffy chases Speedy into the distance. "With friends like the Loco Crow, who needs enemies?".

JUST PLANE BEEP

The Road Runner; Oct 30; MM; Directed by Rudy Larriva; Story by Don Jurwich; Animation by Bob Bransford, Hank Smith, and Virgil Ross; Layouts by Erni Nordli; Backgrounds by Anthony Rizzo; Film Editor: Lee Gunther; Musical Direction by Bill Lava.
The Coyote learns of an "ACME War Surplus Sale" and orders a vintage World War I bi-plane. Among the gags: he props the propeller, which throws him into the sky, and his parachute doesn't work. The plane gets going, but immediately smashes into a wall. Firing the machine guns shear off the propellers. Telephone wires sling-shot the plane into the distance. The Coyote falls out of the plane while dropping a huge bomb. The bomb falls on top of him and explodes. The Road Runner makes his cameo appearance at the end, Beep-Beeping for joy!

HARRIED AND HURRIED

The Road Runner; Nov 13; MM; Directed by Rudy Larriva; Story by Nick Bennion; Animation by Hank Smith, Virgil Ross and Bob Bransford; Layout: Ray Morita and Shirley Silvey;

Backgrounds by Anthony Rizzo; Film Editor: Lee Gunther; Musical Direction by Bill Lava.

The Coyote chases the Road Runner. This time he mails his order to the ACME Company for a snow machine. He puts up signs "Chains Required," then offers free chains and sets up his portable electro-magnet as an elaborate trap for the Road Runner. Unfortunately, the Coyote gets caught in his own snow plow. Other failed attempts in this picture include: a kite with a bomb; parachuting down toward the Road Runner, landing in a tornado; putting an iron road block on the highway, and getting his thumbs stuck, a truck smashing him. He tries the old "dynamite attached to the extended arms" routine and a karate chop that lands him in an oncoming ACME van!

GO GO AMIGO

Daffy Duck, Speedy Gonzales; Nov 20; MM; Directed by Robert McKimson; Story by David Detiege; Animation by Warren Batchelder, Bob Matz, and Manny Perez; Layouts by Dick Ung; Backgrounds by George de Lado; Film Editor: Lee Gunther; Voice Characterization by Mel Blanc and Gonzales Gonzales; Musical Direction by Bill Lava.

A crowd gathers in front of "El Daffy's TV & Radio Shop" watching a live-action bullfight. The proprietor, Daffy Duck, shoos them away and turns off the set. "Everybody wants something for nothing—well, not in my store!" Meanwhile, Speedy Gonzales is having a birthday party in a hole in Daffy's wall. His guests want music, so Speedy turns on a radio in Daffy's store. Daffy is determined to ruin their party and it becomes a battle for Mexican Music.

Daffy changes the station on the radio, Speedy changes it back. This goes on until Speedy uses dynamite to stop the duck. Speedy keeps the music going with a record player, but Daffy cuts the electricity off. Speedy gets a transistor radio, but Daffy confounds them by going down to the radio station and, at gunpoint, broadcasts bad Bill Lava music. Speedy races down to the radio station, ties up Daffy, and resumes the "twist music." Speedy helps the captive Daffy "twist" by spinning him on the record turntable.

HIGHWAY RUNNERY

The Road Runner; Dec 11; LT; Directed by Rudy Larriva; Story by Al Bertino; Animation by Virgil Ross, Bob Bransford and Hank Smith; Layouts by Erni Nodli and Don Shepard; Backgrounds by Anthony Rizzo; Film Editor: Joe Siracusa; Musical Direction by Bill Lava.

What we learn from this film is that the following devices do not help the Coyote catch the Road Runner: an old jalopy (which the Road Runner uses to crash into the Coyote); a giant rubber band; a skateboard with a sail propelled by an electric fan; a time bomb planted in an egg (which the Road Runner sits on, hatching a robot chick who walks to its daddy, the Coyote, and explodes); and a giant skyrocket (which blasts the Coyote into orbit).

CHASER ON THE ROCKS

The Road Runner; Dec 25; MM; Directed by Rudy Larriva; Story by Tom Dagnais; Animation by Hank Smith, Virgil Ross, and Bob Bransford; Layout by Don Shepard; Backgrounds by Anthony Rizzo; Film Editor: Joe Siracusa; Musical Direction by Bill Lava.

A hot weather gag: crazy from the heat, the Coyote imagines Road Runner mirages and disguises a stick of dynamite as a glass of lemonade for the Road Runner, which the bird drinks. Dynamite is disguised as a bird bath; the Coyote tries to drink from a hose and gets the juice turned on full blast by the bird. The Coyote detours the speeding bird into a pipe leading to a cannon. The Coyote gets shot from the cannon, sinking the sun into the west.

1966

THE ASTRODUCK

Daffy Duck, Speedy Gonzales; Jan 1; LT; Directed by Robert McKimson; Animation by Bob Matz, Manny Perez, Warren Batchelder, Don Williams,

George Grandpre, and Norm McCabe; Layouts by Dick Ung; Backgrounds by Tom O'Loughlin; Film Editor: Lee Gunther; Voice Characterization by Mel Blanc; Musical Direction by Bill Lava. Daffy rents a run-down Mexican mansion as a place to rest for the summer. Speedy Gonzales welcomes the duck to the House of Gonzales, but the duck isn't crazy about mice and nails the rodent inside his hole. Speedy crashes out, and Daffy chases him with a hammer back into his hole. Daffy tries to rid the residence of Speedy, employing a plumbing tool, a rifle, a bathroom plunger, grenades. Nothing works. Daffy packs the basement with dynamite, but Speedy tricks the duck into being inside the hacienda when it explodes, sending it into orbit. Speedy comments, "Well what do you know? We got a new Astroduck!"

SHOT AND BOTHERED

The Road Runner; Jan 8; LT; Directed by Rudy Larriva; Story by Nick Bennion; Animation by Bob Bransford, Hank Smith, Virgil Smith, and Virgil Ross; Layouts by Don Shepherd; Backgrounds by Anthony Rizzo; Film Editor: Lee Gunther; Musical Direction by Bill Lava.

The Coyote chases the Road Runner through miles of pipeline, leading to the edge of a cliff. The Coyote falls. Other attempts to catch the bird include: ACME Suction Cups which drag the Coyote off a cliff; a tennis net stretched across the road that captures a truck that runs over the Coyote; TNT sticks on a rope that swings about face, exploding on the Coyote; a skateboard, again through the miles of metal pipe and off a cliff; inhaling helium gas, that permits the Coyote to fly over the bird with a bomb, but unfortunately landing in a cactus patch which deflates the balloon and ignites the bomb that blows up in his face!

OUT AND OUT ROUT

The Road Runner; Jan 29; MM; Directed by Rudy Larriva; Story by Dale Hale; Animation by Virgil Ross, Bob Bransford, and Hank Smith; Layouts by Don Sheppard; Backgrounds

by Anthony Rizzo; Film Editor: Roger Donley; Musical Direction by Bill Lava. Coyote chases Road Runner. The determined Coyote uses a skateboard, which rolls off a cliff, a falcon, which lifts the Coyote into the sky until he struggles free and falls; birds attached to his feet, just as Mercury did in Mythology, until he crashes into the mountainside; a giant hot rod made of odds and ends from the junkyard, doing a wheelie off the cliff, his drag parachute saving the hot rod, not him; a wind-sail on wheels which is blown off a cliff; glue which he pours over the highway. You know who gets stuck *and* run over by the Road Runner steering a steam roller.

MUCHOS LOCOS

Daffy Duck, Speedy Gonzales; Feb 5; MM; Directed by Robert McKimson; Story by Dave Detige; Animation by Manny Perez, George Grandpre, and Bob Matz; Layouts by Dick Ung; Backgrounds by Tom O'Loughlin; Film Editor: Lee Gunther; Voice Characterization by Mel Blanc; Musical Direction by Herman Stein.

In a junkyard two little mice are watching a busted TV set. One becomes frustrated and leaves, the other tries using his imagination to form a picture. Speedy Gonzales helps the little one imagine that "stupid duck" (Daffy) in stock footage from *Robin Hood Daffy* (1958), *Deduce You Say* (1956) and *China Jones* (1959), followed by examples of a "smart mouse" in stock footage from some good Speedy Gonzales cartoons. Daffy is hiding in the TV set, angry over the propaganda Speedy is feeding the kid. The duck hits Speedy with a mallet. The little mouse wonders if Daffy is real or imaginary.

MEXICAN MOUSEPIECE

Daffy Duck, Speedy Gonzales; Feb 26; MM; Directed by Robert McKimson; Story by Dave Detiege; Animation by George Grandpre, Bob Matz, and Manny Perez; Layouts by Dick Ung; Backgrounds by Tom O'Loughlin; Film Editor: Al Wahrman; Voice Characterization by Mel Blanc, Ralph

Jones; Musical Direction by Bill Lava.
Daffy Duck, the good Samaritan,
decides to help the poor starving cats
overseas by sending Mexican mice over
in a Care package. Speedy Gonzales
comes to the rescue by destroying Daffy's car. Next, Speedy tricks Daffy
with a phony Care package full of fireworks that Speedy "Yee-Hah's" into
exploding.

Daffy tricks the mice with an offer of
free cheese in the Care package.
Speedy then chases Daffy and stomps
his foot with a hammer. The mice
escape to the other side of a mountain
crevice. Daffy tries to get across the
divide propelled via a lever, but a boulder falls on him. The duck tries a skyrocket, which crashes into earth. Daffy
tries a catapault which flattens him
against a mountain. The mice ask,
"What can we do with a flattened
duck?" Speedy responds, "Send him
overseas, they are loco for pressed
duck!"

THE SOLID TIN COYOTE
*The Road Runner; Feb 29; LT;
Directed by Rudy Larriva; Story by Don
Jurwich; Animation by Hank Smith,
Virgil Ross, and Bob Bransford; Layouts
by Don Sheppard; Backgrounds by
Anthony Rizzo; Film Editor: Joe
Siracusa; Musical Direction by Bill
Lava.*
The Coyote puts hot tar on the road,
but the Road Runner runs right
through it so rapidly that the Coyote is
backed into the bucket, his feet stuck.
Hopping around the desert with a
bucket of tar on his feet, the Coyote
gets stuck to the tar road and a truck
smashes into him.

He sets up a large mirror on the road
ledge, but his "reflection" plays games
with him, causing him to fall from the
cliff. Falling into a garbage dump, he
gets an idea. He takes a pile of junk
and constructs a giant robot Coyote.
When he turns it on, it works! He commands the robot to walk and it does,
crushing him underfoot. The Coyote
uses the robot to chase the Road Runner, but he gets crushed by its hand,
electrified, and chewed in its mouth.

He makes the robot run after the
speedy bird, but the machine runs off a
cliff. The Coyote ends up in the same
pile of junk he started with.

CLIPPETY CLOBBERED
*The Road Runner; Mar 12; LT;
Directed by Rudy Larriva; Story by
Tom Dagenais; Animation by Bob
Bransford, Hank Smith, and Virgil Ross;
Layouts by Don Sheppard; Backgrounds
by Anthony Rizzo; Film Editor: Al
Wharman; Musical Direction by Bill
Lava.*
Waiting by his mailbox, the Coyote
receives a package, dropped on his
head via air mail. Inside the box is a
chemistry set, and using it, the following gags occur: the Coyote creates
"invisible paint" and paints himself but
the Road Runner still runs him off a
cliff and drops an invisible boulder on
him; the Coyote builds a brick wall and
paints it invisible, but the Road Runner
runs right through it; he next creates a
bouncing rubber formula, covers his
body with it and bounces off a cliff.
Reading about a rocket backpack, the
Coyote creates a "Jet Spray," which
speeds him into trucks and railroad
trains. The film ends as the Road Runner waves goodby to the clobbered
Coyote.

DAFFY RENTS
*Daffy Duck, Speedy Gonzales; Mar 26;
LT; Directed by Robert McKimson;
Story by Michael O'Connor; Animation
by Bob Matz, Manny Perez, George
Grandpre, and Norm McCabe; Layouts
by Dick Ung; Backgrounds by Tom
O'Loughlin; Film Editor: Al Wahrman;
Voice Characterization by Mel Blanc
and Gonzales Gonzales; Musical
Direction by Irving Getz.*
At the El Casa Del Gato, Rest Home
For Cats, the doctors wonder what has
their cats spooked. The answer:
Speedy Gonzales. The head doctor,
Ben Crazy, calls "Daffy Rents" to lease
a "Radar Rent-A-Trap." The doctor
tells Daffy Duck to catch the mouse
and "name your own price." Daffy
brings over "Herman," a robot mouse
catcher, who catches Speedy
immediately.

Daffy is delighted to get the easy money and not have to split it, but Herman wants a fifty-fifty cut. When the duck refuses, Herman lets the mouse go, leaving Daffy to catch Speedy himself! Daffy chases Speedy onto electric wires and gets his feathers burned off. Daffy dresses in drag as a senorita with "Mickey Mouse" ears. Herman thinks he's a mouse and wrestles the duck. Daffy states, "We'll never give up!" Herman retorts, "What do you mean 'we'?" Herman dons a large Mexican hat, joins the mice and throws Daffy out. "It's a sad state of affairs when a mouse can make a machine turn a duck into a chicken on account of a rat!"

A-HAUNTING WE WILL GO

Daffy Duck, Speedy Gonzales, Witch Hazel; Apr 16; LT; Directed by Robert McKimson; Animation by Manny Perez, George Grandpre, Warren Batchelder, and Bob Matz; Layouts by Dick Ung; Backgrounds by Tom O'Loughlin; Film Editor: Al Wahrman; Voice Characterization by Mel Blanc and June Foray; Musical Direction by Bill Lava.
On a spooky Halloween night, Daffy Duck's little nephew is scared of the house down the street because of its occupant, Witch Hazel. Daffy doesn't believe in witches and drags his nephew back to prove it. Meanwhile, Hazel wants to go on vacation and recruits her mouse, Speedy Gonzales, to take her place. She transforms him into a duplicate of her and takes off. "Hazel" (with Speedy's voice) welcomes Daffy in and offers him some tea which transforms Daffy into the four-legged flower-headed creature (with a screw-ball flag on his tail) from *Duck Amuck* (1953).

The film reuses animation of Witch Hazel from *Broomstick Bunny* (1956).

SNOW EXCUSE

Daffy, Speedy Gonzales, May 21; MM; Directed by Robert McKimson; Story by David Detiege; Animation by George Granpre, Bob Matz, Manny Perez, Don Williams, and Norm McCabe; Layouts by Dick Ung; Backgrounds by Tom O'Loughlin; Voice Characterization by
Mel Blanc; Musical Direction by Bill Lava.
On a snow-capped mountain, in sub-zero temperatures, Speedy Gonzales is freezing to death. Speedy decides to ask his neighbor, Daffy Duck, a devout rodent-hater, for fire wood. Daffy gives him some buckshot! The duck brings his wood inside, but Speedy steals it, one log at a time.

Among the many gags: Daffy scares Speedy off with a cat mask, and a knock at his door brings bullets, the duck firing at his mailman who wraps his gun around him. Speedy runs to the log pile, narrowly missing mouse traps, to grab some chocolate covered ice logs. Speedy grabs a real wooden log, and Daffy chases the rodent, getting caught in all the mousetraps. Speedy gets the wood he needs, and begins to build a snowman. Daffy comes after him, but Speedy sends a snowball rolling down the mountain which grows bigger and bigger, flattening the duck. Daffy joins Speedy at the end, in mouse costume. "If you can't beat 'em, join 'em!"

A SQUEAK IN THE DEEP

Daffy Duck, Speedy Gonzales; July 19; LT; Directed by Robert McKimson; Story by Sid Marcus; Animation by Bob Matz, Manny Perez, Norm McCabe, George Grandpre, Ted Bonnicksen, and Warren Batchelder; Layouts by Dick Ung; Backgrounds by Tom O'Loughlin; Film Editor: Eugene Marks; Voice Characterization by Mel Blanc; Musical Direction by Walter Greene.
The Guadalajara Yacht Club annual boat race to Hawaii gains two new entrants: Daffy Duck, who decides to enter for the cash prize, and Speedy Gonzales, a sportsman who is immediately abused by the duck who puts him in a tin can and kicks him away.

Speedy enters in a bathtub with a sail (singing "Hula Lou"); Daffy sets off on a raft (singing "Aloha Oe"). Daffy pulls Speedy's bathtub stopper sinking the tub. Speedy passes the duck on a little raft. Daffy throws him a regulation anchor, smashing the rodent's raft. Speedy lands on Daffy's boat, via a helium balloon and suggests they join forces. Daffy chases him with an axe, Speedy blasting him with water. Daffy tries anvils and baseball bats, and gets stuck in a port hole. Unable to move, Daffy agrees to split any winnings. Seeing a shark swimming toward them, Daffy pushes the raft to the finish line.

FEATHER FINGER

Speedy Gonzales, Daffy Duck; Aug 20; MM; Directed by Robert McKimson; Story by Michael O'Connor; Animation by Manny Perez, Norm McCabe, George Grandpre, Ted Bonnicksen, Bob Matz, and Don Williams; Layouts by Dick Ung; Backgrounds by Tom O'Loughlin; Film Editor: Eugene Marks; Voice Characterization by Mel Blanc; Musical Direction by Walter Greene.
Daffy Duck, a pauper, is begging for coins in Hangtree, Texas, a tough Western town. Mayor Katt, frazzled over that pest, Speedy Gonzales, offers $15.00 a week for a gunslinger who will keep the mouse out of town. With nothing to lose, Daffy offers himself up as ace gunslinger "Feather Finger."

Daffy waits at the border for Speedy, and fires at the mouse when he arrives. Speedy catches the bullets and returns them! Daffy uses a giant mousetrap, and hides in a huge piece of cheese. Speedy grabs the cheese, Daffy jumps out and gets stuck in a rock ledge. Daffy hides in a cannon shell. Though he is caught in another explosion, he also grabs Speedy. The Mayor cheats Daffy on the reward, so Daffy lets Speedy go. The Mayor then beats Daffy up, returning him to his down-and-out-state.

SWING DING AMIGO

Daffy Duck, Speedy Gonzaeles; Sept 17; LT; Directed by Robert McKimson; Story by Sid Marcus; Animation by George Grandpre, Ted Bonnicksen, Bob Matz, and Manny Perez; Layouts by Dick Ung; Backgrounds by Tom O'Loughlin; Film Editor: Lee Gunther; Voice Characterization by Mel Blanc; Musical Direction by Walter Greene.
At the Go-Go club, all the mice are

dancing to Speedy Gonzales's rock-and-roll-guitar tune. Daffy Duck, his neighbor upstairs, is trying to sleep. The duck calls Speedy on the phone to be quiet, then tries to mallet him through the phone lines. Daffy next drills a hole in his floor and drops a grenade into the Go-Go but it pops right out. Daffy drops it again and runs, but no matter where he runs, the grenade keeps popping out, even in a row boat on the lake! Eventually it blows up in Daffy's hand.

Daffy abuses Speedy by dumping water on his head and locking him out of his own club. Speedy grabs the keys, and Daffy chases him. Speedy stops from time to time, trying each key so he can open the club. Daffy uses a vacuum cleaner to pull Speedy out, but Speedy has it stuck in gunpowder and it explodes. In the end, Daffy is back in bed. Instead of sleeping, he has joined the musical fiesta with a pair of cymbals!

SUGAR AND SPIES

The Road Runner; Nov 5; LT; Directed by Robert McKinson; Story by Tom Dagenais; Animation by Bob Matz, Manny Perez, Warren Batchelder, Dale Case, and Ted Bonnicksen; Layouts by Dick Ung; Backgrounds by Tom O'Loughlin; Film Editor: Lee Gunther; Musical Direction by Walter Greene.
A spy being pursued by the police throws his "Spy Kit" out. The Coyote finds it and uses it to help him chase the Road Runner. Wearing a black trenchcoat and hat, the Coyote tries to give the Road Runner sleeping gas, but the bird blows it to the Coyote, who "sleepwalks" off the cliff. The Coyote sends the Road Runner a time bomb in the mail, but it's returned to the Coyote for postage. The Coyote uses Spy explosive putty to cause a boulder to land on his head.

The Coyote raids the city dump to find parts for a spy car. He fires machine guns, uses an ejector seat, and blasts a cannon from the car—to no avail. He uses a remote control device to aim explosive missiles at the Road Runner and it backfires. The Road

Runner uses the remote control to send the Coyote to the moon!

A TASTE OF CATNIP

Speedy Gonzales, Daffy Duck; Dec 3; MM; Directed by Robert McKimson; Story by Michael O'Connor; Animation by Ted Bonnicksen, Bob Matz, Manny Perez, Norm McCabe, George Grandpre, and Warren Batchelder; Layouts by Dick Ung; Backgrounds by Tom O'Loughlin; Film Editor: Lee Gunther; Voice Characterization by Mel Blanc and Gonzales Gonzales; Musical Direction by Walter Greene.

At the Guadalajara Medical Center, Daffy Duck visits a psychiatrist to tell of his obsession with Speedy Gonzales. He not only wants to eat him, but also is beginning to take on the characteristics of a cat. He fears dogs, meows, scratches, competes with Sylvester (a cameo appearance) for Speedy. He has taken up singing to forget but sings on backyard fences, getting the boot! Then Speedy moved into his house and Daffy went wild.

The Doctor finds a high level of catnip in his blood. Daffy goes home and realizes that the catnip factory next door is spewing fumes in his direction. When Daffy bombs the catnip factory, a trio of angry cats beat him up. The Doctor sees his next patient. It is Speedy Gonzales who thinks he is a duck!

1967

DAFFY'S DINER

Daffy Duck, Speedy Gonzales; Jan 21; MM; Directed by Robert McKimson; Story by Michael O'Connor; Animation by Manny Perez, Warren Batchelder, Ted Bonnicksen, Art Leonardi, Don Williams, Bob Matz, and Norman McCabe; Backgrounds by Tom O'Loughlin; Film Editor: Lee Gunther; Voice Characterization by Mel Blanc; Musical Direction by Walter Greene.

At his fast food stand, Daffy Duck serves "Mouse Burgers for cool cats" at 19¢ apiece, using a foam rubber mouse. But El Supremo, a Mexican cat bandit, demands a real mouse!

Speedy Gonzales comes to the door asking for cheese. Daffy puts him in a skillet with onions. Speedy runs, with the duck in pursuit. Daffy chases Speedy into the desert and winds up getting clobbered by a cactus. El supremo now demands his mouseburger at gunpoint, forcing Daffy to don "Mickey Mouse" ears and climb into a giant bun!

The last theatrical DePatie-Freleng/Warner Bros. cartoon.

QUACKER TRACKER

Daffy Duck, Speedy Gonzales; Apr 29; LT; Produced by Herbert Klynn; Directed by Rudy Larriva; Story by Tom Dagnais and Don Jurwich; Animation by Virgil Ross, Bob Bransford, and Ed Friedman; Layouts by Don Shepard; Backgrounds by Walt Peregoy; Film Editor: Joe Siracusa; Music by Frank Perkings; Musical Direction by William Lava.

Warner Bros. decides to re-establish its own animation department, and commissions three cartoons from Herb Klynn at Format Films while the new department is being organized.

The Tooth-And-Nail-Hunting Society issues a challenge to its members: a lifetime membership for the capture of Speedy Gonzales (the only trophy they do not have). But only a "stupid, idiotic, foolhardy ignoramus" would attempt such a challenge. "You called?" responds Daffy Duck, who takes on the hunt! Daffy tracks Speedy to his mouse hole. The duck tricks Speedy into looking into his gun!("Look into the telescope and see a pretty girl!") and the mouse goes wild at the beautiful senorita inside. Daffy is tricked into looking down the barrel, is blasted by Speedy, and the chase is on. Daffy tries his hunting snare, and nets himself. The duck next tries a mechanical mouse decoy filled with TNT which the mouse returns to Daffy to explode. Daffy resorts to "Plan X" dressing as a giant enchilada. The Mexican mice load it with hot sauce, which sends the duck zooming like a rocket! Finally, Daffy tries a jet-powered cannon, and only succeeds in getting fired back into the hunting club!

THE MUSIC MICE-TRO

Daffy Duck, Speedy Gonzales; May 27; MM; Produced by William Hendricks and Herb Klynn; Directed by Rudy Larriva; Story by Tom Dagneis and Cal Howard; Animation by Bob Bransford, Ed Friedman, and Virgil Ross; Layouts by Don Shepard; Backgrounds by Walt Peregoy; Film Editor: Joe Sircusa; Musical Direction by William Lava.
Daffy Duck, on vacation from Hollywood and looking for peace and quiet, is disturbed in his "Balmy Springs" retreat by Speedy Gonzales and his Mexicali Mariachi band, who want to audition for him. With Speedy's help, everything the duck does to calm his nerves ends in disaster. In the pool, he gets splashed; under a sun lamp, he gets baked; playing golf, he swallows the ball! He chases the mice with his golf caddy, and crashes in a sand trap (Speedy shows us the crash again, in instant replay). Daffy finally leaves the resort, but Speedy and his band are in his back seat, driving the duck crazy.

THE SPY SWATTER

Daffy Duck, Speedy Gonzales; June 24; LT; Produced by William Hendricks and Herbert Klynn; Directed by Rudy Larriva; Story by Tom Degenais, and Carl Howard; Animation by Ed Friedman, Virgil Ross, and Bob Bransford; Film Editor: Joe Siracusa; Musical Direction by William Lava.
In the city, a professor gives Speedy a special piece of cheese that can give mice the strength of ten cats. Speedy beats up a robot cat, and the professor entrusts the rodent to bring the formula to the cheese factory. Enemy agent Daffy Duck is assigned to get Speedy and his formula, but all of his super-spy gadgets work against him. Using his rocket belt, the duck crashes through the ceiling; his spy car machine guns knock a telephone pole over his head. His "secret agent glove gun" fires bullets from his fingertips, but Speedy gets him to point at his own head. Speedy reprograms the "mouse tracking missile" to track the duck. Daffy hides at his headquarters, destroying the operation. Speedy tells a secret: "Us good guys always win!"

SPEEDY GHOST TO TOWN

Daffy Duck, Speedy Gonzales; July 29; MM; Produed by William L. Hendricks; Directed by Alex Lovy; Story by Cal Howard; Animation by Volus Jones, Ed Solomon, Ted Bonnicksen, and LaVerne Harding; Layouts by David Hanan and Lin Larsen; Backgrounds by Bob Abrams: Film Editor: Hal Geer; Voice Characterization by Mel Blanc; Musical Direction by Willian Lava.
The first film from the new Warner Bros. cartoon studio under Bill Hendricks, who recieves solo producer credit on all remaining films.

Speedy Gonzales shows his friend, Miguel, a ghost town and a "gold" nugget. Speedy has a map showing where there are plenty more, and Daffy Duck decides to chase them for the map.

To elude Daffy, Speedy ties the duck's tail feathers to the player-piano music roll, and pulls the gringo duck into the music box. Daffy sets up a telephone next to a box of dynamite. When Speedy answers the ringing phone, he tells Daffy "It's for you!" and blasts the duck. Daffy hides in a barrel next to the one Speedy's hiding in, but the duck is so stupid, he throws the pin of a grenade into Speedy's barrel, causing an explosion in his. Daffy chases Speedy into a bar, where a mounted bull-head falls on his neck. Speedy "bullfights" the duck. Daffy finally chases the mice to the cave where the treasure is hidden. Daffy demands the treasure, and they send the cart out loaded with nuggets of cheese! Daffy goes crazy, running through the desert yelling, "Cheese, gold, cheese, gold ..." Speedy wonders what's wrong? "I guess he doesn't like cheese!"

RODENT TO STARDOM

Daffy Duck, Speedy Gonzales; Sept 23; LT; Directed by Alex Lovy; Story by Cal Howard; Animation by Volus Jones, LaVerne Harding, Ted Bonnicksen, and Ed Solomon; Layouts by David Hanan and Lin Larson; Backgrounds by Bob Abrams; Film Editor: Hal Greer; Musical Direction by William Lava.

Daffy Duck is admiring the footprints in cement in front of a famous Hollywood movie palace, scoffing at the tiny footprints of Speedy Gonzales. He boasts about being a better actor than that "rambunctious rodent" just as Harvey Hassenpfeffer, the famous director at Colossal Pictures, drives by. The director "discovers" Daffy and takes him to the studio to put him in pictures.

Daffy is made stuntman stand-in for star Speedy Gonzales. Daffy takes a twelve-foot fall in a "Rock-A-Bye Baby" cradle. Daffy decides to do away with Speedy to get better parts. He pretends to want his autograph, then crushes the mouse in his autograph book and puts him in a library shelf. Daffy takes Speedy's place in a big love scene with his heart-throb, Ducky Lamour. Daffy does all the leaps and climbing to get to her balcony. But when it comes to kissing, the director calls the stand-in, Speedy Gonzales!

GO AWAY STOWAWAY

Daffy Duck, Speedy Gonzales; Sept 30; MM; Directed by Alex Lovy; Story by Cal Howard; Animation by Volus Jones, Ted Bonnicksen, LaVerne Harding, and Ed Solomon; Layouts by David Hanan and Lin Larson; Backgrounds by Bob Abrams; Film Editor: Hal Geer; Voice Characterization by Mel Blanc; Musical Direction by William Lava.

Daffy Duck is tired of Speedy Gonzales constantly singing "La Cucaracha." The mouse decides to send the duck away on vacation. He pours soap chips in front of the window, making Daffy think it's winter. Daffy packs bags and heads south, with Speedy secretly stowing away in his bag.

On an oceanliner, Daffy discovers Speedy and chases him around the ship. Speedy shoves a shuffleboard puck into his mouth. Daffy tries throwing pies, but gets hit with them himself. When Daffy eats, Speedy pulls the old sea-sick gag (a painting of waves rocking back and forth through a porthole). Daffy pulls the emergency whistle to trick Speedy into jumping overboard, then falls for his own trick. Daffy later throws an anvil at Speedy, which sinks the ship. In the end, Daffy swims back to shore, with Speedy in tow, singing, "La Cucaracha."

COOL CAT

Cool Cat; Oct 14; LT; Directed by Alex Lovy; Story by Bob Kurtz; Animation by Ted Bonnicksen, Ed Solomon, Volus Jones, and LaVerne Harding; Layouts and Backgrounds by David Hanan; Vocal: The Clingers (singing "He's Just a Cool Cat"); Voice Characterization by Larry Storch; Musical Direction by William Lava.

English Colonel Rimfire is hunting in the jungle with his 4-wheel drive mechanical elephant and comes acros Cool Cat, "the hip-talking tiger," walking in the sun with his parasol. The Colonel sees this, shouts "I tawt I taw a putty tat!" and shoots. Cool Cat warns the mechanical elephant that someone is after them. The Colonel gets thrown from the pachyderm and Cool Cat befriends it, taking it into the jungle to hide. Colonel Rimfire mistakes a real elephant for his and gets stomped. After a series of backfiring schemes, the Colonel gets his elephant back but it's out of gas! Cool Cat remarks, "They're not making elephants like they used to."

MERLIN THE MAGIC MOUSE

Merlin, The Magic Mouse; Nov. 18; MM; Directed by Alex Lovy; Story by Cal Howard; Animation by Ted Bonnicksen, LaVerne Harding, Volus Jones, and Ed Solomon; Layouts by Bob Givens; Backgrounds by Bob Abrams; Film Editor: Hal Geer; Voice Characterization by Daws Butler; Musical Direction by William Lava.

Merlin, a magician mouse (with a W.C. Fields voice), decides the show must go on despite his audience of only one cat. Putting on a mustache for a disguise, Merlin performs his magic tricks with his assistant, Second Banana. Merlin asks the cat to volunter for his "saw-in-half" act. Second Banana gives Merlin a real saw instead of a rubber one. This causes the cat to get wise and he chases the mice around the theater. Merlin gives the feline a flower pot which is really a dynamite stick. Trapped at a wall, the mice use a rope trick to escape. Merlin then produces a flying carpet, and they take off for their next booking in Peoria.

FIESTA FIASCO

Speedy Gonzales; Daffy Duck; Dec 9; LT; Directed by Alex Lovy; Story by Cal Howard; Animation by Ted Bonnicksen, LaVerne Harding, Volus Jones, and Ed Solomon; Layouts by Jaime Diaz, Bob Givens, David Hanan; Backgrounds by Bob Abrams; Film Editor: Hal Geer; Musical Direction by William Lava.

Mexican mice are preparing a fiesta. When mouse-hater Daffy Duck is spotted, all the mice, except Speedy Gonzales, hide. Daffy asks Speedy what the decorations are for. The mouse plays dumb and the duck gets suspicious. Daffy overhears that they are having a party and builds a rain-making machine to dampen their celebration.

No matter where he hides, the machine-generated rain cloud only rains on Daffy. The cloud soon gets violent, generating lightning and a tornado. The cloud eventually chases Daffy off a mountain. Daffy uses a vacuum cleaner to catch the cloud and falls head first into the party cake. It turns out to be a surprise birthday party for Daffy who begins to cry, the cloud raining on him.

1968

HOCUS POCUS POW WOW

Merlin, the Magic Mouse; Jan 13; LT; Directed by Alex Lovy; Story by Cal Howard; Animation by Ted Bonnicksen, LaVerne Harding, Volus Jones, and Ed

Solomon; Layouts by Bob Givens; Backgrounds by Bob Abrams; Film Editor: Hal Geer; Voice Characterization by Larry Storch; Musical Direction by William Lava.

Merlin and his sidekick, Second Banana, are enroute via locomotive to a performance out West. The conductor throws them off in the middle of nowhere when Merlin is unable to produce his train ticket. An Indian (billed as "Lo, the Poor Indian" in the opening credits) sees Merlin produce a turkey dinner from his magic hat. He chases the duo across the prairie for the magic hat, Merlin using every trick in his repertoire to confound the pursuer. Examples: Merlin steals the Indian's tomahawk and conks him with it; the Indian gets the hat, but Merlin retrieves it by disguising a dymanite stick as a peace pipe.

Arriving at their destination, Pow Wow City, they set up to perform that night to a tribe of angry Indians who chase the mice into the distance.

NORMAN NORMAL

Feb 3; CARTOON SPECIAL Directed by Alex Lovy. Story and Voice Characterization by N. Paul Stookey and Paul Dixon; Animation by Ted Bonnicksen, LaVerne Harding, Volus Jones, and Ed Solomon; Layouts by John Freeman; Backgrounds by Bob Abrams and Ralph Penn; Film Editor: Hal Geer; Musical Direction by William Lava; Produced by William L. Hendricks and N. Paul Stookey.

A contemporary satire on business methods and social behavior. Neither a "Looney Tunes" nor a "Merrie Melodies," it was produced by the new Warner Bros. cartoon department with singer/songwriter Noel (Paul) Stockey (Paul of Peter, Paul, And Mary) and Dave Dixon (miscredited as Paul Dixon in the opening credits). The opening titles are the standard "modern" version, with the words "CARTOON SPECIAL" where "Looney Tunes" would be. Under the credit sequence, a multi-colored rock group plays the "Norman Normal theme."

Norman closes the door on the rock

group, promising we'll "hear it again at the end." Opening another door, Norman meets with his boss who wants him to wine and dine a client. Norman is uncomfortable taking a man he doesn't know to a club he never goes to. Norman goes to another door and consults with his dad about "what's right and wrong." His dad rambles on about his life and tells him to "fit in" and not make waves. Norman leaves and enters another door to a party. At the party is his friend Leo, who walks around with a lampshade on his head asking for "Approval." Another friend starts telling him a joke, but Norman suspects it's "about a minority group. After you tell it, we're gonna laugh and feel superior?" The party's bartender insults Norman for only having a ginger ale instead of a hard drink.

Norman leaves the room, apologizes for the confusion and opens the door to the rock group, then closes the door which is now on his forehead. The film ends abruptly, but makes its point as an animated "think piece."

The song "Norman Normal" appears on Peter, Paul, and Mary's 1967 Warner Bros. album entitled "Album." The soundtrack was produced on the east coast with Dave Dixon as the voice of Norman, and Noel Paul Stookey as all the other characters. Though contractually credited to William Lava, Stookey also provided the cartoon's rock score, a capella, using electronic synthesizers.

BIG GAME HAUNT

Cool Cat; Feb 10; MM; Directed by Alex Lovy; Story by Cal Howard; Animation by Ted Bonnicksen, LaVerne Harding, Volus Jones, and Ed Solomon; Layouts by Bob Givens; Backgrounds by Bob Abrams: Film Editor: Hal Geer; Voice Characterization by Larry Storch; Musical Direction by William Lava.
Colonel Rimfire chases Cool Cat into a haunted house. While the cat hides in the stove, a tubby ghost with a derby hat and a big nose named Spooky comes out of an old trunk. The ghost scares the Colonel and the cat, but he only wants to be friends. Spooky finds the Colonel's hat and gun and tries to

return them, but the two just run when they see the ghost. Cool Cat accidentally gets the drapes tangled on his head, scaring Spooky. The ghost chases Cool Cat outside, until the cat is pooped. "That was a great race we had!" says Spooky. Cool Cat responds, "Not like the one we're gonna have, once I catch my breath!"

SKYSCRAPER CAPER

Daffy Duck, Speedy Gonzales; Mar 9; MM; Directed by Alex Lovy; Story by Cal Howard; Animation by Ted Bonnicksen, LaVerne Harding, Volus Jones, and Ed Solomon; Layouts by Bob Givens; Backgrounds by Bob Abrams and Ralph Penn; Film Editor: Hal Geer; Voices; Mel Blanc; Musical Direction by William Lava.
In this cartoon, Daffy Duck and Speedy Gonzales are best buddies. One night, Daffy walks in his sleep. Speedy sees this and tries to warn the duck about the lake. The cold water awakens the duck, and Speedy offers for five pesos to watch Daffy while he sleeps.

Speedy rigs some string, so that if Daffy walks in his sleep he'll hear a bell. It works once, but a second time Daffy sleepwalks around the string. Speedy wakes up the next morning and finds the duck gone. He trails Daffy to the ACME Construction Co. site, where Daffy is walking around the steel skeleton of the building.

The bell on an ice-cream cart wakes the duck up, just as he is about to walk off the skyscraper. Speedy rescues Daffy with a noose, but the duck falls and gets bounced around the structure, finally landing in Speedy's wheelbarrow. The mouse takes an unconscious Daffy home. The duck awakens, thinking he had a wild dream.

HIPPYDROME TIGER

Cool Cat; Mar 30; LT; Directed by Alex Lovy; Story by Tony Benedict; Animation by Ted Bonnicksen, LaVerne Harding, Volus Jones, and Ed Solomon; Backgrounds by Bob Abrams; Layouts by Jamie R. Diaz. Film Editor: Hal Geer; Voice Characterization by Larry Storch; Musical Direction by William Lava.

Colonel Rimfire and his robot elephant, Ella, chase Cool Cat to Paris, where the cat has entered the Grand Prix road race. The Colonel chases Cool Cat around the track. A well placed oil slick lands the British hunter in the lake. When the Colonel corners the cat, the feline's last request for "a light" ignites a skyrocket blasting Rimfire into space. Meanwhile, the robot elephant wins the race.

FEUD WITH A DUDE

Merlin, the Magic Mouse; May 25; MM; Directed by Alex Lovy; Story by Cal Howard; Animation by Ted Bonnicksen, LaVerne Harding, Volus Jones, and Ed Solomon; Layouts by Bob Givens; Backgrounds by Bob Abrams; Film Editor: Hal Geer; Voice Characterization by Larry Storch; Musical Direction by William Lava.
The Hatfields and McCoys are feuding in the Ozarks. Merlin, the Magic Mouse, and his assistant, Second Banana, are flying over the battle on their magic carpet and get shot down by a stray bullet. Merlin discovers the feud is over a hen and a pig. Merlin returns the animals to their rightful owners, but now the "Feudin' Mountain Boys" blame Merlin for stealing the animals in the first place. They attack the mice, but Merlin uses magic, turning a Hatfield into a chicken!

Merlin and Second Banana run back and forth between the feuding families, until Merlin produces a spaceship from his hat. They blast off (a live-action shot of a rocket launch), "A few more orbits of the earth and we'll be in Steubenville, Ohio, in time for the matinee!"

SEE YA LATER, GLADIATOR

Daffy Duck, Speedy Gonzales; June 29; LT; Directed by Alex Lovy; Story by Cal Howard; Animation by Ted Bonnicksen, LaVerne Harding, Volus Jones, and Ed Solomon; Layouts by Bob Givens; Backgrounds by Bob Abrams. Film Editor: Hal Geer; Musical Direction by William Lava.
Daffy Duck is an assistant in a Mexican scientist's laboratory. The scientist asks Daffy to watch things while he takes a siesta, and, whatever else he does, not to pull the chain on his time machine. Meanwhile, Speedy Gonzales and his mariachi band heckle the duck with a concert outside the window. Daffy tricks Speedy into stepping into the time machine, and sends the mouse back in time, Daffy accidentally going with him.

The duck immediately insults an ancient Roman (calling him a "fathead"). The Roman sends Daffy and Speedy to the lions. The lion chases the pair around Nero's arena, Daffy slicing the lion's mane with a sword (giving him a crew-cut). The lion eats the sharp weapon. Speedy gives the big cat some chili peppers, which sends him shooting like a skyrocket. The pair, chased, fall atop Nero, breaking his fiddle. Nero chases the duck and mouse just as the scientist returns them to this century. Daffy goes to bed, but can't sleep due to Speedy's mariachi band, now with Nero on fiddle!

3 RING WING DING

Cool Cat; Aug 24; LT; Directed by Alex Lovy; Story by Cal Howard; Animation by Ted Bonnicksen, LaVerne Harding, Volus Jones, and Ed Solomon; Layouts by Bob Givens; Backgrounds by Bob Abrams; Film Editor: Hal Geer; Voice Characterization by Larry Storch; Musical Direction by William Lava.
Colonel Rimfire is reading the paper and spots a want ad from the circus, offering $1000 for a live tiger. The Colonel chases Cool Cat into the Big Top and through all the acts: The Indian Snake Charmer, arcade games, the seal act, the human cannon ball, and into a lion's mouth. Cool Cat disguises himself as "Asbesto, the Fire Eater" but the Colonel gets wise and makes him put a hot poker in his mouth! Cool Cat jumps to the high wire, then causes the Colonel to loosen his pants on the trapeze. The Ringmaster has been watching their shenanigans, and, thinking their "act" is great, offers to pay them $500 a week to remain. They accept and Cool Cat divides their first week's wages, "Three for you and one, two, three for me ... "

FLYING CIRCUS

*Sept 14; LT; Directed by Alex Lovy;
Story by Cal Howard, Animation: Ted
Bonnicksen, LaVerne Harding, Volus
Jones, and Ed Solomon; Layouts by Bob
Givens; Backgrounds by Bob Abrams;
Film Editor: Hal Geer; Voice
Characterization by Larry Storch;
Musical Direction by William Lava.*

Ace, a World War I pilot accidentally
lands in the enemy airfield and is
chased by German troops. Back in the
air, Ace is pursued by the Red Baron.
When Ace throws a wrench, Fritz falls
out of his plane, landing on Ace's. They
crash into a barn and a cow flies the
plane! Fritz lands in a U.S. airfield
(live-action stock footage) and curses in
German. Subtitles read: "My momma
told me there would be days like this!"

CHIMP AND ZEE

*Oct 12; MM; Directed by Alex Lovy;
Story by Don Jurwich; Animation by
Ted Bonnicksen, LaVerne Harding,
Volus Jones, and Ed Solomon; Layouts
by Bob Givens; Backgrounds by Bob
Abrams; Film Editor: Hal Geer; Voice
Characterization by Mel Blanc; Musical
Direction by William Lava.*

A hunter searching the jungle for a rare
blue-tailed simian, encounters a specimen named Chimp and his jungle boy,
Zee. He chases them through eagles'
nests and swamps, but they elude him.
Using a blowgun, the hunter hits himself in the rear. Using a skyrocket, he
smashes into a tree.

Finally disguising himself as a
female blue-tailed simian, he gives the
love call and is chased by dozens of
blue-tailed monkeys. Chimp and Zee
swing through the treetops. It looks like
happy ever after.

BUNNY AND CLAUDE (WE ROB CARROT PATCHES)

*Nov. 9; MM; Directed by Bob
McKimson; Story by Cal Howard;
Animation by Ted Bonnicksen, LaVerne
Harding, Jim Davis, and Ed Solomon;
Layouts by Bob Givens; Backgrounds by
Bob Abrams; Film Editor: Hal Geer;
Voice Characterization by Mel Blanc
and Pat Wodell; Song ("The Ballad Of
Bunny And Claude") vocal by Billy
Strange; Musical Direction by William
Lava.*

This is a parody of the Warner Bros.
hit film *Bonnie and Clyde*, Bunny and
Claude are two criminal rabbits who
rob carrots from stores across the country. They are pursued by a redneck
sheriff who follows them to their hideout at Pop's Flophouse. They escape in
their auto, and the sheriff sets up a
roadblock, a giant baby block in the
road! The Sheriff sets an ambush in a
field of carrots, the Sheriff disguised as
a giant carrot. When the Sheriff turns
his back Bunny and Claude kick his
rear and escape.

1969

THE GREAT CARROT TRAIN ROBBERY

*Bunny and Claude; Jan 25; MM;
Directed by Robert McKimson; Story by
Cal Howard; Animation by Ted
Bonnicksen, LaVerne Harding, Jim
Davis, and Ed Solomon; Layouts by Bob
Givens; Backgrounds by Bob Abrams;
Film Editor: Hal Geer; Voice
Characterization by Mel Blanc and Pat
Woodell; Musical Direction by William
Lava.*

Outlaws Bunny and Claude make the
stationmaster stop the "Carrot
Express" train and board the carrot
car. The Sheriff catches up to the train
and hides in a barrel near the carrots.
Claude gets wise, nails the barrel shut
and throws it off the train. The Sheriff
uses a hand car to follow the train, but
Claude uncouples the carrot car and
smashes the lawman. The Sheriff
catches up to the bandit bunnies on
horseback just as they are unloading
carrots off the train. While the Sheriff
reads them their rights, his horse eats
all the evidence. When his back is
turned, the rabbit robbers escape!

FISTIC MYSTIC

*Merlin, the Magic Mouse; Mar 29; LT;
Directed by Bob McKimson; Story by
Cal Howard; Animation by Ted
Bonnicksen, LaVerne Harding, Jim
Davis, Ed Solomon, and Norm McCabe;
Layouts by Bob Givens and Jaime Diaz:*

Backgrounds by Bob Abrams; Film Editor: Hal Geer; Voice Characterization by Larry Storch; Musical Direction by William Lava. Traveling by handcar to Oshkosh, Merlin and his assistant Second Banana enter Rattlesnake Gulch, a western town, and are challenged by a gunfighter. Second Banana pushes Merlin into conflict with the bully, but eventually it's Second Banana who finds himself in the ring with him. Merlin gives his partner a pair of magic boxing gloves and every punch the little mouse throws is a knockout. The gloves think for themselves and keep punching the gunfighter.

RABBIT STEW AND RABBITS TOO

Rapid Rabbit; June 7; MM; Directed by Bob McKimson; Story by Cal Howard; Animation by Ted Bonnicksen, LaVerne Harding, Jim Davis, Ed Solomon, and Norm McCabe; Layouts by Bob Givens, and Jaime Diaz; Backgrounds by Bob McIntosh; Film Editor: Hal Greer; Musical Direction by William Lava. The quick brown fox reads a cookbook "How To Cook A Rabbit" which explains, "first, catch one!" The fox pursues Rapid Rabbit, who runs around the woods like the Road Runner, without saying a word but honking a horn to let us know his presence. During the many chase gags, the fox tries a cannon, but the barrel won't stay in place, firing at the fox; a spring-release mallet which only works when the fox picks up the carrot bait; and a Rube Goldberg contraption which the fox gets caught up in.

A series of Rapid Rabbit cartoons had been planned, but this was the only one produced before the studio closed. Another series, of "Keystone Kops" cartoons, were written and scheduled for production as well.

SHAMROCK AND ROLL

Merlin, the Magic Mouse; June 28; MM; Directed by Bob McKimson; Story by Cal Howard; Animation by Ted Bonnicksen, LaVerne Harding, Jim Davis, Ed Solomon, and Norman

McCabe; Layouts by Bob Givens, and Jaime Diaz; Backgrounds by Bob Abrams; Film Editor: Hal Geer; Voice Characterization by Larry Storch; Musical Direction by William Lava. Merlin looks at a globe of the world and asks his assistant, Second Banana, to help him decide which country to visit. He lets the little mouse throw a dart at the globe, Merlin getting the point in his rear end instead. He then blindfolds the boy and tells him to point and gets a finger poked in his eye! Merlin decides on Ireland and off they go via magic carpet.

Landing on a patch of shamrocks, they are met by O'Reilly, a leprechaun who shoos them off his field. Merlin performs a trick for O'Reilly, but the leprechaun is unimpressed. O'Reilly borrows Merlin's pocket watch to perform a trick, and makes it disappear. He then disappears! They chase the leprechaun all over the countryside, using a large paper airplane, and a sack trap, to no avail. Merlin finds the leprechaun's home, and O'Reilly gives him a sack of watches. As the mice fly home the watches, begin to disappear. The journey ends when they crash into Big Ben. Merlin holds back the closing iris to say "Drat!"

BUGGED BY A BEE

Cool Cat; July 26; LT; Directed by Bob McKimson; Story by Cal Howard; Animation by Ted Bonnicksen, LaVerne Harding, Jim Davis, and Ed Solomon; Layouts by Bob Givens and Jaime Diaz; Backgrounds by Bob Abrams; Voice Characterization by Larry Storch; Musical Direction by William Lava. Cool Cat arrives via dune buggy at Disco Tech singing, "I'm Working My Way Through College." The Cat is jealous of Musclehead Murphy, the schools's greatest athelete ("Wait'll I make the scene—I didn't have athlete's foot for nothing!"). Trying to impress the girls, Cool Cat tries pole vaulting. Stung by a bee, he makes an incredible leap. The coach signs Cool Cat to the baseball team.

Cool Cat goes to bat, and the bee stings him again, causing the tiger to hit a home run! Cool Cat joins the rowing team and the bee bugs him into rowing faster. The bee then forces the tiger into leaping hurdles and making touchdowns. The school becomes number one in sports. On graduation day, the dean awards the sport trophy to the one who made it all possible the bee! Cool Cat remarks, "Well, I'll Bee! Bee-trayed, Bee-littled, Bee-dumb.

INJUN TROUBLE
Cool Cat; Sept 20; MM; Directed by Bob McKimson; Story by Cal Howard. Animation: Ted Bonnicksen, Jim Davis, LaVerne Harding, and Ed Solomon; Backgrounds by Bob McIntosh; Layouts by Bob Givens, and Jaime Diaz; Film Editors: Hal Geer and Don Douglas; Voice Characterization by Larry Storch; Musical Direction by William Lava.
In a series of spot gags, Cool Cat encounters a group of wacky Indians while driving through the desert in his dune buggy. Gags include: an Indian giving Cool Cat a fat, love-lorn squaw, causing the Cat to shout "Indian Giver!"; an Indian painting a face on the paint can, putting it on his head and saying, "Me *Pail*-face!"; An Indian asking Cool Cat, "Why?" with the tiger responding "I thought Indians wanted to know 'How'?", the Indian imitating Groucho. "I know *how*, now I want to know *why*"; an Indian asking the cat to hold his shirt so he "can ride *bare*back Arriving at "Hot Foot (a real jumpin' town)", Cool Cat watches horses throwing "human shoes." He enters a "Topless Saloon" only to find a burly male bartender with no shirt. He plays poker with cow puncher Gower Gulch. The Cat "cuts" out, using scissors to cut his outline in the background. He departs the scene saying, "So cool it now, ya hear!"

1987

THE DUXORCIST
Daffy Duck; Nov 20; LT; Produced by Steven S. Greene; Story and Direction by Greg Ford and Terry Lennon; Co-Producer: Kathleen Helppie; Animation by Brenda L. Banks, Norm McCabe,

and Frans Vischer; Design and Layouts by Robert Givens; Backgrounds by Richard H. Thomas and Alan Bodner; Voice Characterization by Mel Blanc and B. J. Ward; Music Co-ordinator: Hal Willner; Classic Cartoon Music: Carl Stalling and Milt Franklyn.
Daffy Duck, "Paranormalist-at-large", runs commercials for his service ("Spooks Spooked, Goblins Gobbled, U.F.O.'s K.O.ed ..."). He gets a call from Thelma, a sexy female duck with a ghost problem. Daffy heads right over and checks out her kitchen, finding a frozen tundra in the oven, a flaming refrigerator ("Must be the frost-free kind!"), and live-action stock of an express train in her cupboard!

Thelma is possessed, and Daffy's kiss brings the spirits flying. She goes into a trance and begins to speak in foreign tongues ("Ou-yay upid-stay erk-jay!"). Daffy psychoanalyzes her, trying to exorcise the spirit (accidentally reading from "How to Excercise" by Jane Fondue). He removes the ghosts by telling old jokes ("Did you hear the one about the girl who didn't pay her exorcist bill? Her soul got repossessed!"). The ghosts leave her body one by one, but then decide to take over Daffy. Thelma kisses her hero, causing him to spin widly. He falls to the floor, and runs out the door so fast that he leaves the ghosts behind. End: The ghosts chase the duck down the street and into the distance.

1988

NIGHT OF THE LIVING DUCK
Daffy Duck; Sept 23; MM; Produced by Steven S. Greene; Story and Direction by Greg Ford and Terry Lennon; Animation by Brenda L. Banks, Norm McCabe, Mark Kausler, Rebecca Rees, and Frans Vischer; Co-Produced by Kathleen Helppie; Design and Layouts by Robert Givens; Assistant Layout: Lin Larson; Backgrounds by Richard H. Thomas and Alan Bodner; Voice Characterization by Mel Blanc and Mel Torme; Original Song by Virg Dzurinko and Greg Ford; Music Co-ordinator: Hal

Willner; *Original Music by Carl Stalling and Milt Franklyn.*
Daffy Duck is reading monster comic books, and, while searching for "Hideous Tales" no. 177 (It's a veritable collector's item!"), he hits himself with a Godzilla statue clock and dreams he's a performer in a nightclub full of famous monsters of filmland. Stepping up to the mike, Daffy sprays a little *Eau de Torme* (giving him the singing voice of Mel) and sings "Monsters Lead Such Interesting Lives" ("They'll suck your brains, and eat your remains ... "). In the audience is Leatherface, who chainsaws a steak (with an appropriate warning; "Kids! Don't try this at home!"). The Fly, the Invisible Man, Dracula, Frankenstein, The Mummy, even Alfred E, Newman make cameo appearances. Daffy then goes to each table making nightclub patter. When he introduces "Shmogzilla," the giant creature puts the duck in his mouth. Daffy awakens and laughs at the creature on the cover of his comic book who comes-to-life asking, "You were expecting maybe Calvin Coolidge?"

TV SPECIALS AND FEATURE FILMS

The following is a list of Warner Cartoon TV Specials and Feature Films. All of these films were produced by Warner Bros. (with the exception of *Bugs Bunny Superstar*) and feature the famous Warner characters.

Not included here is John Canemaker's excellent two-part documentary *The Boys from Termite Terrace*, produced by CBS for their program *Camera Three* in 1975; Filmation's 60-minute TV movie (for *The ABC Saturday Superstar Movie*) *Daffy Duck and Porky Pig Meet the Groovie Ghoulies* (Dec 18, 1972); and other animated features released by the studio: *Gay Purr-ee* (1963; written by Dorothy and Chuck Jones; Directed by Abe Levitow); *The Incredible Mr. Limpet* (1964); Ralph Bakshi's *Hey Good Lookin* (1982); and *Rainbow Brite and the Star Stealer* (1985).

TV SPECIALS

CARNIVAL OF THE ANIMALS

Nov 22, 1976; CBS; Produced, written, and directed by Chuck Jones; Production Design by Herbert Klynn.
All new animation combined with live action as Bugs Bunny and Daffy Duck accompany musician Michael Tilson Thomas in a performance based on the music of Camille Saint-Saens and the poetry of Ogden Nash.

BUGS BUNNY'S EASTER SPECIAL

Apr 7, 1977; CBS; Executive Director: Hal Geer; Supervising Director: Friz Freleng; Directed by Robert McKimson and Gerry Chinquy; Story by Friz Freleng and David Detiege; Music by Doug Goodwin. 60 minutes.

The Easter Bunny is sick and Granny recruits Bugs to help deliver the baskets of eggs. A surprise ending reveals the Easter Bunny to be a certain lazy duck. (But Bugs and Granny tell us in unison, "We knew it was Daffy all along!") Includes *For Scent-imental Reasons, Knighty Knight Bugs, Robin Hood Daffy, Sahara Hare, Birds Anonymous,* and clips from five others.

BUGS BUNNY IN SPACE

Sept 6, 1977; CBS; Executive Producer: Hal Geer.
The only special to contain no new animation. To cash in on the current *Star Wars* craze, a compilation of science fiction cartoons, featuring complete versions of *Hare Way to the Stars, Hasty Hare* and *Mad as a Mars Hare,* with clips from *Duck Dodgers in the 24 1/2 Century* and *Hare Raising Tale.*

A CONNECTICUT RABBIT IN KING ARTHUR'S COURT

Feb 23, 1978; CBS; Produced, Directed, and "Plagerized" by Chuck Jones; Music by Dean Elliot.

Daffy Duck is King Arthur, Porky Pig plays a varlet, and Bugs is a wise-guy Connecticut wabbit in this all new special. The villains are Elmer Fudd and Yosemite Sam. (This special is also known as *Bugs Bunny in King Arthur's Court*.)

BUGS BUNNY'S HOWL-OWEEN SPECIAL

Oct 26, 1978; CBS; Producer: Hal Geer; Directed by David Detiege, Abe Levitow and Maurice Noble; Story by Cliff Roberts; Music by Harper McKay.

The complete 1966 Daffy and Speedy cartoon *A-Haunting We Will Go*, with clips from eight other classics, including *Broomstick Bunny, Transylvania 6-5000, Scaredy Cat,* and *Claws for Alarm.*

HOW BUGS BUNNY WON THE WEST

Nov 15, 1978; CBS; Executive Producer/Director: Hal Geer; New Animatin Directed by Jim Davis; Written by Marc Sheffler.

In live action, actor Denver Pyle tells how Bugs and Daffy pioneered the West, with excerpts from *Bonanza Bunny, Wild and Wooly Hare, Dripalong Daffy, Barbary Coast Bunny* and clips from two others.

BUGS BUNNY'S VALENTINE

Feb 14, 1979; CBS; Executive Producer/Director: Hal Geer; Animation Director: Jim Davis.

Elmer Fudd is a "stupid cupid" who zaps the wabbit with the love bug. Includes the complete *Hare Trimmed* and clips from eight other classics including *The Grey Hounded Hare, Hare Splitter, Little Beau Pepe* and *Super Snooper.*

THE BUGS BUNNY MOTHER'S DAY SPECIAL

May 12, 1979; CBS; Executive Producer: Hal Geer; Directed by Jim Davis; Story by Hal Geer; Music by Harper McKay.

Bugs has a run-in with a pixilated stork in the bridging sequence of this tribute to mothers. Mostly complete showings of *Stork Naked* and *Apes of Wrath*, combined with clips from *Bushy Hare, Goo Goo Goliath, Mother Was a Rooster,* and *Quackodile Tears.*

BUGS BUNNY'S THANKSGIVING DIET

Nov 15, 1979; CBS; Executive Producer: Hal Geer; Directed by David Detiege; Story by Jack Envart and Hal Geer; Music by Harper McKay.

Bugs Bunny is a diet doctor who prescribes the following cartoons: *Bedevilled Rabbit, Rabbit Every Monday,* and clips from eight others including *Beep Beep, Canned Feud,* and *Trip for Tat.*

BUGS BUNNY'S LOONEY CHRISTMAS TALES

Nov 27, 1979; CBS; Executive Producer: Hal Geer; Bugs Bunny sequences Produced and Directed by Friz Freleng; Road Runner sequence Produced and Directed by Chuck Jones; Written by Friz Freleng, Chuck Jones, John Dunn, and Tony Benedict; Sequence Directors: Tony Benedict, Bill Perez, David Detiege, and Art Vitello; Voices by Mel Blanc and June Foray; Music by Doug Goodwin.

Three all new shorts: *Bugs Bunny's Christmas Carol* (Freleng), *Freeze Frame* (Jones), *Fright Before Christmas* (Freleng).

DAFFY DUCK'S EASTER SPECIAL

Apr 1, 1980; NBC; Executive Producer: Hal Geer; Produced by DePatie-Freleng; Sequence Directors: Tony Benedict, Gerry Chinquy, Art Davis, and David Detiege.

Three all new cartoons by Freleng: *The Yolks on You, Chocolate Chase, Daffy Flies North.*

BUGS BUNNY'S BUSTING OUT ALL OVER

May 21, 1980; CBS; Written, Produced, and Directed by Chuck Jones; Co-Director: Phil Monroe; Music by Dean Elliot.

Three all new cartoons by Jones: *Portrait of the Artist as a Young Bunny, Soup or Sonic, Spaced Out Bunny.*

THE BUGS BUNNY MYSTERY SPECIAL

Oct 26, 1980; CBS; Executive Producer: Hal Geer; Directed by Gerry Chinquy; Story by Jack Envart and Hal Geer; Music by Harper MacKay.

Porky Pig, as Alfred Hitchcock, hosts this compilation of crime cartoons. The complete *Big House Bunny*, with clips from seven others, including *Bugs and Thugs, Hare Lift, Operation Rabbit,* and *Catty Cornered.*

BUGS BUNNY: ALL-AMERICAN HERO

May 21, 1981; CBS; Executive Producer: Hal Geer; Producer/Director: Friz Freleng; Co-Director: David Detiege; Story by Friz Freleng and John Dunn; Music Composer: Rob West.

In an expanded version of *Yankee Doodle Bugs,* Bugs relates his own version of our nation's glorious past to his nephew Clyde, via the cartoons *Bunker Hill Bunny, Dumb Patrol,* and *Rebel Without Claws,* as well as clips from *Ballot Box Bunny, Southern Fried Rabbit,* and *Yankee Doodle Bugs.*

DAFFY DUCK'S THANK-FOR-GIVING SPECIAL

Nov 24, 1981; NBC; Executive Producer: Hal Geer; Produced and Directed by Chuck Jones; Written by Chuck Jones and Michael Maltese; Co-Director and Lead Animator: Phil Monroe.

Using the framing devise from *The Scarlet Pumpernickle,* Daffy Duck tries to sell "J.L." on *Duck Dodger and the Return of the 24 1/2 Century,* plus *His Bitter Half* and clips from *Robin Hood Daffy, Dripalong Daffy.*

BUGS BUNNY'S MAD WORLD OF TELEVISION

Jan 11, 1982; CBS; Producer: Hal Geer; Directed by David Detiege; Story by David Detiege and John Dunn; Music by Harper McKay.

Bugs is the new head of the QTTV Network and presents *This Is a Life?*

along with excerpts from *The Ducksters, Wideo Wabbit, What's Up, Doc?, Past Perfumance,* and others.

BUGS BUNNY/LOONEY TUNES 50TH ANNIVERSARY SPECIAL

Jan 14, 1986; NBC; Executive Producer: Lorne Michaels; Produced by Mary Salter; Directed by Gary Wels; Written by Tom Gammil, Max Pross, and Greg Ford; New Animation Directed by Chuck Jones; Animated by Phil Monroe.

One-hour special with celebrities (David Bowie, Steve Martin, Kirk Douglas, Cher, George Burns, etc.) toasting Bugs Bunny and Warner cartoons. Interviews with Mel Blanc, Friz Freleng, Chuck Jones. Rare pencil tests and cartoon footage.

BUGS VS. DAFFY; BATTLE OF THE MUSIC VIDEO STARS

Oct 21, 1988; CBS; Produced by Steve S. Greene and Kathleen Helppie-Shipley; Story and Direction by Greg Ford and Terry Lennon.

Bugs Bunny is a video disc jockey on the music channel, W.A.B.B.I.T., Daffy Duck is his rival at station K.P.Ü.T. They introduce various song sequences from old Warner cartoons, including "Sunrise in Nutsville" by the Wackylanders; "Any Bonds Today" from the war trailer; and that rock classic "Gee Whiz Willigans." Bugs gets the higher ratings. Clips from *Porky's Poppa, Porky's Poor Fish, Shake Your Powder Puff, Scrap Happy Daffy, Boobs in the Woods, Fifth Column Mouse, Wearing of the Grin,* and many more.

BUGS BUNNY'S WILD WORLD OF SPORTS

Feb 15, 1989; Produced by Steven S. Greene and Kathleen Helppie-Shipley; Story and Direction by Greg Ford and Terry Lennon.

From the "Arthur Q. Bryan Pavillion," the sportsman of the year award is announced. Many clips with Warner characters in sporting activities are shown. The surprise winner is Foghorn Leghorn. Clips from *Raw Raw Rooster, Sports Chumpions, To Duck or Not to*

Duck, Bunny Hugged, High Diving Hare, My Bunny Lies Over the Sea, and others.

FEATURE LENGTH COMPILATIONS

BUGS BUNNY SUPERSTAR

1975; Hare Raising Films, Inc.; Produced and Directed by Larry Jackson; Narrated by Orson Welles. 91 minutes.

A documentary on Warner Bros. cartoons of the forties, featuring interviews with Friz Freleng, Tex Avery, and particularly Bob Clampett. Cartoons shown complete: *What's Cooking Doc?*, *A Wild Hare*, *I Taw a Putty Tat*, *Rhapsody Rabbit*, *Corny Concerto*, *Walky Talky Hawky*, *The Old Grey Hare*, *My Favorite Duck*, and *Hair-Raising Hare*.

THE BUGS BUNNY/ROAD RUNNER MOVIE

Sept 30, 1979; Warner Bros.; Produced and Directed by Chuck Jones; Written by Michael Maltese and Chuck Jones; Production Designed by Maurice Noble; Animated by Phil Monroe, Ben Washam, Ken Harris, Abe Levitow, Dick Thompson, Lloyd Vaughan, Virgil Ross, Manny Perez, and Irv Anderson; Music by Carl Stalling, Milt Franklyn, and Dean Elliot. 92 minutes.

A compilation of Chuck Jones cartoons bridged together with new animation by most of his old staff. Bugs Bunny gives us a tour of his mansion, reminisces about his career, discusses the origins of humor and the chase. In addition to five complete cartoons (*Hareway to the Stars, What's Opera, Doc?, Duck Amuck, Bully for Bugs, Rabbit Fire*) excerpts from eight more are shown, along with an eleven-minute Road Runner compilation consisting of 31 gags culled from 16 cartoons.

FRIZ FRELENG'S LOONEY LOONEY LOONEY BUGS BUNNY MOVIE

Nov 20, 1981; Warner Bros.; Produced and Directed by Friz Freleng; Screenplay by John Dunn, David Detiege, and Friz Freleng; Sequence Directors: David Detiege, Phil Monroe, and Gerry Chinquy; Animated by Warren Batchelder, Charles Downs, Marcia Fertig, Bob Matz, Manuel Perez, Virgil Ross, and Lloyd Vaughan; Production Design by Cornelius Cole; Layouts by Peter Alvarado, Robert Givens and Michael Mitchell; Backgrounds by Richard H. Thomas; Voices by Mel Blanc, June Foray, Frank Nelson, Frank Welker, Stan Freberg, and Ralph James; Music by Rob Walsh, Don McGinnis, Milt Franklyn, Bill Lava, Shorty Rogers, and Carl Stalling. 80 minutes.

This compilation is made up of three acts. ACT I: Yosemite Sam raises hell with the devil in a remake of the short *Devil's Feud Cake* (1963). ACT II: Bugs outwits Rocky and Mugsy, a couple of inept gangsters who hold Tweety hostage. ACT III: Bugs acts as host for a zany parody of Hollywood Awards programs.

Cartoons shown include: *Knighty Knight Bugs, Sahara Hare, Roman Legion Hare, High Diving Hare, Hare Trimmed, Wild and Wooly Hare, Catty Cornered, Golden Yeggs, The Unmentionables, Three Little Bops, Show Biz Bugs.*

BUGS BUNNY'S 3RD MOVIE: 1001 RABBIT TALES

Nov 19, 1982; Warner Bros.; Produced by Friz Freleng; Sequence Directors: David Detiege and Friz Freleng; Animation by Warren Batchelder, Bob Bransford, Marcia Ferti, Terrence Lennon, Bob Matz, Norm McCabe, Tom Ray, and Virgil Ross; Backgrounds by Richard H. Thomas; Voice by Mel Blanc, Shep Menken, and Lennie Weinrib; Music by Rob Walsh, Bill Lava, Milt Franklyn, and Carl Stalling. 76 minutes.

Daffy Duck and Bugs Bunny are rival

book salesmen for Rambling House Publishers. They travel the world finding new places to sell their wares. In the Arabian desert, Bugs encounters Sultan (Yosemite) Sam and his bratty little son Prince Abadaba. Sam forces Bugs to read him stories from books. Cartoons shown: *Ali Baba Bunny, Apes of Wrath, Bewitched Bunny, Cracked Quack, Goldimouse and the Three Cats, Mexican Boarders, One Froggy Evening, Pied Piper of Guadalupe, Red Riding Hoodwinked, Tweety and the Beanstalk, Wise Quackers.*

DAFFY DUCK'S MOVIE: FANTASTIC ISLAND

Aug 5, 1983; Warner Bros.; Produced and Directed by Friz Freleng. Screenplay by John Dunn, David Detiege, and Friz Freleng; Sequence Directors: David Detiege, Friz Freleng, and Phil Monroe; Production Design and Layout by Bob Givens, and Michael Mitchell; Animation by Brenda Banks, Warren Batchelder, Bob Bransford, Brad Case, Terrence Lennon, Bob Matz, Norm McCabe, Sam Nicholson, Jerry Ray and Richard Thompson; Voices by Mel Blanc, June Foray and Les Tremayne. 78 minutes.

Daffy Duck and Speedy Gonzales have been shipwrecked on a desert island for a long time. They find Yosemite Sam's treasure map, but instead of treasure, they dig up a wishing well that transforms the island into a spoof of TV's *Fantasy Island*. Daffy and Speedy welcome visitors whose fantasies come true via footage from classic cartoons. Meanwhile Sam and the Tasmanian Devil work to reclaim their map. Cartoons: *Buccaneer Bunny, Stu-*

por Duck, Greedy for Tweety, Banty Raids, Louvre Come Back to Mel Tree for Two, Curtain Razor, A Mouse Divided, Of Rice and Hen, From Hare to Heir.

DAFFY DUCK'S QUACKBUSTERS

Sept 24, 1988; Warner Bros.; Produced by Steven S. Greene and Kathleen Helppie-Shipley; Story and Direction by Greg Ford and Terry Lennon; Animation by Brenda Banks, Norm McCabe, Rebecca Rees, Mark Kausler, Nancy Beiman, Daniel Haskett, Darryl Van Citters, and Frans Vischer; Production Design and Layout by Robert Given; Backgrounds by Richard H. Thomas and Alan Bodner; Voices by Mel Blanc, Roy Firestone and B.J. Ward; Music Coordinated by Hal Willner; Classic Music by Carl Stalling, Milt Franklyn, and Bill Lava. 72 minutes.

Street salesman Daffy Duck inherits a million dollars from the estate of J.B. Cubish (a la scenes from *Daffy Dilly*), then sets up a ghost-busting service with his pals Bugs Bunny and Porky Pig for the purposes of destroying Cubish's ghost who is trying to take away his inheritance. Cartoons: *Prize Pest, Water Water Ever Hare, Hyde and Go Tweet, Claws for Alarm, The Duxorcist, The Abominable Snow Rabbit, Transylvania 6-5000, Punch Trunk, and Jumpin' Jupiter.*

THE BUGS BUNNY SHOW

ABC TV Network—October 1960 through September, 1962—52 episodes, Tuesdays, 7:30-8:00 pm. Written and Produced by Chuck Jones and Friz Freleng. Theme Song: "This Is It" by Jay Livingston and Mack David.

The second season programs were titled, the first season programs were not. Therefore, for identification purposes, we have listed the production numbers for every episode.

FIRST SEASON

1. #1595; 10/11/60; Jones/Freleng; Bugs Bunny introduces the Looney

Tunes gang; *Rabbit Every Monday; A Mouse Divided; Tree for Two.*
2. #1589; 10/18/60; Jones/Freleng; Rocky and Mugsy plan on taking over the TV business; *Putty Tat Trouble; Wise Quackers; Speedy Gonzales.*
3. #1587; 10/25/60; Jones/Freleng; Guest host Pepe Le Pew speaks about Paris, the city of love; *Wild Over You; Go Fly a Kite; Mouse Warming.*
4. #1591; 11/1/60; Jones/Freleng; Emcee Bugs Bunny gets shoved aside by Wile E. Coyote and the Road Runner; *To Itch His Own, Gee Whiz-z-z, Whoa Be Gone.*
5. #1575; 11/8/60; Jones/Freleng, co-directed by Maurice Noble; Daffy is so desperate to appear on the show he dresses as a Hawaiian, a musketeer, and in knight's armor; *Canary Row, Knights Must Fall, For Scent-imental Reasons.*
6. #1576; 11/15/60; Jones/Freleng, co-directed by Gerry Chiniquy; Daffy plays drums and Bugs imitates "Frankie doing an imitation of Rickie imitating Elvis." Yosemite Sam, trying to sleep, appears and destroys Bugs's and Daffy's instruments; *Long Haired Hare; Sandy Claws; Mouse Wreckers.*
7. #1580; 11/22/60; Jones/Freleng, co-directed by Maurice Noble; Daffy, disguised as Bugs, hosts, but is chased by the sheep dog who thinks he's a rabbit. Daffy finds he cannot remove the bunny suit; *Bully for Bugs, Tweety's SOS, One Froggy Evening.*
8. #1579; 11/29/60; Jones/Freleng, co-directed by Maurice Noble; Daffy wants to host the show and expels all others, including Pepe, Elmer, and Bugs; *My Bunny Lies Over the Sea; Scaredy Cat; Scent-imental Romeo.*
9. #1581; 12/6/60; Jones/Freleng, co-directed by Hawley Pratt; Tweety is host, but in order to be safe from Sylvester, Bugs hangs his cage from the stage ceiling; *Bunker Hill Bunny, Each Dawn I Crow, Golden Yeggs.*
10. #1584; 12/13/60; Jones/Freleng, co-directed by Hawley Pratt; Yosemite Sam is again after Bugs, so he comes to see the "screwy rabbit's" show; *Which is Witch, Mouse Mazurka, Kit for Cat.*
11. #1585; 12/20/60; Jones/Freleng, co-directed by Abe Levitow and Maur-

ice Noble; The host, Porky Pig, is beset by Charlie Dog looking for a master; *Two's a Crowd, All A-Bird, Hasty Hare.*
12. #1586; 12/27/60; McKimson; When Bugs presents George P. Dog (from the Foghorn Leghorn barnyard), Foghorn pushes him aside and introduces the cartoons; *What's Up, Doc?, Early to Bet, Pop I'm Pop.*
13. #1588; 1/3/61; McKimson; Hosts are Sylvester and Junior, who encounter that giant mouse Hippety Hopper backstage; *A Lad-in His Lamp; Doggone South; A Fractured Leghorn.*
14. #1590; 1/10/61; Jones/Freleng; Elmer Fudd is host and tries to sing; *Ant Pasted; Fare Haired Hare; I Gopher You.*
15. #1592; 1/17/61; Jones/Freleng, co-directed Robert Transon and Maurice Noble; Bugs presents an all-Daffy Duck tribute, in which Mama Bear performs "I'm Just Wild About Daffy"; *Rocket Squad, Daffy Dilly, Drip-along Daffy.*
16. #1593; 1/24/61; McKimson, co-directed by Maurice Noble; Foghorn Leghorn presents Miss Prissy, old-time actress, who reenacts her favorite stage roles; *The Leghorn Blows at Midnight; Hot Cross Bunny; His Bitter Half.*
17. #1594; 1/31/61; McKimson; A twist on *Duck Amuck*; an unseen animator draws Foghorn with Rock Hudson's body. Foggy gets even, lassos the animator—Daffy Duck—and beats him up; *Lovelorn Leghorn; Who's Kitten Who?, Windblown Hare.*
18. #1596; 2/7/61; Jones/Freleng, co-directed by Hawley Pratt; Jose and Manuel, the Mexicali Shmoes, are heckled by Speedy Gonzales in the audience; *High Diving Hare, Don't Give Up the Sheep, Stooge for a Mouse.*
19. #1597; 2/14/61; Jones/Freleng, co-directed by Abe Levitow and Maurice Noble; Bugs demonstrates how to draw a cartoon, and how to draw Daffy Duck from a dumbbell; *Mutiny on the Bunny; Punch Trunk; Fast and Furry-ous.*
20. #1598; 2/21/61; Jones/Freleng; A program on music, with interruptions by hunter Elmer Fudd; *Rabbit of Seville, Scarlet Pumpernickle, Stop, Look, and Hasten.*
21. #1599; 2/28/61; Jones/Freleng; Mac and Tosh, the Goofy Gophers are

hosts; *Hillbilly Hare, Hippety Hopper, You Were Never Duckier.*

22. #1600; 3/.7/61; McKimson; Sylvester hosts and tells his son Junior some fairy tales; *The Turn-Tale Wolf; Paying the Piper; Beanstalk Bunny.*

23. #1601; 3/14/61; Jones/Freleng; More fun with Mac and Tosh who spend their time arguing while Bugs introduces the cartoons; *Big House Bunny, Canned Feud, Home Tweet Home.*

24. #1602; 3/21/61; Jones/Freleng, co-direced by Abe Levitow; Pepe Le Pew hosts the show. Yosemite Sam uses the Tasmanian Devil to get rid of Pepe, but his scent defeats them; *Mississippi Hare, Terrier Stricken; Cheese Chasers.*

25. #1603; McKimson; Bugs introduces host Daffy Duck, but Daffy is backstage being chased by the Tasmanian Devil; *Hen House Henry; Curtain Razor, Devil May Hare.*

26. #1604; Freleng/Jones; Rocky and Mugsy take over the show at gunpoint; *Hare We Go!; Foghorn Leghorn, Little Red Rodenthood.*

Second Season

1. Bad Time Story; #1624; 10/10/61; Jones/Freleng; Bugs Bunny reads fairy tales; *Bewitched Bunny, Robin Hood Daffy; Tweety & the Beanstalk.*

2. Satan's Waitin'; #1625; 10/17/61; Jones/Freleng; An elaboration on the short *Devil's Feud Cake* (1963): Sam dies, goes to Hades, but the Devil will spare him if he brings back the bunny; *Hare Trimmed, Roman Legion Hare, Sahara Hare.*

3. Daffy Doodling; #1626; 10/24/61; McKimson; Daffy outwits Bugs for the emcee job; *Hoppy Go Lucky, Lumber Jerks, Weasel While You Work.*

4. Omni-Puss; #1627; 10/31/61; Jones/Freleng, co-directed by Maurice Noble; Bugs Bunny lectures about cats; *Mouse-taken Identity, Kiss Me Cat, Heaven Scent.*

5. Tired and Feathered; #1628; 11/7/61; Jones/Freleng; Bugs Bunny speaks about birds; *Ready Set Zoom, Two Crows from Tacos, Snow Business.*

6. Man's Best Friend; #1642; 11/14/61; Jones/Freleng; A look at dogs; *Sheep Ahoy; Chow Hound; Pappy's Puppy.*

7. Ball Point Puns; #1629; 11/21/61;

Jones/Freleng; Penelope and Penbrooke (the red and black pens) perform for us; *Duck! Rabbit! Duck!, Claws for Alarm; Cracked Quack.*

8. The Unfinished Sympathy; #1630; 11/28/61; Jones/Freleng, co-directed by Maurice Noble and Robert Tronson; A program on music; *Pizzacato Pussycat; Baton Bunny; Three Little Bops.*

9. Prison to Prison; #1631; 12/5/61; Jones/Freleng, co-directed by Hawley Pratt; Bugs as Alfred Hitchcock speaks about crime; *Deduce You Say, The Hole Idea, Bugsy and Mugsy.*

10. Go Man Go; #1632; 12/12/61; McKimson; Bugs lectures about man, woman, and life in general; *There Auto Be a Law; Wild Wife; No Parking Hare.*

11. I'm Just Wild About Hare; #1633; 12/19/61; Jones/Freleng, co-directed by Maurice Noble and Tom Ray; Bugs has overslept, so he hosts the show from his home; *Stork Naked, Going Going Gosh, Touche and Go.*

12. Stage Couch; #1634; 12/26/61; Jones/Freleng, co-directed by Hawley Pratt; Sylvester tells psychiatrist Dr. Bugs of his obsession with Tweety; *Gift Wrapped, Tweet Dreams, Tweety's Circus, A Streetcat Named Sylvester.*

13. Do or Diet; #1635; 1/16/62; McKimson; Bugs talks about a carrot diet while heckling the Tasmanian Devil; *Bedevilled Rabbit, Stupor Duck, Little Boy Boo.*

14. Hare Brush; #1636; 1/23/62; Jones/Freleng, co-directed by Maurice Noble and Ken Harris; Bugs introduces Harry the Brush (from *Duck Amuck*) who explains his role in animation; *Feline Frame-up; Much Ado About Nutting; Duck Amuck.*

15. Is This a Life?; #1637; 2/13/62; Jones/Freleng; Bugs Bunny's life is reviewed with visits from friends and foes; *14 Carrot Rabbit, Robot Rabbit; High Diving Hare.*

16. De-Duck-Tive Story; #1638; 2/20/62; McKimson; Featuring Daffy Duck in his greatest detective roles; *Boston Quackie; The Super Snooper; Dime to Retire*

17. The Astro-Nuts; #1639; 3/13/62; Jones/Freleng, co-directed by Maurice Noble and Ken Harris; Porky Pig in a space suit introduces sci-fi cartoons; *Duck Dodgers in the 24 1/2 Century,*

Jumpin' Jupiter, Hareway to the Stars.
18. Vera's Cruise; #1640; 3/20/62; Jones/Freleng; Sylvester tells of his recent travels through Europe in pursuit of Tweety; *Dr. Jerkyl's Hide, Tweety's S.O.S.; Pizza Tweety Pie; All A-Bir-r-rd.*
19. Foreign Legion Leghorn; #1641; 6/19/62; McKimson; Foghorn is an inept soldier in the Foreign Legion. He explains to his sergeant what made him that way; *The Egg-Cited Rooster; Of Rice and Hen; Feather Dusted.*
20. Watch My Line; Jones/Freleng, co-directed by Hawley Pratt; An elaboration on *Rabbit Rampage*, in which Bugs suffers through various indignities from a mysterious animator, who turns out to be Elmer Fudd; *A Waggily Tale, Scrambled Aches, Rabbit Rampage.*
21. What's Up Dog?; #1644; 7/3/62; McKimson; More dog tales; *Awful Orphan; Don't Axe Me; Mixed Master.*
22. The Cat's Bah; #1645; 7/10/62; Jones/Freleng; Pepe Le Pew recalls the results of a a broken romance; *The*

Cat's Bah; Frigid Hare; Little Beau Pepe.
23. No Business Like Slow Business; #1646; 7/17/62; Jones/Freleng; Slowpoke Rodriguez and Speedy Gonzales are co-hosts; *Red Riding Hoodwinked; Barbary Coast; Double or Mutton.*
24. The Honeymousers; #1822; 7/24/62; McKimson; Bugs invites us backstage, offers us drinks, and invites us to watch a high-rated TV show, the Honeymousers; *Cheese It the Cat, Lighthouse Mouse, The Honeymousers.*
25. A Star Is Bored; #1648; 7/31/62; Jones/Freleng; co-directed by Maurice Noble and Tom Ray; Bugs shows us how animated cartoons are made, telling us confidentially, "I do Mel Blanc's voice!"; *Catty Corner, A Star Is Bored, There They Go-Go-Go.*
26. A Tale of Two Kitties; #1649; 8/7/62; McKimson; Sylvester and Junior discus mice, especially the "giant-size" kind; *Slap Hoppy Mouse; Gonzales Tamales; Cats Aweigh.*

That's Not All

No folks, that's *not* **all!** During it's sixty-year existence, in additon to its theatrical shorts, the Warner Bros. cartoon studio at various times became involved with other projects—for Warners and others—which clearly fall outside any standard categories.

It all began with Leon Schlesinger and his desire to diversify. In the late 1920s, Schlesinger was head of the thriving Pacific Art and Title, a successful company whose primary business was photographing main title artwork and intertitles for silent movies. Schlesinger was an entrepeneur and took a chance backing Warner Bros. in their gamble on sound movies with *The Jazz Singer*. When that film popularized talking picures, Schlesinger, fearing that the title card business would soon die out, accepted Warner Bros. reward of an opportunity to produce short subjects for their new programs of Vitaphone entertainment.

Schlesinger was asked to make films that would promote popular songs in the Warner Bros. new and growing music library and soon thereafter, in the fall of 1930, Schlesinger introduced "Looney Tunes" and "Spooney Melodies." The former series is the basis of this book, the latter was a short-lived and virtually forgotten collection of musical "Vitaphone Varieties." Typical of the series is *Cryin' for the Carolines*, an organ-logue featuring Milton Charles "The Singing Organist." Schlesinger used Frank Marsales to arrange the music and artist Neil McGuire to film abstract visuals using paper cut-outs and double exposures. Schlesinger's success with Harman-Ising's "Looney Tunes" led him to drop "Spooney Melodies" in 1931 for a second series of animated cartoons, "Merrie Melodies."

The producer concentrated on his popular cartoons for the next two years, but in 1933 Schlesinger tried his hand at feature films. He produced a season of John Wayne B-westerns for Warner Bros., with titles like *The Man from Monterey* and *Ride 'Em Cowboy*. One, *Haunted Gold*, featured an animated title sequence featuring cartoon bats and spiders. Schlesinger quickly realized how much easier it was to deal with his pen and ink stars than with flesh and blood ones, and thereafter stuck to his cartoon short subjects.

Schlesinger and his animation studio were independent of Warner Bros., and the producer actively sought outside work for his "boys." Harman-Ising contributed to Paramount's all-star *Alice in Wonderland* (1933), in a sequence of Tweedle-dum and Tweedle-dee telling Alice the story of "The Walrus and the Carpenter" in cartoon form. Bob Clampett directed a technicolor opening cartoon sequence in RKO's otherwise black-and-white Joe E. Brown comedy, *When's Your Birthday* (1937), involving the stars and planets that effect on the earth. In *The Big Broadcast of 1938* (Paramout) Bob Hope introduces orchestra leader Shep Fields who performs "Rippling Rhythm," which is visualized by a cartoon sequence. In it, an athropomorphic "Ripple" of water from the ocean lands on the beach, and jumps on the stage curtain to show Shep how to make music. The live-action musician lifts the Ripple on his baton, and the character plays various instruments including the piano, flute, and violin. The Ripple gets back to the animated beach and leads a chorus of female "ripples" in song.

In 1939, Republic Pictures utilized Leon's studio for their romantic comedy *She Married a Cop*. The story is set in a New York animation studio, "Fay-Fables," and is about an Irish policeman who is tricked into providing his wonderful singing voice for a new cartoon star, Paddy Pig! Schlesinger provided the brief animated sequence in which Paddy woos his girl Peggy in song.

The studio provided main title animation for a couple of Paramount pictures in the early forties. Jack Benny and Fred Allen were rivals on radio and in their motion picture *Love Thy Neighbor* (1940). The title had their "billing" fight it out for top spot, the "Benny" letters chasing the "Allen" letters during the entire credit roll. Preston Sturges' *The Lady Eve* (1941) begins with a serpent in a top hot who displays the film's title on various apples from the tree, then slithers down the trunk, passing the film's credits, winding into the "O" in "Preston," getting stuck on his waist and conked with the "Eve" apple when it falls from the tree.

In 1942, *Leon Schlesinger Presents Bugs Bunny* was the on-screen title for an animated trailer for war bonds, featuring their new star singing "Any Bonds Today." The film, directed by Robert Clampett and animated by Virgil Ross, Bob McKimson and Rod Scribner, was rushed into production shortly after Pearl Harbor and appeared in theaters early the next year. It featured Bugs, dressed like Uncle Sam asking in song "Any Bonds Today?" (written by Irving Berlin). Bugs does a Jolson imitation in blackface, then Porky and Elmer (the fat version) in uniform join Bugs in singing the finale.

Point Rationing of Foods, a six-minute black-and-white cartoon, was produced as a public service by Schlesinger for the government Office of Price Administration. Chuck Jones's unit worked on this special project on evenings and weekends over a three-week period. The film explains, via clever limited animation, reasons for product shortages during the war. The film was released to theaters in February 1943 and was widely praised for its ability to get the message across.

Schlesinger's studio produced a few amusing animated bits to Andrew L. Stone's comedy *Hi Diddle Diddle* (released by United Artists) starring Adolphe Menjou. An opening forward illustrates how reliable an animated male love bird is when attracted by another cute canary. In the finale, the cartoon illustrated wallpaper in Menjou's home comes to life, holds its ears, and runs into the distance when his family takes up singing.

In 1944, Schlesinger lent his star to another studio! Pre-dating *Who Framed Roger Rabbit* by 44 years, Bugs Bunny set a precedent by appearing on-screen with another animated star for another studio. In the George Pal Puppetoon *Jasper Goes Hunting* (1944), Jasper and the Scarecrow come upon a rabbit hole in the jungle. Pointing his gun at the opening, a cel-animated Bugs Bunny (animated by Robert McKimson) pops out to greet the model animated stars with "Eh, What's up, Doc?" (appropriately voiced by Mel Blanc). The scarecrow responds, "Why, It's Bugs Bunny." The rabbit looks around at the unfamiliar surrounding and comments, "Hey I must be in the wrong picture" and dives back into his hole.

In one scene in *Two Guys from Texas*, (1948) starring Jack Carson and Dennis Morgan, Carson tells his psychiatrist of his recurring dream—a Friz Freleng cartoon—that features himself as a shepherd playing a flute to his flock. A caricature of his rival Morgan sings "Everyday I Love You Just a Little Bit More," causing the sheep to swoon like bobbysoxers. The sheep leave Carson, but his carrot-chewing pal, Bugs Bunny, always comes out of a hole to give him some advice. (Bugs tells Carson "Always glad to help a chum!"—then turns to us and says, "Chump, that is.") Carson is disguised as a wolf and sings—but is booed by the sheep and chased by an obese Indian squaw (a running gag in the film).

Jack Carson shared another scene with Bugs Bunny in *My Dream Is Yours* (1949), a romantic comedy starring Doris Day. In this film, Carson is reading an Easter story to Day's young son and dreams a musical sequence (also supervised by Freleng) with Carson and Day singing and dancing with Bugs (dressed in top hat and tails). They do a swing variation on Liszt's Hungarian Rhapsody, asking "Freddy Get Ready." Tweety pops out of an Easter egg in a cameo.

The studio was hopping with activity in the late 1950s, with roughly twenty theatrical shorts a year, production on the weekly network Bugs Bunny Show, commercials for such clients as Skippy Peanut Butter, Kaiser Aluminum, Gillette (with Sharpie the Parrot), and Starkist (creating Charlie the Tuna).

The cartoon studio contributed to four episodes of the Bell System Science Series, a group of special science shows which, after their televised runs became a part of American high schools science classes throughout the 1960s and 1970s.

Gateways to the Mind (1958) is the story of the human senses, greatly enhanced by animation sequences written and directed by Chuck Jones and designed by Maurice Noble. Walking around a motion picture sound stage, Dr. Frank Baxter explains the senses to a group of stage hands, and is helped out by the presence of an animation director and his animator who illustrate various points. The main character animation involves a little man in the "control room" of our brain. He is assisted by Mercury who sends the senses to the brain. This film also features a surreal sequence which illustrates what it might be like without senses.

The Alphabet Conspiracy (1959) sends a live-action little girl into a dream, where she cavorts on a cartoon-like set representing a library and dances with animated letters. She meets the Mad Hatter (Hans Conreid) and the Jabberwock who are plotting to destroy the alphabet. Dr. Frank Baxter enters the scene and explains the science of linguistics. In his speech are three animated segments (directed by Friz Freleng, designed by Hawley Pratt, with voices by Daws Butler), first illustrating an early professor of speech giving his findings. Later, police question a proper gentle suspect and, by the way he pronounces words, pinpoints his home town location. Finally, the animated soundtrack explains how machines of today can read.

Two other shows, *The Thread of Life* (1960) and *About Time* (1962) mainly feature limited graphic animation (i.e. charts, maps, arrows) from Freleng's unit. *About Time* has two brief character animataion segments. In one, a captain and navigator of an old ship (voiced by Mel Blanc) figure their position by using time. The other shows a pair of astronauts flipping a coin to see who goes first in a rocket traveling at the speed of light.

And that's still not all. A few other bits of Warner miscellany are still out there. In 1938, the cartoon staff contributed to Warner Bros. blooper reel with a scene of Porky Pig, dressed as a carpenter, hammering a nail. He hits his thumb and stammers, "Son of a b ... Son of a bi-bi-bi ... Son of a *gun!*" He then stares at the camera, continuing, "Ha, Ha, Ha. You thought I was gonna say "Son of a *bitch*, didn't you?" The cartoon staff had their own blooper reel for three years (1937-1939) in which Leon Schlesinger, Chuck Jones, Bob Clampett, Robert McKimson, and just about everyone on staff appeared in live-action newsreel-like spot gags about the office. In 1972, film historian and filmmaker Joe Adamson obtained Warner Bros. permission to produce new animation of Bugs Bunny for a cameo appearance in his live action/animation short film *A Political Cartoon*.

Warner Bros. characters continue to be a presence in feature films through clips of classic cartoons such as *Duck Dodgers* in *Close Encounters of the Third Kind* (1977), the Road Runner in Spielberg's *The Sugarland Express* (1974), in movies like Peter

Bogdanovich's *What's Up Doc?* (1972), *Clean and Sober* (1988), and *any* film directed by Joe Dante. And, of course, the ultimate feature film homage to Warner Bros. Cartoons, *Who Framed Roger Rabbit* (1988), in which Daffy Duck plays a piano duet with Donald Duck, and Bugs Bunny heckles human actor Bob Hoskins while sharing the screen with Mickey Mouse.

The characters have also been kept alive on television, through Public Service Announcements, in commercials (for such products as Kentucky Fried Chicken and Hershey's Chocolate) and special guest appearances (Daffy Duck guested on *Pat Paulsen's Half a Comedy Hour* (Jan 22, 1970) and Bugs Bunny presented the Oscar for Best Animated Short on the 1987 Academy Awards Ceremony. Chuck Jones even directed a series of Road Runner spots for PBS' educational series, *The Electric Company*, and most recently, Steven Spielberg announced his teaming with Warner Bros to produce a new TV series based on a younger generation of Looney Tunes. Spielberg's 65-episode series, *Tiny Tunes*, will be syndicated in the fall of 1990—exactly sixty years after the released of *Sinkin' in the Bathtub*.

Listing Looney Tunes miscellania can be endless, but it proves that the Warner Bros. cartoons have become a beloved part of American culture—and that the characters' popularity and the studio's success will endure.

The following is a list of other significant shorts—unreleased subjects, films produced for the government, featurettes, made-for-TV shorts, and other miscellaneous odds and ends.

BOSKO THE TALK-INK KID

1929; Pilot film produced by Hugh Harman and Rudolf Ising.
This short pilot film introduced Bosko and helped Harman and Ising establish their studio. On screen, Rudolph Ising is shown sitting at his drawing table and sketching Bosko, who begins to move and talk. Rudy asks his creation why he feels so good, and Bosko responds, "Yeah, I just got out of the *pen.*"

Bosko performs a tap dance, and plays "Sonny Boy" on the piano. Bosko's head pops off his neck, but remains attached by a coil spring. Bosko spins his piano stool to reattach himself. Rudy sticks his pen point on Bosko's rear end, pulls the character into the pen, and deposits him into his inkwell. Bosko bids us goodbye, "Well, so long, folks! See you all later!"

BOSKO AND HONEY

1932; Directed by Hugh Harman; Drawn by Rollin Hamilton and Robert MacKimson; Music by Frank Marsales.
Honey is teaching Wilber to play "In the Shade of the Old Apple Tree" on the violin. Honey telephones Bosko, but he's sleeping like a log. Bruno answers the ringing phone, and Honey orders him to wake Bosko. When Bosko hears Honey's voice he awakens. She invites him over, and tells him to "make it

snappy." Bosko and Bruno bicycle over, and as Bosko approaches, he hears violin music and pulls out his saxophone. Honey greets him in song on the balcony. Bosko takes Honey for a ride on his bike, Bruno tagging along. Bruno sniffs a tree, but the tree kicks him away. Sitting with Honey on a log, Bosko whispers something in her ear. Honey is insulted, but before they can argue, it begins to thunder and rain. Lightning strikes Bruno on the behind. Bosko and Honey wait out the storm under a stone bridge, but a water spout drenches Bosko, causing Honey to get the last laugh.

Private Snafu

From 1943 to 1945, Warner Bros. Cartoons produced 26 "Private Snafu" cartoons for the U.S. Army Signal Corps. They were used as part of the *Army-Navy Screen Magazine*, a film series shown at military bases around the world. Each cartoon is approximately three minutes long and in black-and-white. The cartoons utilized all of Warner's cartoon directors and voice artists and Carl Stalling's music.

Private Snafu is the worst soldier in the army, the one who does everything wrong, even with the help of his magical friend Technical Fairy First Class. The films illustrate in a humorous way what *not* to do to stay alive in the Armed Forces. Many of the films were written by Theodore Geisel (Dr. Suess), and a few are done in rhyme.

COMING SNAFU *June 1943; Directed by Chuck Jones.* This film introduces Private Snafu (*Situation Normal: All Fouled Up*) in the form of a "coming attractions" trailer. The narrator explains, "He's the goofiest soldier in the Army," but he can also be found in the Artillery, the Tank Corps, the Air Corps, and other branches of the military.

GRIPES *July, 1943; Directed by I. Freleng.* When Private Snafu complains about doing KP, waiting in line, and other military procedures, Technical Fairy First Class grants his wish for power. With Snafu in charge of the base, the soldiers become lazy and are unprepared for a surprise attack by the Nazis.

SPIES *Aug, 1943; Directed by Chuck Jones.* Though boasting (in rhyme) about being able to keep military secrets, Snafu slowly blurts out information within earshot of enemy agents (including a lady spy with a radio transmitter in her brassiere). Adolf torpedoes Snafu's ship, sending the soldier to Hades.

THE GOLDBRICK *Sept, 1943; Directed by Frank Tashlin.* The "Goldbrick," a fat, lazy version of Technical Fairy First Class encourages Snafu to goof off while the others drill and do work. Snafu pretends to be sick and limps into "Honorable Booby Trap Hospital" where he is attacked by the Japanese enemy.

THE INFANTRY BLUES *Sept, 1943; Directed by Chuck Jones* When Snafu sings the blues about being in the infantry, Technical Fairy First Class puts the soldier in the Tank Corps. where he runs amok inside an out-of-control tank. Zapped in the Navy, he quickly becomes seasick. In the Air Corps, he crashes a plane into a mountain. Snafu learns that all branches of service are tough.

FIGHTING TOOLS *Oct, 1943; Directed by Robert Clampett.* A Nazi soldier captures Private Snafu who keeps his weapon in such filthy shape that only mud squirts out. Snafu's machine gun, overheats and melts and his artillery gun is loaded with pots, pans, and junk. Snafu tries to escape via jeep, but it won't start. Snafu ends up naked, standing in a Nazi prison camp.

THE HOME FRONT *Nov 1943, Directed by Frank Tashlin.* Private Snafu, stationed in the Arctic, imagines the good times his family is having back home. Technical Fairy First Class shows him his dad building tanks, his mom planting a Victory Garden, Grandpa riveting battleships, and his girl joining the WACs.

RUMORS *Dec, 1943; Directed by Friz Freleng.* Private Snafu mistakes an innocent comment for fact and starts a rumor which spreads throughout the base. Rumors are personified by gremlins which overrun the camp, causing a quarantine for "rumoritis."

BOOBY TRAPS *Jan 1944, Directed by Robert Clampett.* Lost in the desert, Private Snafu encounters a harem filled with scantily-clad women. Snafu attempts to serenade the beauties with "Those Endearing Young Charms" on a piano which has been rigged to explode when a certain key is pressed.

SNAFUPERMAN *March, 1944; Directed by I. Freleng.* Technical Fairy First Class transforms Private Snafu into a super-powered "Snafuperman." Snafu almost destroys the U.S. troops through his reluctance to study manuals, maps, and charts.

PRIVATE SNAFU VS. MALARIA MIKE *Mar 1944, Directed by Chuck Jones.* A malaria-infected mosquito attacks Private Snafu who refused to use insect repellent, netting, and old-fashioned horse sense.

A LECTURE ON CAMOUFLAGE *Apr, 1944; Directed by Chuck Jones.* Technical Fairy First Class gives a lecture, using Private Snafu as a visual aid, demonstrating camouflage techniques.

GAS *May, 1944; Directed by Chuck Jones.* Private Snafu is attacked by an anthropomorphic gas cloud (marvelously animated by Bob Cannon). Bugs Bunny makes a cameo appearance.

THE CHOW HOUND *June, 1944; Directed by Frank Tashlin.* A bull symbolizes the food the soldiers need to eat. Private Snafu represents soldiers who hoard food and waste it. The bull butts Snafu into orbit.

CENSORED *July, 1944; Directed by Frank Tashlin.* All of Private Snafu's letters to his girlfriend are returned to him cut up and censored. Snafu enlists Technical Fairy First Class to deliver his letter, and soon the military secrets contained within are spread to the Japanese enemy who ambush the Americans.

OUTPOST *Aug, 1944; Directed by Chuck Jones.* Private Snafu is bored with his assignment on a deserted island. His companion, a sea gull, finds a Japanese ration can. Snafu's routine report about the can provides information which leads to the defeat of the enemy fleet.

PAY DAY *Sept, 1944; Directed by I. Freleng.* Private Snafu foolishly squanders his pay on souvenirs in the Middle East, on wine and women in the Caribbean, and on a totem pole in the Arctic. Technical Fairy First Class points out how he has no money left for his future.

TARGET SNAFU *Oct, 1944; Directed by I. Freleng.* Malaria mosquitoes are shown preparing for battle. They train through an obstacle course

of fly swatters, DDT spray, fly paper, and maneuvers through netting. They attack Private Snafu and receive a medal of honor.

THE THREE BROTHERS *Sept 1944; Directed by I. Freleng.* Bored with sorting shoes, Private Snafu is shown by Technical Fairy First Class what his brothers are doing. Tarfu (*Things Are Really Fouled Up*) is cleaning a pigeon coop and Fubar (*Fouled Up Beyond All Repair*) is the target for attack dogs. Snafu realizes that his job is important.

IN THE ALEUTIANS *February, 1945; Directed by Chuck Jones.* Spot gags about "the conditions which prevail" in the Aleutians, a string of islands that are the back door to the United States and the front door to the Japanese enemy.

IT'S MURDER SHE SAYS *May, 1945; Directed by Chuck Jones.* Anophels Annie, a haggard old malarial mosquito, recounts her story and how she used to have the world on a string. She started her decline when the Army wised up, put up netting, and devising chemicals to kill her. But with guys like Private Snafu around, she can survive.

HOT SPOT *July, 1945; Directed by I. Freleng.* The Devil spies on Private Snafu and the U.S. troops in Iran transporting war supplies to our allies in Russia. The Devil enjoys the local hot weather conditions and explains the problems of working in the heat.

OPERATION SNAFU *Oct, 1945; Directed by I. Freleng.* Private Snafu sneaks into the heavily guarded Japanese military headquarters. Disguised as a geisha girl, he outwits a general and steals a secret document.

NO BUDDY ATOLL *Oct, 1945; Directed by Chuck Jones.* Shipwrecked Private Snafu and a Japanese General fight over possession of a small deserted island.

COMING HOME *Unreleased; Directed by Chuck Jones.* Private Snafu comes home and tells Army secrets to everyone in town. Because of his loose lips, his troop is ambushed.

SECRETS OF THE CARIBBEAN *Unreleased; Directed by Chuck Jones.* Private Snafu, stationed in the Caribbean to protect the Panama Canal from the enemy meets the local Flora (a beautiful island girl), is beaten by giant insects, and is attacked by howler monkeys and carnivorous plants.

SO MUCH FOR SO LITTLE

1949; A Warner Bros. Cartoon produced for the Federal Security Agency Public Health Service. Directed by Charles M. Jones; Animation by Ben Washam, Ken Harris, Phil Monroe, Lloyd Vaughn; Layouts and Backgrounds by Robert Gribbroek, Paul Julian and Peter Alvarado; Musical Direction by Carl Stalling.

A theatrically released educational film about health, it follows average man Johnny Jones from infancy to old age. Starting with the immunization shots babies should receive, the film shows the perils of disease that can strike at various time in one's life, and how the U.S. Health Department is there to serve—at the 1949 cost of 3¢ a week.

This handsome production depicts childhood diseases as way-out alien disease creatures. The film is basically illustrated narration, but filled with the usual strong Jones poses and imagination.

ORANGE BLOSSOMS FOR VIOLET

May 24, 1952; Vitaphone Novelties; Written by I. Freleng and Charles M. Jones; Music by Howard Jackson; Film Editor: DeLeon Anthony; Voice Characterization by Mel Blanc.

A cast of trained monkeys, in costumes and on miniature sets, are involved in a classic melodrama. The rich and spoiled Harvey and the poor but true Fred are rivals for lovely Violet. Violet is kidnapped, but Fred comes to the rescue in an exciting car chase, and then battles his rival on top of a hot-air balloon. This live-action short subject was commissioned by Warner Bros. utilizing stock footage (most likely from the Mack Sennett library of silent comedies the studio had bought a few years earlier). Chuck Jones and Friz Freleng were asked to edit this footage and write humorous dialogue. They employed Mel Blanc, Bea Benedaret, and Robert C. Bruce to provide voices.

A HITCH IN TIME

1955; Special production for the United States Air Force, #1382; Written and Directed by Chuck Jones; Animation by Ken Harris, Gerry Chinquy, Ben Washam, Abe Levitow, and Richard Thompson; Layouts by Ernest Nordli; Backgrounds by Philip DeGuard; VC by Mel Blanc; Musical Direction by Milt Franklyn.

After four years in the Air Force, airman John McRogers dreams about his future. He's contemplating the advantages all civilians take for granted: a solid gold cadillac, a modern penthouse apartment, a good job, and a beautiful wife. John is interrupted by "Grogan," Technical Gremlin First Class. Expecting to get a lecture on why he should reenlist, John is surprised to find the Gremlin is leaving too. John suggests they get their discharge papers together, but Tech Gremlin is worried that John will "get all soft and sign up again." The Gremlin decides to brief John, so he won't have second thoughts. Zapping in a a two-screen TV set—one screen marked "Civilian," the other marked "Air Force"—they compare pay, jobs, and retirement benefits. John and the Gremlin decide to re-inlist, and the Gremlin's magic wand gives them both officer's uniforms.

90 DAY WONDERING

1956; Special Production for the U.S. Army, #1394; Directed by Chuck Jones; Story by Michael Maltese; Animation by Ben Washam, Abe Levitow, Ken Harris, and Richard Thompson; Layouts by Maurice Noble; Musical Direction by Milt Franklyn; VC by Mel Blanc and Daws Butler.

Ex-soldier Ralph Phillips runs like a tornado from his army camp, Fort Itude, screaming, "I'm a civilian, I'm ME again." Zooming into a clothing store for some civilian clothes, he jets back to his hometown, where his family and friends welcome him with open arms. But things are not all well. When Ralph goes to the old hangout, the malt shop, the teenagers inside make him feel like an old man. All his old girl friends have their own families. Sitting on a park bench, wondering if maybe he should reinlest, he is visited by Pete, the civilian's friend (a little red-haired slicker) and Re-Pete (a pixie-like army recruiter). The two characters compare life in and out of the army. Charged with renewed enthusiasm, Ralph runs back to the army base.

DRAFTY, ISN'T IT?

1957, Special Production for the U.S. Army #1478; Written and Directed by Chuck Jones; Character Layouts by Abe Levitow; Animation by Ken Harris, Richard Thompson, and Ben Washam; Layouts and Backgrounds by Maurice Noble and Philip DeGuard; Musical Direction by Milt Franklyn; Voice Characterizations by Daws Butler.

One night, in a drafty bedroom, Ralph Phillips is dreaming about his future—being an astronaut, winning the $64,000 Question, going on a world tour—and is interrupted by the spectre of a large black shadow. A pixie-like army man, Willie N. List, uses an "ACME Anti-Nightmare Machine," to enter Ralph's dream and compare reality and "comic-strip stereotypes" of military life. He convinces Ralph that his wildest dreams can become reality by joining the "Reserved for You" program.

THE ADVENTURES OF THE ROAD RUNNER

Copyright date June 2, 1962; Directed by Chuck Jones; Co-Directed by Maurice Noble and Tom Ray; Supervising Animators Ken Harris, Dick Thomas, Ben Washam; Story by John Dunn, Chuck Jones, and Michael Maltese; Design by Maurice Noble; Backgrounds by Philip DeGuard; Animation by Dick Thompson, Ben Washam, Ken Harris, Tom Ray, and Bob Bransford; Special Effects Animation by Harry Love; Film Editors: Treg Brown and Joe Flaherty; Voice Characterization by Mel Blanc, Dick Beals and Nancy Wible (uncredited: Richard Tufeld); Music and song "Out on the Desert" by Milt Franklyn. 26 minutes.

Shortly after the success of *The Bugs Bunny Show*, Warner Bros. commissioned a pilot for *The Road Runner Show*. Though a series never made it to prime time, the pilot was outfitted with opening titles and credits (over Jones pencil sketches of the Road Runner and the Coyote), and released to theaters as a featurette, on a double bill with *Lad: A Dog* on Memorial Day Weekend, 1962. This film combines new animataion with footage from two shorts, *From A to Z-Z-Z-Z* (1954) and *To Beep or Not to Beep* (released a year later in 1963). The featurette was later reedited into two unreleased short subjects, *Zip Zip Hooray* and *Roadrunner a Go Go* (which have been shown on television).

The film begins with sunrise on the prairie. A chorus sings "Out on the Desert" introducing the Road Runner and his foe, the Coyote. When the Coyote falls backward off a cliff, the image freeze frames, and the Coyote (voiced by Mel Blanc) explains that he has "a photographic record" of his activities via a series of strategically placed movie cameras. With his projector, we review what went wrong with his latest attempt.

This is all being watched by two little boys (Ralph Phillips, voiced by Dick Beals, in a baseball cap, the other boy in a cowboy hat) who stare at the video screen and discuss the two cartoon characters. "Sometimes I wish he'd catch him," says Ralph. "If he caught him there wouldn't be any more Road Runner. You wouldn't like that, would you?" replies his level-headed friend. A commercial for ACME Batman Outfits (narrated by Richard Tufeld) is demonstrated by the Coyote. The two boys discuss daydreams. "I sometimes think I'm the Road Runner. Beep Beep Zip-Dang!" says Ralph. The other boy recommends a psychiatrist—himself. Leading Ralph to the living room sofa ("I just hope we're not too late") he lays Phillips on the couch while he sits on a chair taking notes. "Okay now just relax and start by telling me some of your simpletons." Ralph recalls his other daydreams, via the entire cartoon *From A to Z-Z-Z-Z* (1954).

The boys return to the TV. Ralph wonders why the Coyote "wants to eat the Road Runner in the first place." The Coyote stops his chase to talk to the boy directly from the screen, telling him, "the Road Runner is to the tastebuds of a coyote what caviar, champagne, fillet mignon, and chocolate fudge are to the tastebuds of a man." He shows us a diagram labeling the different parts of the bird in delicious flavors, including banana, vanilla, salami, chop suey, double martini (very dry) etc.

PHILBERT (THREE'S A CROWD)

April, 1963; Directed by Richard D. Donner; Story by Friz Freleng; Screenplay by Richard DeRoy; Animation Direction by Friz Freleng; Animation by Art Babbit, Virgil Ross, Ken Harris, Bob Matz, Ben Washam, and Lee Halpern; Animation Co-Direction by Hawley Pratt and Gerry Chiniquy; Film Editor: Donald Tait; Title Song by Sammy Fain and Sy Miller; Music by Howard Jackson; Cast: William Schallert, Joanna Barnes. Voice of Philbert: Trust Howard. Black and white. 26 minutes.

In 1961, Friz Freleng conceived of a TV series combining live action and animation. Warner Bros. produced the pilot and it was sold to ABC, scheduled to air Sunday nights at 8:00 pm, but executive politics between ABC and Warner Bros. cancelled all Warner Bros. programming from the network in the early sixties. The program was released as a theatrical featurette in 1963.

A bachelor cartoonist named Griff (William Schallert) lives with his mischievous six-inch cartoon alter ego Philbert. Like Wilbur on *Mr. Ed*, Griff keeps him a secret from everyone.

In the pilot episode, "Three's a Crowd," Griff invites his new girlfriend, Angela (Joanna Barnes) over for dinner. Philbert fears it will break up their "relationship" so he takes drastic action. First he draws a mustache on Angela's picture; next adds hot sauce to her special recipe. Finally, Philbert puts sleeping pill in Griff's drink, causing him to yawn while trying to whisper sweet nothings. Insulted, Angela walks out on him. in the end, Griff thanks Philbert for preventing a terrible mistake.

Other notes; Art Babbit animated the opening titles, Philbert coming off a comic book cover, then dancing on Griff's desk with his office supplies. An early sequence shows Philbert swimming in the fish tank, and getting a sun tan under his desk lamp.

Richard Donner, later directed the feature films *The Omen, Superman, The Goonies,* and *Lethal Weapon* among many others.

ROADRUNNER A GO GO

The Road Runner; 1965; MM; Animation by Ken Harris, Dick Thompson, Ben Washam, Tom Ray, and Bob Bransford; Story by John Dunn; Layout by Maurice Noble; Backgrounds by Philip DeGuard; Film Editor: Treg Brown; Voice Characterization by Mel Blanc; Musical Direction by Milt Franklyn.

An excerpt from *The Adventures of the Road Runner* (1962), featuring the song "Out in the Desert"; the Coyote explaining how he can avoid his last fall; and the catapult gags. Never released theatrically.

ZIP ZIP HOORAY

The Road Runner; 1965; MM; Animation by Ken Harris, Dick Thompson, Ben Washam, Tom Ray, and Bob Bransford; Story by John Dunn; Layout by Maurice Noble; Backgrounds by Philip DeGuard; Film Editor: Treg Brown; Voice Characterization by Mel Blanc; Musical Direction by Milt Franklyn.

Another edited cut down from *The Adventures of the Road Runner* (1962) fashioned with main titles (sans director credit, but unreleased theatrically. The Coyote chases the Road Runner past a Warner-Bros.-shaped road sign.

THE DOOR

June 1, 1968; A presentation of the Campbell-Silver-Cosby Corporation; Produced and Directed by Ken Mundie; Associate Producer: Les Goldman; Music by Clark "Mumbles" Terry.

This is an independantly produced animated film (bearing a 1967 copyright notice) purchased and released by Warner Bros. in 1968. Since this unusual one-shot was animated, the distribution department sold it as part of their group of cartoon shorts. To a skat-singing jazz soundtrack, two American Indians (rendered in watercolor) go hunting. One discovers a door containing images of the future (live action clips of urban blight and war). An atomic explosion ends the scene.

BUGS BUNNY'S CHRISTMAS CAROL

1979; Directed by Friz Freleng; Originally part of the TV special Bugs

383

Bunny's Looney Christmas Tales.
Yosemite Sam is Scrooge, Porky Pig is
Bob Crachet, and Bugs Bunny is a
wacky good samaritan who tries to
teach Sam the meaning of Christmas.

FREEZE FRAME

1979; Directed by Chuck Jones;
Originally part of the TV
special Bugs Bunny's Looney Christmas
Tales
The Coyote (Grotesques Appetitus)
once again chases the Road Runner
(Semper Food-Ellus). Consulting a
book titled "Everything YOu've
Always Wanted to Know About Road-
runners (But Were Afraid to Ask)" he
discovers the bird's weak point—
"Roadrunners love the hot desert.
They hate cold and snow are are easy
to catch in snow drifts." From the
ACME "Whole Roadrunner Catalog"
he orders the ACME Little Giant
Snow-Cloud Seeder ("Makes instant
snow! Capacity: 2,000 blizzards.")

FRIGHT BEFORE CHRISTMAS

1979; Directed by Friz Freleng;
Originally part of the TV special Bugs
Bunny's Looney Christmas Tales.
Over the North Pole, on Christmas eve,
the Tasmanian Devil breaks free of a
crate on an airplane, and jumps out.
He lands in Santa's suit (which was
hanging out to dry), hops into his
sleigh, and takes off.
  Meanwhile, Bugs Bunny is reading
"The Night Before Christmas" to his
nephew Clyde when the Tasmanian
Devil lands of Bugs's roof and spins
down the chimney.The rabbit gets wise
and heckles the Devil, but the beast
eats everything in his house—including a self-inflating rubber life raft,

THE YOLKS ON YOU

1980; Directed by Friz Freleng;
Originally produced for the TV special
Daffy Duck's Easter Special (1980)
Foghorn Leghorn is the foreman of an
egg farm. He is particularly hard on
Miss Prissy, who hasn't laid a good egg
in years. She lays a golden egg, but
fearing she's done wrong again, tosses
it out. Meanwhile, buddies Daffy Duck
and Sylvester are looking for leftovers
in the trashcan. Prissy's golden egg rolls
toward them and they battle over it.

THE CHOCOLATE CHASE

1980; Directed by Friz Freleng;
Originally produced for the TV special
Daffy Duck's Easter Special (1980)
Daffy Duck takes on the job of guarding a chocolate factory in Mexico. The
mayor of the poor Mexican mice offers
Daffy money to buy chocolate Easter
bunnies for their children. Daffy takes
their money and tells them to scram.
The mice enlist the aid of Speedy Gonzales to get their chocolate bunnies.
Daffy chases Speedy inside the factory,
but winds up flattened on the machinery and splashed in the chocolate.

DAFFY FLIES NORTH

1980; Directed by Friz Freleng;
Originally produced for the TV special
Daffy Duck's Easter Special (1980).
Looking for an easier way north, Daffy
Duck decides to hitchhike, but the first
truck he stops is full of hunters and
hounds. Sneaking a ride on the back of
a moving van, he falls off an easy chair,
and into the lake. The duck tries to
mount a stubborn horse. Daffy tries to
swing a la Errol Flynn onto the horses
back, but lands on an angry bull
instead. The bull chases Daffy to the
airport, where the duck winds up in the
deep south—South America.

PORTRAIT OF THE ARTIST AS
A YOUNG BUNNY

1980; Directed by Chuck Jones;
Originally part of the 1980 TV Special
Bugs Bunny's Bustin' Out All Over.
Bugs Bunny recalls his youth heckling
a young Elmer Fudd. Fudd tells us to
be "vewwy vewwy quiet" while he
hunts, and young Bugs ask him "what's
in it for me?" Elmer gets wise and pop-
guns the wabbit, who performs a classic
death scene. Elmer chases the wacky
wabbit off a cliff—but floats instead of
falling off the mountain ("we haven't
studied gravity yet"). Returning to the
present, Bugs bets "Elmer and I are
the youngest people to ever start chasing each other."

SOUP OR SONIC

1980; Directed by Chuck Jones;
Originally part of the TV special Bugs
Bunny's Bust Out All Over.
The Coyote chases the Road Runner
all over the desert, this time using a

with a firecracker; giant flypaper; and ACME Explosive Tennis Balls. The Coyote chases the Road Runner through a pipe line which gets smaller and smaller, shrinking the duot. When they run through the other way, the Road Runner returns to normal height but the Coyote remains tiny. The Coyote grabs the bird's gaint leg, but realizes it's not going to work. He hold up a sign toward us, "Okay wise guys, you always wanted me to catch him. Now what do I do?"

SPACED OUT BUNNY
1980; Directed by Chuck Jones; Originally part of the TV Special Bugs Bunny's Busting Out All Over
Marvin Martian and Hugo, the abominable snowman, capture the earth creature Bugs Bunny using an ACME Rack and Pinion Super Tranquilizing Carrot. On Mars, Bugs turns the tables on his captors turning Marvin into a "Mickey Martian" wristwatch, and tricking Hugo into practicing his frisbee toss—with Bugs aboard the flying saucer—in the direction of earth.

DUCK DODGERS AND THE RETURN OF THE 24½ CENTURY
Daffy Duck, Porky Pig, Marvin Martian; 1980; MM; Produced and Directed by Chuck Jones; Written and Directed by Mike Maltese and Chuck Jones; Production Designed by Maurice Noble and Ron Dias; Master Animators: Phil Monroe; Manny Perez, Irv Anderson, Ben Washam, and Lloyd Vaughan; Key Assistant: Retta Davidson; Graphics by Don Foster; Voice Charactizations by Mel Blanc; Musical Direction by Dean Elliot.
The original 1953 *Duck Dodgers in the 24½ Century* had been a favorite of George Lucas, and many theaters booked that cartoon with showings of *Star Wars*. Warner Bros. asked Chuck Jones to produce a sequel for theatrical release. When he finished this film, Warners had second thoughts, and the cartoon instead became the centerpiece of a TV special, *Daffy Duck's Thanks-for-Giving SPECIAL* (1981).

Duck Dodgers (Daffy Duck) and his

are assigned to protect the Rack and Pinion Molecule—the only substance which can polish yo-yos. Meanwhile, Marvin Martian, about to solve Earth's fuel problem by blowing the planet to bits.

CHARACTER INDEX
BUGS BUNNY

What's Up, Doc? (1950)
Eight Ball Bunny (1950)
Hillbilly Hare (1950)
Bunker Hill Bunny (1950)
Bushy Hare (1950)
The Rabbit Of Seville (1951)
Hare We Go (1951)
Rabbit Every Monday (1951)
Bunny Hugged (1951)
Fair-Haired Hare (1951)
Rabbit Fire (1951)
French Rarebit (1951)
His Hare-Raising Tale (1951)
Ballot Box Bunny (1951)
Big Top Bunny (1951)
Operation: Rabbit (1952)
Foxy By Proxy (1952)
Fourteen Carrot Rabbit (1952)
Water, Water Every Hare (1952)
Hasty Hare (1952)
The Oily Hare (1952)
Rabbit Seasoning (1952)
Rabbit's Kin (1952)
Hare Lift (1952)
Forward March Hare (1953)
Upswept Hare (1953)
Southern Fried Rabbit (1953)
Hare Trimmed (1953)
Bully For Bugs (1953)
Duck, Rabbit, Duck (1953)
Robot Rabbit (1953)
Captain Hareblower (1954)
Bugs And Thugs (1954)
No Parking Hare (1954)
Devil May Hare (1954)
Bewitched Bunny (1954)
Yankee Doodle Bugs (1954)
Lumber Jack Rabbit (1954)
Baby Buggy Bunny (1954)
Beanstalk Bunny (1955)
Sahara Hare (1955)
Hare Brush (1955)
Rabbit Rampage (1955)
This Is A Life? (1955)
Hyde And Hare (1955)
Knight-mare Hare (1955)
Roman Legion Hare (1955)
Bugs Bonnets (1956)
Broomstick Bunny (1956)
Rabbitson Crusoe (1956)
Napoleon Bunny-part (1956)
Barbary Coast Bunny (1956)
Half Fare Hare (1956)
A Star Is Bored (1956)
Wideo Wabbit (1956)
To Hare Is Human (1956)
Ali Baba Bunny (1957)
Bedevilled Rabbit (1957)
Piker's Peak (1957)
What's Opera, Doc? (1957)
Bugsy And Mugsy (1957)
Show Biz Bugs (1957)
Rabbit Romeo (1957)
Hare-less Wolf (1957)
Hare-way To The Stars (1958)
Now Hare This (1958)
Knighty Knight Bugs (1958)
Pre-Hysterical Hare (1958)
Baton Bunny (1958)
Hare-abian Nights (1959)
Apes Of Wrath (1959)
Backwoods Bunny (1959)
Wild And Woolly Hare (1959)
Bonanza Bunny (1959)
A Witch's Tangled Hare (1959)
People Are Bunny (1959)
Horse Hare (1960)
Person To Bunny (1960)
Rabbit's Feat (1960)
From Hare To Heir (1960)
Lighter Than Hare (1960)
The Abominable Snow Rabbit (1961)
Compressed Hare (1961)
Prince Violent (1961)
Wet Hare (1962)
Bill Of Hare (1962)
Shishkabugs (1962)
Devil's Feud Cake (1963)
The Million-Hare (1963)
Hare-Breath Hurry (1963)
The Unmentionables (1963)
Mad As A Mars Hare (1963)
Transylvannia 6-5000 (1963)
The Dumb Patrol (1964)
Dr. Devil And Mr. Hare (1964)
The Iceman Ducketh (1964)
False Hare (1964)
Bugs Bunny's Christmas Carol (1979)

Fright Before Christmas (1979)
Portrait Of The Artist As A Young Bunny (1980)
Spaced Out Bunny (1980)

BUGS BUNNY CAMEOS

All are Warner cartoon shorts unless otherwise noted.

Patient Porky (1940)
Crazy Cruise (1942)
Porky Pigs Feat (1943)
Gas (1944) Pvt Snafu
The Three Brothers (1944) Pvt Snafu
Jasper Goes Hunting (1944) Paramount Puppetoon
Odor-Able Kitty (1945)
The Goofy Gophers (1947)
Two Guys From Texas (1948) Warner Bros. feature
My Dream Is Yours (1949) Warner Bros. feature
Duck Amuck (1953)
Who Framed Roger Rabbit (1988) Touchstone/Amblin feature

PORKY PIG

I Haven't Got A Hat (1935)
Golddiggers Of '49 (1935)
Boom Boom (1936)
The Blow-Out (1936)
Westward Whoa! (1936)
Plane Dippy (1936)
Fish Tales (1936)
Shanghaied Shipmates (1936)
Porky's Pet (1936)
Porky The Rainmaker (1936)
Porky's Poultry Plant (1936)
Milk And Money (1936)
Porky's Moving Day (1936)
Little Beau Porky (1936)
The Village Smithy (1936)
Porky Of The Northwoods (1936)
Porky The Wrestler (1937)
Porky's Road Race (1937)
Picador Porky (1937)
Porky's Romance (1937)
Porky's Duck Hunt (1937)
Porky And Gabby (1937)
Porky's Building (1937)
Porky's Super Service (1937)
Porky's Badtime Story (1937)
Porky's Railroad (1937)
Get Rich Quick Porky (1937)
Porky's Garden (1937)
Rover's Rival (1937)
The Case Of The Stuttering Pig (1937)
Porky's Double Trouble (1937)
Porky's Hero Agency (1937)
Porky's Poppa (1938)
Porky at The Crocadero (1938)
What Price Porky? (1938)
Porky's Phoney Express (1938)
Porky's 5 & 10 (1938)
Porky's Hare Hunt (1938)
Injun Trouble (1938)
Porky The Fireman (1938)
Porky's Party (1938)
Porky's Spring Planting (1938)
Porky And Daffy (1938)
Wholly Smoke (1938)
Porky In Wackyland (1938)
Porky's Naughty Nephew (1938)
Porky In Egypt (1938)
The Daffy Doc (1938)
Porky The Gob (1938)
The Lone Stranger And Porky (1939)
It's An Ill Wind (1939)
Porky's Tire Trouble (1939)
Porky's Movie Mystery (1939)
Chicken Jitters (1939)
Porky And Teabiscuit (1939)
Kristopher Kolumbus Jr.(1939)
Polar Pals (1939)
Scalp Trouble (1939)
Old Glory (1939)
Porky's Picnic (1939)
Wise Quacks (1939)
Porky's Hotel (1939)
Jeepers Creepers (1939)
Naughty Neigbors (1939)
Pied Piper Porky (1939)
Pied Piper Porky (1939)
Porky The Giant Killer (1939)
The Film Fan (1939)
Porky's Last Stand (1940)
Africa Squeaks (1940)
Ali Baba Bound (1940)
Pilgrim Porky (1940)

Slap Happy Porky (1940)
You Oughta Be In Pictures (1940)
Porky's Poor Fish (1940)
The Chewin' Bruin (1940)
Porky's Baseball Broadcast (1940)
Patient Porky (1940)
Calling Dr. Porky (1940)
Prehistoric Porky (1940)
The Sour Puss (1940)
Porky's Hired Hand (1940)
The Timid Torreador (1940)
Porky's Snooze Reel (1941)
Porky's Bear Facts (1941)
Porky's Preview (1941)
Porky's Ant (1941)
A Coy Decoy (1941)
Porky's Prize Pony (1941)
Meet John Doughboy (1941)
We The Animals Squeak (1941)
The Henpecked Duck (1941)
Notes To You (1941)
Robinson Crusoe, Jr. (1941)
Porky's Pooch (1941)
Porky's Mightnight Matinee (1941)
Porky's Pastry Pirates (1942)
Who's Who In The Zoo (1942)
Porky's Cafe (1942)
My Favorite Duck (1942)
Confusions Of A Nutsy Spy (1942)
Yankee Doodle Daffy (1943)
Porky Pig's Feat (1943)
A Corny Concerto (1943)
Tom Turk And Daffy (1944)
Tick Tock Tuckered (1944)
The Swooner Crooner (1944)
Duck Soup To Nuts (1944)
Slighty Daffy (1944)
Brother Brat (1944)
Trap Happy Porky (1945)
Wagon Heels (1945)
Baby Bottleneck (1946)
Daffy Doodles (1946)
Kitty Kornered (1946)
Mouse Menace (1946)
One Meat Brawl (1947)
Little Orphan Airedale (1947)
Daffy Duck Slept Here (1948)
Nothing But The Tooth (1948)
The Pest Who Came To Dinner (1948)
Riff Raffy Daffy (1948)
Scaredy Cat (1948)
The Awful Orphan (1949)
Porky Chops (1949)
Paying The Piper (1949)
Daffy Duck Hunt (1949)
Curtain Razor (1949)
Often An Orphan (1949)
Dough For The Do-Do (1949)
Bye Bye Bluebeard (1949)
Boobs In The Woods (1950)
The Scarlet Pumpernickel (1950)
A Egg Scramble (1950)
Golden Yeggs (1950)
The Ducksters (1950)
The Wearing Of The Grin (1951)
Dripalong Daffy (1951)
Dog Collered (1951)
The Prize Pest (1951)
Thumb Fun (1952)
Cracked Quack (1952)
Fool Coverage (1952)
Duck Dodgers In The 24$^{1}/_{2}$ Century (1953)
Claws For Alarm (1954)
My Little Duckaroo (1954)
Jumpin' Jupiter (1955)
Dime To Retire (1955)
Rocket Squad (1956)
Deduce You Say (1956)
Boston Quackie (1957)
Robin Hood Daffy (1958)
China Jones (1959)
Daffy's Inn Trouble (1961)
Corn On The Cop (1965)
Bugs Bunny's Christmas Carol (1979)
Duck Dodgers And The Return Of The 24$^{1}/_{2}$ Century (1980)

PORKY PIG CAMEOS

Hollywood Capers (1935)
Toy Trouble (1941)
Any Bonds Today (1942)
The Great Piggy Bank Robbery (1946)
The Dumb Patrol (1964)
Who Framed Roger Rabbit (1988)

DAFFY DUCK

Porky's Duck Hunt (1937)
Daffy Duck And Egghead (1938)

Porky And Daffy (1938)
The Daffy Doc (1938)
Daffy Duck In Hollywood (1938)
Daffy Duck And The Dinosaur (1939)
Scalp Trouble (1939)
Wise Quacks (1939)
Porky's Last Stand (1940)
You Oughta Be In Pictures (1940)
A Coy Decoy (1941)
The Henpecked Duck (1941)
Conrad The Sailor (1942)
Daffy's Southern Exposure (1942)
The Impatient Patient (1942)
The Daffy Duckaroo (1942)
My Favorite Duck (1942)
To Duck Or Not To Duck (1943)
The Wise Quacking Duck (1943)
Yankee Doodle Daffy (1943)
Scrap Happy Daffy (1943)
Porky's Pigs Feat (1943)
Daffy-The Commando (1943)
Tom Turk And Daffy (1944)
Tick Tock Tuckered (1944)
Duck Soup ToNuts (1944)
Slighty Daffy (1944)
Plane Daffy (1944)
The Stupid Cupid (1944)
Draftee Daffy (1945)
Ain't That Ducky (1945)
Nasty Quacks (1945)
Book Revue (1946)
Baby Bottleneck (1946)
Daffy Doodles (1946)
Hollywood Daffy (1946)
The Great Piggy Bank Robbery (1946)
The Birth Of A Notion (1947)
Along Came Daffy (1947)
The Upstanding Sitter (1947)
A Pest In The House (1947)
Mexican Joyride (1947)
What Makes Daffy Duck? (1948)
Daffy Duck Slept Here (1948)
You Were Never Duckier (1948)
Daffy Dilly (1948)
Riff Raffy Daffy (1948)
The Stupor Salesman (1948)
Wise Quackers (1949)
Holiday For Drumsticks (1949)
Daffy Duck Hunt (1949)
Boobs In The Woods (1950)
The Scarlet Pumpernickle (1950)
His Bitter Half (1950)
Golden Yeggs (1950)
The Ducksters (1950)
Rabbit Fire (1951)
Dripalong Daffy (1951)
The Prize Pest (1951)
Thumb Fun (1952)
Cracked Quack (1952)
Rabbit Seasoning (1952)
The Super Snooper (1952)
Fool Coverage (1952)
Duck Amuck (1953)
Muscle Tussle (1953)
Duck Dodgers In The 24$^{1}/_{2}$ Century (1953)
Duck, Rabbit, Duck (1953)
Design For Leaving (1954)
Quack Shot (1954)
My Little Duckaroo (1954)
Beanstalk Bunny (1955)
Stork Naked (1955)
This Is A Life? (1955)
Dime To Retire (1955)
The High And The Flighty (1956)
Rocket Squad (1956)
Stupor Duck (1956)
A Star Is Bored (1956)
Deduce You Say (1956)
Ali Baba Bunny (1957)
Boston Quackie (1957)
Ducking The Devil (1957)
Show Biz Bugs (1957)
Don't Axe Me (1957)
Robin Hood Daffy (1958)
China Jones (1958)
People Are Bunny (1959)
Person To Bunny (1960)
The Abominable Snow Rabbit (1961)
Daffy's Inn Trouble (1961)
Quackodile Tears (1962)
Good Noose (1962)
Fast Buck Duck (1962)
Million Hare (1963)
Aqua Duck (1963)
The Iceman Ducketh (1964)

It's Nice To Have A Mouse Around The House (1965)
Moby Duck (1965)
Assault And Peppered (1965)
Well Worn Daffy (1965)
Suppressed Duck (1965)
Corn On The Cop (1965)
Tease For Two (1965)
Chili Corn Corny (1965)
Go Go Amigo (1965)
Astro Duck (1966)
Muchos Locos (1966)
Mexican Mouse-piece (1966)
Daffy Rents (1966)
A Haunting We Will Go (1966)
Snow Excuse (1966)
A Squeak In The Deep (1966)
Feather Finger (1966)
Swing Ding Amigo (1966)
A Taste Of Catnip (1966)
Daffy's Diner (1967)
Quacker Tracker (1967)
Music Mice-Tro (1967)
Spy Swatter (1967)
Speedy Ghost To Town (1967)
Rodent To Stardom (1967)
Go Away Stowaway (1967)
Fiesta Fiasco (1967)
Skyscraper Caper (1968)
See You Later, Gladiator (1968)
The Yolk's On You (1980)
The Chocolate Chase (1980)
Daffy Flies North (1980)
Duck Dodgers And The Return Of The 24 1/2 Century (1980)
The Duxorcist (1987)
Night Of The Living Duck (1988)

DAFFY DUCK CAMEOS

Sahara Hare (1955)
Apes Of Wrath (1959)
Who Framed Roger Rabbit (1988)

TWEETY, SYLVESTER, and HIPPETY HOPPER

Below is an index to all films featuring that lisping alleycat Sylvester. Except for Tweety's first three cartoons, Sylvester appeared in every other one of the canary's films — so, in order to save space, we have noted every "Tweety" cartoon below. Tweety's first three appearances were A TALE OF TWO KITTIES (1942), BIRDY AND THE BEAST (1944) and a GRUESOME TWOSOME (1945). Tweety also made a cameo in NO BARKING (1954). Also noted below are all cartoons featuring the kangaroo frequently mistaken for giant mouse, "Hippety Hopper"

Life With Feathers (1945)
Peck Up Your Troubles (1945)
Kitty Cornered (1946)
Tweetie Pie (1947) TWEETY
Crowing Pains (1947)
Doggone Cats (1947)
Catch As Cats Can (1947)
Back Alley Oproar (1948)
I Taw A Puddy Tat (1948) TWEETY
Hop, Look and Listen (1948) HIPPETY HOPPER
Kit For Cat (1948)
Scaredy Cat (1948)
Mouse Mazurka (1949)
Bad Ol' Puddy Tat (1949) TWEETY
Hippety Hopper (1949) HIPPETY HOPPER
Home Tweet Home (1950) TWEETY
The Scarlet Pumpernickle (1950)
All Abi-r-r-d (1950) TWEETY
Canary Row (1950) TWEETY
Stooge For A Mouse (1950)
Pop 'im Pop (1950) HIPPETY HOPPER
Canned Feud (1951)
Puddy Tat Twouble (1951) TWEETY
Room and Bird (1951) TWEETY
Tweety's S.O.S. (1951) TWEETY
Tweet, Tweet, Tweety (1951) TWEETY
Who's Kitten Who? (1952) HIPPETY HOPPER
Gift Wrapped (1952) TWEETY
Little Red Rodent Hood (1952)
Ain't She Tweet (1952) TWEETY

Hoppy Go Lucky (1952) HIPPETY HOPPER
A Bird In A Guilty Cage (1952) TWEETY
Tree For Two (1952)
Snow Business (1953) TWEETY
A Mouse Divided (1953)
Fowl Weather (1953) TWEETY
Tom Tom Tomcat (1953) TWEETY
A Street Cat Named Sylvester (1953) TWEETY
Catty Cornered (1953) TWEETY
Cat's Aweigh (1953) HIPPETY HOPPER
Dog Pounded (1954)TWEETY
Bell Hoppy (1954) HIPPETY HOPPER
Dr. Jerkyl's Hyde (1954)
Claws For Alarm (1954)
Muzzle Tough (1954) TWEETY
Satan's Waitin' (1954) TWEETY
By Word Of Mouse (1954)
Lighthouse Mouse (1955) HIPPETY HOPPER
Sandy Claws (1955) TWEETY
Tweety's Circus (1955) TWEETY
Jumpin' Jupiter (1955)
A Kiddie's Kitty (1955)
Red Riding Hoodwinked (1955) TWEETY
Heir Conditioned (1955)
Pappy's Puppy (1955)
Too Hop To Handle (1956) HIPPETY HOPPER
Tweet And Sour (1956) TWEETY
Tree Cornered Tweety (1956) TWEETY
The Unexpected Pest (1956)
Tugboat Granny (1956) TWEETY
Slap-Hoppy Mouse (1956) HIPPETY HOPPER
Yankee Dood It (1956)
Tweet Zoo (1957) TWEETY
Tweety And The Beanstalk (1957) TWEETY
Birds Anonymous (1957) TWEETY
Greedy For Tweety (1957) TWEETY
Mouse-Taken Identity (1957) HIPPETY HOPPER
Gonzales Tamales (1957)
A Pizza Tweety Pie (1958) TWEETY
A Bird In A Bonnet (1958) TWEETY
Trick Or Tweet (1959) TWEETY
Tweet And Lovely (1959) TWEETY
The Cat's Paw (1959)
Here Today, Gone Tamale (1959)
Tweet Dreams (1959) TWEETY
West Of The Pesos (1960)
Goldimouse And The Three Cats (1960)
Hyde And Go Tweet (1960) TWEETY
Mouse And Garden (1960)
Trip For Tat (1960)TWEETY
Cannery Woe (1961)
Hoppy Daze (1961) HIPPETY HOPPER
Birds Of A Father (1961)
D'Fightin' Ones (1961)
Rebel Without Claws (1961) TWEETY
The Pied Piper Of Guadalupe (1961)
The Last Hungry Cat (1961) TWEETY
Fish And Slips (1962)
Mexican Boarders (1962)
The Jet Cage (1962) TWEETY
Mexican Cat Dance (1963)
Chili Weather (1963)
Claws In The Lease (1963)
A Message To Gracias (1964)
Freudy Cat (1964) HIPPETY HOPPER
Nuts And Volts (1964)
Hawaiian Aye Aye (1964) TWEETY
The Road To Andalay (1964)
It's Nice To Have A Mouse Around The House (1965)
Cats And Bruises (1965)
The Wild Chase (1965)
A Taste Of Catnip (1966)
Bugs Bunny's Christmas Carol (1979) TWEETY
The Yolks On You (1980)

FOGHORN LEGHORN

Walky Talky Hawky (1946)
Crowing Pains (1947)
The Foghorn Leghorn (1948)
Hen House Henry (1949)
The Leghorn Blows At Midnight (1950)
A Fractured Leghorn (1950)
Leghorn Swoggled (1951)
Lovelorn Leghorn (1951)
Sock-A-Doodle Doo (1952)
Egg-Cited Rooster (1952)
Plop Goes The Weasel (1953)
Of Rice And Hen (1953)
Little Boy Boo (1954)
Feather Dusted (1955)
All Fowled Up (1955)
Weasel Stop (1956)
The High And The Flighty (1956)
Raw! Raw! Rooster (1956)
Fox Terror (1957)
Feather Bluster (1958)
Weasel While You Work (1958)
A Broken Leghorn (1959)
Crockett-Doodle-Doo (1960)
The Dixie Fryer (1960)
Strangled Eggs (1961)
The Slick Chick (1962)
Mother Was A Rooster (1962)
Banty Raids (1963)
Bugs Bunny's Christmas Carol (1979)
The Yolks On You (1980)

SPEEDY GONZALES

Cat-tails For Two (1953)
Speedy Gonzales (1955)
Tabasco Road (1957)
Gonzales Tamales (1957)
Tortilla Flaps (1958)
Mexicali Shmoes (1959)
Here Today, Gone Tamale (1959)
West Of The Pesos (1960)
Cannery Woe (1961)
The Pied Piper Of Guadalupe (1961)
Mexican Boarders (1962)
Mexican Cat Dance (1963)
Chili Weather (1963)
A Message To Gracias (1964)
Nuts And Volts (1964)
Pancho's Hideaway (1964)
The Road To Andalay (1964)
It's Nice To Have A Mouse Around The House (1965)
Cats And Bruises (1965)
The Wild Chase (1965)
Moby Duck (1965)
Assault And Peppered (1965)
Well Worn Daffy (1965)
Chili Corn Corny (1965)
Go Go Amigo (1965)
Astro Duck (1966)
Muchos Locos (1966)
Mexican Mouse-piece (1966)
Daffy Rents (1966)
A Haunting We Will Go (1966)
Snow Excuse (1966)
A Squeak In The Deep (1966)
Feather Finger (1966)
Swing Ding Amigo (1966)
A Taste Of Catnip (1966)
Daffy's Diner (1967)
Quacker Tracker (1967)
Music Mice-tro (1967)
Spy Swatter (1967)
Speedy Ghost To Town (1967)
Rodent To Stardom (1967)
Go Away Stoway (1967)
Fiesta Fiasco (1967)
Sky Scaper Caper (1968)
See Ya Later, Gladiator (1968)
Fright Before Christmas (1979)
The Chocolate Chase (1980)

ROADRUNNER

Fast And Furry-ous (1949)
Beep Beep (1952)
Going Going Gosh (1952)
Zipping Along (1953)
Stop, Look, And Hasten (1954)
Ready, Set, Zoom! (1955)
Guided Muscle (1955)
Gee Whiz-z-z (1956)
There They Go-Go-Go.(1956)
Scrambled Aches (1957)
Zoom And Board (1957)
Whoa, Be Gone (1958)
Hook, Line And Stinker (1958)
Hip Hip Hurry (1958)
Hot Rod And Reel (1959)

Wild About Hurry (1959)
Fastest With The Mostest (1960)
Hopalong Casualty (1960)
Zip n' Snort (1961)
Lickety Splat (1961)
Beep Prepared (1961)
Zoom At The Top (1961)
To Beep Or Not To Beep (1963)
War And Pieces (1964)
Zip Zip Hooray (1965)
Roadrunner A Go-Go (1965)
The Wild Chase (1965)
Rushing Roulette (1965)
Run Run Sweet Roadrunner (1965)
Tired And Feather (1965)
Boulder Wham (1965)
Just Plane Beep (1965)
Harried And Hurried (1965)
Highway Runnery (1965)
Chaser On The Rocks (1965)
Shot and Bothered (1966)
Out And Out Rout (1966)
The Solid Tin Coyote (1966)
Clippety Clobbered (1966)
Sugar And Spies (1966)
Freeze Frame (1979)
Soup Or Sonic (1980)

HENERY HAWK

The Squawkin' Hawk (1942)
Walky Talky Hawky (1946)
Crowing Pains (1946)
You Were Never Duckier (1948)
The Foghorn Leghorn (1948)
Hen House Henery (1949)
The Scarlet Pumpernickle (1950) cameo
The Leghorn Blows At Midnight (1950)
Leghorn Swoggled (1951)
All Fowled Up (1955)
Strangled Eggs (1961)

THE GOOFY GOPHERS

The Goofy Gophers (1947)
Two Gophers From Texas (1948)
A Ham In A Role (1949)
A Bone For A Bone (1951)
I Gopher You (1954)
Pests For Guests (1955)
Lumber Jerks (1955)
Gopher Broke (1958)
Tease For Two (1965)

PEPE LE PEW

Odor-able Kitty (1945)
Scent-imental Over You (1947)
Odor Of The Day (1948)
For Scent-imental reasons (1949)
Sentimental Romeo (1951)
Little Beau Pepe (1952)
Wild Over You (1953)
Dog Pounded (1954) -cameo
The Cat's Bah (1954)
Past Perfumance (1955)
Two Scents Worth (1955)
Heaven Scent (1956)
Touche And Go (1957)
Really Scent (1959)
Who Scent You? (1960)
A Scent Of The Matterhorn (1961)
Louvre Come Back To Me (1962)

SNIFFLES

Naughty But Mice (1939)
Little Brother Rat (1939)
Sniffles And The Bookworm (1939)
Sniffles Takes A Trip (1940)
The Egg Collector (1940)
Bedtime For Sniffles (1940)
Sniffles Bells The Cat (1941)
Toy Trouble (1941)
Brave Little Bat (1941)
The Unbearable Bear (1943)
Lost And Foundling (1944)
Hush My Mouse (1946)

THE TASMANIAN DEVIL

Devil May Hare (1954)
Bedevilled Rabbit (1957)
Ducking The Devil (1957)
Bill Of Hare (1962)
Dr. Devil And Mr. Hare (1964)
Fright Before Christmas (1979)

MARVIN MARTIAN

Haredevil Hare (1948)
Hasty Hare (1952)
Duck Dodgers in the 24 1/2 Century (1953)
Hare-way To The Stars (1958)
Mad As A Mars Hare (1963)
Duck Dodgers And The Return Of The 24 1/2 Century (1980)
Spaced Out Bunny (1980)